The Journey OF AN Apprentice DREAMER

BEHOLD THE KEEPER'S PRACTICE

KAREN C. SILVERSTEIN

AUTHOR AND ARTIST

ISBN-13:978-1478362456
ISBN-1478362456

LCCN: 2013901696
CreateSpace Independent Publishing Platform
North Charleston, SC 29406

FIRST EDITION 2013   BISAC: BODY, MIND AND SPIRIT/DREAMS

VISIT US AT:

HTTP://WWW.EARTHDREAMS.COM   E-MAIL: KAREN@EARTHDREAMS.COM
AVAILABLE FOR PURCHASE: JOURNEY OF AN APPRENTICE DREAMER CARD DECK, IN COLOR OF THE DREAM SEERS. THE SIXTY FOUR KEEPERS ILLUSTRATED IN THE BOOK

PRINTED BY CREATESPACE AN AMAZON.COM COMPANY
MANUFACTURED IN THE USA

FOR MY DEAR HUSBAND most of all:

Jay, who appreciates the dreaming!

And my lovely, dreamy children and their dear little ones,

the grandchildren, who know the dreaming!

TABLE OF CONTENTS

THE DREAMING BEGINS

Dream Journey In The Nemeton Of The Keepers

The Watchers are there as you walk through the woods and brambles. There are others walking—but you do not know them. One of The Watchers stops the group to say, "Life is a quest. This is why you have come. In order to change the world we must change our dreams first." They look directly at me while speaking to all and say, "What is the title of your Dream of the night, Dreamers?"

You think to yourself, Watchers, who are they? And my Dream of the night? You feel off track.

A voice answers you telepathically: "We watch over the Grove. We protect and serve. We watch."

Oh my god! you say to yourself silently. Walking swiftly now, through the trees of the steading, you are feeling the night rolling in and the air cooling. You look to follow the others. Not quite sure where you are going or what you are doing, but moving to do so just the same.

Another voice catches your ear now. A musical-sounding voice that speaks precisely, with poise and diction. Closer now, you can make out the words: "Dream Circle is ceremony. It is power and holy energy." Putting the voice with the person, you are struck by her beauty and the stars in her hair. Who—? No time for questions. The evening program is about to begin as you watch the crowd of Dreamers settle in.

Someone is saying, "Come now to the Inner Circle. Time to step in." Someone has been leading you by your arm and finds you a place to sit. They say to you, "The Keepers of the Nemeton have been preparing for you and for the Dream Circle ceremony. Watch, listen!" They move on to help other new Dreamers. You get comfortable and relax a bit, thinking to yourself, This seems OK.

You knew prior to coming there would be master teachers, and now, looking about, you see the Ancient Ones. The tarot Trump Seers are mingling with the Animal Seers. The Tree Seers are located at the outer edges, forming a circle with their tree bodies. The Grove, you think to yourself. This is incredible! For a long time you have heard stories of them and read about them, "The Keepers." But never, until now, have you seen them or shared the same presence of space. Wow, this is big! Fog and mist are swirling and growing dense. Looking around, you notice rocks and boulders throughout. You can hear the sounds of water but do not see any. There is a fire pit in the center of what is quickly becoming a circle of people, made up of all the "Keepers of the Circle" and the "Novice Dreamers." It is dusk, the time between the worlds. We hear the drumming now. Each Keeper, ready to begin, drums, rattles, chants—all to focus and center themselves in order to build the core of power.

A young man next to you says he is one of the Apprentice Dreamers. He explains that the Apprentices are midway through their initiation and paths as Dream Teachers. The man begins giving basic information about this group, which we are a part of here in the Nemeton. He says, "The Keepers converge when there is a need, whether the need is from human, plant, or animal kingdom. Always there is a balancing to be done. Adepts to initiate. Words to be aired and said. Good words to heal and pray with." Pausing and looking us over, he then continues, "The Master Teachers who are The Keepers take sides with none, as truth is their purpose. This is why you have come, and truth is what the Nemeton contains. It will be mirrored to you in one or many ways. Sometimes this path is not for the faint of heart."

His deep brown eyes penetrate your own. His long pause makes you nervous. You take a slight breath and move your eyes away from his stare. Again you hear his voice, cool and calm. You force yourself to hear his words. "Be sure as to what it is you seek. Each one of you new Dreamers must face up to your own truths, especially the weak parts reflected by the Mirrors of the Keepers. Even if frightened, you must look! Know this: you are safe here and protected. The Keepers are shape-shifters all; they are here for your support and healing. They trust that there will be some of you who will follow in their footsteps one day." His voice trails off some; his tone is softer now. You want to say something, but the words will not come.

Slowly, he says, "Begin to think about your personal dream. Your intention as to why you have come. Which of your dreams wants to be shared at this time? Which healed? Think these things over. Quiet now!" He nods his head and gestures with his hand to the center of the circle.

You shift about and look toward the center. Think of dreams, intentions? You say to yourself, I am not sure…don't know.

The circle has settled for the opening ceremony. We are reminded by one of the Seers that the "Circle of Truth is the shape of harmony."

One of the Ancient Ones draws a large circle in the dirt in front of us. She uses a branch borrowed from the Birch Tree Seer. She holds up this branch over her head after she completes the circle. We are all standing. She looks about the circle at each of us. She says to Keepers and Dreamers alike, "Please step over the line. Step into the Inner Dreaming circle." And so it starts, and you sigh and cry. You listen now to the power of the words of the opening, invoking spirit and the gods and goddesses alike. Asking for support and protections, asking for strong dreams and soul remembrance. Your hands are all joined around this circle. You can feel electrical power surging, going from hand to hand and heart to heart. The Oak Tree Seer has been leading; you hear his deep, booming voice, feel his strength, and sense the soft love sent out to all. Nervous and unsure, heart pounding, you sit down along with all the other Dreamers.

The Yew Tree Seer begins, telling us that the trees of the forest are all interdependent; one depends on the other. You know a little about the yew. In the Ogham it is the twentieth tree, and its attribute in the higher realms is love, made up from all the trees. "Love one another" is what you relate to the words this Yew Tree Seer speaks. You realize we all affect each other.

As you look around the outer edges of this circle, tears come to your eyes. For the beauty of these Tree Seers forming the larger outer circle is awesome. Different tree shapes, sizes, and feelings. Twenty Tree Keepers, master teachers in all their fine greenery. The scene is regal and otherworldly with fog and mist in the trees' branches as the twilight lingers all about.

The Holly Tree Seer speaks up. "I am talking to the New Dreamers…Be aware that the tests are always all around. Both here and in waking reality, all is never quite what it seems. The tests are to keep you in touch with your life path. There might be roadblocks on your path. Do you go on another course, take an easier path? Do you even realize the detour? Are you at all in touch with your soul path at this time? The tests may come in riddles to test your wit and resolve. Tests in the form of colors, senses, glyphs, numbers, intuitions—a whole assortment of symbols only you can decipher. Synchronicities are the keys. Listen to your heart and follow your intuition. You will get through the tests…By being aware!"

The Ash Tree Seer walks about the circle. She is light and beautiful, full of grace. She creates such a feeling that you cannot take your eyes from her. She is talking about energy. "Our bodies are like magnets. The environment responds to our thoughts and feelings. One being filled with doubt and anger may wilt the flowers. Another being's enthusiasm is such that cut flowers last for weeks. Love is such energy. Use it well!" She throws back the boughs of her head, moving with beauty. Her leaves shimmer and shine as she goes.

There is a hush throughout the Grove as we all take in the energy from the Ash Tree Seer. The stars have come out of the now dark sky; they twinkle and glitter. Stretching some, you realize what a fine view of the night sky we all have. Here in the clearing of this Grove, you find yourself thinking from the vantage point of the night sky looking down to Earth… How small this spot, our sacred Grove. How small, but how powerful it feels. Searching the night sky, you find the Bear constellation, Ursa Major, so beautiful. Your thoughts are wandering some…

Then you hear a rather loud rumbling voice. You blink your eyes to see the Animal Bear Seer, and he is out there speaking! Although moving a bit clumsily as he sways about the circle, he has captured the group's attention. His words are these: "Our understanding of our Sacred Dream Circle is this, *nothing is sick!* And everything in your life is a lesson. Understand the lesson, and you have the cure." More quietly than when he started, he moves back to his seat.

The Dreamers begin chatting some after that, wondering about the comments. There is a pause now for break time. People stretch and move about. Good, you think, I need it. Your mind reels. What have I gotten myself into? What do I need this for? This makes you nervous. This would be the best time to get out! To just excuse yourself and leave…Who cares! Getting your things together, you are ready to run! The drumming has started; the Keepers are starting up again. I still have time, you think. You throw your jacket over your shoulders as a cool summer's breeze touches your cheek. The sky has lit up some; the moon is rising.

Then you see her, The Moon Seer Ancient One. Chanting softly, she is a vision of soft light. You are mesmerized! You sit down for a bit longer.

The Moon Seer is saying, "The web we create can trap us if not created in truth. You may ask how I can know my true life's work? Come to me. Study the cycles of the moon. Seed your dreams, thoughts, and ideas at the new moon. Follow my cycles. Talk to me for guidance. Search your heart. Follow me to the Full of the Moon cycle. Search your heart again to know what it wants. By doing this process you will come to know what you are meant to do."

A new Dreamer asks, "Searching your heart is not easy. How do we do this?"

With a swift turn of her head, Grandmother Moon, the Ancient Moon Seer, glows in silver light! We can hear crashing ocean waves as she speaks loudly, clearly. "I move the tides with my breath!" she says. "You will move your heart! You will search. You will dream. This is why you are here! The Nemeton and its Keepers will guide you. Trust them. Create your truth, and the web you weave will not trap you. You will have to work at it. Do your *Dreaming!* Sow your seeds; nurture your intention. We do not give away knowledge easily; we wait to see how you tend your garden. You will move your heart! You must ask for help and you must trust."

Like an explanation point, you hear a huge crash of waves hitting the rocks! But there is no view yet of the ocean's shore. No doubt the ocean is only yards away. Your mouth has dropped open! What happened? There is complete silence now over the crowd. The Ancient One Moon Seer waves her hand. A wolf saunters over to her; she walks with it to the Ancient Willow Tree Seer. The silver light around her shines on the willow and her. Fluffing her cushions, she is comfortable, and the wolf sits next to her.

"Shall we begin?" says the Moon Seer. "We will all go on a journey. This will help those of you new to this work to begin to get in touch with your own personal 'Soul Contract', the one you came into this world with, the contract of your own life mission. Do you know it? The Dreaming work you do here will help each of you to know your skills. Your intentions for this Journey of Dreaming is to find your 'Soul Contract,' view this, ask questions of this, and bring back gifts for yourself to use in this waking reality. You will travel far, Dreamer, back into your own timeline. Make yourself ready. I know just the dream!"

We and the other new Dreamers are sitting quietly now, but with one look at each other, we look around and see the more advanced Dreamers and Keepers are lying down onto their cushions. We realize we need to do the same in order to be relaxed for dream-travel-journey. Once relaxed on our cushions, we close our eyes and hear the Keepers in the background sounding the drums. We are told that we must be ready now to hear the Dream from the Moon Seer, as she will relay the dream clearly, but only once for us to journey into her telling of her dream. This will then spark our own dream encounter of her original dream, while the drumming accompanies all of us.

You feel very excited now to be doing this, and you have come to the realization that you will give your attention to what you can learn from this Grove they call the Nemeton.

INSIGHTS TO THE
KEEPERS OF THE NEMETON

The Nemeton, Sanctuary, the Sacred Grove for Healers is a very special place. One you may not cross paths with often.

The word "Nemeton" is Celtic. It means "a clearing in a wood."

For the ancient Celtic people, the Nemeton was a tree Grove used for ceremony. Some have said that it was called "Nemetona," as was found in old inscriptions. The word may have originated from the Irish name "Nemed," meaning husband of "Macha"; it also may be related to the name "Naomh," meaning "holy." "Nemus" is another Druid word for sanctuary. These sacred groves were widespread until the Romans conquered Gaul and northern and central Europe.

The sanctuary of trees that made up the Grove-Nemeton was sacred space. Within the Grove, druids, poets, musicians, and wise ones assembled to give reverence to their gods and goddesses. This was and is a place to learn, dream, teach, and share experiences.

Our Nemeton is all this, but it is most especially the place of *The Dreaming*: a place of magical energy that draws The Keepers, the Master Teachers of the Dreaming.

This Nemeton consists of three kinds of "Keepers-Seers," Ancient Ones all: The Tarot Trump Seers, The Animal Seers, and The Tree Seers. They make up the "Sanctuary" (this word means "grove") along with the Dreamers who have come to learn their craft of Dreaming. We all need sanctuary; we crave it.

This Nemeton in our work within this book and beyond is a special place of this earth and also the "Dreamtime." A place for healers (master teachers who are the "Keepers-Seers") to assemble and also a place for the Novice Dreamers (those who aspire to the magical arts). It is here among like-minded beings that we can relax, question, dream journey, work, heal, and grow, allowing us to develop into the wondrous beings spirit has meant us to be.

At this time of great changes, the Keepers are so needed and must be treasured. The Keepers-Seers and Dreamers on the path are the light workers. These master teachers come to us in times of need. They reflect—mirror—their truth and wisdom, sending us words of calm, encouragement, and inspiration. They help us to realize we can be more than we have ever dreamed! You are welcome to go to them for support and confirmation, bringing the things you struggle with, need clarity on, or are working on within yourself.

Once you have decided to enter the Nemeton, you will learn about your emotions, hopes, and dreams. Through the dreaming you participate in, you will find ways to the source of your strength. You will learn how to best use the energy available to you in waking reality and the dream world. There is a reawakening that transpires. The Knowing begins to take form and the doorways open. You start to feel less stuck—more empowered. It is hard work, and it is magical.

The Keepers, Trump Seers, Animal Seers, and Tree Seers all relate to each other. They form the "Dream Circle" itself. Trump Seers sit next to Tree Seers or Animal Seers. Their attributes flow together. The newer Dreamers come to the Grove to learn the Dreaming from these master teachers, and a bond is formed with each other through the Dreaming.

Only you can decide which Seers feel best for your magical workings!

The format is this: one of the Trump Seers, Animal Seers, or a Tree Seer becomes your gateway to the dream healing work. "Gateway" means a vehicle that has characteristics that you relate to. This is purposely or randomly chosen by you to work from. This becomes a place to start from and use in your dreamy divination work. These Keepers-Seers are memory palaces to be tapped into for information and healing. The Keepers are your gateways to parts of yourself. You know the parts! The ones that yearn to be set free. Are you dreaming to be an actress, to travel, to dance, write, and paint, to find a new job, to buy a home, to have a mate? There are many others that you may know. The part of you that is daydreaming, "If I only could..." and then allows this to be pushed aside again. Not anymore! Here in this Nemeton you will *dream* with these Master Teachers and nourish the passions that have been important to you and discover new ones. You will learn to Walk Well on your Earth Walk now.

You are ready for the *DREAMING*!

Understand that the timelines will shift and change like in a dream! You are now the Dreamer coming for the first time to the Nemeton, the Sanctuary of the Grove, the place of the Keepers. You are stepping into your own Dreaming life from both past and future, and you are eager to learn the ways of the Dreamer!

Please Now Enter THE DREAM of the NEMETON!

THE MOON SEER - GIVES THE DREAM TITLE:

"My Soul Arrives in a Birch Bark Canoe"

The Moon Seer has paused now, letting her dream title rest a bit and begin to seep into the Dreamers.

You look around this Sacred Grove. Sixty-four Keepers, master teachers all. You are still here; you did not run, not yet. You think that something transpired, caught your interest a bit…Maybe you are even in the presence of something you should know about… The air is calm and still. You notice how the Tree Seers are rooted into the grove; they are holding us all to Earth Mother. You notice the Animal Seers are the sentinels, and the Trump Seers are setting the links and boundaries for the Nemeton. The time feels right. You think to yourself, I have committed these few days to searching my heart, possibly even staying on for the lengthy years of training.

You look at the Ash Tree Seer. "See things through" is the message returned, from looking into her eyes. "Match test for test, your heart is able," is what you hear.

Looking around, you see others are lying down now, getting ready to journey; you do the same. You check with the Dreamer near you, and you both consent to check on each other upon return. The time seems right; the stars are bright. The soft drumming is spreading relaxation across the Grove. The drumming begins to pull you to dreamtime. You think to yourself, My first Dream Journey in this place called the Nemeton, the Sacred Grove, and you are excited.

The Ancient Moon Seer's voice moves in a cadence now, and you are off to do your own inner journey…through the power of Her Dreaming.

THE MOON SEER SPEAKS:
"My Soul Arrives in a Birch Canoe"

I am a young lady or young man of about nineteen years old. I am making a long journey from Scotland to the land across the Atlantic. But you, Dreamer, may be traveling from a different land—your choice now. This is a time of many generations in the past. I left my homeland after having been burnt in the burning times. My last memory was of a wreath floating out into the Atlantic seawater.

My time in the bardo state kept me walking across a vast northern land. Many parts of the land were frozen ice. There were herds of moose, wild wolves, and bears. Sometimes in the ice I would see mirror reflections...images of families living close to the land. I just kept walking and forgetting. There are others walking with me. I do not interact with them. Each of us is doing our own private journey of walking and forgetting where we have come from.

Finally I arrive at my new destination; there is a feeling of No-Time getting here. The thought occurs to me: "It is now that matters."

As I view the landmass, it is lush and so green, wet and rocky along the sea edge. Looking to the hill above, I see a tented village nestled into pine and birch trees. In a wink of an eye, I am there. I see a man who is carving on a large birch tree. He has long black hair with a single braid on one side tied with birch bark and a black crow feather. He feels foreign and fierce to me; his skin is red. He has a necklace on of bones and shells. I feel so pale and frail next to him.

"But your heart is strong!"

I look around, stunned. Who was that?

The man is rattling all about me now. He says, "You must wake up! This is your new home of choice, and you have much to learn!"

I shiver at this statement. Suddenly remembering my pack, I pull out a gift for him. Handing this over, his black eyes hold tight to my blue eyes. I am without breath.

The man explains he is a teacher of this land and he is called One With Trees. He opens my present, which is a small, round wreath woven from ivy and white shells. The man is very pleased. He tells me when the time is right I will find my new family through the center of this wreath. He looks at me piercingly and says, "Do you remember your 'Sacred Contract'?"

Surprising myself, I respond and answer, "Yes!"

"Tell me without delay!" he says quickly.

I begin to feel nervous. He provides me with strength, and I proceed. "I am to learn the ways of being with the land. I am to know spirit is in all creatures and the land itself. I am to learn respect and boundaries for others, and to honor their sacred space and mine. I am to remember my deep connection with the standing people, the trees, animals, and ancient ones gone before me. I am to use my gift of Sight to help others. I am to remember everything I need will be provided for me because I have come to trust and know the Dreaming!"

Quite out of breath, I pause. "One With Trees" is pleased! I want to continue, but he says my list can continue later. He reminds me of My Strong Heart and that I can share this song in my heart with others. He now has me follow him to the birch tree he has been carving. He proceeds to tell me that it is a white birch. He tells me, "You will learn to read the black markings on the bark. You will learn about the core and the heart wood in the tree. You will learn about her living blood, her sap!"

He stops and searches my face; I give him a smile but can not talk. He explains that together we will carve a canoe from this birch. This will be his gift to me. He tells me this will be helpful in my new land with my new people. He tells me the carving process will teach me about my new life. "This Birch Canoe once made will be your gift of 'Soul'!"

I am utterly speechless…

Smiling, "One With Trees" begins to chant this verse:

"You are here Now…

here Now…

here Now…."

Your Dreaming now fades from your mind's eye.

The drumbeats soften; the Seer has stopped. We all come back from this incredible journey of "My Soul Arrives in a Birch Canoe"!

Through the power of the "Moon Seer's" Dream, we are all changed and have much to contemplate.

At last you smile to yourself and make a commitment to stay; this might just be fun!

The Dreaming– An Overview

Dreams are a reflection, a mirror of our own subconscious, sending us information that we can use to track our own life, to solve the questions and mysteries that we are filled with. In our dreams we are both the characters and directors. We learn if we do not like the present movie, we can Dream Journey to change the movie channel. We can dream in information for the future and clear up information from the past. Always working with our own puzzle of who we are and how we can heal as to who we are becoming on our true soul path.

A few definitions:

- Imagination—the ability to deal creatively with reality.
- Dream—from Old English; joy, gladness, music.
- Dreams—a series of images, ideas, and emotions occurring in certain stages of sleep, aspirations, ambitions.

Why dreams? Because we are all intrigued by our own dreams and the mysterious messages that come to us in the night or a daydream. They question us, frighten and delight. When we take the time to reenter these movies of ourselves, we find worlds upon worlds of information. When we learn to pay attention to our "Dream Selves," our soul comes alive with love and gifts beyond belief!

Dream work using the methods in this book becomes a hands-on action plan to assist you in achieving goals and healing. The "Reader-Dreamer" chooses a dream of their own and then reflects on what they want to work with. We learn to work with what the dream-reflections-mirrors are telling us. Staying in the waking reality of now and tracking backward or forward for information. Remember this: the power of the dream always belongs to the original Dreamer. It is this very fact that brings about healing or the change that one may desire.

WHY DID THIS BOOK ATTRACT YOU, DOES IT MIRROR SOMETHING?

We all like to look at ourselves, that is why! Because by looking in the mirror we adjust ourselves. Seeing our reflection, we prepare for putting our best foot (soul) forward or best face (mask) forward. A mask for the current situation.

A Mirror equals anything that faithfully reflects or gives a true picture of something else. From: Middle English, "Mirour"; Old French, "Miroir"—"To look at."

From: Latin, "Mĩrãrt"—"To wonder at." Another Latin word for "Mirror" is "Speculum," giving us the word "Speculate," which originally meant to divine with a crystal ball or "Mirror."

Grooming-Preparing:

Combing your hair—Combing out psychic tangles; Making up your face—Shaving or applying makeup. Applying the face-masks we need to be able to function in the outer world for our world, for our World Work, our Daily Work.

Mirror Work:

"Mirror, Mirror…Who are you?" We keep asking.

Each day we awake for whatever is on our agenda. We make ourselves ready for our career work, house work, and family. Or for friends, leisure time, study time. The selections are long. We wash, dress, hurry or not, we comb our hair. We look in the mirror and put on our appropriate mask. Do we really look in the mirror? Do we connect to the image reflected there? Are we conscious about what reflects back on any given day? For most of us the answer is not really! We do not connect. Do we see someone happy, sad, and tired? Do we even see ourselves at all?

With mirror work we learn to use the reflective surface. From our look in the mirror we can learn to live in the present. We can use this reflection as a message board for ourselves. We learn to become more comfortable with ourselves. Many of us are not comfortable with our own image. Many of us do not even take time to watch ourselves in the mirror. Most of us are too busy making a living, nurturing families, doing, running, surviving. But are we *living*? With all our facilities, are we living with passion, satisfaction, joy? The Mirror knows!

Our reflection can give us a clue as to how we are faring. From your look in the mirror (take a moment to look now), what do you see? Maybe images such as these…

The Goddess or The Warrior
The Young Child, Child Woman, or Child Man
The Maiden or The Gentleman
The High Priestess or The Crone
The Hierophant or The King

What are your images like? Are they happy, sad, or indifferent? Is there another wrinkle or a worry that you see traces of? What are your feelings in the features portrayed from these images you are looking at? Maybe an image like the one described by Mary Elizabeth Coleridge in this poem, "The Other Side of the Mirror":

> MEDUDSA
> "I sat before my glass one day,
> And conjured up a vision bare…
> The vision of a woman, wild
> With more than womanly despair…
> I am She!"

The symbol of the mirror has often functioned as a tool not only for reflection but also as a tool to scrutinize and aid in self-assessment and in subsequent improvement. We are reminded of Narcissus as he stood looking at his reflection at the water's edge, or the story of Snow White. The mirror does not hide anything; it only gives a reflection of the true appearance. The path to self-knowledge is fraught with difficulty. Few are the moments when we look to the mirror to appreciate or admire ourselves. Generally we look in order to assess and then adjust our outward appearance. The mirror can be many things and, importantly, is a productive step toward one's spiritual goals. A Mirror as a tool of divination goes back to the ancient times of the Greeks and the Hebrews who would fill a container with water and then "scry" (divine) by peering into the liquid until an image or vision appeared. It has been learned that the Romans were the first to make glass mirrors. The belief that the soul projects out of the body and into mirrors in the form of reflection underlines an ancient superstition, possibly from ancient Roman times. One such superstition says that breaking a mirror brings seven years of bad luck! However, if one collects the shards and grinds them free of reflection, the bad luck can be averted. In various cultures mirrors were often covered during sleep or illness so that the soul, in its wanderings, would not become trapped and unable to return to the body. In some cultures after a death in the family, mirrors are covered or turned to the wall to prevent the soul of the newly departed from becoming caught in the mirror, delaying its journey to the afterlife.

AS A DREAMER we are reminded of our reflective dreams. Take a moment. Might there be a dream that surfaces? Is there something that you would like to ask of the reflection staring back at you now, in this present time? You may ask, what can the mirror do for me?

The environment responds to our thoughts and feelings. Humans must be aware of how a thought, word, or deed affects the environment. With enthusiasm we choose the positive. How do we attain this energy of enthusiasm? We look into the mirror and search out the light of our souls. We find light in the images that we encounter.

IN THIS BOOK YOU WILL MEET:

THE KEEPERS, THE SEERS of THE DREAMING: Master teachers who will form strong connections with you. They will be teaching you to See yourself and your world with awareness, which will be mirrored onto you and reflected onto you in order to work with and assimilate your dreams. Through the Dreaming within this book, one can truly discover the joy of one's own reflection, and then, should you choose, you may reflect onto others.

Be enchanted with life's shine!

THE KEEPERS consist of: The Trump Seers, The Animal Seers, and The Tree Seers.

The Keepers will help one to find what is shining in their lives that they may use it. Some days our feelings may be darkness or emptiness; please know the appropriate Seer will always appear, helping one through, with magical reflecting lessons.

Through the Dreaming in this book, one is reminded to honor the light of clear mind in each person they encounter of the earth: each creature, four legged, winged, or not, and each tree or plant of the earth. With this clearness of light, consider how your own spirit light and mental clarity may help others.

Mirror Work—Dream Work—Heals the Human Spirit:

When one's soul has shattered, our Human Spirit is shattered.

The soul cannot tolerate brutality. It cannot tolerate abundance of pain and irrationality.

It cannot tolerate being lied to. It cannot tolerate unforgiveness. It cannot tolerate jealousies and hatred. These are all contaminants, poisons for the soul.

In studying the mirrors around our life, one may begin to see where there might be some shattering. Taking time to view those reflections is the hardest part. The Keepers can help us to work toward whatever repair is needed to function with light and love in the present. We never get trapped in the reflected image too long! We acknowledge, learn, heal, and begin to move on with our life path.

Using the 'Techniques Of Lightning Dream Work' by: Robert Moss (See Apendix 1)

Applied with 'The Dream Keeper Images of the Keepers - Seers'

Six Steps:

1) Title of Dream: Title of my day, the Keeper image selected, or dream. Give a title to this as it has become your *dream!*
2) How did I feel when I woke up from this dream? How do I feel about the Keeper image selected and journeyed with? Describe the feelings encountered around the dream.
3) Reality Check: Do any of these Dream Keeper images relate to me now, or the dream I had last night, or the dream journey I just did? Do any actions apply to any future events, or remind me of past events? How does this dream and image relay to my waking reality?
4) What do I need to know? What do I need to know about this dream and the Dream Keeper image or the dream journey that just transpired? Phrase that question for yourself, now.
5) Play the "If it were my dream" game. Ask someone near you, someone in your family, a friend, a co-worker about the dream you had or the Dream Keeper image selected. Get feedback from others. How does this information fit with you? Let the other person tell you the dream from their own vantage point, saying, "If it were my dream, it tells me such and such." Keep only the parts of the dream that feel right to you, as the Dreamer who has told the dream.
6) How will I honor this dream? Suggestions to honor the dream:

   • Draw,paint, write,and create. Or find an object to honor the dream
   • Go back inside the dream through dream reentry

* Share dream with another and make a bumper sticker
Note to Dreamer/Reader: it is helpful to keep a journal on your Dreaming with the Dream Keeper images and journeys taken; also enter the date. The honoring process helps to ground your body with the dreaming and anchors one back into this waking reality.

RECOGNIZING THE MASK IN THE MIRROR:

hat is a Dream Journey? Your dreams are your personal power. We will use the mirror images in this book as your gateway to accessing your dream self. You will learn to track your own Dream Light-Soul Print from the dream images. You will be empowered by this. You are your own director and actor of this Dream Theatre, of the dreams you share and bring to light.

How does the Dream Keeper image you have selected reflect—mirror—back to you? Your assignment is to look for the light, track what was reflected to you. This becomes your Dream Journey.

A few definitions:

- JOURNEY: Means to travel from one place to another. To travel over or through. From Old French, "Jornee." From Latin, "Diurnum" (daily portion) and Latin, "Deiw" (to shine, sky, heaven, god). Suffixed form: "Deiw-yo" (luminous—Latin for Diãna, Moon Goddess).
- IMAGINE: Means a counterpart, an object formed by a mirror.

The Method of a Journey:

Dream Journey work is about collecting information for one's healing work on oneself or for another. The way it comes together is similar to rewinding (tracking) a movie. Picture this: you are ready to play the movie back; you review your movie or, in this case, your dream. This is what we do when we Dream Journey. The word "imagination" means the ability to deal creatively with reality. This is exactly what we use when we participate in Dream Journey work!

Participating in Dream Journey creates the precious present, allowing you to track what the mirror image of your dream and what a Seer-Keeper's image may have triggered in you. These are the components of The Dream Journey, which becomes The Vehicle to learn more about your soul self, directly from yourself. There is no middle man; this technique allows for us to track our own healing light reflections and decide what is useful and what is not. Dream Journey brings magic into our life!

INTRODUCTION TO THE KEEPERS - SEERS:

There are a total of sixty-four Scripted Dreams of the Keepers and Dream Keeper Images, which are the Mirror Gateways to reflect upon and dream with.

1. "The Trump Seers"—twenty-two Dreams and Dream Keeper Images from tarot Trumps
2. "The Animal Seers"—twenty-two Dreams and Dream Keeper Images
3. "The Tree Seers"—twenty Dreams and Dream Keeper Images from the Celtic Ogham

Each of these three gates are *portals* to travel from. They are the "lift off" places. These gateways are dream mirror gates and provide a connection for the Dreamer to both their waking reality and their dream reality. Each portal image, which is a dream mirror, can be used as divination. Using the dream journey work then helps to empower the Dreamer with better choices in the life they are wakefully living and dreaming in.

SECTION ONE
Dreams of the Trump Seers

THE TRUMP SEERS

THE FOOL

DREAM OF THE TRUMP SEER: THE FOOL 0

"Just overwhelmed at times. So much I want to do!" I was speaking with the Hierophant Seer.

He was sympathetic, saying, "You should think about spending the day with the Fool Seer, as he would be presenting his dream to our group this evening! Your timing is perfect; it is still early morning." Smiling, he said, "I will make the arrangements for you to meet the Fool Seer."

At the Dream lodge of some of the Keepers, no one was around. A beautiful, large, round mirror in a golden frame hung on the wall. I went over to adjust my hair. I noticed a small plaque under the mirror that read: "The mirror is meant to reflect the Seeker. What is it you seek?"

Puzzled by this, I looked in the mirror. Looking into my own eyes, I said, "Do you know what you seek?" Walking away, smoothing my hair, I thought, I so much want to understand healing techniques and my dreaming better. I really need to make a Seeker List! Seeing a chair across the room, I headed there. It was made of rosewood, beautifully carved with roses and vines, some in the shape of the infinity symbol. The plush, red leather upholstery was cool and comforting. Pulling out my journal, I wrote down "Seeker List." When I looked up again, the Fool Seer was there. So quiet, I did not even hear his approach. He seemed ordinary to me, not like a fool or an idiot portrayed in tarot at all, just a pleasant fellow in blue jeans and chambray shirt with a winning smile.

I must have had a strangely puzzled expression on my face, because before I could speak, he said in a raspy, deep voice, "Not what you expected?" He was looking me squarely in the eyes. "Maybe you would like me to do something foolish. Perhaps jump around wildly?"

Startled, I looked at him and said defensively, "Why, no! I do not mean to be rude...I suppose I may have had an image of a silly kind of beggar set in my head. I—"

The Seer interrupted me with, "Please lighten up, dear Dreamer. I am teasing and my costume of the Fool is something I use frequently, but I actually have many images. A Fool can come in varied disguises!"

I was laughing a little as I stood. I said, "I am pleased to meet you! I have heard you speak a little. However, to have this time with you is special to me. Thank you!"

He answered with, "The pleasure is all mine, Dreamer! Now let us walk awhile, and you can tell me what you seek!"

"Sounds as if you read the plaque under the mirror. I just wrote in my journal: make a Seeker List," I answered him in a very excited tone. I liked this Seer.

The Fool Seer said, "I am the one who made the mirror and its message!" Then he picked up a basket from a table nearby and handed he to me. He pointed to a note of paper in it. We began our walk, pausing at one of the high points on this mountain of the Nemeton. The views of the cliffs and ocean below were magical. The Keepers sure know the best spots, I thought to myself. The storm from earlier had collapsed, allowing a little sun. We reached, at length, a wide open space at the edge of the wood, before the hill that then tumbled to the cliffs. The wind spun around us as we stopped.

I picked up the paper, and the Seer said, "We will wait here awhile. Read it aloud please!"

This is what it said:

COLOR	PLANET	DAY	FEATHER
1. Gold	Sun	Sunday	Eagle
2. Silver	Moon	Monday	Dove/Owl
3 Red	Mars	Tuesday	Cardinal
4. Blue	Mercury	Wednesday	Bluebird
5. Purple	Jupiter	Thursday	Finch
6. Black	Venus	Friday	Crow
7. White	Saturn	Sunday	Swan

As I finished reading, I quickly asked, "What is this list for?"

Smiling at me, and in a laughing voice, he replied, "Well, it is part of my Fool's list! We will be looking for these feathers on our walk. They will be used as a part of my Fool's costume."

"Feathers? Whatever for?" I answered, confused.

He said, "This will be made known little by little as you help me to prepare for the Dream Of The Fool Seer!"

I was nervous after the comment about helping to prepare. I sure knew nothing about Fool Things!

The Seer was perfectly relaxed. He had one hand over his eyes to shield from the glare, looking intently to the sky, for what I did not know, but of course, I followed his gaze.

"We have until the sun sinks over the mountain." He had pointed to the west and now said, "Ah, she has come!" I looked around and saw no one. Then I heard the cries and realized an eagle was swooping down silently on the wind. The eagle was huge. Her landing was precise. She opened her wings and fluffed them out. How amazing! The Fool Seer went to greet her. I wanted to as well, but I was timid and slow; before I knew it, she had taken to the gust of wind that came by.

The Fool Seer said as he walked back to me, "What an awesome creature!" We both looked as she winged up over the mountain. He turned to me, twirling a feather, "We have received the first gift."

The Fool Seer handed me the eagle feather; it was exquisite. I admired it for a few minutes and then asked the Seer, "What do you mean about, 'until the sun sinks over the mountain'?"

He laughed a bit and said, "Come, let's walk!" We started toward the timberline. I put the feather in the basket. Then the Fool Seer answered me. "'When the sun sinks over the mountain' is my way of calculating time. So we will be tracking the sun as we prepare. Because when the sun is going down over the mountains to the west where the sun meets the water on the beach, that is precisely when my Dream of the Fool Seer program begins! Which of course you will be a part of. Until then we have much to accomplish. This will include what it is you seek!"

We continued walking, but my stomach had clenched. Thinking of looking into the mirror earlier, I had no specific answer as to what I was seeking!.

The Seer must have been reading my thoughts. He said this: "We learn on our dreaming path that the mirror needed is the one within!" I turned my head around sharply and looked at his eyes. He responded with, "Ah! Dear little Dreamer, this is not for you to be worried over! A part of you already existing in the future has already done your seeking, possibly even completing the 'Seeker List'! We will call upon this part of you today as we prepare for the evening's program. But for now, to the assignment at hand." He walked off briskly.

Feeling very confused now, I wondered about my future self already existing. Then not knowing what to do with that, I decided to come back to what was happing now.

That is when I heard the Seer saying, "Come on, boy, I have been looking for you!" I wondered who he was talking to. Then as I turned around, I saw the dog—or was it a wolf? It was trotting over to where we walked along the timberline. He had in his mouth a cloth bag or sack of some sort. Once the animal was in front of us, I saw clearly that it was a dog. He dropped the bag in front of us. The Seer was squatting down, ruffling the dog's neck; there was a lot of affection between the two of them. The Seer picked up the bag, and the dog scampered off ahead of us. The Fool Seer then opened the bag and pulled out six more feathers! He commented on them, "Yes! For the six other days of the week of Carnival! Perfect! That is my guy, 'man's best friend, the dog'!"

The Seer was now walking into the wood. He seemed to be looking for something, picking up pieces of small tree limbs and setting them down again. I came over to where he stood under a huge oak tree. He had selected a certain oak limb. With his knife he whittled at the top, turning it this way and that until he was satisfied with the shaping. Then it dawned on me he was making a kind of wand or staff in which to tie the bag onto. Bravely I asked him if this was what he was doing. He answered with, "I am glad to see you are paying attention, Dreamer!"

I watched as he then put the six feathers into the basket I held with the Eagle feather. Now we had the feathers for the dove, blue bird, finch, cardinal, crow, and swan. I did not remember which day or planet went with which and wondered about the carnival. I figured I would find out later.

The Fool Seer came over to me, swinging his staff with the sack now attached to it over his shoulder. His happy energy and smile were irresistible. I said in a laughing voice, "Where are we off to now?"

He laughed back in a bellowing way, saying, "Well, of course we are on the Fool's Journey! So we are open to many possibilities. As we walk toward the cliffs, I will tell you some of my original history through the images that have been painted of me."

Quickly I interjected, "I would love that!"

The Seer continued speaking as we walked. I held the basket of feathers, and he held his staff with the sack. I thought to myself, This is a comical image.

"The original tarot cards from the years in the late 1400s have depicted The Fool as a tattered beggar or wild man! At that time the cards slowly began to evolve, though there was never one set of rules followed by all decks, but a general pattern developed when the tarot Marseilles came about in the beginning of the late fifteenth century. The Marseilles deck introduced many of the images we are familiar with today. The Fool became a handsome, carefree young man with a sack hung over his shoulder, and a dog, wolf, or cat jumping along with him."

As the Seer recited this last description, I looked to see he was exactly that. He looked at me, smiling, and I broke out laughing!

"What is so funny?" he said.

"Nothing," I answered back, "but you are an exact image of your verbal description!" I was feeling comfortable with the jesting.

The Fool Seer continued, "Well, I aim to please! This tarot Trump may suggest a shepherd walking home, a simple traveler, a court jester, or the Fool!"

"Tell me about the Court Jester!" I chimed in.

"My goodness, Dreamer. I do love your enthusiasm!" replied the Seer. "The Court Jester enigma from the times of Royal Court Kingdoms describes a jester as the only man permitted to ridicule the king and was held in high favor. He was often sent to distribute alms to the poor and sharp words all in one breath. The Fool portrayed in Shakespeare's *King Lear* is an excellent example of how the Fool proves to be the wisest of them all. In the Waite tarot deck, the painter, Pamela Colman-Smith, painted him as a Dreamer, unaware or unperturbed by life's dangers! Of course being a Dreamer, I tend to flow with this scenario!"

We had now walked a good length across the steep part of the hill; I noticed the Seer was checking the sun in the sky, which had moved considerably to the west now. Wind and fog were gathering. The Seer did not express concern as he said, "We may be in for a change in the weather. No matter. The show always goes on!"

At that point the dog we had seen earlier came bounding up the hill and then was nipping and pulling at the Fool Seer. I thought he was being annoying, and it even looked like he was taking bites of the Seer's leg. I was about to blurt out that we need to do something with this dog when the Fool Seer suddenly said, "Hey, guy! What is it? Have you a message from someone, or Spirit? What goes on here?" The dog was still pulling at him some, but the Seer seemed to mind not at all. I found this curious.

The Seer had now separated the dog from his leg and was petting him as the animal calmed. The Seer was sitting down on the dampish grass, rubbing the dog's neck. He indicated to me with a hand motion to sit as well, which I did. Before I could ask anything, the Ancient Seer was speaking. "My friend here needed us to stop and listen awhile. Something we humans often forget to do! Well, Dreamer, I know you have questions about this beast. Let me try to explain how integral this dog is to the tarot Trump of the Fool. The dog at my feet may depict worldly desires, but also sometimes it is my ability to ignore these desires. Sometimes the dog may show himself for a grander purpose. The dog is the pull of the world! Possibly while one is in the free, liberated state of the Fool, one can more easily disregard the 'dog of worldly desires,' which of course becomes a teaching in itself."

The Seer laughed a little as he looked at me with what I realized was a stunned expression on my face. I tried to seem relaxed. He went on with what he wanted to say.

"The attacking dog image on many of the Fool card depictions might be portrayed with a dog, a tiger, or a wolf; they might also make us feel concerned or unsettled. Let me point out that the attacking animal may be viewed as a transformation of values. And when it seems that, I, the Fool, pay no attention whatsoever to this animal and clearly keep sauntering on. This may be an indication of the values of the Spirit, of which I am learning are not the same as the values in the ordinary world!"

I did not know how to respond to what the Fool had revealed about his dog, man's best friend. So I just shook my head up and down as if I comprehended his teachings. I wondered what other tricks he had waiting. As we both stood up, the dog ran off into the mist that was now very thick, too thick to see the sky or the trees. This made me nervous.

The Fool Seer must have sensed that. He said, "Think of this mist as a curtain or a veil. This will be of assistance to the other world workings."

I was not sure where he was going with this. I was lost in the mist! I saw that he put his small sack over his shoulder once more. I thought to myself, All his possessions in one small pack, and the Fool travels and knows not where. I looked up to the sky. Through the clouds there was a slight glimmer of the sun, but then I dashed to catch up with the Seer. I certainly did not want to be left here on this hill in the mist of a curtain or veil by myself!

Now the dog had returned, fiercer than he was earlier.

The Seer said, "Ah! So filled with daydreaming, sometimes am I, there may be something that I have to be made aware of. That is when this fellow comes in handy! Right now he harries us to be aware of the cliff, as we are likely to fall over if we do not stop in our tracks now!"

"What do you mean?" I said to the Seer.

He answered with, "Well, my dear Dreamer, we are literally at the edge of the cliffs. Should we take another step, we will fall into the abyss!" With that the Seer spread out his arm in front of me, making me stop!

I took a deep breath, and my heart was racing as I said, "Oh My!" I looked down and saw a few pebbles fall from beneath my feet. I could hear them skipping below. I could hear the Seer talking to the dog; he was thanking him. I had stepped quite a distance backward from the cliff edge. Now I realized he was addressing me. I had trouble understanding his words, or I did not want to hear them.

"Dreamer!" he was saying, "come stand at the edge with me. We can talk of what it is you seek."

As much as my legs trembled, my speaking voice did even more! "Stand at the edge? Are you mad! You are a mad Fool!" I answered and did not budge from where I was.

The Fool Seer was laughing now. I did not find this funny and was silent. After a moment, I realized what I said may have caused offense and started to say so.

He was already at my side, saying, "Do not worry, Dreamer. I will not let anything happen to you, and certainly we will not do anything you are not ready for!"

Of course I was curious about that "ready for" comment, and I knew I wanted to be ready for everything at this time on my dreaming path. This did not help a lot with the emotion of fear I was experiencing now. Thinking a moment before speaking, I realized how clever this Seer was. Finally, mustering up my courage, I said, "OK! You got me with that! What is it I am not ready for? Because, guess what? I am! There. I have said it!" I held my breath for what seemed like forever. Then I felt his hand in mine.

He spoke softly. "I am taking you to the edge." We walked a few steps; I could not believe I was following him! I was not my self. The Fool Seer said, "Not only am I taking you literally to the edge of the cliff but also symbolically. When we started out this day, you wanted to know what it was you were seeking, correct?"

My answer was a quiet "Yes. OK!"

He replied, "A Dreamer's journey most often begins with the Fool, who is busily traveling into the unknown. In the esoteric circles, the Fool is a symbol of wisdom and enlightenment, often shown as an androgynous figure of a soul about to step into the abyss, before he becomes a human form! Once we are ready to be at the edge of a cliff, the Seeker finds it easier to meet his Dreams! Like a metaphor for anything you may desire in life, if you simply just chase after it, it may evade you. So approach this cliff with open arms and joy, and your dreams will rush to meet you!"

The Seer had paused both in his talk and with the walk! I knew we were right at the cliff's edge. I held his hand tightly and tried to calm my breathing without much success.

The Seer then said, "The Fool is the beginning and the end of everything! That is why his number is the 'zero'—the sacred zero, the continual circle without end!"

I realized I was a bit calmer but wondered what would happen next!

Coming back from my dream thoughts, I heard, "Do you trust me?" Now I was definitely worried again! I did not answer.

The Seer did the answering. "OK! I know you are nervous. However, with just a little faith, we can open amazing new vistas. I would like us to sit down here on the edge of this very solid, rocky cliff, because we will be doing some Dream Journey work, and this is the perfect spot for us to do this!"

I love to Dream Journey. It is my favorite thing, and I am very good at it too! He had me! I felt stronger and answered him, "OK. I do trust you!"

He answered in a heartbeat, "Good! Good, let's sit down here."

He helped me to sit on the rocks that somehow felt cool and reassuring. We sat then in silence for awhile, our legs dangling over the rocky edge of the cliff. I thought about the vastness of the abyss below; a shiver went down my spine. Just then the Seer pointed in front of us. The clouds had been clearing; we watched together as the sun plunged into the misty sea below. I was now much more relaxed; I felt like a very brave soul, sitting on the edge of the abyss. It was exhilarating. I commented to the Fool Seer that I felt as if I could do anything. That is, until I would have to stand back up!

The Seer replied, "When we work with the various images of my tarot Trump, the Fool, we can begin to see that we are evoking stages of the shamanic journey as well as aspects of the shaman in his community. The Fool, for example, may represent the neophyte."

"Well, I suppose that neophyte might just be me today!" I answered cheerfully.

He replied, "I think you may be right. Are you ready to jump into the abyss?"

I froze instantly. "Are you mad?" I cried.

The Seer answered, "I thought we already established that!" He was brave and important in his look, quite unlike his usual expression. I nearly fainted. "*No!* No, my dear. Just kidding! But it is time to Dream Journey! How would you like to go to a special carnival?"

Finally breathing, I answered joyfully, "Why of course! Where is it held?" I asked him.

"It is held here on the Nemeton, each year in December," he replied with a funny kind of smirk.

"December! But it is summer, not December!" I answered curtly.

"Ah! Dreamer, you are on the magic land of the Nemeton. There is no time here; we can shift to whichever timespan we need, and that is the beauty of our work, little one! You may want to think on that when you have time!" He laughed at that. I guess he thought it a funny play on words.

"Well, let the journeys begin!" I said to him, trying to lighten up.

"All right then," he replied. "I arranged with the Hierophant Seer to be our intent, our focal point. He is already at the carnival. Just picture that magenta robe he likes to wear and that elaborate hat. These will act like an antennae for us."

Just then the Eagle swooped in front of us, and we heard her high-pitched cry.

"Music to my ears!" said the Seer. "The Eagle, of course, will be our guardian for our dream flight. Such a nice way to travel, don't you think?"

I really did not know what to think! So much was happening; I just wanted to make sure I arrived at the same carnival as the Fool Seer. Mentioning this to him, he said, of course he would be looking after me. I was not so sure, but I nodded my head yes! We sat in silence as he again gave me the carnival description and that of the Hierophant. Then out of his sack, he pulled a drum. I thought it hard to believe it fit into that small sack on his staff. But there it was, and the drumming was fine!

The last thing I remember was closing my eyes and feeling the cool breeze on my skin. I wondered if I was flying in my dream. The next thing I knew, I heard the drum's three-signal beat, a reminder to return from the journey. And there I was in another reality of the Middle Ages! I thought to myself, the Fool Seer said we would be on the lands of the Nemeton and it would be December. I was not sure about all that, but then I heard someone calling me. "Dreamer! Dreamer!" A tall man in an outlandish hat was waving for me to come to where he was. I was walking down a cobblestone narrow street, there were people everywhere, and I had the feeling I might know some of them. I did not see the Fool Seer. I sure hoped he was arriving at the same carnival. We had come to know each other, and I did not want to lose that connection. Besides, he still needed to tell me why we were even at a carnival!

There were people hawking wares of all kinds, very aggressively. I wasn't interested but did enjoy their period costumes. Now I was close enough to hear the man call me again.

"Dreamer, hello! I am glad you have arrived safely! Come! Oh! I see you have the basket with the feathers. Perfect! We shall be using them very soon. You do remember me, I trust? I am The Hierophant Seer. But of course you do! Come, we will find a quiet place to sip a drink and talk while we wait for our dear Fool Seer!"

I recognized his magenta robe and just followed him through another winding, narrow street. I did answer his questions, but with all the noise and movement, I was not sure he heard. I scampered to keep up with him, almost stepping on his magenta and gold robes at one point. Slowing down to his stride then, I looked at the basket with the feathers. I was not even aware I had it with me! I made a note to myself to pay more attention to details; I might need to know something after all. It was not smart to be so dazed while doing this Dream work; one of the Seers had told me this already.

We arrived at a small garden in front of a quaint inn. We seated ourselves at a table with red rose bushes behind it; they were in beautiful, full bloom. Curious for December, I thought. Looking about, I scanned for details and noted three other tables. One table had two men sipping from large mugs; beer, I supposed. A friendly barmaid came over to see what we would like. The Hierophant Seer ordered beer for us both. I almost objected but decided I might as well go with the flow of this medieval village and carnival. Finally relaxing some, I looked to the Hierophant Seer.

Apparently he was observing me, because he said, "I know you must be confused. You are a trooper, dear Dreamer and, I am told, a fast learner as well. I do hope you are feeling a little more grounded after your jump from the cliffs!"

I looked at him in total shock! "Jump! I did not jump! We used our Dream journey to come to the carnival!" I said quite indignantly.

"Of course you did. Well, no matter!" He seemed to think this quite funny. "The point is," he said, "you have arrived. I would like to tell you about an 'initiatory story,' one where there are final obstacles through which one must pass without hesitation before the portal gate closes. I am reminded of the treacherous clashing cliffs of Symplegades, which 'Jason and the Argonauts' needed to pass. Jason, with the aid of a goddess to the Argonauts, was able to slip their ship through the rocks just before the rocks slammed shut on their ship *Argo*'s stern ornament! Jason used his inner attention to his calling and had an amazing initiation going through that portal!"

I wondered about what the Seer was telling me, not really understanding. More importantly, I did not want to miss catching up with the Fool Seer and so decided to ask about him. "Will the Fool Seer be joining us here?" I asked rather nonchalantly.

The Ancient One answered me immediately. "Oh, yes! He will be a little while collecting the things he needs but will most assuredly be here!" He was smiling and jovial as he spoke. Continuing, he said, "For now, I would like to present you with a little background, so please sip your beer and sit back some to hear my tale!"

I complied with what he said but did wonder how long before the Fool Seer would appear.

The Hierophant Seer began. "The Fool can be related to the gods/goddesses of Greek myth, like Dionysus/Bacchus and Dianus/Diana. The figure may be portrayed as a man or a woman or an androgynous figure. The Fool, or sometimes called the Idiot, represents the irrepressible vital spirit, overflowing and charging across the landscape, carving new pathways. In ancient Greece the word 'Idiot' comes from the Latin, 'Idiota,' meaning a person concerned only with his private affairs, a person or commoner with no interest in public affairs, who is assumed to be ignorant and unskilled. For our purposes, the 'Idiot' represents an ordinary person living in a private world, whether through ignorance, insanity, or rugged individualism, but then by sheer chance is given the opportunity to be:

Saturnalicius Princeps, which means the Carnival King!"

I had been mildly listening, I realized. But now I was really intrigued. Because I knew that the Seer meant that my dear Fool Seer was to be the Carnival King, and that seemed grand!

I knew that the Hierophant Seer could tell that he had attracted my interest, as he continued with his tale. "Well, dear Dreamer, this is why we have come. This is a special event held at the end of December. The seventeenth through the twenty-third of each year. A king is honored for one week at the Carnival of Saturnalia, honoring the god Saturn. This is quite an event; the one chosen is truly admired!"

I looked at the Seer with such fascination and joy; I could barely speak. I said to him in rapid speech, "The Fool Seer will be the Carnival King for this week? Is this what you are saying?"

He answered in a sing-song voice, "There you have it!"

I was so excited I jumped up and said, "Is there something I should be helping him do? I mean, does he need me to fix his robes or something? What about a crown? Kings usually have a crown, you know!" I had been pacing back and forth.

The Seer stood up and then guided me back to my seat, telling me there was more information he should share. He did tell me how nice it was to be excited for the Fool and there would be plenty I could help with. Finally I simmered down.

He continued, "Now it should be noted that the one selected, who becomes the Carnival King, is expected to take on a conscious, intentional step into the irrational, into many chaotic circumstances where all rules are broken. This becomes a teaching for those who follow the tarot, for when we follow the Fool through his journey, he then allows us to also escape our own self-imposed bounds! This break from convention is actually very good for our psychological health." The Seer had paused and looked to me as if to see what I thought.

I then chimed in, asking, "What do you mean, 'where all rules are broken'? I am not sure how that is something beneficial!"

The Hierophant Seer stood and then led me again to my chair. He said, "It is too early to come to any conclusions or benefits just yet. Please do be patient, Dreamer, and listen awhile longer!"

I realized I was making judgments, and winced. I just politely nodded my head yes!

"Often the Fool, the Idiot, is described as whistling in the images. This represents the spirit of vitality. The word 'Fool' comes from the Latin 'Follis,' meaning fool or windbag! The word originally meant bellows. So the Fool is a source of air, of breath, spititus, the unfettered 'vital spirit'! In the Qabalah, according to Gareth Knight, The Fool has the element of 'Air' attributed to him. 'Air,' the spirit of the 'Fool,' is unconfined and it permeates all things.

"Let us think a moment about that in relation to our lives today. There are times in our lives when customary thought patterns have outlived their usefulness. So the time may come when the 'Divine Maniac' is needed! We then can call upon the Fool, and he steps in to be king, for only so much madness can be tolerated! And we are able to undergo needed transformations."

"In Greek and Roman myth, 'The Idiot,' 'The Fool,' is represented by Dionysus, son of Zeus and Semele—for Greeks, Dionysus, and for Romans, Bacchus—the God of Wine. He came by his 'Holy Foolishness' when he was driven mad by the Goddess Hera, Goddess of Woman and Marriage and also the wife of Zeus. She was jealous of Semele, Dionysus's mother tricking them both. Dionysus came to be known as the 'Maniac' for he possessed 'Furor Divinus,' meaning 'Divine Madness'!"

The Hierophant Seer had stopped, with a twinkle in his eyes. I was smiling and said, "I do love this Fool! I even called him mad earlier today! How nice to learn his history. And I see the Greeks had very complicated relationships. Now I'm beginning to understand his makeup."

The Seer replied, "I am so glad to see you comprehend this foolishness, Dreamer!" He laughed and smacked his hand to his knee, apparently thinking this was very funny. I guess I did too, and I laughed along with him.

Just then there was commotion near the gate of the inn, and we heard barking. Next the dog that was the companion to the Fool came scampering over to our table. I petted him a minute, and he took off toward the gate. The Hierophant Seer commented, "Where the dog goes, so goes his master."

Looking in the direction of the Seer's arm pointing toward the gate, there came the Fool Seer with the dog right at his heels. We both got up to greet him, and he was happy to see us.

The Fool Seer, giving me a hug, said, "I see you have met my dear friend The Hierophant Seer! This Seer and I have had a strong allegiance over time, and we have both been part of the Delphic Oracles!" He was patting the other Ancient One on his shoulder. They smiled and shook hands.

The Hierophant Seer said, "The Fool has taught me well and, at times, shown me the importance of exempting oneself from the rules of one's current game!"

I wondered about that comment a minute, as we were in new territory in the life of the Fool. As I looked at these two, I was feeling such appreciation of my training here at the Nemeton. Suddenly, I remembered how we had dreamed ourselves back through a time warp and we were now in a medieval village that was bustling with a carnival! Incredible! I focused myself to what was being said by the two Seers. But I also noticed that the Fool now no longer was dressed in blue jeans and a contemporary chambray shirt. No! He now belonged to the times we were in and had on a colorful tunic in a burnt orange color embroidered with the symbol of Uranus with wide, bouncing sleeves. And he wore tights and soft doeskin boots. I supposed wherever he had been was to the costume shop. He had placed on the wooden table a large satchel in which he was rummaging. Next thing I knew, he had pulled out a beautiful gown of red and yellow silk; draping this over his arm, he told me this was for me, as I would be escorting him through the carnival!

I was speechless! Finally I held the gown to myself and said, "This is like a fairy tale! Thank you. I would be honored to wear this and escort you, but I know nothing of these affairs. You will have to help me through, please! Oh! Here is the basket I brought with the feathers." I moved the basket next to where he had set his staff with the sack tied upon it.

The Fool and the Hierophant Seer both said I had plenty of time to prepare, as I had expressed some anxiety at that. First they told me we would prepare the Crown for the Fool!

I blurted out, "Oh! I want to help with that. Crowns are essential for the Carnival King!"

Both the Seers looked at each other with a suppressed kind of laugh. Something was up.

"Well, Dreamer, hand that basket over here, if you please!" said the Hierophant Seer." The Fool had moved a chair in front of his friend and was smoothing out his hair, and he then sat down in the chair.

I said, "What will you do with these feathers?"

Both said in unison, "Watch and listen!"

The Fool had spread the feathers out onto the table and was straightening them. I could tell this might take awhile, and I sat down to watch and listen.

The Hierophant Seer began another tale. "Over time there have been many painted tarot Fool images with feathers being worn in the hair of the Fool. Possibly indicating a sign of folly, some say feathers in the hair indicate foolishness and feeble-mindedness, even an air-head! Perhaps the oldest surviving tarot deck, from the mid-fifteenth century, is the Visconti-Sforza Tarot which has the image of 'The Fool,' the idiot with seven feathers in his hair. A sign of folly? Some say. However, Herodotus, the Greek historian from the fifth century, tells of the 'Carnival of Saturnalia,' and there the Carnival King wears a crown of feathers. He wears one for each day of the week and, at the end of each day, removes the feather for that day. This is also done at the time of Lent."

I had been sipping my cold beer, but could not resist an interruption! "Why? Whatever are these feathers for?" I said, picking up the list of the feathers the Fool Seer had given me earlier. I was very confused!

The Hierophant Seer said, "Oh! There is much to learn here, dear Dreamer, but I do enjoy your enthusiasm!" I did not think that funny, but they certainly did.

He continued with the feather story. "Feathers, because of their lightness and association with birds, which are symbols for the soul, symbolize the heavens and that which ascends to heaven. This includes the soul and truth. Feathers, as you may know, are widely used by shamans, which assist them through their ascent through the heavens in their journey work."

Now the Hierophant Seer had picked up some of the feathers. He said quietly, as if to himself, "Yes, the Eagle feather. As today is Sunday, the color is gold, the golden day of the sun." Then he placed this feather into the hair of the Fool Seer!

The Hierophant Seer now held the Dove feather, then he said, "This feather of the Dove is for the color silver, but sometimes the Owl feather is used. It is for the Moon, and, of course, its day is Monday!" He placed that feather into the hair of the Fool Seer. Now he held another and said, "This Cardinal feather is the vibrant color red. Its planet is that of Mars, and its day is Tuesday. In the Waite tarot deck, painted by Pamela Coleman-Smith, the Fool's cap has a red feather, a plume of fire, relating to the Sun above and the Mars energy of the warrior, a conduit for true Divine Fire."

I could not help myself and said, "This is amazing. I love this stuff! Look how great the crown is shaping up!"

Just then the Fool Seer got up, pulled out a hand mirror from his satchel, and then proceeded to admire himself. He smiled this way and that, saying, "The mirror knows how to show me off!" We all laughed.

The Hierophant Seer continued with the other feathers, and when he had the seventh one in his hand, he said this: "This is the pure feather of the Swan. Its color is white, which holds all other colors, and the planet it aligns with is Saturn, who rules as the father of time. And, of course, the day is Saturday! The beautiful Swan, the bird of transformation, has a constellation named for her called 'Cygnus' within our home of the Milky Way."

Then the Seer placed the last feather of the Swan into the hair of the Fool Seer, saying, "Ah! How grand! Your crown is complete!"

The Fool Seer looked into the mirror once more, saying, "Yes! A marvelous crown for the Carnival King! What do you think, Dreamer?" He was looking straight at me.

Of course I answered very excitedly, "Why, it is wonderful. I love it. A perfect crown of seven feathers!" I went over to check and touch each one.

The Hierophant Seer said, looking the Fool directly into his eyes, "Now remember each day of this carnival will come to an end, and then gradually the seven feathers will be removed; one for each day from your Fool's head! When the last feather, the white Swan feather of Saturn/Saturday is removed at the end of 'Saturnalia,' you will no longer be king and will then don the cloak of a beggar to show that you have now transformed to the 'Pure Fool.' And of course you will now again assume the role of an ordinary 'Idiot'!"

The Fool turned to me, studied my face a moment, and said, "Do not look so sad, Dreamer. Being an 'Idiot' is not a bad thing! And as you shall discover during this week of Carnival, we will meet and learn from each of the tarot Trump Seers along the way, and I intend to encompass those energies!"

I laughed a little, and said, "I guess my face is showing sadness, but you must realize I am a product of contemporary culture. Not many know of the history of the 'Idiot,' and many have a negative connotation of that word."

He answered with, "This may be true, Dreamer, but this is why you are here to study and learn and to help change people's perceptions, even if just a little! Let me give you some more history with which you can continue to build upon with your Dream Healing Path.

"The Fool is about change, taking risks, having faith, trusting that you will be cradled. He is the archetypal journeyer who moves through all the Trumps, 'I' through 'XXI.' The Fool represents our own internal journeyer on our path through life. He emerges from the abyss and begins his travel through the Trumps to understand the mysteries of life. However, he proceeds without desire and without thinking. He is moving through layers of his psyche. The first archetype he meets is the 'Magician I.' From him he learns about the ability to create, with the waving of his magician's wand, making patterns of reality! Journeying forward he learns from each Seer. He does this not as one who is ego driven but as one following and enjoying his life path!"

"Oh, Seer! How beautiful! I have so much to learn."

He answered quickly, "It will come, dear Dream Seeker, it will!"

I looked across the table to the Hierophant; he was quietly smiling and petting the dog, nodding his head.

The Fool Seer said he had a few more things before we finished preparing for the carnival.

"There are other viewpoints of the energies and personality of the Fool. As you become more versed, you will know when which view is appropriate for each tarot reading circumstance. Beneath the garment of the Fool is the substance, of which the jester is but a shadow that sees the world as a Mardi Gras, a pageantry of divine sparks masked in the garb of fools! The Fool as I am, the number zero, shows me as a circle and represents all possibility. In the circle of all that is, the Fool is whole. Some even say 'holy.' I trust and I am innocent, operating out of perfect faith. The zero is the great unmanifest consciousness of which everything is created. The zero contains all other numbers."

The Fool Seer had been pacing back and forth around our table. He was very worked up during his unfolding speech. As he became silent, he then sat down and smoothed out his hair in between the feather crown. He was a handsome man with an ageless face and gave the impression of a true zest for life. It was easy to be around him; it was healing.

Now the Hierophant Seer said he had a couple of things to add. Smiling at us both, he continued. "You will enjoy this, Dreamer! The French title for the Fool card is 'Le Mat' and is commonly thought to be derived from the Italian 'Il Matto,' the madman. But the word 'Le Mat' also applies to chess as the 'Mate' or 'Checkmate.' The word 'Checkmate' is derived from the Persian and actually means 'The King is Dead'! Now this is not to make one worry; this simply means that the fully evolved Spirit actually now returns to the 'Unmanifest,' as he is dead and must now begin again! This also reminds us that Spirit's aim continually reminds us to be grounded and rooted in our dear Mother Earth who renews us without any thought for herself!"

I replied to the Hierophant Seer in a very triumphant voice, "This is amazing! I will remember that as a bumper sticker at the end of the Saturnalia Carnival and say 'Checkmate' just as the Fool pulls out his last feather of the White Swan!"

Both the Seers laughed and told me that would make a grand finish! Then they hurried me off with the barmaid to change into my beautiful gown.

As I walked back through the ancient inn of this medieval city, I felt like a princess in my beautiful silk gown, with my hair done up very fancy. I walked slowly and put this all into my dream memory bank. Such a wonderful feeling. I could hardly wait to see what the carnival would be like! I now realized that the Fool Trump card might well be the most profound symbol in the tarot. His image brings to mind the court jester, the trickster, and the clown of the modern circus. I had even learned that it was OK to sometimes break the rules and take risks. This was big for me!

When I got to the courtyard, I heard music floating over the railings and gate. There was magic in the air, the sun was at midday, and the Eagle cried, beckoning us to begin! There on the table was the staff and sack of the Fool's. The two Seers both stood near the table and turned when I approached.

The Hierophant gave a quiet applause, saying, "Bravo! Bravo! We have a true Dream Princess in our midst!" I blushed and could not say a thing.

Then the Fool Seer bowed to me, saying in very beautiful speech, "I am so honored, my lady!"

Again my face colored, but I managed to curtsey to them, saying, "I thank you, dear sirs! It is I who am honored by you both!"

"Now," said the Hierophant Seer, "the sack, the bag. You can not forget this!" Giving it over to the Fool Seer, he added, "There are some who say the Fool carries his wisdom in this sack over his shoulders and can retrieve whatever he may need. Other occultists attribute the bag to carrying the four suits of the tarot, which he has at his command if he so chooses!" With a big broad smile, the Hierophant Seer said, "You two make a beautiful couple posed in front of the roses! But you had better be off. I will, of course, see you at the carnival as you journey!"

"Oh!" I exclaimed. "I would like to give you one of the roses!" I ran over and picked one for the Fool and for myself. I could not resist!

Taking it from my hand, the Fool gave me a hug. Then in the Fool's most poetic voice, he relayed this: "He saw the Garden of Eden…and came to a tall, dark tree…and was told to go up near the top of the tree a beautiful woman, like a Goddess of Life…gave him a rose."

A tear sprang to my eye, I was touched. The Fool Seer stood holding the Rose under his nose.

Luckily the Hierophant Seer knew my feelings and said, "I do believe that was said by William Butler Yeats in one of his poems. He was highly influenced by this flower and often used it in his writings, He was, as you may know, an Irish poet and dramatist in the twentieth century, and he was also a part of the occultist Golden Dawn. In fact, the Rose is positioned at the top of the tree in the Golden Dawn Tarot System!" The Hierophant Seer looked at me.

I gave him a huge smile of gratitude, shaking my head a little, I was feeling more composed.

Offering my hand to the Fool Trump Seer, and very much feeling like a Dream Princess, I then said, "Shall we?"

He answered sweetly, "But of course!"

THE MAGICIAN

DREAM OF THE TRUMP SEER: THE MAGICIAN I

you have invited me into your life by choosing my image now. By chance? Maybe. I think not!

Is the energy shifting in your life? Have you decisions to make? Are you listless, bored? Maybe on a holding pattern or stuck with something? Certainly you daydream of new wealth, people, excitement, jobs, and places? Maybe these dream thoughts stay only in your head, and many of us are only going through the motions in life. Feeling void with no sparks in life. Bodies, bones just walking around and around.

What image did you choose? The Magician!

I am the one who has the tools to live a life with passion. Now, in this moment, you will change the energy! Recognize this and you are in the realm of The Magician! Whether you are a new Dreamer or a veteran Dreamer, the Dream journey with the Magician will help you.

* To begin, please hold the Keeper Dream Image of The Magician. Look into the picture. I, the Magician, will guide you.

I invite the Elemental Spirits to sit with me at my Magician's table. Listen closely now. I will set my space this way. You may do likewise!

* I invite the Spirits of:

* Water—"Suit of Cups"—Sprinkle water from a metal bowl.

* Fire—"Suit of Wands"—Light a candle.

* Air—"Suit of Swords"—Open a window to the wind/air.

* Earth—"Suit of Pentacles"—Add a plant and touch it with a quartz crystal.

I honor these Elementals of Spirits! The water is a part of me; I am a part of the water.

The fire is a part of me; I am a part of the fire. The air is a part of me; I am a part of the air.

The earth is a part of me; I am a part of the earth. "We are one! I thank the Spirits!"

In our Dream journey we have now traveled to the Nemeton, and we are gathered in the Grove. All of us are sitting at the Magician's table; the expectations of energy are building. It is awesome to be with the Spirits of Water-Cups, Fire-Wands, Air-Swords, and Earth-Pentacles.

I am gifting you each with a special feather; please hold this awhile. Begin to detect the energy flows with this feather. As you hold it, move it about your body, feel where your energy is the lowest in your body. Which elemental spirit is it? Fire Spirit of Wands, the light of spirit in your heart? Or, Air Spirit of Swords, the winds of change or worry in your mind? Maybe yours is the Water Spirit of Cups, spirit of water our emotional barometer, the water lapping you about in the seas of life. Are tears of joy or sadness marking your cheek? Could it be you feel the energy from the Earth Spirit of Pentacles, calling you for nourishment…a sapling that is underfed in some part of you. Or a part that has become overgrown and needs pruning and release.

Let the feather detect which area needs healing on your body. The feather will find the energy flow. Hold it and decide which elemental spirit is there wanting healing.

See the door open to Spirit in your mind's eye. Daydream here for a moment, and ask for information. Have you been hurt by someone or something? Have you hurt someone or something? Ask now! For help to release the pain or guilt, we must clear the path first, before the magic can happen. There must be release, and we do this through the Elemental Spirits. Now please go to the place you detected on your body that felt low; this is where you are loosing your vital energy. For whichever area you have detected with your feather, decide if it is Spirit of Water-Cups, Spirit of Fire-Wands, Spirit of Air-Swords, or Spirit of Earth-Pentacles; which one? Ask your feather to help you; swish, move the energy spirit you have detected. Move it out! Using strong brisk strokes, ask your feather to assist you.

Now ask for help from your higher self, and ask for the Spirit of All to strengthen you. Dream the threads of health weaving into this place on your body. Dream them strong. Ask the elemental spirit to weave your aura into wholeness. Be thankful and rest.

Pick up your metal bowl of water now and put your quartz crystal into it. Take a minute to select a plant, flower, or herb that you are drawn too. This will call your attention to Earth and earthly things. Put this plant on your magician's table. Asking permission of the plant, pick a small leaf to work with and hold this a moment.

In your Dream you have now become the magician, and you are about changing things into what you would like to have and need. Think! Think very hard on what that is for you. Be very specific. What is it you want to come to pass?

Thinking of this specific intention, tear the leaf from your chosen plant into small pieces. Put these pieces into the metal bowl of water, and add the crystal. This is the elemental Spirit of Water-Cups.

Dream gazing into the water; weigh all the steps of your designated intention. Dream all the possible scenarios. Dream with the plant leaf, the crystal, and the water. Look at the light in your candle. Dream with the light. Breathe the air. Dream with the air. Dream with all these Spirits!

Dream your prayer of intention to your higher self, as to what you want. Make a decision without any hesitation. There must be NO DOUBT!

* BE CLEAR WITH INTENT! Look into the Fire Spirit of Wands in your candle. Realize that the person who wants this to manifest is you. This is enough if you do this doggedly! It gets through to your higher self, and the Spirit of All assists the intent.

Begin to notice the clearing in yourself now; notice if there is more passion in your being. Looking about the Magician's table of spirits that you have set up, decide which elemental spirit feels strong to you now. Which one is calling? Is it Fire Spirit of Wands? Which one?

Call in this spirit; ask for its help and assistance. Do it now!

Offer a Dream prayer to this spirit, and present the spirit a gift offering. Maybe a flower or a pinch of tobacco or lavender. All the while, look into the Fire Spirit of Wands in your candle. Begin to DREAM…Gaze at the old path being torn away.

Do you need help from the "Air Spirit of Swords," slicing, swishing through the air, and cutting away the old path? Or the "Water Spirit of Cups," moving the waves over the old path of emotions, cleaning them out?

Again ask for help from the Spirits. Dream gaze into the bowl of water and the plant pieces floating there. Begin to see new paths shaping as you move the bowl of water. What do you see in these new shapes forming? Take a few minutes dreaming with these new shapes of possibilities. Let this new energy take hold and help you begin to dream the new dream for yourself. Dream journey to the new future path you have chosen. Because you were very clear on your intent earlier; this will be of help now, making it easier to "See Your Future Dream"! Intent is everything; it is what gives us passion in life. If there is anything that needs changing in your Dream, do it now! If there is any harm that is hurtful to others, mend this now. We are in Dream dress rehearsal, and you are in charge. Run your rehearsal and see how it plays. Is it truth and good to those concerned? Make your changes now. As the Magician, I lead you and I protect you. You are in my realm for now, and you have become your own Magician. But shortly you will move on to earthly pursuits and into future dream worlds. My question is this: are you sure about the choices you have made? You are the Magician now for these future events, the ones you were just dreaming and saw in your bowl of water. Be clear with your choices.

You must decide now if you have done the correct dreaming of magic for yourself. There must be no harm done to any involved, be it human, animal, plant, or spirit. You must be certain! There is only a small window of time before the wheel moves again. Once you are certain, we will proceed.

We will journey deeper, Dreamer; as it is time to set your INTENT WITH A DREAM PRAYER! You choose for yourself what should be said. Ask for help from the Elemental Spirits and your guides. In the Dreaming see for yourself AN ACTION PLAN! Ask for details in the Dream of this future event. Come back now, dear Dreamer! You have done your work as a Magician should! Write everything into your journal. Now is the time to HONOR the Dream, to hold the information in a physical way. Draw the dream events that you have seen, and weave these tapestries of events into something concrete. Buy, find, or make a small totem or amulet to hold and honor this dream energy. Thank the Elemental Spirits, of the water, the plant, the crystal, the candle, the air, and your breath. Think of the magic that has transferred into your crystal, and put it into your pocket. Give the water to the plant and wind. Give the fires' light to the night.

* Give thanks and let it be so!

Now, Dreamer, to be clear, I, the Magician, align with many great ones. Hermes, Mercury, Cronos, and Saturn are only a few. I am psycho pomp, and I am able to lead souls across boundaries into new realms. As a Keeper, I am one of the four 'agents of transformation'; the others being: Fortune X, Hermit IX, and Star XVI. I am the teacher one encounters just when they're most needed by you, or when you are ready for understanding. I am the source that leads to a path of change. I am the mediator who is responsible for transforming evil into good.

As you slowly come back from the Dream Journey of the magical place of the Magician's Realm, look into your Dream Keeper Image of the Ancient One-The Magician. Breathe deeply now into your own being, honoring the magical energy that has transpired. Remember you have now had some Dream training with the Magician and are coming to understand that you can be your own Magician in your own right through the workings of your Dreams! Very powerful information has been acquired; hold this so you may build upon what you have learned even as you realize you are here now on the earthly plane. Your path has changed; you have encountered the Magician and will forevermore live with magic and passion in this life!

* MAY IT BE SO!

HIGH PRIESTESS

DREAM OF THE TRUMP SEER:
THE HIGH PRIESTESS II

"Good afternoon, Dreamers!" She said graciously as she moved around the Grove. Everyone was instantly captivated by her beauty, of course, but it was more than that. She gave us the sense of knowing exactly who she was as the High Priestess Seer! But in addition she was able to interact with us all on a grounded level of a Dreamer who is of the Earth, doing what is required to balance us all. She was in command and we loved it!

The High Priestess Seer speaks:

"Dreamers, as a part of your training here today, you will need to know what my reflecting and influencing energy consists of. 'Uniting Intelligence' and 'Essence of Glory' are foremost. I am about the Principles of intuition, self-care, resourcefulness, and integrity. And I am able to hold an inner oasis of source along with the sun and moon. As an Ancient Keeper, 'The High Priestess II' is number two in the sacred Grove. I am the 'Priestess of the Silver Star'!

"I am Earth, Air, Fire, Water, and Spirit. I am the fountainhead found by the moon's light in the desert. I am pure source. Go to the fountainhead to know me. I am your Inner Oasis.

"As you view the tree of life, in the Qabalah I am the Thirteenth path. It is the vertical path of 'The Arrow,' the long path between Spirit and Earth. I am the way of the mystic, who seeks not the manipulation of occult powers but Union with God.

"'Luna,' the moon, is always at my fingertips; she is my symbol. The comb symbol upon my book of wisdom is the 'Energy of the Goddess.' The Goddess is naturally about feminine components: receptiveness and regeneration and the unconscious mind. I use my comb often, combing out psychic tangles of situations, events, or beings. I know about protection, and my transparent veil about my face shields me. It must never be raised before the profane."

The High Priestess Seer stood perfectly still in one spot near the altar of the Grove as she spoke to all the Dreamers. She wore a delicate dress of blue, but I knew this woman was not a fragile lady. Her veil draped over her face was spun of silver transparent threads that sparkled in the afternoon light. Her delicate hands were folded in front of her skirts; her demeanor was friendly but very much in control. After a short pause, she continued.

"My station in the ancient worlds and into contemporary worlds is that of High Priestess. You must know she has always been here, throughout time. You may recognize her by many names, including Isis, Egyptian Goddess of Intuition. The cobra is another of her symbols, with the dynamics of the snake's energy of regeneration. I am the Priestess of the Silver Star-Isis."

"There are other classical names you may know me by: The Oriental Goddess, Kuan Yin, Goddess of Compassion, and Gaea, Demeter, Delphi, and Cyble to mention a few. The Greek Goddess Artemis is the Virgin Goddess of the Hunt and the Moon. I am very much aligned with her. The Roman Goddess Diana is her counterpart; like Isis, Artemis/Diana have come to mean the many energies of the feminine. The Goddess Artemis has often been depicted carrying a pouch of sacred arrows, as she was the huntress who protected animals. The goddess is also a tree, a bear, and the moon. She is 'Woman' moving through the different characters of her life. In Greece at her Temple of Ephesus, she was served by chaste priestesses called 'Mellisai' or 'Bees' and also by eunuch priests. The most popular festival of the Goddess Artemis was held at the Full of the Moon. Worshipers gathered in the wood and gave themselves to her power and to anonymous mating."

"The Goddess Artemis was the guardian of the gate of birth, the divine midwife, and was invoked for assistance in childbirth. 'Goddess Artemis' is referred to as 'The Bear-Ursa Major,' the star constellation. 'The Great She Bear-Artemis' is the guardian of the Pole Star, which is the 'Axis Mundi.' Many refer to Artemis-Diana as 'Alma-Mater,' which means 'Soul Mother.'

"Artemis is also equated with the Christian Virgin Mary, goddess of the bear. She is referred to in Latin as 'Stella Maris'-'The Star of the Sea.' The Sumerian root word of 'Mar' means 'sea and womb'; the name Mary comes from this. 'The Virgin Mary,' the return to one's self, one's inner oasis. Early tarot cards illustrated the High Priestess II as Pope Joan. The female pope! Joan of Arc, some might say! The thirteenth day every month is 'Sacred to Mary'; Mary's Day."

The Seer came to silence and moved to one side of the Grove, where I noticed curtains were set up in front of a small platform. Two Keepers were there as she arrived and pulled each blue silk curtain back one to each side, clasping them with gold braided-rope tassels. There on the small, slightly raised platform were two columns: one white, one black; each one had a silver star on its top. Cushions were arranged, and there she found a place to sit down between the two columns. It was a beautiful scene, but of course the beauty emanated from within this High Priestess. I could hear the sound of the water flowing from the nearby sea. Everything was in readiness. The Seer picked up her book she had there, and I noticed a snake that was calmly coiled next to her. She then she lifted the veil from her face and continued her tale.

"This recent Dream is my gift to you as the High Priestess. I relay it now to you for Dream Journey: *Becoming a Priestess*."

A voice, strong and raspy, is calling is it the wind? You hear howling and blowing while the sea slaps against the shoreline. A rhythm, you think, and you notice a pattern from the receding tides. Again a voice is calling in the wind; but now it is clear, and you hear, 'I am the High Priestess. I am made of Universal Goddess wisdom. Follow me. Follow me to my cave by the sea.' You are sure that you heard this, and again you listen, but the voice is gone.

"Walking against the wind, a Dreamer is there, standing in the shallow tide water, leaning on her staff. She motions for us to gather about her. We are a small group of six or eight. Pointing now to the rocky shore line, she says, 'You will recognize the two strong pillars once there!' Pointing to the entrance to the cave, she continues, 'The Pillars are her supports, a part of her strength. The tops are crowned with silver stars,' she says. There is a hush now. We listen to the waves pounding the rocky coast. Squishing sand between your toes, you feel nervous but excited. Darkness is setting in. The woman, who is our guide, is one of the Apprenticed Dreamers and has long, wavy, black hair. Her dress is rose colored with rosebud embroidery in a twining pattern throughout. Her hair blows in the brisk breeze. The moon's light is coming up over the waters, and it spills over her. She is pointing again now. With her red rosebud lips, we hear her say, 'I have brought you only this far. From this beach to the cave, you must tread on your own. Contemplate your steps as you approach this sacred place. If you are not ready, and some are not, now is the time to choose. Those of you who do not continue to the cave, please know another time will come. No regrets!'

"The Dreamer continues: 'Those that find the cave, at the entrance you will be greeted by another Dreamer, there to help you. The Dreamer will give you a small tablet of paper. On it you will write down what it is you need to release emotionally. Think about this as you walk to the cave. You must do this before you can go beyond the cave entrance. Take your time; write only truth. This release is part of the teaching you will receive on your journey here. Your journey to reaching your own pure source.' With that, the Apprentice Dreamer says, 'Be true to your journey.' She moves off, back the way we had come.

"Some in the group move right off, toward the cave's entrance. Others stand very still, seemingly shocked. Some turn away on the beach and retrace their footprints, back the way they had come. You stand awhile, observing the group. Feeling the others' nerves and questions, but knowing absolutely that your path's direction is toward the cave! You see it clearly now. You focus and walk. The wind picks up; it ruffles your clothing and hair. It feels cool and cleansing somehow, and you pick up your pace on the sand. Hearing the constant rhythm of the waves is lulling and comforting. Going within as you walk, you mediate on your truths. And you wonder what you must release at this point in your life. What? Tossing about several things, you come up with a key issue. Finally you know what you will write.

"Not realizing that you had crossed the great stretch of beach and rocky coast, it is startling to smell other than salt air. The scent is sweet and pungent, one of your companions says it is the scent of roses. Looking about, you see the source: two large braziers at the caves entrance burning the rose oil. Someone—you're not sure who—has given you the paper tablet. Quickly, you write down what you had decided for release. Asking Spirit for help and guidance and thanking them, you fold your paper. The Dreamer who had greeted you is there and shows you where to put your release paper, which is a copper cauldron at the cave's entrance.

"Hesitating and blowing into the fire three times, you sigh; it is done. You watch the flames and follow the smoke that is drifting upward to Spirit.

"'It has begun!' says someone. Another Dreamer guides you. Walking now, your bare feet begin moving slowly on the sandy path of transformation. 'One foot after the other,' you hear the 'Mellisai Bee-Priestess' say, and then she continues, 'In this sacred place you will begin to lift the veil that has kept you in the Dreamer's fog.' Looking about, you literally see fog that is swirling! If the priestess was not there, it would be very difficult to find one's way! Again the 'Mellisai Priestess' speaks: 'You are ready to see as much as you are ready for!'

"Inside the dimly lit cave, there is a sense of calm and protection. Somehow, it feels familiar to you. One of the Mellisai-Bee Priestess asks, 'What do you want from this experience? What do you intend by connecting with your source?' Confused and unsure, you cannot answer! What. . .? A bird, a swallow, flies in front of you! Startled a moment, somehow you begin thinking of springtime.

"You hear the priestess saying, 'The Bird of Spring: the time of flowering love and a sacred time to all Goddesses.'

"The ancient voice in your Dreaming tells you, 'Spring is a much respected, honored time and the swallow holds its memory.' Suddenly, smells of spring flood the air. Memory traces of other ancient times within you are awakened. Your mind's eye is telling you part of why you have come to this cave; because this journey is to regain these past memories. An inner voice says, 'You will remember those feminine parts of yourself that know the pure source of regeneration. Remember, equal sources of dark and light, strength and softness.' Somehow you realize degrees of these memories are being restored to you here in the Cave of the High Priestess. There is a familiarity of the Old Rites of the Goddess, which are being regifted here and now as you knew them once, and it is wonderful.

"Coming back into the present from your remembering, you see the others. They are approaching a floating mist, and there is a figure. You realize this is Her. The High Priestess. You notice the crown on her head made of gold metal with carnelian jewels embedded around the points. Each side has a horn in a crescent moon shape. While admiring this, you hear the Bee-Priestess say, 'They are the Horns of Horus the Bull, the crown of the Triple Goddess.'

"The Bee-Priestess nudges you. 'Remember your offering. Go now,' she says. As you walk, you are trembling. Then from a breeze, calm is felt; you feel it has come from Her. Looking now at the High Priestess dressed in cerulean blue, your eyes do not blink as you stare. You see the cobra snake with jewels on its scales, wound about the feet of the High Priestess. You walk up to her floating form as if in a trance, with tears spilling over your face. You manage to thank her and give her a piece of your hair as an offering. She smiles slightly. Her eyes have connected with your own. There is a power transferring from those deep blue-green eyes to your own. You make a feeble attempt to speak to her. She brings her finger to her lips, for quiet. Telepathically now you are communicating with her. Ordinary Earth words cannot convey what is happening. The priestess tells you, 'In truth you know your pure source. Albeit walking a human path, you may be sidetracked and ignore what you know deeply and at times may not honor your own intuition.'

"This literally causes the lights of your true source to dim. 'The Knowing takes a discipline and a type of courage not many are willing to strive for. You must have a strong resolve to walk this path.'

She stopped with those words and a silence fell, which felt deafening. You are thinking about what she has said and want to speak, but cannot.

"You see the High Priestess take an object out of a beautifully woven round reed basket. It is in the shape of a woman and small…But you realize it is also a comb! 'This has been fashioned from whale bone,' she tells you. Looking closely you see it is decorated with pearls and coral and notice the very refined workmanship. The High Priestess then begins combing your hair with this incredible comb. The High Priestess tells you, 'The Whales are the record keepers and can assist with remembering!' Slowly, deliberately, she pulls out the snarls in your hair. It feels wonderful. The sounds of the sea are in the background with thundering waves creating soothing tunes. Closing your eyes, you flow in the present and your heart is full."

After a long silence of peace…

The High Priestess quietly asked the group of afternoon Dreamers to come back from their Dream Journey, saying, "Slowly coming back from the cave by the sea, remember the things you have learned from the High Priestess. Look at her Dream Keeper Image that is from tarot. Feel your own pure source within. Breathe deeply, and remember the Old Rites of the Goddess. Take a few moments now and remember your Dreaming. Then right here and now, seal within yourself The Knowing. The memories that you have been reminded of through this Dreaming."

THE EMPRESS

DREAM OF THE TRUMP SEER: THE EMPRESS III

A group of us were going over notes we had taken earlier after the program given by The Empress Seer. We had learned so much and wanted to make sure we all had the same information because later on we would be performing a "Dream Theater of The Empress."

Two other Dreamers and I were asked by the Keepers to present this theater for this evening program. All of us were much honored but extremely nervous and wanted to have our collected info all on the same page! The following is a sketch of what we worked with to be ready for tonight:

My fellow Dreamer has been involved with the dreaming path for more years than myself and now is an Apprentice Dreamer. I was happy he would be part of this! The other woman Dreamer, also very experienced, was funny and full of quick wit. I felt we would make a good Dream team for the production, for all involved.

I began by saying, "The Empress III is The Goddess Principle, The Earth mother, with the principles of both extending and receiving love. Her astrological sign is Venus. 'The Empress' is number three in the Sacred Grove of the 'Keepers of the Nemeton.'"

"That is the part we all know," said my friend. "Let me add this. As you view the tree of life in The Qabalah, The Empress is the Fourteenth path. And it is the Illuminating Intelligence, 'Daughter of the Mighty Ones,' according to Gareth Knight."

My other Dreamer friend added, "The Empress is the Goddess principle. She is 'Isis,' the ancient Egyptian goddess of fertility and sister and wife of 'Osiris.' In Greek mythology the goddess is 'Demeter,' the goddess of agriculture, fertility, and marriage. Both are 'Venus,' the creative one, the divine feminine. The Empress is the symbol for humankind to be aware and keep love. The Empress is referred to as 'The Keeper of the Door,' in the Qabalah by Gareth Knight. The Hebrew Symbol of 'Daleth'-'Door' is known as the Pillars of Manifestation."

"Wow!" I said. "Let me get this straight in my notes!"

The other Dreamer added quickly, "She is the 'Gate to the Garden,' which is the flow of spiritual power from the unmanifest to the gate of manifestation. The Empress is also considered to be another aspect of the great feminine side of God; this also appears in the High Priestess. In the form of a rustic goddess, as in *Isis Unveiled* by H. P. Blavatsky, the Isis who is unveiled becomes naked Lady Venus. Also the Christian Rosencreutz believed: The essence is that 'Lady Venus shall awake and be mother of a king.' This is the freeing of Sleeping Venus [Isis]. Does this sound familiar…'Sleeping Beauty Awakes'!" He was very proud of himself after relaying this piece of information, but rightly so.

I said, "My dear Dreamer, this is great and this begins to help us shape our Empress for theater. Hey! I think we can build on the 'Gate to the Garden' line and stage the play in a garden!"

At that point my two friends jumped up very excited. "That's it!" they said. "We will work with that Dream image; it is perfect!" All of us were giving high fives at that point. Still we had to pull more together, but we had a beginning of the weave!

"Another of her symbols is the fleur-de-lis symbol of royalty and of leadership. This is the three-pronged-flame: Body-Mind-Spirit," said my woman friend.

Now our Apprentice Dreamer was pacing back and forth on the grassy knoll where we sat, just beyond the cliffs. You could just see the dream weaving going on in his head as he swung back and forth. Stopping suddenly he said, "Picture this scene…as to what is her underlying makeup. The gate to the garden is this: she opens the gate to her garden selectively for Spirit's purpose. For the purpose of pure manifestation and inherent strength. She then has an opening to the primordial sea, the waters of the unmanifest to the manifest of the astral light, amniotic fluid, and the womb. She is 'The Great Mother,' merging and remerging. The Rose is her flower, symbol of feminine, royalty, and especially the Goddess. The Eagle Seer is her guide, the bird of prey that can rise to tremendous heights. The only bird that can look directly into the sun. The Empress: the symbolic source of spiritual life and light."

"Now I see it!" I said, running to where the Dreamer had stopped pacing. "She will walk through the garden gates of a rose garden!"

"A very special Rose Garden!" my other Dreamer friend said.

"Great!" we all said together. "We have come up with our Dream Play!"

Quickly we kept the creative juices flowing between us, I made notes in my journal. Finally we had the final draft and then worked on the parts that did not flow. It was evening before we could blink. We had decided that the Apprentice Dreamer would be the play's narrator and my woman friend and I would be the actors. We might also select actors from the Dreamer audience as well.

All three of us were very excited as the Dreamers arrived and settled in for the Dream Theater. The Dream was ready and so were the actors. We had made a few props to set the scene of the garden. The following narration is the Dream Theater we presented. The banner had been painted with the Dream Title: *THE EMPRESS and the GATE to the GARDEN.* My Dreamer friend plays the Empress, and I play the woman Dreamer who goes to the garden. The Apprentice Dreamer narrates for us the First Scene:

I glanced at the central hearth fire as I was about to leave for a walk. It was being tended by the fire keepers. I reminded myself of the present time and that I must not stray to far from the heart of our work. Smiling now out in the midmorning light, the sun felt great on my shoulders. Taking off my shawl, I let it flutter in the sun, I knew the sun would change any unwanted or negative energies. Walking a bit, I notice a small garden close by, fenced in and quiet. Perfect!

I notice as I approach the garden that it is filled with roses. Mostly red but other colors too. I catch their scent as I stand next to the arched trellis filled with old-fashioned climbing roses, which remind me of my grandmother. Now I see a small but beautifully designed gate between archways that has a small bench. All are made with rough, twisted wood. Standing a few moments in front of this, I wondered if I should open it. Finally I open the gate, which creaks a bit. A feeling stirs in me about the oldness of this place. The fencing around the garden is made of a short stone wall with a picket fence on the top of the stone on all four sides. Inside the garden I notice there are actually two entrances, one the twisted gate and the other a trellised archway with climbing roses. And the scent! Wow! Looking around I notice how perfectly tended it is. Calm comes over me. I must be respectful while here, I think to myself. Rounding one of the small, grassy pathways, I see a small tree, a rosebush tree. Moving next to it, I lean over and smell the roses. Closing my eyes over one perfect blossom, I see the dew on her red petals. I see the large thorns along her stems. Slowly inhaling the aroma, I have my eyes closed a moment. Sniffing, smiling, I say, "Thank you! You are just what I needed."

Opening my eyes, still bent over, I see an elderly person sitting on a small bench there. I lift up quickly and say, "I'm sorry to intrude on your space here in the rose garden!" I straighten myself and put my shawl back on. I feel as if this person on the bench has watched me all the while. The older person does not respond. Odd, I think to myself as I begin to look for the way out, scanning the garden fence, silently wondering which gateway had I entered from.

"Confused?" I hear this figure say.

Stammering some, I say, "I'm not sure which way I came in."

The person looks at me, still seated, and says, "I am not surprised. That's the usual case with many of you younger ones." The elderly one moves their arms about and continues speaking. "Did you not pay attention to the symbols, or mark your path for return? And I suppose you haven't bothered to check your future path either!" This is what the elderly figure says in a husky, grumpy voice, and pointing. "Over there. The side where the large pine tree resides. She guards the east direction. That is the gateway you entered from!"

As his voice trails off, I feel nervous. My heart is beating so fast. It is hard to reply or know what to do. In a scratchy voice, I finally say, "Again, I'm sorry to have disturbed you. I'll be going."

When I move toward the gate, I hear the voice say, "You're not curious?"

I respond slowly, saying, "I'm, well, I am; but...I need to be getting back to my classes!" I am moving closer to the gateway. I glance suddenly at this figure. I feel our eyes contact for an instant. I feel incredible love. Quickly, I say, "This is such a beautiful garden. I am curious as to who made it?" I had to look around to find this mysterious figure, as she had moved and now was busy using a curious tool and weeding around one of the rose bushes. Honeybees are buzzing about. I still do not have a reply, so I begin to move on.

"I can manage the time factor for you," I hear the figure say. "Sit for a moment on my garden stool."

A little afraid to do otherwise, I find myself following her directions. As she points to the stool, I looked it over. It is a beauty: carved with rose blossoms all over and very polished wood, which is very used and old. Very old, I think to myself. I feel a hesitation.

"Sit, Sit!" the person says, waving her garden tool about.

Looking at her, I can not decide if she is male, female, or what? I do what she asks and sit down.

I am startled back to the present as she says, "The stool is made of rosewood. It was made for The Empress III, just like the garden all made for her."

I start to get up. But the elderly one gestures for me to stay seated. I remain seated.

"You appear to be a respectful young Dreamer, and I can feel your thirst under your quiet disguise. So I will tell you a tale. This garden is the place of dreams, love, creativity, birth, Isis, and Venus."

I can hear easily now as the elderly one stand next to me, and I sit on the stool. I feel uncomfortable sitting there; but I watch quietly as this person puts the garden tool she had been holding next to the fence. I can not help but notice its workmanship. Made of pine, I think as I glance over for a second and look at the huge, old pine tree. This tool consists of a long shaft with carvings upon it that I do not recognize. Lines? Dashes? On the top of the tool is a round, golden emblem. A bird emblem and it gleam in the sunlight. An Eagle, I am certain.

The elderly one seems to be straightening her clothing, all the while looking up into the sun's rays. "Just as I thought," she says. "Look! Up there!"

Squinting in the sun's glare, I catch a glimpse of an Eagle circling and circling around our garden! "Wow," I say. "How amazing!"

"Yes, well, she is making her rounds. Guardian for the Empress, you know!" says the elderly one who walks toward me.

With the glare from the sun, I can not make out the face. Something is different, I feel, but what? As the person approaches the pine tree, she is shadowed in the sun's glare. In a softer light, I see the figure better, and it is definitely female! The elderly one is definitely ancient-elderly as I had thought before, but, curiously, she is young as well.

"Ancient, old, young!" I blurt out, "You are ageless!"

She gives me a half smile. As she walks herself around me, I notice her boots made of beautiful leather, with five-pointed silver stars on the front of each. Her hair is long and flowing, adorned with a simple silver crown with many points. She is really something to look at! I am, well, impressed!

I can hear her speaking but don't quite catch the words. Talking about her necklace, I gather as she holds it out for me to see. It is a half crescent moon, which she holds with her smooth, white hands and red-tinted nails.

Smiling in a calm voice, she offers, "The moon is our divine connection with the feminine."

I hear exactly what she says, however, I am thinking about her perfect hands… Stammering, I asked, "Who was that tending and weeding the garden?"

Smiling at me, she answers, "Well, it was me of course!" Laughing, she picks up her garden tool and looks it over.

Very bewildered, I say, "But your hands…How, with the hard work it takes to make a garden so perfect, do you not show the wear?"

Laughing more now, she sits down on the grass next to me. I am seated on the rosewood stool. I jump up and offer her the stool. She says, "No, my dear. Just sit and enjoy!" I smile a quiet thank you.

"I am the Ancient One, The Empress," she tells me. Somehow I already know. Continuing, she says, "We must give so much walking the Empress path, and while on it always remember balanced Love. Never over give or push too much. Keep boundaries and know your limits of giving. Know that intuitive line of balance, and also know how to receive love. Trust your heart; this is key. Remember to take care of yourself, nurture yourself. Many times do that first, and then tend the others that need your nurturing!" She said these things while fondling her white hands and looking back and forth to me.

Taking in what she was saying, I can feel my heart swelling. The Empress Seer had moved about in the garden and is leaning over a perfect rose, inhaling its scent. She motions to me to do the same. "It smells delicious!" I say to her.

The Empress Seer replies, "Without the toil we give to this Earth, this garden, this rose, the blossom you see here might not thrive so splendidly. Realize we must always give back in order to receive." Continuing, The Empress says, "Roses are by far the most beautiful of flowers. She, the rose, is the essence of Love. The essence of the Goddess, the Empress. The rose is sensual. Her beauty and her scent draw us to her center, just as The Empress does. She is the creative one. Her thorns are her protection."

She is quiet now, walking about the garden with the honeybees following her. I realize the time has passed and I need to get back. I walk toward the arched gateway covered with the climbing red roses.

The pine tree stands tall and proud next to the gate. The Empress is there waiting for me, handing me one perfect rose. She stands there regally. As she opens the gate for me, she tells me this: "The Empress is also the gate to the garden. She opens her gate very selectively. You will do well to remember our garden visit."

With that, my eyes catch hers for one brief but eternal moment. I realize I am going through the gate, back the way I had come, and make a note of this detail. Now, however, I have the scent of the rose and so much to Dream with for I had The Empress III Seer Ancient One within my hands.

The Dream Theater was completed now and the round of applause was heartfelt. We, the actor Dreamers, bowed and bowed again. Some in the audience were saying, "Encore, encore!" My Dreamer-actor friends and I were very touched; I know tears were streaming on my cheeks!

THE EMPEROR

DREAM OF THE TRUMP SEER: THE EMPEROR IV

There it was again, the thunder clap! We were all dashing to take cover from the rain that had begun drenching the sacred Grove. I was feeling disappointed to be moving inside. It is always so special to have our teaching circles out in the open, under the sunshine! I scaled the last step onto the porch as another clap came down from the heavens. Finally my group of four Dreamers found a cozy spot in the lodge where we could continue our lessons with the Tarot Seer, "The Emperor." Watching him, I saw that he not only got our immediate group situated but was directing many other Dreamers as to where they might find a teaching alcove. There were three other Ancient Ones that were working in small groups with the Dreamers. I smiled to myself as I watched him take charge, then I walked to one of the windows and looked at the torrential rains and wind that had kicked up. As I listened to the thunder, I saw one of the branches snap off the nearby oak as a lightning streak appeared above. I jumped back in fear and immediately bumped into "The Emperor Seer"!

He laughed and said, "It is OK! I am sure the storm will be moving on shortly. Look, I see a break in those clouds in the west."

I smiled at him, saying, "Yes, I see what you mean. Sorry I bumped into you!"

He shook his head and said, "Let's join the others."

We crossed the room quickly, smelling the smoke from the roaring fire.

The rest of our Dreamer group had set up near the quartz- and garnet-studded fireplace in a comfy circle. Just as we were about to all sit down together, there was another huge clap of thunder! We all turned and looked out the window and saw quite a spectacular lightning bolt. It contained one main illuminated streak, with several smaller ones branching off each side. It was awesome!

The Emperor Seer then clapped his hands together, saying, "This unexpected surge of energy seems to have changed the rules of the game!" He looked at each one of us intently as he said this.

I shivered at his words and piercing stare. Outside I could hear a roll of thunder vibrating over our warm, dry lodge. The Seer had started speaking; I quickly adjusted to pay attention.

He said, "Sometimes the clap of thunder frightens. Sometimes it awakens large numbers to rally to the call." He paced back and forth as he was talking.

I wondered what he meant about rallying to the call. Just then, one of the other Dreamers asked that very question!

The Emperor Seer's answer was a little sharp, making us all listen. In his deep, booming voice he said, "You know this answer, my dear. Come now!"

Answering him timidly, the Dreamer said, "We should pay attention to the here and now?"

The Seer said, "Are you asking or telling us?"

Finally, in her strong female voice, the Dreamer said, "The present! It brings us to the present!"

"Yes! Yes! Well said, my dear." And he continued, "The sound of the clapping thunder has brought us an unusual sense of possibility."

As if to accent what "The Emperor" said, we heard the thunder boom!

Laughing at that, he said, "Yes, possibility seems contagious today. You must understand, dear Dreamers, that The Emperor is always on call! He uses his fiery energy to act, to make decisions wisely and quickly according to the needs at hand. He is on call, and sometimes things may change as quickly as a bolt of lightening and a crack of thunder. Whether the decision is in the midst of the action of war or making decisions about the state of an Emperor's domain, the Emperor needs to watch for when he 'must use his sense of boldness.' He learns to use his confidence even if the task seems too heavy to bear. When he learns to trust this confidence about himself, his Spirits rise, and this is seen by the others around him. This then, enables all to have a renewed sense in their place in the grand scheme of things.

"A leader must be able to instill trust in his visions and his assessments of situations. He provides shape and form, and he sticks to a plan. A leader sets a direction and also an honest tone. This is what others respond to and follow. In many ways he is a father figure to the many. Sometimes he might need to create order out of chaos. And on occasion his actions may be questioned, and he must always be ready to offer explanations. The Emperor has to be on top of his game and know the big picture of his empire. His shoulders must be strong, as his responsibilities can often be heavy."

There was silence with this last statement as the Seer looked at each of us, scanning us to see how we were receiving this information. But our group was still taking in the download, and none of us was ready to respond. The Seer must have realized this. Suddenly he clapped his hands together as he had done earlier. We all jumped a little.

He was the only one standing and now leaned over us and said, "Come! I do not hear the rain any longer!" We all strained to hear if this was so, and of course it was. "This is a good time for us to go out and survey our domain and find out if there are any repairs required to the Nemeton! Come on! I know you all are comfy and warm, but the others count on us to keep order and stability." He was already out the door. The rest of us had to scramble to catch up to him.

One of the other Dreamers said to me, "How does he keep his energy so high and always on the go?"

I answered in a panting breath as I race walked to catch up, "I am not sure how he does it either. Let's try observing his actions." We both agreed this might give us insight that would be useful for us.

We were out in the wood; I am not sure how we got there as fast as we did. We walked through a tangle of towering oak and pine. I saw the limb from the oak that had been struck by lightning.

I heard the Emperor saying to one of the Dreamers, "Put that on the list: tree clean up. And put a call out to the healers."

Apparently this Dreamer was now the scribe for The Emperor.

The Seer was now saying, "We will make land assessments as to repairs, but we will also go to the Throne Room."

I was at the end of our group of four. The path was narrow here, and I wasn't sure I had heard right. I asked my fellow Dreamer in front of me, "Did he say throne room?"

The Dreamer was laughing when he said, "He sure did! I had heard there was a throne room in the woods, but it cannot be found unless you are invited by The Emperor!"

"Oh my God! You are not serious!" I said, half laughing and half delighted by the intrigue of it all.

The Dreamer in front of me was still laughing. We both picked up our pace.

The ground was sodden after the hard rain. I wished I had put on boots earlier. The sun, however, was poking through the tree canopy, and I was happy for that. Looking ahead I could see the path was wider and realized there was grass underfoot now, not only mud. It looked like a clearing was ahead as well; the woods were less dense in this area. Once we all reached the clearing, the Seer had us sit on the large rocks for a break. Through the swirling wind, water was showering down off the leaves. The water was fine and soft on my head. With the cloud cover again, it felt shadowy. I brushed the sweet, damp hair from my forehead as I watched The Seer walking about in contemplation. I wondered what he was thinking. No one spoke.

Once more we heard the soft roll of thunder, and lightning bolts made their display. The Emperor began in deep soft voice, "There is a full spectrum of possibility that has not existed before now." He continued walking about the wet grass; all of us followed his movement.

I truly hoped we would not get caught in another storm. What happened to the sun? I was deep in my own thoughts. Just then I saw The Emperor was right in front of me, and he had produced a drum that he beat on softly. Quickly I came back to the here and now! I was glad when he walked past me; he continued drumming around the group.

The Seer continued. "The time we are in has announced opportunity to open things that have been dormant. This time asks you not to give up on what lives in your heart and what lives in your Dream." He was looking up now at the tree tops; the sun was making another try. He said, "Look at those light patterns there on the trees, dark and light, round and square." Of course we all turned our heads to the light. "There are those of you that now wear the higher patterns of light, and without the constraints of Earth, you will be called upon to go beyond your present experience. Spirit will give you deep soul insights, and you will be asked to fly higher, possibly move mountains, maybe even dance back and forth between times. You will be given instructions from your own heart to surpass any limitations you thought you had. You are being assisted now on your soul path. You may decide to follow the path of the Emperor, like myself. Or choose one altogether different. Whichever you choose, the things that you learn here about the Emperor will help you to attain what is right for you. Also remember that all the Keepers are about service!"

I looked around the group; everyone was glued to The Emperor. I noticed that the woods were quiet, the birds had vanished, and the squirrels had gone silent. Just then there was a blaze of light from a huge thunderbolt that was very close. As the wind swirled around us, another bolt struck a nearby pine tree, which split and fell just in front of us all! I was clinging to my friend in fear. As the thunder rolled on above, all of us were wondering, what next? The Seer, however, was calm.

He swung his drumcase over his head and picked up the scepter that held the orb of the Moon with the "Cross Patee" on its top. He said in a raspy voice, "I do believe we are hearing from Zeus! Now there is some interesting history." Looking us all over, he said, "Time for us to get moving. Where is the Dreamer scribe? Ah, there you are. Write down this tree as well. The healers are going to have their hands full. Make note of which direction the limbs fell and other things that are of interest. OK...Where were we? Oh, I see, we need to go a little farther, and then we will find the water inlet. Let's hope we can cross the water!"

We all began following after the Seer. I know all of us thought this was nuts, and we were feeling fear. Though no one said so, I was wishing we could have stayed in the warm lodge.

The Seer was speaking and as if to echo my thoughts. He said, "I know what you all are thinking. What is the point of us being out here exposed to this storm? And I tell you that this is the best way to learn what you are made of, to learn about your coping skills, and your self-control. Now let me tell you about Zeus!"

"Zeus maintains order by enforcing his laws, both physical and moral. He does this with 'keraunos,' the Greek name for thunderbolt. In Greek mythology the thunderbolt is a weapon given to Zeus by the Cyclops. Lightning plays a key role in many mythologies, often as the weapon of a sky and storm god. Lightning can be used for instantaneous acts of destruction or used as a divine weapon of manifestation. Zeus is king of the gods, ruler of Mount Olympus, and god of the sky and thunder. His symbols are the Thunderbolt, Eagle, Bull, and the Oak. He is the god of the heavens. Zeus is god of order and fate, and he governs the weather and kings! Those who violate natural law, oaths, justice, hospitality, honor, and so forth are all at risk of feeling the bolt, either as a warning or punishment. As Homer has said, 'A common epithet of Zeus is, "Father of Gods and Mortals"!' This means he is the head of the family. He has both the authority and the responsibility for them. So, you see, this is precisely the same office of the Emperor!" The Seer broke into roaring laughter at that.

We all did the same. Everyone felt much lighter after this story and our walk. Some of the Dreamers asked the Emperor questions. I paused for a moment, looking around at the variety of trees, white birch, oak, ash, pine, all glistening now with raindrops lit by the sun. Suddenly I had a sense of being watched! Looking about, there was nothing. I did hear some birds, so I dismissed the feeling.

Lagging behind, I ran ahead just in time to hear the Emperor say, "Well, my dears, we have arrived at the water. There should be a small bridge to cross, but as we can see, it has been pulled upstream with these wild currents. I suggest that we walk along the water a bit to find a place to cross."

The Dreamer that The Emperor called scribe jotted down the washed out bridge on his notepad. I think most of us didn't mind the walk. We were on an adventure, and the weather was much milder now, plus the storm was moving to the west. A couple of scout Dreamers had sprinted ahead and were now racing back, breathless. They told us there was a place to cross; however, there was someone there who demanded to speak to The Emperor!

The Seer said, "Speak to me? Who is it? No matter, just lead the way."

I ran to catch up. Everyone was in a state of "I wonder this or that." I was instantly brought back to the feeling I had earlier. That sense of being watched! What is going on? I thought with some worry. It took us about five to ten minutes to get to the spot that our Dreamer scouts had found. We all had to walk a narrow ledge along the water's edge, about ten feet above the rushing currents. Some spots were slippery with piles of mud. We all had to pay strict attention to where we placed our feet. Slowing up, we climbed a little higher onto the bank. I could see the scout Dreamers ahead. They were leading The Emperor to a spot at the cliff's edge and were pointing across the water to where we could see several newcomers. All of us were following the direction across the water. This was a narrow spot in this river of water, and we saw our new bridge. I looked down at the water; it was raging and snagging small branches as it passed around rocks and small trees.

The bridge was a huge fallen pine, large enough for us to balance on one at a time to cross the water. I thought, At least the water is not that deep here. But as I watched it swirl, I was nervous. The Emperor told us to find a large branch that we could use as a staff to help us tightrope walk across the pine's trunk. All of us made our staff ready, but quietly there was a lot of grumbling. Then, one at a time, we crossed the tree bridge; it was slow going. I was next to last in our group of four. The Emperor was last.

As I waited my turn, I stood on a thicket of vines, which were at the base of the tree trunk. I could see the white heart wood, raw and exposed. I told the Seer sadly, "I can smell her bloody sap."

He said, "So do I." And then he pulled tobacco from his robe and sprinkled it on the stump, saying a blessing.

I looked across the water and saw the newcomers there. I looked at The Emperor.

He said, "Just keep your mind on what is required of you right now!"

Easier said than done, I thought. It was my turn to cross.

The Emperor, smiled, saying, "You will be across in a jiff. Just dream it!"

Holding my staff and my breath, I headed across. The twenty-foot span felt a lifetime, my stomach in knots, but I made it! The others helped me down and clapped at my tightrope abilities. Before I knew it, The Emperor was jumping down from the trunk, and he walked off toward the pile of branches on the left of the main trunk.

Bringing himself back to our group, he had a huge smile for the Dreamers. But for some reason he was ignoring the newcomers on this side of the bank. The Emperor said, "I am so proud of you all! Each of you used some of your Emperor skills to get across the water. You demonstrated willpower and self-control. You have put yourselves in a position of strength. You can now add that to your experience list!"

The other Dreamers and I were all smiling and feeling very proud of ourselves. We talked about how we had all achieved the tightrope walk. The Emperor walked over to the newcomers. There was a feeling of tension, but none of us knew what this was about.

As I watched this new group of three from a distance, two women and one man, I could not help but feel I knew one of them. They were dressed plainly, but something was different; they seemed too confident, and I was sure that The Emperor knew them quite well. I also knew it was this bunch that had been watching us! The Emperor had been talking with them a few minutes when he then turned and motioned for us all to approach them. Waving his hand this way and that, he was saying something, but it was difficult to hear because the water was roaring loudly. The two other Dreamers and I all looked at each other quickly, hunched our shoulders, and then moved toward The Emperor and the other three. It turns out that we all knew who they were, The Magician, The High Priestess, and The Empress! I thought to myself, what is all the mystery about? And why had they demanded to see The Emperor? I was about to find out.

"Ah, Dreamers!" said The Emperor in a too-jolly voice. "My fellow Keepers would like to say hello. I trust that most of you have met by this time. However, let me introduce to you each of these Ancient Ones. The High Priestess' in all her beauty." She bowed to us. "'The Magician,' whom we often need to call upon in our workings." He bowed to us. "And my dearest, 'The Empress,' my counterpart in this world and others." She bowed to us.

The other Dreamers and I said that we were very happy to meet them! The Ancient Ones all smiled back warmly and shook hands with each of us.

I was left with the hand of The High Priestess in mine, and she did not let go. She had folded both her hands over my left hand. She turned her head slightly but still stared in my eyes and spoke to The Emperor, saying, "This is the one who knew!"

My heart was beating so fast. What had I done? Crazy thoughts were racing around my brain! I looked at her, then back at The Emperor. In a very small voice, I said, "What did I know? Am I in trouble?" I knew all the while it was about the feeling I had earlier in this journey, "the sense of being watched"! I did not dare say another word. Pulling my hand away from The Empress, I waited. My eyes darting from one person to the next, my hands were in a cold sweat now.

All four Ancient Ones started laughing.

I did not think it funny. I blurted out, "What is going on? Is it about the sensing I felt earlier today? Well, I could not help it. Sometimes things like that just happen and I—"

The Emperor had come over to me with one arm around my shoulder, saying, "Dear, dear, let me explain. I suppose today has been a kind of game. All of you Dreamers are learning things very quickly. Each of you receiving lessons from one topic and then the next, training with one Seer and then to the next. In our work we do not give you written tests to find out where you rank. The Dreamer training does not work that way; you all would not be here if you were not capable. But at this point in the program, you are tested. And some of the testing needs to happen incognito, if you will. If we were to say to you, 'OK, here is your test,' many of you would not be able to perform the testing. So the Keepers and I have organized activities that keep the new Dreamers engaged in their learning by the 'Doing' process. We try to keep this as freestyle as possible and work with the circumstances that appear. Then because of our Seer's ability to telepathically communicate, we keep each other informed of our plans. Each of the Ancient Ones has been working with small groups of Dreamers who are really ready for the next steps in their magical training. Today was such a day. And you, my dear, have the gift, which needs honing but is true!"

The Seer had stopped speaking. Everyone was looking at me. I decided to say the first thing on my mind. "So I have been tested about being able to sense something? I had 'a sense that we were being watched,' and then I dismissed it as I did not see anything around. So is that what this is about?" I looked sharply at each one of them; I was feeling mad and angry.

I jumped away from them all and was really ready to say more when The High Priestess began speaking. "Do not be upset with us, little daughter. Yes, this is what The Emperor said it was: a test of your intuitive abilities, which we all can see are strong. We are all proud of you! The teachings on The Emperor's path are about structure, order, and regulation. But sometimes he also needs to count on his gut feelings. Yes, we three Seers were watching and probing here and there in the background. This is what you picked up on. Please remember that the Emperor is also a Warrior and needs to keep his intuitive skills honed. Please forgive us if you should feel in any way manipulated. It is all part of the larger game that we are playing here within this safe environment of the Grove. But trust me when I tell you that this training will provide you with great benefits later in the waking world!"

The Empress had spoken in such a commanding tone with her heart that when she had finished, I could not look at her anymore; because my eyes were blurred with tears. I looked at the fallen pine tree and went over there and sat down on her trunk, with tears dripping down my cheeks I finally said, "I know! And I am thankful." Then silence hung in the air a little while before everyone began moving quietly about. I picked up my hand to wipe away my tears and felt instead the sap of the pine tree. Her blood! I thought I called to the Emperor while I held up my hand sticky with sap and said, "She needs healing!"

"I know," he replied, and next thing I knew, the Magician was next to me.

I got up from the tree and said to The Magician, "She is a beautiful elder pine. I am so sad for her!"

The Magician was a tall man with one of those timeless faces; I could feel his sadness for the pine tree. He looked at me a minute and said, "I will try to save this part for her; it seems she has a double trunk, unusual for a pine, but this may be fortunate for her." The Magician showed me which area he intended to work with, touching the sap that was much thicker than blood and amber in color. He said we need to let her know we are here to help, and that she can hold onto her blood at this point. Then The Magician turned to me, saying, "I could use your help, that is, if you want to."

Quickly I stood right next to him and the tree and said, "Just tell me what to do!"

"All right," he said. "Carefully place both your hands here, then with all your might, talk to the pine and will her to stop the flow of her sap. Let her know you are here to help her through this pain, that she has the ability to live still. Blow your breath onto her bark; call in spirit helpers to assist her now. Let her know she is needed still. Send love to her heart wood."

I took in what the Seer told me and looked around us a moment before we began. I could hear soft drumming and chanting, which was coming from The Emperor and the others. I was ready. The Magician and I exchanged glances, and then we got to work. It felt intense. I felt some doubt for a moment.

Then the Seer next to me turned his eyes to mine, and with his eyes said, "We do not have room for doubt!"

I closed my eyes. With my dreaming I called in spirit helpers of the Eagle and the Bear. They would do the herb collecting and hold the boundaries. I could feel The Magician working with the heart wood of the elder pine. I began to feel a vibration first in the ground under my feet and then from the tree trunk. "What is that?" I called out to The Magician.

Softly, he said, "She is beginning to respond."

Closing my eyes again, I sent dreams of healing light and love to the elder pine, telling her how much we all cared and how much beauty she brought us all. Coming back through the sound of the drum, I sat back upon my knees with thanks! The Magician came back as well. We both smiled at each other.

He said, "She will still need more magical treatments, but I do think she has decided to stay around awhile!"

I jumped up and gave the tree a hug and hugged the Magician as well. I told him I would come every day to check on her. I told the elder pine as well. I gave them both a kiss. On the ground next to the tree were several bunches of herbs. I could hear the cry of the Eagle and saw that she soared above us now.

The Magician said, "You had better get going, I will apply the herbs. The Emperor is already underway, and I know there is still more to do in the Throne Room!"

I started walking away from them, walking backward, looking at the pine tree and speaking to The Magician. I let him know how thankful I was that he had asked me to help. "This was amazing, just amazing!" I said as I ran off into the wood to catch up with the other Dreamers.

Quite out of breath but very happy, I heard The Emperor as he said, "We have just a short way now to the hidden treasure of The Wood; you are all invited to my Throne Room. Onward, Dreamers!"

We all cheered for joy as if we were children in fantasyland. Which, when I think about it, I suppose we really are in a fantasyland! I repeated that out loud for all to hear, and everyone began to make up their own versions of this fantasyland, laughing and joking as we walked.

Noticing that The Empress was still with us, but not seeing The High Priestess, I asked one of the Dreamers about that. I found out that she was one of the healers that had been called to help with the trees and whatever else might need help and healing in the Grove. Just like The Magician was doing. I smiled at that; it seemed the Ancient Ones had the bases covered and their work cut out for them today.

The wood was very dense here, the canopy from the trees barely let in any light, and there did not seem to be a regular path on the upward climb now. We are like a band of bushwhackers, I thought, and I felt for the small knife I kept at my waist. There were huge granite boulders all around, and the silence here was deafening. I was glad when the group paused. I wondered if we might be lost? I was glad I had brought along the staff I had made to cross the river with; it gave me something to lean on. I realized I was tired. I looked up to the sky to see if I could determine the time of day. My stomach was growling. I thought about lunch and realized we did not have any! Still looking at the sky, I saw there were flashes of black. Oh great! Another storm, I said to myself. I looked again, and now the flashes of black were separating, and some swooped around. What the heck? Next thing I knew, one of these flashes was next to me on a tree limb, and it was a Raven, not a cloud! I wanted to scream from fright but was too late; the other Dreamers were screaming! Such a commotion. The birds were now only specks in the sky, yet just seconds ago, there were at least twenty or forty sitting all about us!

The Emperor thought this all very hilarious and could barely speak! Once he settled himself, he said, "We have arrived!"

I heard one of the Dreamers say, "Arrived where?"

My thoughts exactly! Then I noticed a bee was sitting on some small clover near me. But the buzzing I heard could not come from this one bee! I asked The Emperor, "Where was that buzzing sound coming from, and how do we get to the Throne Room?" Everyone shook their head at that.

He responded with, "Patience, Dreamers; watch!" He had lifted his arm and was pointing to a boulder, where we saw a cleft in the huge granite form. Next he walked to the boulder, turned, looked quickly at us, and, with a sideways motion, slid through the cleft! The Empress was right after him! The rest of us looked at each other with astonishment! Then we looked at the boulder and saw many bees were swarming, buzzing, and were traveling through the same cleft in the rocks. Not wanting to be left behind at this point, we all lined up to go through the rocks.

When it was my turn, I noticed that the space was larger than it appeared to be and that there was a definite hexagram pattern at the base of the rock. Before I went all the way through, I looked back the way we had come. I was the last one to pass through the opening. When I looked back, I could see four large Ravens sitting in various places. I realized then that they were the guardians for this place. Everything has been thought out, I said to myself. Next thing I knew, I was through the rock.

Oh my! This is amazing! It really is a throne room! I knew there would be something but, Oh my God! The sunshine poured into this huge space of a circle. It must have been at least twenty feet across. I scanned the entire space. There were flowers growing on the rocks, and a beautiful, small waterfall cascaded down one side. There were birds of all kinds. Humming-birds were everywhere. I noticed that some of the rocks were sparkling and realized they were various crystals growing right there. It took me awhile, turning around taking in all there was to see. My eyes rested on The Emperor. He was standing with the others. He signaled for me to approach them. I did so with much excitement.

"Dear Dreamers and my dear Empress, welcome to my 'Throne Room'!"

We all clapped and cheered.

I noticed that The Empress had a robe over her arm; she walked to The Emperor and said, "My dear sire, let me help you with your robe and escort you to your throne!" She had a big smile on her face as she helped him on with his official garment, and then, like in Camelot, they walked to the throne. The Emperor bowed slightly and was seated, looking around at his subjects and was pleased.

I could not believe this! I must be dreaming! But of course I was dreaming; that is what I do! I broke out into quiet giggles and said, "This is wonderful. I am so happy to be here with all of you today!"

Now The Empress said, "I know you all must be hungry. Please be seated." She pointed to the table in the center of the room. It was piled high with all kinds of meats, cheeses, vegetables, and fruits, and sweets of all kinds! This was a feast fit for a king!

Once we were all seated, The Emperor came and stood at the head of the table. Then The Empress was next to him and said it was time to reclaim his crown. He smiled at that, and she lifted the beautiful crown with the fleur-de-lis on its top and placed this on his head.

We all cheered and said things like, "Here, here! Long live the king!"

The Empress turned to sit at the other head of the table.

The Emperor said, "A toast to the work of the Dreamers. You have done well, and I am sure you will make wonderful contributions as Keepers yourselves one day!" We all clinked our glasses and toasted to each other as we sat down for our lunch. The Emperor said, "I will continue with stories about the throne itself in a few moments, but right now I am famished!"

We said, "Here, here" to that and began to chow.

What a day, sharing dreams and stories around the table. As I was biting into my dessert of honey cake, I heard the bees busily tending to the flowers. I noticed that under our table there was a painted design of a honeycomb, just like the hexagram shape as we entered the Throne Room. Curious, I asked The Emperor to tell us about that.

His answer was this: "Bumblebees remind us that leadership requires vision and building. It is said that that the Greek temples of Delphi had been erected by bees to assist in the oracular vision of the Delphic Oracles. Also many of the garments of royalty have the design of the bee within the weaving or embroidered cloth."

All of the Dreamers contemplated that for a few minutes. Then someone said, "How do you manage your empire so well?"

Quickly The Emperor replied with, "Ah! Strong will! A strong foundation is also key! There are times when it is good to be dreamy, creative, and instinctual; but to control, one must be alert, in touch, brave, and aggressive. One should be ambitious along with the possibility of long-term achievement for the good of the whole. In myth The Emperor may have its origin in the god Zeus, who we spoke of earlier. The Emperor may also be the incarnation of the Sun God, like the Greek god Apollo or the Egyptian god Horus, and he is their delegate on Earth. Another aspect may be that of King Minos, who reigned over Crete three generations before the Trojan War. The Emperor's zodiac ruler is Aries, and he is connected to the god of war, Mars. We would all do well to study their histories!"

Everyone was nodding their heads in agreement.

The Emperor continued as he sipped on his wine, leaning back onto the beautifully carved oak chair. "In tarot, The Emperor IV is the number four. Fours are stable numbers. Four seasons, four walls, four corners. Because The Emperor understands the nature of structure so well, he knows what can and cannot be controlled. To remain in power, he must meet external needs of service, needs that transcend his own personal needs. The Emperor is stability and security, and the number four is his. It is the number of building physical structures, the number of the cube, which is the base of his throne!"

With that, the Seer got up and walked over to where his throne sat. The afternoon sun was streaming in on top of this throne-cube, which had been carved from stone into a work of art. We all admired the craftsmanship and were intrigued by the symbols that were accentuated in the light. I wanted to ask more about the throne, but the Seer had begun moving away and was speaking.

He said, "The Emperor represents structure, order, and regulation. He advocates a four-squared world where trains are on time, games are played by the rules, and commanding officers are respected. He knows how to tie up loose ends and wayward elements. As the regulator, he is often associated with legal matters and disciplinary actions. He is man and the masculine world. He must acquire self-mastery and maturity. He concentrates on goals, is fearless, and has endurance!" The Seer stopped talking and was staring at us all with a slight smile across his face.

I thought to myself, his shoes would be very hard to fill.

Then, looking at me, he said, "Well, I am not always all these things! Every day I must work at what is currently the 'call to service' and do my best! Dreamers! The lesson of The Emperor is this: Whatever you wish to conquer, you must serve! Be it a child or a kingdom!"

By now he had moved away from his Dreamer subjects and was thanking the staff for our wonderful lunch, while taking off his glorious robe to set on the throne. The Empress, now at his side, insisted that he keep the crown on his head. Finally he agreed to that and turned to us and said, "It is time to be back to the lodge! We have other obligations for the remainder of the day and miles to go!" None of us wanted to leave this amazing Throne Room, but the Emperor had spoken!

I watched with admiration as The Emperor led The Empress ahead of us to the crack between the worlds, just like Camelot! Once we were all assembled on the path, I heard the Ravens' calls. The Dreamers and I started back down the way we had come.

Suddenly, The Emperor called to us, saying, "Not that way, please. I know another path." He began leading the way with The Empress next to him in her long, flowing silks that had bees embroidered at the hemlines.

We had not been walking long, when someone said, "The Lodge! It is right there. How have we gotten here so fast?"

I could hear the Keepers all chuckling as they strode away together.

HIERDPHANT

DREAM OF THE TRUMP SEER: THE HIEROPHANT V

It was suggested to me, by one of the apprentice Dreamers, that I speak with one of the Ancient Trump Seers to find some clarity. I had decided this was good advice and began walking through the Grove to the place I was told the Trump Seer should be. With wandering thoughts about how I was building a Dream Healing foundation as a practicing Healer, I walked and was feeling good about what I had achieved. I recalled all the work prior to being a part of this gathering, realizing it was an achievement to be here. I smiled at that revelation! Now here within the Nemeton, I was ready for another part of my healing journey and training. I was gaining confidence. I did recognize some disappointments, some triumphs, but mostly felt joy about "The Work." Yet there was, however, an undercurrent that I could not put my finger on. I was learning so much yet felt doubt and confusion at times. It is all going so fast! I keep thinking, what if this and what if that? How can I ever remember when to use what? Well, I had put off the questions long enough, coming back now to the reason I was walking.

I was in an area of the Grove that I had heard about but had not seen until now. I had been told to find The Hollies, a cute kind of name, I thought. I did not put together until now that this part of the steading was literally made up of holly trees and shrubs, a holly grove! Beautiful trees with spiny, rich, evergreen leaves that were shiny and smooth. Smiling, I thought how magical it is to walk among them. Some plants were covered in bright red berries. Hollies are either male or female, and both bear small, lightly scented flowers. But it is only the female trees that bear the distinctive red berries. I had learned that from The Holly Tree Seer. They are simply glorious, some of them forty feet at least.

It felt so good just walking here that I almost forgot why I had come! I pulled out my post-it note on which my Dreamer friend had scribbled something. It said, "The best time to catch him is before noon, at the Holly Cottage!" I quickly looked at my watch; it was 11:00 a.m. I looked up at the sun through the lush evergreen trees, feeling its warmth and brightness. Looking around, I did not see anything like a cottage.

Then I noticed a path of sorts lined with tall holly trees on each side. I counted ten trees, five on each side. As I neared the end of this path, there was the cottage, made from holly, of course! I could see a couple of people on the porch of the holly cottage. There were a few others approaching from the path. One Dreamer was holding a tray of candles. The Dreamer held out a large white candle to me. I took it, wondering what I was to do. Holding the candle, I looked to the porch and saw a tall man standing there in magenta and gold robes. He nodded to me, and I approached him on the porch. He wore an embroidered white and gold Triple Crown with the roman numeral V on it; the design was beautiful. His left hand held a golden scepter-staff with a triple cross at its top. I was reminded of my dream from awhile back; in my dreaming I met the pope!

Could it be that my dream brought me here now? But my intention was to speak with the Hierophant! As I watched the activity on the porch, I saw The Chariot Seer standing nearby, and he handed a key to the figure in the magenta and gold robes. I was in a daze and very nervous. My ears however received this message: "Before I was The Hierophant, I was the Pope in many of the ancient tarot decks."

I looked at this tall man with the scepter and, in my confusion, said, "Do you mean you are 'The Hierophant Seer'?"

He answered by saying, "I am! And I will not bite!"

The Chariot Seer laughed wholeheartedly at this. I did not know what to say, so I held out the white candle and gave it to the "Hierophant Seer."

The Hierophant responded by saying to The Chariot Seer, "I do believe she has seen the light!" They both had a good laugh at my expense!

Finally I said, "Very funny! Ha-ha! I do admit there are things I do not know, but this is why I have come! And—"

"Oh, my dear Dreamer," said "The Hierophant Seer," "we are only teasing you. Please lighten up! I know why you have come, and I have been expecting you. The Hierophant literally means 'the one who teaches the holy things.' But do remember to keep the humor in the mix; it is important."

By now the Seer had guided me to a wonderful, comfy chair on the porch, and another Dreamer was bringing me tea. I sipped this and looked out onto the hollies and the path, feeling a little less nervous. Scanning the holly grove, I noticed a huge oak off to the left, which made a nice contrast to the shiny evergreen hollies.

From the comfort of my chair, I looked at the beautiful manicured garden just in front of the porch. I noticed that the flower plantings were in groups of five. How interesting, I thought as I looked again at The Hierophant Seer, noting the number five (V) on his crown.

He must have known my musings, as he said, "Five represents the essence of things as they are. In Latin the word 'quincunx' equals five dots that form the quincunx, which is an arrangement of five units in a pattern. This originates from the Pythagorean mathematical mysticism. This pattern is the standard pattern for planting an orchard, especially in France. The number five pattern, the quincunx, is found throughout nature, art, and mysticism. 'Quintessence' is the Latin word for five and nature. Five is also the number of the senses: sight, hearing, taste, touch, smell. So, in part, the Hierophant is part of the world of senses and of 'patterns of meaning,' along with much you will learn about today."

He was looking at me with his head slightly turned to one side. His eyes had that sincere look of one who knows but with a hint of "should I continue on this track?"

I quickly nodded my head yes and said, "It is the patterns of things I am so aware of lately! Amazing that you picked this up while I was enjoying the groups of five flower plantings in the garden!"

He answered, "This is part of who I am. I have the ability to know what needs to be voiced. Come and walk with me awhile in the garden." He began walking down the steps. "Take that basket on the table near you," he added.

As we walked, the Seer collected little stones and wild flowers, placing them into the basket that I held, which I knew, of course, was woven by the Spider Seer. The Hierophant Seer said, "In the Qabalah, I am path sixteen, called 'The Magus of the Eternal.' We can think of this path as a pattern for what is to be and a promise of what will be. A Magus is one who mediates power from one level down to another. The astrological sign of path sixteen is Taurus the Bull, a very strong Earth symbol. In the zodiac the 'constellation of Taurus' is made up in part by the 'Pleiades'; some say the name Pleiades means the 'the sailing ones,' and others say it means 'flock of doves.' The Pleiades are called the Seven Sisters, coming from Greek myth. They were sisters or wives of the Seven Rishis of the Great Bear constellation, Ursa Major. They are the feminine or the form-side aspects of the cosmic patterns held in the Great Bear, which guides their evolution. The Pleiades are mythologically considered to be 'doves,' and these birds are sacred to Venus, which is the ruling planet of Taurus."

There was silence. Finally I said in a slow but sure voice, "Everything is so connected!"

Without expression and looking toward the sky, the Seer said, "A dove is also an emblem of the Holy Spirit." Looking up to the sky were two doves flying overhead.

"Amazing!" I said.

"In the Qabalah, path number sixteen on the Tree of Life travels between 'Chesed'-Kindness and 'Chokmah'-Wisdom. The Hierophant depicts the principle of spiritual authority on Earth. Trump V sums up faith and belief from which any code of conduct or moral standard ultimately derives. Another part of the Taurus constellation consists of the Horn of Taurus, or Horn of Plenty, the 'Cornucopia.' This provides us with a link between the 'Table Round of Chokmah-Wisdom' and the zodiac via the Holy Grail. The early form of the Grail in Arthurian legend was the 'Cauldron of Ceridwen,' who was the 'Keeper of the Cauldron of Knowledge.' She is the Crone of Wisdom, and she represents the darker aspects of the Goddess and has powers of prophecy as well."

I looked at him quizzically but did not interrupt for questions.

Continuing in his even tone, the Seer said, "The Holy Grail is a symbol of high significance, which stresses communality. This represents the many who obtain their source of life and enjoyment from a single, central fount that is never exhausted...'THE GRAIL.' The Round Table and the Horn of Plenty are a central theme, representing evolution through knowledge. The image is one of kings that are all equal but diverse and are all seated at this

Cosmic Round Table." The Seer laughed but was serious when he said, "I have been dreaming for this in waking reality time. And one day not so far away, it will be so!"

I could feel his passion, and I began to understand that the Seer worked toward a goal of evolution through knowledge. I had a shiver at the thought of it all.

The Seer was holding the basket, putting in some stones, looking at violets we had picked and the red berries on the holly we had clipped. Then he said, "Now I know that you have questions for me, so I pass the talking stick to you!" As he said this, he lifted out a key from the basket.

I wondered about the key and wanted to ask but knew he wanted me to get on with my questions. I was nervous; it would really be easier for me to just ask him about the key. But, alas, my response was hesitation. I thought to myself in a flash, a test, to see if I can grab the floor!

"Dear Seer, thank you!" I said. "I want to know about the key that you are holding, however, I will ask my questions first! So here it goes. I have been learning so much by being a part of this Dreamers Gathering. Some days I feel like I know it all and there is flow. Other days I am on overload! My worry is that once I am away from these like-minded Dreamers and working in waking realty and assisting others with their own Dream Healing or soul recovery work that the 'what if factor' will pop up! How will I ever remember when to use what when working with clients, family, and friends? I also worry about the solutions I select. 'What if' the recipient does not agree?"

The question just spilled out of me, and I did not stop to take a breath! I did manage to keep eye contact with The Hierophant Seer while I spoke. Now I turned away, catching my breath and slowing down my fast-beating heart!

There was utter silence. When I looked at the Seer again, he was twisting the key around in his left hand. Calmly, he said in a deep voice, "Each of us is put here in this time and place to personally decide the future of humankind. Did you think you were put here for something less?"

Now as I looked at him, I had tears welling up; I attempted to respond. He just put up his right palm to face me. I did not interrupt. I was breathing hard again.

"Just breathe slowly," he said. "Now ponder this for a moment. If you were living your life from the position of your greatest strengths, what would your life be like?" My mouth dropped open; I could not speak. The Seer said, "Let's walk back to the cottage while you hold that thought." He handed me the key he had been holding. It felt heavy as I held the key and walked back on the path.

Once back on the porch of the Holly Cottage, "The High Priestess" came up to me and said, "Here, sit with me and drink this hot coffee and just 'be' awhile!" She guided me to one of chairs.

The Hierophant smiled and sat down in the nearby rocking chair, saying, "Ah, dear Priestess, always a reflection for your Hierophant, reminding me of how you draw from your vast banks of inner knowledge at precisely the right times!"

The Priestess laughed with him and, turning to me, said, "My little Dreamer, The Hierophant is the initiator, who reflects onto us to test us or challenge us in order to grow. He mirrors for us what we need, and every initiation expands our awareness. If you will notice, the Hierophant holds a staff, a scepter, 'the staff of commitment.' This requires that our mind, heart, and action all share the same intention and focus."

I managed to look around some, but mostly I just looked at the key I was holding and sipped my coffee.

The Hierophant Seer smiled and continued his tale. "The Hierophant presents the lessons of Heaven-to-Earth. Some authorities say that the Hierophant generally represents assistance, friendship, good advice, and religious interests. Others say I represent the first level of understanding. When it appears in a tarot spread, it may be a warning to the querent to reexamine his or her understanding of the meaning of things, of the structure of the world, and the powers that be.

"From the Egyptians we have the image of the Hierophant as a serpent standing on two legs, symbolizing a 'High Initiate' or 'Hierophant.' He wears a disc with a ram's horn upon his head. Further Egyptian symbols express the idea of life, animation, being, the idea of reunion. The Hierophant equals 'The Initiate of the mysteries of Isis' and is seated between the columns of the sanctuary. He leans upon a triple cross and makes the sign of esotericism with his left hand. As a contemporary religious symbol, the three cross bars of the cross interpret as the 'Papal Cross.' The three cross bars represent the Roman Catholic pope's triple role as Bishop of Rome, Patriarch of the West, and successor of Saint Peter, chief of the Apostles. The word 'Esoteric' means admitted to the inner circle. Esotericism, being an element of initiation of knowledge that must be kept secret and only accessible to those with the proper intellectual background. Esotericism is not part of a single tradition but is used in a vast array of traditions."

As the Seer finished saying this, he was staring at me intently.

I felt a burning, and my face was flushing red. "*What?* Never mind. I get what you are saying!" I said loudly.

Both the Hierophant and the Priestess burst out laughing and said, "Just relax. You are OK!"

Looking back embarrassed, I said, "I thought about what you said, living my life from my greatest strength!" Looking at them both fiercely, they both responded very calmly, which should have made me calm but did not. I continued: "From my greatest strength I have the ability to connect to peoples' needs, sometimes before my own. I am able to dream ahead possible solutions to their problems. I am able quickly to see new ways to rearrange a room, what to put into a painting, see into a life. Many times I am able to dream transfer these insights as a gift to another. I suppose I am now realizing that my life would be different if I did this with a larger focus, using the 'Staff of Commitment,' like the High Priestess mentioned. By living my life like this, I would be living my Bigger Story!"

Not realizing it, I had stood up and was pacing the porch, flipping the key from one hand to another. When I stopped speaking, I was not sure what to do. I set the key on the nearby table.

The Hierophant had gotten up and was clapping; so were others. I stood in place, my gaze flitting from one person to the next.

The Hierophant lead me to my chair, saying, "She does know how to grab the floor when she wants too!"

Everyone laughed at this—even me! Snuggling into my chair and sipping coffee, I looked around the porch now and realized there were more Dreamers that had joined our group.

The Hierophant said, "Let's go back to your 'What If' questions!" He was standing next to the table and emptying the basket we had carried earlier of holly clippings, stones, and violets. On the table was a clear, round, glass vase; as he spoke he arranged these items into the vase. He spoke in a comforting voice, and it was fascinating to watch him set up the flower arrangement, turning the vase this way and that, making an artful arrangement. I pulled myself back from daydreaming to listen, sitting up straighter in my chair.

The Seer said, "We finally go through some of the trials of life and begin to build a future and often we may be struck with 'What if'…everything you have been working for is taken? Maybe it is stolen, vanishes somehow. And what if, what if? And our mind reels!"

There was utter silence. We all sat waiting to hear what the Hierophant would say next. He looked at all of us. My mind was certainly reeling.

Very calmly he picked up the pitcher of water and poured this into the flower arrangement. He picked up his creation and smiled as he admired the beauty. Setting it down, he turned and said, "You may be asking, how can we be free of this fear? And The Hierophant, as the wise teacher I am says, there are two ways: one, either give up that which you fear to lose so it no longer holds power over you, or, two, you may consider what you will still have if your fear actually comes to pass in this reality." He stopped speaking and looked around at each of us. "After all," said the Hierophant, "if you did loose all you'd built you, would still keep the knowledge and the experience and the Dream of this, would you not?"

Each of us slowly nodded our heads in agreement to this, but none of us knew quiet what to say.

Turning to the Hierophant from where I sat leaning on my chair, I said, "Trust! Trust in my staff of commitment and the number five; pay attention to the patterns of meaning! That is what comes to me."

The other Dreamers all began to add their own thoughts. One said, "I often find solace in my various Dream Journey experiences!" There was quite a lot of enthusiasm generated.

The High Priestess said, "The sign of Taurus is an Earth sign and is connected to the Hierophant, meaning a holy man, initiate of heavenly realms. What one needs to realize is Taurus has the purpose to bring the spiritual down to Earth. He symbolizes a connection to the divine, which answers many a human voice. The Hierophant is the universal principle of knowledge. He teaches us about faith within us and our families and extended communities. Trust faith in life, and when we have challenges that require us to go deeper, we use faith within our own selves."

The Hierophant Seer was standing at the table now. He picked up the large, white candle I had offered him early in the day and nodded to me as he spoke. Lighting the candle, he looked at the sun that was directly overhead. We heard the bells toll twelve times. It was noon.

Quietly, he said, "I was called 'The Pope' once, in another faraway time. 'The Pope' energy represents a masculine energy and several other things. 'The Pope' represents sound. Remember we talked about the senses! Sound for the Pope is the ability to listen when spoken too. And to be able to talk to the heart of others, so they in return listen to us. As the Hierophant, he teaches one how to listen. He is the awakened one, and he mirrors your inner spiritual self."

"The Pope is a bridge between the causal realms, Heaven, and the physical world, Earth. As the Hierophant, he is the great manifestor...His primary role is to illuminate!

"The Pope is a spiritual guide. He may actually represent anyone who guides us in our walk of life. This could be a counselor, parent, and a friend. Call on the Hierophant, as there are many that can be of help. There are many who are 'soul sick,' and this great illuminator can assist."

The Hierophant Seer was still standing at the table. He had picked up the small stones we had gathered earlier. Looking at me, he said, "How are your 'What if's?"

Laughing in response, I said, "I am really feeling much better! After all, you showed me how to understand the 'Staff of Commitment'! And I will forever trust in my own experience of knowledge!"

"Excellent, my dear Dreamer!" he said, chuckling.

Now he was placing the small stones we had found on our walk around the holly flower arrangement in the glass vase. Setting them in patterns of five, I noticed. As he looked at what he had made, he said, "Just like the beauty of these male and female holly clippings and the delicate purple violets, we enjoy viewing them for a time, and then their beauty changes into something else. As Dreamers we must learn to stay in the present and use what is offered to us while there. Whatever the offerings are in that moment in time. Always trusting in the ever-flowing cup of the Grail!"

"Well, Dreamers! It is noon!" said the Seer.

The small Dreamer group began to move about, getting ready to go have their noon meal and move into the rest of the day. I was smiling but stayed seated for a few minutes, wanting to assimilate my experience of the Holly Cottage and The Hierophant Seer. Looking up, The High Priestess and The Hierophant came over to me, linked arm to arm.

The Hierophant leaned over to the table and picked up the key that was shining its golden color in the sunlight now. The Hierophant put the key in my palm and said, "Why don't you dream on the female partner key to this golden one, and I believe its color to be silver!" My ears heard what he had said, but my mouth could not speak.

The two Ancient Ones looked at each other and said, "Yes, it is time for lunch!" So gracefully they moved down the steps and away from the cottage.

I called after them, saying, "Thank you, and thank you!" I could not tell if they heard my words, but surely their hearts knew my thanks! Then I looked at the golden key and then down the path; all the others had gone. My senses were busting. Female partner key, which is silver? Dream about it? I just finished getting a few questions answered and was already posed with more. I left the cottage and walked slowly in the sun-filled path. Viewing the trees, an idea glimmered, and I thought maybe the trees would be of help for this new dream? Ah! Such is a Dreamer's life!

THE LOVERS

DREAM OF THE TRUMP SEER: THE LOVERS VI

osters had been placed all around the Grove:
>A Dream Theater in the Round Presentation
>"THE LOVERS"
>The Main Lodge—8:00 p.m. Tonight

So of course, all of the Dreamers were buzzing as to what this was all about! I had been asked by some of the Seers to collect some things to be used for props, and I was happy to do so. This offered me an advantage to be a part of this gala night! The weather was cooperating with mild temperatures, and I heard we would have a starry night sky over our outdoor stage, very good news. This will be fun. I had a list of things to bring by 5:30 p.m. Greenery, flowers, candles, arrows, wings, large sword. A swan, an apple tree! What on Earth? Well, I will just find them and not question. I will know soon enough. As I went about my mission, I had different dream scenarios about the tarot card of The Lovers. Would the Ancient Seers portray the "Star-crossed lovers of Romeo and Juliet"? Maybe it would be "Adam and Eve"? I could not wait to find out.

I was dashing about, collecting the task assigned to me, when one of the other novice Dreamers found me. He looked at my pile of props and said he had been asked to assist me. I was glad for the help. I asked him to find the Swan Seer and The Apple Tree Seer and then meet me at the theater. In the meantime, though, he helped me carry all the other things to the staging area. Then he was off to bring back the Seers. After putting everything down at the edge of the round stage, I looked about for the cast but found no one, as yet. I looked at my watch; it was still five minutes to six. I saw some Dreamers setting up chairs and cushions for the audience, and I was sure the cast would be here in a minute. I was standing in one of the aisles and then walked up the couple of steps to the round stage and observed; then I decided to move the prop items to the center where a long wooden bench sat. As I took in the view of this outdoor theater, I realized there were five aisles, like spokes of a wheel, that connected to the stage with steps. I mused about how the performance would be done, then I saw a group of six Seers coming down one of the aisles, laughing and carrying on, not aware I was on the stage. Then, down another aisle, came my fellow Dreamer, who had The Swan Seer and Apple Tree Seer with him; all were smiling. Turning, I could now see who made up the cast of six. The Lovers: the male God half and the female Goddess half, the pair, which made The Lovers a whole! Then there was "The Emperor" and "The Empress" and "The Sun" and "The Moon." Very interesting, I thought to myself.

One of The Ancient Ones called out, "The props look great. Let's get to work!"

The Emperor nodded a hello to me as I got close to where they were all pulling things out of their bags. Costumes, drums, sage; they had come prepared. The Empress smiled at me and thanked me for collecting everything. She moved quietly like a deer might; she was secretive. Some said stubborn and unpredictable. I wanted to be just like her. Then The Lover-God called me over and told me that we were going to create a garden effect with the greens and flowers. Quickly, I followed his instructions as to how they would like it set up.

As I worked on this, I asked The Lover-Goddess, "Are we recreating a Garden of Eden?"

She laughed and said in a cheery voice, "That is part of it!"

Smiling back at her, I said, "I knew it! I did!" Looking up then, I saw on the other side of the stage the Dreamer who had gone for Seers was now helping The Emperor; both were carrying a huge rock onto the stage. I stopped what I was doing and said, "What is that for?"

"Never mind that," said The Emperor. "Bring that beauty of a sword that you found!"

I answered with, "The sword…whatever for?"

"Just bring it, please, my beauty!"

I gave it to him in an instant.

The Emperor held it, turning it over and admiring the workmanship. Then he said, "Yes! This will make a fine Excalibur!" Next he proceeded to place it next to the huge rock along with greenery. "That will do," he said. "It looks just as it should, being lodged into the stone!" Hearing this, I knew that somehow King Arthur would be making an appearance!

At the center of the stage was another Dreamer; she was being twirled about by The Lover-Goddess. The wings I had picked up were being tied onto her back. With her long, white, flowing gown, yellow hair, and angelic face, she certainly looked the angel that apparently she would be portraying. The Seer showed her how to fold the wings over herself and told her that once they were set up she would do that. She was to sit at the end of the bench, trying to be just part of the scenery, camouflaged until her cue.

This is getting more and more interesting, I thought to myself. Then The Lover-Goddess called me over to help her. The Apple Tree Seer was there, and The Lover Seer was asking her to move her branches about, like so! Which the Apple Tree Seer was happy to do, and then she gave me a wink. The Seer was searching in her bag; finally she pulled out what she had been looking for. Three Apples!

The Apple Tree Seer said, "My own fruit is not quiet ready and certainly not that red! Someone must have painted the apples."

I laughed at that and said to her, "This must be The Forbidden Fruit!"

She laughed and said, "You got it!"

Then, with the string she had, we tied them to the tree. Now The Swan Seer was next to us and asked The Lover Seer where she should set herself up. The Seer had explained to her about using her wings as camouflage, like the angel, until her cue. Then she showed her where she could sit on the bench.

Now, on another part of the stage, I saw The Sun Seer conversing with The Moon Seer and The Lover-God Seer. I walked over to them to see if there was more I could do. One of them said, "Sage. We need sage going all about the stage, for starters. Then I will tell you how to make clouds for later."

Looking back at The Sun Seer who had given me this instruction, I said, "Clouds? What will we do with clouds? Not to mention, how we will make them?"

His only response was a wave of his hand, meaning for me to get on with it!

I could hear The Moon Seer saying as I left, "Which phase shall I be? First phase, Gibbous, Full?" I tried to keep an ear to what they were saying, but I needed to set up my smudging of the theater and did not want to fall short with what had been asked of me.

Walking about the aisles and the spaces where there was seating, I drifted the thick sage smoke all about. From this vantage point, I caught a good view of the production on stage. Additional elements were being put in place, like the snake for the garden scene. The Dreamer stagehands were testing the lighting. This was amazing; just a few simple props made all the difference! I could hear some of the actors going over lines as I continued my counterclockwise sage walk, spiraling toward the stage. I was asked to leave the smudge bowl under the bench at the left side; I was almost to that place now.

Suddenly there was a big commotion, and a few Dreamers came running down the aisle with long poles that had material wrapped about them. I wondered what they were for.

One Dreamer, out of breath and excited, said, "Never thought we would get these made up in time, but here we are." She was saying to the cast of Seers, "And we have twenty-three minutes to spare!" She clapped her hands with the other Dreamers, all proud of themselves.

Then "The Lovers" came to the center and said, "Dreamers, dreamer crew, listen up! This is how it will go!" The Seers proceeded to tell the cast of characters where they would stand and when their cue was. At this point they all said it was now or never, and all were confident that they could pull off a good show. They were laughing about the fact that there had not been much rehearsal in real time, but in dream time they had gotten it!

Now The Emperor came around to much of the cast and gave them each a long staff with a banner at the top, which had a beautifully painted image of The Lovers and the other Ancient Tarot Keepers. He explained that the cast would stand in the small bunch of pine trees nearby, waiting for the audience to be seated. Then, to the sound of a drum and holding their banners, the cast of *The Lovers* would file down each of the five aisles and run up onto the stage. He then showed them the stands that had been placed around the entire stage for holding the banners. The Emperor said he would act as master of ceremonies at that point, and possibly at other times. He would say at the beginning: "Welcome, Dreamers. Let the Dream play begin!" And with that, he said to all the cast, "Hurry now! The audience will be here any minute. To the pines!"

Before I left the stage, The Sun Seer came over to me and draped me with a beautiful bluish multicolored shawl. I asked what that was for, and he explained that I would be the cloud maker, using my shawl to move the smoke. He showed me where I was to seat myself on the left side of the bench. Underneath the bench was a large brazier with several pieces of lit charcoal. He explained that on cue I would get the sage smoldering in my smudge bowl and then, with my shawl, move the smoke into appropriate clouds for the correct effect in the play. There was another brazier there with charcoal and water, and with that my fellow Dreamer would create mist when needed!

"Oh, my!" I said to him, "I sure hope I can do this right!"

"No hoping, Dreamer. You are my weather girl, and we will trust that things will go just fine!" said The Sun Seer. He continued, "We will be working together, and it will be great!"

Laughing at him, I answered, "You had better not mess with Mother Nature!"

He liked that and then said, "Go, go to the pines. It is time!" The Sun Seer ran, holding his banner, and I trailed just behind him.

As we got to the pines, quite out of breath, I nudged the Seer. "We just made it! The theater is filling quickly. Look!"

The fanfare was building. The drumming, softly in the background now, was provided by some of The Keepers. The voices of the audience were in high gear with anticipation for the dream theater event of the season. The night air was cooler, and the star field in the sky was amazing. The First crescent moon had risen, and I thought about The Moon Seer and what she might portray.

I heard some rustling behind me and turned to hear The Emperor say, "OK, troupe! This is it; as soon as the drum gets to the crescendo, I will start down the aisle, and you all will follow within a minute at most! Hold your banners proud, those of you carrying them. Places, places!"

I looked around at the cast. Everyone looked nervous, especially me, and I did not even have any lines! As I looked around, I found them all so beautiful; I felt like we were medieval troubadours! The players were all taking a last deep breath. I was so excited to be running down the aisle with this cast of Dreamers.

The drum was at the correct pitch! The Emperor began his walk, holding his banner proudly. Once he was almost to the stage, everyone else followed down the five aisles, with the pentacle shape providing protection. We all merged at the same time onto the stage. The main players with the banners, which depicted the images of the Ancient Keeper's "The Lovers" were deposited around the stage. Like magic the air currents softly caught the cloth of the banners and waved them slightly in the air. The audience cheered and clapped at that. The stage had been set, the cast was in place, and the magical workings had begun.

Standing now in the center, The Emperor held out his hands and said, "Welcome, Dreamers. Let the Dream play begin!" The whole audience clapped loudly and some whistled. After a moment, he continued, "And now I introduce to you, 'The Lovers'!"

There was more clapping as The Two Lovers moved hand in hand to the center stage. They were bowing and enjoying it! They then separated to different sides of the stage. In the meantime, The Sun Seer had signaled me to begin making clouds. The sage was already smoldering some on the brazier. Then, with my shawl, I began dancing the smoke about, making the best clouds that I could! One of the other Dreamers was helping to make mist in the other brazier; this created a mystifying backdrop for The Lovers as they spoke! The audience was clapping loudly.

The Lover-God was holding a mirror and saying, "The mist within this mirror is making cloud patterns; the mirror is alive like it is a passageway, a doorway. I see a woman from a past time, but she fades in and out. Why, I am feeling such anger that I do not understand! Hush! I hear someone, a woman; something about her words, the softness, makes my anger vanish like the mist." He waved the mirror in front of himself, as if to reconnect. He then said, "Anger: mist so very hard to control, contain, or define!" Again he heard her, but this time he recognized the words. He held the mirror close, he needed to be certain he heard.

The clouds swirled as the voice came, saying, "Seeking your destiny is like looking into a mirror. It is me you seek, your other half!"

The Lover-God moved about the stage, now saying, "My destiny? How could you know what I seek? Who are you, and where are you? You are only tricks in the night air!"

From across the stage I was moving with my shawl, dancing clouds of confusion across the stage so that The Lover-Goddess could make her entrance! She danced and turned, floating in between the clouds as if she were an apparition, then stopped. The stage lighting was directly on her.

In a firm, deep voice, she said, "It is me you seek! I am your other half!" She looked at him directly. She spoke to him with honey and smiles but then shot him a glare that surely had no honey in it!

The Lover-God cringed some as he heard this. Horrors of times past flashed in his mind. What was happening? He pushed it down. "Stay with the living now," he said to himself.

His other half continued, "Throughout time we have been soul mates, lovers, sisters, brothers, mothers, and fathers. In harmony or not, but we always come back stronger than before, and with more wisdom. For in our separation comes the desire to reconnect! True lovers can never really fall short, and they can never get it just perfect. No one is keeping score."

In a booming voice, she demanded, "Look in the mirror and you will see the other half of yourself that is me! Whether it is Inanna and Dumuzi, King Arthur and Guinevere, Adam and Eve, Romeo and Juliet, or Apollo and Artemis. As The Lovers, you and I combine all the elements into a balanced whole. Your lover's destiny is what you choose it to be! Stuck in past turmoils or pining for something lost, do you think everything is equal and all is on par with everything else? Get over it!"

The Seer was quiet for several moments, with her hands on her hips and staring at her other half as he took in her meanings. He looked like a little boy. The audience waited with baited breath!

The Lover-Goddess began walking slowly toward him. Now she was speaking in a soft, musical voice. "Let us Dream of this destiny as a process for personal development, a time to shift to the next level. This will require some adjustments of our personal outlook in order to move up the ladder." She walked away some, and, pointing, she said, "The staircase is there. Our task is to take a step up!"

The stage lights dimmed away from her; I made the clouds thick again. The Lover-Goddess floated to the other side of the stage and began walking up the staircase! The lights shifted to the other side of the stage, and the lighting was now on The Lover-God. He began walking wildly around and around at first, and then the staircase was in front of him. He climbed the first step! The lights dimmed, and the clouds moved in! The audience was clapping loudly. There was much whistling and hooraying. I walked to the bench and sat with my shawl around my head and shoulders until I was needed.

Then The Emperor came to center stage as emcee, saying, "Dreamers, follow the thread backward in time, and we will visit the lives that have been tied within the 'Lovers Knot'!" The lights were a little dimmer on the Emperor as he spoke. "The Lovers represent the impulse that drives us out of the garden and into adulthood. This might manifest as curiosity: Eve, Pandora, and Psyche. Or it may manifest as sexual desires. The manifestation is sometimes as a duty, heeding the call to something larger. When The Lovers appear in a spread, it typically draws the querent's attention to whatever impulse drove her from home, to whatever impulse made him move out. To what made him accept the call in the first place! That original impulse should be honored and understood. If appropriate, the call should be renewed. The relationship with the garden is needed, be it in exile or absence. Lovers, friends, adversaries: each one teaches us; each one stretches us. Each can kill us. Each can break our heart."

The Emperor's voice had been so penetrating that no one in the audience dared to move. The lights faded out on The Emperor, and now we were in the garden. Through the clouds and fog, I created. We began to see The Garden of Eden. The Lover-God was walking toward the apple tree. We could see the Snake lurking there nearby.

The Lover was speaking. "The image of the male and the female are drawn together by Love." Now the lights were on the tree, and we saw Eve standing there so innocently, looking about. Lover-God spoke to say, "Love can present a theme of 'choice' or 'temptation'! As I, Adam, have been witnesses! Then overpowering energies may force us from The Garden!"

At that point we saw Eve take a bite from the forbidden fruit!

Adam spoke. "No matter who we might be, we can become Love's victims!"

Now I puffed up the clouds as much as I could, and somewhere in the background there was a clap of thunder! The lights dimmed.

The Lover-God made an appearance as narrator and had these words to offer: "Love and sex are riveting subjects!" He walked about the stage, moving his hands to accentuate his words. "And as you would expect, the 'Tarot-Lovers' represents both. The urge for union is powerful, and in its highest form, it takes us beyond ourselves."

In the background near the bench, a soft lighting hovered as the angelic being slowly unfolded her wings and stood up for all to see.

The Seer continued, "So when that is the case, we may want the blessing of an angel that may help with the bond of the two lovers."

We now saw the lights highlight the Angel in white standing behind him. Softly we heard her say, "For The Lovers: may they have both blessings in Dreams and in waking life."

The lighting faded from her to The Lover Seer once more. "Sometimes in one's divination draw of The Lovers, there can be an indication of a moral or ethical crossroads. A decision point where you must choose: your personal beliefs or another's. To do this you must know where you stand. For some this may become the dilemma!"

The stage lighting was fading, and I brought on the clouds and the fog intentionally as a gust of change.

The stage setting was medieval, with a knight on a white horse crossing the stage. They stopped near the huge rock that had been placed earlier. I could see that the knight was our Emperor! He circled the rock and then his hand was on the sword. I swirled the clouds a bit more for effect.

We could hear a voice telling him, "The sword was his to bear. All he had to do was to remove it!" The voice said, "Arthur, you will be made king when it is in your hands!" The voice belonged to Merlin (our Magician Seer).

The lighting dimmed around them, and my clouds rolled to center stage. There on the bench sat Queen Guinevere, our Empress. The light shown on her gleaming, strawberry-blonde hair. She was a vision, but a vision in deep pain.

The Lover-God arrived as emcee and said, "I give you the Lovers of King Arthur and Queen Guinevere!"

I moved the clouds in a rolling motion around the queen. The audience clapped with enthusiasm.

Guinevere said, "I am Queen of Summer Country in my own right, and it is a woman's right to choose her champion. I had such hopes, was so young in my love. The years have moved swiftly. The marriage was no worse than most, mine to King Arthur, The House of Pendragon. There was love once. Amir is lost to me, my son dead. I am barren. I will bear no child now. I can no longer weep. I would not, I think, have chosen this path, would I? Had I only known the entanglements. I am Queen of Camelot and Avalon with Arthur my King." She stopped and stood up. The soft mist blew in. "Is it you, sire? Do you hear my words? Or is it only myself out here in the garden under the starry field of the heavens!" She turned and he, King Arthur, began toward her slowly. The Queen said, "Which of us has all things he may desire, my king?"

The lighting faded from Guinevere, and the clouds swirled. The bluish lights fell onto King Arthur.

King Arthur said, "I hold the sword Excalibur, entrusted to me as a mere lad. I heard your words, my Queen. I love you still; a different love, but love it is. All things one may desire, you ask. This is hard. This sword was entrusted to me by The Lady of the Lake. With an oath I swore to defend our Mother who provides for us, defend you, my Queen, with my last breath. All women I have sworn to defend! Yet the times, the ways, change. There are wicked among us, searching for this sword and the hallows that hold the treasures of Mother. The twisted ones push us. It is a double-edged sword. Amir, gone from us Guinevere, my Queen! Morgaine, my sister and heavenly twin! Who is she really? Guinevere, you and I, are we lost? Oh, the pain of it!"

The stars twinkled brightly, and the clouds shifted. There were tears in the audience now.

The Lover-Goddess came to center stage. As emcee she was solemn. There was light drumming in the background. She threw her hands and head up to the starry sky, her dark curls cascading down her white neck, her lips bloodred. The First Crescent Moon began shining down. "I speak to you now as Morgaine. My name, pray that you know, means 'Sea born, offspring of the Sea' Morgaine! I am sworn to the Goddess, High Priestess of Avalon. I am thy Priestess, O Mother! Use me as best thy will!"

The Moon Seer appears as a silver crescent now and says, "Crescent, expansion, growth, struggle, opportunity. The time in the cycle that you gather the wisdom learned at the New Phase. Communicate your intention. Light a candle. Commit to your goal!" She fades from view.

Morgaine continues, "It is torment, it is madness! But it is done; he has chosen. Though it was his plan to follow the path of the flowering tree, he has gone another way with this woman. And in many ways, like the fruit tree, she has fulfilled him. He chooses her and that is his path. Whatever one's choice, it should not be made lightly, as the ramifications will be lasting. Wishing for harmony, union, there are many choices to be made. And difficult decisions are made not necessarily about love." She walked about the stage, stopping next to one of The Lovers' banners. Looking up to the image, her lips were smiling, bloodred. She said, "*Ah!* The Twins, sign of Gemini; theirs is the attribute of communication, or should be!"

Morgaine continued her stroll about the stage. In and out of the misting clouds and fog she walked. The audience was spellbound, as was appropriate.

"O Mother! Hear my prayer!" She stood peering into the eyes of the audience. "But sometimes there is separation. The sword is an attribution of The Lovers. The sword cleaves, cuts, separates. It is through the sword that we know ourselves as individuals and as unique beings. The dilemma of The Lovers: the tension of separation facilitates our desire to reconnect. We seek what we are missing to make us whole. True marriage consists of knowing you are simultaneously united as well as separated. This must be so to work. The Lovers are the royal exalted marriage of The Emperor and The Empress. Without separation there can be no demonstration of love.

"It is time that you hear me. O Mother! I thank you, the Goddess, without ceasing, for having put it in my heart to escape persecution. For having blessed me with thy will!"

Morgaine stopped suddenly! The lighting shifted to something near the bench. Moving slowly, unfolding in the blackness, was a Swan!

Morgaine said, "It is you. You have heard my calls! The Saxons tell of the 'Swan Knight,' 'Lohengrin,' who came from the mountains where Venus lives in The Grail! Can this be so? I wonder…You are him! 'The Knight of the Swan' and the servant protector of woman! Was it all for nothing? Do I dare cling to the Goddess for hope?"

The Swan Knight moved gracefully around the stage; the clouds I made engulfed him and Morgaine. We could hear him say as the lights dimmed, "Not all was for naught; many have grown and healed with Mother. I protect you still! Peace be on you always! There must be Trust!"

We could see that Morgaine had lit a candle as she walked into the black night!

The drumming had gotten a little louder. The audience was whistling and clapping, and some were tapping their feet. The Lovers were certainly invoking feeling tonight!

An array of spotlights lit the stage! The Sun Seer, our emcee, walked to the center and began narrating. "Dreamers! We have followed the threads backward in time to the hearts of lovers; long gone, or are they? And there are others we did not allow time here to be with us! Like our treasured tale of Romeo and Juliet, 'The star-crossed lovers,' doomed from the start, some say. Astrological in origin, with the belief that the positions of the stars ruled peoples' fates. In their case, working against their relationship! Is this true? It must be you who decides! You are the one holding the Dream!

"The Lovers is a confusing tarot, as it is ruled *not* by an emotional water sign but by airy Gemini! In Sanskrit the air is called 'Prana,' meaning 'Breath of Life.' Vital energy filled with desire and love. This is what keeps us alive! To 'The Lovers, The Ancient Ones,' our breath of life…we thank you! Dreamers, I do believe the entire cast should now hear your welcome for them!"

As if the Sun Seer had to encourage the applause! The Dreamer audience was wild with joy! Standing up now, they clapped and whistled their thanks! The Sun Seer then announced each member, and they took their bows. When he came to me, he said, "Our Dream Weather Girl, the Cloud Maker!" As I bowed, he continued, saying, "Clouds may symbolize a veil over something, or possibly a cloud bringing fertile rain. Moods of the sky can also reflect the weather within us. Thank you, Cloud Maker!" I blushed, head to foot, from all the attention, but I was very proud.

But of course the largest bravos were for The Lovers! They stood hand in hand and then bowed and walked to the center of the stage. The staircase was there. They turned to move up the stairs and, with a backward glance, said, "We both need to stretch and walk up the ladder of our Dreams!"

The Dreamer audience was beside themselves! The lights dimmed as the Dreamers called, "Encore! Encore!"

VII

THE CHARIOT

DREAM OF THE TRUMP SEER: THE CHARIOT VI

Walking the winding path down to the water, I was speaking out loud, maybe too loudly, but I could not help it! "Why do things stand in my way? Sometimes there are so many obstacles. I can't take it!" I could hear the sounds of the water lapping the shore now. Tears were dripping down my cheeks. Was anyone around? I did not care! I screamed again, "*Why?*" I could hear that as an echo back to me. I sobered up some and tried to center myself. The beach was in sight now. I needed to think! My ideas are good, I just get things going and feel I am on a roll with bringing something to fruition when…Bam! Someone, something, falls in my tracks, and I have to stop and take care of that! I began tracking back in my life all the dreams I had started to realize that then got put on hold! Lack of time, lack of privacy to pursue them, lack of dollars, lack of enthusiastic energy for the project in the end! "Well, I am tired of *lack*!" I said this quite loudly and turned around in my tracks to see if anyone was there. Thank goodness, no! I did see a figure a long way down the beach, but he or she was certainly too far to have heard! The roar of the waves clapping the shore was very loud; there was no way to have heard my ranting and raving!

I walked the shoreline, with quiet tears streaming from my eyes; they were salty like the ocean water. Here and there I saw small crabs digging into the sand. Carrying their shell houses on their backs, they could retreat whenever they wanted. I smiled at that, thinking how nice to have such a simple life. Walking barefoot, the water was soothing to my body, and I could see the tide was ebbing in now. I watched as a few crabs moved with the waves back out to sea. I thought of some people I knew who had been able to make their voices heard or their work seen. What did they do that helped them get accomplished? What am I missing here? In front of me was a huge piece of driftwood, looking like a sea creature. This would be a good place to sit for a while until I could ease the confusion in my head some.

Thank goodness I had free time this afternoon and two more days before I needed to give my dream presentation! My group of Dreamers had been given an assignment: Present Your Future Dream, illustrating what the Dreamer sees for himself when finished with the training here at the Nemeton. Some of the group had already done their part, and the results were just incredible! How could I ever compete? The waves were lapping in faster, and the tide was coming in, but I liked sitting here on this sea creature and decided to stay put for awhile. I had no idea what I could possibly present! The salty tears came back.

Something like thunder was sounding above the wave noises. What on Earth? I jumped off my sea creature of driftwood and stared into the western sky. I held my hand above my eyes to deflect the sun's glare. Whatever it might be, it was racing directly toward me. Half in the water and half on the beach, the water sprayed in all directions. Then it stopped. Not five feet from me stood a two-wheeled chariot drawn by roan horses. One was chestnut and one was blue, which looked whitish with dapple black flecks. A strong, furious, Mars-like warrior stood inside the chariot. He was in full armor, a shining crown was upon his head, and his left hand held a scepter with the orb of the sun and the reins that held the horses. His right hand held an olive branch. His breastplate of armor had engraved stars upon it. The canopy of the chariot was green with the astrological symbols for Cancer the Crab on each side. In the center was a silvery crescent Moon. I thought it interesting that the crab symbol was there after just seeing them on the beach. The whole picture was overwhelming. I took a minute to read the face of this warrior, but I could not discern anything! Why was he here? I gave him my coolest stare, not knowing what to do.

The Mars Warrior had stepped off the chariot and was rubbing down his horses. I could tell that he treasured them. The blue roan's green blanket matched the color of the canopy. There was a symbol embroidered in the center; it was the symbol for Mercury, The Messenger. Very beautiful, but, I wondered, what is the message for me? Outwardly I was trying hard to give an indifferent expression, with barely a smile on my face, striving to be calm.

Suddenly he was speaking to me! "Some might see a smile on your face, but I know there is sadness lying underneath."

"Why do you say that?" I said in an annoyed tone, a touch breathlessly.

In a laughing response, he said, "Pushing the limits of one's comfort zone is not easy. Just like recognizing that we may ask for help; that isn't easy either!"

I could feel anger pushing up; it was all I could do to hold it in. I was adamant when I said, "I need to leave now!"

He was busy adjusting the reins and the bridle pieces for the horses; both horses nudged him fondly. In a sturdy, even voice, he said, "Many get stuck along about now; the path is not for everyone. Dreamer's choice, it always is!"

I had walked away from him, but that last remark did it! "Stuck! Who are you? I did not ask for your advice!" He stared back at me fiercely. Though there was warmth underneath, it unnerved me. I looked away. He said, "Well, of course you must know who I am! Ah! But maybe an introduction would help. I am 'The Chariot VII Seer,' at your service and your current guardian. To watch over and keep watch, it is my duty to be as a sentinel and protect those who have been called and are ready to move on in their path."

As he was staring at me, I began to feel something I could not explain. I finally answered, as if I had been put under a spell and there seemed to be nothing I could do to stop it. Responding very quietly, I said, "But I did not call you!"

He looked at me in a queer way, like a father might, and said, "It was not your out-loud words that got my attention!"

After that statement I crumbled to the sand beneath my feet. The blue roan was right there; his foot pawed at my hand. When I looked at him, I could feel unbelievable love. With tears, I said to the Seer, "What did you hear?"

The Chariot Seer replied with, "Ah, my dear little Dreamer, I have heard the blue veil of sadness around you! The time has come for divine intervention! Your time of suffering can end. The emotions that have surfaced are healthy. Right now there is nothing to do but ride the wave a little as this purging takes place. Keep afloat and the shift will come. Storms are difficult, but they do end!"

As I looked at him, my heart felt more open. I was beginning to realize he was genuine and there could be something to learn from him. I decided that it would be best if I let go of my stubborn tendency of not asking for help. This was big for me. Feeling the wind, I saw a little whirlwind blowing sand around. New energy, maybe? Before I could loose my nerve, I said, "Seer, what is it I should do right now? I have an assignment to complete and do not even know where to start! My feelings get—"

The Seer stared at me intently. But in a calm voice, he said, "One thing at a time! First you must realize that your lifeline to your source of strength is within you, and you can continue making this stronger. Remember we are magnetized to the reality we choose, so be thoughtful with what you want. Use these questions to guide yourself: 'What is your passion?' 'What brings you joy?' Reach for the stars, my dear! Answer these questions, and your purpose will be revealed. Then once you have that in hand, no matter what, stay the course!"

The Seer had been standing next to his two horses. As he finished speaking, I could feel three sets of eyes on me. A shiver went down my back. My feet were covered with the incoming tidewater. I could not speak.

The Ancient One sensed this and said, "Let's walk down the beach awhile. Why don't you hold the reins and lead the way."

Silently I nodded my head OK and took the reins from him. The horses and the chariot trailed behind us, walking slowly.

We walked into the sunlight of the western sky. It felt good to move, and I was feeling very comfortable with this chariot warrior.

The Seer began speaking. "Let me share a few things about the life of a warrior. A light warrior is constantly scouting the energy. Be it light or dark, it is around us at all times. Once detected, a warrior's code is nonaggression; one waits until legitimately challenged or called, and we yield when at all possible. We learn discernment and negotiate our movements with an impeccable vibration of energy, which is based on no distractions or loss of focus. Once engaged in action, a charioteer warrior is able to see with the eyes of faith in the Light. We learn there is no room for doubt; doubt dilutes."

I was still holding the reins. I said to the Seer, "I feel like I have been off on a wrong trail. I can see there is so much for me to learn! You have it all together. It is easy for you!"

He responded with, "*Oh!* I see. 'The poor me routine' is what you will try!"

I did laugh at that and then said, "No! I do not want to be sorry for myself. There is just a lot that I need to do! And you have already done it all!"

Stopping then, the Seer answered, "Let me tell you something, dear Dreamer. I always remind myself of this: just because you have arrived, does not mean you are no longer on the journey!"

I laughed very hard and told him that I would be sure to remember that when I arrived!

"Well then," said the Seer, "we have much to do, and the day is moving quickly." The Chariot Seer stopped suddenly; he put his hands on both sides of my shoulders and told me this: "First and foremost. Be who you came to be, my child. You must step into your power!"

I nodded my head but could not speak; his words stayed in my head. We resumed our walk.

The Seer began additional lessons in rapid succession. I was mesmerized. I had to really trust my dreaming skills that I would remember everything!

The Ancient One was relaying in a strong voice, "The Chariot is fire and yang energy. Some key words would be: conquest, willpower, discipline, bravery, victory, and honor. The Chariot is the vehicle of the Hero and is used for new adventures and to celebrate his triumphant return. Within the chariot the Hero is mobile yet secure. To the ancients an archaic term for 'chariot' was 'wain'; a horse-drawn cart, which was built by a 'wainwright' of skill and reputation. Today the name Wainwright is a surname to many. It is especially important that the hero master and control the raw animal energy of his horse-drawn cart, the two horses. One is physical energy and the other is spiritual energy, which pull in different directions. The Charioteer needs a steady hand on the twin reins to be able to move through whatever he encounters. From Greek myth we have the image of The Chariot associated with the Greek god 'Mars' or Roman god called 'Ares.' Originally the god Mars was associated with green vegetation, now associated with the color green, also fertility and vitality. He was called upon at the beginning and end of war season, which was March through October. 'Mars' was called the god of action. This was translated into 'the god of Marches' and 'the March God.' This referred to that month in which nature began to move, change, and march into a new season: the month of March, the beginning of the spring season. There is a term for the date of March fifteenth on the Roman calendar, which is, 'the Ides of March,' meaning a turning point. It was on March fifteenth in 44 BC that the Emperor Caesar was assassinated."

"Wow!" I said to the Seer. "When I first saw you earlier, I thought, Mars warrior! But I had no idea of all the history."

"Yes!" he said. "And there is a great deal more. Let me continue. The chariot is associated with the astrological sign of Cancer but also with the sign Aries because this corresponds to the God Mars, which rules Aries. Mars was the first month in the pre-Julian Roman calendar. The birthday of the God Mars was celebrated the first of March, with festivals through the month.

"I would like to now talk about the vehicle of the chariot. In tarot circles there are different viewpoints; all of them have merit. The four posts of the chariot represent the four elements: Earth-green, Water-white, Air-blue, Fire-red. The posts are also related to the temperaments of man. The hero standing in the middle of the four elemental posts is a symbol of governing the Anima Mundi."

The Ancient one went on without skipping a beat. "In the Qabalah, The Chariot is path eighteen on the Tree of Life. This is summed up in these phrases, 'Child of the Power of the Water' and 'Lord of the Triumph of Light.'"

Perplexed, I looked at the Seer. He looked back, saying, "In essence our task on this chariot path is to get our purpose clear and bring that into manifestation on this plane!"

I answered, "I could sure use some of that knowledge. Where do I sign up?"

The Seer was laughing, but then he turned serious and said, "When a Dreamer's destiny is *not* moved forward and worked out, the results are rarely welcomed. The first task is to have a clear channel to bridge the abyss that separates us from our true purpose. Only then can our destiny filter to the dense levels in this physical plane. As cosmic beings we are immersed in the waters of manifestation, which is there for us all, but many of us simply do not know what to do. We have amazing light encoded within us. Our task is to act as mediators and brighten the waters with our encoded natural light. The danger lies in the light 'being dowsed by the very water we are in,' or obscured in some way. This may be, possibly, because one takes their standards of action from the dictates of another. When this is the case, the incarnating Spirit has lost touch with their true responsibility, which is the Truth of One's Own Light! There can be a trap here of replacing one's own light with the authority of another."

The Seer was silent as he looked at me a few minutes. Then he said, "What is the message here? I will tell you! Know your intention! Know your direction! This is how one can manifest the movement of the wheels that support 'The Chariot,' which holds the King or Queen of Light! On this path we learn about our own movement. Also the driver must be able to control the reins of the chariot. There may be danger of reaching too high, going too fast. Or simply being unprepared for the ride. We choose our path carefully, having done our map Dream work ahead of time, my dear Dreamer! And So It Is! And the movement begins!"

The orange solar disk in front of us was radiating warmth. The Chariot Seer had looked at me in such a way that I knew this was not the time to interrupt on his flow. He was looking directly at the sun and then had this to say, "The ancients had a depiction of the 'Sun itself as a Charioteer driving a team of four horses.' This relates to the 'Immortal Chariot of the Sun of King Solomon.' King Solomon had made himself a chariot from the wood of Lebanon, expressing the essence of mysticism, which was: 'that man is his own fate and the maker and controller of his own destiny.' The history of the chariot runs deep. From the Greeks we have 'Helios,' The Sun god of Greek myth. He was portrayed as a handsome god crowned with the shining aureole of the Sun. He drove the 'Chariot of the Sun' across the sky each day to the Earth, circling Oceanus and through the World-Ocean. And he returned to the east each night. The Nordic people of Denmark relate the story of the 'Trundholm Sun Chariot,' which depicts the huge sun in a cart-like chariot being pulled by a mare." The Seer stopped for a minute and turned away from the warm rays.

Then he said, "Yes, the threads of myth-history are certainly intertwined. The Chariot is the conqueror who, in his mobile throne, occupies the center of the four elements. This is the man who has vanquished and directed the elementary forces, and he is in victory. In victory as a man, yet performing the function of God the creator. He is mobile; he has learned to pass from one world to another."

We had come to the ragged rock jetty along the shore. The Chariot Seer took the reins from me without saying a word. He smoothed the blankets on the horses and patted them. Then he readjusted the reins to the interior of the chariot. What was he up to? I wondered if he intended to be off.

I was about to ask, when he climbed into the chariot and, offering me a hand, said, "I believe it is time for you to assume the reins of power!"

I was so startled, I did not speak or move for what seemed like forever! Finally, I answered with, "You mean me?"

He roared with laughter and said, "I do not expect you to perform miracles, but, yes, you!"

I was laughing as I got into the Chariot, but on the inside I was so nervous. This was something very new to me!

The Seer said, "Are you ready? Let's turn her around and follow the shoreline back down the beach!"

I said, "OK, let's go for it!" We began slowly, with the Seer guiding me. He let go and I held the reins. I felt unsure, but it was good!

The lessons continued with the Chariot Seer saying, "On this point of the Chariot path, you are entering an entire new path. Your old personality can no longer hold the growing force of your Spirit. You are in progression toward personal change. You are mobile within your chariot."

He paused and asked me how I was doing. I answered with, "OK!" I could not say more; I was too involved with leading of the horses!

The Seer seemed to understand and said, "You are doing fine. Just take a deep breath and relax some!" He continued the teachings. "Your subconscious has opened and become active. There have been many choices for this transformation. You have developed your armor, which acts as defense against any vulnerability. You are protected and equipped to meet challenges, now becoming the master of expressing your life! Learning balance and understanding the power of Spirit within yourself: all these things you have learned through your willingness for self-examination. Part of the magic you have acquired is the effective use and power of words, deeds, symbols. As you have come to understand these things, you have been forced to grow. Now you are able to create from what you have gained!"

We had gone quite a distance along the beach. I was in a dream and under a spell, I was sure! Yet, when I looked at my hands, it was me doing the directing, communicating to the roans go left, go straight; this was amazing, and I liked it!

Coming out of my dreaming, I heard the Seer saying, "Well, Dreamer, how do you like assuming the reins of power?"

In a very strong voice, I answered, "Let me think. Well, yes! I like it and could easily get used to this!"

The Ancient One was laughing as he said, "You could, could you? Let me caution you with this. The chariot is very much about your ego, your conscious mind, and your self-image in relation to the world. So a Dreamer must be certain of their focus and how it not only serves them but the spirit as well. Remember your true path. Earlier we talked about two questions. 'What is your passion?' and 'What is your joy?' So, Dreamer, as you are learning to drive this chariot and understand your movements, I do not think you will have any trouble finding the answers you seek!"

We had gone a long way down the beach. The two roans were trotting at an even clip, and the dunes curved upward toward the path back to the main Grove. I slowed the horses some and said to the Chariot Seer, "It is getting late. Would you like to have your chariot back now? I am very happy to have had your teaching company this afternoon. Thank You!"

He looked at me a little surprised and said, "It has been my pleasure! I would, however, very much like it if you would drive me directly to the Grove, if it is OK with you?"

I replied, "OK? Are you serious? Of course! I cannot wait to show off!"

The Seer was laughing as he said, "Go for it!"

As we went up onto the grassy hill, I felt a surge of confident energy. With a big smile, I said to the Seer, "I think I know what I can present for my assignment of a Future Dream!"

The Seer looked back at me radiantly and said, "Well, of course you know, Dreamer! And remember, once you have that focus, 'No matter what, stay the course!' You have it now, and you are learning motion!"

VIII

JUSTICE

DREAM OF THE TRUMP SEER: JUSTICE VIII

There was much commotion on the back veranda of the dining lodge after breakfast; I went out back to find out what was happening. I discovered several carpenter Dreamers there building something; I began asking questions, of course. To my delight they were building a dais, a throne for the Lady of Justice, as they so sweetly put it. Thanking them for their time, myself and two other Dreamers who were curious decided to track down this Lady of Justice. We wanted to find out in advance what she was planning.

The Dreamers and I set off to find the Tarot Seer of Justice VIII. We were intent on becoming involved and helping with whatever the Ancient One's plan might be. I said to the women while we walked, "The lessons I received the most from are the ones that I actually assisted in helping the Seer set up prior to a program." Both of the Dreamers agreed that hands-on work was the best teacher!

One of the women said, "The Keepers are the stewards of the Earth, and whenever I am invited to work with them, it is an honor and a privilege." I was delighted with her comment and told her so.

It was a misty summer morning, which added to the mystery of Lady Justice.

When we arrived, the mist had turned to light soft rain. We dashed onto the veranda of the lodge. No one seemed to be around. However, there was a beautiful sword sitting on the rocking chair next to the door. I was about to go into the lodge, when a few of the Keepers came into view. The next thing we knew, The Strength Seer, The Temperance Seer, and The Justice Seer all burst through the door.

The Seer of Justice walked over to the rocker with the sword on it. Looking at us, she asked, "What have we here? A Dreamer delegation, maybe?" She was laughing along with the other Keepers.

The Dreamers and I exchanged glances. Here we go, I thought to myself. But out loud I answered, "Not exactly. More like a few curious Dreamers wondering if you would like any help with the event you are planning?"

There was another roar of laughter from the Seers. The Dreamers and I were laughing as well, but we each felt a slight unease.

This was quickly erased when the Strength Seer said, "Do you suppose they are psychic? But, hey, I like that. Dreamers who are willing to help. This could be beneficial!"

There were a few moments of silence, with the other Dreamers and I not knowing what to say. We watched The Justice Seer as she looked over the sword that she had picked up. It was about thirty inches long of gleaming silver. The hilt had a cross piece forming the handle that had been intricately carved with ancient symbols. There were rubies and emeralds set within the design. I wondered to myself, how ancient it must be.

Someone was speaking; I came out of my daydreaming and realized that The Temperance Seer was asking Lady Justice, "Does that feel comfortable?" The Seer was helping Lady Justice with the scabbard belt, which held the sword in place at her waist.

She answered, "Yes! Yes, this feels fine, thank you." From the rocker she now picked up the crown that had been underneath. Placing this over her arm, she said, "Ready, everyone?" Looking at her fellow Keepers and then at us the Dreamers, she said, "Well, if you mean to be of help, we had better get going! Then from her skirts, she produced a pad and pen and gave it to me. She told me to make note of the items she would require. Next she asked, "Have the posters been put up?"

One of the other Dreamers said, "No, I haven't seen anything."

The Seer replied, "Make that your job, please. Display them in the dinning lodge and the other usual places."

The Dreamer answered, "Yes, of course. And what does the poster say?"

The Justice Seer said, "I thought you Dreamers knew, being psychic and all!"

The Seers all laughed at that! Coming back to her self, The Justice Seer produced a flyer of what the poster would be:

Past Life Dreaming

With Lady Justice

Hall of Judgment

1:00 p.m. @ The Main Lodge

Today

The other Dreamers and I all oohed and said that this was perfect. It would definitely pique the interest of the entire circle of Dreamers!

Walking along the woodland path, the sun glistened on the raindrops that clung to branches and grass. Everyone was chattering about the current doings around the Nemeton; we were all feeling happy to be here. Arriving at the Main Lodge, we found a bevy of activity. In a nearby field, a tent was being arranged in case of inclement weather.

But now with the sun out fully, I said out loud, "Maybe we will not need the tent."

The Justice Seer answered, "It is fine to leave it in place. For now, with the flaps down we can get our program organized and keep the mystery going. Later, should Father Sky agree, we can roll up the flaps for the program time. In the meantime we have much to do."

She asked me to see the list I had been writing as we walked, and she dictated what to write. Looking this over a minute, then looking around the tent, she said, "Yes! This will do just fine as the Hall of Judgment!" Now she began telling me where she would like the incense placed. The braziers should be along the two main entrances, one on each side of the aisle. Flowers! She wanted there to be many flowers. They would be helpful because the subject matter would be somber. There were many other details that she wanted me to attend to as well. I walked with her around the tent, noting various things.

We were near the dais when the Seer said to me, "I would like you to be my assistant during the program, especially at the last half when the Dreamers begin to participate. How does that sound to you?"

A surge of excitement came right through me, and I quickly answered, "I would be honored."

The Seer went on with, "Of course you will have to have the proper gown. The Temperance Seer will help you with that." I nodded my head yes! Then she began to explain that near the end of the program she would be seated at her dais, which would be upon the third step level. She told me that this indicates that fully administered justice can be reached only by those who have reached the third degree in their studies of the Mysteries. I knew I would be pondering that for awhile.

Next she explained that I would be in charge of the cards and escorting various Dreamers to her for judgment. I asked the Seer, "What cards do you mean?"

The Ancient One answered with, "Tarot Trumps, of course! Let me explain. At the base of my dais will be a large clay bowl, with the Tarot Trumps inside. The Dreamer will have been brought to me by you. They will be playing the part of their deceased self and are now here in the 'Hall of Judgment' to receive judgment; pronounced by me! They will stand before me and ask this question of intent: '*What* is my current lesson from this past life?' This judgment will be in the form of one of the Tarot Trumps' that they have just selected from the clay bowl you have offered them. Their judgment-sentence is the card that they receive. This becomes their 'Current Life Lesson' from the 'Past Life' of the tarot card they selected. The Dreamer is then encouraged to dream with their card to gain any insights on their own Karma. And should they want to take this further, they can make a small sculpture from nature to represent this and offer that 'Karma Sculpture' to a fire ceremony!"

All I could muster was, "Oh! My! This is really going to be something!"

The Seer responded with, "It will be fun! Let's get going on the preliminaries!"

Everything had been made ready. It was now 12:45 p.m., and the Dreamers had filled the Judgment Hall. There was quite a buzz of excitement in the air. I thought to myself, they are all very brave! I wonder how they will all be later.

Now the soft drumming became a drumroll, with chanting and chimes. The Dreamer audience was seated. At this point the Keepers filed in and filled the seats in the front reserved for them.

I was standing near the Justice Seer, The Temperance Seer, and The Strength Seer. The Temperance Seer winked at me. I thanked her again for the help she provided in getting me a beautiful gown, an Egyptian-Greek-looking garment, which would help me play the part.

The two other women Dreamers who were attending the Seers with me would also be next to Lady Justice. We were all very nervous.

The drumming was softer. We began walking down the main aisle, and the standing audience was clapping. Once in the front of the dais, we fanned out, facing the audience. Each of us gave a small bow and sat upon the benches to either side of the dais. The Dreamer audience, still clapping, took a minute to quiet as the Tarot Seer of Justice bid them to be seated. As I looked around our space, which had now become The Hall of Judgment, I admired the burning braziers, the added candles, and of course the flowers! All was as it should be. Even the tent itself added to the atmosphere. We had added long, flowing, colored-fabric streamers at various places, just so. The sides of the tent had been rolled up. The sun was out; all was well.

The Justice Seer was saying, "Dreamers, let us open our circle!"

Standing in a circle, we sang. Afterward, The Justice Seer offered protection and opened our session.

Once everyone was seated, the Seer began explaining her program. Lady Justice stood in the center of the Dreamers seated in a semicircle; she was very regal. Her gown, also of Egyptian-Greek design, was a deep emerald green, sleeveless, and low cut. She had a wrap of deep cobalt blue silk over one shoulder. Stunning and graceful, she moved about as she spoke. Only occasionally using hand gestures, there was a slight smile on her face. She was painting the history for us with herself in the lead role. The stage was being set. The audience of Dreamers was definitely responding. As I looked over the crowd, I saw that she had them enraptured.

In a smooth, serious voice, the Justice Seer was explaining the twenty-second path in the Qabalah, by Gareth Knight. "This twenty-second path, Justice, is known as the 'Path of Karmic Adjustment.' Here we learn about the effects upon the personality. The aspects of the teachings may be likened to a Judgment Hall, the place of cosmic balance. The best analysis of the twenty-second path relates to the 'Egyptian Book of the Dead,' particularly the judgment scene. Later in our program we will participate in a 'Judgment scene for Dreamers'! The Egyptian Judgment Hall is where each individual was judged after death and, according to the result, either went onto a life of bliss or was annihilated!"

There was a large out cry from the audience at that. The Seer continued, "To the Egyptians, the thought of death was awful, so it was really only the very unworthy that were totally annihilated. Most were fortunate to have only the unworthy parts of themselves eliminated. Facing judgment is difficult. The personality does not want to do this, and the individual may find it difficult to face certain truths about themselves. What does one do about this challenge? A person, who is committed to their soul path, has the answer in working on their 'Redemption.' This means the ability to face up to the situation 'Within Oneself,' coupled with the 'Willingness' to change what needs changing."

The Seer looked around the Judgment Hall in silence. There were murmurs here and there, and she wondered if they were getting nervous yet. Then she picked up where she had left off. "Easy to say but, as you know, hard to do, for it requires ruthless honesty. Once the person has accomplished this, they can learn a certain mastery over the parts of themselves that need purging or changing."

There was definitely a change in mood now from the Dreamers as they each thought over the judgment of themselves. I sent them all love. The Dreamers who were on the bench with me seemed to be doing something similar as they smiled at me and then the Seers.

The Justice Seer said, "This afternoon I am your Lady Justice, and this"—pointing with her hand around our tent hall—"is the Hall of Judgment! Now let me tell you about the 'Egyptian Judgment Hall of Osiris'! It is the place where balance is performed. Osiris was the judge of the Dead and the King of the underworld. This is the region of the Dead, or the Dead-Land, and is called 'Tat.' Here the deceased come and declare their innocence and purity, called 'Redemption-Declarations.' These are forty-two negative affirmations, called The Forty-Two Declarations of Purity.' This is done before coming to the final judgment by Osiris. At one end of the hall sits Osiris."

The Seer walked to one end of the hall. One of the Seers, the Hierophant, was there, representing Osiris. Then the Seer walked to the other end of the hall. There stood the Temperance Seer, representing the Goddess Maat.

The Seer said, "This is 'Maat,' the Goddess of Law and Truth." She continued explaining how the deceased walk through the hall doing their 'Forty-Two Declarations of Purity.' "The deceased arrive at 'Maat,' the Egyptian Goddess of Absolute Law. She is the feminine counterpart of the recording god, Thoth. Maat considers the weighing of the heart. To the Egyptians the heart was considered the location of the soul. The deceased people with good, pure hearts were sent onto 'Aark.' The unworthy were devoured by the Goddess Ammit, the lioness. The deceased person stands before Maat, and the heart of the dead is weighed in the scales."

Lady Justice brought over the Strength Seer, who held the Scales. I noticed the scales were imprinted with the Greek letter of alpha (beginning) on one and the letter omega (ending) on the other.

The Justice Seer then pulled me forward and said to the audience, "This Dreamer represents the deceased." I was not so sure I liked this role! I walked with the Seer as she relayed the story of judgment. "The deceased stands before The Goddess Maat"—played by the Temperance Seer. "She is beautifully robed, and her headdress is made of ostrich plumes. Maat, staring into the eyes of the deceased"—played by me!—"asks for the heart to be put onto the scales." She did not take her eyes away from my own, then continues, "Maat says, 'In the balance scale I will place my symbol.'" She took a feather from her headdress and placed her symbol of 'Maat' into the scale. Now the Goddess of Right and Truth paused.

The Justice Seer continued relaying the story. "The weighing is usually performed by 'Anubis,' the 'Opener of the Ways' and the god who brings the souls into the Judgment Hall. The God 'Thoth' records the results of the weighing, and the justified soul is lead by 'Horus' from there to Osiris for the final judgment. 'Horus' is accompanied by his consorts Isis and

Nephthys." The Seer took my hand, and we walked up the three steps of the dais. She put on her crown, took her jeweled sword from its scabbard, and sat on the throne as Osiris. I continued standing as the deceased.

The Justice Seer continued, "The deceased is brought to the feet of Osiris, whose name is 'Lord of Winds.' The deceased says, 'Hail, Lord of Winds. Save me. I have purified myself.' Thoth then asks the deceased, 'What is thy condition?' The deceased replies with her condition. Osiris is brought forward to then receive her and declares a new life for her and promises that subsistence should be provided for her from the 'Eye of Ra'!"

The entire Hall of Justice was held in an anxious silence! The Seer moved from me and the other players, and we seated ourselves on the benches. The audience of Dreamers was clapping loudly, and some whistled! It seemed they were happy for me, the deceased, to have been declared a new life! The Justice Seer was smiling to the crowd as she said, "We all love to see life go on, don't we."

More clapping and comments of "Yes! Yeah!"

She was holding her arms up now for silence. She continued, "This whole process is to remind us that the god-forms are aspects of the soul itself and that it is not other external entities that decide our fates! We must ask the questions of redemption for ourselves. On the path of the 'Higher Mysteries,' there are many tests. Much is weighed in the golden balance; many efforts are rejected. We must be willing to do our own work if we expect to pass the tests.

"The Justice Trump, represents the 'right order' of the universe, especially balance, whether in the physical world or in the spiritual world. Achieving such balance is not a simple matter of numerical equality, for fair, just, use of the scales requires a steady hand and a good eye. This skill can be finely honed, like the sword. True justice tempers measurement with wisdom. Masculine discrimination with feminine compassion. Male with female. Fire with Water.

"This Justice card, as we have just witnessed, is a reminder of the judgment of the soul in the Hall of Osiris. It teaches that only balanced forces can endure and that eternal justice destroys with the sword that which is unbalanced. Sometimes the image of the Goddess of Justice is portrayed with a braid of her own hair twisted around her neck. This may subtly imply that man is the cause of his own undoing, the hair knotted at the neck!

"Many Justice Trump images are portrayed with pillars in the background. The pillars have a purpose: they separate two different conditions. As an initiate of the 'Mysteries,' the candidate stands between the pillars, between the 'Balance of Justice,' and it is there that he names and explains the significance of the pillar parts. This is a test that one must be well prepared for, and the adept must not fail!"

The Justice Seer had been standing in the center of the Hall of Justice. She now paused and was looking about, as if to determine how well the Dreamers were all listening. She stood there in full justice regalia, beautiful robes, crown on her head, and sword in her hand. The smile on her face indicated she was being received. Now she walked down one aisle and picked up with her lecture.

"In the history of the Justice Trump, the number placement of this card has been shifted within the twenty-two trumps. Mostly Justice is attributed to the number eight trump, but sometimes it's number eleven or number twenty. Justice is also considered one of the three cardinal virtues represented in tarot. The other two cards are Temperance and Strength.

"The Greek philosopher Aristotle gives an account of what 'Justice' meant in pre-Christian times. His idea was not about karma. Rather, Aristotelian justice is about fairness in transactions between people. The just person takes only what he or she is fairly entitled too. It is about not cheating, being greedy, or taking advantage. Justice is to find the proper mean between any extremes."

"There is more Greek history," said the Seer. "The Greek 'Goddess Themis,' daughter of Uranus and Gaia, was considered the organizer of 'communal affairs of humans, particularly assemblies.' Her name 'Themis' means 'law of nature.' The ability of the 'Goddess Themis' to foresee the future enabled her to become one of the 'Oracles of Delphi.' She was called in some myths the 'Goddess of Divine Justice.' Many classical images of Themis did not show her blindfolded. Because of her talent for prophecy, she had no need to be blinded. Nor was she holding a sword, because Themis represented common consent, not coercion. Themis presided over the proper relation between man and woman, and the basis of the rightly ordered family. The Greek oral poet Hesiod, eighth century BCE, mentions Themis as the first recorded appearance of Justice as divine personage. Some trump images of Justice portray the Goddess of Justice as being blindfolded, because this was thought to avoid favoritism while making decisions.

"It is the Greek 'Goddess Athene,' the Roman 'Goddess Minerva,' who holds the 'Scales of Justice.' She is the goddess most closely associated with a well-balanced mind. The function of the scales is weighing, beginning and end, intention and consequence, therefore weighing 'means and ends.'

"Some accounts say that the scales are about our life, our karma, being weighed. The scales are usually seen as being held in the left hand, the unconscious forces of our lives. There are many references to the scales in the Bible. The god of knowledge who weighs our actions…However, it is important to recognize that God is within us, and we can be guided by our own discrimination and knowledge. Especially that we have our own free will. Justice is usually seen holding the sword of discrimination in her right hand.

"Let me say to you Dreamers who read the cards, when Justice appears, a Reader may say, 'This is your karma!' This might sound trite, at first look, but actually this is the meaning of the card!

"But that is not the whole story. It is important to take into account the surrounding cards. This is the only way to get a true reading on the querent's current karmic pattern and then, of course, Dream scenarios to help them to resolve and enhance that karmic pattern."

The Seer was now walking toward the center of the Hall of Justice. She said when she stopped, "The astrological sign for Justice is 'Libra,' and the element for Libra is 'Air,' which alludes to intellectual activity. Remember the ostrich feathers in Maat's crown headdress?"

The Seer pointed to the Goddess Maat. "Remember that everything has meaning and significance, and the feathers are a symbol of Air. The intellect and truth of Maat are symbolized by her feather plumes."

The Justice Seer had now climbed the three steps to the dais. But she did not sit. She motioned for me to come forward to assist her now. By this time it was late afternoon. She asked that the braziers be turned up and that the incense be relit. I picked up the clay bowl of tarot cards and moved next to her. Looking out into the Dreamer audience, I could see people talking quietly, and I could sense their curiosity. The Ancient One of Justice was ready.

"Dreamers, for this last part of our program, we are offering class participation. This becomes the 'Past Life Dreaming, With Lady Justice'! May I introduce my Dreamer assistant!" She patted me on the arm. "She is holding a bowl filled with Tarot Trump cards. We will demonstrate first, to show you all how your 'Past Life Dreaming' will work." The Justice Seer now sat upon the throne with her crown on and her sword in hand. "Here is the procedure:

*My assistant will lead any willing Dreamer one at a time to me seated upon the dais.

*The Dreamer will be playing their deceased self, and they are now in the Hall of Judgment to receive their judgment, pronounced by me!

*The Dreamer will stand before me and ask this question of Intent: 'What is my current lesson from this past life?'

*The Dreamer reaches into the bowl filled with 'Tarot Trumps' and hands their card to me, which I read out loud.

*The card selected becomes the Dreamer's judgment, which is their 'Current-Life-Lesson,' from their 'Past-Life.'

*The card selected becomes a teacher for this lifetime.

*The Dreamer may, on their own, Dream with this card and enter into the lessons to be learned.

*The Dreamer may possibly want to use simple, natural materials to make a 'Karma Sculpture' of this past life and work with that or possibly even offer it to a Fire Ceremony."

The Judgment Hall was totally quiet. Then the Ancient Keepers began a soft drumming, and we heard clapping as everyone got into the excitement of participating in their own judgment!

The Justice Seer stood up a minute and said, quoting Yeats, "In sleep we enter upon the same life as that we enter between death and birth." Then she announced, "Let the Judgments begin!"

IX

THE HERMIT

DREAM OF THE TRUMP SEER: THE HERMIT IX

The snowflakes falling outside my window were huge. I wanted to see them closer, so I went out onto the covered porch. Reaching out, I caught a few, each one different and beautiful. I was sad to have them melt on my hand. Breathing in the cool mountain air was invigorating; the silence was amazing! The white blanket was doing a fine job of slowing us down some. Maybe the blizzard conditions have passed through, I thought as the wind had stopped. I listened again to the silence. I looked at my watch; it was past midnight now.

In a gathering two days earlier on Monday, we were informed that a huge snow front would be coming and we all should be prepared. The Keepers said, "We have been through these before, and we can do so again." They told us there were plenty of food supplies in the Grove and firewood too. However, we were all asked to help out with stacking the wood into the sheds along the main lodge and to bring extra wood for our own cabin stove. Also to help the kitchen staff in preparing foods ahead that could be heated easily. One of the Keepers said to check the kerosene lamps for readiness and to pick up snowshoes from the barn; there are plenty of pairs for everyone. We were all very excited and worked at a feverish pitch to be ready. An Ancient Seer said the old sleigh would be prepared and available with the horses; but mostly we would stay within the main lodge and our cabins. There were cheers about the idea of a sleigh ride!

We all worked well together, and in no time we were ready for what might come. Of course it had been winter for a month now, and there had been many snows. But apparently this one was different; it was the big one.

On Wednesday morning the first flakes arrived along with hollowing wind. It was fine; we were ready. The power did go out just as dinner was finishing, around 7:00 p.m. After that, the generators ran for the essential things only. It was not a big deal; we used the fireplaces and stoves anyway, and kerosene lamps and candles were our kind of light source. A few of the Dreamers were too nervous with the winds and decided to stay in the main lodge with sleeping bags. Not me! I really wanted to tough it out in my cabin, so I hiked back there with my friends. We didn't need the snowshoes yet, but our flashlights came in handy. It was only a half of a mile, maybe less. However, the wind was wicked cold, and going up hill was a challenge. My Dreamers friends and I occupied the three cabins on the top of the hill set in a semicircle, with adjoining grass and outdoor furniture. The cabins were protected by pines and white birches. From here you could see over the cliffs to the sea; I loved this spot! We all made it back before the worst of the storm hit. Saying our good nights, we agreed we would meet at eight thirty the next morning to head back to the main lodge. This was a fine arrangement; I was ready to get cozy and do some reading for the evening.

I stayed out on the porch for awhile longer. I noticed the snowdrift sculpture not to far from the porch looked more like some of the cliffs near the sea. I wondered how deep the snow was. Feeling a chill, I knew I had better go back inside. Now it was 12:30 a.m. The last few hours by the glimmer of the kerosene lamp, I had been reading and note taking from the book given to me by The Hermit Seer. We were to have had an intensive private meeting this evening, but of course these plans were changed now. She told me to keep the material for now, and after the snow we would re-set our date.

After picking up my journal and a cup of herbal tea from the stovetop and checking my lantern, I snuggled into my bed again to review. The wind muffled through the rafters for awhile, apparently not done haunting my cabin. At times the tree limbs near one of the walls could be heard rapping, at least I trusted that was the source. This is a strong little cabin, I will be fine, I thought. I went into my review. Which read as follows:

THE HERMIT IX—"The prophet of the Eternal" and "The Voice of Power"

This Trump holds the principles of: Completing detail and depth; Able to go within self; Likes space and time alone to reflect; Astrological sign of Virgo and element of Earth.

The Hermit is number nine in the sacred Grove and is the Light Bearer and the one who shows us the way on the path. The Ancient One, The Hermit, has an internal wisdom that she draws upon. She reminds us of our own inner light and teaches us to be the wise leader and light the world. The Hermit bears the Staff of Faith for safety and protection. This staff is mentioned in the Bible in the twenty-third psalm: "Thy rod and staff they comfort me."

There are several things from Gareth Knight in the Qabalah: The Hermit is the twentieth path on the tree of life. Between Chesed and Tiphareth. It is given the Hebrew letter: "Yod," "A Hand," meaning the means of action and the symbol of creative and directive energy.

Virgo, the Virgin, for the Hermit is associated with the Divine Sea of Yod in the Qabalah. This recalls the doctrine of Immaculate Conception. Also know that the Virgin Birth has been attributed to many others besides Christ. We may consider the Virgo's soul energies as the Divine Mother. Some say this may also be related to the Quest of the Holy Grail. The Hermit is, "True will of spirit, not just of the individuality, but is manifested in complete control while in Earth."

Again the wind howled and rattled the window some. I got up and pulled the outside shutters tighter, closed the windows, and pulled the curtains across. Then I stoked the embers in the small stove and refilled it with wood, stacking it like a log cabin. It took to the fire quickly. I smiled and jumped back into the goose down bed, feeling happy. My lantern glimmered and I got back to my notes.

Virgo is the astrological sign that commits to details, organization, and, foremost, beauty. How we do these various things reveals who we are. Does one's Earth Spirit walk their path in the beauty way? Are you paying attention, walking and talking truth? How do you fare on these points?

I stopped here a few minutes and realized I liked the attributes of this Hermit. I liked what she says about how we do various things "reveals who we are." I was getting sleepy and knew I had better finish this up for the night. I read the last section.

Many times it is necessary to go to that place of introspection. Look deep within yourself; go to the darkest part. Can you be alone? Will you find within yourself that divine spark and light your own way? This is the place the Ancient Hermit knows well. "Some instances may require a time with the Dark Night of the Soul. This allows one to search out the divine sparks of primordial wisdom."

I put my journal down. What is she talking about? The Dark Night of the Soul…Can I be alone? I am alone now in this storm, aren't I, and doing just fine! Just then the entire cabin seemed to shake a bit from the wind. I snuggled deeper into the covers but looked to the stove to make sure it was still going, which it was. I will have to ask when I see her. I mean, really! Straightening out the covers some and turning out my lamp, it wouldn't take me long to be in dreamland, I was sure. I heard the wind and pulled the goose down comforter over my head.

It was dawn or shortly after when I awoke. Pulling my head out of the covers, I found it was cold! I knew I had better get the logs into the stove before the embers faded. Piling on my long, thick, terry robe didn't seem enough against the chill, so I worked quickly. Finally the logs were catching. I got some water into the kettle for instant coffee and opened the cloth napkin that held several biscuits. I am not one to be moving so early in the a.m.….But I did not want to freeze either! Furthermore, there were images flashing, dream scenes I realized. I see cliffs and a black sky, am I by myself?

Sipping my early coffee and nibbling the rolls, I had pen in hand and wrote down the following dream as the scenes came to me, titled "Dream of the Hermit IX":

"How can this be?" I ask. The night was pitch black; the wind was cold. No one is there to answer me! Again, I say in a loud voice and afraid, "How can this be, that I am so alone?" Walking to nowhere I know, talking to no one who is there. Concerned and nervous for my situation, I scream out again, "I am so alone. I am not sure what direction I should go!" Throwing up my hands and head back and feeling desperate now, I look above in the black sky. My eye catches a glimmer of something. Standing there in the cold wind, I shiver but continue looking skyward. And there, twinkling in a universe far away, are nine bright stars! A slight smile crosses my lips; I feel there is company now. As I stare into the night, one star becomes a shooting star! "Wow!" The wind is swirling and I shiver again. Thoughts of alone begin creeping back to me.

Suddenly, I feel a presence! Now I am truly afraid out here in…where? I do not even know where I am. What is this place? I begin walking backward slowly. I am certain something is staring at me. A moving figure? I'm not sure. I keep moving backward slowly.

Backing up with my walking, I hit a hard surface. Feeling with my hands, I can not see a thing; it is so dark! But I realize it is a huge boulder-rock. Now what? I think to myself, I'm trapped! Looking up to the sky now, the nine stars twinkle and provide very slight light. There are shadows; something moves. I hold my breath. I think, I do not even know how to protect myself! Not even a stick do I hold, no less a club. Again in the shadow there is movement. I have no place to run. I scream, "Who are you? What do you want?"

The head was dark like the cloak; the air hung silent between us. I wanted to run! Motionless, I was glued to the granite rocks, heart pounding and voice gone now. The figure shifts; there is no sound, but I nearly feel the breath from it! A hundred images cross my vision-scape: wolves, bears, nameless monsters! What can I do? I try to find a breath. It is hard but comes…Then the moon rises over the head of this monster. In its left hand it holds a staff. My heart is beating out of my chest. Staring in disbelief at this creature, I can not tell what or who it is. I notice now the snake on the staff, which seems to be winding its way off! Wanting to scream, all I can do is shiver from cold. I point my finger toward it and say, "The snake!"

Abruptly the moon rises brighter, and the being whips off a cape of midnight blue and then proceeds to drape it over me. Over my shoulders, in fact! Looking at the cape, I see the inside is the color of gold. I realize that I feel warmer, but I am confused.

A woman's voice begins to speak. I hear her say she is The Hermit Seer, one of the Ancient Ones, and she is answering my call.

"My call?" I say, "I have not called you!"

"But I heard and I am here," is her reply. "Do not trouble yourself about how. Our work begins!" She continues, "Your soul has expressed the need. You have connected through the twinkle of our Nine Sisters in the sky; they are some of the Divine sparks. I'm here to help you rekindle your spirit. You've been through a dark night, a dark time. I am the 'Light Bearer'; I am the 'Threshold Guardian,' one who can help with obstacles or things that must be overcome. The one who can show you the way on your path."

The Hermit takes her staff and holds it up. It glows like a small sun at the top, giving off a lot of light. There are various glyphs tooled into the length of it all around. I notice her hands are beautiful as they hold this magical staff. Her left hand is pulling to open one side of her inner garment, and then her hand rests upon her hip. Now her abdomen begins to glow so brightly it illuminates the whole place. I am in awe! I scan quickly around, using all my vision. We are on a high mountain plateau. Jagged terrain, rock, and fir trees abound. I see the snake has coiled at the feet of the Hermit, looking less dangerous now.

"The light makes such a difference! It's nice to see where I am." I say.

"And where is that?" she replies. I try to answer and cannot. "As I thought! No matter," says she. "This is why you are here." She had taken the staff and poked it gently at my abdomen. I am surprised, but oddly not afraid. The Hermit says, "Do you see the beauty in this place here in the dark?" I look around and tell her that I do. "What about here?" she says, poking me again in the abdomen. I don't know what to say. She swishes a little to the side, but still holds the staff to my chest. "Here!" And she jabs the staff at my heart! "Here is where it counts!" she says.

Now I am in fear!

I have been walking sideways in order to get a bit away from her. But now I have realized that I have come close to the cliff's edge! Using all the strength I can muster, I take my hand and lay it upon the staff! Firmly I move the staff away from my chest. The Hermit has locked her eyes on me. Then with a voice from within, I say, "I know about beauty in my heart! Sometimes my heart breaks for the beauty I see all around this Earth. Sometimes my heart breaks that others do not see the beauty or respect what it offers!"

"Ah! You do have a voice after all," she says. "Had to push your limit there, but you found it, your voice!"

My stiff shoulders relax some; my glaring eyes do not soften. Quietly, I ask, "Why are you here?"

The Hermit's eyes are soft and compassionate. There is a hint of laughter about her lips. She is resting now upon the staff. "Have you looked at yourself?" says she. I look down at my middle and see that my abdomen has a small but pulsating, golden glow.

"How? Did—" and I look up into her eyes.

"I am here," says the Hermit, "to not only help you with the path you have chosen this lifetime but, most importantly, to allow you to create your own light! I am here to guide you for using the power of your intuition, introspection, and strength for time alone. As of late, you have come far and are learning the powers of attention to detail. Now is your time to shine; do not hide your light! There is not time for you to hide!" Again she jabs my abdomen but lightly.

Now I do not feel fear, but release. With that, my heart within begins to sing! "This all feels like such a Dream," I say to the Hermit.

"Is it? What is a Dream?" she replies.

The hour is quickly becoming twilight, and now she has taken swift steps away from me. I look down quickly at my middle that was still glowing. I look up and see her yellow flowing hair and midnight-blue cape, just before she descends from this beautiful mountain place. "Wait!" I say.

She responds with a laugh; and I hear her say, "When you light your own way with the help of the Divine Sparks, you'll realize you are learning your soul path through your own creation. You then create light! This in turn manifests in many other lights upon the ley lines of Earth Mother. Remember your alone space. Remember your sign is the sign for Fire and of Earth, the color ray of yellow. You are the beauty of Earth; keep your lamp always lit. You are the voice of power!"

And she was gone! It was a dream. I blinked my eyes as I said, "Was it?" But didn't I then see the snake slithering away, having shed its skin?

"Oh my Goddess! What was this? I suppose the Hermit Seer, kept our meeting date after all. In spite of all the snow, we met. This is incredible! Now I have to dream with this all again in order to understand what happened." I put my journal down and lay back in the warm covers, trying hard to believe what had happened...It was all so real.

I may have dozed some but was awakened to pounding. Disoriented, I looked around. Then I realized there was knocking at my door! Quickly I jumped up and threw on my robe; I pulled the door open to find my friends there. Very fast I came back to this present dream of being in the Nemeton.

"You are all dressed! What time is it?"

They all replied at once, "Late. Eight forty-five a.m. Thursday!"

"Oh my! I will be ready in five minutes. Please wait."

They agreed and said to hurry; they would stay on the porch.

I dashed about, threw things on, combed my hair, checked the stove, got my pack, put my snowshoes on, and looked around. My Dream Journal! Got that and was out the door. My friends were teasing me about being snowed under a snowflake. They went on all in good fun!

Walking was a winter wonderland of sunny, delightful views. Roofs were covered like they were vanilla frosted, two feet deep. The snowshoeing was not bad once I got the hang of it. Jokingly I said, "What century are we in?"

Everyone laughed as we arrived at the main lodge, with Dreamers mingling on the porch, saying that breakfast was started. If we had not shown up soon, they would have searched.

We were all happy to have gotten through the night and be back together. The laughter and story telling was spreading fast. I was hungry and ate, but I could not wait to find the Hermit Seer. There was much information being given about the power being out. It could stay that way for several days. Not to worry, we have everything we need. But do conserve everything and keep the wood stacked and...so many housekeeping things. I was listening but not...Where is she? I kept scanning the dinning hall. Nothing. Then when I was about to help out with some chores, I saw her. The Hermit Seer winked across the room, and I knew we would meet again by day's end.

THE WHEEL OF FORTUNE

DREAM OF THE TRUMP SEER: THE WHEEL OF FORTUNE X

The Keepers informed us at the end of our morning's dreaming, "Please gather in the main lodge midafternoon. And be in party mode, as we will just have some fun. We are under the astrological influences of Jupiter, after all!" This is what was said, and, of course, the Dreamers all cheered!

I arrived a bit late and saw everyone at one corner of the lodge and spilling out onto the lawn. I could hear the Dreamers singing and carrying on. I pushed ahead to see what this was all about. Once up close, I saw who was causing such a ruckus. It was The Wheel of Fortune Seer.

There was also someone acting as a hawker might at a carnival. He stood to the right side of The Wheel of Fortune Seer, saying things like, "Step right up. Come and take your chance. Spin the wheel!" Now I realized the hawker was The Oak Tree Seer. The Dreamers were delighting in his antics! He was definitely working the crowd.

As I watched, I saw The Wheel of Fortune Seer perform an amazing feat. She had somehow expanded herself and shaped herself into an actual wheel, almost the same as a roulette wheel in a casino! Then I noticed that to the left side of the Wheel was The Spider Seer. I thought that was interesting in some odd way. She was holding her distaff.

The noise level was worked up now, and no wonder. One of the novice Dreamers was trying their luck at spinning the wheel. There was much advice coming from the crowd. "Make a wish," someone yelled. Another said, "Turn the wheel with your nondominate hand!" Still another said, "Spin it for your destiny!" Finally the novice spoke up and said, "it's only a game of chance." I wondered about that. Then she spun the wheel hard, using her nondominate hand.

Interesting, I thought, and I wondered about that.

I heard drumming off to the side, and the Oak Tree Seer said, "And the answer from the oracle is…!"

The Dreamers were silent while holding their breath, waiting for the wheel to stop its spin. I watched in awe and could not imagine how The Wheel of Fortune Seer could possibly change her shape into an actual spinning wheel, just as if she were at a carnival! But then the Seers were able to pull off so many feats of illusion, I had lost count.

The Oak Tree Seer's deep voice brought me back from my reverie. "So, my dear novice, what has this game of chance brought to you with the stop of the wheel?"

The very nervous Dreamer novice stepped up close to the stopped wheel to find out exactly what the image was that her hand had stopped upon. We were all waiting for her to share it with us. In a timid, quiet voice, I heard her say, "It seems to be at the bottom of the wheel, resting against an old man, on his hands and knees. I do not know what this means? There are a few words, saying, 'Sum Sine Regno.'"

Many of the Dreamers tried to get closer to view what she was describing. I decided to just stay aside and see what was next, even though I, too, wanted to know what it all meant.

Then, out of the blue, the roulette wheel of fortune disappeared before our eyes! In its place was a beautiful woman; she looked like a goddess. We were all in awe of this transformation, and when she began speaking, there were whispers among the Dreamers. "Could it be?" Was one of the comments. "Now I understand," was another. It was all still a mystery to me.

The goddess woman could be heard now, and she said, "I am the 'Goddess Fortuna.' Fortuna who spins at random, changing the positions of those on the wheel. Some suffer, some gain. I am the 'Goddess of Fate'!"

There was a momentary hush in the crowd of Dreamers. Someone finally said, "What about the scripted words and the old man image?"

Then we saw the novice Dreamer come to the forefront. "What does it mean, the old man at the bottom of the wheel? And the words, 'sum sine regno'?"

Quietly, and in one motion, all heads turned to the 'Goddess Fortuna.' Without any expression on her flawless face, she said this, "The old man at the bottom of the wheel was once crowned at the top; he has been around the wheel in a cycle. The words in Latin, 'Sum Sine Regno' translate to 'I Am Without Rulership' or 'I Am Without Reign'!"

The Goddess Fortuna looked about the group, watching the Dreamers take this into their psyche.

It was quiet; then we heard the novice Dreamer crying! She said, "This must mean that I am finished somehow!" She began to cry more and ran off.

Next we saw The Wheel of Fortune Seer going after her. She told the other Dreamers, "I will take care of the novice. Please!" She said, "She will be fine. Go on and enjoy the rest of the afternoon! Remember the wheel reminds us of the willingness to take risks, to change, to move. Go and have fun!"

The Dreamers began to disperse. Some were laughing, and some were still staring in puzzlement at the whole situation.

As the Seer turned to follow the novice Dreamer, she caught my eye and then nodded to me, inviting me to follow her. I did. I walked up to the novice who was still weeping some and put my hand out to her. She took it, a bit reluctantly.

The Wheel of Fortune Seer said, "Let's walk awhile along the cliffs; it is not far and the sun will warm us as we go."

The novice Dreamer and I followed her. I asked her what her name was. She said it was Fatima. We walked awhile without talking; the sun sure did feel good on my shoulders.

Finally, Fatima said, "Please, dear Seer, help me to understand. Is something awful going to happen to me?"

The Seer responded by saying, "No! No! This is a teaching for us all. For none of us may be in control of all the phases of the turning wheel at all points in our lives. However, we can choose 'how to react during those tough phases.' We can learn to be creative; that is what Dreamers do! Of course The Wheel of Fortune, when it is turning, is about chance and karma. It is a game of mastery, concerning that which is given and that which is taken away. Just as there is an endless turning of life, seasons, years, fortune, and death."

At this last word, "death," I could feel the novice shiver, and I did too.

The Seer continued. "First, the words, 'I am without reign'! said by the old man, does not necessarily mean a physical death. He has gone a cycle around the wheel. All needs to be looked at in the big picture; one should be very present with their intent when they spin the wheel. The Wheel of Fortune is the Great Spinning Wheel of creation and change, bringing to us the energy of all possibilities!"

At this Fatima turned and gave the Seer a big hug. The Seer laughed, and I did too! We were looking at the Dreamer novice, waiting for her to speak. "What?" said, Fatima. "I just feel relieved is, all!" We all smiled at this, knowing she had lightened up.

At the edge of the cliffs, it was so beautiful. The ocean, with its deep, aqua-blue waves down over the rocky ledges. Behind us the trees of the Grove, and the mountains beyond. This Earth is a treasure, I thought to myself and came back to listening to what the Seer was saying.

"The lesson of the wheel is to hold one's self in the center and 'Watch' what turns the wheel. Make note of that. In times of accomplishment, 'Remain balanced.' In times of tragedy, 'Remain balanced.' Being at the center, one is able to hold the key to fortune.

"Some decks of tarot have human images lying against the wheel. Others depict animals. Still others are entirely different. Since the image with the humans around the wheel is more common, let me talk of that. Besides, it was a human old man, which you responded to earlier."

Fatima answered, "I guess I did at that."

We laughed!

"One of the oldest decks, the 'Visconti-Sforza,' illustrates the Wheel of Fortune trump with a blindfolded female figure at the center of the wheel. This is 'Goddess Fortuna.' At the top of the card is a king on a throne, with the words 'Regno,' 'I Rule.' On the left is a young man rising, with 'Regnabo,' 'I Shall Rule.' On the right, another man falls headfirst, with 'Regnavi,' 'I Ruled.' Underneath the wheel, an old man crawls on all fours at the bottom, with 'Sum Sine Regno,' 'I Am Without Rulership.'"

Continuing, the Wheel of Fortune Seer said, "The Goddess Fortuna is she who turns the wheel whereby men and women suffer the vagaries of those 'two imposters, failure and success'!"

Fatima and I just stared at the Seer, not knowing how to respond!

The Seer said, "Don't worry. This kind of view of the world was very prevalent in the Middle Ages. Today some of this still applies. However, the cyclic aspect of this energy, the Wheel of Fortune, should lead us to consider the universal principle of cycles, in relation to time, space, and circumstance. When we are able to do this, with the results of the wheel turning, we can Dream better choices. Man does not stand still; neither can time. This energy can also call to your attention recurring patterns in life. The energy can also allude to the mystery of life, to seek higher consciousness. The Wheel signifies the perpetual motion of the universe and the changing cycles of human existence."

We listened attentively as she went on. "On the Tree of Life, the Qabalists say, 'The Wheel of Fortune' is path number twenty-one. 'Intelligence of conciliation and reward, it receives divine influence.'

"This means that the potencies of this path are responsible for the ideals and aspirations that capture the imagination of man. Think of this like the ideal quest for the Holy Grail. What the search is for may not clearly be known, yet with the energy of this path, man becomes 'The Seeker' who, of course, is questing. But the quest is for the 'Inner Quest'! This energy brings about an immense desire. There is a link between this path twenty-one of desire and vision, to path number thirty-two, the path of coming and going into and out of physical form. This is 'The World XXI Trump' and the path of rebirth. We must make mention here that rebirth can not happen without desire; which of course is 'The Wheel of Fortune X' Trump!"

I said to the Seer, "I guess I really didn't know much about this wheel. Somehow I thought it was just ones turn of luck as it went around!"

She smiled at me and said, "Yes, most people do not go below the surface image. But then this is why you are all here at this gathering, to go deeper in your Dreaming. We are here to learn the history and the stories and to commit them to our hearts. To have them available when they are needed in dream healing work."

The Seer went on. "The Wheel of Fortune card is the symbol of the wheel of birth and death. There is an emphasis on cyclic rebirth. In essence, the Wheel of Fortune is a symbol of the evolving destiny held within the soul. The circular shape of the Wheel of Fortune reminds one of evolving and of the desire of the soul for life and realities in the higher worlds. It is also reminiscent of the 'Round Table.' In modern life this might be the roulette wheel. The real wheel is a reflection of the image of 'Chokmah,' wisdom, The Wheel of the Zodiac, which is the 'Round Table of Arthur.'"

Fatima and I were both amazed at how so many Dream threads wove together!

"The goal," said the Seer, "of a human being is to become as kings-all-equally-seated about this table. This energy can occur through the assistance of the planet Jupiter, which is the ruler of this path, and of course with its innate desire as 'The Seeker.' It is a fundamental occult law 'That whatever one gives, so will one receive.' So, thus far, what have we learned?" She looked at us, not expecting an answer.

Thank goodness, I mused.

"There are two basic principles: the principle of balance, ascending and descending and a hold of balance in the center; and the principle of 'The Wheel' as a line. A line without beginning or end, a symbol of eternity.

"Other principles also come into play in the history of the wheel. One of the best known is that the 'Wheel of Fortune' symbolizes Fate. 'Fate' is shown spinning the thread of destiny. The image of the distaff or spindle motif is associated with the 'Web of Fate' in many cultures. For tarot, the 'spinning wheel' and its myths may have been translated into 'The Wheel of Fortune X' Trump image!"

Laughing, a little, I said, "Fate. This is what we are all curious about and surely worry about!"

The Seer nodded her head and said, "Let me tell you something of 'Fortuna' from Roman mythology; with the Greeks she was called 'Tyche.' Fortuna is the goddess of fortune. She was the personification of luck. She was sometimes represented as veiled or blind. She is also the 'Goddess of Fate.' Her father was 'Jupiter,' and she had no lovers or children. Her name derives from 'Vortumna'–'She who revolves the year.' The earliest reference to the 'Wheel of Fortune' occurs in Cicero, in Pisonem, circa 55 BCE. Over the Roman world, Fortuna was worshipped at many shrines. Fortuna was not always positive; she could be: 'Doubtful Fortuna'–'Fortuna Dubia,' she could be 'Fickle Fortuna'–'Fortuna Brevis,' or 'Evil Fortuna'–'Fortuna Mala.'"

Fatima sighed and said, "What a rich heritage you have, dear Wheel of Fortune Seer!"

The Seer replied, "I am honored that you are both so willing to learn. Let me now take you to the Middle Ages," said the Seer. "The Wheel of Fortune images were vivid, and many were printed in medieval manuscripts. In addition, the wheel was portrayed in the huge stained glass windows in cathedrals all around Europe. Like the beautiful rose windows of the cathedrals in Amiens, France. The design of the wheel characteristically has four shelves, stages of life, with four human figures usually labeled. I shall reign, I reign, I have reigned, and, at the bottom, I have no kingdom. Medieval representations of Fortune emphasize her duality and instability. Wheel of Fortune in Latin is 'Rota Fortunae,' or 'nature of fate.' Dear Fortuna, who spins at random, is changing the positions of those on the wheel. Some suffer, some gain."

We were all sitting on the edge of the cliffs. The Seer reminded us of that fact. She said, "It is a little scary looking over this edge, isn't it? Well, I am here to tell you that in life we all live a little on the edge! It is said that 'Fortune favors the bold, the brave!' This means the goddess of luck is more likely to help those who take risks, take actions, and develop their skills proactively. Think about that," she said to us.

"We all go through ups and downs in life. Our brains have a file cabinet of disappointments, and our hearts have a similar file. Many of us base our future on these disappointments. However, we have the ability to trigger and integrate the 'Success region of our brains.' We can activate this by what we do! For instance, begin your day thankful that you awoke with your breath; some did not. You succeeded in going to work; many do not have jobs. You drove there in a car; many had to take a bus or walk. Remind yourself of success everyday, and remind others of theirs instead of failures. This is how we change, how we re-pattern and help the brain with restructuring. This brings in new light and awareness to each of us.

"The 'Edge' of succeeding is booby-trapped for humans. This is where sabotage may come into play. Pay attention! Notice when you feel like backing off something you have been striving for or destroying your goal in some way. This is actually a sign from your inner-self and the universe saying to you, hang in there, press harder! You are at '*The Edge*' of succeeding!

"Often humans do not want to succeed fully. It feels more comfortable with only a little success. There seems to be fear in more success. So we may sabotage. Here at this time on Earth, there are many spirits of light ready to help us succeed. They will assist those who assist themselves, moving vibrations to help one succeed in whatever their 'Heart Mission' is asking them to accomplish!"

We were quiet, listening to the waves pounding against the rocks below. So very soothing. We heard the screech of the Raven in the air.

The Wheel of Fortune Seer stood up, saying, "Ah! Magic is in the air. Time to move along on the wheel as the wheel's nature is to not remain still for long!"

We all were about ready to leave, when Fatima said, as she looked over the edge of the cliff, "I am ready to take the leap of faith, to take a new spin around the wheel!"

I replied, saying, "I know what you mean. I feel energized. I feel like The Seeker!"

The Seer was smiling, saying, "Good! Just as long as you do not leap over this cliff's edge!"

XI

STRENGTH

DREAM OF THE TRUMP SEER: STRENGTH XI

The wind was wild, and the rain was pouring down in waterfall fashion. This afternoon's program had been planned to be out in the Grove. However, with gale force winds blowing, that was not our plan now. For the last couple of weeks, the weather had been so fair and perfect. This storm really put a damper on the Dreamers, especially the newer ones. I just kept telling various novices, "This too, shall pass!" I thought of the 'Wheel of Fortune Seer' and how she had taught me about the turnings of the wheel. I was in the main lodge, and it was so dark from the storm that the lights had been turned on. Someone was getting a fire going in the fireplace, which would be lovely for us all.

I was standing by the large Palladian series of windows that looked out to the Grove with the cliffs beyond. I thought about the ocean and how the waves must be swelling and knocking the shoreline hard. I could see the path that lead over the cliff wall and down to the beach. My stomach grumbled; snack and some tea sounded like a good thing.

I suddenly saw some Dreamers at one end of the Grove outside. What on earth were they out there for now? In this weather? I could see their coats blowing in the wind; somebody's hat flew off and was gone. One, two…It looked like there were four of them. They were standing around one of the trees of the Grove. Which tree, I'm not sure. Straining, I was able to see more clearly; long, thick branches were swaying so hard they almost looked like they might take off. Now I heard thunder. Looking up to the sky, I saw lightning striking, with some bolts coming down and hitting the grass not far from the group around the tree!

"Oh! My God!" someone cried out.

Many Dreamers had gathered now at the windows. We were all very concerned for the group outside. "Who are they?" "Which Dreamers?" Someone else said, "Look, it is the Lion Seer!" Then another Dreamer said, "There, look, it is the Oak Tree Seer and the Magician Seer!"

I was glad they were so observant. It was hard for me to tell who was who.

"But what are they doing?" said another.

We all stood silently, watching from the warm, dry lodge.

I said, "Maybe I'll go out to see if there is something they need!"

Someone answered me, "No! This is something they need to do on their own!"

We all turned around to find The Emperor Seer standing near us with his arms crossed and looking like a ruler!

"What are they doing?" I asked.

"You will all know soon enough," he said.

We heard the thunder crack and looked out the window. The lightning was bolting near the group with the tree. Now we could see there was another figure standing against the tree. We had all concluded that the tree was the 'Alder Tree Seer' in its physical tree form, one of the protectors of the outer rim of the steading. The figure against the tree was slight and female; she had one hand against the tree. As I watched her, I got the feeling she was holding up the tree. Curious! I thought to myself.

"Oh my Goddess!" I heard someone say.

We all turned and looked intently out the window. The Dreamer who had spoken was standing there, pointing out the window to the group at the Alder Tree. I did not know what she was pointing at.

"The colors, do you see the colors?" Another one of the Dreamers was saying this with such excitement that we were wanting to know what he meant.

I looked out at the tree as did all the other Dreamers. "Nothing. I see nothing!" I said.

Just then the thunder cracked very loudly; a few of us jumped at the crashing sound.

"Watch!" someone said.

We all were transfixed by the tree! Suddenly we saw quite clearly a purple haze, like a transparent cloud, all around the tree! It was especially under the tree, connected to the trunk and the small woman whose hand was against the tree. It was only a flash, but we all knew that we were seeing something incredible! I watched the woman; she was calm and serene. The tree had stopped swaying and blowing; it now seemed strong and steadfast. This was such a contrast to the storm that was still on the other side of the tree's canopy. As I watched the sky, I saw a few more small lighting bolts, but the wind was slowing, and I began to see yellow brightness coming out of the eastern sky. The storm was moving out; it had run its course. I heard some background sounds in the lodge; this brought me back to attention. Concerning the group of Dreamers who were out in this storm, I looked around through the window down toward the Grove, and the Seers were not there. They had gone, but where? I felt myself jolted back to this reality. I had let myself get caught up in the doings of the moving storm and lost track of the main players, 'The Seers,' and this was a teaching to me! One of my guides had worked with me about where to put my attention, my focus. It is hard to remember that all the time!

As I got myself into the waking reality in the lodge, I realized that the other Dreamers had moved out to the porch. I ran to catch up. I saw raincoats being shaken out and hung up on the pegs; boots were lined up along the ledge of the porch.

Someone was wrapping the Magician Seer in a blanket. He said, "Ah! That feels great!"

The Oak Tree Seer had on a blanket and was headed inside, saying, "A good glass of spirits will warm me up!"

The Lion Seer said to one of the Dreamers, "Thanks for the blanket. It is the fire that I need now!"

Most were already in the lodge, laughing and carrying on, and asking so many questions at the same time. I started to go in as well and looked back to the porch for a moment. There were several Dreamers gathered around someone sitting on a bench. I turned and walked over to them; three women Apprentice Dreamers and two men were talking quietly to the woman sitting on the bench. "Drink some more tea!" said one. Another had some apples and cheese on a plate.

I could not see the woman on the bench very well, as her head was wrapped in a towel that she was briskly rubbing about her head. I watched in amusement as she removed the towel and flipped her head back, shaking her long, black hair. "Nothing like storm rain—washed hair; it brings out the shine!" Now she was combing her hair, saying, "I had better make sure I comb out any kinks that might have picked up. Ah, this is good!"

She stood up and took some apple and cheese as she joked around with the group. She was the small, slight woman I had seen under the 'Alder Tree.' Very delicate, but her energy felt powerful! She turned now and we were face-to-face. With her eyes on mine, I felt serenity.

Smiling, she said, "Why don't we all go inside where it is warm." Her eyes never left my own. Someone handed her a cup of tea. She then asked me, "Could you please carry my bag?"

Of course I said, "Yes!" I was still not certain which ancient seer she was. I knew we were about to find out.

Once inside we all settled around the huge stone fireplace, warm and cozy. The other Seers who had been outside were there joking with the Dreamers.

When the delicate Seer was next to the circle, The Magician Seer said, "Please take this seat! We are all anxious to have you tell our dream story of 'The Grove in the Storm'!"

She nodded at him and took off her wrap, her blouse in sepia tones of georgette silk had woven into the design an image of a small woman standing next to a Greek-looking column with a huge Lion seated at her feet. Her left hand was on the column. The Seer got herself comfortable and sat down, spreading out her deep Dioxazine purple–colored skirt. The whole room was silent as she set the stage for the story telling.

The Seer spoke: "What an afternoon! This was not our original plan for you Dreamers!" There was some laughter in the crowd at this. "However, as the Keepers of this sacred Grove, we realized we needed to do some unexpected work. There is a teaching here that will unfold to all of us in time. First let me introduce myself, as I have not yet had the honor to work with you all! I am called 'The Strength Seer XI,' number eleven Trump. Although, some of you may know me as the eighth Trump from your studies. We will get to that later!"

I was sitting fairly close to her and wondered about the bag she had given me. Embroidered on one side was a fierce looking lion. I was curious about that.

Now she said, "I want to thank the other Seers who were all so supportive of 'The Grove in the Storm'!"

At this, the Lion Seer, the Oak Seer, and the Magician Seer all stood up, bowed, and made light jokes of her serious thanks. We were all laughing.

Then The Emperor Seer said, "Come, come. Let the 'Strength Seer' continue. There is much to be disclosed."

Disclosed? I thought this was an odd word. What does he mean, disclosed?

The Strength Seer held up both hands. Looking at each of us, she said, "'Why were you out in such a storm?' you are all wondering, speculating. I will begin with reminding you of the first days when arriving here in the 'Nemeton.' We had a briefing about our sacred Grove and what it is we are gathered for; it was explained then that: first, we were to expand and ground our own healing through Dreaming; second, learn how to teach the Dreaming in our own waking realities to those we come in contact with, and third, through the Dreaming, 'See' into the future for the benefit of 'Earth' and to 'Keep a balance for her' by making better choices." She looked to the group, saying, "I trust you have remembered these things!

"In the early days of our gathering, we made it clear that the 'Dreaming Path' is the absolute path of integrity and light and to let no impurity enter your being. We spoke about various energies that are always present and learning to recognize which are beneficial and which are not. One day many of you will be selected to be a 'Keeper of the Nemeton.' This is an honor and a tremendous responsibility! We touched slightly on the subject of protection in those early days of this gathering. This is what we will talk of some now. The other Keepers and I are always in touch with each other, especially during gatherings like this, about the energy vibrations that we are detecting. As one of the Keepers, detecting energy is a huge part of one's training!" She looked coyly at the other Seers, as if to get feedback from them. I saw the Lion Seer shaking his head at this. The Seer was now standing and moving her hands expressively, and then she began to walk about the room.

The Strength Seer said, "Early this morning I began to feel a storm of some sort brewing. And I did not think it only had to do with the weather! So after feeling the strength from the morning's coffee, I went out to the Grove. It was not raining yet, and there was only a slight breeze. I walked among the gracious Tree Seers who, as you all know, are the outer rim of protection for our sacred Grove. I knew that if there was some sort of threat, they would make me aware of it." She paused and looked around the room as the Dreamers got slightly nervous about what she had said. As the group calmed, she said, "It did not take too long to find out that the 'Tree Seers' were concerned. Some of them felt there was an energy that was trying to plant negative influences and making a segue into our inner teachings.

"As I walked among the Tree Seers in their physical form as trees, I felt a unity and a beauty beyond belief! Just as I got close to the 'Alder Tree Seer,' we all heard a rumble of thunder. The 'Alder Tree Seer' said, 'We can deflect this! We need your help and a good plan!' I was looking at this beautiful old Seer; his height must be fifty feet at least, and his canopy just as wide. 'Me? You want me?' I said to him, feeling so tiny in comparison to him. 'Yes! You are the "Strength Seer." I have seen what you can do!' said the Alder. I laughed at that but knew he was serious and that I had been called. With that last thought, we heard a huge crack of thunder!

"'OK,' I said to the Alder and the other Tree Seers. 'This is what we will do! First we should get a few other Keepers to assist us. Which ones do you think for this situation?' I asked the Alder Tree Seer. Before he could speak, I said, 'I would like the Lion Seer with me.'

"'I assumed so,' said the Alder. 'Also I think the "Magician Seer."'

"'Yes, of course," I said.

"One of the other Tree Seers spoke out and came over to us in their human form, saying to us all, 'I would like to be a direct part of this!' It was the Oak Tree Seer.

"I clapped my hands, saying, 'Great, great!' So the four of us devised a plan that would work with the physical weather storm as a way to deflect this unwanted energy. I was selected to stand with the 'Alder Tree Seer' under his canopy, holding against his trunk, offering my energy of strength. Meanwhile the Alder would use his branched antenna system to send back into the universe what we did not need! The Oak Tree Seer would hold us to the Earth for grounding, and the Magician Seer would watch our backs and use his incredible tools of magic!"

There was complete silence around the fireplace in the lodge. Except for the hissing and cracking from the logs in the fire, no one spoke. The Strength Seer was looking around the room; her story was being felt in different ways by each of us.

Finally, I broke the silence, saying, "I suppose we all take for granted the beauty and the safety of this place. It is hard to think there are those who would want to ruin that!"

"Yes, yes!" Other Dreamers were speaking up, saying similar things.

Then the Strength Seer said, "It is part of the way of our world, but we have contained things, and we are OK! This is a teaching to us all not to let those negative influences unbalance us. This is the end of the tale from the Keepers' 'Grove in the Storm' dream…"

And she started to say something else but became silent. Suddenly we were all interrupted by someone joining us. The Strength Seer was moving over to give a big hug to The Alder Tree Seer who only just now came into the circle in his human form.

He was laughing when he said, "Not only did it take me awhile to dry out, but that purple haze was a bit hard to let go of!"

We all roared with laughter. The Lion Seer rolled on the floor!

Someone said, "We are happy to see you!" Another Dreamer said, "Come and get warm by the fire!"

The Alder Tree Seer stood by the fire, saying, "Of course you know the alder wood makes the best firewood. But enough of this story. I think you are all waiting to hear more from our source of strength here, the beautiful and dainty 'Strength Seer'! She has much to teach and share."

All of us stood up and clapped our hands, saying, "Yes, yes! Please continue!"

The Strength Seer stood up and said, "I would be happy to, but first let's break for a few minutes."

We all agreed, and the Dreamers and Keepers walked around outside and in, sharing what we had all gone through.

I was talking to one of the Dreamers when the Strength Seer came over to me and asked me for some help. "Of course, what can I do?"

The Seer said, "Follow me, and bring the bag I asked you to hold."

I did as she said. We were next to some tables across from the fireplace. She asked me to bring the vase of flowers over to the table and one of the large candles. I put them on the table. She took the bag I had been holding and pulled out various tarot cards, then she spread them out on the table. They were all images of the Tarot Trump Strength XI (11) and some that had Strength VIII (8) all depicted a little differently by the various artists.

"It is a beautiful display, dear Seer!" I said.

She agreed, cocking her head this way and that, changing the positions of a few of the trumps. Finally, she said, "There. That should do it. This visual display will be helpful as I speak about Strength."

With that, we walked back toward the fireplace. One of the Keepers was drumming softly to bring everyone back together for the story of The Strength Seer.

The Strength Seer said, "When you have unloosed the winds, then you must abide by their blowing, whatever they may tear down!"

We were all quiet as she let this statement sink in. The Lion Seer was seated at her feet in his animal form; it was quite a picture. I thought of the Seer standing out in the rain and winds and how incredibly brave she was and how she was able to loosen the winds for all of us just a little while earlier.

She began again. "I want to tell you something of the connection to the Qabalah and strength. On the 'Tree of life,' Strength is path number nineteen. 'Daughter of the flaming sword, leader of the lion.' The planetary ruler is 'Leo the Lion.' This path is: 'One of the great force, the main girder of the individuality.' Many images of the Strength Trump depict a Woman as strength, holding apart without effort, the jaws of a lion. The Lion is a common symbol representing the uncontrolled forces of nature. This is also a symbol of the Fire sign, Leo the Lion, and is an important constellation in the esoteric astronomical systems. The start position on the zodiac for the constellation of Leo is the same as on the 'Tree of Life,' representing the first formation of individuality from 'Chesed,' which means 'kindness and love.' These things are part of the attributes of Strength.

"The Hebrew letter glyph that represents strength is the 'serpent.' So on path nineteen, the serpent and the flaming sword may also be linked to Adam and Eve and the Fall from the Garden of Eden. The allegory of the human race falling into the worlds of form. The nineteenth path is the way of coming into activity of the human soul after its initial projection into Form in 'Chesed,' kindness-love, on the 'Tree of Life.' Remember that Adam and Eve were prevented from returning immediately to Eden by an angel with a flaming sword.

"Strength, like its ruling sign Leo, is a trump encompassing courage and high energy. It represents both the Lion's roaring energy and the Maiden's steadfast will. In some cards she opens the lion's mouth; in others she shuts it. In some images she appears to be holding up a column, with a calm Lion at her feet. Both ways she proves that inner strength is more powerful than raw, physical strength and that forces can be controlled.

"The title 'Strength' is a translation of the French title 'La Force,' appearing on the Tarot de Marseille cards. Three cards from traditional tarot depict cardinal virtues: Fortitude or Strength, Temperance, and Justice. 'La Forteza,' or 'Fortitude' from the Old Italian, has a couple of versions of her image. In the most predominant of the early Italian decks, we see a lady holding a column. In addition we find the figure, usually female but not always, subduing a lion. So the image of Fortitude as a serene woman passively subduing a lion without apparent physical effort has a big impact on our senses. In Aristotle's thought, Fortitude represents moderation in our responses to fear and pain. Fortitude-Strength offers determination, strength of character, a need to pick one's battles and see them through. Strength endures disappointments without being defeated, always looking to the goal."

The Strength Seer had stopped speaking for a minute. She was observing the Dreamers about the room as they sat fixed in thought. Quietly she said, "I know there is so much to take in, but hang in there. That is what strength does! When one realizes they have gained strength, there is an inner spiritual force that comes to your consciousness. One feels connected to spiritual growth and the ability to accomplish his or her heart's desire.

"There have been various numberings assigned to this Strength Trump. The placement of the virtues was one of the reasons different communities altered and adapted this. In the Waite-Smith Deck, the placement of Strength and Justice were swapped. Waite's became Strength VIII and Justice XI. He did this in order to make a better fit with the astrological correspondences he used. He also introduced the 'lemniscate' as a part of the image, with the woman closing the lion's mouth. The 'lemniscate' is the sideways-shaped figure eight curve. This comes from algebraic geometry; lemniscate refers to this curved figure in mathematics as the symbol for 'Infinity.' In Latin, 'Infinitas' means 'with out end.'

"The absolute creative force is represented by 'La Force.' It brings both liberty and courage. The image I like to portray most often is the one of the Maiden sitting or standing near a pillar or column, which is partially broken, but not quite, as she offers her support to mend things. Of course the lion sits near her feet. To me the image is pure strength and support. There are times, however, when the image needs to be male rather than female. Other times it is showing only the lion that is being subdued. Interestingly the 'Strength Trump' is one that traditional interpreters have had the most trouble with, precisely because Strength is usually represented as a woman! The decks that show a female with a pillar-column instead of a lion are perhaps reminiscent of the pillars of the temple brought down by Samson, for the lion. Making the female the hero!"

The Seer stood up and said, "Why don't we take a look at the table set up by the window to see the various artists' depictions of *me!*"

"Yes! Yes!" We all laughed and then jumped up to have a look at the display. There were many ooh's and ahh's! This really helped all of us to understand what the Seer had been relaying to us. Some of the cards were very old and priceless, I was sure.

I wanted to tell the Seer how much I had enjoyed these lessons. As I got close to her, I overheard the Magician Seer saying, "It has been such a pleasure to work with you once again! Real strength never impairs beauty or harmony; it bestows it. This is what we have learned from you today, my dear Seer!" He then gave her a slight kiss on her hand, like the true knight of magic that he was.

Before I could get up to her, the Oak Tree Seer was talking with her. He had this to say: "A healer, whether good or bad, can draw strength from someone or something by the mere touch of the hand. Or give strength! You are the true 'Goddess of Fortitude,' giving and giving and enduring despite all obstacles, endlessly. I have seen you do this so often, and I want you to know I am thankful!"

The Strength Seer reached over and, with tears in her eyes, gave the Oak Seer a big hug.

Before I could say anything, the Alder Tree Seer had pulled me gently by my arm and said, "Let's get in there and hug them also!" I was honored to be included. My message for myself was to press on, not giving up on dreams.

XII

THE HANGED MAN

DREAM OF THE TRUMP SEER: THE HANGED MAN XII

It was early morning, and I was taking some time to sit on the porch rocker at my cabin and catch up my journal notes. What an amazing view I had from this particular angle. I could see over the top of the orchard into the foothills of the mountain range, green pastures in some parts, dense forest in other areas. The sun was just beginning to spread its warmth as I rocked awhile, sipping coffee. I could hear the birds and noticed the bees in a nearby morning glory vine. This was perfect! Staring across the hills, I began to realize there was a lot of activity behind the orchards. Everyday there was something new going on in the Grove. Sometimes it had to do with the care and maintenance of the grounds, but my sense was telling me this was Dreamer activity. Why not? I thought, I have free time. I grabbed my things, then headed toward the stream. Once there, I took a minute to look around and get my bearings. I thought, I just need to find out what the Dreamers are doing at the top of the hills!

I knew that there were other paths to get where I wanted, but going along the stream would be most direct, although it would be a steep uphill climb. This isolated path walking through the woods was one of my best ways to think. And to assimilate "the work." As the path got away from the stream, the rock cliffs became more prevalent and steeper. The physical activity felt good to me, after so much classroom and dream journey time. At this point I really needed to pay attention, as I did not want to lose my footing along the hill. Finally the area smoothed out some, more grass, less surface rock. Then I began to hear the noise of a hammer.

Walking now was easy, in the tree line, where the sky meets earth. I still heard the hammering, but no one was in sight yet. Looking at the trees, I could see that many were apple. I wondered if this area had been an orchard at some point. These trees were old and gnarled, not at all like the pruned orchard below. Beautiful, so beautiful were the twisted branches and knotted trunks; I could feel energy from them as I walked. From a distance I saw a few Dreamers that I knew. They were cutting wood, taking limbs off a tall narrow tree. Once I was close enough to speak, I asked what was going on. Were they here to collect firewood?

One of the younger fellows laughed a little and then said, "I wish it were so!" The other Dreamers all laughed at that, joking between themselves.

Finally I said, "Hey! I don't get it!? Please tell me what you are up to!"

"All I know," answered one of the women Dreamers, "is that we are to prepare this tree for the 'Hanged Man Seer.' He gave us these detailed instructions, which includes a diagram of the tree to use, and how tall the cuts should be for the vertical section, and how wide for the perpendicular crossbeam. It tells how deep to dig the hole to put it into and all kinds of other details! The thing is, we all feel creepy about this. I mean, this contraption will be what the 'Hanged Man Seer' gets hung on!"

The woman Dreamer then handed the diagram to me, her mouth tightening at the corners. I looked up to the tree line; there were shadows across the mountains to the north. Then the wind came, and a mist of rain began to fall. I looked again at the woman; the black waves of her hair seemed untouched by a single raindrop. Not knowing quite what to say, I said, "The Ancient Ones are here to teach us. I am sure that there is more than what it might seem to be at first!"

One of the other Dreamers, called out, "You are always the eternal optimist!"

I just hunched my shoulders. Then I offered my help. The four Dreamers were happy to have more help. I was studying the diagram of the Hanged Man's hanging post. Strange name, I thought to myself. That is what the others were calling it, but to myself it felt more like a cross! I noticed that many of the words on the old diagram were written in Latin. Not being a Latin scholar, I did not recognize them. One, however, caught my attention, it said, "Patibulum" or "Crosspiece." As I looked at the drawing, I saw what the crosspiece was. A drawing of the rope that was looped over the top: this was for the foot, I realized, as the man is hung upside down. Yes, this was a little creepy, I thought quietly to myself. Studying more of the drawing, I noticed that the crosspiece showed green leaves, and looking closer, I even saw that there was one golden apple. Curious about that, but somehow relieved as well, I definitely wanted to know more. I looked around to find out what else had to be done.

One of the fellows came over to me and said, "Quite a drawing! It looks like it has been done on ancient parchment from a thousand years ago!" His tone was one of knowing.

I did not dispute him, saying, "This is amazing! What else do you need to get done?"

He said they could sure use the help. I noticed that he had a saw in hand and a coil of thick rope. With a pause, I had another thought: I have walked this dream, and there is something so familiar here.

A fellow came up just then and said, "Are you ready?"

As I looked at the man, daydreaming to myself, I knew that, yes, something is familiar. Trying to pay attention, I nodded to the man as the Dreamer introduced me to the Hanged Man Seer. In a fragile voice, I answered, "Pleased to meet you!" Shaking his hand, I remembered what one of the Keepers had told me about the energy of a healer: "a healer, good or bad, can draw or give strength to someone by the mere touch of the hand!" And with the touch of the Hanged Man Seer, I definitely felt him providing strength to me, in a good way! With one glance from him, I was blushing.

Thankfully he looked away and said to the Dreamer next to me, "Let's get going." Then, turning to me, he said, "Would you like to come?"

Quickly I answered, "Of course! And where are we off to?"

The Seer replied, "To find the right piece of wood for the 'Patibulum'!"

He began to say more, but I interrupted, saying, "I know what that means! It is the 'Crosspiece' for a cross! Oh, I am sorry!"

They both laughed at me but were pleased at what I had said. Holding up the diagram, the Seer said, "I am glad that you noticed the name on the diagram."

Answering, I said, "The drawing is beautiful!" To myself I wondered how he knew I had looked at it, since I had not seen him earlier.

The Seer went on to mention that I used the word "cross," in my explanation.

"Well, it seems like a 'cross' of some kind to me! I heard some of the others calling it a 'hanging post,' What would the right word be?

The Seer laughed again as he began walking. Pointing to the direction we were to go, he then said, "Let's get into the woods some; we will talk as we go!"

The fine rain had turned to a thicker mist, and the wind was still stirring. Clouds swirled and the sun was making another appearance. From here in the woods, I looked back to the open mountainside and could see that many other Dreamers had arrived and were bustling around the area. Some were setting up chairs, and others were raking around the hole that had been dug, for the post, I figured.

The Hanged Man Seer apparently saw that I was perplexed and just then began talking. "This will make a perfect spot for this afternoon's occurrence of the 'Arcanum XII.' I decided that for the Dreamers to really understand my tarot energy that an enactment of 'my hanging' would best serve the Dreamers, so we will have another one of our famous 'Dream Theater in the Round' extravaganzas!"

All I could think to answer was, "Oh, I see!"

The Seer in a laughing voice answered, "Well, I think a bit later that you will truly see!" He seemed to think this comment was very funny and went on awhile laughing.

I asked the Ancient One, "What have you decided to call this event?"

He answered quickly. "Why, I think this sounds good, 'The Arcanum XII Affair'! What do you think?"

This time I was the one laughing as I answered him, "Yes! It gives an air of intrigue!"

The Seer responded with, "Exactly!"

The Dreamer we had been walking with had moved on ahead some. As I looked around, I realized that this was the direction that I had arrived from. The cleared grassy area now held some of the old and twisted apple trees. Many of them looked as if they would provide an abundant apple crop for the fall season, and I wondered if anyone came way up here to pick them. The sun was decidedly warmer, and as I looked up to the clear sky, I saw a couple of hawks circling near one of the trees. Just then the Dreamer with the saw and rope popped out from behind some of the trees. He was waving his hands for us to come to where he was.

As we arrived at the trees, the Dreamer said, "I think I have found the wood we need!" He was pointing to a tree that had been felled by nature. The Dreamer began pointing out the quality of his find to the Hanged Man Seer. He said, "This apple tree must have come down in yesterday's storm. The break is fresh, still sappy. I think this limb would make a perfect 'crossbeam'!" He was holding the limb up for the Seer to check over.

The Seer seemed pleased. "Yes! Just a little trimming for the ends, and please leave on these leaves. Why, I see there are even a couple of apples on the branch! But let's trim two of them, keeping just the one. Perfect! We have our 'crossbeam'!"

I was smiling too, clapping my hands for the find. "How nice, made from an apple tree! Wow, the limb will make a beautiful 'Patibulum'!" I said to the Dreamer and Seer both. Then I suddenly felt a little strange about my jubilant reaction to a hanging tree; my smile faded and I stepped back a bit.

The Hanged Man Seer, noticing this, spoke to me with a soft pat on my shoulder. "Hey, dear Dreamer, don't be sad. There is much to learn through my so-called demise! First let's talk about the 'patibulum' or 'crossbeam.' Patibulum comes from Latin and means 'horizontal beam.' This beam was most often referred to in the construction of the crosses that were built for 'crucifixion' in the ancient Roman times. From Latin, 'cruci' means cross, and 'fixion' or 'ficere' means fix or do). But other civilizations have built them as well. The crosses consisted of two pieces the 'patibulum'-crossbeam and the 'stipes'-post. The word 'stipes' is from Latin and means 'post or tree trunk.' In botany the word 'stipe' means a stalk that supports some other structure. So these are the components of a cross. Of course the most famous cross is the one used for the crucifixion of Jesus Christ."

The Hanged Man Seer had taken a pause and was in the process of both thanking and blessing the apple tree. When he had finished, he said, "Her sweet magic will support me!"

I smiled at him and nodded my head in agreement, knowing there were probably other levels to what he had said. In the meantime we both watched as the Dreamer trimmed the branch to the correct length, carefully allowing the green leaves and the one small apple to remain, just as the Seer had instructed. Once he had it ready, he tied it with rope and then hoisted it to his shoulder for carrying.

We got back to the hilltop where the "Arcanum XII Affair" would take place. Scanning the hillside, I saw that the Dreamers had been busy in our absence. The area was all set up with aisles between every twelve chairs, in a half moon design. At the top center was the vertical beam; the "stipes" were all set within the hole that had been dug. I wondered how long before show time. I turned to see the Seer talking with other Keepers.

Deciding I was hungry, I sat down front and center and began munching away on my snacks. Just in front of me on the ground was the altar made up with a beautiful red cloth with many colored ribbons. There were two women Dreamers that I knew who were setting the final touches on the altar cloth, with lit candles and other mementos that Dreamers wanted to share. I told them it was beautiful and gave a calm presence to our gathering. They were pleased that I had noticed. The space had not been set with smudge yet, so I had enough time to finish my lunch; eating during our circle was not permitted.

I was about to get up, when the Dreamer I had been with earlier came and sat down. He said, "Everything looks great! It was nice to have you along for finding the cross-beam."

I answered, "I really enjoyed being a part of it. Why it was not put up yet?"

Smiling at me, he said, "The Seer would take care of that, and he will be explaining the crossbeam during his program. We have about a half an hour before our Dream theater guests arrive. For now, though, could you please come with me? The Hanged Man Seer would like to speak with you."

Jumping up from where I sat, I said, "Of course! Lead the way!"

In a moment we were with the Seer just at the edge of the hill where the tree line started. He was explaining something to a few Dreamers who held trimming sheers. He turned to us when he realized we there. "Great! They will make sure the path to the stream is clear," he said, as the other Dreamers with the trimmers, went off down the path.

"Now, my dear Dreamer," he said to me, "how would you like to assist me at the end of the program?"

With a huge smile, I said, "It would be my pleasure! What will you have me do?"

Taking me by the arm, he led both me and the other Dream fellow over to where the crossbeam sat on the ground. The Seer then explained that at the end of his "hanging per-formance," one Dreamer would help him down from the post. Then, looking at me, he said I was to have a wet cloth waiting, which I would then lightly bathe his face with as he still sat on the ground. Once done he would rise and be standing. Next I was to lead him to the stream for more renewal with water. The Seer added that I was to announce an invitation to the Dreamer audience to come along if they chose. Staring at me, his eyes were dark and unreadable, but of course I consented. He was pleased with my answer. "OK! Let's get ready for the 'Affair,'" said, the Ancient One.

The soft drumming had begun; the Dreamers were gathered. Next the Keepers came in and took the front seats reserved for them. Smelling the sage and the clean mountain air, I took the seat near the center I had been given. I found a small bowl of water and a clean cloth under the chair.

The drumming provided a beautiful presence now; the chatter was stopping as the Dreamers brought themselves to the present. One of the Dreamers approached the center. He was dressed like a knight might be, very gallant and tall. He held a rather large brass gong. I was glad I had taken along a colorful skirt this morning, which I quickly changed into before the drumming started. I felt as if I were participating in a pageant that held important messages for us all.

The Knight Dreamer held the brass gong out in front of him, gonging his beater two times for two o'clock. Then he announced, "The Keepers would have you all stand to open the circle!"

We all complied quickly as the Hanged Man Seer led us in blessings and protection. Then the Strength Seer led us in song. I noticed the Hanged Man Seer had managed to break away; he was getting ready, I realized. Now the Knight Dreamer asked that we all be seated. One of the women Dreamers was circling us all with sage.

The Knight Dreamer said, "Welcome to the Arcanum XII Affair!" And he gonged once more ever so loudly!

Heads were turning to the back of the space of the half moon–shaped chair arrangement. There were comments like, "Oh my God!" and "What the heck?" Then I saw the Hanged Man Seer dressed like a troubadour might from Shakespeare's time. With green tights and a loose shirt tied at his waist, he looked like a man might from the Middle Ages… except for what looked like a scene from Hollywood, with the actor portraying Jesus dragging his cross! The Seer was dragging the crossbeam! It was absurd! It got everyone's attention. It was a brilliant entry!

Finally the Hanged Man Seer was in the staging area. The Dreamers were still buzzing, and the Seer had set the crossbeam down next to the stipes. He was holding out his arms, calling for us to settle down, which took a moment. Walking back and forth, smiling and beaming good energy to the crowd, he said, "I know what you are thinking: Was that heavy? Are you afraid?"

The crowd roared with laughter, probably because his comments were true! The laughter was good, and everyone loosened up. In the background a couple of fellow Dreamers had attached the crossbeam to the stipes; the cross was in place.

The Seer was still walking back and forth. He added this, "I have been through this countless times. I have learned how to work it, you might say!" There was more laughter. I was smiling too as we all heard him say, "With the great turn of the Wheel, I have developed Strength to be at this point on my path. Now is my time, and maybe yours as well, to create a 'Scared Map,' re-envision self. This is what we are here to understand tonight!" His dark, piercing eyes were circling the Dreamers; he stared for a few moments as if to let that penetrate.

Standing now very calm in front of the crossbeam, he continued. "I am thought of as one of the dark Trumps by many. The Hanged Man, The Devil, The Tower, Death, and The Moon have this connotation. To many these may be so, but they have only looked to the surface meanings. As Dreamers, we are committed to go deeper with our studies and our dreaming. You are all beginning to realize that the deformative process is a necessary one. It is through the breaking away, the letting go of the old, that new truths take root."

As I felt the beautiful outdoor space, the air was very still. I thought it must be holding the truth of the words of the Hanged Man Seer, slowly releasing them to our group of Dreamers so that they may understand what they needed to work on for themselves.

The Seer began once more. "Later we will experience the 'hanging' together. For now let me get into the background and history of this 'Arcanum XII.' Crosses! It has been said that many of the Hanged Man tarot images done over time depict a 'Tau Cross.' I would suggest that you look at some of the old tarot drawings to understand the designs. The 'Tau' image has the crossbeam very near the top, and some indicate a loop effect at the top. 'Tau' is the

Greek name for the letter *T*. The Tau Cross is seen as a symbol of redemption through the act of reversal. The lesson of the Hanged Man XII may be that an impossible or unacceptable situation can be saved by reversing it and then viewing from a new perspective.

"The Tau Cross is similar to the Egyptian hieroglyphic symbol of the 'Ankh,' which means 'eternal life.' *Crosses* mean various things. A direction at a crossroad, crossing over something, crossing a challenge. Or the weight of a 'cross that one bears' and possibly crossing to a new height. A cross in general is about all that changes and all that stays the same."

The Seer had been sitting on a stool in the center stage. Now he was up and moving around, waving his hands in an excited fashion. "From Gareth Knight on the Qabalah, we have various symbols: the Hebrew letter 'Mem'/'Water' element and Tree of Life Path number twenty-three. Colors are Deep Blue/Sea Green. Attribute is 'Spirit of the Mighty Water.'"

"The twenty-third path in the Qabalah travels the Sephiroth, of which there are ten on the Tree of Life, connecting 'Hod' with 'Geburah.' 'Hod' is referred to as 'The Water Temple of Hod.' One of the principles of water is reflection, and in Hod lies the principle of the higher worlds. The power of this path teaches man to use his mind with the true plan of evolution. In life the human reaction to difficulties has been a willingness to 'hang the other man.' The lesson this path teaches is, 'Go hang yourself'! Esoterically, the man hung upside down is one of sacrifice. Another lesson indicates the values of the 'higher worlds' are the reverse of the 'lower worlds.' The lesson of 'Spiritual Law': 'You get in life what you put into it.' A key to this path comes from the element of 'Water Reflecting': 'As above; So below'! The energy of the twelfth Trump is much like the ancient symbol of the 'Seal of Solomon,' representing the combination of opposites. An upright triangle, 'Fire,' and an inverted triangle, 'Water'; when these are overlaid and have inscribed a circle around the two triangle symbols, we have the 'Seal of Solomon.'

"Eliphas Levi made a profound connection between the Tarot Trumps and the Hebrew alphabet. He offered his insights as correlation as a key to the mystery of the ages. Levi also likens the Hanged Man to the ancient Greek myth of 'Prometheus, the Eternal Suffer'! There are some views that suggest that the inverted figure denotes the loss of spiritual facilities. In some Hanged Man images, the figure has one leg folded and arms folded behind the figure. Levi surmises that this symbolizes the symbol of 'sulfur,' and, according to Levi, signifies the accomplishment of 'Magnum Opus,' which from Latin means 'The Great Work.' Referring to alchemy and the 'Philosopher's Stone,' this stone is thought esoterically to be capable of turning base metals into gold. It is also thought to be the 'Elixir of Life'!"

The Hanged Man Seer used his voice well, projecting with deep resonance for spark, using body language to make various points. Walking back and forth along the aisles, he had started again. "Prometheus, yes! Let's get to the history of this Greek who has been connected to me! Prometheus from Greek myth was a Titan, son of 'Iapetos' and Klymene' and brother to 'Atlas.' He was known as a champion of humankind and for his wily intelligence. He stole fire from the God Zeus and gave it to the mortals. Zeus punished Prometheus for his crime, having him bound to a tree on a high, rocky mountain top. When Prometheus betrayed Zeus for humanity's sake, he knew the consequences, and it happened as he foresaw. On the orders of Zeus, 'Hephaestus' chained him to a tree on Mt. Caucasus. Each day a great eagle ate at his liver, which then grew back each night, to then have the same thing happen day after day! Prometheus was in an eternal punishment. Some stories tell this lasted from thirty years to four hundred thousand years! It has been said that Prometheus is torn by his bitter thoughts during the day, but at night he rests from his grief. His ego consciousness and life are destroyed and reborn repeatedly. Finally, after much time, Zeus allows the Greek hero 'Hercules' to shoot the eagle and free Prometheus from his chains, some thirteen generations later. Because the bonds of Zeus are irrevocable, even by him, Prometheus wore a ring made from his fetters and set it with a stone from the mountain. Since that time people have worn rings set with stones in commemoration of Prometheus's sacrifice on their behalf!

"The original play of *Prometheus* was written by the Greek poet Aeschylus; this was his seventh tragedy play written in the years 470 to 472 BC. He was recognized as the father of Greek tragedy.

"Centuries later, the romantic English poet Percy B. Shelly, who lived from 1792 to 1822, wrote a beautiful poem of tribute to Prometheus, called 'Prometheus Unbound' in 1820. It was a poem of tragedy based on the Greek poet Aeschylus. In his poem there are many passages of dreams that came to Prometheus while he was chained to the tree on the rocky mountain. 'Panthea' comes to him, saying, 'Dream, dream, with an echo of her voice repeating; follow, follow'!"

"So you see, my dear Dream students, that Prometheus was a Dreamer! Prometheus was a supreme craftsman, and he instructed humanity in all the arts and sciences. He taught the sacred art of 'Metallurgy,' which is the study of physical and behavior of metallic elements. He also instructed in the art and craft of metalworking.

"Prometheus is the archetypal traitor, who betrays the established order in favor of a new world, and he is the patron of all such traitors. First, he betrayed his kin, the Titans, in favor of Zeus and the Olympians. Later Prometheus, the supreme trickster, betrayed Zeus to the benefit of mortals! When we look at the Hanged Man as the 'Hanged Traitor,' this represents the unavoidable torments of overturning an old order and of a voluntary sacrifice for the sake of spiritual rebirth.

"I would like to look at the word 'Traitor' a moment. In Latin it is 'proditor,' and Greek it is 'prodotes.' In a basic sense, it means to thrust, project, and, in a more developed sense, it means to reveal, to uncover. We realize that one side's traitor is the other side's savior, and in many cases the traitor betrays the old regime to the intended, new regime. The Hanged Traitor is unique in that it represents a voluntary reversal of fortune, a voluntary sacrifice for the sake of the greater good, for which Prometheus is the prototype! Prometheus was changed by the ordeal, for after he was freed, he was made immortal. Likewise, the Traitor, hanging head down, cannot escape from the Wheel. As you may recall, the Wheel of Fortune precedes this Trump. But he can discover its hub, where the gods reside. He can learn to transcend his fate by sacrificing himself; this, then, makes him sacred. The hanging is a dazzling moment, dreamlike and clear. Connections he never understood before are made as 'he hangs.' Mysteries are revealed!

"Comparisons have been made with Prometheus as the rebel who resisted all forms of tyranny epitomized by Zeus! For instance, the church, monarchs, and patriarchs. Prometheus is also compared to the French Revolution and to Christ. Also there is the comparison of the human ability to heal ourselves.

"In medieval Europe there were special punishments for criminals, especially traitors. The traitor was beaten while hung by the heels. If the traitor was dead, his corpse might be hung and abused in the same way! If the traitor was not available for insult, he might be painted in the upside down pose, and this was then posted. They called these paintings 'Shame Paintings'! This method of punishment was used in Italy, Germany, Scotland, and in England. In England it was called 'baffling,' and this punishment continued into the twentieth century!"

The Hanged Man Seer had spoken about this last part in a very fierce tone and now was surveying his Dreamer audience, looking for reaction, which he was getting! There were comments of "Oh my God!" and "That is unbelievable!"

Now the Seer was laughing and saying, "You had all better watch out...Make sure you know what you are doing before betraying! The symbol of the Hanged Man, some say, is related to 'Judas Iscariot,' who was one of the twelve original Apostles of Jesus. He was the one designated to keep account of the money bags. It is 'Judas' who turns over Jesus to Pontius Pilate's soldiers with the 'Kiss of Judas.' In the Christian view, it is said that the guilt-ridden Judas later committed suicide by hanging himself with money bags. Some images of Trump XII illustrate money bags in the paintings.

"There is another view to also consider, from an account of the Hanged Man by Margaret Starbird; the Hanged Man is thought to be one of the Knights Templar. Stripped of honor, prestige, and armor, the Templars were subjected to heinous tortures, including sexual tortures, by the Inquisition. A man hanging by one leg may be a euphemism used in literature to represent the genitals! Some say that the crossed leg is a representation of the fleur-de-lis, the emblem of the Merovingian bloodline.

"Some Hanged Man images show a tortured Templar man holding two bags of gold, representing the monetary treasure of the suppressed order. The image may suggest the genealogical 'family jewels' of the royal bloodline!"

The Dreamers had whisperings and laughing comments about the Templars and the family jewels, but they settled down quickly to glean more from this amazing Seer!

"Another beautiful analogy of the Hanged Man is that of the 'Fisher King,' the 'wounded king' from King Arthur legends. In the varied stories, there are knights who travel from many lands to heal the 'Fisher King,' but only the chosen can accomplish the feat. The 'Fisher King' had been wounded in both body and spirit; his kingdom suffered and the land became infertile. He was a 'hung man,' suspended, until such time that his wound could be healed.

"T. S. Eliot, poet of 'The Waste Land,' used the 'Fisher King' theme and tarot images within the poem and mentions the 'Hanged Man' in one verse.

"Now we travel to Northern Europe and learn about Norse Mythology. Paganism during the Viking Age tells of 'Odin,' who was considered the chief god in Norse Myth. His name is related to 'Oor,' which means 'fury, excitation, and mind.' He is associated with wisdom, war, magic, prophecy, trickery, and the wild hunt. Odin was the 'god of Occult Wisdom' for Seers and sorcerers. From as early as 100 BC, 'Odin's Cult' performed various shamanic feats, including human sacrifice. Odin's best known shamanic undertaking was called 'Odin's Ordeal.' This ritual was enacted as an attempt to gain knowledge of and power over the 'Runes Stones' used for divination. The 'Runes' were considered a magical element of divination—their nature is that of timeless mysteries—and came into being with the 'Nine Worlds out of Ginnungagap.' These were the 'Nine Realms of Existence.' These magical workings are unique to the Teutonic/Germanic people of Northern Europe."

"As you might imagine, this would be an amazing achievement for Odin! To enact the ritual, Odin hung himself on the 'Yggdrassil,' World Tree, in order to gain illumination. He hung for nine nights, during which he received neither food nor wine. Odin had also pierced himself with the point of a spear. Upon completion of the ritual, Odin was able to recognize the Runes and make them submit to him as their 'Rune-Master'! The theme of this myth corresponds with many shamanist initiation rites among many peoples. As we can see, the 'Hanged Man XII' can be related to the visions of a shaman's initiatory journey. He who can understand his own higher nature will receive a great awakening!

"In French the name for 'Hanged Man' is 'Le Pendu,' which means 'to hang'! The word 'pendant' comes from this and means anything hanging. 'Le Pendu' is derived from 'Pendre,' meaning 'undecided state'! Now isn't that interesting! The Hanged Man does not hang by his neck or arm. No! He hangs by one foot! Feet are a symbol of moving forward into the future. The Hanged Man has decided consciously not to take any further steps at this time. He is suspended, hanging and contemplating his options. He is undecided! Now, looking to the sequences in the tarot, we have: the twelve position being between the Trumps, backwards to 'Strength XI' or to self-realization, or moving forward to 'Death XIII'! Of course there are lessons to be learned in repeating cycles of death and rebirth. The Hanged Man is suspended between duality: conscious of his past deeds. Yet taking no action, he is contemplating. Taking no action sometimes is a stronger statement than taking action. It may be wiser 'to do nothing' until all aspects of an issue have come to light. It is a fallow time and requires patience. The truth will later be revealed! When we are in the Hanged Man position, we can discover what it is we are doing with our life and how we might proceed from here. This can only happen when we allow rest for our body and mind. We come to realize that we have created our own bondage conditions. Our story of our life requires a lot of energy to maintain; only we know how we can change what needs changing! When viewing many of the tarot images of the Hanged Man XII Trump, some depictions show that his eyes are closed, because his journey is an inward journey. His hands are behind his back because this is a time of not doing!"

The Seer paused and lifted his hands above himself as he said, "And that, my dear Dreamers, is my tale of the 'Hanged Man'! Now with the help of my two Dreamer assistants, I will perform for your journeying benefit, 'My Hanging'!"

There was wild applause! The Dreamers were cheering; everyone loved this amazing Seer. The noise settled, and we watched as the Seer was about to assume the hanging position. We were told to journey with him as he went through this experience. He told us he would hang for twelve minutes and the Keepers would accompany the ritual with their drums. We stood or sat while holding our breath until the Dreamer assistants helped him to be hung! Then there was *dead silence* a few minutes before the soft drumming started. We dreamed with the Seer as he went through his ordeal; we journeyed with him and for ourselves as well! This was incredible; I knew my own experience would help me to change into a better Dreamer healer!

The drumming was slowing; it was time to come back. The Dreamers assisted the Hanged Man Seer back to the ground. I arrived next to him and bathed his face, neck, and hands with the cool water as he sat a moment. Then he was ready to stand, and there were cheers and hoorays! Everyone was so very happy to have him back! Now the Seer had me announce that all Dreamers were welcome to follow him down to the stream for more ritual cleansing!

Before we could continue with our walk, a Dreamer came up to the Hanged Man Seer and presented him with a pouch filled with "Runes" that had been carved from an apple tree, she said. The Seer was very touched and pleased, then thanked the Dreamer. A large group of us began our walk down the path past the apple trees, headed for the stream. The Hanged Man was in good spirits and joking with many of the Dreamers who were following, laughing, and talking happily!

DEATH

DREAM OF THE TRUMP SEER: DEATH XIII

This had been one of those late night, informal discussion groups going until 3:00 a.m. in the small pub of the main lodge. We were still in the grip of winter, and our daily Dream work usually just switched gears to informal talk about what might be on a Dreamer's mind. Tonight we seemed to still be in the grips of the Death Seer, who had been the main venue for the day's Dreaming. This one line from The Death XIII Seer kept going around in my head: "Learn to count upon death...Visualizing possible changes to family and home affects those around you. Thus the bridge is built that leads beyond the veil."

I had that on my mind when I entered the pub; about ten Dreamers were already there, deep in discussion while they enjoyed the sipping of a friendly spirit from the barkeep. The group was laughing about the irony of it all, as someone said, "No matter what you do, you die! What is the point anyway?" Others joked and said, "Careful, the spirits dwell here in the pub. They may inquire about you!" So the conversations went back and forth from serious to funny. What else could we do with such a topic, I wondered?

The Death Seer was not in the pub at the moment; though someone said he was sure to arrive. A couple of us were reviewing our notes from the workshop earlier in the day. This is some of what we remembered from, DEATH XIII Trump Seer in the Grove:

The Qabalah, from Gareth Knight, refers to The Death Trump as the "Child of the Great Transformer" and "Lord of the Gates of Death." Death is the principle of: rest, rebirth, creation, destination, renewal, release, detachment. It is an astrological sign of Scorpio, the element of water.

The Death Seer, during our session in the Grove, had said, "Death is the one we turn to voluntarily or with a push. Change is always around us; the seasons change their venue. A child is born, grows; there are changes in one's interest, people, careers, homes. The little deaths are always there moving us on, preparing our way for the larger death. "Upon the planes of form, death and birth are two sides of the same coin" (From Gareth Knight).

"The Seer had been precise, matter of fact as he spoke. That is what was unnerving to me," I said to the bunch in the pub. Someone else recalled this, saying it was their favorite part! Before he could relay his notes, I interrupted with, "How can any of this be favorite?" Of course all of us laughed. What else can you do with this subject!

Then he said, The Seer had told us this: "The Ancient One of Death may be shown to us in a skeleton form. The significance is that the basic structure of the body is that of the skeleton, upon which all else is built. The bones of who we are! Our memory lies there within the bones. Often the death figure is shown as a symbol that is holding a sickle/scythe. This is a harvesting tool. Plants, flowers, people, are planted; they grow to abundance and are then harvested. Then there is rest!" Then the Seer looked at us a few minutes and added, "Ah! But the mystical red roses grow again, and again!"

The Dreamer who relayed this also added, laughing quietly, "Remember? Do you remember that?" We all nodded our heads in agreement.

Another Dreamer relayed: "In the Qabalah on the Tree of Life, Death is path number twenty-four, 'Imaginative intelligence.' It is given the Hebrew letter 'Nun,' The Fish, and 'Mem,' Water. 'Mem' is also used for 'Woman,' as I recall. The Seer then held up a tarot card of 'Death' and said, 'We can refer to one of the Three Women on this card, Maiden, Matron, and Crone, though all one in the same. The point to remember is she travels on the twenty-fourth Qabalah path, the lightning path."

One of the woman Dreamers in the pub said she had that card with her and pulled it out for all of us to look at closer. After awhile another Dreamer said, "The Death Seer mentioned something called, 'The Cosmic Doctrine.'"

And said, "This gives an explanation of the seven types of death. Here are the first and the seventh: 'The first death' is the vortex of the plant-tree world; things grow to a culmination, then release. They drop leaves, and seeds grow again. 'The seventh death' is the 'Lightning Flash.' This knows birth and death and birth of the personality. Here on the seventh death we come to know our soul. We gain a confidence in the future. A knowing is realized and, rather than giving into the voices of apathy, inertia, and cowardice, We move on and on again."

All the Dreamers in the pub had bits and pieces to say about that; some were in friendly, heated discussions, and others just laughed and sipped their drinks. The mood was high energy.

One Dreamer, in a quite loud voice, added, "The Death Trump has deities associated with it; two come to mind: Pluto and Hades. Death is irrevocable, and no one, not even a god, can bring back from the dead someone whom Hades wishes to keep!"

There was a silence one could slice with a knife for several minutes. I had a chill on my back. Others were sipping their drinks.

Out of the dark of the night, someone else said, "Oh my! So somber, so sad! Come on, Dreamers! It was your choice to be here!" Then there was high-pitched laughter!

All the Dreamers turned to the entryway, and there in his/her (this body could adapt) human form was The Death Seer! He wore a long, black cape and black boots; his eyes looked black as pitch, and the sockets seemed to be darkened with coal. He stood there diffidently staring and holding his long sickle. There was not a breath in the entire room; he really had put fright into the whole pub!

Finally, after what seemed like days, one of the Dreamers said, "Please, Seer, join us! Would you like a drink?"

The Death Seer said, "But of course! A little sip from the spirits can't hurt!"

Then someone found a chair and the Seer proceeded to remove his cape. Once it was off, some of the Dreamers began to laugh. We all tried to get closer to see what was so funny. The Seer then turned around for all to see his costume of a basic black leotard. On it, painted in white, was a skeleton! It was crazy looking and everyone loved it! He walked about, modeling for all to see. We were all hysterical with laughter!

He had removed the skintight mask from his face and looked like a normal guy. Except I thought, He is The Death Seer. At least he has a sense of humor, and the Goddess knows we need that!

After a little bit, the Seer said he had a few things to say. "Dreamers, you are as initiates here in the Grove, learning, growing, and stretching. You are learning with the death topic that each of you is going through an 'initiate's ego-death' of your own. It is normal to feel terrified of this impending death. It is dissolution of the personality, and each of you has no way of knowing the outcome. Death is a confrontation of the unknown; it will feel horrifying. You may try to resist, but at this point you cannot. There will be the end of what you thought you knew, and finally one succumbs. There will be resurrection, and, as an initiate who has now gone through transformation, you will still look back, grieve, be saddened for the life that is gone. This is the price that must be paid for transformation!"

The Seer had of course grabbed our attention in such a way that none of us was able to move. Again the silence was thick! He searched each one of us, as if to say, "You will come to me one day." I was squirming some in my chair, and I saw others doing the same.

Just then the Death Seer called out, "Barkeep, please give them all a round on me! Yes! That's the ticket! Hey, Dreamers, come on now! You all learned a long time ago how to live every day to its fullest, even though death may be just over your shoulder! It's what we do; we are Dreamers! And know this, throughout the tarot system of symbolism, there is *no* exact reference to birth! This is because birth is death and death is birth! So there you have it!"

The Seer then clapped his hands, and we all laughed the best we could and began to say good night. The hour was 3:00 a.m., after all! Still, with all that had transpired, we had fun!

As we were leaving, the Death Seer mentioned a Dream assignment for the night: "Dream of your own Confrontation of Death. Tomorrow we will share these dreams!"

The following is the Dream that came to me that night. I call it "*Confronting* Death!"

The dishes are put away. My house feels in order. I have given time freely. I have helped my husband, children, mother, father, brother…The list goes on. Busy with career and everyday work. Outside now, relaxing, walking; there is something on the wind's voice. Fog is forming out there in my back woodland space, calling me. It feels eerie, forbidding somehow, but I keep walking. My mind reels over the loose ends of the day. Answering the call, I am walking now out into this fog, with the wind's voice pulling me. The moon is showing her evening face and lights the way over the pond to the hazel tree there. Proud, beautiful, hazel, already shedding her leaves! It's only late August, but the hazel nuts are growing rich. Before I know it, the harvest time will be here.

Shrugging my shoulders from the cool evening breeze, I rub my arms for warmth. Birds, nesting for night, fill the air with songs. Again something on the wind's voice pulls me….to the water's edge. I see the clear, still surface like a mirror. It is beautiful with the fog around the edges drifting, skimming the surface. The quiet is broken by a crying sound, but I don't know from where. Afraid now, I am ready to run back into the warm comfort of home. I start but then notice a figure in the surface of the water. Hard to decipher…I look again.

The voice on the wind is crying, whaling now. I say out loud, "What is it? Who are you?"

The answer comes back, clearly in a woman's voice, saying, "It's the Keening!"

I say, "Who are you?"

The cries are loud now. The voice says, "Keening—the cries; the lamenting cries are for the death of someone." Now I am ready to bolt! "Try as you may," the woman's voice says, "But you are here now between the worlds, cannot go back, and cannot go forward. You need to look at what is now."

Thoughts rush around my mind with the words "change, change" continuously bouncing around. I want things to stay as they are in most ways. But, death—that scary word!

"Death! I don't have time for this," I say out loud.

The woman takes a form now. With the light of moon, I see her, a floating half image of woman and half surreal, eerie goddess. On the voice of the wind, I hear her say, "You don't have time for this, and yet I am here. I am the Ancient One of Death, part of the White Moon Goddess! My sacred number is thirteen and, oh yes, you will have time for me."

At hearing her words, I crumble down to the ground. "This cannot be real!" I say, "Why are you telling me this? Why?"

Over the wind I hear the cries. "The Keening. It gets your attention!" says the Ancient One of Death. "Does it not?"

I look her right in her face, a transparent face, an illusion, I am thinking. But out loud, still looking into her face, I say, "Am I dying?"

The Ancient One of Death smiles lightly and answers, "Not in the way you think. Your physical form will be here sometime yet. But there is change on the horizon. With my help and your Dreaming, you can be more prepared for possible events of the near future. Walk with me to the hazel tree," says the Ancient One. "This tree is one of wisdom and protection. Some believe the hazel nuts hold special powers." She picks a few to munch on and offers some to me. I shake my head to say no thanks. "Suit yourself," says she. "Just put these in your pocket for now."

As she does this, I notice a beaming in the night sky. "Mercury the Communicator," is what she answers. "A good one to consult," she says.

The Ancient one nudges me to walk more. At the pond's edge we now stop, standing in swirling fog now. Something out of an eerie movie, I think to myself.

The Ancient One of Death seems calm and pleasant somehow. I watch her as she skims small, flat stones across the top of the pond. She gives me some to do the same with. I throw a few, but they do not skip across the top like hers. "It takes many years of practice to make them skip and many years to make friends with death. Practice for the biggest transition we will ever do comes with paying attention to the smaller deaths in our lives. One should start by making friends with these changes, mini deaths, and you will be skipping from fear in no time!" says the Ancient One of Death.

My thoughts are in a swirl with gaping questions by this time. "What changes?" I ask.

"Start here." She throws a rock into the water, and a new image of a woman appears. "This is The Triple Goddess."

Looking closely, I see three figures in one and three heads. "But they are skeletons!" I scream.

"So it is," says the Ancient One. "We all need a support system don't we? The bones carry our memories of who we are, our DNA, our exact blueprint. We can learn much about ourselves if we can only get past the fear. This is you! Your ancestor self. Look at her! Feel her joy; feel her pain! She can guide you now for the changes that will come. The Triple Goddess: the Maiden, the Matron, the Crone. The Crone is the waning moon death aspect of the Great Goddess in the Greek pantheon, which held dominion over the land of the dead. You may want to think of her as Grandmother Skeleton Woman!"

The Ancient One of Death is looking right at my eyes as she speaks. "You are ready to handle this information. You feel the restlessness, and you are ready for more depth of knowledge! This Triple Goddess is you, all three in one. She is here to help on the timing of things, much like the seasons and the way the trees drop their leaves. These are some of the things she can teach you. This kind of study takes discipline and strength of heart. But the payoff is this: you will receive calmness and a sense of wholeness that cannot be gotten except by being true to yourself and doing the study of change!"

The fog is lifting, the keening has turned into the animal noises of the night. The Ancient One of Death is being called by the midnight. She then tells me, "Our work is done for a time."

I stop her before she moves on, to say, "But where can I find you? I may have questions."

Staring with, dark black eyes that are kindly, she replies, "You can find me in your Dreams, and journey to my sanctuary in the Sacred Grove. Look for the guardians there. They will help; you only need to ask."

With that, she is gone! I never thanked her!

I stand there in a fog, between times…Then I hear someone at the house calling my name. "You should come in now, it's chilly," they are saying. I know that voice from my everyday world.

Slowly I respond, "I am coming!" And I follow that voice on the wind back to my warm home. But I am still in that other world, with part of me wandering in the night, conversing with the Ancient One whose sacred number is thirteen.

I will keep always the image of her transparent face and, when I need her help, find her in the Grove. Now I looked forward to the morning session of sharing and doing the "Lightning Dream Work" that would provide me with the answers I needed.

.

XIV

TEMPERANCE

DREAM OF THE TRUMP SEER: TEMPERANCE XIV

I awoke in a sweat with the feeling of terror! Was that real or just a dream? Trite question, I thought to myself. I am a Dreamer after all! I should be able to make sense of this feeling…realizing that the terror came from my other reality, the Dream world! I got out of bed and looked through the window and saw the dawn, the rising sun in mostly pinks and purples, coming between the twin peaks of the eastern mountains. Too early to get out of bed, I wrapped the blankets around me and put my journal within reach. Remembering that I had gotten up from my left side, I resumed that same position, trusting that my dream body would be enticed to go back into this dream! I knew that by re-entering this dream I could retrieve some answers. My intension being to discover what felt so terrifying.

The blankets were still warm; I was grateful. It did not take me long to snuggle into the down comforter and track the dream, which for now I have titled "What Was The Terror?" My dream tale is this:

I was a young mother in ancient Scotland, living in a time of war and hardship beyond description. There were invaders after my family, its land and the grove. I had to find a place to hide my children before the next round of attacks. My oldest child was a boy of eleven years. I needed him to be in charge of the two smaller girls. I knew he was strong and capable. But he is only a child, I said to myself, crying as I packed supplies they would need. In my head I was going over the route we would take to the small cave that would serve as a temporary hiding place, a small home for the three: eleven years, eight years, and five years. Babies, just babies all! With tears in my eyes, I packed.

My eleven-year-old son said, "Don't cry, Mother. We can do this! We will be fine! Don't you remember how we stacked the wood and made other things ready a few weeks ago? I will take good care of my sisters. They are strong! We know how to cook some, and this is a protected place! And I know that you will rejoin us in a day or two!"

I turned around and embraced this child that I was now asking to become a man. As my tears still flowed, my son used his hand to wipe them away. Who is the adult here? I was thinking to myself.

We were off! A muddy, icy path through the wood, but the children all kept up. As we got to the rock ledges, my son was like a mountain goat, going ahead to check the path and then doubling back in order to help the younger ones. Looking to the left, about thirty feet above, I could see the narrow crevice. Just enough room for us to squeeze through. Everyone was inside.

Then I heard the noise. It sounded like thunder within the Earth! Quickly I pulled the branches in front of the crevice and was inside. My son was already tending the fire with the younger ones. I began to light the rushes in the wall niches for extra light. Interesting how the glow of light brings us comfort, I thought to myself. The walls of this ancient cave had paintings on them. I had been here many times over the last few months, but I was always in a rush and never really paid much attention to these renderings in russets, reds, and blues. Now, however, I was drawn to one in particular. I looked at the children briefly; they were fine. My youngest daughter was running about the fire. Playing a game with the fairies, is what she told me. I turned back to the painting, but it wasn't there!

Looking all around, I was puzzled and said out loud, "Where did you go?"

I got an answer I didn't expect! "Over here."

I turned around to find this amazing ,vibrant woman talking and playing with the children!

"See, Mother," said my son. "We will be fine! This is 'Temperance,' the Ancient One Trump XIV. She told me she would be looking after us when you go to the sacred grove near Loch Maree."

I wanted to speak but could not. Elder Grandmother always told me that the children would be protected. I had not put enough faith in the things she taught me. Our everyday life had been safe and beautiful then. All that I held dear was being challenged now, we were being invaded, and our beliefs were being stamped out. The invaders wanted nothing left of the Goddess; the Druid priest and priestess were clear about how careful we must be now. My own mother, a wise one and "Dreamer" for our clan, had been killed as an example to the wrath from these warring invaders. She had told us many months ago to make ready a place to keep the children safe. I did not believe her! And now she is gone!

My Elder Grandmother had taken me aside and said, "We must do as your Mother has said. 'The Dreaming' is true!" She told me this with such conviction in her eyes…and I loved this elder, and of course I did as was bid. We made this cave ready. In the doing of that readying, I was back and forth many times, often in the cover of night, in order to keep the place secret. My husband and father were on the far side of the Caledonian Forest, where the Scotch pines grew to a hundred feet. Most of the men and women warriors were there; this was the place of the worst fighting.

I was deep in thought about all the things that had changed our world. Then I heard my son speaking to me. "Mother, aren't you going to say hello to 'Temperance'?"

Coming back to this reality I said, "Yes, of course!" Now I realized that she was the exact image that had been on the wall. Moving away from the wall and toward the fire, I held out my hand in greeting to Temperance. Still in disbelief, I grasped hers. I said, "Hello and welcome! Please excuse me; I have had a lot on my mind! I see now that my Elder Grandmother has given me many truths."

Still holding my hand, the Ancient One said, "Yes, quite a lot, but then that is why I have come. To help you through what I can." She began moving away from the children. I turned to check on them. "They will be fine!" she said. "Let's sit over here awhile where we can talk."

The cave had grown warm now. I looked around at all the provisions that had been stashed. I saw the bearskins and those of fox and deer. Piles of wood and flints and cookware and foods had all been organized. There were pots of herbals and herbs still drying on lines overhead. This would make a fine temporary home. I was glad that I had listened and had done all that I possibly could over the past few months. But all that time I spent making ready, I really never thought we would have to use it!

Wiping the tears that had sprung to my eyes, I looked at the Ancient Seer. In a quiet voice, I said, "My grandmother and mother have told me stories of the Seers, and, at the time, I only half listened and half believed! I wish truly that I had paid more attention! Now my mother is gone...If only I had more faith in the things she tried to teach me. Many times I was difficult and would say awful things about the old ways! Now she is gone!"

Looking at the Temperance Seer, I felt her compassion. It was hard to keep my control, but I must tell her what I could...Continuing, I said, "My grandmother is still here, I hope! She stayed behind with other elders to do blessings. They would not leave our village until that had been done. They were also checking the ley lines in the Dreaming for the warriors of our clan, so they would be able to track their way back. This is what they stayed for! I thought them crazy and pleaded that they leave with me and the children. Then we heard the thunder over the earth, the invading battalion army fleet on their thundering horses. Everyone figured at that point they were a few hours from us!" I was frightened and I was quite out of breath from recounting this to the Seer.

She reached over and said, "Take a moment, my dear. There is much to do in little time. I feel that if we regroup what the most important things are at this time, we can make a difference!"

My mouth was open. I closed it and took a deep breath. Thoughts of what was most important began flooding my brain. I had gotten the children to safety. I needed to go back for the other elders and my grandmother. I needed to go to the grove and collect anything that might suggest the Druids had been there.

The Seer suddenly spoke up, saying, "Yes, now we are making progress!"

I answered, saying, "But I did not say anything out loud!"

"Oh, my dear, you will get used to the telepathy with time. I am sure your Grandmother used it with you!"

I just shook my head slightly, again wishing I had paid more attention years before, when they tried to train me in the Dreamer's arts!

"It's quite all right," said the Seer. "I am sure you picked up more than you give yourself credit for!"

I answered briefly, "I hope so. I never really believed truly, until today. And with you here, you have given me new hope and strength!"

The Seer smiled warmly. "Now what is first on the list still to do?" said the Seer. "And most importantly, what is the terror that I am sensing from you?"

How did she know that I felt such terror? I wondered at this, with a lengthy pause, before I spoke. With my eyes on the brink of tears, I said to The Temperance Seer, "I am terrified for the children! Not me, being hurt or any of that, the children! How can I leave them and know that they are safe? I know that I must do these other things for the good of all, but they are so small!" The wetness was over my cheeks now. I wanted to sob but would not dare let the children hear.

The Temperance Seer had my right hand in hers as she said, "My dear girl, this is why I am here! And it is also time for you to give your trust to your young son! I feel what you are going through is what is called the Dark Night of the Soul. It is what dreamers, healers, and mystics often go through for the growth on their path. Let me explain."

I looked back at the Seer, puzzled and yet very willing to hear what she would say.

Someone was calling my name and saying, "It is OK! Wake up. I am here. Everything is fine!"

Suddenly I jumped up out of the warm comforter and out of the bed. I was disoriented. Staring at the woman seated on the edge of my bed, I blurted out, "Where am I? What is going on?" I looked about and said, "This is not the cave! And the children!"

The woman had gotten off the bed and was comforting me now, saying, "Dear, dear, I know what has happened. You were talking in your sleep. You have been dreaming in two places at once. I will explain: you are here as a part of the Keepers gathering in the Nemeton." She waved her hand about the cabin, and I followed her hand movements as she smudged with sage. I began to recall the familiar things about the room. Then she added, "Also, you have been back in time to an ancient life in Scotland, where you were attempting to keep your children safe in a cave!"

I looked at her stunned. Two places at once? As I began to ground myself, I smelled the sage, and sighed deeply, half collapsing on the bed. I held my bent head with two hands and then slowly looked up, saying, "You are her! You were in the cave with me! You were a painting on the wall, and then you were in person!"

She answered in a strong voice, "Yes, I am one and the same, and I am The Seer Temperance! And we were together in that past life of your dreaming and now again in this lifetime."

With that realization I began to weep, saying, "But what has happened to the children? What is it I should do now?"

"Dear Dreamer, you will be fine. The children were kept safe in that life because of the care and choices you made at that time. In this life, right now, you are reconnecting to lessons you received then, so you may be more fully awake to the teachings for your current waking lifetime."

The Temperance Seer was handing me tea to drink and a biscuit. After a moment my heart felt more normal. With a little munching, somehow I reentered the dream in my mind and went backward in time to that hidden cave in Scotland.

I looked at the Seer intently. I needed her to help me make sense of all of this. Then I said, "As I recall, you were about to explain something about 'The Dark Night of the Soul.' Would you please go into that now?"

She nodded her head and, with a big smile, said, "Yes, of course! You appear to be ready now. But before we go over that part, know the dream life in ancient Scotland is a part of you, and you can reenter this life when you feel the need. Now, however, let us get to the lessons in this Dreaming Life!"

The Seer continued, "If you recall, in your dreaming of that life, you were terrified something would happen to the children if you left." I was nodding my head yes. "A mother's relationship with her child is multifaceted. At a fairly young age, the mother begins to wean the child from her breast, then putting the child from her arms and teaching the child to walk. This is a 'dark night' feeling for both the child and the mother, as the child is beginning to give away his childish ways. There are many stages of this throughout childhood. The child is tested in the dark so they may acquire strength. The child is beginning to trust in self. It is a huge lesson. Spirit teaches the soul to learn to walk alone. The soul begins to learn of its three aspects: will, intellect ,and memory. The Dark Night of the Soul is a test to see whether the soul will turn back at a crucial moment. The word 'crucial' is from the Latin 'crux,' meaning 'a cross.' Some say this is the most difficult moment, the darkness before dawn. Will the soul pass the test? They must try."

The Seer had paused and was scanning my reaction so far. I looked back and said in a raspy voice, "So what you are telling me is that my fear is: can I let my child go to learn life on his own little by little? And my other fear is: what then will I do, without him, for myself? Is this what I am to learn from this dark night?"

"Well, you certainly pick up speed fast!" said the Seer. She got up and got my sweater and said, "It would be good for us both to walk awhile. The sun is out brightly now. I believe I hear the water calling our names!"

Still in a dream trance, I followed the Seer out of the cabin. The Temperance Seer had put on a wrap as well, but her angel like wings were peeking through. She slung her bow over her arm and held an arrow in her left hand. As we walked, she twirled it around. We were silent for a few minutes. Finally, she said, "Go ahead, and ask me!"

"Ask what? Well, I am curious about the bow and arrow," I answered.

She had a quick step, and her long, silky hair was trailing as she walked. I picked up my speed so that I could hear what she was saying.

"I, Temperance, the XIV Trump, am associated with the sign of Sagittarius. In the Qabalah this is the Tree of Life Path number twenty-five. 'Daughter of the Reconcilers' and 'Bringer Forth of Life.' This path allows the soul seeker the first glimmer of mystical higher consciousness. However, before one is able to work with this mystical energy, there is a purging that needs to happen. The seeker usually goes through what is called The Dark Night of the Soul. Leaving behind what does not serve now in the outer worlds. During this process one learns to invoke the 'Inner Light' as a guide to use in the darkness." The Seer paused and stopped walking for a moment; she lifted up my chin and said slowly, "This is what you went through in your terror of letting your child do what he must: grow up!" She began walking again, I raced to keep up. I heard her saying, "Sagittarius is associated with the 'Centaur,' a creature symbolizing half god and half beast, which man is! The most notable in Greece was the 'Centaur Chiron,' who consented to die that Prometheus might have eternal life.

"The image of Sagittarius is portrayed as the Archer." The Seer held up her bow to me. "In this context the archer may be considered as the 'Individuality' who is marking its prey. The 'prey' is the 'Personality,' and an arrow is speeding into it, causing 'Divine Love.' Temperance reconciles the vehicle of man the individuality and the personality. This is why Temperance is called 'Daughter of the Reconcilers.' This is what brings new birth, 'Bringer Forth of Life.' There is another image of Sagittarius, 'The Archer,' which is linked with the Roman 'Goddess Diana,' the Huntress. To the Greeks she was called the 'Goddess Artemis.' Her 'Hunter's Bow is the bow of promise,' which brings new revelations, new life. In the Greek myth of Artemis, she is found traveling in the wood in her annual apparition. This was a moment in time in which she renewed her virginity by bathing in a sacred source. From her right hand she pours water from a cup, making fall the liquid on her sex that she has covered with her left hand. 'Atteone,' a Greek figure who in myth was raised by the 'Centaur Chiron,' was watching her from a distance with longing. Once she realized this, she was furious! Shooting her arrow into 'Atteone,' the Goddess Diana changed him into a deer. She made him into a mild-mannered animal as a symbol of temptation. He has forever since remained her companion."

"Oh, dear Seer," I said. "These are beautiful stories! I am so happy that you appeared in my dream!"

Laughing now she said, "Which dream?"

I laughed as well. We had walked the winding path down to a quiet, secluded cove. When I looked back up the hill above the water's edge, the sun was shining brightly between the paths to the twin peak mountains.

Apparently the Seer had read my thoughts, because she said, "After testing, you are shown a path to Glory. See the path between the mountains? You enter the world of Spirit on the path of the Temperance. An important question to always ask is this, 'Does this path have heart?' You can always be guided by your answer here."

The Ancient one was now at the water's edge. She told me to get comfortable on the sand or sit on the rocks. She said the story she was about to relay needed to be entered as a dream, and this way I could track with her. I nodded my head yes and took out my pen and journal and spread a light blanket that we had brought. I watched the Seer as she set out two vases, one with a Moon image and one with a Sun image. She seemed to be looking about as she did this, as if she was looking for someone.

The Seer looked at me hard and said, "I am counting on you to be in this dream tale as an 'observer only'; you are not to speak or interact in any way!"

Meekly, I answered, "Yes, of course."

The Seer smiled and said, "I tell you this for your own good, for any interruption could change the flow of the magical workings that I will be doing!"

I smiled back and said, "OK! I will be a watcher! I understand." I did not really understand; however, I certainly would not interrupt anything the Seer would be doing. My curiosity was certainly in high gear at this point. I looked at The Temperance Seer, and she was checking the two vases. She had made a small fire in the pit nearby. I did not see any reason for a fire, as it was getting to be quite warm. I turned to look at the sun that was directly over head. I could actually trace some of the sunbeams right down to where we were. That was odd, I thought, but amazing. I looked over to The Seer; she was in a meditation, and I wondered how soon she would tell this "dream tale" as she had put it. I did not dare to say anything!

Then I heard a whistling of some kind. Oh gosh, I thought. Someone might be walking along here, not knowing that the Seer was doing her thing! Maybe I should jump up and check and get them to go away. The whistling was stronger now; I almost got up when I saw what looked like a hologram, with many bright colors, a person within it, swirling down the hill slowly. What the heck? I almost got up, but the Seer was looking in my direction, and her hand was up, palm facing me. I thought better of moving or of speaking. I was frozen to my spot on the blanket!

I heard The Temperance Seer speaking in a very normal voice, but this scenario did not feel so normal to me! The hologram was definitely a person now! I heard her say, "My dream tale is about our 'Trump Seer the Fool.'" She was looking at me as she said this. "This is a part of his tale on his continuing Spiritual path." The whistling was strong all around the hologram. I was mesmerized!

Just then The Fool Seer materialized in the place where the hologram had been! Now The Temperance Seer was relaying her dream tale. I could not take my eyes off the whole scene! She was saying, "After 'The Fool Seer,' the zero Trump has gone through his 'Dark Night of the Soul,' he begins to wonder how to reconcile the oppositions he has been facing." I watched the Fool act out his wondering on this dream stage of where we were. All the while I listened to The Temperance Seer continue with the story.

She said, "His oppositions between the material world and the spiritual world were causing him confusion and sometimes worry." I watched as The Fool played out this dilemma. "Now at this point in his wonderings," said Temperance, "he comes upon an angelic winged creature standing with one foot in the water and the other on a rock." Temperance played that part! She continued the tale. "The radiant creature pours something from one vase with a Moon image painted on it into another vase with the Sun painted on it. Drawing closer still, The Fool sees that what is being poured from one vase is very red. Then he sees it is fire! A bluish liquid pours from the other. Then he sees it is water! The two are blended together!" Both actor Seers did this with feeling. "The Fool asks the angel how she can mix fire with water. The angelic being answers, 'You must have the right vessels and the right proportions.' The Fool watches with wonder. 'Can this be done with all opposites?' says the Fool. 'Indeed,' the angel replies. 'Any oppositions, fire and water, man and woman, thesis and anti-thesis, can be made to harmonize. It is only lack of will and disbelief in unity that keeps opposites, opposite!'"

The Temperance Seer continued. "That moment, The Fool begins to understand that he was the one keeping the universe at bay, always holding life-death, material world and the spiritual world separate. Now he realizes that all it takes is the right vessels and the right proportions and, of course, the mixing of the two!" I watched as The Fool portrayed the mixing and blending; he was serious and comical at the same time!

With a smile and laugh, The Fool said, "Mixing the Fiery Red and the Watery Blue… What happens? You change your belief, and you then create a magical 'Violet-Energy Color'!" Still with the big smile on his face, he looked straight at me and then bowed! So did the Temperance Seer!

Very excited, I stood and clapped and clapped, saying, "Bravo! Bravo!"

Then, before I could say a word, the hologram swirled, and The Fool moved away within its beautiful colors. In a whisper, I was saying, "That was just amazing!"

The dust began to settle, and The Temperance Seer was right next to me, saying, "'The Fool' was happy that you enjoyed our dream tale. He said he looks forward to his time working more with you when you are ready."

"I am so impressed!" I said to the Seer, "I had so many questions to ask him!"

She was laughing. "If you could only see the expression on your face! I told you there would be magical workings!"

Responding to her, I said, "That is an understatement!"

Collecting our things and putting out the fire, I stopped and gazed at the twin peak mountains with the path between the two. Turning around, I saw The Ancient Seer was also looking at the mountains. I said to her, "That path you mentioned between the mountains takes an awful lot of training, doesn't it?"

She answered, "The path to glory always does! The two mountains represent the conjunction of opposites. On the Temperance path, we begin to learn how to unite wisdom and understanding."

We were walking back to the lodge. The Seer continued her teachings. "Temperance is also about psychological wholeness, a man's union with his anima, inner woman, and a woman's union with her animus, inner man. Often the androgyny of the shaman must be used when becoming a soul guide or a messenger between the worlds."

I responded quickly, "I had not thought about the shaman aspect."

Temperance shook her head. "Shamanic work is a big part of the Dreaming. How much you use it depends on the type of Dream work that most calls to you. Think about this as well: Temperance is a mediator and has a motto that is 'Nothing in Excess.'"

"I love that motto!" I said.

We were near the lodge now, and many Dreamers were strolling about. The morning sessions were over, and the dining hall at the lodge is where everyone was headed.

"One more thing," said Temperance. "To be temperate is moderation and self-restraint when called for. On the surface Temperance may seem unexciting, but her attributes are deep within her, and that is what is important. She is the calm within the eye of the hurricane, the still point that brings everything into balance. Of course, I know you are wondering about my angelic wings. My feathered wings are both for protection and transcendence. This allows me to be a liaison between heaven and earth."

"How did you know that was a question I had? Oh! Right, the telepathy thing, of course!" I said with humor. "Dear Seer, I do not want to stop. This has been great! Especially the help about the Dark Night and getting in touch with my past life. And the tale of The Fool and You! I shall never forget today!"

The Seer looked at me and said, "I do believe you have let go of some fear and terror today. Call on me if questions arise. Ah! We are back to the lodge. Dream strong, Dreamer!" She was on to something else.

I called after her, saying, "Thank you!"

THE DEVIL

DREAM OF THE TRUMP SEER: THE DEVIL XV

"Don't be used in the dreaming of another!" The things I saw were not clear, but the viewing kept coming. I filed them in my memory bank and would have to wait for the future to catch up with that.

But that phrase about dreaming, what on earth did that mean? I let it go for now. I was going over in my head the things I had brought with me for the small circle of Dreamers gathering for a twilight class with an Ancient One. He had asked us to meet at one of the odd cabins near the cliffs. As I walked the field to the cliffs, there was not a breeze or cloud in the sky, and the colors were changing into peach and purple. I loved this time of day between times and worlds. Looking up again, there was a lone raven winging over the field silently.

I had brought scrying items, a crystal ball, cornmeal for the water scrying, my journal, and extra crystals for any who may want one. A footpath led deeper into the wood and westward through the oaks and evergreens. At the clearing I saw the cliffs, steep, gray, and jagged, they rose up suddenly. Another part of the Nemeton I had not seen. A very private area with the huge trees on one side and the cliffs on the other, with the smell of freshly mown grass and an outside campfire. I thought about how I love this place.

But where is this cabin? I walked toward the evergreens, and then I saw it. Having been named Cliff House, of course it was built right next to the cliffs, like an extension of them. The sun burned low on the horizon, and the tall spires stretched long shadows across the camp. This will be perfect! I seemed to be the only one here so far. I supposed I should go in to set up, but it was so glorious out there! I decided to take a little more time, and as I walked around the grass, I could hear the raven. I wondered what he was seeing.

Something shifted; I began to get visions again like earlier. People screaming. Are they being burned? I don't know if that it? Then I am running, running! Men are galloping after me! I stopped my walk, and shook myself! This made no sense; I could feel a knot in my stomach. What was this all about? And what was the sudden fear that I felt too? As I looked around these beautiful grounds, this thought occurred: maybe knowing we would be meeting with The Devil Seer was giving me the creeps! Could that be it? The knot was still there. I thought to myself, This is silly. But something made me think this may be a karmic knot of some kind. And maybe that is what has me so unnerved. I do not even know this Seer! I said to myself as I walked toward the Cliff House. I am being completely unfair. I mean, I have greeted him casually and he is certainly friendly enough. Mind you, when I have seen him around the grounds, he has not been in the traditional Devil garb! Just an ordinary-looking Seer, I thought. So what is going on here with me? Shaking my head, I said, Enough. Time to set up and be ready for the class. I walked up the five stone steps to the cabin.

There were lots of windows in the main room of The Cliff House. I was glad for that and opened several for circulation before I smudged. Standing in the center of the room, I took out supplies from my Spirit Bag To Go and got to work setting the altar cloth on the floor in the center of the room. So this is the Cliff House, I thought as I lit candles. The illumination of the flickering light showed sparse furniture in the room. I noticed the walls were embellished with ancient and cryptic symbols. I looked outside. Twilight is short here, I thought, and the night and cold will come quickly. The smell of the sage was cleansing and definitely grounding for me. Goddess knows I needed that!

I stayed with my task of setting the space, cleansing the space. Dream circle is sacred work and needs honoring. We are all held between the worlds in our work, and the Dreamers need to be safe. The circle is a place of protection, and I intended to make it secure! As I walked around, I called in Spirit and the directions, and then I sealed energy with blue light. I was feeling much better!

I heard some noise from the back door; I turned and then saw The Devil Seer with an armload of firewood. He nodded and said, "Hello! I figured we would need to get the fireplace going; it does cool down at night!"

"You are so right," I said. "The fireplace is always so important! I have just finished smudging our circle. Please let me know if there is something you need or I can do anything." I was speaking in the most cheerful tone, trying to keep the feelings from earlier at bay. I was, however, glad to see he was not dressed in Devil garb! I saw that he was looking at me intently; I hoped he had not read my thoughts. I smiled and began fluffing my cushion on the spot I had chosen to sit.

He still stared and then said something odd, "Diana e la bona Dea."

I didn't know what he meant. All I could say was, "I am sorry. What was that?"

He responded quickly, "Diana e la bona Dea. It means 'Diana the Good Goddess.' Looking at you I am reminded of Diana, from long ago!"

My face was turning crimson, I was sure. I said, "The Goddess Diana. I'll take that as a compliment!"

He answered with, "It is meant as one! And I thank you for the care you have taken to make our space sacred."

I nodded and said, "You are welcome!"

We were both silent for a bit. He was getting ready for the night. I was feeling more comfortable and wondered if I should mention the visions I had earlier.

Before I could speak, the Ancient One began talking to me. "There will be some this evening who will have trouble facing this Devil energy. And I will undergo some shapeshifting into the part I need to play for the Dreamers to learn this lesson fifteen. It would be helpful to me to know that someone was here to assist in any situation as the devil plays out his role. I need a strong Dreamer, and that would be you! That is, if you are willing?"

"Me?" I answered back quickly, very surprised. "What can I do? I am really not sure…"

The Seer looked at me just like any ordinary man, tall, handsome, and striking with his black hair smoothed back. High cheekbones accentuated his deep, obsidian eyes. An ordinary man, except that he was the Devil! As I thought these things, I had my fingers crossed behind my back so he could not hear them! Oh, my Goddess! What do I do now?

He was smiling and laughing a little as he said, "Please relax, and I will not bite! I only play a role here, and my heart within is the same as yours! Now let me tell you something. Women are the master Dreamers; it has always been so. And from what I have heard tell, and what I observe, you, dear Dreamer, are among the best! Think about our work here tonight like this: we are all living in multiple layers of light, a holographic reality. All of us are vibrating at different frequencies and dimensions. Each person weaves their light into the hologram as they are able. We then weave together to become one body of work, all important, all separate, and all one. This special Sacred Grove supports us all, and the Master Teacher and the Apprentice Dreamer both need each other."

I had tears in my eyes as I said, "Of course I will assist you! Please tell me what is needed."

His answer was, "Be the Dreamer that constructs the dream paths for our work. And hold that energy, much like when you set up the circle with the sage smudging. But you know this! Also there needs to be a warding for the circle. I have asked another Dreamer to help with this warding as well. You will be just fine. You are more than ready for this responsibility at this point of your journey. And I will always be able to assist, if need be. Thank you!"

All I could do was nod my head yes! Now the other Dreamers were filing in, laughing and shuffling their things around, making themselves ready for the "Twilight Devil Class," as I had heard it called all day around the Grove.

The Dreamers attending here tonight were strong and well along on their path of heart, or they would not have made it to this class. We were expecting seventeen dreamers, a nice size group of varied backgrounds and abilities. I just hoped that none of them would freak out with this heavy work! Looking around the room, the space could accommodate us all nicely; we had about ten minutes until we would open. I looked at the Devil Seer. He was joking with some of the crowd. He doesn't feel so creepy, I thought to myself. And the knot in my stomach has eased. I began a very quiet drumming so that I could center myself and begin dreaming the pathways for our work. I had already spoken with the other Dreamer who would be helping with the warding of the circle. I had worked with him before and felt confident about our assignment for tonight. I began weaving flows of Spirit to shield my own source from others. Embracing the soft drumming, I wove a soft flow of light that would help keep the Dreamers vibrating in similar frequencies and be grounded for this encounter with the Devil!

Everyone seemed to be settling down, and we were ready to open. I counted the Dreamers and realized that we had fifteen instead of seventeen. Interesting, isn't it, how things turn?

I invoked and set the blue light around us and connected to my crystal in the center of the altar upon the purple cloth.

The Ancient One did a beautiful opening, and we all felt charged for the night. With the twilight almost gone now outside, the glow from the fireplace was welcome. The Seer walked back and forth around the room. He told us that first we would get background information about the Devil. And then he would see what was triggered. He said he knew that his "devil persona" was a tough one to understand. But understand we must, as this was one of the major testing areas on the path to completing the Dreaming. "At least on this level," he said with a laugh. No one seemed to be laughing, I noticed. I think everyone was nervous! That included me, but I had to push that away. I was entrusted with the dream pathways for the night, which was more important.

The Devil Seer began: "A naïve assumption could be that everything and everyone is just pure Spirit and casts no shadow!" He was looking around the room for responses—nothing! "Come now, is this the world that we all know, without any shadows?" The Dreamers began to whisper some. Then the Seer, in a booming voice, said, "I don't think so! Now let me hear from those totally pure in spirit, and let us check you for shadows. A show of hands please!" There was lots of mumbling around the room, and then the laughter started. The Seer said, "What, no one is so pure? Just as I thought!" There was a lot more laughter as he pranced around the floor. Then the lessons got underway.

"The Devil is the title given to the supernatural being who in many mainstream religions is believed to be a powerful, 'Evil' entity and temper of humankind. He is commonly associated with heretics and infidels and other unbelievers. The name 'Devil' derives from the Greek word 'Diabolos,' which means slander or accuser. In mainstream religion, God and the Devil are portrayed as fighting over souls of humans. Whenever we mention the Devil, powerful images spring to mind. Often the image is similar to the 'Greek God Pan.' 'Pan god of Nature' in Greek mythology is god of shepherds, flocks, and hunting. He has the hindquarters, legs, and horns of a goat. Some images also have cloven hooves, very much like a faun or satyr. He is the god of the fields and groves. He is connected to fertility and spring. His name originates from the word 'Paein,' which means pastures. Some say he was the son of Zeus, others say Hermes. The worship of Pan was begun in Arcadia, Greece. Pan's greatest conquest was that of the Moon Goddess Selene. Pan is merely one form of a horned god who was worshipped across Europe by witch cults.

"The Greeks have another god who is considered grotesque; this is the 'God Hephaestus.' As the tale in myth goes, he fell at sunset and became lame in his legs. He was Zeus's son; this angered Zeus and he cast him from heaven. Another version says he became lame during the rescue of the Goddess Hera, whom Zeus had chained to a storm. The God Hephaestus was the god of blacksmiths, sculptors, metals, and fire. Being lame gave him a grotesque appearance in the eyes of the Greeks. He is the blacksmith to the gods, and his symbols are a smith's hammer and an anvil."

The Ancient One had stopped for a moment as he was panning the crowd. Then he said, "Are you all getting this character? Am I painting the picture strongly enough?" He held up his hand as he strode around, saying, "Let me go on! The Devil represents material creation in all its manifestations, including sex as a means of natural generation and fire as a means of artistic creation. These things manifest as technology, art, crafts, and the alchemical Great Work. All these things are necessary for life and may help with enlightenment. Too much fascination and it can entrap us, keep us chained. Then by one's ignorance and reluctance to see what has happened, it may keep oneself bound."

"The Devil-human-beast and god in one is Nature! Realize there is power and beauty in our instincts, appetites, and drives in the material world. But Nature as a part of our psyche is mostly unconscious. The shadowy components of ourselves mostly are not recognized or disowned, and we may unconsciously project parts of this shadowy self outward onto other people or the world at large.

"This Trump XV calls on us to confront our shadow, not to deny or destroy it, just acknowledge its reality, understand its nature, and reorient it toward the good.

"We can look at the Devil as a source of illusion that creates an impediment to further progress. As the Devil heralds a confrontation with the shadow, we find the shadow personifies everything that the subject refuses to acknowledge about himself. The challenge of 'Diabolos' is not to defeat the Devil within but to confront it and integrate all parts of ourselves. When we *do not do* this, we may be prone to make someone or something the Scapegoat! This term, as you can see, came from the Goat God Pan! The Great God Pan, the principle of generation in Nature, became the scapegoat for Christianity. Creativity also has its dark side, for ungoverned creativity may be diabolical. The confrontation with the Devil can make us aware of this danger. Pan is called Pamphagos, All-Devourer, as well as Pangenetor, All-Begetter. He is neither wholly evil nor wholly good; he simply is and lives his life in nature!

"The horns on 'Diabolos'-'Devil' are symbols of the life force. In addition to the goat horns of Pan, there have been many other images expressing the horns. Like the Devil, the horn is bisexual. With one view as phallic and penetrating, and another view as hollow and receptive, as Jung explains. The God Hephaistos is linked with Plato's 'Demiurge God,' demiourgos-maker, or Craftsman-God. In later Gnostic thought, the Demiurge became an evil god, akin to the Christian Devil. The Cathars equated the Devil with Demiurge. As you recall, the God Hephaistos was thrown from Heaven because of his deformed legs. This story recalls the fallen angel Lucifer, who was thrown from Heaven for challenging Yahweh and is identified with the Devil. 'Lucifer' means 'Light-Bringer' and, like Prometheus, he stole the fire from Heaven but for his own aggrandizement."

The Seer looked around the room and said, "Lets, take ten minutes." And he quickly left the room before anyone could question him. I thought that odd.

The Devil Seer had been going fast and steady, and everyone was caught up in his charisma and his smooth way of relaying the history. He had us all spellbound, I was sure of that. What a gifted orator he was. But I agreed everyone was in need of a break. I decided to take a look at the pathways I had woven for our Dreaming. It would be easier to do now before we got busy again. As I scanned the path flows, the Dreamers' temperaments appeared fine. Everything seemed in good shape. But I had the feeling that was all going to change. The Dreamer who was doing the warding with me came over and told me all was well on his end. We joked about some of the things that had come up during the session. I looked at my watch and began soft drumming to call the Dreamers back to the circle.

It was not too soon either. We all heard some noises out on the porch and felt the wind whipping around. The lighting flickered and the windows rattled some. What is going on? A storm must be coming through. I wondered where the Seer was. Quickly I looked at my fellow warder; he got my drift, and we were on top of the sealing work. Our eyes met periodically, and we kept up the drumming. The Dreamers were laughing and joking but on edge.

Then he was there. He was not who we had earlier; he was the 'Devil'! I mean the one we all know from our childhood stories, the frightening ones! Oh my Goddess! I said to myself. What am I to do now? I could feel the fright among the Dreamers. We had been having a very nice style of lecture on devil lessons, but this was entirely different! I suddenly remembered the 'Dreaming Pathways' and tapped into them. They were thin and loosing energy. I quickly pulled in my weavings around myself and then began to secure the weaving of the dream paths for our group to work. I felt shaky but better.

Scanning the group, I felt I needed to shift the energy for the Seer. I started to talk to the Dreamers about our new guest. "Dreamers! Hey, everyone, let's settle down. The storm outside is passing! As you can see, our guest, 'The Devil,' has arrived! Let's give him a hand and welcome him to our circle."

The Seer began to walk to the center as he was lightly applauded. There was a clunking noise as he came, the lights still flickered, and it was hard to see him.

I relit the large center candle. Turning around, I was face-to-face with The Devil. I masked the shock of what I saw. I nodded my head to him and went back to my seat. I said to myself, Dear Goddess, above all, guard for the darkness, as it eats ever at the night…He's just a man, an ordinary man.

He walked awkwardly around the circle, as if seeing it for the first time. There was utter silence but for the wind in the oaks and pines.

"Ground us, dear ones," I said silently to the Tree Keepers.

Abruptly he stood still and laughed. Nothing seemed funny to any of us. In the candlelight now, we all got a good look at him. Ghastly, with horns, greenish and scruffy, and he had a beard. He was more than six feet, but he hunched with female breasts and translucent bat wings. Like a gargoyle on an ancient cathedral, he was grotesque. His beady eyes were looking at the Dreamers' reactions, like he was waiting for someone to faint.

I was truly surprised that it was not me! I looked around at the Dreamers. They were holding themselves together, barely! I looked at my crystal for support. There was another roaring laugh. I looked as the Devil was fingering the chains around his waist.

He was hovering over me and then said, "Do you consult the Oracle for your fate or mine?!"

My only answer was a long, despairing breath. He turned away. Thinking himself very funny, he was laughing again. Let him find another victim, I thought to myself. Though I suppose I should not have thought that.

He stopped at a woman Dreamer, one very skilled in past life work; she was icily serene in blue silk. The Devil just stood there, playing with his chains. He asked her what her work was.

She answered with, "My work is to Dream, so I can help others live their lives."

The chains were noisily shifting from hand to hand; he seemed willing to indulge her. Then he turned on a dime. Almost yelling, he mocked what she said. "So you dream things for others, and then do you do the living too? How cute is that! How convenient for those who seek you out!"

She cried out, "It is not like that!"

He responded with, "How do you know what to dream? How can you possibly know what a seeker may need to live his life?" She started to reply, but he shouted back, "Be silent unless I ask you to answer!"

The Dreamers in the circle were getting restless, eyeing each other. I wondered where he was going with this. Maybe I should say something before things get out of hand! I looked at my dream paths. The flows were running thin, and I began breathing more light into them and myself, turning the reds to purples and blues.

The Seer walked away. He asked her what her name was.

She replied with icy tears in her eyes but a strong voice, "Deana. My name is Deana; and you have no idea of how I work!" He turned quickly. That cold lady's stare of hers did the work.

Then in a voice from the first Devil, the more-like-a-man devil we had a while ago, he said, "We are all tested with our calling. We need to be certain of our path, learn how to hold the reins like in driving the chariot." He was not so tight jawed or bristling now. He went on speaking in an even tone but moved like Pan. He said, "After having a look at me now as the devil from the stories of history that you may relate to or not, I needed to have you all look at someone else and their shadow side so we could see what they are made of. I tried to turn you from your abhorrence of my appearance to look at another person's situation. I used the 'Scapegoat' approach on this poor dear here, and I lashed out! I have walked this dream with her before, and I knew she was up to it! Deana, thank you! You were a good sport!"

Everyone clapped lightly at that. There was a huge sigh of relief in the room. The Seer held up his hand, and everyone settled down. "Dreamers, remember things are not always what they seem!" He was still walking around, but the Devil did not feel as frightening, at least for now. I was happy that he was not fingering that awful chain! The Seer continued, "Remember also that the soul thinks in images! Earlier as I came into the room in my 'Traditional Devil attire'"—he pranced about some to show himself off—"many of you felt horrified! Some possibly flashed back to a long-forgotten memory of an encounter with the Devil. Yes, images invoke power! It is here on the fifteenth path that we learn to confront the demons that we may be living with, although many times we are hardly aware of their presence. So how do we do this?" He looked around the room a minute, then he said, "Relax, I'll try not to scare you too much!" There was a little weak laughing.

"There is something you must all get at this point in your dream training. You are healers with considerable skill, and you will be called to some harrowing circumstances requiring your help, which you will answer. But it is this that you must remember for your own protection! All of you…Please say this: 'I can keep myself untouched, unless I let something through'!"

Then he had the Dreamers say it together out loud. Everyone was in deep thought with that statement. I knew that it was something I would keep in my tool box.

"Now let's move on. No hand-painted tarot Devil images have survived from the ancients. Only printed versions have remained. Isn't that interesting! The absence of any hand-painted forms of the Devil suggests that in the Renaissance period the evil qualities of the Devil were taken seriously, and it was preferred that this card be hidden and not on display. In the meantime the weeds may flourish with the good-growing crop. The parable from the 'Tares and Wheat' illustrates that the wheat grows to a greater height than the tares. To try to eliminate the tares during growth would be a difficult task and injurious to the growing wheat. But at harvest time, the wheat ears, having grown higher, can be easily harvested. So the point is that there is always a counterbalance, a good and a bad. We all know this. What we need to learn is to recognize how to best work with the circumstances.

"Evil, the dark, is present not only within the world but within each one of us. The Devil's presence is as close as God's. It seems sad that some only give credence to the promptings of evil rather than good. The choice remains ours, always. One can get caught up with the Devil and, like in Dante's 'Inferno,' actually become like prisoners chained. But remember, says Dante, 'The inhabitants are there by their own free choice.' Hence, the Delphic adage, 'Man, Know Thyself'!

"Some say that the Devil, the brutal repugnant bully of the Middle Ages, embodies the Inquisition. His big ears are trained to catch any hint of heresy; his chains are designed to bind the hearts and minds of the people. He looms, ready to enslave the entire human race. The Devil's image is powerful!"

The Seer strutted himself around for all to see! Some of the Dreamers began laughing at his antics. Suddenly he shrieked, "How dare you laugh at me!" Everyone cowered back! Then the Seer said, "Don't you see what I am doing here? It is called manipulation! The act of manipulating in order to turn the wheel to one's favor is an art, and the world is filled with these devil-like personalities." He was glowering around the room.

I decided to take a chance and asked, "How should one handle this type of thing?"

He answered with, "Finally, someone is braving up! Handle is a good word. What often works for me is just my palm raised, almost to their face if possible, saying, 'Ouch! That hurts!' Usually that is sufficient. Sometimes humor is the best thing to defuse the situation. Humor almost always does the job. What you do *not* want to do is 'play word war games'! This will almost always not be in your favor with someone who is being confronted with devil stuff! It is the cool rational power of dream observation and thought untainted by emotion or desire that will save the day! Dream ahead your answers to one caught up in devil games, and test them out in the dream space before using them in waking space!" He was quiet for a few moments.

The Seer was near the fire, adding new logs; in the flickering light, he truly looked menacing and creepy! Yet as he spoke, he was the more ordinary man that had started off our evening. How did he do this? I wondered silently. The shape-shifting into such a character must be very difficult. I don't think I could do such a thing.

Now The Devil was ready to continue. He looked around and said, tapping on his chest, "The Devil, that is me! We all have preconceived ideas of who or what it, he, or she, may be! Every society has its equivalent evil, bad, or anti-god image. Throughout history the Devil has been utilized by the Christian faith to obtain good behavior and absolute obedience. Thus keeping the minions in line through manipulating them with the threat of an eternal Hell. There are variations on a theme of the Devil, but generally he is male with a lizard-like tale, horned, club footed, winged, and with a serpent-like penis!" He made some lewd gestures, and everyone was hysterically laughing. The Seer said, "I am not finished, so listen please! The Devil has the power to chain us to false identities created in the past. The chain that binds is simply that: our own karmic link in this world with all thoughts, feelings, and doings shackled to the devil. The devil is the voice that tempts us back into old habits, obsessions, and neuroses.

"Guilt can be another important interpretation for the Devil. Symbolizing our guilt about anything; guilt at being happy, alive; guilt at being not right, guilt because we want something. And there is much more. He is also a Habit!"

One of the Dreamers answered out loud to that statement, saying, "Yes! I will drink to that! I certainly know about habits!" The whole group was buzzing around with similar comments.

"Well, Dreamers, let's plough through! The Devil is the part of you that struggles in chaos. When you reach the fifteenth trump, 'The Devil,' in your study, there is struggle for truth amid seeming contradictions and incomplete information. But through this are glimpses of light. That which we fear is no more or less than our own shadow; the shadow being the dark, undesirable part of ourselves. When it surfaces, we often explain it in terms of the devil. Some may even quip, 'The Devil made me do it'! We are dividing our very selves in half when we give in to this. A confrontation with the Devil, internal or external, should alert us to the fact that it is time to change our attitude.

"We need to embrace our shadow in order to transcend it. When we learn to come to terms with our inner Devil, we become tolerant. Of course, this requires deep commitment. It is generally easier to leave things as they are. But for those who wish to realize wholeness that comes from integrating matter and spirit, the Devil can help provide gifts."

Looking around the fire-lit room, the Devil Seer said, "Dreamers, do you see your own shadows? Are you able to confront them? This may be a good exercise to do in small groups: dream on your devil shadows! Yes! This is your assignment and, next time we meet, we can compare dreams. In the meantime remember that Devil is a mirror, one that may mirror an image of us. We may recoil from the hideous face in the mirror...seeking to blame anyone but ourselves! Some interesting information: 'Devil' spelled backward, interestingly, is 'Lived'! The word 'Devil' is 'Devi' in Sanskrit, which means 'Goddess.' Some say, 'the Devil is the curse of those who have abandoned the Goddess'!"

The Seer said, "I think that is a wrap. Dreamers, we have made it through the night! We will close the circle now and later finish with a celebration for making it through. Maybe we could find some devilish music! Shall I change my attire or remain as I am?" With that he began a few bows and said, "Gotcha!"

Everyone was in high gear, proud that they had gotten through the night. We had a beautiful closing in front of the fire; afterward things shifted and relaxed. I pulled in my light energy and warding, tying off the flows for the class work; my fellow Dream warder did the same. We felt good about the evening. The Dreamers joked that we were sure to have a "devilish night"!

I was putting my things away when The Devil Seer came over to me. He had shape-shifted into an ordinary Seer. I joked with him, saying, "The Dreamers took a vote and wanted you to stay in traditional Devil attire!"

He quipped with, "I can always accommodate, should the need arise! But first I would like to thank you for holding the Dreaming for the group! You did a great job, and we would not have had such a smooth ride if you had not been so present. It is very much appreciated!" He had a big smile on his face.

My eyes were sparkling as I took his hand and said, "It was my pleasure. Learning to become a Seer, a Keeper, is hard work, but it is made easier when I can learn from someone like you!"

He was touched, and then he said, "I need to have some dinner before I can think about celebrating!"

I agreed and we met up with some other Dreamers on our way to the dinning hall. As we walked, I asked him, "What do you make of this statement that came to me in a dream? 'Don't be used in the dreaming of another'!"

He answered with, "Let's do the process."

At that point a few Dreamers were adding their "If it were my Dream...!"

THE TOWER

DREAM OF THE TRUMP SEER: THE TOWER XVI

Steaming vapors were all around, whispering, thirsty; the storm had ended. There were vague siftings and glimmerings from the forest. Walking past the swampy pool, I recalled hearing this pool was credited with having the ability to collect and reflect the thoughts of those that had gazed into its rippling face. Pausing at water's edge for a moment, I peered into its depths. Controlling my expression and thought, I did not want to deposit anything. Ready to leave, I felt a tug from the surface of the water. I realized the pool was reflecting to me…

A deep, watery, voice said, "They were here, the couple; they had stopped to exchange wishes with each other. They knew they had to experience The Tower but were reluctant. Once they had reconciled this, they asked about directions in the dream…"

The words drifted away. This is the Oracle, I thought, and I stepped away from the pond quickly! Feeling confused, maybe frightened. What could this be about? I walked fast to get away, then suddenly stopped right in my tracks. What am I doing? Let me think! I won't be able to just let this go. What to do? I saw a huge boulder a few feet away and climbed up on it.

From the vantage point of this boulder, I grounded myself and then looked around the area. This was really a beautiful spot in the Grove, and with the winds moving out the storm, I felt more comfortable. I looked over to the misty pond not more than fifty feet away. The sun was glowing on it now at midday, and the mists were moving away. My interest in the cryptic message about the Tower was strong. I decided to go back and see what else I might discover.

The willows lined part of the pond with shading limbs hanging over the water. A wise Dreamer must be in control of her emotions, I thought, not let them be in control of her. I stood near the edge a moment, thinking over what to ask. The sun's warmth felt supportive on my back. Before I could utter a word, the mirrored surface shimmered, and I saw dark eyes as deep as the pond!

She spoke: "Why have you come? What is your desire? And if I like your answer and it is true, I may grant your wish. Dream truly, Dreamer!"

Instinctively I backed up! I was not expecting to be asked anything! At least not just yet! The water shimmered like when a rock is dropped into it and sends out ripples from the center. I thought about my own center. What do I feel about this tarot Tower Trump? My first response was fear. I feel fear! I decided to answer with that!

"Dear Oracle of the water, I acknowledge you as an Oracle, and I ask you for your help! I am a Dreamer Apprentice traveling the Tarot Dreaming now. I did not know until I walked by your banks earlier that I have come to learn about the Tower Trump, but it is what is true. My desire is that I am fearful of this and desire to understand this fear!" There. I said it. I was not quite sure how it all sounded. I kept backing away from the water's edge.

The Water Oracle spoke: "You have backed away quite enough, Dreamer! Please come and sit on my grassy bank for a minute, and I will dream on your request."

It was quiet; I looked around to see if anything or anyone was near. Nothing. Feeling uneasy, I wondered, Is the Oracle going to continue? Maybe I should just head on back to the lodge. This all feels so unreal, I thought. At least the sun is out, nice and warm.

Then she spoke, thin and liquid, floating in the cool calm of the void. "Strange things happen in the wilderness, Dreamer. Especially just when you thought you were all alone! This encounter with the Tower is not by chance. You are ready to move through this path sixteen now. I am to give you some assistance on your path as you travel to meet the Ancient Ones of The Tower."

There was silence, but I was not sure if I felt relief with her answer to grant me information about the Tower. I was feeling very doubtful about this arrangement. I mean, was I just to sit down here on the grass, or was I to search in the woodlands for the Tower? What if someone else came? How could I explain I was talking with the pond, for 'Goddess's sakes! What if...

"Enough of the what if's!" a loud voice rang out. "It has been decided, and you will begin your transformative Tower work, my Dreamer Child, and you will be just fine! So spread that blanket next to me now and look into my depths. Put one hand into my waters and cleanse; make yourself ready for this first part of this journey."

Taken aback by her comments, I was still a few minutes, but I pulled out my blanket and sat down quickly. I sure did not want to get this Oracle miffed. I cleansed with the water as she had asked. I am as ready as I will ever be, I thought to myself. In my pack I had tobacco and gave an offering to the Water Oracle for her help.

She answered, saying, "That was very thoughtful of you. Thank you, Dreamer!" I could see her eyes like I had before; they were even darker and deeper than the pond itself.

The Water Oracle began. "Later you will be with the Tower Seers, but for now I will inform you about the symbol of the Tower itself. The word for 'tower' in French is 'tour.' Which means a wheel, and it may be equated with the Gaelic word 'torr,' meaning a conical hill and a castle. There is also an Egyptian word for fortress, 't'ra.' One of the surnames of the Greek God Apollo was 'Tortor'-'Tower of Towers.' The Cornish name for 'tower' is 'lug.' In Scotland and in French Brittany there are plentiful remains of round 'towers' known as 'brochs.' Sometimes circular towers were called 'peels'-'pauls' and sometimes called 'duns.' The fabled stronghold of King Arthur, now called 'Tintagel,' was alternatively known as

'Dundagel.' The Scotch 'broch' or 'peel' served as a sanctuary from wandering marauders and materially justified its title 'Burok,' 'Broch,' or 'Peel' as a 'High tower and a Refuge.' As a rule, the Celtic Round Towers were built without mortar. As Christianity spread across Europe, it is not unlikely that in the cathedrals the great central spire was understood to symbolize the Holy One."

The Oracle had stopped, as the wind blew through and ruffled her surface. I realized that there was so much history concerning this tower image, things I had never thought of concerning a tower. I began to think about the tower image a little differently.

Now, in a more musical voice, the Oracle went on. "The tower may be a prime symbol of our discontent and the quest for mastery, for power. Towers are masculine, symbols of transformation. They rebel against nature, using 'fire,' will, then combined with 'air,' intelligence, to raise the material universe upward against the pull of gravity. Towers exude pride and a sense of power, the ambition and ability to rise above the natural state. When a tower is built, the builders seek their own elevation. The physical elevation of these structures includes the triumphal power of the builders. This would be the essence of the story of the 'Tower of Babel.' Where the pride, rebelliousness, and genuine power of humanity was rebuffed by God.

"I would like to briefly mention a few impressive towers from antiquity. The Egyptian 'Obelisk at Luxor' is thirty-three hundred years old and commemorates the reigns of the pharaohs Ramses II and III. Given to France as a gift, it now stands in the Place de la Concorde in Paris. The 'Colossus of Rhodes' was built on the Aegean Sea about 300 BC. It was one of the 'Seven Wonders of the Ancient World' and inspired the French sculptor Auguste Bartholdi to create the 'Statue of Liberty,' which stands in the New York harbor. The 'Lighthouse of Alexandria' was built about the same time as the Colossus, third century BC, on an island of Pharos, on the coast of Egypt near Alexandria. It was made of white stone blocks and stood four hundred and forty feet high.

"Practical, modest towers have been built through out the ages. For example, bell towers, church towers, lighthouses, clock towers, watchtowers, and towers of castles. Towers have been built to increase communication over distances, much as lanterns and bonfires provided for in ancient times. In modern times these would be: radio, TV, and cell phone towers. There are control towers at airports and harbors that guide planes and ships. Towers rise! They point to distant goals, and they are symbols of success!

"So, my dear Dreamer, there you have it: a small overview on towers! Something to get your wheels turning for the next part of your journey! I have taken you as far as I should. The rest of the journey you will discover on your own, with some help from the 'Tower Seers'! So before you are on your way, is there anything that you might need to ask or say?"

As she finished speaking, there was a large ripple on top of the water that emanated from the water's center and spread to the pond's edges.

I was a little stunned with all the information. I needed to stand up and move a little to gather my thoughts. I paced a few moments on the grass; finally I realized what I needed to ask. I smoothed the hair from my face and said, "The couple. You mentioned a couple had been here! Something about them knowing they had to experience the *Tower*!"

Quickly the Oracle added, "Once they reconciled this, they asked for directions in the dream!"

"Please, Oracle," I said. "What does this mean?" I could hear laughter rippling in the water.

She said, "Mean? Why, this is what you will discover on the journey you are about to take! I recall your desire was to learn about your fear as you travel the path of the Tower! I grant you protection and insight on your travels. As you walk to the tower, it may be wise to dream this: 'Why does the tower need to fall?' Off with you now! Travel into the noonday sun; the dream path will be made known to you!"

I felt confusion and was apprehensive but knew that my work here was done. I gathered my things and looked into the sun; I turned and thanked the Water Oracle for all that she had provided.

She answered, "Think about your question as you walk, 'Why does the tower need to fall?' You may discover something, and it will help to prepare you for the Tower Seers! Remember to use your senses; this will keep you on the correct path. Now off with you and onto your fear, Dreamer! We will talk again!"

I looked at the water as the wind skimmed the top, and quietly I said, "Thank you!"

I began walking the path. To myself I said, 'Thank you, I think...' What am I getting into with this journey to the Tower? And she had said, 'onto your fear'! This certainly is dangling a wonderful carrot...Am I crazy?"

The sun was my guide, and it sure felt great; at least I was happy for that. The woods were not as dense in this part of the Nemeton, and this made me happy. I began on a winding, upward trail and didn't know if this was correct. It was fairly steep here. I could see a crest in the hill and decided to get to that before assessing my whereabouts. What had the Oracle said? Use my senses? Senses for what, I wondered...None of this was making much sense! As I climbed I was getting very much winded. How steep this is! Almost to the top, I grabbed onto the sapling birches for support.

Once at the top, I leaned over with hands on my thighs to catch my breath, which took a few minutes. I put my pack down and began looking around. Wow! This is an incredible view. I can see clear to the sea, the higher peaks behind and a glimmer of the main lodges, the apple groves too! Then I started to think, At least I will know which way to go back to the lodges from here. But where do I find the tower and the path that gets me there?

Suddenly I began to smell something....Smoke! Smoke! Oh my God, is there a forest fire? How do I get help for that? We do not use cell phones here! I started pacing around in circles, trying to determine where this smoke was coming from. Trying not to get too panicky, I took some deep breaths. OK, Spirit, I could use some help here, please! I saw a few hawks not far to the left, circling. Then I saw the dark clouds rolling and remnants of lighting in the sky. How odd, I thought. The sun has been so bright here! Next I noticed several streams of white smoke curling like ribbons into the sky. As I looked downward, I realized where the fire was. It seemed to be coming from a lone tree on the hillside opposite from me.

I could smell the smoke a little stronger. What had the Oracle said? Use your senses! I picked up my pack and walked, almost ran, toward the tree! Could this have anything to do with the tower? But what? And I had not even had time to think about the question, 'Why must the tower fall?' No time now; let me just get there!

I was surprised how fast I got down and then over to the hill with the smoldering tree. I thought from this hundred-foot distance that the tree actually looked like a building. How unusual it was. I saw someone running about. As I got closer, I realized that the tree actually looked like a kind of tower. Had I come to the tower? I needed to be clearheaded now and cool with my emotions, clear about finding out the facts. There was a stillness that clung to the surrounding hillside. Yet the fire was lapping at the huge tree with many branches still intact. The trunk itself was the tower. Windows had been carved in the trunk, and flames came from the three windows. The trunk looked as if it were built from layering stone upon stone, just like a tower castle might look. Its height must have been eighty feet at least, and there was a definite interior space, as its circumference must have been twenty feet! This was a truly amazing structure.

Suddenly I caught myself…This is the tower, and it is on fire! What do I do about that? I came back to that reality. Then I saw off to one side a woman standing there, waving her hands, definitely distraught! I began to walk toward her. Something made me stop in my tracks. What is going on? I said under my breath. Then I felt the energy of the Water Oracle….Her message was this: "Uncontrolled thoughts are troublesome when you walk in a dream. You must control them if you mean to continue. Remember your training, Dreamer; you must ask permission! To step into another's Dream is very dangerous unless she knows you and expects you!"

With a surprised voice I answered, "Oh my goodness. Thank you, Oracle! I really needed that reminder!" I took a moment and focused on myself planting my feet firmly, as if a tree I rooted to the earth. Then in the dreamscape I asked permission of the woman Dreamer near the tree.

She responded quickly with, "Granted, Dreamer. We have been expecting you. Before we can dream forward with this dream, there are things required of you. First, a Dream traveler must Dream their image in place: their particular stance, their clothing, their dress, shoes, shawl. The Dream of the way they wear their hair. All these must be dreamt firmly into a single image that becomes your transporter between the worlds. You are quick, Dreamer. I can feel that you have done image work before your Dream walking here. This procedure provides something for the Dreamer to ground with. As I said, your dream image becomes your transporter between the worlds. You know this, Dreamer; I can feel this transpiring…I am the 'Woman of the Tower Seer.' Welcome!"

Silently I let out a sigh of relief. Then I scanned myself again, like the Tower Seer had said, so that I could be certain of what I looked like. I was brought into the tower dream space quite unexpectedly by the boom of a thunder.

The Tower Seer was saying, "The energy begins to weave around you, forcing and becoming tight. Sometimes we are not even aware or choose not to be. The weave builds, the pressure builds, and suddenly it can explode in every direction!" She seemed to be explaining the circumstances and asked if she might sit down, nodding to me to do the same.

The tree was burning nearby. How was it that she was so cool, just sitting there for a few minutes as if this were ordinary?

"You have done well, Dreamer," said the Tower Seer "To have gotten this far on your path work in such short order speaks highly of you! A leaf may fall from its tree at its proper time and does not complain; it knows that it is part of the whole plan. This much you have acquired."

I smiled and thanked her, which made me more comfortable. However, the way she stared, her face in shadows, made me alert to other issues that were sure to come. The Tower Seer was standing now and was observing the "tree tower," looking this way and that. I looked along with her. I found it interesting that the flames seemed to be contained within the tree tower. I noticed a large golden crown set askew around one of the main limbs on the left side.

Then I stood up, crying out, "Look! There is a man falling from the tower!"

The Tower Seer replied with no emotion, "Certainly took you awhile to notice, and yes, the man is falling, and he is my other half."

I could not help myself and said, "Shouldn't we do something?"

The Seer turned. "We will get to that in time, but as a lesson on the tower." As she spoke, the lighting struck again, and the figure of the man was held frozen in space.

I looked at her in disbelief! The set of her jaw said to me she meant to have her way. I tried not to look at the man.

The Woman Tower Seer was speaking. "Sometimes in order to reach a goal worthy of pursuit, one must turn away from others, temporarily. This is something one may encounter while tower building.

"Let me begin with the basic lessons of the Tower Trump XVI. This trump has to do with what we think of ourselves and how these illusions are easily shattered. The Tower itself represents false ego. The self, the will, the ego mask is a principle in man that makes him feel separate from others. When at point sixteen on the path, the individual may discover they have been living by a false ego identity. Then the Tower is blown and falls, the illusion destroyed." The Seer stared right through me. I was uneasy and could not speak. Still looking, she said, "To continue…When the Tower is blown and falls, the crown that sat on the top begins to topple. 'The Crown' represents the 'Crown Charka.' It is said that the crown charka is the seat of spiritual experience. The lighting bolt is heaven-sent, and a spiritual awakening can occur. However, sudden change is a shock to our system, though the experience may be very enlightening." The Seer had paused and was checking on my reactions.

I said to her, "I can recall times in my life when there was sudden change, a possible tower experience, but I am not sure about the spiritual part!"

Quickly she said, "As you travel through this path sixteen, there may be some pieces, some flashes of insight, for you that will help."

I glanced at the man who was still in a freeze-frame of falling.

The Seer saw me and said, "Please do not worry. He is fine. Just think of this as when you have clicked the pause button while watching a movie. We will get to him!"

The Woman of the Tower began her lessons. "The Tower symbolizes a false rigidity attached to the heart. When the 'Lighting Bolt' comes from God, it is a time for learning life lessons. This is the Lightning Flash from the higher source of power. 'The Tower' is a vehicle for the spirit in the form of a building: 'The House of God.' In some old tarot decks, the Tower card was called 'The House of God' and thought to be linked with King Arthur and his knights and the Holy Grail. According to Sir Thomas Malory's account of the incident in *Le Morte d'Arthur*, Sir Balin smote King Pellam with the Grail spear, which he had discovered in the Castle Tower. 'There with the castle roof and walls broke and fell to the earth.' Also the flame-like towers and pinnacles are suggestive of the 'City of the Sun,' which may be equated with Camelot, the wonder city of King Arthur. One of the great features of this fairy city was its magic portal. 'There was,' said Tennyson, 'no gate like it under heaven.'

"The Tower when referred to as the 'House of God,' as in some decks, has been stricken by the hand of God. The heirs of King David's royal house lament that God has forsaken his promise to them. How long will God abandon his chosen one? His crown is in ashes, his citadel, tower, in ruins: "You have rejected and spurned...your anointed. You have renounced the covenant with your servant...you have broken down all his walls, you have laid his strongholds in ruins." This is Psalm Eighty-Nine, verses thirty-nine through forty-one.

"The Tower card is most closely linked to Mary Magdalene herself, for 'Magdala,' in Hebrew, means 'Tower' or 'Stronghold.' The descendants of Israel's royal house, David, whose citadels were ruthlessly demolished during the 'Albigensian Crusade,' were rumored to have been descendants of Magdalene, the 'Vine of Mary' and as well the 'San Raal,' Royal Blood, of King David and of Christ. Mary Magdalene the Magdal-elder."

(Watchtower of the flock: by Margaret Starbird) The Tower, the Stronghold is one.)

The Seer was standing now and looking to the sky. We could see streaks of lighting quite far off. I wondered if it would rain. Paying attention again, I spoke to the Ancient One. "There is so much that I do not know! This history is so fascinating. It also seems to help me with the fear I have had of this Tower Trump!"

The Seer looked at me with surprise but laughed. "Well, I am happy to help you work through your fear!" She was looking at the lighting again and said, "Lets move onto the Lighting Flash and see how you feel about that!"

Suddenly I was apprehensive.

"The lighting bolt sometimes takes the form of the zodiacal sign of Scorpio, and the tower may be considered a phallic emblem. This trump is popularly associated with the fall of man. The lighting flash may also represent the loss of virginity: 'the bolt that ruptures seemingly impenetrable defenses.' Lighting is a common symbol of masculine virility, which can illuminate or destroy. Lighting may burst through the earth and open a passage to the underworld, for it represents the descent of celestial illumination, an unpredictable gift of the gods. Also being hit by lighting is thought to confer instantaneous shamanic initiation, as the experience blasts open the gates to the underworld. This shatters structures and sows the seeds of new life. Some say that the celestial fire descends from the Pole Star, which is the Omphalos Caelestorum, Navel of the Heavens, out of the clouds, which usually surround it, down through the tower, which is the pillar of the World Axis, into the mound, which is the Omphalos Mundi, World Navel. The theory goes that this is intended to establish the union of heaven and earth. In old tarot decks, The Tower was sometimes called 'The Fire' and the 'World Navel' and often is associated with fire. For example, the central mountain is often shown as burning, or a 'Burning Tree' grows on it. This fire represents the heat generated by the awakening Kundalini."

The Seer had walked close to the Tree Tower, and seemed to be examining the flames that came from the lower window. I was astounded that she did not show any effects from the heat! I asked her, "How is it that the heat does not affect you, Seer?"

There was a queer smile on her face as she answered, "This is what I have chosen, the lighting, the heat, the fall. But then there comes the seeding and rebuilding, which I have become masterful with. So I move on. I know how to take the heat!"

"Wow! What strength you have. I could certainly do with some of that."

She was smiling as she answered, "Have you ever heard of the 'Burning Bush'?"

I nodded my head yes, saying, "Just the name. What is the story?"

"I am about to tell you!" she replied.

"This story comes from the 'Book of the Penitence of Adam'/'The Burning Bush.' Seth was permitted to reach the gate of 'Earthly Paradise' without being attacked by the guardian angel with his flaming sword. And he beheld the Trees of 'Life' and 'Knowledge,' which had joined to form a single tree, said to symbolize the harmony of science and religion in the Qabalah. The guardian angel presented Seth with three seeds from this tree, which he was instructed to place in Adam's mouth when he died. From these grew the 'Burning Bush,' which God used when he talked to Mosses. The 'Burning Bush,' burnt, yet it was not consumed! This story from the Bible is in the book of Exodus, chapter three, verse two."

The Seer was looking at me with my face full of wonder. I said, "So with the Tower energy, you have been able to conserve your core energy and not be consumed, is that correct?"

She was nodding her head and saying, "Very good, Dreamer. On the outside it may look as if there has been total destruction, but when one Dreams well, they learn to burn away the old forms and rebuild the new!"

The Seer continued. "The Tower became a powerful symbol for the poet Yeats. While writing some of his later poetry, he actually purchased and lived in an old tower.[1] An image can be seen of a tree with a Lighting Bolt that was pasted in the back of Yeats's 1893 notebook! So as you can see, Dreamer, the Tower has been significant to many. Now where was I? Oh yes, my other half!"

I did not catch what she meant until I realized she was walking to the other side of the tree. I jumped up and followed just in time to see her turning her palms outward. The lighting made a backward track into the sky, and the man continued his fall! I was aghast! But as I watched, the man just seemed to get right up as if this was a usual circumstance. And then he walked over to us both, dusting himself off as he moved.

The Woman of The Tower greeted him affectionately, and then she turned to me and said, "May I introduce The Man of The Tower!"

With a formal bow to me, he said, "It is an honor to meet you, Dreamer!" And then he shook my hand.

Dumbstruck, I answered, "Likewise!" And I shook his hand.

The Woman of The Tower then said she would be turning the lessons over to her other half.

The Man of The Tower said, "I am happy to get on with the teachings. The Tower is about matter ascending to Spirit, but there is a flaw in some towers. And like the 'Tower of Babel,' they may stand too tall, with much towering ambition, which makes a rigid structure and separates the occupants from the heavens. The tower's crown is intended to call celestial lighting to consecrate the sacred marriage consummated in the dome, and so it does. But the heavenly blast is so strong that the artificial structure disintegrates, exposing and freeing its occupants, who tumble into the abyss. For the bolt is directed at the edifice, not its inmates!"

The Seer was looking at me with a smile but looking for my reaction.

"I can see," I said, "that you both have a lot going on with this 'Burning Tree Tower'!"

Laughing at my comment, he continued. "When the divine lighting destroyed the 'Tower of Babel,' some said that human language became confused. The man and the woman here represent emotions when they are turned upside down by the bolt. There is history telling of 'The Titans,' seven of which were associated with the flood. The word 'Tityn' means 'Divine Deluge.' Babylon owed its foundation to those who were saved from the deluge. These were the giants who built the 'Tower,' and they were astrologers. They had received instructions on a secret wisdom of the Heavens. The giants were the astrologers in whose temples were kept the records of all great periodical upheavals. Their motto being: 'As above, so it is below; that which has been, will return again.'

"The 'Tower of Babel' is one such astronomical temple. It was also called the 'Temple of the Seven Lights' and the 'Celestial Earth.' It was an edifice embodying the knowledge of antiquity. It is said by the history of the Jews that 'Nimrod,' was not man but a 'Gibbor,' Kibor, a giant on Earth. And it has been told of 'Nimrod' that God was the Lord of Heaven, and he was the Lord of Earth. And to that end, God might no longer be able to hurt him by a flood of water, as he had done in the First Age. He ordained the building of the marvelous work of the 'Tower of Babel.' Wherefore God, to confound the said pride, suddenly sent confusion upon all mankind, which were at work upon the Tower. All spoke one language.

Now it was changed into seventy-two different languages, so that the workers could not understand one another's speech. And with this reason, the work of the said Tower had, of necessity, to be abandoned."

Shaking my head excitedly, I told the Man of The Tower, "I always wondered about the Tower of Babel. How fascinating about the language being confounded! I wonder if the expression 'speaking as if they were babbling' comes from this."

The Seer answered with, "I am sure it must. In the Qabalah, the Hebrew letter that symbolizes the 'Tower' is 'Peh'-'Mouth.' It is said that 'Peh' acts as a vehicle for 'The Word,' which is the 'Manifestation of Spirit.' I am sure that you have heard this statement from the Bible, in the Gospel according to John: 'In the beginning was 'The Word,' was God. The Word and The Word was with God, and The Word Was God!'

"In the Qabalah, the Tower is path number twenty-seven, the 'Principle of Manifestation' containing both the 'Positive and the Negative Pillars.' It is also a reminder for balance and to build one's Foundation True. This is essential in occult work to secure a balanced personality. The interior must be secure or the tower will be built on an insecure foundation." The Man of The Tower stood unbothered while looking at the 'Tower Tree' still burning. With the afternoon sun now low in the sky, it was truly something out of a dream! Meeting my eyes quickly, he said, "We still have much to cover, dear Dreamer." He sat down on the grass, and the Woman of The Tower sat next to him. They made a nice couple.

"After the encounter with the lighting flash, the truth arises. Flashes of insight appear and summon you to change. This higher challenge demands that you break out of old structures. You have opened yourself as a deserving channel for the new, and the universe has begun to respond. Experiencing truth, however, can be disturbing. To know the truth, you must be in a position of freedom. Adopting freedom does not come easily. Freedom will upset the circumstances of your life. The Trump Tower may be moving you to higher levels of vibration. Part of this lesson is learning acceptance. The Tower represents a place to be isolated in order to understand. Isolation has two forms: Solitude and Imprisonment. Both teach that matter and form are the ruling principles of existence.

"With solitude, we must face ourselves. Some may rant and rave. But we find no answer in raging emotions. The answer comes as a lighting flash of insight; we begin to accept we have made our own prison. Until we understand why we created it, we cannot escape our prison. Once we can come to terms with that, the lighting flash is upon us! The Tower falls and we are hurled into the unknown.

"Sometimes the Tower may fall on us because it is someone else who is attacking the personality. When we examine this for facts, we may see that it is another's idea and perception that something is wrong with us, even though we may have been feeling fine. Remember to always consult your feelings first. Follow with the reality check and the whole of the 'Lighting Dream' work process!"

The Man of the Tower reached over and took hold of the hand of The Woman of the Tower. He continued, saying, "The Tower is about renovation. When one is drawn intuitively to this Trump XVI, be aware that you may have a natural ability to heal, renovate, and restore ideas, people, buildings, organizations, and environments. You are a natural architect, designer, and builder of visions."

Both of the Seers stood up and walked slowly past the 'Burning Tree Tower.' They were holding hands. As they got close to the crest of the hill, they motioned to me to come closer to them. I felt such admiration for the way they were able to live the drama of the Tower and still be so in love with each other and life. Standing close by them, I could feel their hearts.

The Man of the Tower said, "You are welcome to stay as long as you need to contemplate your own Tower experience! It has been a pleasure to be dreaming with you, Dreamer!"

I said back enthusiastically, "Yes! It has been great! I would love to stay awhile. You have really both helped me to understand some of the fears I have been holding. A little extra 'Tower Time' would be perfect! Thank you!"

The Woman Tower Seer said she had a bit more to add. "Another concept is that the Tower actually is *not* struck down! The crown of the roof opens to receive 'The Lighting Flash,' the higher source of power! 'The Man and the Woman are the positive and negative pillars,' which are being cleaned and renewed to the 'Heartwood Interior' of their own inner Tree Tower. Then they are building and restructuring their selves with the new seedling that has been set. The Man and The Woman of The Tower thus install themselves as the now regenerated King and Queen of the Wood, looking toward the Grail Castle of Camelot!"

Both the Ancient Seers were readying to leave. Before they did, I said, "When you stopped next to the pond of the Water Oracle earlier, I believe that you both recognized your individual positive and negative pillars and pledged that you would help to balance each other within the Tower! Am I right?"

The Woman Tower Seer giggled a bit but said, "You are close, Dreamer. We each have to find what balance means for us. Everyone is different, and each tower is unique, just like you, dear Dreamer!

"Now remember when you are ready to leave this dream you must recall your physical image strongly in order to make the shift. Your need should be in place with a strong intent to return to where you choose! Strong Tower Dreams, child!"

"I remember and I will! And thank you!"

And before I could say more, they were strolling quickly down the hillside. I turned and began to contemplate The Tower as my own. This amazing tower just might help me to wake up!

DREAM OF THE TRUMP SEER: THE STAR XVII

everal of us decided to camp in The Starfield for the night. We were very excited; the warm summer night in the Nemeton was perfect to await the "Stella Matutina," the Morning Star of Venus. Of course The Star Seer would be among us!

A few of the Dreamers and I arrived early on the grassy hillside of the cliff that overlooks the sea in order to set up a campsite area. The staff of the Nemeton had brought all our supplies: sleeping bags, firewood for the campfire, and food of course! We also would have a campfire cook! All seventeen of us were very excited, and a night like this would feel carefree. I thought to myself, I had done much of the hard path work already and The Star XVII Trump work will give me the feeling of a light at the end of the tunnel, with much completed!

The cliff area was such a sight, with the music coming from the waves of the sea below. It was slightly breezy but very warm. The placement of the campfire was perfect for our work, and the huge boulders to the right blocked the winds off the water. I set up my sleeping bag near the campfire. I arranged the altar for the group with a velvet, cobalt-blue altar cloth and a star grid of eight clear quartz and nine sapphire crystals. The Star Seer had given me these along with eight candles, star maps, and star deity cards to put around the altar. The cloth had silver threads woven through the blue, and with the sparkling star deity cards, it looked awesome! The staff had placed several torches in the area to be lit later on. I walked over to the edge of the cliff and stood awhile just taking in the beauty and giving my offering of prayers with tobacco. When I turned to leave, I saw chiseled into a large granite and quartz boulder these words:

THE STARFIELD
"May those who spend time here among the stars
be blessed with hope and be illuminated with light!"

How beautiful, I thought, wondering then about the many other Dreamers who had come before me. Looking out to the sea, I enjoyed the pink and purples of sunset sparkling on the water. Hearing the laughter and the smell of the fire, in a moment I was back with the other Dreamers.

The Star Seer had arrived. She was beautiful in her blue and magenta robes embroidered with silver lines of the star constellations. Her blue-black hair held a small diadem with stars fashioned from diamonds, aquamarine, and sapphires. She was from another world and this one at the same time. Smiling at me, she said, "The altar is perfect!" Saying thank you to her, we both filled our plates with the great smelling food. The Star Seer said, "We have about an hour before we get into the program. In the meantime let's enjoy this heavenly star field in the purple sunset!" She stepped out of the dream I was viewing and became a regular person enjoying good company and the warmth of the fire.

The light was fading as I sipped my hot chocolate and felt the anticipation growing. Now the Ancient One, The Star Seer, had asked us all to join in a circle on the grass to open our Dreaming with the stars. We stood together hand in hand. I could feel my heart racing as she voiced the words to open and protect our sacred circle; it was beautiful. We sang the song of Gaia, and then everyone settled down just as the first stars began to show themselves in The Starfield.

Time felt different here. Then the Star Seer stepped back into the dream. With artistically designed stars sparkling on her diadem, she was otherworldly. I looked up into the deep blue-black and felt a surge of energy from the twinkling above. The torches were now lit, and the candles were glowing; so were the Dreamers around the circle.

The Star Seer began, telling us that we would be learning about The Star XVII Trump as we all participated in a ceremony. There was complete silence after that; everyone was wondering what she meant. Quietly now The Seer was in mediation for a few minutes. As she came to the attention of the Dreamer circle, The Seer said, "We will all participate in bringing in the star energy by invoking the 'Star Deities of Inspiration'!"

Standing now and looking around at each of us, she asked me if I would pass out the eight star deity cards randomly, but that there was one which she would do herself. I gave her the cards; she took one and gave the rest back to me. I then passed out the seven left around the circle.

The Star Seer told the group, "Those of you with the cards, study the words of your deity for a few minutes. When I call on you to recite the invocation you received, be ready and use your best strength of emotion to invoke your deity! I will begin with the deity I have chosen. Once we have done this, our ceremony will have begun and the work will commence!"

There was a slight murmur of words around the circle of Dreamers. Everyone was getting charged.

The Ancient Star Seer walked to the center of the circle. The night was cooling, the candles and torches were gleaming, and the music from the sea of rhythmic waves felt reassuring. The Seer with hands above her head asked that we make the same calling gesture as she. Looking up into the infinite star-filled sky was awesome. This is what our Star Seer presented: TO THE STAR DEITIES of INSPIRATION.

The Star Seer said, "I INVOKE The 'Goddess Rhea'! The first of the eight star deities this evening. 'Goddess Rhea,' The Divine Lady of the River of Heaven, whose starry body forms the Rainbow Bridge, the Milky Way. 'Goddess Rhea,' please come! We call you! Rhea of Greek myth, daughter of 'Ouranos'-'The Sky' and 'Gaia'-The Earth. Rhea! Mother of the stars and gods! We call you! I light a candle to you, 'Rhea' the Goddess of the Milky Way Galaxy, Home of our Earth!"

The Dreamers stood hand to hand, with heads to the Starfield above, connecting to the dream of the stars above. Quietly, softly, we all noted the shift in the heavens; our hands held us together tightly. The Star Seer had joined the Dreamer circle.

The next Dreamer, a woman, began her invocation. "I INVOKE The 'Goddess Ariadne'! She who is the 'Crown of Stars' of the 'Corona Borealis'! 'Goddess Ariadne,' please come! We call you! Ariadne of Greek myth, daughter of Minos of Crete. Ariadne, deserted by Theseus, whom she loved! Dionysus found her and brought her comfort. He took part of her crown for the heavens, which he flung into the night to become there after the 'Corona Borealis'! They shine their light eternally for those in need; look only to the stars of the north at night! We call you! I light a candle to you, 'Ariadne' the Goddess of the Corona Borealis!"

The Dreamers looked to the northern stars; they noted a twinkling and knew it was true! The Dreamer then joined the circle.

The third Dreamer, a man, began his invocation. "I INVOKE The 'Goddess Sopdet-Sothis'! The Goddess of the Star Sirius, the brightest star of 'Canis Major,' the Greater Dog. 'Goddess Sopdet-Sothis,' please come! We call you! Sopdet of Egyptian Myth, wife of Sah, the Orion Star, a sister to Isis and the mother of the Star of Venus. Sirius, the earliest astronomically recorded star. 'Goddess Sopdet-Sothis,' who is goddess of the waters of inundation. She who is goddess of fertility and the New Year. She who is part of 'Canis Major,' appearing the brightest in summer skies and known as the 'Dog Star-Sirius.' 'Sopdet,' the goddess who foresees the rise of the River Nile and distributes the rich silt of fertility! We call you! I light a candle to you, 'Sopdet-Sothis,' Goddess of Sirius!"

The Dreamers instantly felt the energies of the Goddess and the bright star Sirius, the Dog Star. The Dreamer joined the circle.

The fourth Dreamer, a woman, was ready. "I INVOKE The 'Goddess Kore-Persephone'! The princess 'Andromeda,' maiden of our sister galaxy. 'Goddess Kore-Persephone,' please come! We call you! Kore-Persephone of Greek myth, daughter of Cepheus, king of Ethiopia and his wife Cassiopeia. Her cruel parents gave her for sacrifice to a hostel sea and to the sea monster Cetus. They said her fate, as beautiful as she was, would be to relieve the peoples' hurt by submitting to her own. She was laid arrayed in white, like a bride, upon a rock of the sea, expecting death. She was chained to a rock! Perseus, returning from triumph in battle with the head of the Gorgon Medusa, sees her and is horrified. He cuts a path through the air to save her. A duel with the sea monster Cetus ensues. He rages in battle but triumphs. He rushes to Andromeda to unchain her and is struck by her beauty and pledges marriage. Admiring her beauty and her locks of hair in the light, he flings this image to the heavenly skies to appear forever in the night! Andromeda's name in Greek means 'Man.' The word 'andreia' means 'courage.' The Goddess Kore is another name for Persephone; 'Kore' means young maiden. The Goddess Kore-Persephone, the innocent maiden, the returning goddess, the one who brings the changing seasons! We call you! I light a candle to you, 'Kore-Persephone'!"

The woman Dreamer rejoined the circle. All were still as they saw the night sky glimmer with the beauty of 'Kore-Persephone.'

Now the fifth Dreamer, a man, was beginning his invocation. "I INVOKE The 'Queen Cassiopeia.' In the north next to the Pole Star Polaris is where she sits to make amends to her daughter. 'Queen Cassiopeia,' please come! We call you! The Ethiopian Queen, the seated woman. Cassiopeia, 'She of the throne.' In Greek it is the word for 'Throne'-'Support.' In Sanskrit it is the word for 'Throne'-'Dharma'-'that which is established firmly.' Hyginus, writing of 'Cassiepia,' describes the figure as bound to her seat and secured from falling out. She goes around the Pole Star with her head sometimes upside down. The five brightest stars create the shape of an *M*. This is known as the 'Celestial M' when above the pole, and the 'Celestial W' when below the pole. From Queen Cassiopeia come the enhancement of beauty and objects for adoring the body, such as gold and jewels. Remember, she was the vain queen who boasted about her beauty. She also chained her daughter, Andromeda, to a rock as sacrifice because of her vanity. As punishment, Poseidon condemned her to the celestial ring, to be forever in her 'Throne,' bound to the 'Pole Star,' Polaris. It is said that she bids men to give her gold in trade for her seer-ship! Dreamers, we can learn from her to keep our hearts humble and to be kind! We call you! I light a candle to you, beautiful Queen Cassiopeia!"

The man Dreamer stood quietly in the center a few moments, as if he was making sure we all understood the message he had given. Then he rejoined the circle.

A woman stepped forward to present her invocation of the sixth star. "I INVOKE The 'Goddess Callisto'! The Great Bear and Goddess of 'Ursa Major,' part of the Big Dipper. 'Goddess Callisto,' please come! We call you! Goddess Callisto, daughter of Lycaon, king of Arcadia. The Great Bear Ursa Major, which never disappears below the horizon, is always visible in the night sky, all night, every night of the year. One version of Greek myth tells us that the Great Bear is identified with the Goddess Callisto, a paramour of Zeus. The Greek mythographer Apollodorus says that Callisto was turned into a bear by Zeus to disguise her from his wife, Hera. But Hera saw through the ruse and pointed out the bear to Artemis, who shot her down, thinking she was a wild animal. Zeus sorrowfully placed the image of the bear Callisto into the night sky where he could see her forever shining! The name 'Callisto' in Greek is 'Kalos'-'Beautiful'! The seven stars of the 'Great She Bear,' never below the horizon, guide man on his paths. We call you! I light a candle to you, 'Goddess Callisto'!"

The woman Dreamer lit her candle slowly and rejoined the circle of dreamers. The circle of Dreamers was entranced by the beauty they saw from the 'Great She Bear.'

Now a man came to the center of the circle to do the seventh invocation. "I INVOKE 'The 'Goddesses of the Pleiades'! The Seven Sisters, please come! We call you! In Greek myth, The Pleiades, 'Doves of Heaven,' the seven daughters of the Titan "Atlas" and the sea nymph 'Pleione,' were born on Mount Cyllene, Greece. It is in this hour that these sister goddess appear! Their names, from eldest to youngest, were Maia, Electra, Taygete, Alcyone, Calaeno,

Sterope, and Merope. Merope, the sister of mystery who remains hidden, we beckon you all! The Pleiades are an open star cluster in the constellation of 'Taurus.' They are among the nearest clusters to Earth. Their mother's name is 'Pleione,' which in Greek means 'Sailing'; her daughters are the 'Sailing Ones.' The name of Pleiades must come from their mother. Another version of the name says 'Pleiades' means 'A flock of Doves.' The seven sisters are the guardians of the 'Axis Mundi' and are the brightest stars of the pole encircling 'Ursa Major.' The seven sisters, the 'Goddesses Pleiades,' were companions of Artemis. We call you! I light a candle to you, the 'Goddesses Pleiades'!"

The man Dreamer lit the seventh candle. The air was still. The candlelight and the starlight all became magical! The Dreamer rejoined the circle.

It was now my turn. As the last woman, I would light the eighth candle. I took a deep breath before I began my invocation. "I INVOKE The 'Goddess Virgo Astraea'! Goddess of Justice'! 'Goddess Virgo,' please come! We call you! 'Goddess Virgo,' who is daughter of Zeus and Themis. But also known as 'Astraea' in Roman myth, daughter of 'Astraeus, Father of the Stars.' Virgo we know as the virgin goddess of the dawn. The goddess Virgo, portrayed as justice, holding the scales of 'Libra.' She is also portrayed as the maiden who, in her hand, bears the gleaming ear of corn 'Spica'; in addition, she is seen as the virgin with her sheaf of wheat belonging to 'Ceres.' Virgo is the second largest constellation in the sky. She is often identified as the 'Goddess Dike,' goddess of moral justice, and her mother, 'Themis,' was goddess of divine justice. The name 'Astraea' means 'Star Maiden.' She was a celestial virgin, and 'Astraea' was the last of the immortals to live with humans during the 'Iron Age,' the final stage in the world's disintegration from the utopian 'Golden Age.' Fleeing from the wickedness of humanity, she ascended into the heavenly skies to become the 'Constellation Virgo.' At the end of the age, Astraea shall return to us! We call you! I light a candle to you, 'Goddess Virgo-Astraea'!"

I lit the eighth candle, and we all looked to the star field of the night sky and enjoyed the amazing light show that we had called in! The Star Seer came to the center of the dream circle, and I rejoined the Dreamers.

She said, "Dear Dreamers, I acknowledge you! Now you have successfully brought in the Star Deities! Let us all look to the heavens in silence for the inspiration to aid our cosmic purpose, for our star maps are here. Together we have lit the candles to honor the fire of the stars. Together we give thanks to our 'Star Deities of Inspiration'!" A bell was struck eight times. "Our ceremony has opened this space; our work has begun! Let it be so!"

The Star Seer suggested we all take a break. There was a buzz of excitement among the Dreamers. Everyone seemed to be really starstruck by now! Before long we settled down and resumed the evening, seated around the central fire. I felt the star fire from the stars of the night were connected to each of us. Looking around the group, I knew that many had similar feelings.

The Ancient Star Seer's otherworld dream glow was touching each of us. She began: "Look to the star fields, Dreamers. There in the quiet starlight, one can find passive guidance. As you peer within the darkness, you will find the light you need!"

I thought to myself, So many times I have stared into the star-filled sky, wishing and hoping for something. With what I am learning here tonight, I will be ale to do this with more knowledge and focus.

The Seer continued. "The ancients generally regarded stars as living entities. Sometimes they were heavenly angels, sometimes legendary heroes. Sometimes the stars were the souls of the unborn or the souls of the dead. The star might be referred to as 'astral'-'starry,' which is a body made of star stuff called 'ether.' This 'ethereal body' is what the Gnostics referred to when they spoke of Jesus or other holy persons who radiated 'starry bodies of light.' Some cultures have traditions that locate a person's soul within a star, even assigning an eternal soul to one of the stars in the heavens. Some traditions tell of psychic dangers attributed to perilous passages in a person's life cycle; they may make a statement like, 'When a man's star is low...' Jewish scriptures maintain that 'Every affair, in which man is engaged here on Earth, is first, and indicated by above by the angle of his star.'"

The Star Seer had stopped momentarily, her blue-black hair shining with the starry diadem upon her forehead, a vision of beauty on this night. Some Dreamers were commenting quietly on the angel star information. In the background a bell was rung, and we focused again on the Seer.

"When most of us think about the image of a star, it is usually the five-pointed shape, like the pentacle. This probably comes from the stars' natural prototypes: the five-pointed star in the apple core and five-petaled flowers, like the apple blossom and the rose. All of which were originally sacred to the Goddess. The pentagram is the most universally recognized star shape. In tarot it is used in the suit of 'Pentacles.' The five-pointed star is used widely on flags and in the military. In Wicca and in alchemy, the pentagram represents the microcosm, with the saying: 'As above, so below!' There are, however, many stars of various points.

"'The Star XVII Trump' represents the entrusting of oneself to Fate, who is viewed as a benevolent force. The Star Trump then symbolizes 'Hope,' which is supported by the 'Goddess of Hope,' 'Spes' or 'Elpis.' In Roman myth, 'Spes' was the 'Goddess of Hope.' Traditionally defined as 'The Last Goddess'—Spes, ultima dea—meaning that hope is the last resource available to man. In art, 'Spes' was depicted hitching her skirt while holding a cornucopia and flowers. 'Spes' personified hope for good harvest and for children. She was invoked at births, marriages, and at other important times. Her equivalent Greek goddess was named 'Elpis.' The energy of this goddess and the Star Trump represents the conscious mind's willing surrender to the unconscious, giving oneself over to the flow.

"The Star Trump also contains the energy of the 'Goddess Rhea,' the goddess of flow. Goddess Rhea, from Greek myth, was also called the 'Mother of gods'; she was mother to Demeter, Hades, Hera, Hestia, Poseidon, and Zeus. Rhea was wife to 'Chronus,' Father Time. Greek myth says his name means 'Time.' He is usually portrayed as an old, wise man with a long, gray beard. The Goddess Rhea represents progressive destiny."

The Star Seer paused a few minutes and looked around our group, making sure we were all with her. Satisfied, she went right on with more amazing star stories.

"This story gives us interesting insight into the myth of 'The Three Wise Men,' who followed the star of Bethlehem at the time of the birth of Christ. The story may actually come from the three stars in the belt of 'Orion.' For the Egyptians, this rising announced the coming of 'Sothis,' the Star of Osiris, also called 'Sirius'. Sirius is the brightest star in the sky and whose coming heralds the annual flooding of the Nile River in Egypt. Early symbols for the 'The Star XVII Trump' indicate it was the card of the astrologer. The Three Magi, astrologers in all likelihood, followed the Star of Bethlehem, Jupiter, for two years. The star card is the card of hope. The Magi tracked the star to find the birth of a king and a new regime in life. '*Jupiter is the planet-star of good luck and abundance.*' The star which brings hope!

"From the Qabalah, by Gareth Knight, the Star card is path fifteen on the 'Tree of Life'-'Dweller between the Waters.' The star helps with being able to see through the darkness of where its soul has come from. Knowing it is part of the collective consciousness. Trusting that all the 'Divine Sparks'-'The Stars' will perfectly adjust to the ley lines on the collective. This is the 'Sight of the Spider's Eye,' which is the web within each human eye! Every man and every woman is a star. 'I am the Alpha and the Omega.' The Egyptian 'Sky Goddess' was called 'Nut' or 'Nuit.' Her name means 'Night.' It is said of her: 'Coverer of the sky, she who protects, Mistress of all. It is she who holds a thousand souls.' 'Nuit' is said to be covered in stars, touching the cardinal points of her body. 'Nuit,' the goddess of resurrection and rebirth.

"From Greece we have the myth of 'The Star of the Muses.' These are stories of sacred women or female spirits in groups of nine that actually occur everywhere in folklore and myth. For the Greek myth, it is the Nine Classical Muses. The Nine Morgans of Celtic paradise, and the Nine Korrign on their sacred isle. Medieval superstitions sometimes called them 'Mares' or 'Maers,' who dwelt in the wild woodlands. Some say the sprites would settle on the top of bodies of sleeping men, choking off their breath, and then taking away their power of speech. Hence the name of 'Mare'-'Night-Mare'!

"To the Celts, the 'Pleiades' were associated with mourning and funerals, since the star cluster rose around the time of 'All Souls' Day,' a festival devoted to the remembrance of the dead.

"In Aztec mythology, the 'Goddess Citalicue' wore a star garment, and it is said she created the stars along with her husband, the 'God Citalatonac.' Both are said to be related with the first pair of humans, 'Nata' and 'Nena.' Another Celtic myth is about 'Arianrhod.' This is from the Welsh; the name 'arian'-'silver' and 'rhod'-'wheel' together create 'silverwheel.' 'Arianrhod Keeper of the Silverwheel of the Stars.' 'Arianrhod' is a woman from Welch myth in the Fourth Branch of the Mabinogi. 'Caer Arianrhod' is the name given to the 'Corona Borealis'-'The Crown of Stars.'

In Australia the Aboriginal Yolngu gather at sunset to await the rising star of 'Venus,' which they call 'Barmumbirr.' As she approaches, in the early hours before dawn, she draws on 'her rope of light' attached to Earth. Here is the decorated 'Morning Star Pole.' With this the people can communicate and remember their dead loved ones. 'Barmumbirr' is also a creator-spirit for the 'Dreaming' and sang much of the country into life!

"Many of the Star Trump cards depict artwork with an eight-pointed star. This comes from the association with the star of 'Venus' and her eight points. The eight-pointed star is the 'Star of Isis,' symbol of Aphrodite, Rhea, and Sophia. This eight-pointed star is also the 'Star Shield of Inanna,' and according to Jung: 'the eight-points represent completeness of the individuated self.' The star is often colored in red for emotion, or yellow for intuition. The 'Goddess Inanna' is the goddess who descends into the underworld to confront her dark side, which is her twin sister, 'Ereshkigal.'"

"Venus in astrology is the ruling planet of Taurus and Libra. Venus is the second brightest object in the night sky after the Moon. Venus is the planet of Friday and is the bright morning star, spring through autumn."

"'Divine Goddess Dana,' Star Goddess of Atlantis, is related to the Virgo zodiac sign. In astrology Virgo is the maiden representing 'Persephone,' the Roman daughter of the 'God Demeter,' the wheat-bearing maiden. In Egypt, the star 'Virgo' was part of the zodiacs called 'Denderah and Thebes,' holding a distaff marked by the stars of the constellation 'Coma Berenices,' 'Berenice's Hair,' for Queen Berenice of Egypt. In Syria, the 'Goddess Ishtar' was called the 'Queen of Stars' and related to Virgo. Venus is associated with copper, and she is the star who is the 'Mirror of the Goddess'!"

"The word 'Virgo' is Latin for 'Virgin,' probably related to 'Virga'-'Virgate,' the word for 'twig/switch' or 'rod/wand.' The Greek counterpart is 'talis'-'a marriageable girl.' The derivatives of the Latin word 'tales'-'tally' means 'detail.' Virgos are well known for paying attention to detail. From 'Maniluis, first century AD, Astronomica,' it was said: 'The Virgin-Virgo will study and train her mind in the learned arts. She will give not so much to the abundance of wealth as the impulse to investigate the cause and effects of things. From her tongue which charms the mastery of words, comes a mental vision which can discern all things. In her early years there are many who have a bashfulness sort of handicap; holding back their gifts. Time however, allows Virgo to mature deeply and she then gives her gifts freely'!"

The Star Seer had been seated, but she was standing now, studying the night sky. We all waited in anticipation for what she might say. She walked around our starlit temple, then stopped, saying, "The eight-pointed star holds importance in many cultures. The American Indian has the myth of the 'Dawn Star,' the eight-pointed star of the Planet Venus, the 'Morning Star' of hope and rebirth. The Shawnee describe a crone grandmother a female deity called 'Our Grandmother'-'Kokomthena,' whose partners are the stars. It is said that the stars have the special gift of giving rainwater to the Earth.[2] In other legends, the creator placed Grandmother Spider in the sky to keep the webs in good repair. Native legends tell of 'Star Spider Woman' weaving the universe by day and then unraveling her web at night. The world would end when her web was finished. Pueblo Natives say 'Spider Woman' wove east to west and then north to south to determine the Earth's center. Several times Star Spider Woman destroyed the web of the world and remade it. She saved only those wise ones who kept contact with her via the invisible strands spun to the tops of their heads. Some say 'Grandmother Star Spider Woman' lives among the star constellation we call 'Scorpio.'"

The Ancient One stopped her lecture, and we all held our breath. She asked us all to stand and to look at the 'Heavenly Starfields' for a few minutes. Then we were to share what we felt that star energy may be teaching this evening. The night air had gotten decidedly colder, and I put my blanket around my shoulders. Everyone was very quiet; we heard just the waves lapping at the shoreline below the cliffs. A few of the fellow fire keepers were stoking the campfire, and the scent of pine drifted; I was thankful. We heard soft drumming, and someone struck a bell a few times. We resumed our circle. The Dreamers hesitated with sharing. I decided to offer my ideas first. The Star Seer gave me the floor.

"For me the essence of the star symbolism is about things that may feel unreachable. The stars themselves are beyond our grasp, with more in the skies than we can ever see. We associate stars with light and also with the divine. I feel them to be the lights of heaven. I have always liked this great expression: 'Aim for the stars!' This is so true; somehow they bring us peace and good wishes!"

Everyone clapped! I was honored. Now the Star Seer selected another to share their insights.

A man Dreamer began to speak. "When I look at them, I feel hopeful! To me they personify that wonderful word, '*hope!*'

All the Dreamers said, "Yeah to that!"

The Star Seer said, "Dreamers, you have all done well here tonight in our 'Temple of the Stars'!" All of us were all glued to this amazing otherworld Dreamer—The Star Seer, who was literally gleaming now with twinkling starlight! Somehow she was able to bring down starlight right into our circle. Incredible! Now the Seer said, "Please, each of you, come one by one and pay your respects to the 'Central Flame of the Stars.' The star deities have come to you for this purpose. Now you may begin your own mapping of your own starlight of hope! I can only hold this starlight energy for a short while. Please begin!"

The Dreamers took their turns and paid their respects as closely as they would allow themselves. This was simply amazing! I do not think any of us will ever be the same! I know that for me there has been an incredible charge of ascension and hope!

The intense starlight began drifting into the chill of the midnight air. The Star Seer then transformed back to herself, and we began closing our evening star dream ceremony.

The Star Seer said, "The stars of our temple ceiling reflect the stars in their orbits. We have invoked many of the Star Goddess energies this evening. But in order to gain their knowledge, you may not succeed unless you can first awaken the Goddess within yourself! So make sure that you make this your task. They are there and willing to help with your star maps; you only need ask for help with your awakening!

"Now, Dreamers! The hour is late, and we intend a little more 'Dream Work' with the dawn's first light! As you are all aware, we will greet 'Venus,' our morning star! So now let us close our circle for the evening and give thanks to all that have participated!"

With the closing, the Dreamers drifted off into small groups to chat or, like myself, drifted quickly into starry dreamland. I was excited for the early morning, to have the opportunity to feast my eyes on the star map of Virgo (the constellation is called "Spica") and to greet the "Stella Matutina"-"The Morning Star of Venus," "The Dawn Star"!

DREAM OF THE TRUMP SEER: THE MOON XVIII

Walking the beach in the sun was very rejuvenating. Along my way I was collecting shells that spoke to me. I paused for a moment to watch the crabs scurrying in the sand. Up ahead of me I noticed several Dreamers. I moved along to say hello. Four Dreamers had rakes and other garden tools, and I noticed there were piles of sand tinted a bluish color. "What are you all doing?" I asked.

One of the tall fellows, who was holding a rake, studied me a minute and then turned back to his raking, saying, "We are making a 'Moon-Painting'!"

Very puzzled, I answered, "A 'Moon-Painting.' What does it mean?"

He was working meticulously in the sand, creating a large circle design. Still working, he said, "Why, yes! A 'Moon-Painting' for the 'Moon Seer' of course! She will conduct her Moon program here on the beach in the early evening. Didn't you hear the announcement? Anyway, to know more about the painting, we could use some help. Are you interested?" Leaning on his rake, he had stopped his circle raking and seemed to be checking over his work. He looked over to me with a big smile.

I smiled back and said, "I would love to help! What shall I do?"

The Dreamer introduced me to the others, whom I knew somewhat. Then he explained that the painting would portray the 'Eight Phases of the Moon'! I told him that sounded so exciting and that the Moon for me was a constant companion, but as yet, I had not met the 'Moon Seer.' The Dreamer told me I would soon have that opportunity; she would be on the beach within the hour. In the meantime, he told me where to rake and how to make the crescent shapes. I found out that the blue sand was our paint for the design work. This large painting had a twelve-foot circumference, and each of us had a section to paint using our rakes.

All of us kept checking the paper drawing, which we were copying from and onto the sandy beach; we had to get everything just so! Every now and then someone would make a mistake, but we all just laughed and started over.

One of the Dreamers said, "Sand painting is easier to work with than many other mediums. When you mess a section up, all you have to do is rake it out!"

I was told that the blue sand would be layered on at the end of the drawing-raking process. We were all really having fun and learning a bit as we placed the various crescents of the moon.

We just finished the blue sand layering and were admiring our handiwork, when the 'Moon Seer' arrived. Not saying anything to us, she walked around the painting, analyzing our work. Finally she said, "Yes, Dreamers, this will work very nicely! Let me help you make a few minor adjustments." She took one of the smallest rakes and touched up in several areas. Then she walked around again, nodding her head admiringly. We all felt very proud! Looking at us, she said, "This is terrific! Now I need to collect a few shells to put around the outside edges."

I spoke up to say, "Earlier today, I collected these!" And I showed her what I had in my bag.

Smiling at me, the Seer said, "Great! This will do it!" Then she walked the circle of the "Moon Painting" and placed the shells. Next she asked one of the guys to bring something over. We were all curious about the large silver chest that she had placed at the bottom of the painting. We asked what it was for and what was in it. But she would only say that we would find out tonight. Then The Moon Seer stood back and said, "You have created something of beauty today. Thank you!"

Everyone clapped! We all said this was truly a work of art! One of the Dreamers took out a camera and began snapping pictures, saying, "Once the tides get going, and the elements, the painting will begin to fade! It will be fun to have our work saved on film!" We all clapped at that and posed in the various phases of the Moon! The Ancient Moon Seer was in every photo!

Like so many of the days and nights here in the Grove, the time went quickly. It was just after supper, and the Dreamers started to arrive on the beach. There were some chairs that had been set up and a campfire near the painting. Many of the Dreamers brought blankets and bedrolls. It looked like there might be quiet a few camping for the night! But then it was midsummer, and the solstice was not far off. A few Dreamers were going around lighting the torches and stoking the fire. The hour was twilight, and the sun was doing its setting over the ocean waves in the west. Many were watching as the colors turned from orange to mauve and purple, rippling its glow across the water. What a beautiful sight!

On the rocks was the Moon Seer. She was in mediation as she 'Called Down the Moon'!

I looked at her now and realized that she was literally the ancient Moon Goddess. She had long, silvery hair that blew with the wind; her silver, filmy, net gown looked like it had been woven by moon-fairy fingers from the moonbeams themselves! With her arms outstretched, she was chanting quietly, an ancient moon chant to be sure. Then the skies grew darker from the fading sun. I could hear the lapping of the tides. Looking around, I noted the Dreamers admiring our creative Moon-Painting. The Drumming had been started by several of the Seers. They indicated that we turn to the "Moon Seer XVII," who stood on the rocky ledge. What a feeling as we all joined in with the drumming. The Full Moon began to show her face, rising in the eastern sky. We drummed a little more as the Moon Seer came to the center of the circle. She performed a beautiful opening with songs and protection. We all sighed and laughed some as her program got underway.

The Moon Seer, in a booming voice, said, "Dreamers, come with me by the light of the moon to the 'Palace of the Night.' There you will come to know me, your 'Moon Goddess'!" The whole crowd clapped at the amazing energy that had been created. The stage on the beach was ready.

"Now let me tell you what I can about your 'Moon Goddess'! The Moon rules the night and the dark that resides within us. She rules the oceans and all that may feel like tidal waves within us. She teaches us about time and the cycles of time and how to change." The Moon Seer fluttered like a willowy form as she walked about talking, teaching. Her eyes and hair were luminous like the moonlight. "First I want to thank the fine artists who made this painting!" She pointed now to the sand painting, which was lit by candle and torchlight. "The painting is called, as most of you know, 'The Eight Phases of the Moon.'" She laughed a clear, soft laugh. "Because of my strong connection to astrology, we will have a few insights, here and there."

The Seer continued. "There are eight phases that happen to our moon each month, phases that are cycles of time and energy. This has been so for eternity. I will mention them quickly. For a deeper study, please consult me at another time. This cycle is for twenty-nine point six days. The 'Eight Phases' are as follows:

-NEW , dark of the moon, = Beginning, seeding, birth, emergence.

-CRESCENT = Expansion, growth, struggle.

-FIRST QUARTER = Action, expression, growth, breaking away.

-GIBBOUS = Analyze, prepare, trust.

-FULL = Fulfillment, illumination, realization.

-DISSEMINATING = Demonstration, distribution, sharing, introspection.

-THIRD QUARTER = Realignment, revision, integration, cleansing.

-BALSAMIC = Transition, release, transformation, renewal.

"When you walk around viewing the 'Moon-Painting,' you may want to dream yourself into one of the phases, to see how it feels. Start at the 'New Moon,' the dark circle you see at the top!

"The Moon in astrology refers to the feminine principle, either in ourselves or others. It is about our emotional needs. Here is an expression that makes a lot of sense. 'Where the Sun acts, the Moon reacts!' Look to the Moon in your natal chart to see where she falls; this may help you to determine where you feel secure. The Moon in our chart shows how we protect ourselves and feel comfortable and safe. The Moon is the radiant darkness behind the light!

"In astrology the zodiac symbol for 'Cancer' is represented by the Moon. The elemental sign of the Moon is Water and is symbolic of the maternal principle of nature; this was recognized by pagans as the origin of life. Also the zodiac symbol for 'Pisces' has an image that represents two crescent moons: one waxing and one waning.

"There is fascinating history with astrology from the ancient 'Chaldean Astrologers' of Babylonia in the sixth century BC. We know that the eleventh dynasty, known as the

'Chaldean Dynasty,' consisted of mythologies of ancient Summer, Assyria, and Babylonia. The 'Chaldean Astrologers' were members of the magi, astrologers, sorcerers, enchanters, and magicians. They were soothsayers, but advanced mathematicians as well. The 'Chaldean Astrologers' defined themselves as 'Moon Worshipers,' calling the zodiac the 'Houses of the Moon'! This is unlike modern astrologers who make their observations from the placement of the Sun rather than the Moon. So as you can see, in the beginning, astrology systems of divination were based on the Moon's course through various houses. Today the bulk of astrologers assign planetary ruler-ship according to the ancient Chaldeans."

The Seer had walked over to the campfire and stood gazing a few minutes. Then she looked up to the radiant Full Moon. Turning to the Dreamers, she said, "What magic she holds!" Then she reached into her pocket, put something into her palm, and threw it into the fire! The fire crackled and sparked into red, blue, and purple hues! Speaking again, she said, "A small salt offering to her radiance!

"Let me continue. Because of the Moon's involvement with the oceans tides, which come in cycles, there is a connection to a woman's monthly menses cycle. Some ancient believes held that the woman's cycles of 'lunar blood' was supposed to give life to every human being in the womb. From these beliefs the Moon became the prime symbol of the 'Mother Goddess' everywhere."

Standing quietly, her hands on her hips with her filmy, silver gown catching the breeze, she was a vision to behold. The Moon Goddess said: "You must be wondering...So what does this information have to do with tarot? I will tell you! The Moon in tarot, *in a tarot reading*, is about cycling through phases! The card may suggest change for the querent you are working with. Of course the surrounding cards always give the larger picture.

"Now there is so much I need to share. You all saw me at the start of the evening on the rocky ledge! What was I doing?" She asked this general question to the Dreamers.

Someone came back with, "You were Drawing Down the Moon!"

With soft laughter she answered, "Yes! Yes! Now let me give you some background here! Drawing Down the Moon, also know as Drawing Down the Goddess, is a ritual that is central to many Wicca traditions. During the ritual, a coven's High Priestess enters a trance and requests that the Goddess or Triple Goddess, symbolized by the Moon, enter her body and speak through her. The High Priestess may be aided by the High Priest who invokes the spirit of the Goddess. During her trance, the High Priestess speaks and acts as the Goddess. This is performed under a Full Moon, and all involved stand within a circle drawn on the ground. The members of the coven, which can be no more than thirteen, stand about the circle. Some solitary Wiccas perform the ritual as well. They also stand within a drawn circle, under full moonlight. The solitary Goddess will stand in a 'Goddess Pose,' both arms held up high, palms up, body and arms forming a *Y*. They will recite a charge, or chant!

"From Thessely, Greece, ancient 'Thessalian Witches' were believed to control the moon. According to 'literary tract': 'If I command the moon, it will come down; and if I wish to withhold the day, night will linger over my head; and again, if I wish to embark on the sea, I need no ship, and if I wish to fly through the air, I am free from my weight!' In all likelihood, the 'Calling Down of the Moon' can be traced to pagan earth-based religions, with rituals just as I have just described."

The Moon Seer had paused, with everyone clapping! I looked around the group, and all were in high spirits. The Moon Seer, realizing that, said, "Now, dear Moon Dreamers, we will not be doing any rituals here tonight! We have much more to discover."

Everyone was laughing, but they began to settle down.

Standing in front of the Moon Painting, she went on, "The Moon symbolizes the last trial before rebirth, the final plunge into the unconscious sea. There may be confrontation with sea monsters before the new dawn. We are at the edge of the ocean, the deep salt sea. Its brine is bitter, poisonous, yet the very stuff from which we are made and from which life has come. Our 'Ocean Baptism' is rejuvenating; yet if we do not leave it, we will wither and die. The sea represents the watery depth of the unconscious, within which everything dissolves and loses its form. Boundaries vanish; the ego is lost, and shifting moods and confusion reign. But the sea must always be faced. The nature of the Moon is most clearly seen in the ebb and flow of the ocean, the salt sea. The sea surrounds the earth. It is to the sea that the Sun returns eastward during the night and the Moon during the day. It is from this that we understand that the saltiness of ocean is essential for the alchemical transformation work that one does with the Moon! The demands of the 'Moon Mistress' cannot be ignored. The Moon can churn the unconscious depths and calls up primitive images. This can be a potent source of inspiration and creativity, or it may be overwhelming. It is with this that we may call on the shape-shifting shaman and make a plunge into the new. With the Moon we operate in a more instinctive realm than we are accustomed to, and courage is required to progress into the unknown. The Moon is of the night; vision is inadequate and it is necessary to rely more heavily on the other senses: hearing, taste, touch, smell, and the lower senses, as do the dog and the wolf. With the Moon energy, we continue with our courage!

"The Moon represents the unconscious, and salt is one of its aspects. Salt is the spark of the 'Anima Mundi,' World Soul, which is dissolved in the dark depths of the sea, as Jung has said. It is, however, no ordinary salt; it is 'Sal Spiritual,' Spiritual Salt. The salt of the philosophers; the alchemists. The ocean holds the chaotic primordial waters, which contains all four elements, the source of all life. When you look at the elements of the Moon, you see they are feminine, lunar elements of Water and Earth; which oppose the Sun's masculine solar elements of Fire and Air. Both share the quality of being hot and are a force of action and separation.

"The Moon has animal symbols that it is associated with. The 'Crab' is portrayed very often in tarot images. It is associated with the zodiac sign of 'Cancer" the Moon rules 'Cancer.' The crab is also associated with danger, its claws, and illumination, because it sheds its shell, and with rebirth. The crab can run backward or sideways. It may advance onto land or reach for the deep. It is said that the crab depends on the Moon and waxes and wanes with it. The crab is also 'new beginning,' for Cancer holds Summer Solstice, when the 'Dog Star' is at its highest point and the sun begins its retreat. Canines are another common tarot image, and Canines play a big part in Moon associations. As symbols of vigilance, dogs are often found guarding the gates of the underworld. Black dogs are especially associated with the 'Goddess Hecate.' Dogs can be spirit guides between worlds. Canines have established many connections within the Major Arcana and are associated with the underworld because they eat carrion. It is said that the dog that carries the souls to the underworld is named 'Lupus,' Wolf, or 'Feronius,' Fierce. It is thought that the dogs may represent the conscious mind, 'scenting and intuiting' the unconscious. Thus the dogs in the Moon are held spellbound by her."

The Ancient Moon Seer was silent and looking to the Moon glow above us. Turning back to the Dreamers with much enthusiasm, she said, "I need to tell you more of the Goddess that is so much a part of the Moon's being! But first I will tell you of a 'Moon God'! Images and folklore of the Moon may come in part from the 'Epic of Gilgamesh,' in the time of ancient Mesopotamia. Gilgamesh was in search for everlasting life. In his journey he found himself between two huge mountain passes. Standing between these peaks, he saw two lions. He became afraid, as it was night. Seeing the Moon, he lifted his eyes and began praying, 'O Moon God Sin, protect me!' It is said that the God Sin listened and he was protected. On many images of the Moon tarot, mountains are shown with the moon above. 'Sin a lunar God' is a Sumerian, Mesopotamian god of the moon, circa 2600 to 2400 BC, a male; 'Nanna' is the female, 'The Illuminator,' the House of Great Light. In the Sumerian culture, there is a triad of power consisting of 'Sin,' the Moon, and 'Shamash,' the Sun, and 'Ishtar,' Venus. 'Sin' wore a beard made from the stone 'lapis lazuli' and rode a winged bull. He was worshipped in Babylonia and Assyria. In the country of Turkey, there is a city named 'Harran,' Carrhae; this is an ancient city of Mesopotamia and noted for the temple of the 'Moon God Sin,' from 53 BCE. It is said that Adam and Eve set foot in Harran after they were expelled from the Garden of Eden! So you see, my dear Dreamers, that the Moon has not been exclusively female!"

After the laughter settled some, the Seer continued walking with her carved scepter that had a large Moonstone set on the top. This could be any century from long ago or the future. There was a sense of the cycles of time without time when she was in charge.

"From the Greek myths, we have several Moon Goddesses. The first one I will speak about is the 'Goddess Selene.' She is associated with the Full Moon, and she rules the heavens. We honor her tonight!

"Selene is the Titan goddess of the moon and daughter of the Titians, 'Hyperion' and 'Theia.' In Roman myth, the moon goddess is called 'Luna,' which is Latin for 'Moon.' Selene played a large role in the raising of her pantheon. The most likely meaning for the name 'Selene' is connected to the word 'Selas,' meaning 'Light.' The name Selene is the root of 'senenology,' which is the study of the geology of the moon. 'Heilos,' the Sun, is Selene's brother. After Heilos finishes his journey across the sky, Selene, freshly washed in the waters of 'Earth-circling Ocean,' begins her journey as night falls upon the Earth. The Earth then becomes lit from the radiance of her immortal head and golden crown!

"Another Roman goddess was 'Goddess Diana.' She was goddess of the hunt but also the moon. Diana was daughter of Jupiter and Latona. Her Greek counterpart was named 'Goddess Artemis.' She rules Earth and was referred to as 'Goddess of the Light' and was associated with the 'Waning Moon.' It was her duty to illuminate the darkness.

"The Greek 'Moon Goddess Hecate' rules the underworld, is associated with 'Persephone,' and is associated with the 'New Moon,' the dark of the moon. Some say, 'The Moon belongs to Hecate.' She is the daughter of 'Asteria,' the Titian goddess of the star. In her role of 'Queen of the Night,' she was both honored and feared. Hecate was usually accompanied by an 'Owl,' a symbol of wisdom, and often depicted with her 'Sacred Dogs.' Some images depict her as a beautiful woman with three heads. She had the ability to see into several directions at once: past, present, and future. 'Hecate's name means 'far-darter' and 'bright and radiant.' She was called 'Goddess of the Crossroads.' 'Hecate' is the goddess of the witches. It is said that 'her powerful witches may be either hostile or helpful on our quests'!

"Well, I suppose that depends on what it is we are questing!" quickly cautioned the Moon Seer.

"Aglaia was the ancient name of the Hebrew 'Moon Goddess.' 'Agla,' the Hebrew word, is one of the 'Secret Names of God' and is much used in Hebrew magic; it means, specifically, 'Moonlight'!

"The 'Moon Goddess' in pre-Islamic Arabia was represented by a 'moon emblem' for the entire country; even in current times there is a 'lunar crescent' on Islamic flags. Originally this 'Moon Goddess' was called 'Manat,' and she was considered the 'Old-Moon-Mother of Mecca.' She once ruled the fates of all her sons, who called her 'Al-Lat, the Goddess.' Now she has been 'masculinized' into 'Allah,' who forbids women to enter the shrines that were once founded by the 'Priestesses of the Moon'!"

The Dreamers all whispered at these revelations, wondering how it could be.

"The Egyptian hieroglyph 'Mena' means 'Breast and Moon.' An Egyptian belief says from the breasts of the 'Moon Goddess' flowed the 'Milky Way' and all the stars. In Egypt once a year, a sow was sacrificed to the Moon and Isis. The sow was thought to be a primordial keeper of time, and so was sacrificed to mark the time. The Egyptians also believed the inundations of the river Nile to result from the 'Tears of the Moon Goddess,' which, falling into the river, swelled its flow. In some tarot images, these 'tears' are seen as dropping from the lunar face!

"The metal 'Silver' is related to the 'Moon' and is regarded as the moon's metal. There are medieval superstitions that say, 'A woman should not pray to the male god for any special favor, as she would not likely receive it from that source. She should pray to her own deity, 'The Moon,' by means of a piece of silver.'

"From the Middle Ages in Christian Europe, there are accounts in folklore of women who prayed for favors not to the Christian God but to their deity the 'Moon Mother' and swore oaths to her. They baked cakes for the 'Queen of Heaven,' the moon, called 'moon cakes'! In French they were called 'croissants' or 'crescents'—still popular today!—and were baked for their lunar holidays. Today modern 'birthday cakes' are descended from the Greek custom of honoring the monthly birthday of the 'Goddess Artemis' with lighted 'Full-Moon-Cakes!' The ancient Greek Mother 'Europa,' well-known mother of continental Europe, actually means 'Full Moon'-'Europe'!"

The Moon Seer paused and smoothed her dress. Finding a stool that had been placed in front of the 'Moon Painting,' she sat down gracefully. She had this to say: "Now we travel to the other side of the globe to Mesoamerica! It is here that we find the 'Maya Moon Goddess.' Traditional Mayans of Mesoamerica, from circa 2000 BC to 250 AD, believed the moon to be female. Although there were some who believed in a 'Male Moon God,' this was not prevalent. In the Moon's female form, it was believed that the Moon's phases were accordingly conceived as the stages of a woman's life. She is naturally associated with sexuality, procreation, fertility, and growth. Everywhere in Mesoamerica she is associated with the element of water, wells, rainfall, and the rainy season. In addition the 'Maya Moon Goddess' represents a moon of illusion of duality. 'Maya' is said to have two functions: 'avarana'-'covering' and 'vikshepa'-'throwing out.' One hides reality, and the second deceives us into believing that our fulfillment lies without. This type of thought may present the moon with a source of fear. Primarily the Moon card in our work helps us to reveal and then to pull in and bring change."

Now the Ancient One of the Moon was walking about in the circle of Dreamers, waving her moonstone scepter, catching the moonbeams as she glided around us. She would be fairy-like and then solemn from one facial expression to the next, a master of the art of change. "Remember, she said, "night is only the other half of day, and to some it may feel awful, but it fills the soul with wonder. It is not fearful, and we can learn to treasure the darkness the night skies provide. Without night there would be no sweet sleeping or dreaming!

"Let's continue," said the Seer. "The souls of the dead are said to reside on the 'Moon,' and the same souls are said to descend from the moon to take on new incarnations. Therefore it is said that the 'Moon' rules the astral plane of ghosts, spirits, and dreams! There is a folktale that says, 'The Moon collects the neglected dreams and memories that have escaped from people while they sleep, at dawn they are returned to the Earth as dew!' I really like that one!" said the Moon Seer.

"In our work here at the Nemeton, in these beautiful groves of old, we are on a spiritual journey. When we reach the path of Trump XVIII, we realize many things. The tests have been hard, but we have kept going. Working this path, we see we can truly encompass intuition and psychic abilities. The Moon reminds us to dream our dreams! She can teach us to release and then to rebirth. It is here that we learn to contain our own source of light. When the cycle is in the 'New,' we use that light to plant our seeds and dreams! The Moon is seductive, and some say she represents illusions because her light is only the Sun's refection; to those I say it may be that the positive and negative factors need recalibrating, as we can not have light without dark; we always need to look into the mirror, do we not? Please know the Moon's cycles and call on her to plant you gardens. Follow her phases as you undertake any magical workings. Let her be your gateway to your fantasies, the mysteries, and dreams!

The 'Moon' is a symbol of all that is psychic. Learn to use your talents; have fun with that. Most magicians use the energies of the 'Moon' in their work. Do remember that in a tarot card reading, the 'Moon' showing itself may suggest it is a time to do some magical work!

"Ah! My dear Moon Dreamers, it has been a grand night under the light of the 'Queen of Heaven, the Moon'! I travel, as you know, by moonlight, and the hours have passed. But before I move to my next phase, I would like to offer you some moonbeams! I have a silver chest here next to this marvelous painting, and it is filled with moonbeams for each of you!"

The Seer motioned to me to help her with the chest, which I was happy to do. The entire group was up and walking and excited to see what was in the silver chest! The Full Moon had moved perceptibly in the sky since the start of the evening. I was sorry to see the night coming to a close! We had the cover of the chest open now as everyone stood quietly and breathless.

I was standing close to the Moon Seer. Nudging me lightly, she said, "Dear Moon Child"—she meant me—"please reach in and make your selection!"

I did as she asked; the silver trunk was sparkling with moonbeams of actual Moonstone Crystals! I pulled out one that felt special. Then I said to the entire Dream circle, "I thank you so much, dear 'Moon Seer.' to me you are my 'Grandmother Moon'! Hey, I do think we all need to thank this Ancient One, The Moon Seer! Don't you?"

The entire crowd was clapping loudly and saying, "Thank you, dear Seer" and "Thank you, Grandmother Moon!" Each Dreamer, full of love and smiles, in turn selected a Moonstone Crystal. I turned to see the Moon Seer smiling, and there were definitely 'Tears of the Moon' falling from her sparking eyes! I reached over and gave her a kiss on the cheek; she hugged and kissed me back.

Then she said, "It has been a wonderful night!"

I agreed with her, nodding my head, saying, "It is all because of you and how much you give us all!"

Smiling, she looked at the Dreamers on the beach, all having a great time, checking out their moonbeam crystals. I could see the mood had been set and the Dreamers intended to keep it going awhile. Turning with a quizzical smile, the Seer said, "Walk with me awhile, child!"

I answered, "I would like nothing better!" We moved off down to the edge of the sea; the Seer's white wolf joined us. We were barefoot, enjoying the salty waves rolling endlessly across the sand.

We could hear some music now and a song: "Dance! Dance! Dance! By the light of the Moon. Prance! Prance! Prance! In the light of the Moon. It will soon be Sun-day, when no fairies can play! Dance…"

"Oh! I do recall that one," said the Moon Seer. "Those are the words of that old, old song of childhood from the Moon Fairies!"

I laughed; we both did and continued our moonlighted walk on the beach, watching the white wolf running into the waves.

XIX

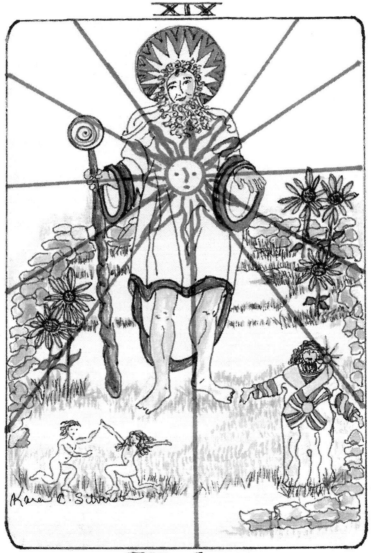

THE SUN

DREAM OF THE TRUMP SEER: THE SUN XIX

Dreamer's training is complicated, is what I was thinking about as I dressed for the day. How do I explain what it is like to do tracking or dreaming for healing another? A Dreamer has to focus on their path. Various dreaming paths are like highways, in a sense. The training is that one must be able to drive on more than one highway at once. "That's it!" I said quite out loud, looking around to see if anyone was there, knowing I had a private cabin to myself. My program for today was light. This made me happy as I walked out the door with my pack. And glad for the Sun drying the last remnants of rain.

Feeling full of vitality, I walked now along the apple orchard with the sun radiating onto my back. I was bursting with enthusiasm and started laughing and skipping along like a child. Then I stopped to look about, wondering if anyone had heard my silliness. I thought, This extraordinary sunny day must be enticing me to dream for insights on how I am feeling. I looked around for a spot in the apple orchard to hide from the world awhile. Over on the crest of the hill, I saw the beehives and a beautiful stone wall; this felt like the perfect place for the morning.

Quickly I was there, smiling at the bees that were busy drifting from flower to flower within the stone-walled garden. The stones had been fitted perfectly in dry-wall fashion. It was about three feet tall and made a nice square on three sides, with the forth side having a wooden trellis arbor full of red roses. There were sunflowers and lilies of all kinds. Yes! Throwing my head back and laughing again, I knew that this was the place to relax and contemplate. Around the outside walls of this garden, the apple orchard spread over the field. The trees were planted in groups of five: "quintessence," the essence of things as they are. So perfect. I realized it was warm, and I liked it. I sat on my blanket and looked up at the Sun, with its rays touching my back. Then I got busy snacking on hard-boiled eggs, bread, and apples I had picked. Feeling contented, I began thinking. What was the insight I wanted to know about earlier?

Deciding I wasn't sure, I laid back and listened to the bees, so busy with their collecting. I just let myself receive the energy from the Sun. Before I knew it, I had fallen into a deep Dream sleep. The following is what I recorded in my journal:

THE TEMPLE OF THE SUN

My dreamscape takes me to ancient Greece. I seem to be a tourist on a sightseeing trip. I marvel at the white ancient ruins and feel good in this sunny place. I stop and read something under a sign that says, 'The Temple of the Sun.' The sign says this:

"'Sol' is the Latin word for Sun, and 'Sol' is the star at the center of the solar system. The Earth and other planets orbit the Sun. The color of the Sun is white out in the solar system, but when viewed from Earth, the color turns yellow due to atmospheric scattering. The Sun orbits the center of the Milky Way Galaxy approximately 26,000–27,000 light years from the galactic center. The Galactic Center is the rotational center of the Milky Way Galaxy. It is in the direction of the constellation Sagittarius. The 'Milky Way' in Latin, 'Via Lactea,' is derived from the Greek, 'Galaxias.' It is a spiral galaxy, which is part of a group of galaxies in the universe. Its special significance to humanity is that it is the home of our solar system.

"The Sun plays a big part in the zodiac, which turns through the phases of the zodiacal wheel. In its passage each day into night, it represents an alchemical process. It is a transformative power, part of a psychic life force. As the solar disk appears over the horizon, we enter the 'Citrinitas,' yellowing, in which the matter is ennobled. When the Sun reaches the zenith, 'Rubedo,' reddening, is achieved, which is the highest state. Then its magic gives way its light to the Moon until the next day.

"In astrology the Sun is ruled by the number one, and the Moon is ruled by the number two. The astrological symbol for the Sun is a circle with a dot in the center. The colors for the Sun are orange, gold, yellow, and amber.

"In alchemy we have the imagery of 'The chemical wedding': The Sun-King, whose element is sulfur and gold, and The Moon-Queen, whose element is mercury and silver. 'The chemical marriage' is an important theme of alchemy, symbolizing the union of male and female."

I can't believe what I have come upon—just incredible!. Having finished reading the sign, I took a minute to look around. The Sun was bright now with quite a glare.

Looking again to the sign, which was hard to read due to the glare, I began squinting some and felt the information on the sign begin to change. I was puzzled, but then I saw that it said to please move onto the next site, "The Garden of the Rising Sun." Interesting. I thought this sounded exciting.

As I was walking in the direction of the arrows, I heard voices, music, and laughter. Curious as to where this was coming from, I found nothing. Now I smelled sweet scents of flowers, roses possibly. What was going on here? I kept walking and I began to see beautifully made stone walls with a lush garden within the square interior. Below the walled garden, I found steps leading down; it had various levels. Could this be an ancient outdoor theater garden? Is it an amphitheater? Puzzled, I turned around and found the sign that said, "The Garden of the Rising Sun." A soft breeze and the scent of the roses captured my imagination again. I heard children's laughter. I turned quickly in the direction of the garden and saw a young boy and girl leaping about the walled garden, so enjoying the sunshine and the day.

Looking again, I cried out loud, "Why, they are naked!"

As if in response, there was laughter, but not from the children. It was a robust male voice, but whose? I looked down to the small amphitheater. There was an ancient-looking man standing there in white robes, with a band of golden laurel on his head. He was motioning to someone and saying, "Please come down!" I looked around; there was no one there. I pointed to myself as if to say, me? His response was, "Yes, you, please!"

I was stunned! However, I began to walk down the grass steps of the theater, turning once or twice as I heard the children laugh. What is this place? I thought to myself. And this man. Why, he looks like something out of a Greek tragedy. Why am I here? What is "The Garden of the Rising Sun"? I knew that something had been shifting when I was reading the sign earlier, but what?

Next thing I knew, I found myself at the ground level, grassy floor of the amphitheater, and I was standing face-to-face with a *Greek*! He now was laughing at me!

"Who are you?" I said in the strongest voice I could muster.

His face was quite red from his laughing, I guessed, but it was a kind-looking face. He was straightening his white robes that were trimmed in golden threads in the design of the sun's rays. He had a big clasp over his left shoulder, also of a sun design, that gathered the folds of his robe. I cocked my head to one side, waiting for him to answer. In a deep, clear tone, he said, "Please forgive me. I could not resist the humor I saw in your surprise at the children! I am at your service for the day!" I did not know how to respond, so I just shifted my feet around some. He continued, saying, "I believe that earlier today in your world, you asked for insights about 'this extraordinary sunny day!' Please, let me introduce myself. I am Apollo." Then he held out his right hand to me in greeting.

Stunned for a second time, I was finding words hard to come by. But my hand did go out to clasp his. This is unbelievable, I was thinking to myself. Finally, out loud with our hands still joined, I said, "Apollo? Like in Greek mythology, Apollo?"

He had a roaring laughter response to my greeting, and when he calmed, he said, "Why, yes! Do you know of him?" Laughing again. I felt highly embarrassed and began to explain that I was not in the habit of meeting ancient icons from myth! Apollo said, "My dear, you are a Dreamer. Anything is possible!" Now I was the one who laughed! Tears were rolling down my cheeks. Apollo said, "Let's find a sunny place to sit for awhile, now that we have broken the ice!"

Once we were seated on one of the grassy steps, I smiled and said, "I am really happy to meet you. I suppose that I am not on an ordinary tourist trip!"

Smiling back at me, he said, "No, dear Dreamer, you are on quite a different trip here!" He was laughing some as he said that. I wondered at the meaning of that. But he went on to say in classic Greek orator mode, "Insights on an extraordinary sunny day. Apollo, your hero"—he pat himself on his chest—"resides in Greek and Roman mythology. He has been recognized as the god of Light and the Sun. His energy is about prophecy, truth, healing, music, and the arts. He is the son of Zeus and Leb. Apollo as the Sun slays the python of darkness. He has a twin sister, the chaste huntress Artemis. He was a patron of Delphi and an oracular god to the Temple of Delphi. His son was Asclepius, the god of Healing. Hermes created the musical instrument, the lyre, just for me, Apollo." Apollo had paused.

I was stunned at the beautiful information. In my usual graceful way, I blurted out, "Oh my god!"

Apollo just smiled and said, "Oh yes! Apollo was also identified with the Greek God Helios, god of the Sun. And his sister, Artemis, was equated with Selene, goddess of the Moon!".

Having collected myself somewhat, I said, "You are amazing! I just want to ask, why have you chosen me to share all this with? I am so honored."

Apollo, in a clear voice, said, "The honor is mine! Your dreamways are open, my dear, and you are a lover of the ancient ways, which need to be preserved and passed on to true Dreamers such as yourself!"

"I am so flattered," I said. "I have so many things to ask! Wait until the others hear about this! I do want to know about the children in the garden up above." I swung my arm in the direction above us.

Apollo was smiling and snickering some as he said, "Soon. You will see soon! But first there are a few things I need to add and explain. Then there is someone I would like you to meet!"

Like me to meet? There are others like him? I was thinking to myself, Who? Meanwhile Apollo had continued speaking. Quickly as I could, I tracked back to his words.

"First, The Sun, the supreme cosmic power, is the heart of the cosmos. In most traditions, the Sun is the universal Father, with the Moon as Mother. The Sun is constantly rising and setting; its rays can be vivifying or destructive. The Sun symbolizes both life and death and the renewal of life through death. In astrology the planetary sign for the Sun is a circle with a central dot. It means in astrology: life, vitality, the heart and its desires."

"I love this Sun history," I said quickly, clamoring to hear more.

Apollo smiled but did not loose track of what he wanted to say. "The day 'Sunday' has an interesting background," he went on. "Sunday, as it is known in modern times, is the seventh day of the week. In very ancient Egypt, the seventh day was Saturday, which was the day of 'Sut'-'Saturn.' An ancient culture called Sabien was the originator of Sut, and in time Sut was turned into a solar god. Then his day became *Sun-day*, the day of the Sun. A little later, the early secular church founded by the Roman emperor Constantine set aside the day of the Sun, 'Sunday,' for the worship of Jesus.

"There are ancient stories of 'The Two Waters,' which are interesting." Pausing, he looked at me as if to ask if he should continue.

I said, "Please go on!"

He continued. "The Two Waters provide the fertilization of the world. This consists of 'The Pool of the Sun' and 'The Pool of the Moon.' The double waters were said to issue from a mount called 'The Rock of the Horizons.' This rock marked the first of the Solstices and later the Equinoxes. 'Shu,' Mars, was the god of Solstices. He was the Smiter or Divider of the Heavens. The ancients believed this is how the two great planets were arranged in the Heavens. The very roots of our religions are found in the Luminaries and in the Stars. It has been said that the wisdom that rules over all comes from the 'Hidden Sun,' which is a 'Spiritual Sun' as an immense super-solar force. To understand the roles of the Sun and the Moon, think of it this way: the Moon should be considered the background of life and the Sun the germinating factor.

"In *The Divine Pymander of Hermes*, we are told that, 'If we would see God we must consider and understand the Sun, consider the course of the Moon, and consider the order of the Stars'!"

Apollo had been walking back and forth in front of me as he spoke these last words. He was a gifted orator, and I was truly mesmerized as he spoke. Sitting there on the edge of my seat, I wondered what other amazing things I would learn about. So when there was silence, I felt disoriented.

Apollo was looking up at the Sun, just staring, possibly meditating, I thought. As he looked back at me, he said, "Noon. Yes, it is noon, and our friend should be here soon. Oh! Let me just add this, the Central Spiritual Sun and its manifestations of Light appear much greater at certain periods of world change. This change is upon us now. May the soul of man be reawakened through this knowledge, issuing from the planets, stars, and astrology. May man be reawakened to the Golden Age of Mystical Knowledge in our time."

The Sun God Apollo reached his hand over to me and pulled me up from where I had been sitting. "Come!" he said. "There is someone who wants to meet you!"

I got up somewhat reluctantly and told Apollo, "I could sit and listen to you all day. It is wonderful, the knowledge you are relaying to me!"

"Yes!" he answered. "And you are a fine Dreamer Apprentice!"

We had reached the top of the amphitheater and were almost to the walled stone garden. I began to hear laughter again; the Sun felt so good on my back. I saw the little children running and playing and, yes, still naked! But there was someone else also in the garden. A man, a considerably large man, who had his back to us, but he was making the children laugh. As we got closer, I could see he was juggling what looked like stars, over the heads of the children. He was clothed in a yellow robe that draped clear to the ground. The robe was embroidered with a design of an orange setting Sun, with gold metallic threads woven through it. Very beautiful. I thought quietly, Who is this? Apollo and I were now within the stone walled garden; the scent of the rose was all about. The sunflowers were heavy with their seeds, drooping their faces with the weight. I walked carefully past the white lilies, not wanting to disturb them.

Then the man in the yellow Sun robe turned and said, "At last we meet!" He was looking straight at me. He walked the short distance across the grass of the garden, while the children ran off in another direction. Not sure what to say, I looked quickly at Apollo.

Apollo stepped up now and said, "Dear Dreamer, I would like you to meet The Trump Seer, the Sun." The Sun Seer stepped forward and took my left hand, kissing my hand and my sapphire ring. He said he was delighted to know me. All the while I felt such warmth and love radiating out from his being; I became slightly overwhelmed, even dizzy. Then he patted my hand a moment, saying, "Take all the time you need, my dear. Sometimes it is hard on humans when their 'Light' is activated to another level as they interact with me. Do not worry; you will take it in easily."

"Wow!" I said. "I guess I was not expecting that. I am, however, honored to meet you, dear Sun Seer."

Apollo was laughing, "Remember what I told you earlier? You are a Dreamer; anything is possible!"

I laughed back at that, looking from one amazing being to the other. The Sun Seer's yellow robe had a different sun designs on the front. It was in orange tones that turned into to pink hues with magenta accents, all threaded with golden metallic threads. The design was of the rising sun. So incredible!

As I looked up, he greeted me once more, saying, "Welcome to my Garden of the Rising Sun." There was a beautiful smile on his smooth, round face. How old must he be? I was thinking, Beyond all time as I know it! We all walked over to an arbor that was laden with red roses, scented red roses. How wonderful.

Apollo and The Sun Seer were talking and laughing. Old friends, I was sure. Apollo turned and said to me, "It has been a pleasure for me to know you! I must be off now. The Sun Seer will see to your every need, sharing his wisdom with you. As I told him, your dreamways were open!"

Surprised, I said, "Oh, Apollo, I wish you would stay."

Answering quickly, he said, "Alas, I cannot, little Dreamer. But call on me at any time. My dreaming threads are open to you."

I ran over to give him a big hug. "How can I ever thank you for all that you have done on this extraordinary sunny day?!"

He answered by saying, "Keep the stories alive; keep the Dreaming strong!" And with that, he ran back down the hill.

I turned around to find The Sun Seer standing close by with open arms. Realizing the tears were brimming in my eyes, I forced a smile.

He gave me a hug, saying in a musical tone, "There, there, child. You will meet him again."

I answered somewhat shyly, "I know."

The Sun Seer continued. "Well then, on our journey we finally arrive at the 'Garden of the Rising Sun.' Let me tell you about this magical place." My ears began to perk up, and he went on. "This garden sanctuary is protected by Apollo. It is here with our consciousness that we receive illumination." The Seer was pointing now to the rising Sun on his robe, saying, "This Rising Sun represents the consciousness reborn and the dawn of a new world. The Sun, in case you did not know, is the source of all life to the world!"

He was looking at me intently. I answered by saying, "Illumination! I need a lot of that!"

The Seer smiled and went on. "Let me tell you the story of a traveler that I have known over time. This traveler awakens at dawn to find that he is not where he thought. He may be in his present lifetime, and there have been disappointments and hard lessons. As he walks along the 'river of his life,' he is comforted to discover a serene garden. A walled garden, with many flowers. The Sun is bright overhead. He hears child's laughter. A joyful child appears and takes the traveler by the hand to view extraordinary things: flowers, grass, seeds, insects. The traveler, being with the child, realizes that here under the Sun, he feels simply and purely happy. The child asks him many questions, plays games and songs. Finally the traveler asks the child, "Who are you?" The child says quite simply, "Why, I am you! The new you!" The traveler realizes that the garden, the Sun, and the child all exist within him. And that he has just met his own 'Inner Light'!"

Standing up quickly, I exclaimed, "Oh, dear Seer! This is just how I felt as I started my day, walking through the apple orchard to the little garden. This is amazing!"

He was laughing now in response, shaking as he did with laughter and radiating love and warmth all at the same time. "Well then, where was I?" said the Seer. "The Sun makes one aware of spiritual realizations. All things are illuminated with the Sun in your garden. Conscious and subconscious are brought into synch. Here we find love, wisdom, and spiritual transformation."

"Yes!" I said, "it is beginning to make sense. But the children…why naked?"

The Sun Seer smiled and said in a joyful tone, "I was waiting for that! These are the 'Children of the Sun' and represent spontaneous creativity and complete innocence of the new conscious mind. They are our illuminated masters, natural and pure, dancing the dance of life. They are the fraternal twins who harmonize the opposites through their sacred union. They are the Logos and Eros reborn. Though the garden seems to be a friendly place, it also has its trial. For the Sun may also scorch as well as comfort us, and excessiveness can turn anything into lifelessness. So as in all things, there must be balance. The children must be made aware that the stone walls are their boundaries and are the visible material world. The children are the positive and negative elements that have awoken to spirit and have moved from the material world to the divine world. The Sun has provided the renewal of their bodies."

I shook my head in his moment of silence, knowing that I had much to assimilate now.

The Seer continued. "In the Qabalah the nineteenth Trump known as 'The Sun XIX' is path number-thirty on The Tree of Life. The Sun is 'Lord of the Fire of the World.' This pathway on the Sephirah travels to 'Hod,' majesty, splendor, glory. 'Hod' is where form is given. It is supported by the Archangel Michael and is said to be the sphere in which the magician mostly works. The magician in his work may grasp a certain type of energy that he wants to use. But it doesn't actually have a physical form. So he will find an object and then transfer the energy into that. This symbol-object becomes something that can be used in the future for ceremonies and the like."

"Wonderful," I said. "So helpful to the work of a Dreamer!"

"I figured you would like that aspect," answered the Seer.

"Back to the Qabalah for a moment. The Fire in the Sun is referred to as 'Divine Reason.' The Sun shining without an end causes life to wither and die. So its pendulum swings back and forth: Day into Night and back again. So must there be with man; it is balance it is 'Divine Reason.' This is the beginning of The Great Hermetic Ray, the path of wisdom."

The Seer went on with the lessons. He too was an amazing orator. He allowed me to relax and open my heart. "To Christians," he said, "the Sun is the 'God the Father,' ruler and sustainer of the universe, radiating light and love. The Sun is the abode of Archangel Michael. For the Egyptians, the rising Sun is 'Horus,' with 'Ra' as the zenith and 'Osiris' as the setting Sun. The right eye is the Sun and the left eye is the Moon. In Egyptian myth, the Goddess 'Hathor' gave birth to the Sun. To perform this feat, she took the form of a Nile goose. The Sun god became the egg of the goose, appearing from the branches of the sycamore tree, which is the Goddess Hathor's sacred tree. In Scandinavia, the eye of the god 'Odin/Woden' is the all-seeing eye. Here the Sun is depicted as the sun-snake."

"Oh my gosh!" I said.

The Seer just kept going. "India has the story of 'Garuda,' the golden-winged Sun bird. He represents the sunny, hot, dry season. Garuda is always in perpetual conflict with the serpents. From Greek mythology, we learn about eagles who are associated with the Sun, as they are in many other cultures. But now I will tell you about the Greek hero 'Prometheus.' His name means 'forethought.' He is a 'Titan' known for his intelligence. He stole fire from the god Zeus and gave it to mortals for their use. Zeus then punished him for his crime by having him bound to a rock. Then every day the eagle would come and eat out his liver, only to have it grow back to be eaten again the next day."

Jumping up from the stone bench, I said, "Get out of here! That is awful!"

"I know, I know," said the Sun Seer. "Now you are getting an idea of all the stories I have to live with." He thought that quite funny and carried on a bit before continuing with his sun tales.

"Much of the world's stories about the Sun associate the Sun energy with the masculine energy. Now I would like to tell you about some cultures that associate the Sun with female energy."

I responded with, "I had no idea that the Sun could be feminine. You see how programmed we can become."

The Sun Seer shook his head and went on. "The Arunta people who live in central Australia, west of Queensland, have a story of a Goddess called 'Arunta Sun Woman.' Her story confronts the erroneous stereotype of the Sun as a universally male image. There are other similar stories: The Sun Sister of the Inuit, the Allat peoples of Arabia, the Story of Arinna in Anatolia. Japan has the story of the Sun Goddess Amaterasu, a Shinto deity. Her name means, 'that which illuminates heaven.'"

I had become teary eyed while the Seer was doing his Sun telling. I realized how much I needed to learn in order to have the right Dream stories when doing my Dream healing work. The Sun Seer saw this and said, "Do not be so hard on yourself, Dreamer. You know more than you think." I blinked my eyes some and felt heat from his presence.

"Let me say now, The Sun Trump card XIX is a positive card. Remember, after the night comes the light. There is glory, gain, triumph, pleasure, truth, success, and many other things to be had. This card can help with discoveries made fully conscious and wide awake. It is a card of intellect and clarity of mind. The Sun also suggests happiness: in love, marriage, and life in general. There is clarity of vision and artistic flair with this energy. It also signifies commitment. Oh! Also in regard to the children and the child-like essence of this card, you might inform a querent that there may be a most welcome babe on the way. The Sun Trump is simply one of the luckiest cards in the tarot deck!"

The Seer had been pacing as he spoke; now he stopped directly in front of me with his arms held out to the sides. This allowed me to see his robes with the embroidered sun design very clearly. Beautiful, just beautiful.

I stood up and said, "Bravo! Bravo! I do so love the Sun and especially so, as I have come to know you, dear Sun Seer."

The Sun Seer made a grand bow to me and to all in the garden; it was just amazing. Then he put his arm over my shoulder and said, "Let's take a close look to what is here in this garden!" As we walked, he spoke of this: "The energy of the Sun has the power to oppose or neutralize negative attitudes, including fear. Always keep that knowledge close; you never know when you may need to call upon me for that! The Sun is faith, not just hope."

I looked back up at this huge man with the round face and happy smile and said, "I thank you."

And with that his face turned bright red! "Oh, dear Dreamer, I do think the Sun is getting ready to set. My colors are changing!" He was standing between two huge sunflowers that were dwarfed next to him. I gave him a big hug and a kiss, and his face colored to deeper oranges and reds. Before I could blink or ask anything, he simply smiled and then set beyond the hills!

What had just happened? "Oh my Goddess. I need to thank him again!" I said with much confusion. I felt a chill and turned to look around for my blanket.

Next thing I knew, I was rubbing my eyes sitting on my blanket in the walled garden with the roses and the apple orchard beyond. Again I felt a chill. The Sun was setting now. No wonder, I thought. The Sun! Was that a dream? Where am I? Have I been here all day? I got up quickly and gathered my things; I need to move. Was I in Greece? And Apollo?

I definitely need to journal all this, but first I needed to do some Lightning Dream Work! Then I got going down the path to the main lodge. I was certain to find a Dreamer there to share with. As I walked, I recalled that I had started out my Dream as a tourist on a trip in Greece! What a trip!

JUDGEMENT

DREAM OF THE TRUMP SEER: JUDGMENT XX

I sat on the grass of the hillside, enjoying the between times, the time of day when the sun is setting and the moon is rising, an opposition in the cosmos. From my vantage point, I had a most incredible view of these two objects. The water of the ocean below picking up the sun's pink and purple reflecting rays made all feel right with the world.

I put my journal down and stretched out myself on the still warm grass. The clouds above were rolling about in whimsical ways; it was fun reading them. Sometimes I could see animals, sometimes faces or tree shapes. Feeling the wind was cleansing, I wanted to stay awhile and let some of the day's events release. I had been doing past life work, and knew I had many things to integrate.

Daydreaming on the hillside, I recalled what one of the Keepers had said during the class earlier in the day. "With this training, like a cosmic mirror, the memory of the soul will come alive!" Other Dreamers and I were training to journey through the flame of a fire. Once we had protection set and a clear intention of what we wanted to 'Dream Journey' for, it was a very exciting afternoon.

My dreaming went like this: I am with the guardian guide I had chosen to work with, Hermes, the Greek god of travelers and boundaries. He is also a guide for souls in the other-worlds. We enter a theater where there are seats arranged for us; there is a purplish glow all about. I realize this is the Violet Flame. It is growing strong and bright. As I focus with this, I look at Hermes; we both feel safe and secure. After a time, I notice a large screen. Scenes of my life begin to flicker on this screen. In my intention for this dreaming, I had asked for three past lives that would be helpful to me in waking reality now. I was very excited to see what would be presented. It was not long before the figures came into view. I saw some of the Keepers from my present Dream work begin to move across this movie screen; I knew many of them. Now I had a view of an ancient Greek temple.

Hermes nudged me and said, "Recognize anyone?"

Looking again, I saw a simple girl with a basket entering the temple. I knew her to be myself! I reached over to let Hermes know, "It is me!" He was smiling.

Suddenly there was noise, or music? I came right out of this past life! Quickly, I grounded myself and closed the Dreaming portal. I knew there was something on this plane to pay attention too. More music. Why this sounds like a trumpet! I said to myself, What is going on? Still partly in my past life dream, I called out to Hermes, "Are you there? Hermes are you still around?"

Standing up, I looked up to the skies; the clouds were swirling again. I definitely heard the sound of a trumpet!

Then through the mist came Hermes, saying, "I am still here, Child! It seems you will need me to stay awhile."

"Well, yes! Of course you will stay. How else will I figure out what is going on here!" I answered him in a curt voice.

"No need to get worked up, dear! You have gotten 'The Call'!" He had answered me in a laughing voice, and his words made no sense at all.

"The Call! What on Earth are you talking about? I really need some grounded Earth information now!" I said. Just then we heard the trumpet sound again. I put my hands over my ears and screamed, "Hermes!"

I had closed my eyes. When it felt OK and quiet, I opened them slightly. There was a violet haze blazing from the sky, as the sun was now setting. It was beautiful, but I felt nervous. I cried out in a soft voice, "Hermes! Are you still here?" Now I heard other voices. I turned to see that Hermes was here but engaged in conversation with…with an angel? One that held a trumpet! What is this all about? And what had Hermes meant when he said I had gotten 'The Call'? More curious than afraid or nervous, I decided to check this out. I marched myself over to where they stood.

Just then someone else appeared, and before I could speak, they did. "That was a marvelous introduction, my man, Hermes! And the Angel was great on the trumpet. I am assuming that you are the Dreamer who has gotten 'The Call'!" This man had turned to me and spoke directly into my soul, or so it felt.

Not knowing what they were talking about, I cracked a small half smile and turned to Hermes, pleading with my eyes for help.

Thank Goddess! He took the floor, saying, "Dear 'Trump Seer Judgment,' allow me to introduce our promising 'Dreamer' who I am sure is honored to be learning the ways of Judgment from one of our most prominent Seers. I am afraid that from her response to the sound of the trumpet, she has still to be enlightened about 'The Call'!"

The Judgment Seer laughed a little but responded with, "I quite understand. She will learn by what she will experience here tonight. The Dreamers have gathered a bit higher on the hill. Shall we join them?"

My mouth had been open to speak several times. Nothing, however, was spoken! Finally as we walked the hill, I pulled Hermes's arm and said, "You both were speaking as if I weren't even here! Please! Tell me, what have I been 'Called' for?"

Laughing at this, Hermes took my arm in his and said, "The Call, the summons which can not be ignored!"

I stopped in my tracks and said, "Judgment, *oh my*! I am being called to death! That's it!"

Again laughter. Then Hermes said, "No, my dear, you will not be dying this evening! This summons teaches us about changes and how things are resurrected. It is more of a 'Call for Magic.'"

I released my grip on his arm and sighed a little, saying, "Am I then to play the role of the 'One Called' for the 'Judgment Seer'?"

"Bravo!" answered Hermes. "Now we had better catch up to the group and be ready to participate."

I smiled some and did some deep breathing. At least I would not die tonight, I thought to myself and almost said that out loud. But we were just in time for the opening circle, so I laughed at myself and my own fear, quietly!

The opening was very beautiful for "An Evening With Judgment," as the event had been named. The Judgment Seer was showing the Dreamer group an assortment of Judgment Trump cards, which had been painted by a variety of artists. They were arranged on a small table near the central altar. He asked us to look them over and notice the common thread of the cast of characters.

In a booming voice, the Judgment Seer said, "Dreamers, call out what these characters are!" He then tapped me on the arm, handed me a tablet, and said to make notes. I did as well as I could. Soon the answers were trailing off. The Seer said to me, "Let's hear that list, Dreamer."

I walked to the middle of the group and began. "Well, we have the Angel, the wings of the angels, the mountains, and clouds. Of course there are crypts, the trumpet, the banner or the red cross, the people in the crypts, and some cards show water or trees. Some show a wise old king. I think that these are the most common images."

The Judgment Seer smiled at me and I handed him my list. He looked at it briefly, saying, "Well done!"

The Seer held up his arms, the folds of his emerald-green, silk robes were gracefully draped about him; the golden threads of the embroidered astrology symbols glittered as he moved. Now he was softly drumming, and then he said, "Dreamers, in just a while, we will enact the Arcanum Number Twenty, and I would like you to think about which character you would like to play!" He stroked his long, silver-gray bread as he spoke.

"But, for now I will present the history behind myself, The Judgment XX Trump." He bowed slightly to the applause, holding onto the simple gold crown that was upon his head. The skies above him were swirling with white clouds and shafts of violet light from the last of the setting sun. Then he set down his drum upon the altar. Everyone had seated themselves on cushions. The candles and braziers had been lit.

I could feel the breeze upon my arms and pulled my shawl closer. I wondered where Hermes had gone. I knew he was here; I could feel him. And I knew he would be a big part in what was being presented tonight. I reminded myself to set another time with him to continue my past life work that had been interrupted in Greece. Quiet, I said to myself. The Seer is ready!

"Judgment! Well, the earliest records of this tarot trump were from 'Sermones de ludo cum aliis,' circa 1500; Bertoni, circa 1550; and Garzoni, circa 1585. At that time this trump was called 'Lo Angelo' or 'L'Agnolo,' meaning 'The Angel' rather than Judgment. As we can see in these various cards' images, the angels are prevalent. In many interpretations of the twentieth trump, the angel is identified with the 'Archangel Michael' who in Christian traditions blows the trumpet to call the souls home on Judgment Day. The 'Angel' is the divine messenger. In some Christian traditions, the angel is thought to be the 'Angel Gabriel,' who first appears in the Book of Daniel in the Hebrew Bible as a messenger from God. In some traditions he is regarded as one of the Archangels or as the 'Angel of Death.'" The Seer paused at this time, looking about the group, reading their reactions.

For myself, I felt nervousness and wondered, What am I afraid of? Then I shook this away as the Seer continued.

"The Archangel Michael, Saint Michael, is considered in many Christian circles as the 'patron saint of the warrior.' To the Hebrews he is described as the 'Prince of Light,' one of the leading forces of God against darkness and evil. Saint Michael is also associated with the planet 'Mercury,' the messenger. In the religion of the Seventh-Day Adventists and the Jehovah's Witnesses, both believe that the Archangel Michael and Jesus are the same being. Some say that the XX Trump of Judgment is modeled after the Christian Resurrection before the 'Last Judgment.' These believers say, 'The final Judgment Day, Day of the Lord,' will take place from God after the resurrection of the dead and the Second Coming. Some relate the Judgment Trump to the Apocalypse, from the Book of Revelations, the last book of the New Testament Bible, attributed to Saint John. This book records a vision of the events that herald the end of the world!" The Seer paused and said, "Wow! Is there any account of what happens next?" He held up his hands to say no comments. Quietly the Dreamers had concern.

"I will now tell you about a Greek myth and the 'archetypal angelos' of the 'God Hermes.' In Greek mythology 'The Olympian God Hermes' is the messenger of the gods. He is considered the god of flight and the god of boundaries. He is the son of Zeus and Maia. The equivalent Roman god is 'Mercury.' Myth tells us that Hermes knew the art of interpreting hidden meanings, and he delivered messages from Olympus to the mortal world. He is said to have invented 'Fire,' a parallel of the Titian Prometheus. He also invented the syrinx and the lyre. In our study of the Arcanum, Hermes is often correlated with the 'Magician Trump' because of his ability of transformation. This same ability applies with the 'Judgment Trump.' As we will learn in our lessons here, from images on a sixth century BCE urn, we see Hermes using his wand to raise a soul, to lead it to its final destination!"

The Seer had paused. I noticed the Dreamers were now very engrossed in the story telling. I was especially happy to learn more about Hermes.

"Hermes is the Emissary of Hades, who touches the eyes of the dead with his golden wand and then guides their souls to the underworld. Hermes, along with Hades, Persephone, Hecate, and Thanatos, were the only gods who could enter and leave the underworld without hindrance."

"Hermes has been referred to as 'Psychopompos,' which is Greek for 'Guide of Souls.' This can also be an angel or deity, and their responsibility is to escort newly deceased souls to the afterlife. Their role is not to judge the deceased but simply to provide safe passage. In many cultures the 'Shaman' also fulfills the role of 'psychopom.' In psychological terms he awakens us to a new life on Earth, achieved through new consciousness. Now our dear Hermes not only leads souls to the underworld, he also shows them the way back! So he is also the Redeemer, rescuing souls from death, and the Deliver, who raises the dead from the underworld. I would say this is a good man to know!"

The Trump Seer Judgment seemed very pleased by this last comment, and the Dreamers were all chuckling a little. The Seer continued: "Now we know that Hermes is a redeemer, but let us make this clear: this redemption is getting back something of one's own. In this case of Judgment, what we are getting back is the 'integrated self'...that which is most truly ours. The myths of Hermes reveal his ingenuity, creativity, mental and physical quickness, as well as his friendly nature.

"The 'Egyptian God Thoth' is equated to Hermes. Hermes-Thoth-Trimegistus, the 'Times Three Hermes,' was the master of all arts and sciences, 'Ruler of the Three Worlds,' 'Scribe of the gods,' and 'Keeper of the Books of Life.' Hermes is also considered the 'Trickster,' representing the duality of our reality. His lessons are learned by tricking you! He is also linked with the magician Merlin. In this case, lessons are taught by magic to help you see through the illusion of both Time and Emotion!"

With his dark, unreadable eyes, The Judgment Seer scanned the faces of the Dreamers, checking their energies. He seemed pleased. "Hermes was known as the 'Father of Alchemy.' When the God Zeus, his father, appointed Hermes the 'Divine Herald,' he awarded him a 'Copper Helmet' with two small wings and a pair of 'Winged Sandals' that could carry him across water as well as land. Of course we know that these 'Winged Sandals' were special and allowed him to fly between the mortal and immortal worlds!"

The Dreamers were excited by this and called out, "Yea, Hermes!"

Everyone settled and the Seer said, "I want to mention that Hermes is also the god of travelers, orators, literature, and of poets! His symbols—"

Suddenly there was commotion from behind our Judgment Seer and laughter from the Dreamer audience. Then with a gust of wind and mist, my dear guide Hermes stepped through the worlds and made himself known to us! Everyone cheered!

The Judgment Seer, half laughing himself, said, "And what is it you are doing?"

Hermes had been parading up and down, showing us all his Winged Helmet, putting it on and taking it off for us to admire! "Well," said Hermes, "I thought some modeling might be in order. It is always nice to see things firsthand, would you not agree?" As he did this, he was lifting his feet for everyone to see his Winged Sandals. The Dreamers became hysterical with laughter after that!

The Judgment Seer, who could barely contain himself, now said to us all, "Dreamers, I give you Hermes! Please do show us your 'Caduceus, the Rod of Hermes,' while you are at it!"

Everyone was standing and clapping; it was wonderful. I thought to myself, He sure knows how to lighten the mood, given the serious content of "An Evening With Judgment."

Now the Seer stood next to Hermes with his hand on his shoulder and said, "I would like to mention that the 'Caduceus' is what has come to be known as the staff of the physician in medicine. The wings symbolize air-transcendence and the wand is power. The two serpents are healing and poison, and illness and health. The two great opposites." Now Hermes was holding his staff, the 'Caduceus of Hermes,' and showing off the beautiful features. The Dreamers were laughing again and the Seer said, "Hermes, the floor is yours!"

Hermes said, "Thank you, my dear sir! The important thing to know here"—he pointed to the staff—"is that this winged staff with these two snakes wrapped around it was originally an astrological symbol of commerce for the 'Messenger of the Gods,' yours truly! So when it is shown and used, there is Magic to be heeded. Originally this staff had only two white ribbons around it, which wound into a figure eight; we know this as the symbol for eternity. Then in the seventh century, the caduceus became associated with medicine; based on my 'Hermetic Astrological' principles using the planets and the stars to heal the sick. This rod with the two entwined serpents suggests a DNA double helix. And it is likened to the Kundalini in yoga. So, my Dear Dreamers, this 'Rod of Hermes' is especially magical in that it is also a symbol for immortality! As you can all see, I have come on the winds of time, and I am still here on your Earth plane!"

Well, the whole group was standing in applause and joy with that! I was laughing to myself, thinking, That's my guide! I always am taken by what he manages to do for everyone who comes in contact with him. Finally the Dreamers settled.

The Judgment Seer was clapping along with everyone, saying, "We are 'Dream Walkers All.' We have much to learn and be thankful for from this 'Sage of Old'! I would like to share some of his other symbols, including the tortoise, the lyre, the rooster, and, of course, his wonderful way with those he comes in contact with!" Now Hermes had taken off his Winged Helmet and held it over his heart, bowing to the Seer and then to the Dreamers.

The Judgment Seer said, "Thank you! Thank you! One of the core elements of this Trump of Judgment is about the 'Patterns of Life.' The ripples of your actions spread across the 'Pattern' to change the weave of one's life threads; many times the Dream weaver is not even aware of what has changed. Yet the Dreamer stands in the heart of this web of their 'Pattern.' The key learning is: which way should it be woven? Should there be a missed thread or warp, the Dream weaver could fail and fall, then all could fail and fall. But do we just freeze and stop what we are meant to weave? Or do we learn to trust our intuitive judgment, knowing that we are skilled at the threads of our life? We learn that things change, even the ways of gods and heroes. Dreamers, please do know how to say: 'This is in my hands now, my decision! Mine'!"

Just then we heard the blare of a trumpet! And we were all bathed in moonlight. I looked around at the Dreamers, their bright eyes wide with disbelief! The trumpet sounded again! What was this?

The Judgment Seer held up his hands and said to us all, "The Threshold Guardians are summoning, reminding us, calling us to be the 'Watchers, the Dream Keepers,' so others may learn from us. Remember when lightning cracks, thunder blares, or the trumpet sounds and suddenly everything is disrupted, the only thing to do is to center the self and take control. Instinct kicks in, and we pay attention! The lightning may reveal something in the shadows. You have a wake-up call. The trumpet has now sounded. You have all received 'The Call'!"

Everyone now was very quiet, not knowing what to expect, including myself. The Seer had walked slowly about the group, looking into the eyes of each of us Dreamers. With his last words, "You have received The Call," he stopped directly in front of me! I was panic-stricken! He had put his hand on my shoulder. I felt a sting, my arm went numb, and the feeling traveled to my heart! I wondered, Am I to say something? I've nothing to say; my brain is numb. Am I to be called for this judgment thing? Am I to face my death? I had spun away in my inner dream world.

Slowly I could hear Hermes saying, "When the fog clears…" To myself I felt woven into a barrier. I was safe in this dream bubble! But then again I heard the voices. I knew I had to face this "Call," whatever it was.

My eyes were wide open now. I could not tell you how much time had elapsed. I could not speak' but I was aware of everything going on. The Seer was speaking; he held the cast of characters list I had written earlier. He was quickly casting the Dreamers into the scene of the Twentieth Trump Judgment! Using the most common images found on the card, one of the Dreamers had now become an 'Angel,' another 'The Trumpet,' of course! Mountains, Clouds, Trees were cast, and then there were the two Crypts! And he did not leave out the 'People-Souls' who were rising from the crypts. Everyone was in good spirits while this went on. I thought that odd, but then walking a Dreamer's life was not the usual! I laughed at my own joking.

I realized that Hermes was next to me; he gave me a clap on my back, saying, "It is time to be back in this space, Dreamer! Did you have a nice flight?"

I answered with, "Flight? Oh…My flight to my Dream world!" I began laughing and asked him, "Have I been gone long?"

"Long enough! There must be some fear needing to release. I am certain, however, you will gain a new understanding about Judgment, because your soul has agreed that you must answer 'The Call'!"

I nodded my head and said with a tiny laugh, "Maybe my soul has agreed, but this body is still having a hard time!"

He gave me a quick hug, saying, "It is part of your Dreamer Life."

I answered with, "I know, I know! What do I have to do for my part?"

Hermes said, "For now, just listen. And when the Seer asks you certain questions about being ready to answer you're calling, I will be with you should you need help!"

I felt better already! Then I looked around at the stage setup of "The Judgment Trump XX."

The trumpet sounded again, and the mists of clouds swirled. Through the clouds came an angel with beautiful wings, who landed in the middle of our Dreamers. The trumpet sounded once more.

Then "The Trumpet," a Dreamer in disguise, began to speak. "I, 'The Trumpet,' tell you that in ancient Greece the trumpet was called a 'Salpinx,' a long, straight war trumpet. It was associated with the elements of fire and water. Two primary opposites, just like that of the sun and the moon. These opposites are part of the knowledge of the 'Judgment Trump XX,' part of the makeup of the energies of this Arcanum XX. The trumpets are among the oldest musical instruments, dating back to 1500 BC. The primitive, penetrating sound of the 'Salpinx'-'The Trumpet' represents 'The Call.' The summons which can not be ignored!"

Now the Judgment Seer came forward. He said, "In the ancient Greek legend of the Trojan War, it is said that Achilles's mother, worried for his safety. So she dressed him as a girl and hid him among the women in Lukomedes palace. He was discovered by Odysseus, who sounded the 'Salpinx.' Achilles automatically grabbed weapons, since he could not ignore the summons. This was the call to leave his mother's protection and take on adult responsibilities. Such a call may come from inside or outside, but in either case it summons us to advance in our development. If we ignore this, we sink back into stagnation, and are perhaps never called again!"

The Seer continued. "Judgment and the trumpet call may also represent God's promise of Life after the Death of this Life! Some say, 'The trumpets are sent to awaken the human family that has been buried alive for centuries. 'Awake, O Sleeper!' The trumpets herald a new day for enlightenment for man and woman, a new millennium of joy and harmony. The sound of the trumpets is for 'Reveille,' not for 'Taps.' When the trumpet calls from the Archangels, you are being called to the light. Your soul is calling you to ignite your Central Sun, your Heart Center!"

All the Dreamers were making quiet comments with each other. Our gateways were opening to our soul selves. The Seer had stopped now in front of a green-eyed woman, whose stare at him was definitely not meek. He stopped smiling at her; with another glance from him, she turned away. The Seer had the ability to look right through to one's soul. He was speaking about 'High Magic,' which is 'The Great Service,' as he walked over to where I stood. Nervous, I lowered my eyes as if sleepy, but of course I was not. He was talking about the Qabalah.

"On the Tree of life, The Judgment Trump XX is path number thirty-one on the Sephiroth between 'Malhuth' and 'Hod.' Path thirty-one is called 'the path of perpetual intelligence' because this path regulates the Moon and the Sun. This path of Judgment is 'Spirit of the Primal Fire.' Fire is about the awakening of the Spiritual will in Man. This path of Judgment is esoterically associated with the 'Hearth Fire.' This is about the building of a home and the raising of a family according to spiritual principles. 'The Hearth' is 'The Altar' of family life.

"The regulating of the sun and the moon is about the supreme symbols of radiation and of receptivity. And it is also the relationship between 'the leader' and 'the led.' In esoteric traditions, man has often been guided by the 'Inner Plane Beings,' such as: Hermes, Merlin, Narda, Isis. They are invaluable. Remember to call upon these guides of wisdom. These guides can teach one about leading or when one should be led!"

The Keeper of Judgment was walking about; I knew he would soon be before me. I wanted to remember every word of these teachings. I silently filed and sorted as much as I could. I would examine things later to make sure that I understood all.

With one glance from him, I knew he would ask about my "Call"! Blushing, I turned my head. I was happy to find Hermes next to me, just as he said he would be.

The Judgment Seer was a man of tall stature. In his emerald green robes, he made an imposing statement. He walked toward me, his hands were folded within the sleeves of his robes, and I felt humbled by his presence. He was saying this: "Those who are called are not perfect. Those who hear the call are not perfect, but they are authentic, impeccable, and wise."

His eyes stared into my own. I had to work at keeping my glance steady. I could feel support from Hermes, and I held the ground.

The Seer asked me, "What is it that summons you, Dreamer?"

I answered in a voice that seemed not my own, steady and firm: "I am called to advance my spiritual development; this is my path and time. "

I detected a slight smile, but his eyes were unreadable. He continued: "Dreamer, have you a true understanding of what you are committing your Dreamer-self for? Are you divided in any way against yourself?" The Seer paused.

I took a deep breath. Somehow through Hermes's presence I knew what to say and did so in a voice as smooth as silk. "My heart is true, and I know the work I must do. I know the support of my guides in this plane and the Otherworlds. I am undivided in my commitment!" I gave a silent sigh; I kept my eyes locked with those of the Seer.

The Keeper of Judgment signaled to Hermes, who blessed me with his magical "Caduceus." Then the Judgment Seer said, "You may pass! May your awakening be true to your choosing. Be who you came to be, my child. You must step into your power!"

I looked at the Judgment Seer with tears in my eyes and said, "I thank you, and I will work to the best of my Dreamer-self. I pay honors to all who have walked this path before me. I acknowledge you as an Oracle, and may the Sun and the Moon shower you with blessings. I thank you for your help!"

The Seer and I both bowed to each other, with our eyes locked. I could feel a transfer of strength. I kept a straight face as we rose back up. My arms were folded within my shawl, and I felt renewed and proud to have answered "The Call"!

The trumpet blared again! The Dreamers clapped! There was still much to share and learn. The night was young with brilliant starshine.

The Judgment Seer was now ready to teach the additional segments on judgment. I was very happy to have completed my part; I must say I felt pleased with myself! And thanks, my dear Hermes!

"Let us speak of Awakening," said the Seer. "The Judgment card, when drawn in a spread, can be a positive or a negative influence. Sometimes the card indicates decisions which must be made and also may show which decisions will change the life patterns for the better. The 'positive-awakening' means renewal, joy in accomplishing, renewed health, and vitality. The 'Negative-loss' is guilt, fear of change, fear of ill health, and sometimes fear of death. If one refuses to make the decisions which must be done, this will cause much delay in advents. The Judgment Trump is about 'Awakening.' Whether this be a positive or a negative teaching, awaken we all must!"

Now the Judgment Seer moved to the edge of the group of Dreamers. The evening was darkening, however the fullness of the Moon provided amazing light. I wondered what would be next.

The Seer continued, "To 'The Majestic Mountains,' who hold the background! Pray tell, what might you share as a symbol on this twentieth trump?" The Seer held his arms outstretched wide as he spoke in deep, earthy tones.

"The Mountains" spoke: "We, as the symbol of the mountains, portray strength and help to reach beyond one's ordinary landscapes. We remind the diviner to reach for the heights!"

"To the Mountains on high, we thank you!" said the Judgment Seer. The Seer continued: "To 'The Clouds,' who are a part of this life on Earth! Pray tell, what might you share as a symbol on this twentieth trump?"

"As Clouds we are often painted within the scene of Judgment. Clouds reflect the moods of the sky: stormy weather clouds, whimsical sunny day clouds, dreamy clouds, sometimes mysterious or frightening clouds. These clouds may teach us to check in with our own 'Inner-Weather'!"

The Seer said, "Dear Mountains and Clouds, we thank you!"

The Seer continued, "Dear Dreamers, now I would like to hear from one of my favorite images, and that would be 'The Crypts'! Pray tell, 'Crypts,' what might you share as symbols on this trump twenty?"

"As 'The Crypts,' let it be known that I also go by the name 'Sarcophagus,' which in Greek means 'Flesh Eater.' The sarcophagus is a funeral receptacle for a corpse. The Greeks carved this sarcophagus from a special Trojan limestone, which was thought to dissolve the flesh of corpses. Therefore the 'Sarcophagus' represents the dissolution of the old life, which has been accomplished by the preceding Trumps. It is believed, esoterically, when the word 'sarcophagus' is broken down as 'S-arco-phagus,' we have in Latin 'Arco-Arca.' The word 'Arc' means in the midst of an ocean. But when we look into the word 'Arca,' we find that this is a box, including a coffin, or a coffer holding hidden treasure. From this has derived the word 'ARCANA,' meaning the secrets hidden in the 'ARCA'!

"Many myths refer to the primordial couple floating in an 'Arc' on the cosmic womb, representing the seeds of the next creation. The sarcophagus represents the bronze cauldron of rebirth, as talked of in many cultural myths."

The Dreamers and The Seer alike clapped and cheered after this accounting! The Seer said, "Yes, this is one of my favorites, still. Crypts, we thank you!" There was much laughter at that.

The Seer continued, "Earlier we had angelic information, but there is more to be said! The Angels! 'Angels' and 'Crosses,' please, pray tell, what might you add as symbols on this trump twenty?"

"As Angels, we exist in many varied images because we have the ability to carry out divine wishes, commands, and edicts. Angels can be a part of whichever god or goddess you choose. The 'Wings of the Angel of Judgment,' which are a part of me, are an effective tool to help one through the upward journey of the Spirit. Some may see this as the 'Tree of Life,' with Judgment being the Path of Fire.

"Some Angel images also show a banner or a flag with the emblem of a red cross on a white background. Most think this is 'Saint George's Cross,' originating in Genoa, Italy, prior to the year 1190. In the year 1190, it was adopted by England, as a benefit from the protection of the pirate attacks in the Mediterranean Sea. Later during the Crusades, it was adopted by English soldiers, particularly by the 'Knights Templar.' In the year 1277, the red cross became the official flag of England and Wales.

"The Cross symbol also reminds us of the Greek Goddess Hecate, who is in charge of the 'crossroads,' where all important decisions are made. Let us remember the crossing of a threshold as well and the consequence of choosing a direction at a crossroads. Another way to look at the cross symbol is about hidden truths and motives that may be uncovered by 'cross-examination.' Crosses can also be an X—which is a cross that has been turned on its side. An X marks the spot! In ancient Greece the word for 'Light' is 'Lux' and is represented by the letter X!

"Some say that the equal-sided cross is a visual reference to Mars, by way of the 'Magic Square of Mars,' which is five times five. Some tarot authorities believe the banner with the equal-sided red cross is the 'Square of Saturn' which is three times three. 'Saturn' is the Roman god of agriculture and justice. This becomes a study in itself of esoteric numerology. We, the Angels and Crosses, have spoken!"

The Seer said, "Angels and Crosses, we thank you!"

Again there was much clapping from the Dreamers. The Seer then turned his orientation to the next cast members and continued. "'Awakened Souls,' please, pray tell, what might you share as symbols on this trump twenty?"

"As 'Souls' who have now awakened, the learning of judgment becomes the awareness that there is no death, only a change of form. We call this 'Spiritual Rebirth'; we learn the unity of all things. We transcend, and judgment provides us with resurrection. The judgment path becomes a new cycle. At Trump XX we come onto our path consciously. This is the path of Fire of Light. We learn that we can become the Light; in order to ascend, one must internalize the Light. I will tell you, Dreamers, this experience is about becoming and 'Being Love.' Make your own 'Heart Light'! Ask yourself, Have I done the best I could? Am

I loving? Do you feel Light Hearted? When you follow this path, you are changed forever, 'Your Heart Is True'! We rest."

There was much applauding, and I heard whistling too! Then the Judgment Seer said, "Well done. Bravo!" He too was clapping. The Seer now turned to us all and said, "I believe our cast of Judgment has done a great job helping us all to understand the intricate parts of this trump. I honor you all! Now as a summary, I shall say these things: In the Judgment card, there is redemption in the vibration that has been set up by 'The Call' of the summoning of the trumpet. This sound resonates from deep within the our unmanifest selves, which brings with the sound a previous secret knowledge. Just as on Earth in spring the flowers are called, so too are we called to join with Spirit.

"In our everyday lives, the tombs, the crypts are also part of our 'Samskara.' A Sanskrit word that has to do with rituals consisting of 'Homa'-'fire sacrifices.' In our work we need to remember that 'Rituals' are 'Rites of Passage' and that they mark stages in our lives. From within the 'Crypts-Tombs,' we rise up and we break old patterns; we become new and we are 'Awakened'!

"Now I thank you all, Dreamers, for this 'Evening With Judgment'!"

We heard the trumpet blare, and our amazing Seer walked off onto the hillside with the starry night and the moon showing the way! I had tears in my eyes. I felt beautiful and Light Hearted! Then I felt a presence…"Hermes, it's you?" I said with joy and tears.

He answered in a clear, beautiful tone, "You have done well with your dream weaving, Dreamer. Your soul has been reawakened, and your heart is true. Step into your Power, Dreamer!"

There was quiet, and then I heard: "We will meet again in that beautiful temple in Greece!"

The lavender mist swirled, and he was gone but still in my heart, as was this eve!

THE WORLD

DREAM OF THE TRUMP SEER: THE WORLD XXI

It was decided that just before dawn would be the best time for the World Trump to be honored. The bonfires were made ready; the tables for the feasting afterward were being tended. I began to fret about this time that was chosen. I do love the morning once I get moving into the day, but the getting up part is hard for me. I mean dawn, and just before? What were the Keepers thinking? What hour are they speaking about? I had better take a deep breath. I can do this, and of course there would be music and dancing! Then the Dancer would come who was the…"Center of the World."

Some of the Ancient Ones say she is the "Keeper of the Keys." So much excitement as we bring the Arcanum together. Some of the group had coined the name for the event as "The Dawning of the World." The artist Dreamers had been busy making beautiful posters; a couple of us collected them and were now placing them around the Nemeton. We still have time before the Dawning!

In the meantime, after leaving dinner, I took a walk to unwind some. So much had happened through this segment with The Trump Seers; it felt good to walk and organize my dream thoughts and get some perspective on the teachings of the Seers. The training has been arduous; however, I would not trade this experience for anything!

The waking up for predawn Dreamer work went smoothly for me; which, of course, shows me that when I love what I am doing, nothing stands in my way! I was walking with a few Dreamers to where we would meet the "Dawn" on the Eastern Hill. We walked without flashlights, dark as it was. We had come to know these mountains of the Nemeton, and our night vision was working well. The clear night with starlight and the full moon were, of course, to our advantage.

One of the Dreamers was talking about how they had become confident of their intuition through the dream training work. He had this to say: "Signs of reliable intuition, for me, convey information neutrally, unemotionally. It feels right in your gut." He smiled at his revelations, and I told him that his point-by-point description was very helpful.

Then I said I had one thing to add from my experience. "True intuitions never put me down as a person, or put down whomever the intuition may be about. It is simply information coming to the surface." A couple of the Dreamers said they knew just what I meant.

Now we were on Eastern Hill Mountain. The entire hillside was illuminated with light! What on Earth? I thought to myself. I looked about to get a sense of where the light was coming from.

There were huge candelabras and torches set up within the central grassy area that held the altar. This of course was the stage for the event the "Dawning of the World"! Then all around the grass was a circle of trees that framed the grass center. On the trees were blue velvet drapes that had been painted with the Sun and the Moon, and various planets and star constellations. This effect created a beautiful theater. One of the painted images on the blue velvet drapes was The Milky Way galaxy, which was amazing. Within this was a rendition of the constellation of Cygnus, "The Swan"! Also sometimes referred to as the "Northern Cross," it was especially impressive, I felt. I had learned that Cygnus, the celestial swan of classical myth, is perhaps the oldest constellation in the world. And the elegance of the blue velvet background and the candelabra lighting—well, it felt as if royalty were coming. Leave it to the Dreamers to transform anything!

I was looking around in awe of the beauty, when a Dreamer came up to me, saying, "Hey, let me help you with that."

Startled some, I came back down to earth, and said, "Oh! I had forgotten what I was carrying!"

He laughed and said, "I will take at least half of these bundles. Follow me then, to the center circle."

I just nodded my head. I was carrying bundles of laurel. Yesterday I picked as much as I could, and so did the three other Dreamers I had walked here with. We had been told by the Trump Seers of both the Sun and the Moon to pick the laurel, as it would be used this morning for the World Trump Seer. The other Dreamers and I walked up the hill to where the center circle was; chairs and cushions had been arranged around the center. The grassy area below the altar was being raked carefully. Looking around, I saw other preparations going on. I noticed a small quartet of musicians: one violin, one viola, one cello, and one flute practicing; the music was familiar, maybe "Scheherazade," by Rimsky-Korsakov?

I put down the laurel along with the others; someone was scurrying over to where we stood. In a rather direct, booming voice, they said, "Of course you picked this at twelve o'clock noon, and you were careful to ask permission first, then picking only a little from each plant! I know that you did. I am just going over what I had said, and yes, I see that the grass has been raked and made ready for the wreath that will encircle our special guest. Come! We need to get on with the weaving of this wreath!" We all just looked at each other and followed the breathless speaker. This was the Trump Seer of the Moon, and we each had to move fast to keep up with her. She governs the plants on Earth and, of course, expects us to be respectful when we walk upon their sweet beauty.

The Moon Seer was saying that a little later she would tell us about the significance of the laurel that had been selected for the wreath. She was busy laying the laurel boughs around the grass, when she suddenly stopped and looked at us and said: "Ah! Dear Dreamers, you have done well. Good predawn to you all! However, the light of the cosmos has its own timing and will light this sacred circle should we be prepared or not.

"We have much to consider as we weave this wreath. Keep these things in mind as you work at the weaving. First, ground yourself in 'All that is-Gaia.' We are part of a crystalline magnetic 'Ley Lines' with Gaia. What we send out, she will give back. Be mindful of your Dreaming while you weave. Dream in balance for the mirror image of the female and the male that is within each of us.

With the weaving of the laurel, we help the crystalline grid realigned with Gaia. Breathe in your expansion of light and the love of who you are!"

The Moon Seer then stepped aside so we might do our weaving. She then said, "The hour still belongs to me in the darker half of this night to day. Now I intend to call in the feminine energies to be held within the circle of this wreath, which I will anchor into the Ley Lines of the grassy knoll of Gaia. There they will remain for the use and support of our dear 'World Trump XXI Seer.'"

We watched a moment as the Seer did her magical calls. We knew we could not let ourselves get distracted, as the wreath needed weaving. I was truly feeling inspired and humbled at the work we were achieving. We had been shown a chevron weave pattern. Now that the last section was coming together, we could see how nicely it would dovetail with the side the other Dreamers were working on. And of course it all moved in a clockwise progression. Ah! We met up and connected; the wreath was done and beautiful!

Other Dreamers had been arriving, selecting their seating areas, and admiring our handiwork. I was definitely feeling proud of the weaving I had done and took the compliments graciously. In the far background were the bonfires and the feast tables. Coming toward the center where the wreath was placed were four aisles, and I realized there were animal guardians at the ends of each of these. I thought to myself, They are guarding the Spiritual Center of the Earth, the one who embodies the wisdom, The World XXI Seer. This is an awesome realization!

There was soft drumming now; the Dreamers had settled for the opening of our circle in this incredible landscape of the Dawning of the World. I looked for a moment at the night sky and realized the same stars had been mirrored and painted onto the velvet blue drapes that surrounded us "As above, so below,' I whispered quietly to myself. All the Seers were here. The opening was beautiful, and now the Moon Seer would continue with the teachings.

"Let me introduce myself. I am known as the Moon Trump XVIII," she said with diction and grace. The Dreamers gave her a huge round of applause. "There are some who call me 'Grandmother Moon.' Yes! Yes, I know most of you well, and you have all worked hard about learning how to cycle many things. And here tonight you will learn how to pull these teachings together in a balanced way. My job tonight is to help you keep your feminine energies strong. *Yes!* Even those of you in male bodies will be able to mange this to a lesser degree! So before our 'Dancer' arrives to teach, share, and, of course, dance, there are preliminary things one should know. A man, or a woman, when working magical work, must be aware of the power of woman, then honor that. The woman is a vessel that when trained well knows how to hold the Dreamscapes and how to hold energies to travel in the Dreaming. This work must be incredibly focused in order to move energy for various purposes in Dream healing. This ability to hold the space is highly prized. From ancient times, women have done the work to hold group energy. Tonight my part of the story will unfold the Dreaming vessel of the 'Spring Queen,' which is 'Gaia-Earth,' and the 'Corn King,' which is the 'Sun,' and it will be unfolded a bit later. For now I will supply you with some of what you need to be 'Way Showers' in your future dream healing work. As Dreamers we learn to read and write 'Light,' communicate with 'Light.'"

The Seer had been walking around the wreath as she spoke, sometimes making hand motions or nodding her head. Now she had stooped down and was touching the 'Laurel Wreath,' saying it had been beautifully made, with care and intent. She stood up and turned. Walking about the wreath slowly, pointing to it, she said, "This wreath has been woven from 'Laurus Nobilis,' and it is the symbol of strength of life. In classical Greek-Roman myth, a wreath made from laurel is sacred to Apollo. It is the symbol of both triumph and peace and, because it is evergreen, represents immortality!"

The Seer looked deeply at all of us and then continued. "But as you might have noticed, this wreath is not the common round shape. No, this wreath is another shape entirely; for it is an 'Ellipse,' and shortly it will contain the 'Dancer'! The name ellipse is the name used when it is a circle surrounding a dancer. The shape of an ellipse represents development rather than an endless circle. The ellipse unites two poles and brings balance.

"Divine figures from classical times are often portrayed as surrounded with elliptical nimbus or halos, which represent their divine radiance. Some images of Roman or Greek gods and goddesses depict a 'Mandorla,' which is the Italian word for 'almond' or 'kernel.' The mystical almond is a symbol of a precious kernel hidden and protected by a tough, nearly impenetrable shell. This, of course, represents the difficulty of the initiatory path in spiritual workings. But this also shows the sweet rebirth that occurs once one has gained entry to the 'Mystery'! The 'Mandorla' shape is used to depict sacred moments that transcend time and space. The 'Mandorla' is also the shape and representation of the vulva, which, of course, is a symbol of the 'opening gateway' of a new life. Some esoteric thought says the 'Mandorla' shape is the shell of an egg, with the embryo within. This, then, becomes the 'Philosophical Egg of Alchemy,' in which an androgyne is incubated.

"As we will see, the 'Spring Queen,' the 'World Trump,' is a culmination in the ultimate mystical union of the 'Androgyne,' a unisex figure who dances in the center of the Tarot Trump card image. It is here we learn the 'World Trump' is about regeneration."

The Moon Seer had paused and was looking over the Dreamers, her silver hair glowing with moonstones woven into the wisps. The last rays of the Moon glimmered above, which would be setting not too long from now. The Seer glanced at the radiance from above; she was ready to continue.

"The 'Ouroboros' serpent symbolizes eternity and is depicted in some images around the 'World Dancer.' This symbology shows life as a serpent that incessantly creates and devours itself. There is a 'Hermetic' maxim that says: 'Nature delights in Nature, Nature contains Nature, and Nature overcomes Nature.' The World card can teach us that when one has come to a place of growth around the circle of life, they will know how to then unite on a higher plane.

"The World Trump is the alignment of the axiom, 'As above, so below.' We learn that we are the beginning and the end. The universe is at our command, and we are in balance with Spirit. The lessons of emotions have been harnessed, and lessons of attention and discrimination are now a part of us. We are able to master what we wish to accomplish. There is now balance with strength, and we can overcome fear or weakness. The World card has trained us to truly understand the laws of nature. We have received a gift. The 'Woman shown in the image is Nature,' and she invites you to dance.

"The dancer on the World Trump also corresponds to 'Isis,' the Egyptian Goddess of Eternal Feminine. Yet she is also 'Rhea,' the Greek-Titian Goddess, daughter of 'Ouranos' and 'Gaia,' wife of the Titian Kronos and the Queen of Heaven. Some say 'Rhea' is simply another form of 'Era,' the 'Earth.' She, like her daughter 'Demeter,' is the undeniable 'Earth Mother.' All these comprise the energies of our dear 'Arcanum the World.'

"The image of the 'World Dancer' is often painted in the nude, Showing she is in her natural state, following her inner natural light. Nudity represents the absence of shame, a 'symbol of truth.' This is the meaning of the term, 'Isis Unveiled.' This equals the fact of the 'Truth Unveiled'!"

The Moon Seer then said, "So now, my dear Dreamers, I have given the first part of our lessons concerning 'The World.' This information has provided the feminine side of the XXI Trump. So you may come to know what this tarot card is the various 'Goddesses of the Night' who have been speaking through me! But turn yourselves now to the eastern side of this mountain; the rays of light are beginning to show themselves!"

Everyone was in very high spirits, with cheers and bits of laughter. Then there was a large round of applause as the Moon Seer said, "I give you over to the rising 'Sun Seer Trump XIX'!"

So much excitement! Within a few minutes, we saw the 'Sun Seer' walking on the hillside; he seemed to literally come out of the physical sun! He was standing next to the Moon Seer. They greeted each other in a warm embrace. I thought to myself, This is like an eclipse of the sun, in a way. But no time for that aspect now, I thought.

The Moon Seer was clapping, with hands held high and a huge smile upon her face. She said, "Dreamers, 'The Sun' who is 'The Corn King'! The floor with the 'Laurel Wreath' is yours, my dear friend!"

The Sun Trump Seer, did some fancy bowing and kept saying, "Thank you, my dears. Thank you!" He was dressed in bright robes of the rising sun, in watercolors of pinks, peach, and oranges melding into yellows. So very tall and majestic, I thought to myself, and everyone loves him!

The Sun Seer said, "Come, Dreamers, let's continue into our lessons of the 'Keeper of the Keys.' We have much to do before the 'Dawning of the World'!"

The Seer walked around the perimeter of the circle, admiring the blue velvet drapes with the images of the sun, the moon, and constellations. He nodded his head, saying how beautiful it all was. The candelabras shined a warm glow upon him. Now he was ready, and so were we!

"Many of the old early tarot images of the mid-fifteenth century depict the 'World Trump' as an encircled city surrounded by sea, which is held up by angels or a regal woman holding a scepter, or standing upon an encircled city. These images are similar to the painting depictions of Christ or the Virgin Mary, which are within a vesica-piscis, sometimes with the world at their feet.

"The image of the central woman is symbolic of the eternal dance of 'Shiva,' the Sanskrit word meaning 'Auspicious One.' Shiva is a major Hindu god/goddess. It is said that all the while 'Shiva' dances, the world continues to rotate…She therefore gives us life!

"When we are ready for the teachings of the World Trump, we come to understand that we have the ability to do anything; everything is an offer. There are no limits here, only possibilities!"

There was a huge round of clapping after that comment. The Dreamers must be ready for their possibilities, I thought. The Sun Seer was near the center of the wreath, the ellipse, quietly observing the Dreamers and this beautiful Eastern Mountain. In the background we could hear the musicians playing to his cadence.

The pitch in the Sun Seer's voice seemed mellow and rhythmic as he began again. "Tarot scholars have observed that the number of the 'World XXI' is the union of one plus two. It is the union of the dancers of 'The Empress II' and 'The Magician I,' which is that of the Greek 'Aphrodite,' the Goddess of Love, and 'Hermes,' the Messenger of Zeus. From their union, Greek myth tells us they had a son, Hermaphroditus. When he was grown, the nymph Salmacis fell in love with him at a pool where he bathed; she grabbed him and he could not free himself. She prayed to Zeus that they would never be separated. Her prayers were answered, and the two were united into a single being: the first 'Hermaphrodite.' This myth reflects the inseparable union granted as a gift of the gods.

"From Roman mythology is the story of the Roman god 'Janus,' who is the god who reigns at the end of 'Saturnalia,' the holiday of 'Saturn' at the end of December. The god 'Janus' is who the month of January is named for. Janus, who is the universe, is always moving, whirling in a circle, like our dancer, the World. There is an alchemical mystery in the nature of Janus, for the ancient physicists said he comprises both Apollo and Diana, which represent the Sun and the Moon!

"Macrobius, a Roman grammarian and philosopher who flourished in circa 430 AD, mentions the god 'Janus' as having twelve altars and authority over the first day of each month. He said Janus rotates in the heavens, and the twelve altars will always return to the place where they began. The World Trump is very much related to the 'circling' like Janus.

"In artwork Janus is often portrayed with a 'Key' and a 'Rod,' which are his emblems as 'Gatekeeper.' With the Rod, he discourages those who are not allowed to enter. With the Key, he opens the gate. Sometimes Janus is shown with a pair of Keys.

"Dreamers, we know of course that Keys are for opening, but in our esoteric work, there are other levels. I would like to explain. A Key is a symbol of binding and loosing; it closes and it opens. Specifically in esoteric thought, the 'Silver Key' loosens and the 'Gold Key' binds; they are alchemical dissolution and coagulation. Keys are symbols of liberation and initiation. The 'Silver Key' represents the 'Lesser Mysteries,' and the 'Gold Key' symbolizes the 'Greater Mysteries.' These keys are associated with 'Janus as the God of Initiation,' for he oversees the endings and the beginnings of everything. Janus holds the 'Keys of Power,' allowing access between gods and mortals.

"Keys are also the attributes of 'Hecate,' the guardian of the underworld. Another 'Key-Bearer' is 'Diana Triformis,' who looks three ways and is the female counterpart to Janus. Unless we brave to view Diana-Hecate's third face, it is said, we may not know our true destiny. Therefore it is said that keys often come in threes. The third key, after the gold and the silver keys, which is usually hidden from our view, is the 'Diamond Key'! 'Jana' is the female counterpart to 'Janus.' 'Jana'-'Diana Triformis' and 'Hecate Triformis' are the Lunar Goddesses, which are a part of the 'World Trump.'"

Now we had quiet for several minutes as the Sun Seer walked about the wreath calmly.

"Let me tell you more about the male counterpart, 'Janus.' His work is to guard the gates of the temple, so his image is shown as holding 'Rods' or 'Wands.' This is found in many art depictions of our World card. The Rod, or Magic Wand, or the Caduceus of Mercury-Hermes, is a symbol of masculine power ,and Janus uses it to drive the unworthy away from the gates he guards. Esoterically the staff is the 'Axis Mundi,' The Rod-The Tree, at the 'World Navel.'"

The Sun Seer had been walking about the rectangle shape that surrounded the center wreath, stopping at each of the corners, giving each of them a little attention. He had been silent awhile. Suddenly, with a very deep voice, he boomed these words: "There are always four! *THE SACRED FOUR.*' Originally the heavens were said to rest on the 'Four Corners,' or 'Quarters of the Universe.' Some say the four sacred elements of Earth, Air, Fire, and Water were symbolized in these four corners. Many illustrations of the World card portray the 'Wards of the Quarters.' In many cultures, these wards are used in sacred paintings. 'The Wards of the Quarters' may be these: Four Elements, Four Animals, Four Faces, Four Winds, Four Planetary Signs. Each culture attributes different images, or beings, with unique symbology.

"The 'Wards of the Quarters' are referred to by some as 'Tetramorph,' and its purpose is to define the quarters of the Cosmos. The Earth, the Heavens and the Abyss; each are divided into four quarters. Isn't it interesting how these four wards are arranged in relation to the Arcanum XXI? As you can see, the World Dancer is always in the center of them all. She therefore represents the 'Quintessence,' from the Latin words 'Quinta,' meaning fifth essence, and 'aether,' meaning a pure air substance. So our 'Dancer is the Fifth Element-Quintessence,' and this is the goal of the alchemical work of the 'Magnum Opus,' which means 'The Great Work.' The World Trump has concluded the Trump journeys and sums up a transfiguration to a higher plane of knowing.

"The Tetramorph of four principal animals can also represent four principal shamanic and yogic paths that are found at the Axis Mundi. These would be 'The Bull' and 'The Lion,' for the 'Chthonic Path,' the Earth path of the underworld. For the 'Celestial Path,' 'The Eagle' and 'The Winged Horse' are the symbols. Sometimes the Snake is used for the Kundalini Serpent and takes the place of the Lion.

"Some tarot scholars describe the 'Scared Four' corners with the images of the four animals of the Apocalypse, which are 'The Man,' 'The Lion,' 'The Bull,' and 'The Eagle.' The four figures placed at the corners represent the four letters of the sacred name and are the symbols of tarot: The Scepter/Wand-Yod-Fire-passion; The Cup-He-Water-emotion; The Sword-Second He-Air-intellect-man; and The Pentacles-Vau-Earth-material substance.

"As we can see, the 'Tetramorph' has represented the four suits of the 'Minor Arcana,' which is made on the bases of the elements. Also there is a representation for the potentials of the 'New Personality' on the threshold of fuller development. There are *Four Gods Who Rule These Potentials*:

Poseidon, 'Lord of the Earth,' Pentacles-Physical Reality; Zeus, 'Lord of the Fire,' Wands-The Bolt from the Blue, Creative Imagination; Aphrodite, 'Goddess of the Water,' Cups-Love and Emotion; and Athena, 'Goddess of the Air,' Swords-Intellect, Wisdom."

"Well, my Dreamer friends, the predawn light is growing stronger! Let me just walk about our card that we have painted and made together here on this wet, dewy grass and enjoy what we have done. Yes, yes! The four corners are lined up, but they need filling!"

Then the Seer picked the appropriate Dreamers to be animals for each of the three corners. For the fourth corner, he selected a Dreamer, one of our wisest male Dreamers to hold that space, as Man. Everyone was pleased with these selections. We were encouraged by the Sun Seer to walk around the rectangle on the grass with the Laurel Wreath in the center. There were many compliments for the living painting we had made; there was a sense of mutual admiration, and this was good.

Thinking about all our trainings and all I have done while here, I realized that in this Grove, I feel strong; my head is clear on this Eastern Hill, and now I am learning how to contain the lessons. The light of the Grove was turning from gold to greenish yellows; I drank it in!

Looking around, I saw that everyone was having a small break. I was glad; we needed a pause. These thoughts ran through my daydreaming: Watch for passages today. There will be thresholds, crossings from one realm into another; notice what is inside to outside, woodlands into meadows, upstairs into basements. Watch for glimmers of light, shiny objects. Maybe sunlight reflecting onto moonlight which catches it!

This was random, but I would pay attention. This is what Dreamers do!

As the sunlight became brighter, the mists that had been hovering around our hillside began moving some; now there was music in the mist! The musicians of the quartet were taking the lead, and the sound was heavenly. We have all been trained to listen to the drummers at our gatherings, and certain drumbeats indicate a time to focus our dreaming attention. That was what was happening now! The Dreamers got seated and settled, and then the drumroll became very strong, still with the background of the violin, viola, cello, and flute; they were creating a magical mood on this mountain. The sun drifting through the floating mist was perfect!

Then from the top of our elliptical wreath, The Moon Seer and The Sun Seer came hand in hand, smiling and calling out fond names to all. They both clapped along with the Dreamers in the audience. There was such an excitement from the crowd, and it took a little time for the attention to shift to the Keepers who were our emcees and teachers for this amazing event. Everyone knew it definitely was becoming morning!

Our Goddess the Moon Seer held out her arms high, saying, "Dreamers! Dreamers!" She laughed and shook her head; her voice was barely heard over the clapping and cheering from the crowd. She began again, but now the Sun Seer joined with her, and together they gave their introduction for the event's star attraction!

"Lady Dreamers and Gentleman Dreamers! Our star for this Dream Theater. THE DAWNING OF THE WORLD, our WORLD TRUMP XXI SEER!"

Everyone was standing, cheering, and clapping! We could hear the music again, and the mist was swirling strongly. Then as if in a dream (no pun intended), she came, dancing as she did so. I remembered what we had learned earlier about Shiva dancing the motion of the world; this is just how it felt, as if we were all part of an incredible cosmic rotation in the dance! I remembered my earlier daydreaming: watch for passages, thresholds, crossing from one realm into another. This was it! The World Trump Seer, with her ability and wisdom, was helping us to move through the realms of experience and showing us the dance of passage. My daydream came again: watch for glimmers of light…I quickly looked and saw the Sun Seer reflecting his light to the Moon Seer, who graciously was catching these rays. Wow! This was indeed a special moment!

Taking a deep sigh, I tuned into the music and the Dancer! She was definitely a vision, floating through the mists, touching the dewy grass here and there. She wore a mantel of rose-red silk and nothing else; she was in her natural state, the symbol of truth!

I noticed that in her right hand she held a golden wand with a gold key attached, and in her left hand she held a silver wand with a silver key attached. Around her neck hung a small diamond key! Incredible, I said to myself. She was moving around the Grove now, admiring the beautiful blue velvet drapery painted with the cosmos, dancing as she went, and sometimes greeting the Dreamers there. Her long, reddish hair flowed with the breeze she created with her dancing; the red rosebuds as her crown enhanced and framed the beauty that she was.

The drumming grew louder. The Dreamers settled and the Dancer of the World moved to the center of the Laurel Wreath. She stood silently in the center; we all held our breath as we now were able to see our Living Painting of the World completed!

It was so quiet; it felt to me as if the literal world had stopped. Which, of course, she had! I thought to myself, I will cherish this moment forever. Suddenly we heard the cry of a bird…An eagle was circling overhead, giving us a look over, showing us the larger picture, I thought! Everyone had turned their heads up to see this majestic sight.

Another cry came from the Eagle, piercing the silence. And with that, the Dreamers added their cries and cheers, and of course the clapping was nonstop for awhile!

The Sun Seer held his hands high. The drumming helped us to refocus, and the energy shifted to the center of the wreath.

The World XXI Trump Seer said, "Dreamers, I thank you for holding the energy for me and creating such an incredible space in this Grove to do our work. As you are all coming to know more deeply than ever now, 'humanity can be sustained and preserved by the visions of the Dreamers!'"

Just then we heard the eagle give another cry. She circled and then glided away, and we all laughed a bit!

The World Seer continued. She was looking to the heavens as she said, "Thank you, dear Eagle, my friend! Wow! How beautiful she seems to have flown right into the center Sun!" There was a silent pause…And then she turned her attention to each of the Dreamers in the Grove.

"Our still point of strength…The Sun and the Moon and the Stars shine through us, and we through them. What we come to understand is that the light of understanding that we seek is our own light! I am your Map of Heaven on Earth. Please remember to consult me when your light feels dim, and I will help you strengthen and mend that light with the Ley Lines that connect us all! I know the dance between appearance and reality. I have the codes! After all, I am the 'Keeper of the Keys'!"

The Dreamers had been in a very intense focus. After that comment, there was laughing and everyone lightened up and smiled, relaxing now for the lessons that were to come.

The World Seer continued, "In the Qabalah, as the World, I am path thirty-two on the Tree of Life. My astrology symbol is that of Saturn, the image of a crescent moon with a cross on top. It is said of me in the Qabalah: 'Great One of the Night of Time.' The thirty-second path is: 'Administrative Intelligence,' because this path directs and associates the motions of the seven planets. I can tell you that walking this path can be likened to Persephone's descent into Hades with Pluto, the king of the underworld. Lewis Carroll's story of *Alice in Wonderland*, may be the modern-day version of the Goddess Persephone. The goddess of the grain and of the spring. Persephone, daughter of 'Demeter,' is our 'Earth Mother.' Demeter was the Greek Olympian goddess of agriculture, motherhood, and the afterlife. Her husband was Zeus, father to Persephone.

"Persephone, as a young maiden, was carried off by Pluto as she gathered flowers near the cave of Hecate. Pluto gives Persephone a pomegranate, which she eats. This is a symbol of femininity and fructification. By eating this fruit, she binds herself automatically to Pluto!

"Persephone's mother, 'Demeter,' is grief stricken at her abduction. She cries endless tears at not finding her daughter and cannot be consoled. Then Demeter unleashes her wrath at the world and withholds grain from mankind. Her anger is heard by her husband Zeus; he then requests Pluto to send Persephone back. Pluto does comply, but it is at that point that he feeds her the pomegranate, whereby she becomes doomed to the lower world. However, an agreement is made between Zeus and Pluto, whereby Persephone would spend one half of every year in the lower worlds of Hades, and the other half in the upper worlds. The lesson we can learn here is that only by descent into the underworlds is new life possible; this requires death to gain rebirth."

The World Trump XXI Seer had stopped for the moment and was checking the Laurel Wreath. Then she stood upon it at the top and said, "Stay with me a moment while I walk the ellipse of this wreath. I will walk clockwise."

She walked slowly, and the Dreamers were watching her every move. All wondered what she was going to tell us. She walked to the top of the wreath where the crossed red ribbons were, and she stopped.

I watched carefully as she looked out to the Dreamers in the Grove. Her strawberry hair cascaded, and her stance at the top of the wreath was firm. By this time it was a bright and beautiful new day. The lights from the torches and the candelabra had been dowsed. I could smell sweetness in the air as the musicians played a peaceful backdrop melody.

The World Seer said this: "Dreamers, we are at an important gateway to understand here. This wreath symbolizes much of what we need to understand. As you can see, the pieces of laurel were started here." She pointed with one of her magical wands to the starting point. "You all watched as I traveled the path of the wreath, and you watched when I stopped!" She looked around to see the Dreamers' reactions, which, of course, showed they all agreed so far.

"Let me explain. My World is about endings and beginnings! This wreath was started from one point and then stopped from where it started. This story from Roman/Greek myth will give you a better idea. In the World card the holiday of 'Saturnalia' comes to an end. This is the Roman feast to the 'Temple of the God Saturn,' which is held in December each year at Winter Solstice. 'Saturn is the Roman god of agriculture and harvest, justice and strength. To the Greeks, 'Saturn' was known as 'Cronus,' Father Time. Saturn is the namesake of the day of the week called Saturday, and Saturn is the son of 'Uranus,' for Greeks, or 'Callus,' for Romans, and 'Gaia' or 'Terra,' the Earth. In astrology the sign of Saturn often stands for the Father. 'Saturn/Cronus' represents limitations; for all things have endings, but there are also beginnings. Saturn energy may affect us by delaying rewards until they are earned! Saturn rules the 'Golden Years' of old age and retirement. Astrologically it is said that Saturn can impart serenity and wisdom of the Earth itself, to those of his choosing.

"As you may recall from the lessons a little earlier, it is the Roman god 'Janus' who reigns at the end of the holiday Saturnalia, who then starts 'Anew' around the circle. Always moving, stopping, and starting, this is the 'World's' energy. The World-Wise Woman! This is who I am! I hold the keys of Heaven and the keys to the Abyss, and I can point the way into the new Aquarian Aeon, where the return of the 'Golden Age of Saturn' awaits!

"'The Golden Age of Saturn,' from Greek myth, is the 'Golden Age of Man'! This was a time when man and the world were perceived as an ideal state of utopia. Some refer to this as being the 'Silver, Bronze, and Iron Ages.'"

"My friend and fellow 'Keeper of the Dreaming,' 'The Fool Trump Seer,' also dances at the carnival of 'Saturnalia.' Just as do I, the woman of the 'World Trump'! We both dance the eternal dance of 'Liberated Life'!

"The Dancer in the World card is a symbol for the transfigured 'Fool' who has done his journey through all twenty-one trumps! Dancing combines rhythm and spontaneity. Dancing is creation! You are aware that in many myths a god or a goddess dances the universe into existence.

"Rhythm and time represent the two fundamental dimensions of the universe. 'The Cosmic Dancer' knows instinctively how to choreograph and balance. As the 'World Trump Dancer,' I am grounded in the reality of this life, yet I am also very much connected to the universal flow of Spirit. Many of the World card images portray me as androgynous because I represent the reconciliation of opposites. I have been able to dance the world and, as a result, become a reborn child who then grows to maturity with balance and grace. Constant dancing is what sustains the universe!"

The World Trump Seer then pointed to the drummers and the quartet with her silver wand. And on that cue, the music became a kind of waltz! She then glided and swayed around the Grove, turning herself this way and that, with the Dreamers sometimes stepping into the dance with her. This was enthralling and invigorating to all of us; it was about having fun! I thought to myself, It is really about enjoying this journey we call life! I truly felt the sacredness among us in the Grove. Now the music was softening, and the flute went on alone.

The World Seer was back at the center of the wreath and said this: "As the World I trust to impart the fulfillment of the ancient promise of peace on Earth. In my symbol of a female figure, I remind us to be co-creators with God and to remind us all that our human destiny is to care for our 'most sacred vessel, our planet Earth'! My message is about a restored world to its highest degree. I am in the center of the ellipse, and I stand for truth!

"Dreamers! It is believed by many that this 'Golden Age' will return! Through our Dreaming, may I, the 'Arcanum of the World,' help to usher this into being! May you, through your hard work of dreaming and truth, be a part of this 'Golden Age'!"

The World Trump XXI Seer was taking her bows, all the while laughing and giving thanks. All the Dreamers were cheering and could not wait to greet her! Then the music floated, and a beautiful waltz began. The World Seer danced with each of the Four Wards of our living painting! The four corners of her world and ours were thrilled about that. She started off her dancing waltz with the eagle, and it was wonderful! All the Dreamers joined in and were dancing with each other. As The World Seer danced with the four corners of the world, the work of the Dreaming felt so right!

The drumming grew louder, and someone announced about the feast being ready, saying, "Dreamers, the Dawn has come along with the World Dancer, and now I invite you to 'Break-Fast'!"

There was a huge cheer that came forth from the Keepers and Dreamers alike! It seems that food always makes people happy. The noise was simmering, and we could hear the mellow music being played. Gazing to the top of the hillside, I saw the Moon Seer was with the World Seer; they were laughing about something, and they seemed like sisters to me, as I could feel their love for one another. Musical tones grew into a beautiful waltzing mode, and many were dancing. I thought I would give the World Seer a little time before I greeted her with my thanks.

I was about to go over to one of the feasting tables, because of course I was starving, when I noticed the Fool Seer was next to the World Seer. I was just close enough to hear him say to her as he bowed most graciously. "May I have this dance? To honor your Dawning of the World!"

She most beautifully replied, "I would be most honored, kind sir!"

They moved off, twirling and swaying. They were truly instep with each other, a beautiful sight for all!

Then as they waltzed past me slowly, I heard the World Trump Seer say, "Watch for me by dawn light, dear Dreamer!"

Section Two
Dreams of the Animal Seers

ANIMAL SEERS

BEAR

DREAM OF THE BEAR SEER

find myself as a young girl walking the woodland hills of the mountain. I have come here to be alone, time to myself. I cannot shake a sadness I feel. Tired now from the hike, I scan the woods and notice a small clearing with a tall, straight tree growing there. Moving closer I confirm that it is an ash tree. Feeling magic with this place, my thoughts linger in the dark sky, but it feels safe to me. Sitting now at the base of the ash, I am weeping slightly, wondering, What is this sadness I cannot shake? There is a scent of smoke… And off to my right I see a campfire. It must be the Seers, I think and I am excited. I want to join these Seers of the mountain. But somehow now I cannot move. Then I hear noises, see shadow things, and lighting in the sky. I am afraid for some reason, and I am crying more. I wonder if I am dreaming…

I am drifting back in time through other lifetimes, now. Again I feel my cheek and the tears there. Talking out loud now, I say, "Such sadness for a young girl." I hear rattling and again notice lightning in the sky.

My senses are picking up a voice. Then I hear it: "Let the tears come; they are cleansing." Putting the voice with the large figure nearby, I am apprehensive. The shadows loom to one side of this figure. I see now a bear, huge, but with a human feel. Confused, I hear the bear voice go on to say, "I am the 'Bear Seer' of the Nemeton."

"Nemeton?" I question.

"You are in a sacred grove of the Ancient Ones. Dreaming has brought you here. There are lessons here for you to learn."

"Lessons!" I reply, "When will it change? The hurting, the conniving, the slandering, the killing. Each generation does it a little different, but it is still the same. When will people learn? Life after life, will it ever change?" I ask. "I'm so sad. There is not much respect for others' boundaries or spaces. Shouldn't it be a person's right to just be who they are, not trying to arrange others solely to suit ones needs!"

Standing quiet close now, he puts his hand to his lips and says, "Sh. Hush." Looking at me intently, he says "Listen!"

I strain to listen. I hear nothing and tell the Bear Seer.

"Exactly," is his reply. "You hear the peacefulness of this woods. Mother Earth is there for us. Talk with her, and ask her to help with this peace you are after….many of us are after. Listen! Listen to the small things with your family and others in your life. You have much you can teach and share in this life. First listen! When you have acquired wisdom to share, first figure out who will hear you and if you will be heard. Play the split-second-dream-scenario game. Think from the other person's moccasins," said the Bear Seer.

"What do you mean?" I ask the Bear Seer.

"Well, can they 'bear' what you have to say? A pun here, you know! Lighten up a bit! What I mean is this: from their moccasins, their point of view. You may want them to understand something from a larger picture than they may presently have the scope to hear. In the split-second scenario, consider this: Is the timing right? Are they working at all on their inner-self for the better? Will my words of insight or wisdom be heard? Do not waste your own energy on those who do not hear at this time. Maybe they do not 'Hear' because of the word 'Ear'; placing an *F*, it becomes 'Fear.' Try to sense what the fear might be. Then choose evaluate your timing with good words, checking if this is the appropriate time before you speak. Or are they caught up in some kind of fear? Maybe not open enough right then to hear you. Be patient; you will connect with those who will hear your cries for peace. Teach them that peacefulness is found by doing peaceful things, especially in and with nature. A wonderful healer our nature, our Mother Earth."

As the Bear Seer was speaking, he was very animated, moving about this way and that. I am fascinated by the large shadow that he cast in the moon's light.

Bringing me back from my slight in attention, I hear the ancient seer say, "Amazing isn't it? My shadow! It is me and it is not. It reflects me and protects me. Our shadows hold our dark light; we all have this. Our makeup is part bright light, part dark. Many times we do not want to face the dark part of us. It takes time and love to know our shadow selves and know that we could not survive without the dark. This energy is part of the survival of the fittest. Of course it must be tempered with the bright energy.

"I feel this is what has made you so sad of late. You are able to see the truth line in others, their bright potential. Yet you witness their brightness overrun by their darker shadow self. For many, that dark shadow is a pattern they do not know how to change."

"Bear Seer," I interrupt, "you are so right! I seem to know how to keep my bright light, bright! I want to shake some of these people that I encounter! 'Just change the picture,' I say. They do not seem to hear or care! Some do. Not enough. Not enough!"

The Bear Seer goes on to say, "Dear Dreamer, just keep coming back to nature, walk with the ancient standing ones, the trees, the rocks, and all of Earth Mother. She will guide you, first working in small ways, with your family, your friends. Teach thankfulness and not to be wasteful of natural commodities and personal energy. Teach them about sacred space and boundaries. You have been learning so much as a Dreamer, while doing your training here, and now others are learning from you. Do not be sad, little one. Remember trust and patience."

Turning my head, we can smell the smoke again; looking toward the campfire, we can see the elders making their space ready. Listening, we can hear the drumming starting slowly, quietly. Looking back to the Bear Seer, I smile and say, "I have learned to go deeper within myself, because of you, dear ancient one! You have touched my heart with your faith and love for me."

He stands up now, so big, towering over me. He reaches for my hand. The Bear Seer hands me his bear rattle, saying, "The ceremony is about to begin, Dreamer. They are waiting for you."

I thank him and look toward the campfire. Smiling now, feeling lighter, I shake the rattle softly. It awakens me with its beauty. Again I see lightning in the dark sky. Looking back over my shoulder, I see the Bear Seer moving slightly closer to the wooded area. I see his amazing, big shadow following next to him. How nice to have met him this evening, I think to myself. I will call him Bear Shadow!

He stands tall and proud and offers these words before he leaves: "Bear was powerful in Celtic lore. The word 'Art' means 'Bear, Stone, God.' Also the name 'Arthur' means 'Bear man.' You might think of me with this connection, along with King Arthur, of course! Also in France, there is a 'Bear Goddess' by the name of 'Artio' or 'Andarta.' She is a very powerful goddess from the region of Lourdes, France. You may sometimes want to call upon these aspects of 'Bear Medicine.' Remember me too in the constellation of 'Ursa Major-The Big Dipper,' which has seven bright stars. In this constellation, half the year the 'Bear' lives above the North Star, for 'Spring-Summer'; the other half the year the 'Bear' lives below the North Star, for 'Autumn-Winter.' In addition, the 'Goddess Artemis Calliste,' the beautiful 'She Bear,' is guardian to this pole star, 'Axis Mundi.' So as you can see, I am always available, when you know where to look!"

He is gone in a blink of an eye. The evening's shadows are all about, and I can no longer find Bear Shadow. I am saddened. Then I smell the smoke and sage and know he will never be far, should I need his counsel. I look at my newly acquired bear rattle and walk slowly to the evening's events, rattling lightly and begin a new dreaming with my own shadow self. As I arrive at the evening campfire, I feel more whole and glance to the dark sky to find The Big Dipper. A smile crosses my lips as I feel Bear Shadow still there.

BEE

DREAM OF THE BEE SEER

I went walking in the Grove quite early this morning, wanting to spend some quiet time before our Dreaming began. Moving through the circle of trees, I could tell someone had already tended the beautiful fireplace made of huge granite and quartz crystal stones. Some even had garnet crystals in them. It was an unusual freestanding fireplace; one could walk all around it. This fireplace was not a part of any building; it stood on its own in the Grove. It had a small chimney of about eight feet, and there was a huge horizontal lintel stone, with two tall, vertical stones holding it up. The overall shape was that of a hexagon. From the way the stones had been laid, I knew a master craftsman had done this work. Four or five people could stand under the hearth easily. Looking around from where I stood on the crest of a small hill, I drank in the beauty of this special place. The design of this Grove was both beautiful and practical.

When the Dreamers come here, which is the Heart of the Sacred Grove of The Nemeton, they usually enter from the east. I realized that being at the eastern entrance at this point in the morning allowed the sun to shine brightly onto the fireplace, which made the quartz and garnets gleam and sparkle. I knew this automatically drew the Dreamers to it.

I walked over and stood with my back to the blazing fire; it felt wonderful. Warming myself and enjoying the energy that was emanating from the center where the altar was set in the Grove, I was feeling all the love of the Dreamers working here together.

Standing now next to the altar, I noticed that the altar cloth itself had been changed. Curious, I looked closer. The design on the cloth was of small connecting hexagrams. "Why, it looks like a honeycomb!" I said out loud, not quite realizing that I had.

Then someone answered me. "Why, yes, it is!"

I turned around to see a woman standing there, holding a bunch of golden-yellow candles in her hands. Smiling at her, I told her how beautiful it all looked and that I liked the candles she was holding. She was of medium height with graying hair swept off her delicate face. Her face was ageless, hardly a line or wrinkle, a timeless beauty.

Answering my thoughts, she said in a laughing voice, "It's the honey. I eat it daily ,and I use honey cream for my complexion!"

Surprised, and laughing a little myself, I said, "I did not mean to stare!" "

It is fine, my daughter. Why don't you help me finish arranging these candles? They are a gift from the Goddess Aphrodite, and the wax was gifted by the bees, and was made into candles by the 'Melissae Priestesses'!"

"So I guess that you are The Bee Seer," I said to her.

"No guessing, my child. You know that it is so! Say always what you mean, and use clear words and conviction when you speak. Our voice is important!"

Taken back a bit, but knowing that she was right, I smiled and said, "I am very pleased to meet you!"

She smiled back, and said, "Likewise." Then she handed me a bunch of the candles to be placed around the altar and the Grove. When we had finished, we looked around the sacred space, admiring the beauty of our handiwork. We turned, smiling at each other, quite pleased with ourselves.

The Honey Bee Seer said, "I have some Melissa tea brewing near the fire. Come and join me for a while." I nodded my head, and we found a cozy place to sit near the fire. She told me, "It seems we are meant to be visiting some, before the other Dreamers arrive."

I agreed. Looking at her, I was entranced by the light that she held. "I love the honey-bees!" I said, "They are so focused and industrious; they really are a marvel. What else do I need to know about their energy, Ancient One?"

There was a slight smile on her face as she held out my tea cup. "Honey?" she asked me.

"Of course!" I said quickly, helping myself to generous spoonfuls.

I watched her as she smelled her cup of Melissa tea, holding the cup with two hands. She took a sip. I copied her actions; it was wonderful! The Seer began to speak; her voice was dreamlike. "The Melissa plant, or Bee balm, which is the common name, is a favorite of the bees. I dried this Melissa tea from the plants in my garden."

"The tea is delicious! Thank you!" I said to her.

"To continue," said the Bee Seer, "the bee is the symbol of tireless activity. It represents a good work ethic and being diligent at a task. The bee's hard work is connected to the beehive, which symbolizes order, industry, and wisdom."

"Wow!" I said to her.

The Seer continued. "Throughout history, bees have provided food, honey, and drink, mead. Their hives offer an analogy of a peaceful society, where each member has contributed to the good of all. They are important to humanity, pollinating our fields and orchards. Because of the honeybee, we have beautiful flowers and fruit. The bees give us so much. Bees also provide us with sweetener and wax. The wax is used to preserve and to illuminate. Some cultures see them as messengers between the worlds. In ancient times it was important to 'Tell the Bees': tell them anything that was important, lest they take offense and swarm away. Bees are seen as industry and harmony." My eyes stared in amazement at all the things I was learning. The Bee Seer smiled and poured more tea into our cups. "It makes me happy to see how much you are enjoying this!" she said to me. "The honeybees are masters at communication. Let me tell you about their dancing!"

"Dancing?" I said.

"Listen!" She said, "Bees perform a 'Waggle Dance,' which is an elaborate mode of communication used by the bees to signal hive mates about the location of food and potential new nesting sites. This dance takes the form of a figure eight and is performed by the worker bees on the vertical surface of a comb near the entrance to the hive. As the worker bee moves along the line in the form of a figure eight, it 'Waggles' from side to side. Then it returns to the start point, and the sequence is repeated over and over again. This definitely gets the attention of the hive, and they proceed to pass on the information. That is the 'Waggle Dance'!"

"This is astounding!" I said in a rather loud voice.

The Seer just laughed. Then she became a little serious and said, "This is a good time to talk about the number eight and the number six. Eight is the same shape as infinity, for one thing. Eight is also associated with the planet Saturn, karmic debt, and the sign of Scorpio. It is related to the Water element and is a fixed sign in astrology. It also means power and sometimes sacrifices. The other number for bees is the number six. The hexagon is a six-sided shape and the shape of their honey combs. It is associated with the planet Venus, love and beauty, and the sign of Virgo, which is the element of Earth and a mutable sign in astrology. It also means reaction and sometimes responsibility. When we add the numbers eight and six, their sum is fourteen. The number fourteen is the number for the 'TEMPERANCE SEER' in tarot. Very interesting! Is it not?" She was giggling a bit as she said this!

I wanted to say something, but the Seer just waved her hand a bit. Then she said, "Let me go onto 'Beekeeping.' Beekeeping has been taking place for several thousand years. In Latin the word for beekeeping is 'Apiculture,' and 'Apis' means Bee. The bee keeper is called 'Apiarist.' The place hives are kept is called an 'Apiary.' The Honey industry existed in the Holy Land at the time of the Bible, and beekeeping has been around since at least 900 BC. The domestication of beekeeping was well developed in Egypt. Honey pots were found in the graves of the pharaohs, such as Tutankhamen. In addition the ancient Egyptians used honey for embalming the dead. In Egypt the image of the bee denoted royalty.

"French royalty used the bee image as well. At the coronation of the Emperor Napoleon, the robes he wore were embroidered with the honeybee image. In the east, for Buddhism, honey plays an important part in the Festival of Madhu Purnima. As the myth goes, Buddha had made peace among his disciples in the wilderness. In the myth there is a monkey who brings him the gift of honey, to honor the peace. To the Buddhists the buzzing sound of the bees is associated with the raising of energy, leading to Nirvana."

The Bee Seer stopped for a moment, adjusting the golden clip that held back her hair. I could not help staring; she looked so young. "What?" she said.

I replied, "It is just that you are so beautiful and seem so young!"

Tossing her head back and laughing, she said, "Remember the honey pots of the Egyptians?"

"Yes?" I answered, wondering.

Laughing again, she said, "Embalming. You know, it really works!"

"Let us continue," she said. But, I was still wondering about her comments. "The Greeks have contributed such rich stories and myth surrounding bees! Remember 'Melissa'?" I nodded my head, yes. "Melissa was a mountain nymph who saved Zeus from his father, 'Cronus,' while he was trying to devour him. She hid with him and fed him milk from 'Amalthea,' the goat who plundered the beehives' honey for its sweet strengthening. 'Cronus' became out-raged when he found out and then turned her into a worm. Zeus felt sorry for her and turned her into a Queen Bee instead, to be forever connected with honey. Greeks believed bees to be a bridge between the natural world and the underworld. Bees were said to be the souls of nymphs, priestesses, who had been in service to Aphrodite during their lifetimes. 'Aphrodite's temple at Eryr' had the symbol of the Golden Honeycomb. The priestesses of this goddess were called 'Melissae,' which means bees. Often they were accompanied by eunuch priests known as 'Essenes,' which means drones."

Looking at me with a twinkle in her eye, she said, "Do you know where the name 'Hon-eymoon' comes from?"

I answered, "I have not a clue!"

"Well, my dear, I will tell you!" She said, "In Greece bees are referred to as 'Hymenop-tera,' or 'Veil-Winged'; this is like the 'Hymen-Veil' that covered the inner shrine of the God-dess's temple. It was here that a High Priestess would officiate; she bore the title of 'Hymen' and ruled over marriage rituals and the 'Honey-Moon'!"

"Oh my Goddess!" I said with a laugh.

The Seer joined me in laughing. Then she continued. "Honeybees are feminine aspects and are very sacred to the Goddess. In the physical world within their Hive, they live in a matriarchy ruled by a Queen. The Greek 'Goddess Demeter' was addressed as the 'Pure Mother Bee.' Demeter is the goddess of grain and fertility. She is the preserver of the Earth. From Israel, there was a matriarchal ruler named Deborah, and her name means Queen Bee."

"The Celts associated the bees with wisdom. The Druids felt the Bee symbolized the sun, the Goddess, celebration, and community. In Medieval Europe, abbeys and monasteries were centers of 'Beekeeping.' From the gifts of the bee, candles were made of the wax, and 'Mead' was made from fermented honey, especially in colder climate areas where grapevines were hard to grow. In early Christian times, some monks built beehive-shaped huts symbol-izing a harmonious community. Other tidbits from Western culture: 'Bears' are depicted as eating honey. The word 'Honey' is a term of endearment in most of the English-speaking world."

The Bee Seer paused some, looking at me with a twinkle in her eyes. "Of course you know about their life in the hive, right? Well, let me just mention a few things about the basic community. A hive consists of a 'Queen Bee.' She is selected from the larvae by the worker bees and fed a special diet of royal jelly, a protein-rich secretion from the glands of the female worker bees. As a result of the difference in diet, the Queen will develop into a sexually mature female. She is usually the mother of all the bees in the hive. She is continually surrounded by worker bees who meet her every need.

"The 'Worker Bees' are all nonreproducing females. They protect the hive and build the hive. The worker bees do the gathering and the pollinating. They are also strong fighters if needed.

"The 'Nurse Worker Bees' are the ones who care for the Queen. The worker bees' work is never done and goes on and on, usually in a most peaceful manner.

"The 'Drone Bees' are the male bees. They develop from unfertilized eggs. The drones have two reproductive functions. One, they convert and extend the Queen's single unfertilized egg into ten million identical male sperm cells. Two, they serve the Queen and mate with her. The Queen's mating with the Drones is done while in flight, sometimes at several hundred feet in the air. It is thought that only the strongest Drones can do this, thus passing on their genes. Drones do not gather, pollinate, or construct the hive. They are defenseless and without stingers. Their purpose is mating. The life expectancy of a Drone bee is about ninety days.

"Bees have been the symbols for goddesses, queens, kings, popes, conquerors, and secret societies. The Bee's Wisdom is vast. Bees are associated with the goddess; they are about understanding female warrior energy, reincarnation, communication, concentration, fertility, and prosperity."

The Seer looked about. I wondered what was up. Then we heard voices and saw that other Dreamers were coming into the Grove. Our special time together would be coming to a close.

"Oh, my dear, don't look so sad. I know it feels like you have been around the world with bee stories, and we have! But I am certain that you will know how to find me again when all this info settles and you are then buzzing with questions!"

I leaned over and gave her a warm hug. She smelled as sweet as the Melissa flowers that she grows. It was getting a bit louder, and we could hear the soft drumming. Standing up now, The Honey Bee Seer told me she would be leading the dreaming this morning. Then she asked me if I might assist her in certain parts. "You are developing your voice nicely now, like the Bees, Dreamer!" she said to me ever so sweetly.

I would be her Bee Priestess Dreamer for the morning! Of course I said yes! And was all smiles for the morning's dreaming session.

Karen C. Silverstein

DEER

DREAM OF THE DEER SEER

Walking during the break, I found the evening air was revitalizing and grounding. I really needed that to bring me back from the journey work the circle of Dreamers had done. Our intent had been to travel back to an ancient lifetime and discover gifts from that life that may be helpful to one's own work now.

Upon returning from break, I came close to the hearth fire in the center of the Grove. There was a lot of commotion. The voices were flaring between several novice Dreamers. There was a heated disagreement. Something about the best way to transfer a soul? Looking around the circle, I saw how uncomfortable the group was getting. The Ancient Ones, the Seers, had not returned as yet. Quickly I remembered my dream journey from earlier. The Deer had come to me, and I learned so much. So I focused on my dream of Deer Medicine! Silently I retracked my dreaming. This is what I found.

Deer can be found in almost every area of the world and in many sizes. They are able to go for long periods without water and still maintain their strength. Deer have a very keen scent and are swift, graceful, and masters at being gentle. They are about abundance, intuition, dreams, and good listeners. They are accepting of others and have well-developed psychic powers. Also, deer are associated with regeneration because of their ability to shed their antlers each year. The Deer is the goddess of the woodland and the Stag is the lord of the underworld, who has an understanding of the cycle of death and rebirth.

Coming out of my dream re-entry, I could still hear the loud voices. This is not appropriate for this space, the center of our work. This is our sacred space and should be regarded as such. It should be kept free of negative energy; I really wanted to shout and to tell them to keep quiet! I wanted to scream at them to take it somewhere else! I was wondering what they were even doing here if they did not know these basic skills.

Standing near my blanket, I realized the time was growing short. Soon the new session would start. The Seers would be here, and I knew they would not tolerate this. I was not a novice Dreamer anymore; I had to try something! I spotted on the altar the beautiful deer antler I had brought, and I reached over and picked it up. The altar etiquette says: do not touch things on the altar without permission. This antler belonged to me. I began feeling a rush of reentering my dream of the ancient past. I was the Deer Goddess of the Woodland, wearing a soft deerskin garment. I was holding this very same antler. The Spirits told me the antler was one from the right side of the deer and was used for healing. The Spirits reminded me that deer are rather shy and able to blend inconspicuously with their surroundings. Working now in two worlds, I moved quietly to the area where the arguing was going on.

"Deer Medicine is gentleness," the Spirits told me, "and their eyes show compassion."

Taking this in to myself, I began looking over the top of the antler on this earth plane. At first I did not notice too much, just a few eyes of the novices darting about. I kept up my medicine work, of holding calm love and gentle energy.

I used my eyes to send love and compassion. One of the novice Dreamers caught my glance, and he smiled slightly at me. I could sense a feeling of fear in him. Maybe fear that his point of this argument was not correct? I was not sure; maybe it was something deeper, and he was triggered by the topic? Well, this part may be something for later, I thought to myself. The point is I will use my deer medicine, sending out love and compassion; this will help to melt fear. My eyes became deep black pools of love and kindness; I looked at these Dreamers, maintaining that dream as I held the antlers and examined the situation.

Spirit said, "Remind him on the dream-plane to stop pushing so hard!"

I transmitted this. Now I noticed the noise level was lower. Yes, something was changing! The Dreamers who had been so disruptive were moving apart. A few of them came over to me to admire the beautiful antlers.

One of the Dreamers, a young woman with long, strawberry blonde hair and a pretty smile said, "When I realized you were near us, your magic was already at work! The power of your gentleness made me see that we were being too loud and pushing the limits with our disagreements." She looked at me with searching eyes; I knew she needed an answer. But it might not be the one she wanted.

Speaking in a level voice and keeping eye contact, I said, "In my dream of what transpired, we all have opinions that we need to express. As Dreamers we learn discernment. We take in the larger picture, and we do a quick dream to the future. If I say this, they may say that, and it might cause such and such to happen. Then we make a quick assessment: is this the right time, place, etc.? If it were my dream, I would take these things into consideration. And remember too this is our 'Dreamers Sacred Space'; we want to keep the energy clear."

The young woman looked at me with some shock and tears in her eyes, saying, "I have so much to learn. Thank you."

Turning to go, the man who I had made eye contact with earlier stopped me and said, "You are a beautiful Deer Woman. I would love to learn more about your medicine."

I looked at him a bit startled, but Spirit whispered in my ear, "It is your time, my dear."

I smiled at the man and said, "I would be happy to share what I know."

The young Dreamer continued, "I had such anger earlier; your tone, while speaking with the woman Dreamer, seemed to calm me, and my anger just vanished! I could not help but overhear." He was gazing at me, waiting.

Silently I checked the time to see if we had enough time to chat before the main program started back up; we did have a while. Looking at him with a steady gaze, I felt like the "Deer

Woman, Goddess of the Woodlands." I began sharing some of my recently learned Deer Medicine.

"Deer are sensitive and clairvoyant and make quick decisions. In Egyptian lore, early paintings of deer are shown with 'Isis.' In China, the 'God Lu-Hsing' was the god of success and wealth; he was represented by the deer. Greek lore tells us about the Greek goddesses: Artemis, Aphrodite, and Athene. And there is the Roman Diana. The Deer was sacred to them all. Fawn skins were the mode of dress for the Greek Orphic Devotees. I should also tell you about the 'Stag.' The Greeks brought the stag to the temples and believed the stag could identify medicinal herbs and plants." I stopped and took a breath as I looked above the man; there was the image of the Deer Seer from my dreaming and the Deer Seer of this Grove.

I was ready to jump up and turn over this lesson to her. She shook her head, saying to me telepathically, "No, you are doing fine. Please continue!"

Turning some, I said to the Dreamer, "Where was I? Oh...Let me see. In Celtic lore 'The Stag' plays many important roles. The God Cernunnous wore an antlered headdress. This same god sometimes went by the name 'Dagda'; he was also referred to as the 'Horned One.' The stag symbolized the virility of the warrior, the Sun, and fertility."

The drumming could be heard softly now. I paused and looked at this young man who was becoming a more experienced Dreamer. He was staring at me intently. I blushed some. Then, I said, "I believe that is all we have time for now."

The Dreamer looked at me, his eyes now gentle, and said, "You have gifted me more than you know. I treasure this time. Thank you!" He reached out his hand to shake mine; I thanked him for the compliment.

We turned our attention now to the circle of Dreamers who had reassembled, ready to continue the afternoon session. The drumming was now quite loud; it certainly got us all to come back to center and focus! Smiling to myself, I thanked the Spirit of the Deer Seer, who had helped me through these teachings.

DOG

DREAM OF THE DOG SEER

As I stood there watching from afar at the two men speaking, I wondered, Is that King Arthur? Or maybe it was the Hierophant Seer? The other one, I was sure, was the Fool Seer, as I could see a dog there jumping up to him and nipping at his ankle as well. There was definitely a lot of commotion coming from them. Curious, I came closer and said, "Hello!"

They turned and greeted me as well. "Hello, hello!"

They had spoken in unison; the hound even stopped its yipping and biting for a minute, staring at me intently. The Fool Seer leaned down and was petting him. "Ah, I see, young fellow. I suppose you were trying to get my attention for this young Dreamer." The Fool Seer was looking up at me, smiling! The dog was quiet, sitting crossed legged in front of the Seer.

I looked back and said, "I did not mean to interrupt."

The Hierophant Seer answered. "No, no, we were only talking about the Greek Delphic Oracles and what contributions they have gifted to the Dreamers!"

I smiled at them both. Then the hound was up and jumping about, he then would run off a bit and then would come back. We all laughed at his antics! Now he was jumping at me!

"Hey, what is going on?" I asked him as I nuzzled his neck. His hair was soft and warm, and up close now I realized that he might be part Labrador retriever and part, well, just hound!

The Fool Seer said, "He likes you and it seems he wants you to walk with him!"

"Me? Walk with him?" Shaking my head no, I said, "I do not think so!"

Just then the dog jumped lightly against me and then sat there wagging its tail, his warm eyes melting my own.

Looking up from the dog to the Fool Seer, I said, "Would this be OK with you?"

Both the men laughed, and with twinkling eyes, the Fool Seer said, "Please, go and enjoy yourself!"

With that, I started a slow run with the hound bounding after me and before me. I looked back, saying, "Thank you!" Waving to them with a smile on my face, the dog was quite a bit ahead now, I called out, "Wait up!" He scampered back some but then was off in the lead again. My eyes stayed fixed to him.

My breath was rapid; I noticed this path was all uphill. I stopped to rest a moment and looked around. Realizing this was a new path for me in the Grove, I felt a sense of excitement. The tree line of the forest off to the right was very thickly wooded. There was ivy growing up some of these huge trunks. Looking around, I did not see the hound anywhere. Somehow I was not concerned; I knew he would find me! Just then I heard something off to the left sounding like water. But the sea was the other direction. Again, splash! I moved off into the woods. Walking downhill some, I found the Hound, happily swimming about in a small pond! I just laughed and found a nice, large rock near the water's edge to sit on. I took off my shoes and dangled my feet in the cool water. "This is wonderful refreshment for one of these dog days of summer!" I smiled as I said this.

Next thing I knew, I was having water sprinkled on me from Hound. I threw my head back with giggles, watching how he shook himself literally from head to tail; it was amazing. Once he was certain that most of the water had been shaken off, he came next to me on the grass to sun himself.

I reached down and petted him and was reminded of such a feeling of comfort. "You are beautiful!" I said to him, ruffling his head.

The Hound looked right at me and said, "Do you know why they call the hot summer months of July and August the Dog Days of summer?"

Not at all was I surprised that he spoke. I simply answered him, "No, I guess I don't know!"

"Well," said Hound, "these months of July and August are the ones that the 'Dog Star Sirius' rises and sets."

"Oh!" I said. "And I suppose I should acknowledge you as the Dog Seer, rather than be calling you Hound. Sorry for that!"

The Seer replied, "I kind of like the name Hound. It is fine with me, whichever name you use! I have lots of stories and teachings to share. Are you game?"

"I thought you would never ask," I said. "Do go on, The Dog Seer." Or maybe Hound sounds better, I thought to myself. Looking at The Seer, I saw that he was rubbing his paw, licking it too. I just had to ask, "Why do dogs do that?"

The Seer said, "Dogs are able to heal their wounds by licking and rubbing them. This healing ability has led to the belief that if a dog is placed by the bedside of a sick person, the person would be healed. There is a strong connection to the healing power of dog with the Celtic God 'Apollo Cunomaglus,' the 'Hound-lord' who is strongly associated with healing. Also the dog can heal emotional wounds in humans. King Arthur had a pet dog that he depended upon named 'Cafall' or 'Cabal.' In Celtic myth, hounds are frequently mentioned, often in regard to the underworld. The dog is a very powerful guardian in both waking reality and the Otherworlds."

The Dog Seer got up and walked some in the shallows of the pond. He was drinking and then he was sniffing around. I called out to him, "I am aware of the loyalty and faithfulness of dogs!"

The Seer came back and said he was glad I knew, and continued. "Dogs are also companions, understanding of doubts, and are full of love and protection. They are watchful and can smell trouble from a distance."

Hound was seated near me again and telling me about a dog's lineage, and I was twisting small grasses as he spoke. "The dog is a domesticated subspecies of the wolf, 'canis lupus,' and it has been the most widely kept working and companion animal in human history. There are hundreds of breeds. Archeological evidence indicates dog's domestication between fourteen thousand to seventeen thousand years ago." The Seer was quiet a minute. I looked at him and told him how much I loved hearing all this history of his lineage. By this time, the Dog Seer was in human form, but he had a pelt of an ancient canine over his shoulders.

He began speaking again. "The dog is related to the wolf, which of course is a hunter, but the dogs of today do not need to hunt. Some think that the dog's soft, limp ears are a result of atrophy of the jaw muscles, because when it was a hunter originally, the jaw was shaped differently. A dog's vision is equivalent to red-green color blindness in humans. Their field of vision is similar to humans. However, it is their sense of smell that is really amazing! For a dog's smell is twofold; it can distinguish two types of scent. One, an air scent, from a person or a thing that has recently passed. Two, a ground scent that remains detectable for longer periods.

"Dogs also have a 'Sprint Metabolism' that can generate large amounts of energy for a short period of time. Then they 'cool down' by panting, and the spleen collects more red blood cells for their energy resource.

"When you begin to observe and study the dog, you will find that different breeds have different qualities. The herding dogs were originally used to assist the laborer and provide protection. Other dogs are bred to hunt and retrieve. Of course many are mixed breeds. I would venture to say, all of them have an amazing ability to love and bring joy!

"A few of the contemporary stories are, television's *Lassie*, 'Toto,' Dorothy's dog in *The Wizard of Oz*, and 'Krypton,' who was Superman's pet. And in the Harry Potter novels, we have 'Padfoot,' associated with the wizard Sirius Black."

The Seer had a laughing smile as I looked at him, nodding my head in agreement.

He went on. "From the Greeks we have the story of 'Argos,' the faithful dog of Odysseus in Homer's *Odyssey*. This faithful dog waited for his master's return to Ithaca for over twenty years, while most presumed Odysseus dead. When his master finally returned, it was said that as soon as Argos recognized his master, he dropped his ears and wagged his tail. Having fulfilled his destiny of 'Faith' by laying his eyes upon his master once more, he released a final whimper and died."

"Oh! My goodness, such a sad story, but I suppose it is uplifting too!" I had tears in my eyes as I said this.

The Seer smiled and nodded his head yes. Then he continued. "In another Greek myth, we have 'Cerberus.' He was the hound of 'Hades,' a god in Greek mythology who ruled the underworld with his brothers Zeus and Poseidon. 'Cerberus' was a monstrous three-headed dog with a snake for a tail and snakes down his back like a mane. He is referred to as a 'Hell-hound.' His job was to guard the gate to 'Hades' and ensure that spirits of the dead could enter but none could exit! And that no living person could come into 'Hades.'"

"No way! I don't like to think of dogs as threatening!" I said, standing up,

"It is OK, my dear," the Seer answered. "It is important to learn all sides of a being's nature. There are needs for these things at times. Come and sit back down."

Looking into his soft, brown-black eyes melted any fears I had; I sat back down.

"It is good to be reminded that in many cultures the dog is the guardian of the mysteries. He can be a fierce protector, defender, when that is needed. Just think about dogs you have known that have carried on barking and snarling until they have sniffed out someone or something new on their turf. They are amazing guardians and deserve our highest appreciation. The dog is the guardian of gateways and the underworld. In English tales we have the story of the 'Black Dog,' the one who guards the gateways to death. Just as a dog guards his master and protects in this world, he does the same for his master in the Otherworlds, protecting and guiding the soul of their dead home. The dog is a keeper of boundaries between this world and the next. For the Egyptians, a dog is a guide to the hawk-headed solar god to keep the sun on its right path, which is sacred to the Egyptian, This dog or jackal-headed god is 'Anubis.' The dog is also associated with the Greek's 'Hermes,' as messenger god. In Scandinavian myth, the god 'Odin' has two dogs and two ravens as counselors."

There was silence. Tossing a few small stones into the water, I said, "The depth of man's best friend is really something. I suppose I have really taken the dogs I've known for granted!"

I could hear a sigh from the Seer. He responded, "Most people do, but then this is why you have come to this Sacred Grove of the Nemeton, to scratch under the surface of that granite!"

I laughed a bit at his comment as we sat here by this pool of water.

The Seer continued, "I am reminded about the ancient connection between dogs and water. Many of the Celtic goddesses were depicted with dogs as companions. Lakes, pools, and the sea were seen as gateways to the Otherworlds, whether that be dreamtime or life after death. The waters were places of healing and renewing, and the dogs were the guardians from one realm to another.

"Well, my dear, we have been enjoying this private healing pool for some time now. I can see the sun's shadows are shifting and the dragonflies are buzzing. Shall we walk back to the main Grove?"

I nodded my head yes, and we climbed up to the path. "It feels good to be moving," I said as I dusted off my skirt.

The Dog Seer put one hand on my shoulder and said, "In my experience for everyday living, my best gift to myself for guidance is my trait of 'Loyalty' for others but mostly for myself. In my dream of offering advice, I ask, when confused, 'Am I loyal to myself with this?' Whatever that may be, practice one's Loyalty to Self and one's personal Truth."

I looked back at him with my eyes shining and said, "I will always remember that and our time here together."

We walked a bit more, and the Seer said, "I really do not mind if you call me 'Hound'!" Then he started sniffing at the air. "Do you smell that?"

I sniffed and didn't smell a thing. I started looking about. The next thing I knew, he was in dog form, scampering off into the woods on the trail of mystery, I was sure. How happy I felt to have learned so much in this amazing day. I began sniffing again, but now I could smell something. The evening campfire had been stoked, and it was calling me home. I thought, I'll bet "Hound" is there already!

Karen C. Silverstein

DOLPHIN

DREAM OF THE DOLPHIN SEER

Swimming, yes! That is just what I need! I was in my room changing into a swimsuit as fast as I could. Pulling down a towel from the shelf, then gathering a blanket and some snacks, I was out the door and on the path that lead to the beach. The sun on my back felt great. I was feeling a bit drained after the morning's session; I had been working with some of the novice Dreamers who were trying hard to be on track with our Dream work. Some of them just were not ready for the higher realms of our healing work yet, mostly because they were not taking the work seriously. I felt a concern for them.

These Dreamers needed to receive clear messages from me about healing themselves. So by using the "If it were my dream" method with the ones who asked for help, I then provided a few possible dream scenarios. As I watched them take in this added dreaming, I was encouraged. Standing up from our circle work, I was tired, and knew I needed to close some circuits here with the work we had done. In my dream weaving I called on my animal guardians to help me disconnect the energy work. Once done, I looked at the bright sun and smiled. Then I suggested to the group that we take some afternoon time-off. Everyone thought this was a great plan, and all of us began to go our separate ways.

Thinking about these Dreamers, I saw such sparks and promise for their potential. Some, though, had a hold on a lot of negative energy. Thinking about this, I reminded myself that we all have some; I cannot judge here. The teaching for me is to share with them my own experiences and dream-ways to face the hard challenges of life that then allow us to cross over to more positive lifestyles. Wanting the light is one thing, but it takes constant work to change. It takes hard work and a belief in your path! We must all stoke our own hearth fires to becoming a part of the light flow that is so freely given to those who study and work in earnest. Yet there may be some here who will not make these positive transitions at this time on the planet. I am learning that this is quite all right; there will be many other chances or timelines to do this.

The sounds of the waves were lulling me to the sea. How beautiful this place is! The tide was out, and I could see the rocks easily on the small island now. The rocks formed a circle with a pool of water in the center; I just loved this little grotto. In my dreaming I often use this sacred pool as a portal for a journey. Looking at the beach, I found a secluded spot away from most of the swimmers and sunbathers. I spread out my blanket and let myself to just drink in the light from the sun and feel the salted air on my skin. Well, I am definitely hot enough now, I thought. I scanned the water, holding my hand over my eyes, which helped to cut the sun glare. I felt like a seafarer searching the seas, looking out over the horizon line for an expectant ship.

Then something just beyond the rock grotto with the pool caught my attention...What the heck! I watched water stream into the air, and then there was nothing! Suddenly, again more water spraying, but now there was an arch of something...a dolphin! It was definitely a dolphin performing graceful jumps not far from the small rock island. I was so excited! I took a deep breath and plunged into the water; I needed to be with this amazing sea creature. It was a distance to get out to this island with the rock grotto, but I felt I could do the swim. I said to myself, If I am meant to be with this dolphin, it will be so!

After my first rush to get a distance out toward the island, I changed from the breast stroke to the side stroke for a while, which allowed me to rest and look about some. I saw that I was only about fifty feet from the rocks. Not that far, but the last stretch was hard. I was happy when I climbed upon the rocky shore of the little island. I stood for a few minutes and looked around, smoothing the hair back off my face; I was still breathless. Realizing that there were no "sprays" in the surf, I felt disappointed. Finding a place to sit down, I looked back at shore. Wow! This sure gives me a different perspective of the Grove, the Nemeton, I thought. There it was, all nicely nestled on the top of the hill above the cliffs. From a passerby on the sea, it just looked like another part of a beautiful shoreline. A natural piece of Mother Nature that they saw as they passed by. To our Dream Family, it was so much more. This place gave us a place to anchor, to ground. It was a private jewel by the sea, and we were the different gems being molded in the dreaming we held here.

The tide was still way out; in some areas, not far off, I could see sandbars. But mostly this was deep water. Looking at the shore, I saw some of the Dreamers and waved. The rocks were smooth here, from all the water action. Still no sign of the dolphin. So I stretched out on the sun-baked surface. I figured within a half an hour I would need to be heading back to shore.

Just as I was comfortable, I heard her. Sitting straight up, I looked off to the right. She was performing her acrobatic feats. I admired the way she could leap out of the water, easily reaching twenty feet! Now I began to hear her music, deep humming sounds that were coming near the rocky edge. Then it was gone! Deciding it was now or never, I climbed down into the deep. The water felt colder than it was earlier. Shivering a bit, I got myself moving about, just doing easy side strokes, not far from the rocks; I still needed the grounding comfort that they had provided for me. I turned onto my back and just floated. The rays of the sun felt as if they went right through me into the sea. I liked that. Then the waves peaked a bit, and next thing I knew, the dolphin was floating right next to me!

Looking into my eyes, she said, "You are brave to come out here on your own!"

I managed a small laugh, as I turned myself around while treading water. "I had to! I just needed to meet you and learn from you...if that is good with you?" I knew that I had asked with a sense of longing.

Quickly, the Dolphin Seer answered, saying, "I am happy to meet you and teach what I can. Are you ready, Dreamer? We will begin with the breath!" Then she turned and dove deeply into the blue-green waters. I just stayed there, not knowing what to do.

I felt relived when I saw her surface. She began talking immediately. "The breath is all-important to man and dolphins and all creatures. The thing dolphins know intuitively is how to control the breath. Our breathing can release our emotions and help us reach altered states of consciousness. As I recall, earlier today you were full of emotions with the Dream work you were doing." I wondered how she knew this. "Why don't you give those emotions away now by blowing them out with your breath?"

I immediately did what the Dolphin Seer suggested. After a couple of minutes, I looked at her and said, "I think this is helping."

Smiling at me, she responded with, "The salted seawater helps with negative energies as well. But let's move on. If you are able to breathe in a rhythm, like a dolphin, there is much you can learn. So let me show you how to ground yourself to the land first and get your sense of the firmness of the rocks. Do this in your mind's eye, breathing in your rooted source. Next, picture this wonderful, light, sun-filled air filling your lungs and all of you, making yourself ready to go into the depths. Practice this a few times. Once you feel a confidence in the rhythm you are developing, we will travel together through the water. Do not worry. I will protect you, and I know how to monitor the body for endurance."

"My goodness," I said. "This is something!"

"I know that you are a bit afraid. Don't be! I am here for you!" said the Seer."

So I practiced the breathing and then let her know I was ready. We dove into the deep blue together; there was barely a sound.

"Just hold onto my side if you like," said Dolphin. "I will take you to places that existed before man walked the lands, and I will show you our primordial beginnings. This helps one to know more about what the world is made of, how things were and came to be today."

We traveled so quickly. I saw many amazing landscapes, and I saw animals, both land and sea creatures, that existed before time as I knew things. The waters were clear and full of life. I had my eyes wide open, and my breath was not a problem. I was swimming with a dolphin and entranced!

I could hear sounds traveling through the waters, and then I saw that we were entering a whole ring of dolphins! OH! MY GOSH!

The Dolphin Seer told me, "You are within the 'dolphin pod' now, and there will be some here that will share and teach along with me."

I swam around on my own some, letting all the dolphins know how much I appreciated this time. One of them said to me, "We encourage others to follow the rhythms of the universe and to hear the Voices of the Ancestors for what has come before." I nodded and thanked him.

Another called out, "Dolphins are among the most intelligent creatures on Earth. They have dwelled in the oceans of the planet for more than three million years!"

I kept going around in the pod. One ancient being said, "Stop a moment!" I did and she revealed this amazing story from Greek myth. "Dionysius, the god of wine and mirth, was voyaging across the Mediterranean, disguised as a traveler. The sailors aboard the ship had evil intentions and, not knowing the true identity of their passenger, planned to kidnap Dionysus and sell him as a slave. Once Dionysus discovered this plot, he used his divine powers to fill the boat with vines and the sounds of pipes. He caused leopards and lions to appear and changed the oars of the boat into snakes! In order to escape from this madness, the sailors leapt overboard into the sea. Here the God of the Ocean, Poseidon, changed them into Dolphins, forever destined to help sailors guide their boats. Thereafter 'The Dolphins' were the messengers of Poseidon."

I was awestruck. "Thank you! What a wonderful story," I said.

"I have a little more to tell about Greece." This message came from another ancient being in the pod.

I swam over quickly. "Please share." I said.

"Well, it has been said that the constellation in the heavens, 'Delphinus,' the dolphin, was put into the sky by Poseidon in gratitude to the dolphins for finding his bride, 'Amphitrite.' Also, in ancient Greece, to kill a dolphin was punishable by death, as dolphins were seen as the messengers of the gods. There are also many tales of the friendships of boys and dolphins. To the Greeks it is the dolphin who guides the souls to the Isles of the Blessed. Dolphin has both solar and lunar associations, being connected with 'Apollo Delphinos,' the light of the sun. It is also associated with the feminine principle and the womb, between 'delphis,' dolphin, and 'delphys,' womb. There is another strong connection with the 'Goddess Aphrodite,' the woman of the sea."

This incredible creature swam off quickly. I called after him, "Thank you!" I swam on to another of the pod.

"I have news from various cultures!" I swam close to this dolphin's side to listen. "A Hindu myth tells that the Dolphin is one of a few creatures that herald the goddess's decent from the heavens. The Inuit people of the Artic attribute whales and dolphins with the divine creation. In ancient Sumeria, dolphins were connected to 'Ea-Oannes,' the deity of the sea. In Egypt the dolphin was an attribute of the 'Goddess Isis' and helped to guide souls in the underworld. From the land of the ancient Celts, the dolphin was attributed with 'well worship' and the healing powers of waters. The dolphin image can be found on many of their artifacts. For many cultures across the world, the dolphin is a symbol of protection and its image brings good luck."

I could swear I saw a smile across the face of this amazing creature. There was silence now in the pod. "Thank you! Thank you, all! This is all so wonderful, I am grateful!" Swimming off slowly, my heart was full.

The Dolphin Seer was there to greet me. "How do you feel?" she said to me.

"Feel?"

Realizing that I sounded confused, The Seer said to me, "Why yes. Feel about being under the water all this time!"

"Oh!" I said. "I am fine." But thinking about it, I was also surprised, as I had nearly forgotten about being in the deep water! But knowing I was in a magical place, I then added, "I feel wonderful!"

Smiling at me, she said, "Time for us to head back."

I nodded my head yes! We were back in the blink of an eye! All the way back to the spot on the beach where I had left my towel!

"Now that was nice and convenient!" I said.

"Let's dry off some and then sit a few more minutes," the Seer answered. I realized now that the Dolphin Seer had changed to her human form, and she was just as beautiful.

"It feels a bit strange being on land now!" I said to her.

"True, I know what you mean," she answered.

The Dolphin Seer continued. "Even today dolphins are thought to possess mystical powers; this makes me glad and proud. Healers and patients alike use dolphins to help heal ailments of all kinds. Remember the sounds that dolphins make? Well, those sounds release endorphins, the body's natural pain-killing hormone. Healers who know how to work this in humans can achieve results doing sound releases. Sometimes these sounds produce feelings that can bring intense happiness and excitement. Some healers believe that 'Dolphins' act as channels for 'chi,' the life-force energy associated with many healing modalities.

"Observation has shown that dolphins with their sonar and telepathic abilities can sense internal conditions in others. One can see this when watching mothers with their young. There is essential nurturing that takes place with mother and baby when she teaches the baby when to breathe. Gradually, she holds the baby underwater and teaches about breath. While holding the baby for longer and longer periods, all the while she is guarding and sensing the condition of the baby's young body. Young dolphins nurse with their mother for the first year and continue to stay close to her side for several years."

"Oh my Goddess! I just love you all so!" I could not help myself with responding!

The Seer laughed, saying, "Well, to go on just a bit…Dolphins can teach us 'Image work,' to picture a goal, something that we want, and hold that, just like the breath. We trust that it will be accomplished without undue effort, just like the breath!"

There was quiet now. I was trying to process some of the afternoon's events; it had been too extraordinary for words really. Finally I realized the Dolphin Seer was speaking, and I tried to listen. Although I was still in the dream, she was patient with me.

"So, to sum these things up, what would you say?" The Seer said, looking at me with deep, blue-green eyes.

"Well, this is what I have gathered," I said. I recited my mental list to her. "Communica-tion, change, freedom, trust, balance, harmony, and understanding rhythm in your life, also using the breathe for physical and internal means of movement or to travel."

"I am impressed! However, do take a breath for yourself now." The Seer then said, "Let me also add a few more: wisdom and the water element. And, of course, MAGIC!"

With that, she stood up quickly and prepared to go back to the sea. Giving me a warm hug, she said this has been a wonderful afternoon! I agreed and I gave her my heartfelt thank you! She then crossed over some rocks in her human form, and then crossed over as a dolphin and into the blue-green sea. I felt sadness for her going. But such appreciation and very glad too. I picked up my things and saw the tide had really come in now. I turned and headed for the Grove. I was starving! I wondered what was for dinner.

DOVE

DREAM OF THE DOVE SEER

It was dawn with the light just coming over the hill. I am not usually an early riser, but when I heard the cooing out of my window, I knew I had to get outside early and just walk. It would be good to get my feelings and thoughts in order before the busy day. I heard the sounds again. I knew it was the Morning Doves. What were they up to? Why did I need to follow them?

The dew was collecting on my boots as I walked up the hill. The grass was neatly cut here, a wide, green meadow with a few rocks cropping out. The wind was lightly blowing, I was glad for my jacket. I noted various wildflowers I would like to pick, but not now; I wanted to get up to the hillcrest and feel the sun as it arrived for the day. I heard the cooing again. Looking through the tree line, I still did not see the doves. It was getting brighter; I ran the last few yards and stopped, quite out of breath. I leaned over with my hands on my knees, to let my heart slow down, and there they were, the doves. They were quiet now, feeding in the warm morning sunshine. I smiled at them; they did not seem to notice. Of course, I said to myself, They are busy, and they are ground feeders! I could feel messages from them however, reminding me of their contact with Earth Mother and for myself to keep grounded. By doing so, I would be able to receive her creative possibilities. I sat down on the grass and drank in the newly arrived sun. "See, I am grounding," I said to the doves as I picked at a few blades of grass.

They made cooing noises back to me. I lay back onto the grassy knoll, staring at the sun, which had dawned the new day. This is one of the "Between Times," the Dawn and the Dusk, which I loved, and both of these times were good to connect to the source. It was "dawning on me" to ask Spirit for help with my current dreams. I closed my eyes. The sun felt wonderful on my face. I began to journey into a daydream...

I was in my dream but heard the cooing again; it was so close. When I opened my eyes, the dove was right there! Turning over on my side, I propped my head on my elbow. Now I was eye level with this beautiful creature. As I admired her, she felt female, I noticed something odd on her left leg. It looked like a tiny scroll. What on earth? Is this...?

The dove cocked her head to the left, and she began talking to me! "It is a 'pigeon post,' and you may open it. I have carried a message to you."

Sitting up quickly, I was taken aback, but, smiling some, I said, "A message for me?"

"Please open it," she said.

Taking her leg carefully, I saw a small cap on the top of the post. I opened this and, pulling out a small piece of very thin paper, I said, "Who would send me a message in this fashion?"

The paper was so delicate and translucent; I took care as I unrolled it onto the warm green grass. In a beautiful old English text, which was hard to read, the message said, "The Greek Goddess Aphrodite was born from an egg brooded over by a Dove." I repeated this over in a quiet voice a few times. But what does this mean to me? I thought.

When I looked up again, the dove had gone. In her place was The Dove Seer! Standing just a few feet away, in human form, she was adjusting her incredible feather cloak. It was, of course, made of pinkish-beige dove feathers with tiny seed pearls stitched in interesting designs throughout. She only stood about five feet tall; however, one could feel the love and warmth emanating from her.

Realizing that my mouth was gaping open, I quickly stood up, straightened myself, and tried to seem composed. Standing there, I towered over her. Even though I am five feet six inches tall, I felt ungainly somehow.

The Dove Seer stood watching me; I was uncomfortable and did not know what to say.

She folded her arms in front of her, and the cloak glimmered with its beauty. Laughing slightly and cocking her head to the left, she said, "I won't bite!"

I smiled faintly, trying to relax. Breaking the uneasy silence, I said, "But why have you come?"

The Dove Seer stared at me without emotion and said, "You have read the message from the dove's pigeon post, carried by 'Aphrodite,' who is my 'Carrier Pigeon,' a homing pigeon. She assists me with my communications. We certainly got your attention, did we not?" I attempted to speak; she waved her hand. "You ask why I have come. Why don't you remember? You have been asking for a sign to help with your creativity. I can assist you with that. Shall we continue?" Smiling, I nodded my head yes and answered in the strongest voice I could manage. The Seer suggested that we walk over the hill and find a spot to converse.

By now the sun was warming everything as early morning had broken; the wildlife was busily taking care of its needs. From this vantage point on this grassy knoll, we could see the ocean over the cliffs to the right and the Grove of Nemeton on the left. Inspired by what I saw, I said, "It is so beautiful and perfectly peaceful that it brings tears to my eyes."

"This is only one of the reasons that I am drawn to work with you, my daughter," said the Dove Seer. We found a spot to sit down for a while. The Seer spread out her dove cloak for us. I hesitated to sit. She told me not to worry, that it was incredibly strong, and the energy it would give to me might be helpful. It was so soft. I felt very regal as I sat down with this amazing teacher.

"Where do I start?" I heard the Dove Seer say. "There are so many symbols...White Doves symbolize purity, as I am sure you know, but also restoration and peace. The Christians and the Jews use the dove as both peace and love symbols.

"According to the biblical story, after the flood Noah released a dove to find land. The dove came back with an olive branch in its beak. Since that time the dove with an olive branch has been a symbol of peace. Seven doves appeared at the time of Jesus's baptism. To the Christians the three dove iconography symbolizes the Holy Spirit. Sometimes in Christian weddings doves are released, as they are associated with love, peace, and pacifism. The Olympic Games promote this symbol on their banners. Dove is also the emblem of the Knights of the Holy Grail."

"This is such wonderful information! I am really glad you came to me," I said to the Seer. "But tell me, how did you realize I need help with my creativity? I do not recall specifically asking for help."

She answered me, saying, "We have noted, my rock pigeon dove friends and I, that you were talking to us as we cooed around your cabin lately. Whispers of things you long to do, to make, sometimes upset that you were not achieving these things. The carrier pigeons/the doves have the ability to 'Home' over long distances. Sometimes they would return to me with this information, no matter where I might be, as they do for many who are on the healing path. The birds have the ability to detect the Earth's magnetic field. Using this as a map mechanism, we can track those seeking help."

Staring at her some at this startling information, finally I said, "Wow! I am impressed. I do feel kind of stuck lately. I have so many art projects and life projects I would like to do, and lately I just do not seem to make headway!"

The Seer answered by saying, "This is a time of nurturing and gestation for you now. Possibly a time to make peace with yourself about something." I looked at her grey eyes reflecting what she was telling me. She turned her head and then pointed to the sky. "Look at the dove hovering over the water. Do you see it?" she said.

"Yes, I see it," I answered back.

"I mean, do you see the halo? The three-rayed halo?" the Seer said to me.

"Oh my gosh! I do! I see the halo! It is incredible. Does it mean something in particular?"

Quietly the Seer put her hand back in her lap and looked at me intently. There was silence. I wanted to say, Is it a sign?

The Dove Seer looked at me with her eyes twinkling. "Why, my daughter, it is meant for you, and it means Creation!" I could not think of anything to say. Taking my hand in her own, she said, "It is quite all right. We have plenty of time to work with this gift!"

A gift…I thought to myself.

The Dove Seer picked up her teachings again. "Now let me think a minute. The dove is a bird of prophecy, and, curiously, we just had one arrive especially for you! The dove in divination can help you to 'See' what to give birth to in your current life. Now remember, earlier we spoke of a gestation time; it seems that we are now moving into the birthing time. So it would be wise for you to reflect on this now. Be honest, and remember, we often receive what we ask for!" I sat back a bit, wondering. There was not time to go deeper just then. The Dove Seer continued, saying, "The dove lays two eggs, and the number two is the traditional number for the feminine and creative energies. The Dove is the symbol of the Goddess, brooding over the waters of creation. She helps with 'The Goddess Within.' The dove is a primary symbol of female sexuality. This, I believe, brings us back to the message that was sent to you by my dove with the tiny 'pigeon post'!"

I pulled out the tiny message written in old English text, and I read it to us both in a smooth but excited voice. "The Greek Goddess Aphrodite was born from an egg brooded over by a Dove." I put the scroll on the grass and anchored it with a few pebbles. My eyes turned to look at this amazing woman.

The Dove Seer was relaying that "Aphrodite," who is the Greek goddess, is really the same as "Venus," being the Latin, Roman counterpart. "In the Sumerian culture she was called 'Inanna.' They all have these characteristics: love, desire, the creative mother, fertility, imagination, and beauty; their color is green; their flower is the white rose and vervain; and their stone is Lapis Lazuli. The Goddesses day is Friday, their direction is the west, and, most importantly here, their bird is the 'Dove'! So my dear," said the Seer, "our dear little dove has done us a wonderful service brooding over this amazing Goddess." The Seer then tapped my shoulder, and I realized she was referring to me!

Then she continued her tale. "I would venture to say they are very endeared to one another! I am sure you have seen countless old paintings of various goddesses that were surrounded by the doves. The 'Dove' is an amazing creature that has been with us forever and has been a continuing symbol for the goddess, whichever her name. Also, the bird is her communicator and guardian for love and peace. The dove is the symbol of 'the life Spirit, the soul': the passing from one state or world to another. Doves are sacred to all Great Mothers and Queens of Heaven.

"They depict femininity and maternity. They are symbols of renewal of life. A dove is the emblem of the Greek Goddess Athene. Also an emblem for the Great Mother in the Minoan culture. To the Chinese, doves symbolize longevity, faithfulness, and orderliness. To Egyptians, a dove is a symbol of innocence. The dove is the emblem of the Knights of the Holy Grail.

"Here is one last story for you. In northwestern Greece there is a small city named Dodona. There within is the 'Oracle of Dodona.' According to a fifth-century historian, it is among the oldest Hellenic oracles. In the Egyptian town of Thebes, two priestesses had been carried away by Phoenicians. One was sold in Libya and the other in Hellas. These women said they were the first founders of places of Divination in their country. They pledged they would continue their work. Then the story tells of two black doves that flew from Thebes, Egypt. One came to Libya and one to Dodona; the latter settled on an oak tree. And it was here human speech was uttered by a woman, yet a dove, saying that a 'Place of Divination' declared from Zeus must be made there.

"The people of Dodona understood that the message was divine, and they therefore established the 'Oracular Shrine of Dodona.' the people of the village called the woman 'Dove' as she performed her oracle work because when she spoke she sounded strongly like the very bird itself."

After a few moments of silence, the Dove Seer then said, "My work in the Nemeton is about Love, Beauty, Creation, Communication, and Peace. Other attributes would be Deep Understanding and Gentleness. The 'Dove' is a spirit messenger between the worlds, and we are very instinctive and sensitive to emotions. One thing you might like to remember, my dear one, is to call upon dove when you are doing deep healing work with a client. Dove can assist in releasing trauma stored in our cellular memory."

There was silence between us for a while. Our eyes, however, stayed connected for several minutes. I knew the Dove Seer was transferring healing messages to me, which would be revealed at the right times. I was bewildered, but much honored.

The wind picked and stirred some, then the Seer stood up, saying, "It is time to move into the rest of the morning!"

We started walking down the hillside. I turned to look at that magical spot on the grassy knoll for just a moment, and then I turned to express my thanks to the beautiful The Dove Seer; she was already flying off! But I did feel her saying, "You are welcome!"

DRAGONFLY

DREAM OF THE DRAGONFLY SEER

The rain had been hard during the night. I loved the way it sounded hitting the roof, lulling me to sleep. I slept soundly, but did not have any dream recall this morning. I always am disappointed to not catch the dreams of the night. I was, however, looking forward to daydreaming today! The Dreamers have all been so busy with the workshops and healing practices, and it becomes very tiring. I was happy that I had the morning free to just be! Rather than go for the morning meal with the others, I had decided last night to bring back bread, cheese, and an apple for this morning. I would breakfast myself once I arrived at the Sea Pool, and I was excited!

I had everything in my pack: journal, shawl, food, water, and tobacco for the Spirits. So why was I still looking around my room?

I got to the Sea Pool in no time. The sun was trying hard to come out from behind the clouds. Realizing that this place is so incredibly beautiful, I was smiling from head to toe! Tall limestone cliffs were covered with lichen and barnacle rock shells. The sea was off to the left some. I could hear her, but not see her. Looking up I spotted nine points in the spiked cliff in front of me. I supposed that if I were at the top, I could probably dive right into the sea's whitecaps! Windy mists were above the floodwaters; it was so beautiful. I pulled my sweater closer around myself as I began to inspect this ancient, mystical place. I took my sandals off and walked on the wet sand, which mingled with shallow sea pools. There was a lovely marsh area with grasses and reeds in many variations of the color green. Seafoam green was most prevalent, but the new shoots of the reeds in lime green were the prettiest.

I had brought a small basket for the treasures I knew that I would find. Walking among the grasses, I collected little shells, rocks, and bits of colored glass that had been washed in from the sea. It was a beautiful start for the day. I saw a flicker of something near one of the rocks, then saw the pelicans there chasing after their morning meal. Looking at the few things in my basket, I decided to climb the bank and find a spot to rest and have my own breakfast. Opening my thermos, I quickly poured coffee and drank it half down. Looking at the huge rocks and cliffs around this Sea Pool, I could see black lines etched into the rocks at least ten feet up from the sandy floor. Wow, I thought, The tide really comes in high here. I had heard stories of this being a kind of grotto, where the faerie beings and urchins came.

Also, I had heard, it was not the place to be in the night! Looking around at the natural beauty, everything seemed perfectly normal to me.

I spread out my purple shawl to rest upon, then stood up a moment to straighten my little perch. As I was looking toward the grasses, I saw them, The Dragonflies! There must have been thirty or sixty or more. Buzzing around so fast, I really could not tell how many, so I sat down quietly and just enjoyed the show. Pulling out my journal, I made some sketches of these dainty creatures, the dragonflies.

In between I admired the rocks, the grasses, and the way the sun's light and the shadows played the scene; I made sketches of these too. A feeling came over me, a flicker of a daydream of being a part of something in an ancient grotto. What a private treasure I had for the morning. Well, this was not an actual grotto, maybe just the outer area of a grotto! A grotto in the true sense is a small cave. But this spot sure did get the floods of high tides like a grotto would. Looking again at the limestone rocks etched with water marks, I thought again about grottos. I remembered that they often contained a well or sacred spring.

With my knees bent up and my arms wrapped about them, I watched the dragonfly air show.

I remembered that they can fly at speeds of thirty miles per hour and that they can spot their prey from forty feet away. As nymphs they are in the water; at maturity they move to the air. They are creatures of two elements, two realms: water and air.

Looking up at the sun and embracing its warmth, I was happy. Thinking of the ancient cliffs here, I thought how ancient dragonflies are as well. In my daydreaming just now, I was given messages about dragonflies having been estimated to have been on Earth for over 180 million years! Dragonfly is one of the most adaptable of insects; they have two pairs of wings, but if need be, they can fly with one pair. What incredible information.

It was warmer now, so I walked down to the shallow Sea Pool for some wading. Folding my skirt over my arm to keep it dry, I enjoyed the soft sand and laughed at the little sand crabs scurrying around, digging themselves into the sand. I felt that I was in the canvas of a Maxwell Parish painting, and it was delightful! I could hear a kind of humming and turned to see the dragonflies were all around me.

One of them held the light, and its wings looked like jewels. I heard someone saying, "Our realm is light, and our coloring reminds us of our true colors. This is our territory; it is the height of summer, which is our most powerful time! What brings you to our cove?"

Stepping back, my reverie gone, I stammered to say, "Where are you? And who are you?" I did not see anything, and again the voice came.

"Dragonflies remind us of our light and how we can reflect this light in powerful ways. Now, tell me, daughter, is this some of why you are here?"

Nodding my head yes, I was afraid to do or say anything else!

The humming from the huge ban of dragonflies turned into a beautiful melody and complemented the constant sound of the sea. A breathtaking creature, part woman, part sprite, part dragonfly, was walking now alongside of me. As the music played and her eyes met mine, I relaxed. Of course this was the "Dragonfly Seer," and I was happy to meet her.

Speaking in a tone that sounded like a flute, she began. "Some Native Americans believe dragonflies represent swiftness, activity, and pure water. It is said that they are a symbol of renewal after a time of great hardship. Some Native stories tell of dragonflies representing the souls of the dead." She was looking at me harshly, maybe checking for my response; I couldn't speak. The Seer was in seafoam gauze and cerulean blue robes. With an even tone in her voice and darting eyes, she said, "Will you walk with me awhile, daughter?"

Of course I answered yes, although it was more from head nodding, than from my voice!

The Dragonfly Seer went on. "In some places in Europe, dragonflies have been portrayed as sinister. Some have said they darted about so quickly, biting, causing injury. They were given names like 'Devils Needles' and 'Ear Cutters,' referring to the injuries. Dragonflies in Japan are symbols of courage, strength, and happiness."

As the Seer was saying this, I smiled and realized I was fine and began feeling very happy for myself this morning. In her musical voice she now continued, swirling and dancing through the shallow water where we walked. She was talking about the traditional uses of dragonfly as medicine. The Seer also said some parts of the world use the larvae as food.

"Oh yuck!" I said out loud.

She just laughed! "Dragonflies are symbols of immortality and regeneration," the Seer said.

We both looked around the cove; it was teeming with activity. The dragonflies were flitting about in the green-blue water and the sea foam in the pools. "I am not sure if they are dragonflies, sprites, or faerie beings," I said to the Dragonfly Seer.

She answered, "We must remember that all water is one, whether in a stream, pool, lake, or sea. All water is connected; it is the way of the Mother. So the creatures that live among its realms are all connected as well. There have been stories of old told about the interchangeability of the small ones, the faerie. The important thing to remember is these beings can aid you in replenishing your energy, because they have abundant energy themselves. But of course you must be of pure intent and highly respectful while working with this realm."

Wide-eyed, she looked at me; she was tracking something as she stood very still. "Do you hear that?" she said, turning around and looking toward the tall limestone cliff. I looked where she did, but I did not hear anything and told her so.

"The training of a Dreamer is to know how to listen, Dreamer!" I was taken aback slightly, but there was no room to answer as she continued. "Oriental stories speak of an ancient time when dragonflies were related to real dragons and to connections with the Faerie Realm."

Tilting her head and holding out her left arm, again she said, "Listen! This may become a link to incredible nature spirits to work our dreaming with. Come and follow me quietly!" I did as she asked. She was headed toward the more open area of the cove and kept looking up toward the high, spiny cliff.

I just kept quiet and followed. I reached for my small pouch of tobacco to give as an offering, should I need it, and I handed some to the Seer. She smiled and so did the Goddess, sending mist to wrap us close to this cove and shut out most of the everyday world.

The tide was coming in. I had no sense of the time; the sun was blocked now with the sudden fog and mist. I looked around the cove, which was turning quickly into more of a grotto! The fog was swirling. I was uneasy and stayed close to the Dragonfly Seer. What was happening. . .I did not know. The Seer looked again at the spiny cliff and pointed to it with her hand. I followed her gaze.

Then she said, "The best of dreams show only one path among many! The weather is turning; there will be rain soon." She was pointing now to the high cliff with the jagged edges. This was the cliff with the nine points that I had noticed upon arriving earlier. "It looks like a dragon, does it not?!" She continued, "In China, dragons symbolize power and are connected to the number nine. Nine is the largest single digit. This is considered lucky. The Chinese Dragon has nine spines and nine attributes. There are nine forms of dragons, and dragons have nine children. The number nine is the number of The Emperor." I was in awe as she told this story. She was not finished.

She was silent a moment, then said, "Shush. . .Did you hear that?"

I did not hear anything but the crashing of the waves. I noticed the tide climbing high, quickly now. I grabbed my pouch and journal. Slinging this over my back, the Seer held out her hand with the tobacco, sprinkled some against the rocks, and motioned for me to follow her upward climb. Of course I did so instantly, but I was becoming even more apprehensive. We rested on a fairly wide ledge for a bit.

Once the Seer and I relaxed, she continued. "Dragons are most often depicted as composites of other animals. The word 'Dragon' comes from the Greek 'Drakon' and means serpent or great worm. They are found throughout the world in all forms. Christianity has made them seem evil, but this is not so; 'what they are is powerful'! They are the guardians of treasures and of 'Waygates.' The Basilisk Dragon breathed fire and could kill with a look from his eyes! The name 'Basilisk' comes from the Greek 'Basiliskas' and means 'Little King.' It is a legendary reptile reputed to be king of serpents. One of the earliest accounts is from 'Pliny the Elder's Natural History,' written in approximately 79 AD. In England, Geoffrey Chaucer also spoke of this dragon and called it 'Basilicok.' The famous Leonardo da Vinci from Italy included a 'Basilisk Dragon' in his 'Bestiary,' which, in medieval times, was an illustrated volume describing wildlife along with moral lessons. Leonardo said of this dragon: 'the being was so utterly cruel that when it cannot kill animals by its baleful gaze, it turns upon herbs and plants, and fixing its gaze on them withers them up.'"

The Dragonfly Seer paused, as she was almost to the base now of the nine-pointed spiny cliff. She jumped from one of the rocks across the water to another larger rock and reached out her hand for me to do the same. I was fearful; it was quite a stretch. I looked at her, and she just waved her hand as if to say, Hurry now! After looking at the tide waters rising, I held my breath and took the leap across! I was fine; the Seer had my hand in hers. We had a wide section of rock now to climb upon, and we were out of any danger from the rising tide waters. Thank the Goddess! The beautiful grotto was being engulfed now, but the fog was not quite as thick here. My heart was racing!

The Seer had us sit a moment there on the rocky ledge and told me she needed to relate more about the dragon. "According to some legends, 'Basilisks' can be killed by hearing the crowing of a rooster. In another tale, the 'Basilisk' can be tricked and killed by having it gaze at itself in a mirror! This story comes from Warsaw, Poland, where a man killed a dragon by carrying a set of mirrors."

She turned suddenly and laughed a roaring laugh! She said to me, "Well, you can close your mouth now! Trained in dreaming, one can put any meaning into the words; take care in the ones you choose!"

I moved my head so as not to stare at her. In a small voice, I said, "Dragonfly Seer, why have we gotten so heavy and dark about the dragon just now? Only a little earlier there was lightness and even music from the dragonflies buzzing about!"

She turned and looked at me with gentleness. "There are histories, patterns, to everything. As a Dreamer, one needs to know as many sides as they can absorb. Sometimes there is dream smoke, and as a Healer it is very important to know what is behind the smoke. So, as one who is teaching, I must present various parts of my makeup, both light and dark. Then it is up to you to use the teachings as you see fit. My daughter, I am 'Dragon,' but I am also 'Dragonfly,' sprite and fairy!" I smiled at her and nodded my head.

We continued our upward climb; it was easier now, not being on the sheer cliffs. Looking at the grotto, which was now covered with water, I still felt the magic it held earlier. We were at the top. The sun poked back out from the clouds, but it was definitely cooler, and I could feel a mist against my face now. The Dragonfly Seer was right next to the tall cliffs; I noticed there was a large cleft in the rock next to her. I stood there not knowing what to say or do.

She said, "Stand at the crossroads if you will, but if you'll not choose, I'll move on without you!" And with that she was gone!

I was flabbergasted! Totally surprised, I looked about, and I saw a group of dragonflies in the grasses, but they moved off in a moment. I looked back to the rock; way at the top I saw the nine spines. The Dragon!

I thought, Could it be? I looked at the long cleft in the limestone cliffs. Could it have opened? Is this part of the grotto inside? Is that a 'Way-Gate'? Has she gone to the Dragon? Is she the rocky Dragon?

Just then there was a blaze of light from the sun, and a few dragonflies went past me. I was reminded of my own light and how I could reflect that light in powerful ways, as the Seer had said earlier. I would remember my dark side as well. What did she mean when she said, "But if you'll not choose"? I had tears in my eyes; I had come to know the Dragonfly and did not want her gone just yet!

The tide was coming in quickly; I knew it was time to get back to the hearth fire. I took out my tobacco pouch and gave thanks to the "Nine-Pointed Dragon" and, of course, to the Dragonfly Seer! I could feel her laughter and her thanks. I knew now that I could re-enter this dream at a later date and with intention choose to follow her through the crack in the rocky spine of the dragon, if I dared! I had so much to think about, dream about. Adventures are sure amazing in this dreamland.

THE EAGLE

DREAM OF THE EAGLE SEER

Sitting in a circle on the grass felt wonderful in the early morning light. We each had our own blanket and sense of our own space, but the feeling of connectedness was strong with our Dreamer group of four. The Eagle Seer was a tall, thin man and used his hands expressively to accentuate his words as he spoke. He seemed to be able to take off and really fly with a theme, focus, and then go for the kill (punch line) and next, without any effort, soar on the thermal winds, just waiting for us to take in what information we could. He so captivated his audience! I thought to myself, He really is very much like the eagle himself!

Silently I began going over some of the attributes I remembered about Eagle. Throughout all cultures, the eagle is associated with the sun and solar light. The bird's ability to soar toward the heavens makes one think of strength, authority, and inspiration. They are a universal Spirit and about wisdom. Eagles often mate for life. The eagle's vision is truly amazing; it is eight times greater than humans. They are able to see sideways as well as forward. Their hearing is also excellent, and they use this as well as sight for hunting. Eagles have great control over their very large wings. When they see their prey, they scan the landscape and only when favorable do they swoop down for the kill. In summation, eagles teach us to soar above, recognize opportunity, and act on it!

I came back from daydreaming. All eyes were turned toward a loud sound, the high-pitched cry of the Eagle! The Seer was pointing to a low mountain to the left; we all watched the eagle as it flew without effort toward a solitary white pine tree. "See how it connects with the element of Air? In your work, practice this connection with the element of Air with other attributes of Eagle, and this will bring you some illumination. Eagle is a form of Spirit," he said.

"Look! He is almost to the tree. It would take us a morning's walk to arrive where he has in just minutes," said the Eagle Seer, who also seemed to want to be on the wind currents in the sky himself. All four of us Dreamers nodded in agreement. Leaning on the grass with one hand, I noted that the morning dew had gone and the wind was picking up some too.

The Eagle Seer was telling us about the Greek mythology of Zeus. "Eagle was sacred to Zeus. He would shape-shift into the eagle to get help with controlling the thunder and the lightning, for his various causes."

We all listened, enraptured. He continued now about Scotland. "The wise ones talk of the 'Scottish Airts,' the four chief winds. They often called upon Eagle for help with this.

The Druids' shamanic ability to work with or control the elements for their purposes was really something! They might call up a magical mist or a cloud bank to conceal something. Possibly call the winds to free or change something. Eagle could be called upon to scout for the weather conditions: both physical weather or maybe the conditions of an invading army." Looking at each of us intently now, the Seer said, "What is it I am trying to convey? Can someone tell me?" He flailed his arms all about as he spoke. There was silence! Not one peep from any of the four Dreamers, although we did look at each other in desperation.

Seemingly without a clue as to what he was after, I hunched my shoulders up and answered, "I don't know!"

"Ah! But you do!" he replied, still very worked up. "What is our dreaming? I will tell you," he said without taking a breath. "It is about scoping out the weather conditions, the lay of the land! Dreaming possible scenarios, focusing on opportunity, and then seizing that opportunity! Remember, all change and creation must begin in the dream world first, before it can manifest on the physical plane."

His voice was a piercing cry, like that of the eagle. Very suddenly, before our eyes, he took to the air. We were all astounded! However, in our hearts we knew it was this Dream Seer's right.

Everyone was quiet now; each of us was feeling a bit inadequate at our "not knowing" the answers the Seer was looking for. The Eagle Seer was soaring while we each began to assimilate his teachings.

As I watched him glide in the sky, I said to my Dreamer friends, "I feel as if he has provided each of us a truth about ourselves and that we must trust in our own ability to dream on goals and recognize the opportunities that come!"

The others nodded their heads yes. Someone said, "It is high time I got serious!" Another Dreamer said, "It was good that he shocked us and took off! I have been very complacent. Now I know I cannot take things for granted. I will not squander my time here!" One Dreamer said, "Heck! I want to soar…just like him!" All of us had stood up by now, and we were laughing. I think we were getting the message and had a new sense of commitment.

There was a gust of wind, and suddenly the Eagle was back! Walking toward us now in human form, I could see he was happy with our small group and with himself. I noticed that his eyes flickered to the huge white pine tree on the low mountain. I followed his gaze and saw the other eagle perched there on its top.

As if he had not been away at all, slowly the Seer began saying, "Mohawks legends say an Eagle sits atop 'The Tree of Peace, the White Pine,' ready to cry out at any sign of danger. The Eagle is our ally. Dreamers, you must work hard to learn what I know. Should you choose to follow this dreaming path, you will be tested, time after time. It is the Eagle who can provide you with strength and swiftness. You will be challenged; the eagle will give you courage and keen sight. There will be times when you will feel as if you have nothing. Eagle can help you with creation of something new, rising above with magic, sometimes above the material to the spiritual. May you learn about your own power and soar as eagle does with dignity and grace."

There was silence now. The Seer was standing tall and watching the other eagle in the white pine tree. The Dreamers were all standing with hands over their brow to shield the sun's glare. They also watched the tree and the eagle on its top. The Eagle Seer spoke now in a deep, serious voice. "There is something you must each do for me, Dreamers!"

"Of course!" we all called out together. "Anything. What is it?" we asked together.

He looked at us each individually for a few minutes, and then he directed the same scanning kind of look to all four of us. Finally he spoke. "Yes, I feel you are ready! But do you? Ask yourself, Can I truly commit to the Dreaming? Can I trust in my ability to see the bigger picture, the larger story of me? This is your homework, Dreamers. Each of you must search your hearts on these important questions. We are at a new crossroads now; decisions need to be made. Use your intuition to know which road to take to your future self. Eagle can help you to study your own lay of the land, then help you to act and swiftly choose!"

The Seer was very still. I had to blink my eyes to make sure he was actually there!

Of course he was…as he searched us, each one, with his eagle's eyes. Then he said, "Please dream on this 'Dream Commitment Proposition' carefully this evening! Then tomorrow at eight a.m. we will meet here on this hill, rain or shine. Be Ready, be Prompt, come Knowing. What is it you want at this particular time? Have it written out. In four sentences, without rambling, tell me what you are committed to in dreaming. Tell me your dream plan of your larger story, and know it in your heart! By doing this, Eagle will have begun to teach you about the higher truths that live within each of you!" He was in the air before we could say a word.

Again each of us was shocked! This Seer did not believe in nonsense! I really did not know what to do as I watched him glide in the air without effort. Air element…he had said something about that early on. I knew I had better check that out; maybe it would help me.

One of the Dreamers said, "The Seer sure has high expectations of us!"

Someone else said, "We should each expect the highest from ourselves!"

I said to the Dreamers, "The Seer has given us a tall order and a short timeframe. But you know something? Sometimes when I am under the pressure to do something, I do my best work! I say, just keep the positive energy flowing and call on Eagle for courage and strength to get this done!"

Everyone cheered. We all decided to head back for lunch, and we knew we would be busy until we each saw this through! All four of us hugged and wished each other "Sweet Eagle Dreams"!

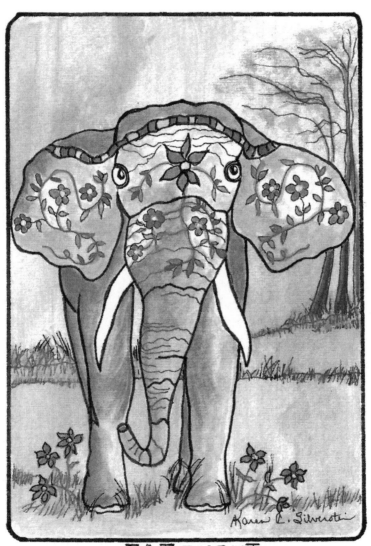

ELEPHANT

DREAM OF THE ELEPHANT SEER

So many people live lives of quiet desperation. Lives in which events and circumstances don't turn out the way they had hopped, planned, with expectations that are not realized. When their physical lives are pleasant, they are happy for a short while. Many fill their time with running from event to event. Or buying things that are diversions, or maybe moaning about lack and limitation. So many experience a great deal of sorrow, unhappiness, and pain. Beyond their surface appearance of smiles, they are "Soul Sick"! These were some of the words that left us hanging on a thread as we stopped for a break.

Soul sick! Soul sick! I could not get these words out of my head! The Dreamers, who had gathered, were on a thirty-minute break. The Ancient Ones had been leading the morning program. The topic they presented, "Soul Sick, Dreams for Healing," really had the Dreamers wound up.

Thinking of so many people that I work with or know, I wondered how we could remedy soul sicknesses for others? I found myself dreaming as I walked out to the meadow. The world would be a more enjoyable place overall if men and women had a way to tap into themselves, connecting with their true life path. Knowing why they were here. Then working at that life contract, fulfilling whatever that may be. I did realize that sometimes the ruggedness of life becomes a distraction. This is the hard part, I thought to myself.

I had not realized that I was walking in the wildflowers of the meadow until something tickled my leg. Reaching down, I picked some of the blue cornflowers; so many were growing there. As I looked around the field, there were daisies, black-eyed Susans, jewel weed, buttercups, Queen Ann's lace, and many that I did not know the names of, all beautiful! I walked about collecting a small bouquet, which I would add to the altar later. Admiring my handiwork, I looked around to see where I might find a spot to sit for a while. Then I saw the Elephant Seer grazing in the grasses, and I thought he might give me some insight on our topic of "Soul Sick"!

Walking over to him quickly, I was astounded by his size once I was next to him! "Hello, dear Seer!"

He looked up while munching on the grass. How much he must need to eat for his size, I thought to myself.

"Quite a lot," was his answer. Of course he was telepathic!

Smiling, I said, "I hope I am not intruding on you?"

"Not at all," was his response. "How may I help you?" He was swaying back and forth. Then he reached his trunk over to me as a sign of a handshake greeting, I suppose. "You suppose right, about being telepathic. Why don't we go over to the shade of that large oak, and we can chat," said the Elephant Seer. Once there, I asked him immediately his thoughts on our "Soul Sick" topic.

The Elephant Seer responded by asking me if I knew the story of "Siddhartha". I said that I had heard of the name. The Elephant Seer had knelt down under the oak tree. He was still so large! The Seer continued the story. "In the second century in Nepal, Buddha's mother tells how she had dreamt of a white elephant entering her womb. Buddha's mother's name was 'Maya,' and in the dream she was to give birth in Devadaha, in ancient Nepal. Buddhist texts say she had Immaculate Conception, for when she awoke from her dream, she was pregnant. 'Queen Maya' was married to her cousin King Suddhadana. Tradition stated that she go to the homeland of her father in Nepal to give birth. En route, she had to stop and give birth early; she was in the foothills of the Himalayas. The birth was in the Lunbini Grove, which is where her son, the Buddha, grew up and lived until the age of twenty-nine.

"His mother, 'Queen Maya,' died seven days after the birth of her son, whom she had named 'Siddhartha,' which means 'He who achieves his aim'! As the story goes, a woman who dreams of a white elephant entering her womb will give birth to one as 'select as the elephant' is among animals. He will be a Buddha who understands the meaning of 'Dharma.' This word means 'One's Righteous Duty.' Dharma also relates to the higher truth or ultimate reality of one's universe."

Turning to me, and now in human form, the Elephant Seer was saying, "So, my dear, without this amazing dream from 'Queen Maya,' there would be no Buddha and no Buddhism!" I just sat there truly astounded, not able to do more than nod my head! The Seer went on. 'Siddhartha,' please remember, means 'He who achieves his aim'! Well, this is quite something for people to live up too. Fulfillment in life is a huge task for most of us. So, yes! Many are 'soul sick,' but maybe not entirely so. There are many stories of Siddhartha relaying how on his journey he would find many distractions, temptations, and obstacles in his path. Does this sound familiar?" He looked at me with huge, black eyes.

Again I nodded yes. The Seer went on. "The point is that we all may get sidetracked from hopes, wishes, goals. Let's give ourselves a break and ask, Am I truthful to myself? Am I loyal to myself and others? The list goes on from there: Am I loving, kind to others? Am I able to feel happy at whatever I may choose to do? This is the secret. We do not need to be a Buddha or on a particular religious path to fulfill 'Dharma,' 'ones righteous duty'! This, in my dreaming with Spirit, is 'To Be Happy'!"

I looked at the Seer and smiled, saying, "You are so right. But the ones who are stuck and very sidetracked...How do we help these souls?"

He smiled and said, "We encourage them! We give them a new dream or revamp a dream they have had. Then with gentle but firm dreaming, show them the dream track so they may get back on. Using our creativity we create a good dream-hook and help them match to what they want. We show them by example, and we dream with them. However, it is up to that person to want that path, or track, and up to them to do the work required. When dream healing with others, always remind and reinforce that it is 'In the Dream Journey' where the ideas are born and in the waking dream world where the contentment and happiness comes!"

I replied, "You are amazing, dear Seer! It seems so simple when I hear your words."

He said, "No, it is not simple! Everyone's life is complex, and sometimes there are things we need to overcome. This is where the wisdom of the Seers can really become of use. Teach those you are helping to use our resources! Remember the attributes that you learn from each of us here in the Nemeton, and apply them to the life situations. I, for one, am very good at moving obstacles in the paths!" I laughed at this, realizing the sheer size of him!

"I will tell you the story of Ganesha," said the Seer. "Ganesha is a Sanskrit word for elephant. This is the Hindu God of Wisdom and Success. He has the head of an elephant and the torso of a human. He emerged as a deity from the fourth and fifth centuries and is one of the most worshiped deities in Hinduism and Buddhism. He is revered as the 'Remover of Obstacles' and widely known as 'Lord of Beginnings and Lord of Obstacles.' He is a patron of arts and science, and is honored at ceremonies and invoked as a patron of letters during writing sessions. 'Ganesha' has one broken tusk, his left tusk. It is said this indicates his ability to overcome all forms of dualism. This allows for a mastery of the soul."

There was a pause, and I quickly said, "I love this being!"

The Seer went on. "Elephants embody strength and power. They have poor eyesight but are able to rely greatly upon their sense of smell with their trunks, which becomes a symbol for higher discrimination. 'Do things smell right?' They check out what they smell. Elephants are great communicators. They are able to communicate over long distances, receiving low frequency sound, infrasound, which travels through the ground faster than it can travel through the air. The elephants' sensitive skin of their feet and trunk picks up these resonate vibrations from the ground. This ability aids them in navigation. They often lift one leg, face the source of the sound, and then drag their trunk along the ground, which gives them more contact information."

"Oh! This is truly incredible!" I said.

Smiling at me, the Seer went on. "It is also good to know something of the way the elephant community lives," said the Seer. "The females, when mated, are in pregnancy for twenty-two months. All members of the tightly knit female group participate in the care of the young. The cows live in a herd, led by a wise old cow; the young and the mothers all support each other. Males usually have their own herd. Their lifespan may last eighty years. Elephants are affectionate to one another and are very loyal. They help each other when sick or wounded.

"Many cultures have elephant stories. To the Christians, the elephant was a symbol of Christ as an enemy of the serpent, trampling the serpent underfoot. Also the elephant symbolized chastity, because it was thought they showed no sign of passion. The ivory tusks symbolized purity. If an angel was seen riding an elephant, it represented the power of God.

"To the Greeks and Romans, Elephant was an attribute of Mercury as intelligence. 'Pliny,' an ancient Roman scientist and historian, said, 'The elephant is a religious animal, worshipping the sun and stars and purifying itself at the New Moon, bathing in the river and invoking the heavens.' To the Romans, Elephant was about longevity, immortality, and victory over death. For the Greeks the word 'elephant' actually means 'Ivory'!"

The Elephant Seer had paused. I noticed various things about his human form. He wore a gray shirt with a beautiful, flowery design.

Staring at me just then with his intense black eyes, he continued his tale. "The species of elephant is ancient. The predecessor to the elephant is the 'Woolly Mammoth.' The first species known is probably one hundred fifty thousand years old. Because of this, they are keepers of ancient wisdom."

The Elephant Seer stood up and shook himself a bit. I stood up and stretched out my limbs. The next thing I knew, The Seer had become the elephant again, in all his huge glory! He swayed his trunk down to the grass and said, "Hop on! I will put you onto my back and walk you back to the Grove, if you would care to?"

Breaking into a laugh, I said, "I would love to have a lift and would certainly enjoy your company on the way back! Wow!" I exclaimed. Within a second I was sitting on top of the most majestic of animals, holding on and trying to sway as he did with each huge step. It took me a moment to get my bearings. It felt great, sitting up so high into the trees. I felt on top of the world! From this vantage point, I admired his large head and realized how intelligent and how filled with wisdom this creature is. Looking at his huge ears, I realized how strong was his ability to listen to people who sought his help. What an amazing, loving being! I could hear small branches crunching as we walked into the woods past the meadow.

"Well, that is very nice!" said the Seer, having heard my thoughts telepathically! "I would like to remind you of some of the other characteristics we mentioned. First, Remover of Obstacles! Then strength, discernment, loyalty, commitment, patience, and also help with Soul Evolution. Did I leave anything out?" he asked.

"I thought you were telepathic!" I said in jest.

"Because that is what I was thinking!" He gave out a huge roar from his belly and trunk and said, "Well, of course I am…most of the time!"

We both laughed at that. From my high vantage point, I could see the roundness of the trees that made up the Grove and the green, lush grasses around it. So beautiful! I thought, How happy I am to be a part of this amazing Dream Weaving work. I felt I had acquired so much to work with for those who may be "Soul Sick." I remembered what the Elephant Seer had said about "Dharma"—"One's Righteous Duty"—and tapping into this to find the higher truth or ultimate reality of one's universe. I vowed to use this for myself and to help others do so as well.

It seemed we were back in time for the second part of our Dream work session in just a blink of an eye. I thanked The Elephant Seer for all that I had learned from our time together under the shade of the old oak tree.

"You are welcome!" he replied. "And you are a treasure for me to hold near my heart. I have witnessed your sincerity and hunger for the ways of the Ancient Keepers."

With one last hug and a kiss to his cheek, we went into the program.

GOAT

DREAM OF THE GOAT SEER

Why am I always being sacrificed? Here it goes again! I am laughing about this trait of mine, which rears its head in my thoughts as we are in the midst of the Keepers Meeting. We have done so much with our gathering of the Dreamers and the Keepers of the Nemeton. Will no one hear me! Saying these things to myself, getting myself so worked up, I stand and begin to pace. I suppose "The Night of the Long Dream" must have its own space in this dream telling!

Let me start at the beginning…

I looked around the Grove; it was ready. The Keepers were arriving for the night-long session. I, The Goat Seer, was in charge of this session. A few of us had gotten to the Grove earlier to prepare. I had selected three other Dreamers to help me, along with The Hierophant Seer, The Raven Seer and 'The Apple Tree Seer.' We smudged and cleansed the Grove. Remembering the teachings of the ancient Greek Seers, we had branches of Laurel strewn about. The Herbs of Lavender and Chamomile were burning in the braziers. I was holding a bundle of fleece lamb skins to be placed around for the comfort of The Keepers during the dreaming. Suddenly, I had a vision, a daydream of an ancient story. Calling the three Keepers and the Dreamers to listen, I related this story.

"The Romans had a god they called 'Faunus,' a half-human and half-goat creature. It had horns that resembled a goat's and was goat-like below the waist, with hooves that were cloven. He was one of the oldest Roman deities, a good spirit of the forest, the plains, and fields.

"The God Faunus kept a sacred grove close to the small Roman town of 'Tivoli,' originally called 'Tibur', along the banks of the river Anio. Here Faunus revealed the future in dreams and voices that were communicated to those who came to sleep in his precincts, lying on the fleeces of sacrificed lambs, or goats. This was the 'Incubation Ritual'!" Looking at these Keepers with a hint of laughter, I said, "Of course you all know about this! But to continue, this is the practice of sleeping in a sacred area with the intention of experiencing a divinely inspired dream, or curse! So I ask you, 'My fellow Dream Keepers,' please say words of thanks to the dear goats and lambs who have given us their fleece that we may dream in comfort this long night! And being the Goat Seer, I am in charge here, and I will go first!"

They all laughed as I handed them the fleece to be spread about the Grove. Taking my bundle and holding it above my heart, and then above my head, I said, "I thank you for your spirit. May we all dream true!" The other Keepers moved about the Grove, thanking and making things ready. I felt very glad indeed to be able to participate in such an amazing gathering. The sixty-four Keepers had come from far and wide to honor our ancient practice of dreaming, teaching, and healing. We had all gotten the call through the Ley Lines of our Earth Mother, and she needs us now, more than ever. All of us came, some at great peril or hardship. But now that we were here, I wanted to make this "Night of the Long Dream" special and make sure that we all remembered those who had blazed the Dream Trails before us. So I was glad to have shared my Roman deity, the "Faunus myth"!

The evening air felt cool. I noticed the mist was rising in the mountains now. With the darkening sky and the fog, I began sensing dreams in the mist. The Apple Tree Seer lit the large oil diffuser, having placed the essential oil of Laurel in its bowl, to scent our air and Dreams. She was walking toward me now and had one of her branches in her hand.

Holding it in front of me, she said, "Shall I add this to the fire now?"

I smiled and said, "Yes, let the dreams begin!"

She answered, "And the magic of the Apple, as well!"

Someone called out, "Look, the fog has cleared some, and we can see 'Capricornus' in the night sky now!"

The constellation of Capricorn! We all turned our heads upward and marveled at its beauty. I stepped up in front of the fire and said, "This must be my opening!"

Everyone laughed! A voice called out, "Well, I am glad to see that you recognize your own Constellation of the Goat!" More laughter!

"OK! OK! I see that we are in high spirits! Yes, I am 'The Goat Seer.' Good evening!" I was looking up at the constellation while the Dreamers got settled. Then I told them, "Did you know that this constellation 'Capricornus' is also called 'Amalthea'?" Looking around the Grove, I could see that there were some who did not.

"In Greek myth, 'Almlthea' was the 'tender goddess,' a nurturing goddess. It is said that she was the goat-goddess who suckled the infant god Zeus in a cave in Cretan Mount Aigaion, Goat Mountain. It is also said that her horn, which came off of her, offered food and plenty to those in need. Her horn then became called 'Cornucopia,' or 'Horn of Plenty'!"

Sensing the interest from our group, I shared a few other things. "As Dreamers learning to be healers and possibly one of the future Keepers, it is very important for you to learn and really know these stories from each Seer you work with. A Dreamer simply is prepared with his or her bag of tricks! One never knows when you may need a particular tidbit of story information, which could just be the dream-hook for someone in need of a dream healing! Dreamers, you must also know that I am the Keeper of abundance, independence, and sure-footedness. Also I can help remove guilty feelings and provide a deep understanding of the energies of nature. Of course, call on me with help in scaling and reaching new heights! I am also proud to say I am one of the most gifted in agility. You never quite know when these traits might come in handy, but they are good to know. Now there you have it, Dreamers!"

Everyone clapped and cheered and was thanking me for this short introduction. Looking about our sacred space, I sensed that the Dreamers were ready. So, holding out my hands, I said, "Let's stand and do our opening of this sacred space, hand to hand, heart to heart."

HAWK

DREAM OF THE HAWK SEER

The smell of leaf mold and moss filled my senses as I walked with my Dreamer friend. She was saying, "Did you notice how the Seers in our last group session had looked around the circle, trying hard not to meet each other's gaze?"

Tracking my dream thoughts back to class time did not take me long. I looked at the Seers in my dream, and I did notice an undercurrent of energy; something was going on. I answered my friend, saying, "You are right! What's up?" We had been walking briskly in the noonday woods, not paying a lot of attention to what was around us. Now suddenly we were at a fork in the road, with a huge, beautiful oak tree separating the two paths. My Dreamer friend and I stopped and looked at each other, bewildered.

My friend looked at me and said, "This is the first sign from the Goddess!"

We both just started laughing! Both of us sat down quickly, happy to be taking a little free time to sit and relax with the oak tree.

I mentioned to my friend, "Some of the sessions are really intense: the journey work, the practical information, on and on! But you know something? I would not have it any other way!"

Laughing with me, she nodded her head in agreement. Settling on the warm grass and leaning against the huge oak felt perfect.

Tracking back to our earlier conversation, I said, "What do you think is up?"

My friend said, "I cannot quite put my finger on it...However, I did notice that some of the Dreamers in our group were missing this morning! I know that we can attend the sessions that we want, however, it seemed that we had developed a small circle within the circle, and I thought we had a special bond. Maybe I imagined that? It is just odd that three Dreamers were not there. Do you think the Seers know something that we should be concerned about? Also, do you keep in touch with any of these Dreamers?" she asked, looking very intently at me.

I answered, "Not really. I have wanted to. I've wanted a bond to develop, but so far I've only had casual conversation with most of them. Hey, listen, do not be too concerned," I answered. "If there is a situation, we will know what to do when the time presents itself."

We were quiet a bit. Then, through the canopy of the trees, we heard the cry of the Hawk.

Turning to my Dreamer friend, I said, "Another message from the Goddess!" As we both laughed, we both looked at the Hawk, watching it land in a nearby tree, and there it remained very still. I began speaking very quietly, not taking my eyes off the Hawk. "The Hawk teaches us to be observant, to look at the whole picture from above. When Hawk sends out a cry, we need to listen for messages, whether good or bad. And to hold onto that awareness! We must also be responsible with insights we might receive.

My friend replied, "They are such fearless birds and will take on poisonous snakes, tearing off their heads! Dreamers who work with Hawk medicine should keep this attribute in mind and make sure they use it appropriately."

Nodding my head in agreement, I added, "Hawks, along with some other birds of prey who hunt snakes, are called 'Ophiophagy,' from the Greek word meaning 'snake eating'! Isn't that something?"

She responded, saying, "I think that this is a reminder for those who work with Hawk medicine to be aware of snake as well."

I nodded my head in agreement with her. "Look!" I said, pointing my finger toward the Hawk as it flew suddenly from its perch.

We were captivated as the large Red Tailed Hawk began moving closer to us. As it moved, it grew in size to a man! Now in his human form, The Hawk was speaking to us. In a calm, strong voice, he informed us that he was the Hawk Seer and would like to dream with us!

Dazed, my friend and I just looked at each other! We answered, "Why of course!"

The Hawk Seer immediately began to tell us about his ability to soar and glide on the air currents. He spoke about his home territory and how he guards it. Just then he changed shape and instantly flew up toward the sun! We were startled to see that he was back in the blink of an eye.

"I am a solar bird of power, the 'Royal bird of Spirit.' I am the swift messenger for the Greek God Apollo, as well as the Roman Sun God 'Mirthra.'" He was speaking in a warm, inviting tone. "In Celtic oral tradition, I am listed as the oldest animal, called the 'Hawk of Achill.' The Hawks became excellent messengers for the needs of the Celts.

"The Egyptians have a sky god called 'Horus'; the name means 'high' or 'distant.' The God 'Horus' had the body of a man and the head of a Falcon-Hawk. He was a heavenly deity, with its wings in the sky and the sun and the moon in its eyes. You may have heard of the 'Eye of Horus.'" He continued, saying, "The hieroglyph of this is an Egyptian symbol of power."

Looking keenly at us a minute or two, I admired his strong, lean build. I noticed hawk feathers were painted on his blue jean, contemporary shirt. He was ready to continue.

"This symbol's name in Egyptian is 'Wadjet,' and she was a solar deity. Her eye saw everything! The eye was that of the eye of the Peregrine Falcon. The right eye, including a teardrop below it, was 'Wadjet' the Sun. The mirror image of this eye, the left eye, was the Moon. This Eye of Horus became an important symbol of the unified land of Egypt. The symbol was also used in the funerary rites of renewal after death."

As the Hawk Seer spoke, he had shape-shifted into each of these role images: Egyptian, Celtic, Apollo. He was truly amazing! Then we heard him say, "Hawk is a deity of swift justice to the Hawaiian people."

The forest was slowly settling itself for sleep; it was getting late. Something made me think of the earlier conversation my friend and I had about the Dreamers who had not come for the afternoon session. I decided to take a chance and ask the Seer about this. I explained that we had hoped a bond was forming, and yet they did not attend the class. I added that we had the feeling the Seers who were present might be concerned.

The Hawk Seer looked at me with piercing eyes; long and hard he looked. It was hard for me to hold his gaze. I wondered if I should not have mentioned this; I felt nervous.

Then in a quiet voice, he said, "This path is not for everyone. The Dream of the Seers is to have a strong, vibrant core of Dream bringers. The work is tough; it is demanding and requires discipline. One must be able to bend like the Willow and sometimes roar like a Lion. A Dreamer must have the ability to fly off to retrieve messages and then, most importantly, be able to return and transfer the message to the one needing healing with good words. Words that the one receiving healing can take into themselves on their own level of receiving. Words that are positive and for the highest good of all concerned!" He stopped what he was saying and just looked at us both.

So many thoughts and questions were going through my mind but now. How should I respond? I said simply to the Seer, "The Dreamers who were absent earlier were rethinking their commitment? Is this what you are telling us?"

He looked back, saying, "We are still early on in our training, and surely this is a good juncture for many Dreamers to examine why they want to be doing this work. There may be some who are searching these questions before they make a decision to see the path through or move on. Some may wait until another lifetime. The choice is always hard and theirs; there is no judgment on this. Each of us are light workers who are spinning threads of light to support, mend, and heal. We need to be sure that we can sustain ourselves strongly for the right reasons of love and truth. Remember, it is always easier to break something than to repair. Each of us must find our own path!"

It was getting onto dusk; The Hawk Seer told us how much he enjoyed our dreaming together. And before we could blink, he was gone.

My friend and I just looked at each other, both feeling inspired but realizing there were many questions that he had opened for us. I thought to myself, He really did not answer my questions about the other Dreamers the way I expected. But then, I could see he did not have to; time would tell what had happened with them. What I learned is I need to concentrate on my own skills and use what I learn from the Hawk's traits, applying this for my own support first and then for the support of others' healings.

As he flew off, we did hear him say, "Trust your insights! Study my lineage and that of snake!"

Gathering our things together, we thanked the old oak tree for her comfort, and we walked back to share the evening meal with the other Dreamers. Both of us were very thankful for our afternoon spent with the Hawk Seer. Looking through the trees, we saw the sun was setting bright orange. Just for an instant, The Hawk Seer glided in front of it.

My friend and I smiled, and we both said, "There goes the 'Solar Bird of Power'!"

HORSE

DREAM OF THE HORSE SEER

While here at this steading, the Dreamers help out with various chores. We all have needs: things need to be taken care of in order that the whole group runs smoothly. Some of the class work taught today was about the behind the scenes of running a program. We learned what it takes to put together a teaching program. If we want to be teachers, we should know how to do our lesson planning. As teachers we should be aware of various pitfalls when leading a group, like possible chaos situations that might crop up. For instance a Dream teacher may have rented a space for their program and then find the grounds staff is outside the window with a loud lawn mower! Or one of the students attending the class develops a problem that begins to interfere with the class as a whole. What is a Dream teacher to do? We learned that to know how to focus the group's energy is the most important thing, no matter what the peripheral influences may be.

I am walking from class with all these thoughts running through my head, on my way to the field where the horses are grazing. Now, the Horse, I think to myself, is such a powerful animal. We could all learn from the way they survive together!

I had signed up to help with the feeding of our herd of horses. It smells so sweet out in the field; the sweet grasses are getting tall at this time in the summer. I do not really know much about taking care of these animals, but I am excited to learn. When I arrive to the fences of the paddock, the Stable Master is there. He shows me where to find the oats and mash that are to be given to the small herd on the left. I look over and notice four mares and one stallion, which has a beautiful grayish-flecked black coat and long, rippling black mane. They are grazing, but when they see me, their heads lift up. The stallion comes over to the open gate of the paddock and walks through; the mares all follow. I put their feed into the trays and fill the water in the troughs. Taking out my apple, I sit on one of the fences and just watch them. I will give the core to the stallion when done.

The horses are focused while they eat. I think about how powerful they are, how they can run like the wind. I also notice how this small group remains so conscious of each other. As I look beyond the fence to the field, I see the rest of the herd. I notice the white mare with her young foals; she is grazing herself but very mindful of her young.

Turning back to the paddock, I see the beautiful gray-and-black stallion is looking at me; he moves closer. I feel his wonderful energy. He begins talking with me as if he were human, as if this were the most natural thing to do.

"When man discovered that we, the horse, would allow them to ride upon our back, all of civilization began to change. From that moment on, man learned how to travel and that the horse could assist in agriculture and also in wars. But I think what intrigues man most is the freedom we horses can provide—and the sense of power men feel when they ride upon us!"

I look at him. Smiling, I tell him it is very nice to meet the Horse Seer!

He acknowledges me and my greeting with the blinking of his long eye lashes. Then he continues speaking, all businesslike. "There are legends that speak of the clairvoyance of horses. Many are true," he says. "I know that Dreamers are interested in this, but I feel that at this point in time, Horse can teach you, Dreamer, about what it is that gives one power to be a leader."

Very intrigued by his comment, I ask, "How can I learn this?"

The Horse Seer had shape-shifted and is now in human form, smiling. He begins telling me he would be honored to share as much as he can for today, and then, of course, the rest of the study would be up to me.

THE HORSE SEER says, "First, a Dreamer must learn to Balance their Shields." Staring at me, he says, "A Dreamer's shield is an important tool for healing work. The shield represents the knowledge one has gained with a particular ally. In our work here today, your ally is the horse. We will dream journey to do this. Let us get comfortable here on the grass with the noonday sun; this is perfect!"

I get settled on a blanket he provides, and the Seer begins his drumming. He tells me to have an intent of "bringing a vision to my horse shield." I hear him say, "Enter the darkness and find the light...Go to the north. The place of wisdom. The people are in need of this. But know that power is not given lightly but only awarded to those who are willing to carry responsibility in a balanced manner. Horse has the power to run! Run now with horse. Fill your shield and run!"

Suddenly in addition to the drumming, there is the sound of galloping! Looking to see where this is coming from, I am shocked to find that it is from me and also the Grey Horse Seer! I am a horse! A wild, white mare, running with a stallion; the running is amazing. I am exhilarated and really in disbelief!

Then I hear, "Believe it! How else can one balance their horse shield?" The stallion Seer is speaking to me, and now we have slowed and are doing a walk.

I say to him, "I felt as though I was flying through the air and could reach the heavens!"

He is laughing some. We have come now to the edge of the woodlands after having run through the meadow. "It was good for you to experience a run! I would like to continue the lessons," he says.

"Horse is movement, travel, intellect, wisdom, nobility, and light. It is dynamic power: swiftness and magic. Horses are ridden by heroes; horse is also about fertility and the power of the ruler. The riding of a horse renews our sense of power. Let me tell you some other interesting facts. 'The Four Horses of the Apocalypse' are War, Death, Famine, and Pestilence. The Buddha left his home on a white horse. For the Chinese Taoist, horse is an attribute of 'Ch'ang Kuo,' one of the eight immortals. In Iranian symbolism, the stallion is solar power, fire, and the warrior. In Ireland the Irish 'Goddess of War-Macha' was said to have run on a horse against the fastest horse known while she was pregnant!"

The Seer stallion has related all these things with barely taking a breath and is now laughing at me some. He says, "That should catch you up a bit on horse energy! Where is your shield? You must put all this into your shield, my dear. That is how you will retain what you will learn here today!" Again he is laughing.

I say, "What is so funny?"

He just says, "Your face…I suppose you are overwhelmed, but really you can do this!"

"Well, I do not find it funny! I am trying!"

He answers me by saying, "That is fine to try, but what we need here, as someone who is 'learning to lead,' is *doing*! Leave your doubts behind, put your intuition in gear and that into your shield, my dear Dreamer. You can! And you will *do*!"

I want to cry, really; but I do not dare. The Seer had handed to me earlier a beautiful circular shield made of white horse hair. On its reverse side is smooth leather: red ribbons and sinew hold it to a wooden rim. It is beautiful. I transfer what I am learning into it and hold it tightly. I lean forward some and said to the Seer, "I thank you for this and will cherish it always."

Shaking his head and smiling, he says, "You are welcome! Now I would like to relate a little more. I do see there is rain and maybe a storm coming from the west. Let's move toward the cave just over there."

I follow him, even though I do not see or feel the impending storm he speaks of. We sit in front of the cave entrance, and he continues his tale.

"Epona, Goddess of Horses. The name 'Epona' means 'Great Mare' and is from the Gaulish language. 'Epona' was a beautiful goddess much revered in the Gallo-Roman religion of the first through third centuries CE. 'Epona' was a protector of horses, donkeys, and mules. Originally a Celtic goddess, she became accepted by the Romans who had invaded the lands. They saw her as a protector of their cavalry. Some say the goddess and her horses were the leaders of the soul in the 'afterlife ride.' It is said she carries the keys to the underworld and always rides a white horse.

"In England there is a giant chalk horse carved into the hillside turf at Uffington, in southern England. This dates from approximately 1400 BCE, which is too early to have been 'Epona,' who appeared a millennium or so after; yet some say this may have influenced her being anyway. The Welsh 'Goddess Rhianon' rides a white horse and has many attributes of 'Epona.'

"In Ireland it has been said that 'Epona' was a dream goddess. Many children were told to be good or Epona would visit them with nightmares! Of course some say the word 'nightmare' is attributed to her because she rode in on mare horses!

"'Epona's image is usually portrayed in sculpture or paintings as a maiden goddess riding a white mare. She rides sidesaddle usually, sometimes with a foal. Other images show her standing among a great many of horses; she is both fertility and abundance.'"

Just then we hear a huge crack of thunder, and the wind whips about. We pick up our few things and run into the cave, getting only slightly sprinkled. I am amazed that the Horse Seer has the foresight of this storm. There is another huge crack of thunder, and the sky lights up with huge lightning strikes. I say to the Seer; "I love a thunderstorm, but how nice that we can be in the cave and not get soaked! It is lucky that it was close by!"

The Seer stares right through me as he says, "Luck...Well, I know this cave and am here from time to time." He moves into the cave some and starts tending a fire with the wood, which is neatly stacked on one side.

This is curious, I am thinking. Really like it has been planned or something. Again the storm is hurling wind; the rain comes down in huge sheets. I run to the entrance to watch. Now there are bolts of lightning, one after another, and they light up the whole sky! I call to the Horse Seer to come and watch. When he gets here, we hear a huge thunderclap, which makes me jump some. "Oh my gosh. This is incredible!"

The Seer says, "It certainly is. And of course it must be him up there, you know!"

"Him? What are you talking about, and who is up there?" I say in a very puzzled voice.

"I suppose I should tell you about the Greek myth!" He says, "You must have heard about 'Pegasus,' I am sure. Well, 'Pegasus' is a beautiful horse with wings, and he can fly, soar to great heights. His parent, 'Medusa,' bore him from the blood of her severed head. Then when 'Perseus' killed 'Medusa,' Zeus felt sorry for him and favored him and gave him much attention. Zeus had 'Pegasus' help him to carry his thunderbolts through the sky, as he was the amazing flying horse!"

Another huge thunderbolt flies across the sky! I look at the sky, and then all the Seer and I can say is, "This is amazing, really amazing!"

The Seer is all smiles and then adds this: "In contemporary life we talk of energy, in a car for example, as having 'Horsepower'! Which is the name given for units of measuring power. Well, just look at the power up there!"

We both laugh and enjoy the sky show for awhile; it is great. Then the Seer moves to the campfire, and I follow him. The warmth that it is now throwing off is wonderful. I sit down, and from some magical cupboard, the Horse Seer hands me coffee and crackers to munch.

"This is so perfect, and thanks!" I am enjoying my snack and looking around the cave, while the Seer brings over a few logs. My eyes have adjusted now to the dimmer cave light, and I can see there are drawings on the walls. I jump up in a rush when some in particular catch my eye. Standing next to them now, I see the image is of several horses, one of them white, and one black. Quite loudly, I call out, "Oh my....Have you seen this? I mean these ancient drawings here on the wall are of horses! Seer, come and look!" He is coming over, but then I say, "Well, of course you have seen them. You have been here before, and I suppose this is really your cave!" This realization hits me now and I just sit down right there.

I look up at him, and he answers me, saying, "I suppose it is my cave! I hope you like it!"

I jump up and am full of laughter. "Like it? I love this place! Imagine that: I am in the cave of 'The Horse Seer'! Am I dreaming or what?"

"Speaking of dreaming…Time for you, Dreamer, to transfer this energy into your newly acquired 'Horse Shield.' I will help you with this." He has me sit near the fire; the outside storm seems to be moving off. "Now," he says, "slowly re-enter our dreaming of this day. And as you hold your shield, let this dream information collect into your shield. Good, good!" I am doing what he asks. I recall the details, and it is just beautiful, frame after frame of dream scenes of our day. Next the Seer is guiding me again. "Dream of the paddock from early this morning," he says, "and we will go there together."

The next thing I know, I am sitting on the fence, staring into the black eyes of the gray-black horse! I flutter my eyes and ask the horse if I was in a dream. I do not hear anything very loud, but I am sure he says, "Of course you are, Dreamer!"

Smiling, I jump down from the fence. There on the ground is the most beautiful "Horse Shield," the one with white horse hair and red ribbons. I pick it up. With tears in my eyes, I give the horse a kiss and thank him immensely! He takes the apple that I offer and then rides off toward the back meadow to join the herd. The tears are streaming still, ones of joy and gladness! I hold my Horse Shield tightly to my breast, glad I will have this to lead with.

Karen C. Silverstein

HUMMINGBIRD

DREAM OF THE HUMMINGBIRD SEER

I detected the concern behind her casual glance as her eyes swept the outdoor classroom. I could feel a thread between the Seer and the new Dreamer attending. I looked around to see if anyone else picked up anything, but it did not seem so. I must track in my dreaming for what might be going on here, but before I could continue, the Hummingbird Seer was going on with the class and told this beautiful dream story:

I am walking in the woods at midday; it is a very warm summer day. I notice the denseness of the woods, the light and the shade, the smell of the leaves and earth as I walk along the path. The tree canopy makes this woods feel like a much-protected space. But, what I like the most are the amazing colors! I find a few beautiful pebbles and pick some dainty purple violets. Not really thinking about much at all, just enjoying nature. Reaching down to pick up a feather, I am delighted! It is small, tiny really, and green! What bird could this be? It can't be tropical in this part of the world. Walking along, I see more green and some red feathers and pick those up as well. I see rocks the size of a small bench and decide to sit down awhile. Looking over the feathers I have found, I'm puzzled. Then on the ground in front of me, I see it: a small, tiny bird! Feathers are coming out of it, and its stomach is hanging out from the body. It is dead! I drop the feathers and scream, Oh my Goddess!

What has happened? It is a small Hummingbird, and it is dead! Sobbing now, I am so sad! How can this be? What can I do? Wiping my eyes some, I begin to say a prayer: "Dear little one, may you go softly back to the Mother. You were loved by many while you were here." Taking out a bit of tobacco as a part of my prayer, I sprinkle it over the tiny creature. Still crying, I begin looking around for a stick to use as a digging tool, so I might give the little one a simple burial. I find a proper stick and begin to dig a hole behind the rocks.

"Pick it up!" I hear someone say. I look around, and nothing, nobody, is there. Disregarding this, I begin again.

"Unless you hold it, you will not feel it!"

Standing up, I say, "Who is there? Who is talking to me?" Trembling some and shaking my digging stick, I am determined. Who is there? Suddenly, from the branches of the wild apple tree, a mist of yellow green light comes floating down to the ground. Astounded, I catch my breath and drop my stick.

"It is quite all right, daughter. I've come to attend to this small Hummingbird with you." Blinking my eyes, I watch as this beautiful light turns into a magnificent woman adorned with a shawl of colorful feathers in greens, with some touches of red near her throat. Why she looks—

"Just like the colors of the tiny Hummingbird." The woman finishes my sentence! "I am 'Hummingbird Woman,'" she says. "And I am very moved that you cared enough to offer ceremony for this little one."

She reaches down and picks up the bird, handing it to me. I hesitate a little, but I do take the bird from her petite, graceful hands.

"What do you feel?" she says.

"Why, she is so light!" I answer, looking at the woman's eyes.

She smiles, and says, "Your feelings?"

I look down at the bird that I hold and feel joy. Looking at the woman, I say, "Joy! I feel joy, but sadness. I am so sad for her!"

"Ah! Now you are beginning to understand!" she says to me. Then, reaching over to my hands, she separates the tiny stomach from the body. Holding this near me, she says, "Eat this!"

I pull back in disbelief, saying, "What do you mean?"

She answers, "I mean for you to eat this tiny stomach!"

I answer, repulsed, "I cannot!"

She looks at me, and with her small voice and her eyes, she says, "You may not be ready. I will go."

"Go! Ready?" I say. "You just got here. I do not know why. Ready, ready for what?"

Again with her emerald-green eyes, she says, "We on the dreaming path go through trials in order to have the veils lifted, yet again, but you may not be ready."

With tears rolling down my cheeks, I answer, "I feel I am ready. I am afraid sometimes, but I do not let that stop me with my learning."

"Oh," she says. "Maybe this is about trust and intuition? Can you use your intuition?"

I nod my head yes. I am still holding the tiny bird.

Now, again she asks, "How do you feel about this?"

I say, "The stomach?"

"Why, yes, my dear. What does your gut tell you?"

I think a minute. She must have a reason; she seems so true. I have been asking for a guide, and I might learn much. But I don't know.

"Hummingbird Woman" looks at me and says, "It is OK. I will be going." The green light begins to swirl.

"*No!* No!" I scream. "Please, please do not go! Really…stay!"

She looks me straight in the eye and says, "Eat this!"

I comply.

The scene shifts some, and I find myself walking on the same path as earlier, but with company. "Hummingbird Woman" is with me and tells me that by eating the small stomach of the bird, I will receive the bird's medicine. I will come to know the bird's attributes and habits. These things will become very useful for the healing work I will be doing. We walk on and she talks on; I listen, entranced. There is no limit to her knowledge. I am still in disbelief about having eaten the tiny stomach, however, I am fine. In fact, I've never felt better, I think, smiling to myself. Trying to write notes as she speaks is difficult.

She looks at me and, with a finger pointing to her head, she says, "Use your ears. Listen. Just listen."

I put my writing things in my pack.

After a while, she tells me that time is growing short. She needs a Dreamer such as me to pass her knowledge onto; she tells me I will become a part of the lineage. Then she says, "You are ready now to hold the gifts and to teach in your own right. There is much to share. We will make the most of our time together. In the near future, there is someone who you will be able to help with 'Hummingbird Medicine.'"

I am very curious about that last statement. The Humming Bird Woman is ready to leave; however, she lets me know that we will meet often. I just need to keep a look out for her green mist! I thank her and we part for now.

"This was my Dream sharing of initiation," said the Hummingbird Seer. The Hummingbird Seer was then silent a bit. Others asked her about her experience, and the class moved onto other topics she wanted to cover.

Later, while still in her class and on break, my day-dreaming of this dream told by the Hummingbird Seer came back. Now it finally occurred to me that she had given us the story of how she became a Seer herself! It is such a beautiful story; I smiled as I thought about it. Present now as the class was about to resume, I saw the new Dreamer. I remembered that earlier I wanted to track something about her. Focusing, and asking permission in the dream-time of this Dreamer, I discovered that she would need some help in the fairly near future with a physical ailment concerning her stomach! It was then I made the connection of the concern behind the Seer's glance as her eyes swept the class at the start of the day.

Just then my eyes met those of the Hummingbird Seer, and an understanding took place. I then knew I would learn much from her and I too could become a part of the lineage, but first I needed to study very hard. I knew I must learn as much about the attributes and habits of the Hummingbird as possible!

I was paying attention to the present class now; the Seer was mentioning some of her most notable attributes. She said, "Hummingbird has the ability to heal by using light as a laser from her mouth. My amazing makeup has endurance for long journeys and the ability to fly into small places to heal. I am one who can bring happiness, love, and joy to others!"

I smiled at her as our eyes met, and we touched on another level. Yet I did not kid myself. There was much to do, and I knew there would be tests, but I was fine with that.

LEOPARD

DREAM OF THE LEOPARD SEER

This evening consisted of small dream circles sharing, conferring on things learned. Walking back to my room after dinner, I met several fellow Dreamers. All were excited about our ongoing dream adventures. They were deciding which circle they would join later, and they asked me my thoughts. All I could answer was, "I'm not sure." I began moving through them and said, "See you later!" I was tense with overload and in need of space, alone time! Next thing I knew, I decided I would not participate in any of the circles. Feeling a little guilty about my decision once I reached my room, I plopped down on the bed and thought maybe a nap would help. Or should I go to something? No! I said firmly to myself. Take a little care for you! I flashed back to all the various Dreamers I had helped lately.

Time to reflect and have quiet and time to work on some of my own fears that have been cropping up as of late. Lying on the bed awhile felt so good. Outside my window, I could hear a few of the evening animals nestling in for the night. The orange-and-purple sunset was giving away to bluish black. Through the cabin walls I heard some laughter not far off. I was happy the Dreamers were enjoying this special time.

But my eyes would not close to sleep...jumping straight up, I grabbed my wrap. I knew I would feel better outside with the Moon.

Walking some, I reflected on the New Moon. It is the dark of the Moon, which does not give out light but reflects energy just the same. Traipsing near the huge granite cliffs was not as easy in the dark. I looked up to the bright starry sky for support. Something told me to use my spirit eyes. I began doing this and felt better. I stopped for a moment to just look around; in front of me was an interesting crack in the rocky cliffs. This looked like an entrance to a cave. Suddenly my dreaming brought me to a memory of "The Temple of the Moon"! This is a beautiful place in this reality and the Otherworlds. Part of the Inca civilization, it is located in the Huayna Picchu mountains near Machu Picchu in Peru. But why should this be coming to me now? I have never been there in waking reality, although I would certainly like too. I wondered, Why now?

Standing there in my dream, I felt in two places at once: here for my work in the Grove and also at this amazing "Temple of the Moon." I could feel a slight breeze near me, and a presence, but saw nothing. I moved off my stance some, and then the starlight shifted onto the rocks. I saw what the breeze had been. It was a Leopard; fear gripped me! We caught each other's eyes and stared.

Pulling my wrap tighter and beginning to move backward with one foot, I heard a voice, "Do not go just yet!" Looking around for someone but knowing it was the Leopard, I froze in place. Looking straight at this huge predator, I did not know what to say. So, I just stood there looking terrified. She looked calm and sure of herself. (I knew this was a female, dark of the Moon and all.) She had a rather long body and short legs. Her head was massive. From what I know, she very closely resembles the Black Panther.

In a raspy voice, I heard her say, "In case you were wondering, I can move in a run at thirty-seven miles per hour!"

My mouth dropped open; I closed it and just looked at her and her beauty. I was intrigued by her and her glorious spots. To myself, I said, She can read my thoughts. I decided to just ask her! "So, you can read my thoughts, is that so?"

She answered quickly, "Sometimes."

I lowered my eyes to the ground but knew she was looking at me, or maybe through me! I was not sure what to say.

Then I heard her talking. It was a soothing voice that she was speaking in. "Certainly you know that I am The Leopard Seer?" I nodded my head in acknowledgement. "Not much of a voice, have you? Oh well! That's OK! Let me just go on for a while. I am sure that if you have something to say, it will come out. Seems it is your time, Dreamer, to learn my facts!"

I only stared. Now she was in human form, with dark black skin and silky black hair that flickered when the starlight fell on it. Her clothing was tight and close to her body, like a runner might wear black spots on beige, a second skin. I figured she was always ready to sprint if need be. Now she was ready to continue.

"The Leopard is an old world mammal and the smallest of the big cats. We are very solitary, and aside from mating, interaction with others is infrequent. We live mainly in the grasslands near woodlands and forests. Generally we are nocturnal but sometimes active during twilight or dawn. Leopards are very good at stalking their prey and do so silently. We hunt best at night and sometimes will store our prey in trees. We are agile, solitary, and secretive. We know how to blend with our environment when we need to be out of sight."

Listening to the Seer speak about her attributes made me feel more comfortable with her. I was able to put aside some of the initial fear that I had when she initially showed up on the cliffs. Looking now at this beautiful creature, I could hear that she was summing up her characteristics.

"So the Leopard is: power of invisibility, intuitive, elusiveness, ability to hide, family secrets, understands stalking, good climber, trusts inner self, strength, power of silence, understands one's shadow side, and very sensitive to touch and beauty."

The Seer stood up and stretched her legs and paced about some. I moved about as well, stretching my back and then looking up at the brightly lit sky. I suddenly knew that this Seer was the one who could help me understand the fears that had been popping up for me over the last few days! I swung myself around, ready to get to my questions. But when I saw the Seer, she had changed; she was now the fearsome animal once more. I heard her laughing at my surprise!

"Don't worry! I am able to interchange at will. Still the same being, either way. Oh, my dear girl, do not be afraid!"

She pranced around some and then was in human form once more. She said this: "I am sensing that part of the reason for our evening together is to help you get through some of your fears." I smiled a weak smile, and told her that I did want to talk about fear.

"Good, good!" she said. "First let us talk about Panther, who is very similar to me. Panther is secretive, silent, and graceful like her sister, the Leopard. Those working with this ally will find power in silence as goals are pursued. She is also solitary by choice. She tells little but listens. Like Leopard, she is careful not to share too much information, only enough to ease curious minds. All large cats have binocular vision. Each eye can work singly, providing greater vision. Panther-Leopard people have broad vision. We also have incredible hearing-clairaudience, which is something that may develop, working with me as an ally. These animals and many people that carry their traits enter this world enlightened; most people have to work at that. The auras of both cats are mystical, and both find power in darkness. Both the Leopard and the Panther are connected to the Moon energy; this is the symbol for the feminine. Black Panther may be more aligned with the New Moon, which is the dark of the Moon. These cats have an understanding about death and can teach people not to fear it. For out of death comes rebirth. Working with me will help one to understand the darkness and any fear that might bring. Aligning with leopard or panther helps with an inner knowing."

I was feeling more relaxed as the Seer sat regally, legs crossed on her rock perch and hands crossed as well. She did not show expression, but her energy certainly drew my attention. She began again.

"In Greek myth we have a story of Dionysus, the Greek god of wine and intoxication, who the panther nursed back to health. Panther may have helped reawakened Dionysus's abilities that may have been closed down. And helped him to overcome fears of darkness and death. Dionysus had to overcome much before he could take his place in the heavens.

The Leopard teaches us to confront our dark side and reassures us, being our guardian throughout. In Greek art, Dionysus is often shown riding a Leopard or a Panther. In ancient Roman art, there are similar images of this same god, but it's known to the Romans as Bacchus."

The ancient one stopped speaking. I told the Leopard Seer, "Thank you!" I was really learning so much. She smiled at me in human form now. With the fur and head of the leopard resting on her shoulders, there was a powerful image that came through her light force. I felt that I could not take my eyes away from her.

She then spoke: "There is an energy that wants to transfer between us, and it will happen. Before that can take place, we need to go back to the fear you are holding. Are you ready to work on that now, my dear?"

I was nodding my head yes! But had no idea where to begin. I said out loud, "Where do I start?"

She smiled and said, "Simply start from where you are right now. You are here in the center of this beautiful, sacred Grove, doing important work to help our Mother Earth and her beings. This is big!" She looked at me with eyes of compassion.

I braved up to speak. "I will be honest and say I am afraid that many Dreamers are endeavoring to do more than could ever be possible!"

Looking at me intently, she said, "Please share with me what makes you fearful."

Speaking quickly, before I lost my strength, I said, "Sometimes I feel I do not know enough to help the people that come to me. I am fearful that I may not give them what they really need to heal. I am fearful of my own energy levels not being strong enough. There is so much sorrow in the contemporary waking world, and we as Dreamers have big goals, visions, stating we can help to make a difference in the world. But speaking from my own dream…I am fearful of the time going so fast and not accomplishing enough! I am—"

"Whoa!" said the Leopard Seer. "Let us take this a little at a time, please!" Then she went onto this: "First, what do we do with Fear? WE LISTEN! We learn to use the adversary of fear as a catalyst. We learn to live a less-stressful life by becoming more aware of self and what components cause any LACK and LIMITATION in us that might allow us to become victims of FEAR! Take apart the word FEAR; what do we have? Remove the letter *F*, and we have EAR!"

The Leopard Seer was silent and searching me for reaction; well, I was dumfounded! On she went, not taking her eyes off me for a second.

"Dreamer, think like this: in every situation, break things down to its simplest state. For instance, with the word FEAR, we use the EAR in fear to HEAR what is really going on! If we think of ourselves or situation in regard to what we lack or what limits us and we are honest about this, we are usually able to remove the fear as just another obstacle. Everything has a cause and an effect. So we need to listen to our fear and know what the cause is to the best of our ability. The fear then eases away, and we are able to live less stressfully."

The Seer was quiet; I was trying to digest what she had said. The breeze was picking up, the damp air from the night was setting in, and I felt a chill on my shoulders.

The Leopard Seer put her arms on my shoulders and said, "We have done quite enough for one evening! Remember this: when Leopard or Panther enters your life, it is a time of new beginning, expanded awareness, alternate realities, and the working to eliminate fears. All these things bring rebirth. If you remember to ask, the Leopard or Panther becomes your guardian, your protector!"

I smiled as bravely as I could and thanked her, knowing I had much to digest.

"Dream on these things as you drift to the Otherworlds in your sleep!" she said. With a quick wave, she was gone.

It was silent; it was night. Looking around the rocky ledges, I was reminded again of the "Temple of the Moon" and smiled to the darkness and the temple for the lessons I had now received. I headed back to my cabin for a night of rest and dreaming, feeling more at ease.

LION

DREAM OF THE LION SEER

I awoke from the dream, thinking, Am I the Lion, or with him? The thought of what she had said felt like a bee sting. In the dream we had been standing under the moonlight, which glowed over the water on the beach. She held a scepter covered with sapphires and aquamarines; sea foam and mist were her robes.

I could not see her face. Who was this woman? I had told her it was my time to roam! I needed change; the pride was fine without me for a while.

"And the young ones?" she asked.

"Oh! It does not matter!" I had said.

"Oh, it matters!" she replied in a stinging voice! Continuing, she said, "Use this night to search your convictions, your plans. Life is a circle; men are lost when they forget that woman is the circle."

"I am the Lion!" I screeched at her. "I have been the male guardian, the sentinel—"

She held up her scepter, and I became silent. I gave my voice to her.

"I know these things," she said. "You have been our strength!" The goddess with her scepter continued. "You are a wonderful leader; it is a difficult role to play. Someone, something, commanding your attention at all times. This is the life you choose. This incarnation comes with obligations and patterns of karma, as all lives do. I am not suggesting that you not go! I am saying to search your soul! What is it you are after? We all come with the right to use our free will, and we can choose to use it to alter a karmic pattern that we may not want. We may become someone vastly different from the person we have been, the same, yet different, possibly more in touch with our dreaming soul path. Yes, our 'Lion Pride' depends on you for strength. But you may learn something if you ask the lionesses to show you how the Feminine Lunar energies might help you at this juncture in time."

There was a long pause; I did not know what to say. It was awkward.

Then the Goddess said, "Think of the 'British coat of Arms' that has the Lion and the Unicorn engraved upon it. This is said to represent the Sun and the Moon. This is a symbol of two energies in harmony. Yes, you are the Lion," she said.

It was morning! Was I dreaming still? *No!* No. So much to do before the day's program. I had better get going. Yet, I am the "Lion"...Or am I? The dream was with me strongly!

Looking at my watch, I thought of the "Lion Headed Coronus" as time and destiny devouring all things. The sunrise was oranges and purples. Again an ancient symbol of Lion came to me. The Egyptian "Akeru" gods were the supernatural lions who guarded the gates of sunset and sunrise.

The dream! I must honor the dream! Walking briskly down to the beach, I would give an offering to the sea and my gratitude to the goddess of my dream. I felt like the early morning light was out just for me, the orange, gold, and pinks. The sound of the waves was soothing. The dream was beginning to take on new meaning as I reached the beach.

Hurry, hurry, I kept saying. She may be there! Walking down the hill to the water, nothing! I saw no one! An ache of disappointment came over me; I really thought she would be here. So many things I wanted to say, to explain, and ask. Leaning down now to the water, I offered the wild flowers I had picked, laying them onto the sea foam. I watched as they bounced around in the waves. I thank you, Dear Goddess of the Sea. I trust you will come to me again!

Hearing something near the rocks, I turned to see. My heart was racing. Could it be the Goddess? There on the rocky ledge were two cats. The seagulls above were circling and making a racket with their calls. The one cat just sat there; the other moved about. I walked over to see what was up. The sun was out strongly now; the warmth was on my back. I was glad. Once I arrived at the rocks and was closer, I realized this was a huge cat. However, the cat just sat!

I was totally surprised to see the "Scepter" lying on the sand. The goddess scepter, of sapphires and aquamarines, but the Goddess? Looking around, I did not know what to think. Then the cat that had been quiet and indifferent began purring, and he made me think of "Cat Sith," the Scottish Faerie cat. Legend says at times it may be transformed into a witch or wizard. The cat's purring became louder. Curious about this creature, I said, "So, my beauty, who are we today? I had leaned over and picked up the jeweled scepter. Not expecting an answer, I got one just the same!

"I can be your Strength, your council of wisdom, if you allow me to tame you!" Now she was the goddess of last night! But now I saw her lioness face. I was in awe of her odd beauty, wondering if this was actually a vision. "Strength?" I said out loud. "Like the 'Strength Tarot Seer'! One image I have of her is of a woman taming a lion." Musing to myself, I thought, I must meet with her. Looking back to the Lion Goddess, I handed her the scepter and said, "I had thought you were The Goddess of the Sea."

She answered, "All women goddesses are connected to the Sea, governed by the Moon, and we are rhythm and flow. This is what gives us our strength."

The cat that had just sat silently nearby had now grown into a huge lion. In between licking his paws, he said, "There is that word again!" He was speaking to the Goddess with the deep-black pools in her eyes.

The Lion Goddess answered. "Strength worries you?"

"No, no!" He answered. "You do know that Lion is the King of Beasts, thought to be both good and evil. So many times, the lion is the Lion God of war. Lions are the guardians of doors, gates, treasures, even the Tree of Life. 'Leo the Lion' is on the astrological zodiac for July twenty-fourth to August twenty-third. The list is great! Shall I continue?"

Then there came a pregnant pause, which held for awhile, and I felt sad. I listened to them banter once more.

"What is it, Lion Seer? How may I help you?" I said to the Lion Goddess with dew in her eyes. I was barely audible but needed to offer help.

"Help? I suppose, well, with balance. That may be it? Could it be that simple?" said the "Lion Goddess."

I tried to keep the conversation going. I looked back and forth to each of them. "Last night, Goddess, I thought about what you said. Convictions, plans, wanting to roam. Well, it does matter, to the young ones."

The Goddess added, "You are right! The pride needs to see that their leader is part of the workings of the pride, the community. But what I also realized is that a leader must show their human frailties at times and ask for help and support." She was looking at the Lion with sympathy.

He responded, "I can teach them about speed, teamwork, stalking, intuition, initiative—"

"Lion Seer! Stop and think!" said the Goddess. "What is it you are after now?"

Shocked by the demanding tone in her voice, I was concerned but said not a word.

The brave Lion, laden with sadness, stared into her eyes. In a strong voice, he answered, "Balance!" He then sat back down on the rocks and rested his head on his arms.

Smiling and with the sun in her hair, The Lion Goddess reminded me of the Egyptian Goddess Bastet, a feline-headed deity who guards against evil. Or of the Sekhmet lioness, the fiercest hunter known to the Egyptians, who had a very strong cult following and was often dressed in red, the color of blood. I watched now as the Lion Goddess adjusted the red shawl around her shoulders. As she stood up, she said to the "Lion," "We will help you tame with balance!"

Hearing the drumming, the three of us looked at each other, smiling. With thankfulness, I handed my hand to each lion and said, "To balance! May it not be too painful!"

Laughing, the Goddess Lion said to the Lion Seer; "All good leaders must learn this in time. But tell me, legend says Lions are known to sleep with their eyes wide open! Is this true!"

He answered, saying, "You are my lioness, and you have known me under many a Moon. I do believe you would know!"

We were all laughing now as we dashed up the hill to where the ceremonies were beginning. The Lions seemed ready to enter a new dream! And I, for one, wanted to see how this dream would go!

OWL

DREAM OF THE OWL SEER

What a wonderful evening we had! Some of The Keepers presented Dream Theater for the entire dream family that was gathered here in the Nemeton. One end of the Grove had been bustling all morning with Dreamers making a simple theatre in the round. In the afternoon the dream presented was, "Dreamers Make a Difference." The theme of the dream was quick scenarios of Dreamers working with and healing those who inquire about dream healing. Some portrayals were serious, or sad, or just realistic tips. Some were very funny! The intention of the dream theater was to be a way to learn from our master teachers in a lighthearted, instructive method. It was wonderful to view the interaction with the audience, made up of novice Dreamers, Apprentices, and Keepers. Some of the Ancient Tarot Seers reminded me of the old troubadours or bards, with their flare for story telling or poems. And their costumes were amazing! I felt the best part was the impromptu actors who were called upon at random from the audience to act out a character in the dream scenario. This was great fun, and everyone was a good sport about participating.

I was among several other Dreamers who were straightening up our space and making the altar ready for the next morning's dream sessions. We were all in high-spirited dream mode, laughing and sharing the early evening events. "It was fun live theater!" I said.

"Certainly was, and needed, too, for lightening up our energy bodies!" said one of the women Dreamers I had come to know and treasure.

"Are you ready to walk back?" I asked her.

"Yes! And look at that Moon! So large and bright, it almost touches the cliffs next to the beach!" She answered quickly, and then added, "The moonlight must be amazing over the water now, and I would love to see it!"

"Yes! Yes! Let's head to the small part of the cliff where we can take it all in!" I answered her.

Wrapping my shawl tight against the damp evening air, we were next to the cliff in a few minutes. It did not take us long to scale this low area of the rocks, and of course we had the moonlight to light our way!

My friend said, "This is perfect, as I have some private things I would like to share with you, if that is OK?"

"Of course!" I answered as we found a nice place to relax. "But first, let's just take in the Moon in all her glory and thank her for her radiance and the abundance she brings!" I said.

We were silent for a while, just listening to the waves lapping against the beach, feeling the tides waxing and waning. It was truly marvelous.

I felt a breeze and shuddered a bit. I was about to say something, when my friend said, "Did you hear that?" She looked a little startled.

"I don't think so. But I feel something!" We both looked at each other. Clutching our wraps, trying to keep brave, looking at each other, we knew something was going on!

Suddenly there was another breeze, and then a hushed voice spoke, "Owl's flight is silent! I am the Owl Seer, come to join you Dreamers; I am the Keeper of the 'Moonlight Vision'!"

My friend and I were frozen in place on that rocky cliff, not believing what we saw under the moonlight.

"Well, ladies! Is this OK with you?" said the Owl Seer.

My friend and I were so stunned at the owl's appearance; we had not blinked or uttered a sound. Muttering a bit, I said, "Yes, of course! We were just surprised when you came!"

"I seem to get that response from many when I show up!" She was chuckling at this comment. She was still in her owl form, looming nearby. "But, my dears, Owl can bring us dreamtime visions, inner knowing, and acceptance of the dark, the night, the shadow within and without. In honoring her we receive Truth. We can invoke owl for the ability to keep silent and the will to hold onto that which must be kept secret."

Smiling weakly, I said, "Please join us!"

"Here, please have a seat on the blanket," my friend said as she spread out a place for us all.

"Ah! Now we are the triple goddess under the moonlight, as it should be!"

She looked at us with huge, black-centered eyes rimed in yellow gold. They were so piercing that it was unnerving, and I looked away. I looked instead into the moonlight. I noticed my friend was doing the same.

The Owl Seer broke our reverie, telling us a short poem from the book *The White Goddess* by Robert Graves:

> The New Moon is the white goddess of birth and growth;
> The Full Moon, the red goddess of love and battle;
> The Old Moon, the black goddess of death and divination.

"How nice! I like that; it helps to understand the moon energy better!" I said quickly, hoping to change the somber mood I felt.

My friend nodded her head in agreement. She said, "Dear Seer, please tell us more about Owl energy, and why do so many fear the Owl?"

Now the Owl Seer was nodding her head. She had changed from bird to a beautiful, age-less woman, with long, white hair. There was a soft smile on her burgundy lips, and the same dark, black eyes with the yellow rims looked at us both, feeling softer now. "I thought you would never ask!" She cackled! "I have so much to share with you on this full moon night. Wisdom! Owl is the symbol of the feminine, the moon, and the night. Because of its association with the moon, it has ties to fertility and seduction. The owl is the bird of magic and darkness, of prophecy and wisdom! To answer your question about why people seem to have a fear around the Owl, this would be my dream. Owl is a bird of the night, the darkness, the night hunter. The darkness is what is feared by so many. The owl has also been a symbol of the darkness within, the secrets that humans may hold. Owl has the ability to see what others may miss. Their medicine gift is the ability to not be deceived by external appearances. Owl gives us the ability to discover the truth in a given situation. Owl has a keen perception of everything going on, at all times. They are able to focus with sharp clarity. People with owl medicine may be clairvoyant or psychic. Their intuition is accurate and precise. They are not gullible and can see past a lie or scheme, to the truth beneath." The Seer gazed at us and paused.

Feeling a revelation, I said, "You know, these characteristics are definitely what might make some nervous or afraid!"

I could tell from my friend's response of "Yes" that she was picking up the same thought.

The Seer said, "I would not be surprised that if someone was not being forthright, the energy of the Owl might make them feel concerned!" The Owl Seer continued. "Owl also stands on the threshold of the Otherworlds, reminding us of the ever-present reality of death. But we must remember that death is also a gateway. In our own death, when we come through it, we realize that it is simply change. Owl can teach us about detachment of the physical, and through those lessons we gain wisdom for our next rebirth."

The Owl Seer stood up and was now walking some on the rocks, standing so close to the edge in some spots that it made me cringe a little! Then I remembered she was the Seer with amazing sight and could fly if she needed to.

My friend and I stood up too. It was nice to have a little break. I noticed that the Seer was walking in a circle counterclockwise. "Why are you doing that?" I asked.

She answered, "It is called 'Widdershins.' In Scottish Gaelic it is 'Tuathal,' meaning left-hand-wise. It means, 'a direction opposite to the usual.' Walking counterclockwise, left, three times, confounds any evil that might follow. And you ask, Why do you do this? I will share this with you: I was picking up a slight presence, possibly because of talking about death. So rather than feel any of that, I simply change the energy. Walking 'Widdershins' confounds and disperses!"

"Oh my! I will certainly remember to use that!" I said, "Thanks."

"Why, of course," the Seer answered. "Now let us continue. Owls are an order of birds of prey classified as 'Strigiformes,' of which there are two hundred species. Most are nocturnal and solitary. They hunt mostly small mammals, insects, and other birds. A group of owls are referred to as a parliament. Much of their hunting strategy depends on stealth and surprise. Owls' bodies are an aid to them; their dull feather coloration can render them almost invisible. Also, the serrated edges on the leading edge of the owls' 'remiges,' feathers on wings, muffle the owls' wingbeats, allowing flight to be practically silent. Owl's sharp beak and powerful talons allow it to kill its prey before swallowing it whole."

The Seer looked at us to see how we were handling this information. I did not want to let on any discomfort, so I just nodded my head. She went on. "When an owl grows old and cannot fly or is injured, its off spring and others in the community come and pull out the oldest feathers from its body and constantly care for it until it has recovered its strength. Owls are sometimes referred to as 'Night Eagles' by Native Americans. Hopi Native Americans have taboos that surround owls, having to do with evil or sorcery. Other Natives see the Owl as the carrier of the Elder's spirit upon death. The Mayan and Aztec and other Mesoamerican cultures saw the Owl as a symbol of death and destruction.

"To the Eastern Indians, the Owl is seen as a harbinger of prosperity. As you can see, in many parts of the world, owls have been associated with death and misfortune, likely due to their nocturnal activity and of course their screeching calls!" The Seer laughed and gave us a screech demo!

We laughed and my friend spoke up, saying, "I feel so bad for them!"

"Not all is gloom and doom!" said The Seer. "There are associations with wisdom and prosperity. Frequently the owl is a companion animal for goddesses. In a Hindu Myth, the barn owl is considered to be a vehicle of the 'Goddess Lakshmi,' the goddess of wealth. So it is lucky to have an owl, a form of the goddess, residing near your house. Egyptians used an image of an owl for their Hieroglyphs, for the sound of the letter M. Egyptian hieroglyphic writing is called 'the alphabet of the birds,' which means 'Divine Language.' In medieval France there was a term called 'La langue des oiseaux' which translates to 'Language of the birds.' There was actually a secret language of the 'Troubadors,' connected with the tarot!"

"That is so fascinating!" my friend said.

The Seer continued. "In France, the word 'Hiboux' means 'Eared Owls' and is a symbol of wisdom. The word 'Chouetts' means 'Earless Owls' and is a bird of ill omen. To the Celts, birds in general are thought to have a 'charm with their voice,' but especially the Owl, who could produce magic charms with the song in its voice. The Celts felt the owl represented prophetic knowledge. To the Celts the Owl is most often associated with the 'crone' aspect of the goddess. The word 'Cailleach' in Scottish Gaelic means owl. Sometimes the owl was called 'The Night-Hag.'

"In the Celtic-Welsh Myth, in the stories of 'Mabinogion,' the Owl is considered cursed. The first owl was a woman, but before becoming the owl, she was a woman named 'Blodenedd,' born of flowers. She was wife to Lleu Llaw-Gyffes. However, she fell in love with another man and plotted to kill Lleu. Lleu's guardian, 'Gwydion,' turned her into the first owl, saying, 'You are never to show your face to the light of day...You will not lose your name but will always be called "Bloden-w-edd."' The addition of the 'w' in her name changed her from a woman of flowers to an Owl!"

"That is such an amazing story!" I said, anxious to hear more.

The Owl Seer said she had many more tales. "From the Mesopotamian-Babylonian culture, there is a preserved terracotta relief, dating from the second millennium, 1950 BC, called the 'Burney Relief,' named for the former owner. The image portrays a nude, winged goddess figure, with Eagle's talons, flanked by OWLS, and perched upon Lions. She has been identified as 'Lilith,' the first wife of Adam. To the early Christian Gnostics, the Owl is associated with 'Lilith,' the first wife of Adam who refused to be submissive to him!"

"Yeah! Lilith! Good for her!" I just could not hold back this outburst.

The Seer cried with hysterical laughter at this! We laughed with her. Finally composed, she told us, "In Finland, the Owl is viewed as a symbol of wisdom but also imbecility, presumably because of its dumb stare!" We all laughed at this as well.

Leaning back on the rocky crest of the cliff and straightening her skirt, The Owl Seer was staring at the Moon. We followed her gaze. She said, "What a beautiful celestial planet, the Moon!" Turning toward us, she said, "Owl can see the Ley lines of Mother Earth, the places of power around the globe. When we have more time, we can consider this topic for dreaming! Owl can help with your sight: physical and psychic. An owl's hearing is just as keen as its eyesight! Did you know that?" The Seer seemed to be coming back from a reverie.

Looking at the Moon again, she said, "Let's travel a Ley Line to one of the Greek myths. Owl was associated with Athena, Minerva to the Romans. Athena was a bird goddess, and the Owl was known to rest on her shoulder. Athena was the Goddess of Wisdom and was portrayed as the figurehead of Jason's ship, the *Argo*, from the story of Jason and the Argonauts, whose mission was to retrieve the Golden Fleece. The ship was built of oak from the sacred grove at Dodona. It was known that Athena could speak the language of the birds, and her presence would be helpful to the ship's mission. The Romans had priests who were called 'Aguar'; their mission was to interpret the will of the gods by studying the flights and actions of the birds; they too knew the 'language of the birds'!"

"Oh! Dear Seer, how will I ever come to know all the stories and teachings you bring? It is just amazing to me!"

She just looked at me and said, "One day. One day! You are doing just fine!"

My friend was anxious to tell us something. "Please do," said the Seer.

Smiling some, she said, "I can contribute a very small story!"

"Yes!" I said.

She continued, "'Owl' is the name of Pooh Bear's wise friend from the English author A. A. Milne!" There was silence. "What?" my friend said with worry!

The Seer and I smiled. The Seer said, "No! That is great! It just is contemporary and brought our dreaming into another dimension. It is wonderful; we need contemporary too!"

Again we all laughed! Then we were all quiet, each of us, as the triple goddess energy was deep within our own dreaming. It has been a magical night; I knew it was getting late. I realized the Moon had moved some in the dark night sky. We could now see moonbeams were glazed across the top of the low tide.

The Seer said she just had a few things more to say. "The Snowy White Owl is magnificent. Like other owls, she hunts at night. Her method is quiet; she sits, and she waits. When a snowy owl moves into an area new to her, she does not proclaim her presence. Quietly she goes about her business. This is her gift: the ability to be nonthreatening in spite of her ability and power. She accomplishes her tasks with timing and skill, not through intimidation.

True strength is gentle, and this is what the Snowy White Owl teaches." More silence and then she went on. "Owl medicine is clairvoyance, stealth, silent, and swift. It is secrecy and a messenger of secrets and omens. The energy is of shape-shifting and a link between the world of dark and light. Owl is patient and has a comfort in its shadow self. Owl is wisdom and freedom. Well, my dears, it is getting late!" said the Seer.

We were all climbing down the rocky cliff, but of course we gave our thanks to the Moon for her supporting role. Once we were on the path back to the cabins, I could not help but ask the Owl Seer, "I thought you would have turned from your human form and flown off by now, Dear Seer!" Then I wondered if she might take offense to what I had said.

"Flown off? Why, no, not yet! This has been a special time for me to be with you both and to enjoy the Grove with you as a human! I thank you for that." Then she said, "As an Owl I help cast off any fears of the dark, and I come for you to experience the truth in the night." She handed each of us one of her beautiful feathers. We both thanked her for them and the amazing evening. "We three have felt the Moon together. Now harness that energy with your feathers, and hold the power for wise and future use!"

She was spreading her arms out like feathers for us to see; it was beautiful! We were thanking her again. She simply looked at us and said, "My night is just starting!" And she was gone without a sound.

My friend said, "I guess we will talk of ordinary things tomorrow. Owl is magic!"

RAVEN

DREAM OF THE RAVEN SEER

I was so happy to be walking on the cliffs after the high-energy intensive that dealt with the realms of death and transformation. These cliffs are the most removed from the Grove. It was only noon, bright and sunny, and I had plenty of time before my next class in the early evening. I had packed a lunch and a jacket in case it turned windy or cool on the rocky precipice I wanted to climb.

Dreaming back to the classes, two days now, I had been involved with the Keepers.

I thought, Am I searching my heart? Maybe…Studying with the Seers is hard. They expect much. They had put us, the Dreamers, on the spot for many things. The dream image transfer work came easy for me, which was helpful in the afternoon's work. I was climbing higher on the cliffs now and could hear the sea and her waves crashing the rocky shore. One more foot hold, and I pulled myself up higher still. The view! I took a deep breath and I could see the full expanse of the sea now, a beautiful, foamy, greenish blue, with large white-caps rolling in along the shore. Standing up here, the sun felt glorious. I shielded the sun's glare with my hand over my eyes, looking around. This is perfect! No one will find me here.

Shaking my blanket some, I sat to relax as I ate my lunch and flipped through my journal. My thoughts wandered back to the dreaming of the morning class.

I could still hear the words of The Tower Trump Seer: "Face my own death to live; what is needed is dying to live!" With that I just shut myself down. I could not get anything more from the rest of the class. I saw other Dreamers shaking their heads and talking with the Seer. I got nothing; I tuned out. The Seer's eyes met mine; I turned away. I could not wait to leave!

Now on my back and enjoying the sun and my sandwich, I decided it did not matter. I noticed the sun seemed to have a flashing quality. I lay down for a while on the warm, quartz-layered rocks. The flashes came again, and I felt a cool wind brush over me. Startled, I sat up.

Now I heard a croaking cry. What is it? I thought. "Well, if you are trying to scare me, you have!" Having said this loudly, I consciously pulled in my energy of protection and rolled my shoulders back.

Just then, at the cliff's edge, about twenty-five paces to the west, I saw a tall figure, a man in a cloak of black-blue plumage. His head was bent over the front of his chest, and his arms were crossed over his chest as well. The cloak shimmered with long, black feathers that were beautiful but a bit creepy, I thought. He was so very tall. Taking a deep breath, I said to myself, "Black can mean many things, but not necessarily evil."

The man opened his arms, and out flew two ravens! I was aghast! The sunlight was flashing all around me. The cloak was wrapped about him; it shimmered as he walked toward me.

Well, so much for my hideaway, I thought to myself. Quickly I stood up. My heart raced as he walked toward me. Time stood still; I was receiving flashes of information as he walked!

I am dreaming…I see a Raven Banner for a King. I am in ancient times, ancient wars. Images of Knights with the symbol of the Raven. Raven on the Coat of Arms for the Isle of Man, Scotland, and something that felt Norse. Another image: Raven is closely linked with Odin, the Norse God of Scandinavia. Raven in the battlefields of ancient European wars, going for the blood of the fallen.

The dream scene changes to that of ancient Gaul, France. Raven is woven into the Bayeaux Tapestry with a Norman Knight holding a Raven Banner. Raven with King Arthur, and then after his death, seeing his soul take the shape of Raven.

Images of the Tower of London that has had Ravens roosting there for thousands of years! The Ravens there are known for their warding abilities. Within the Tower, the Ravens are tended by The Yeoman Warders of the Tower. Legend has it that Britain will fall if the Ravens ever leave the Tower! The longest resident Raven was named Jim Crow, which lived there for forty years!

OH! My Goddess! I blinked my eyes and pulled myself back from this dreaming!

Shaking some, I reached down on the rock for my jacket. While bent over, I saw the black-blue feathers at my feet! Quickly, in one swift motion, I pulled on my jacket and moved backward. With my arms covering my chest, and staring at the man, I heard him say, "You did well. You are a talented receiver. I see that you are shaken. I mean no harm. Raven has been so typecast!"

The handsome man's face turned to one side a bit, and he had a slight grin. I thought, Does he expect me to laugh? I couldn't.

He continued in a smooth, comforting voice. "Raven does not have to be the dark side."

Looking straight at him and taking a deep breath, in a quiet voice I asked, "Why are you here? I did not ask for you!"

The tall man carefully removed his black plumage cloak, folded it carefully, and laid it onto the rocks. "May I sit down?" he asked.

"It's free space," I replied.

"You did not ask for me? I wonder why?" He laughed. I did not find this funny.

Just then several Ravens flew closer and perched on rocks nearby. They were making very distinct calls and a few more had come to roost as well.

"They are very vocal birds," said this large, angular man. He seemed almost normal now. There was perspiration on his brow from the hot sun. His face was kindly, and his mouth smiled some when he spoke. His dense hair was as blackish-blue as his plumage cloak.

Realizing I did not feel threatened, I decided to trust those feelings. I did, after all, know that he was the Raven Seer.

Paying attention now, I heard him say, "Ravens have alarm calls, chase calls, and flight calls. And sometimes they make a snapping noise with their beaks." Looking at me quickly, he continued, "Ravens are good at problem solving. They may call in wolves or coyotes to a dead animal. The canines open the carcass, making it accessible to the birds. The ravens watch the canines as to where they bury their food and then remember locations of these caches. Then they literally steal from each other! It becomes a game. Some then travel farther from the territory to prevent this. They are very smart!"

We heard a commotion on the rocks where there were about eight ravens perched. "See the pair off to the left?" My eyes followed to where the Seer was pointing. "They are mates, and they mate for life. Then they defend their territory. I think the chatter we hear is the setting of boundaries for the visiting flock. The Raven's power of speech is very important."

"Why are you telling me this?" I asked.

"What holds you back?" he answered me.

"Holds me back? What are you talking about?" I responded.

"From discovering your demons," he said with a curt smile. Feeling uneasy, I was not sure how to answer. He replied to my silence, "OK! Now we are getting somewhere. I do believe this has struck a chord with you! Not having an answer is really unlike you. We need not worry; we can tame whatever demons need taming."

Now he was laughing at my expense, which didn't make me feel any better! But my thoughts did wander to what demons I might have and not want to admit to, but I sure did not want to say that!

The Raven Seer continued. "I must say again, you did very well earlier, receiving information about Raven. Where did that come from, I ask you?"

I was confused and did not know what to say.

"Please let me help you," he said. "One of my Ravens attributes is getting, receiving, information and then transferring it to those who are able to receive it and are wanting it. So it seems to me that you do have a start of a relationship with Raven. If it were my dream, what I might suggest is that you may use me to discover demons for whatever may hold you back from the growth you are meant to do at this time in this safe place of the Nemeton."

Deep in my being, something had clicked. I knew I could feel safe and face my fears with this guardian teacher and feel better for having done the work.

The Seer looked intently and said, "Come on now. I know you like magic in your life, and I can assist you with that. I can be your courier to find information or carry energy for healing. You can wear me as a cloak to keep you invisible and protected when needed. Remember, Ravens are true magicians and can help us shape-shift for balance! I see that twinkle in your eye and the start of a smile at the corner of your mouth. Come on. Give yourself this gift!"

I wanted to smile, but I had to keep it in for some crazy reason. So I could feel in control, I suppose. I managed to keep a cool, expressionless face. Looking straight at him, I said, "You are the Raven Seer."

He looked at me quizzically. "Why yes, My Dear, I am!"

I replied, "I will work with you!"

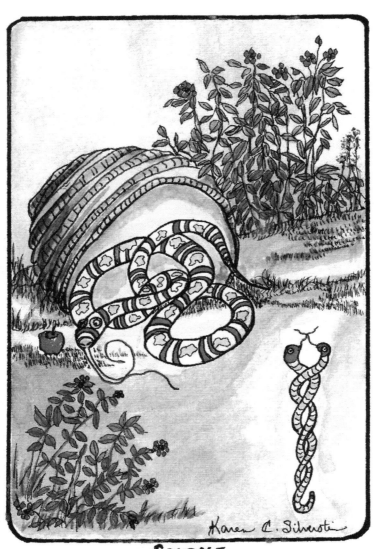

SNAKE

DREAM OF THE SNAKE SEER

I was on the edge of the wood, picking raspberries, my favorite! Reaching for a clump at the back side of the bushes, my fingers got pricked. I moved myself around for an easier reach, and then I seemed to get myself caught up in some brambles. So I put down my basket and began to untwine myself. It was one of those hot, hazy summer days, just made for taking things easy and slow. OK! Finally now I was free of the prickly brambles! Relaxing and looking at the view from this high spot on this northeastern crescent of the hill, I noticed how the sun lit up the Grove at midday. I saw some bustling activity below. Dreamers were just finishing the noon meal, and everyone had some time for themselves until 3:00 p.m. I had chosen to just grab a sandwich and come to explore another part of our Nemeton. It felt great to be way up here. I could see the ocean beyond the Grove, and as I turned about, I could see the mountain peaks in deep, verdant greens with touches of blues and purples. I felt as if I were a sentry for one of the corners of our world!

I'd picked off the brambles and some other round, prickly balls, seedpods for something, I supposed. I looked around for another spot; most of the grass was pretty tall, resembling hay. Seeing a sunny area of flattened grass a few yards away, I rummaged in my basket and took out my blanket. I decided that I could pick more berries later. It was definitely lunch time! Arranging my journals to one side of the blue-and-yellow blanket, I was ready for a quiet afternoon. The few berries I picked made a nice little dessert.

Lying on my stomach, I began going through my notes. In our morning session, we had been talking of the ancient Egyptians and other Eastern cultures that have contributed such rich history to all of our lives. Someone had said, "Light and its energy are both motion and mind. Light comes from the action of the Spiritual Sun, which was symbolized by the physical orb, the sun, which we see each day." I was not really sure what that all meant.

Closing my journal, I turned on my side. Looking at the grass, I saw there was something odd, a small, grayish looking piece of paper, very thin and transparent. I picked it up and saw immediately that it had scale markings. I dropped it and said, "Oh my God! It is a snakeskin, maybe one that has just been shed!" I was panicking now! I never did like snakes. Looking around the grass, I did not see anything, and I breathed a sigh of relief. Now I just felt edgy...I started packing up my things into my basket. I shook out the blanket and started to put it into the basket.

Then, there it was. I froze! A rather large black snake, wet looking, was curled right inside the basket! Jumping back, I dropped the blanket. As I looked at this creature, it stared right back at me! Suddenly I had this image of the snake turning into a bluish cord that connected to my solar plexus. I began to feel lightheaded and fearful...

Then I heard a voice! "Wait a minute, my dear, we are not ready to dream journey yet!"

I had been looking at my stomach, and now I looked up to the sound of the voice. I saw now a tall figure, thin and angular. Not really male or female, I thought to myself. This person was dressed in various shades of blue-black leather, which wrapped tightly about them in interesting patterns with lapis and sapphire jewels attached here and there. I was mesmerized by the beauty presented. Gradually I came to realize this was the Snake Seer, and I felt only slightly better.

The Snake Seer smiled at me and handed me some raspberries. "Are you feeling better? I suppose that I gave you quite a start, showing up the way that I did! However, when it comes to snake medicine, I have found that the quickest way for those who are called is to just get on with it. Surprise can assist with cutting through the fear that a healer may have of our species!"

I did laugh a bit at that, and some tension started to release. "Well, there was a definite element of surprise! I must tell you that I do still have fear. I have always been fascinated by snakes but always squeamish and fearful!"

The Seer was looking intently at me with deep blue-black eyes that held my gaze. "It is understandable," said the Seer. "Some human healers may not pay attention to what it means to connect to snake medicine. It is important to study and gain insight and prepare for the connection. It should never be done casually, without advance training. Not all are called to Snake, and not all are ready for this opening!"

"The opening? What opening are you talking about?" I said, a bit worried.

The Snake Seer watched me and seemed shocked by my comment. The Seer went on. "The awakening of one's kundalini energy, of course! This is where the fear comes from. This process is an initiation to own life force! The spinal energy, which is called 'kundalini,' spirals about the base of one's spine and opens when we face the fear of it; this is where the snake resides. Facing the fear of this energy with its incredible power, makes one realize the amazing abilities they possess, which allows one to be connected to their own healing and to helping others to heal. However, we may be fearful of our power or timid about putting this energy to use. So, my dear Dreamer, you have been calling, and I am here! Do you feel ready to begin a little training? Best not to get analytical here: use your gut instinct. Yes or no!" The Seer simply stared and did not seem to care what answer I would give.

Although I was stunned by his directness, oddly I also felt calmness. I held my hands to the back of my spinal column. I nodded my head. "Yes!" I said to The Seer, "I want to be awake!"

The Snake Seer had no expression on his face, just nodded, gave me more raspberries, and said I should drink some water. "It is good to have eaten lightly. This is helpful when we dream journey deeply to connect, heal, and awaken."

I began to ask questions, however, the Seer asked me to wait until we had done some work.

The Snake Seer began, saying, "First, let me provide some background information about my species, the elusive, mysterious Serpent! Snake medicine often comes to you at a time when you are heading for change. You are ready to explore the mysterious, voyage where you have never gone before; this might be in the physical world or in the depths of the mind and soul. Once we have gone over this information, I will ask you about taking a personal journey to your own serpent energy, OK?" said the Seer.

I answered, "OK! Yes!"

We found a spot to settle down for our Dream work. I spread out the blue-and-yellow blanket, once more thinking to myself the Seer coordinated nicely with the blues of his outfit. As I sat down, I picked up the translucent, shed snakeskin I had found earlier. Holding it up to the sunlight, I said, "It is a marvel!"

Looking at it, the Seer said without expression, "This is a good place to start! Snakes-Serpents are connected with renewal and regeneration because of their practice of shedding their old skin and growing a new one. People with snake medicine know the power of renewal. Snake sheds his skin, leaving it behind and slithering away completely renewed. Snake people can do the same, shedding their dull layers to reveal a brilliant new self underneath. Snake medicine is rare and a gift. It is most often offered to the person using the approach of fear!" The Seer looked keenly at me as he said, "Sound familiar?"

Smiling only a little, I answered, "I guess it does."

The Seer continued. "A person with snake medicine will find that they are fearful of this shadow animal most of their lives. They survive many venomous snake attacks, in waking reality from either a physical snake, or many times from a snake in the dreamtime who is trying to connect life teachings with them that may be past lives or from Otherworlds. Once the person realizes that they have survived, they conquer their fear and are opened to the awakening of the teachings of the Serpent-Snake."

My curiosity was really piqued now…In my mind's eye I was recalling several dreams I had had about being bitten by snake or some kind of snake ceremonies. Some were from years ago; others were very recent. I realized I was anxious to hear more; I pulled my attention back to what the Seer was saying.

"Let's talk a minute about the snake's attributes. They are known as reptiles, and their skin is made up of scales. The scales are clean and dry, and the snake must shed its skin at least once a year. They are cold-blooded, and the air temperature decides their body temperature. If the air is too cold or too warm, the snake will die. Snakes hibernate in the cold weather. They use small, hooked teeth to grab and hold their food. Each side of the snake's lower jaw moves. This lets the snake eat food bigger than its mouth. Snakes sense odors with their tongues. There are a few poisonous snakes, but most are not harmful and will only attack if provoked. The snake has a special sense organ in the head that reacts to heat put out by another creature. If you have snake medicine, this could indicate sensitivity to the auras of others. Snakes have tremendous speed and agility. Before a snake sheds its skin, its eyes cloud over; this gives the snake a trance-like appearance. Many mystics and shamans believe that this indicates the ability of snake to move between realms of living to dead and back again.

"We spoke earlier of the 'kundalini' energy. This stems from Eastern traditions and is sometimes referred to as the 'Serpent Fire,' which lies coiled at the base of the spine. This energy is released as one grows and develops. Throughout the ages the Serpent-Snake has been a symbol for creativity and sexual energy. This energy can teach us about greater perception and how to apply your intuition."

The Seer had come to a pause. I began thinking about how snake energy might be helpful to me with my intuitive senses.

Now I could hear The Snake Seer saying, "I do believe I have gotten your attention. Could be that you are beginning to connect to your rare gift at last!"

Laughing at this comment, I said, "It is as though I am able to feel this medicine in an entirely different light!"

The Seer's response was, "Good, very good." The Seer continued. "Snake venom has an association with healing, like some medicinal herbs, plants, and fungi have a similar association. Some have the power to heal; some provide expanded consciousness through divine intoxication. To ancient healers and shamans, the snake was one of the wisest of animals, considered to be close to the divine. This divine aspect, combined with Earth properties, connects the snake to the afterlife and immortality. From culture to culture, the mythological symbolism is twofold. Sometimes positive, other times negative."

I spoke up at this point, and said I felt that there was more negative and that this bothers me!

The Seer looked a little sad and said, "This may be so, to some extent, however, this is partly why I have come to the Dreamers; all of the Keepers here at this gathering are working to pull the old teachings back, so that we may offer a more balanced view of all Earth's creatures. We are striving for a time of harmony now!" Then the Seer continued about the symbolism. "In the worldview of the Christians, which is large, a negative symbol would be that of Adam and Eve. From the book of Genesis, the story tells us The Snake tempts the woman, Eve, to eat from the forbidden tree, Tree of Knowledge. She succumbs, eating the fruit of the Apple, the fruit of good and evil. Then she shares this with the man, Adam. Aware now of their nakedness, they use Fig leaves to hide from the sight of God. God finds them and they are banished from the Garden of Eden forever!"

"Oh my God! You are right!" I blurt out. "The poor snake! And now its image is that of evil, just from this one story!"

The Seer was laughing. "Relax, relax. There are many other stories to counter this one! There are several stories of Serpents and Sacred Trees. Some are called 'Chthonic' or Earth Serpents, who are the guardians of the sacred trees. In the Greek myth, 'Ladon' coiled around a tree in the garden of Hesperides, protecting the Golden Apples. The Norse myth has the dragon-serpent, 'Niohoggr,' eating at the roots of 'Yggdrasil,' the world tree. In Mayan myth 'The Vision Serpent' of rebirth sits at the top axis of the world tree. Most likely the oldest image of two snakes entwined around a rod, limb of a tree, is that of the Sumerian fertility god 'Ningizzida.' This image has become widely known as the god of healing and magic, the caduceus. The Sumerians regarded their serpent deities as dualistic and often had male and female aspects, yin and yang. The Sumerian language itself does not differentiate between masculine and feminine genders but, rather, active and inactive genders.

"In both the Buddhist and Hindu beliefs in India and Nepal, Snakes-Serpents are referred to as 'Naga.' 'Naga' is the Sanskrit word for a deity in the form of a snake. A female naga is 'Nagi' or 'Nagini.' Both Buddhist and Hindu cultures have stories involving the 'Nagas.' To Hindus in India and Nepal, the Nagas are considered nature spirits and protectors of springs, wells, and rivers. Also guardians of lakes, seas, and of treasures. They are also thought to bring disasters such as floods and droughts. According to traditions, Nagas are only malevolent to humans when they have been mistreated. To the Buddhists Nagas are the servants of 'Viru-paksa,' one of the 'Four Heavenly Kings' who guard the western direction. The Nagas act as guards, protecting the divas who reside there. 'Mucalinda' is one of the most notable of the 'Nagas' and, with seven heads, was the king of snakes. He shielded the Buddha from the elements and protected him with his hood while he meditated under the Bodhi Tree.

"Many notable fully-enlightened Naga also transmitted and/or transported 'Terma' into and out of the human realm that had been elementally encoded by adepts. The phrase 'Terma' can refer to fully enlightened Earth treasures and intentions, or mind treasures. They may be part of physical objects that, when discovered by one who is studying, trigger a recollection of the ancient teachings, but sometimes it may be transferred randomly. The 'Terma' may also be held in the mind stream of thoughts, which may come to fruition in one's life, or held for a future incarnation at a more beneficent time."

"Oh my gosh! These Naga snakes are really impressive. And I love all the positive energy that they are about!" I said this with such enthusiasm to the Seer that his comment was a smile of pure joy! There was not much nonsense with this Seer, only the work. He continued on.

"Let us talk of guardianship. Serpents are represented as guardians of temples and other sacred sites. It is the nature of snake to defend. Rattlesnakes and Cobras frequently hold and defend their ground with threatening displays and fighting, rather than retreat. Therefore they are natural guardians. Snake is both solar and lunar, life and death, good and evil, light and dark. It is phallic and the procreative male force. The presence of serpent is almost universally associated with pregnancy. It accompanies all female deities and the Great Mother. Serpents or dragons are the guardians of 'The Thresholds'…temples, treasures, esoteric knowledge, and all lunar deities."

The Snake Seer stood up and stretched for a few minutes; I did the same and was reeling with all this new information but said nothing.

The Seer sensed that I was pensive, and asked me, "What is on your mind?"

I answered by saying, "I need some time to integrate what I am learning. However, I do feel much more comfortable with my fear!"

"Good," was the only answer. The Snake Seer continued, "There is so much. Let me talk some of the Celts. For them serpents are associated with healing waters and wells. The serpent is associated with the 'God Cernunnos,' the god of fertility and virility. Snake is an emblem of 'Bridgit as Mother Goddess.' Women with hair of serpents, such as 'Erinyes' or 'Medusa,' signify the powers of enchantment and magic; they hold the wisdom and guile of serpent. Sometimes to the Celts the serpent and the dragon symbolized trouble, noting that when they appear, strife and infertility follow. In King Arthur's dreams of dragons and serpents at the time of the conception of his son, Sir Mordred, he was actually foretelling of his own death by his own son, Mordred, in battle many years later.

"At the time of the Bible, the Gnostics knew the Serpent and the Tree were divine images. Later the Hebrews and the Persians perverted and degraded the serpent image. Calling it the 'Archaic Snake,' a malignant deity. The Bible has misconstrued the snake image in its interpretations. So now we have the mythical dragon or serpent very misinterpreted. The serpent is one of the 'Four Directions' of India, the animals that guard one of the four corners of the Earth. The other three being the Eagle, the Cow, and the Ape. There is a Kamite Serpent, a seven-headed Serpent of Darkness, whose seven heads are the seven Constellations.

"The Greeks have so many stories of Snakes! First let's talk of 'Ourobros.' In Latin this means 'tail-devourer.' The image of a snake swallowing its own tail is an ancient image and is thought to symbolize eternity. It is believed to have been inspired by the Milky Way. In Gnosticism it symbolized eternity and the soul of the world. In 'Alchemy' the 'Ouroboros' is a purifying sigil, an archetype and a basic mandala of alchemy.

"Other Greek myths tell of 'The Python Serpent.' This snake was the Earth-Dragon of Delphi. She resided at the Delphic Oracle, which existed in her cult center for her mother, the Earth, Gaia. Pytho is the name for the place. This site was considered the center of the Earth and was represented by a stone, the 'Omphalos,' or naval, which Python guarded. The stone denoting this location was considered the 'Naval of the World.' On the slopes of Mount Parnassus, 'Pytho' became the Earth spirit deity and was an enemy of the Greek Olympian deity 'Apollo.' Apollo slew 'Pytho' and remade her former home and oracle as his own. This brought profound change to the religious concepts of the culture. There are various versions of the 'Pythons' birth and death at the hands of Apollo.

"The Greek Goddess of Childbirth and Midwifery is 'Eileithyia.' She is also linked with the Minoan culture. She is older in history than the 'Greek God Cronos,' who was father of Zeus. She is very closely associated with 'Artemis' and 'Hera.' There is a 'Cave of Eileithyia' near Amnisos, Greece. This was the birthplace of 'Eileithyia,' and she was a serpent. She was the savior of the city of Sosipolis. In the second century AD, she was seen by a traveler named 'Pausanias' caring for a serpent that was fed on honeyed barley-cakes and water. At a crucial moment in a war when the Elians were threatened by forces from Arcadia, 'Pausanias' saw that a child was placed on the ground between the contending forces who then changed into a serpent, thus driving the Arcadians away in flight. Since that time her image is often shown as bringing children out of darkness and into light! The Greek Healer 'Aesculapius' was not a serpent god, even though he was very much connected to serpents."

There was silence for just a moment. The Snake Seer's black eyes penetrated mine; I felt we had a transpiring connection between student and teacher on an ancient level. Just as quickly, he was back to his lessons of the snake.

"For the Aboriginal people of Australia, we have the 'Rainbow Serpent.' This important mythological being is seen as the inhabitant of permanent waterholes and is in control of life's most precious resource ,'Water'! It is known as both a benevolent protector of its people and as a malevolent punisher of law breakers.

"The Aztec culture has 'Coatlicue.' Called 'the Mother of Gods,' she was an Aztec Goddess who gave birth to the moon, stars, and 'Huitzilopochtli,' the god of sun and war. She is also called the 'Lady Serpent,' patron of women who die in childbirth. The word 'Coatlicue' means 'The one with the skirt of serpents.'"

The sun was much lower in the afternoon sky. It was getting cool, and I noticed The Snake Seer had put a blanket across his shoulders. I was remembering what had been said about air temperatures for the reptile species. I got up and walked around our grassy spot, then I said, "This has been amazing. Not in a hundred years would I ever think I would be interested in the comings and goings of snakes! But listening to you this afternoon has given me a whole new insight and appreciation of this mythical being! I am so thankful to be able to understand a little better about this medicine."

The Seer had also gotten up and was helping me to gather up things into my basket. The Seer stopped and looked at me with love, saying, "How is your level of fear? I am sensing that your kundalini energy is very fired up, and that is a wonderful thing! The caution here is to know when and how to use this medicine; it will take time to balance this for your personal use!"

I was nodding my head in agreement, and I said, "I am not afraid of you! Or of all these beings that you have told me about. But if I were to see a snake unexpectedly, most likely I would be scared out of my wits! And that is the truth!"

The Seer laughed and laughed! "Well, it may take a little longer than I thought, but you will make a fine Snake Healer or Seer one day! Do you want me to get back into the basket?"

The Snake Seer was beside himself with laughter on this comment! I did not find this so funny! What an afternoon it had been.

SPIDER

DREAM OF THE SPIDER SEER

O n an early evening walk, I found myself by one of the lodges where the Seers had been staying. The sun was bright on the western part of the large porch and the dew sparkles on the grasses where I was walking. How peaceful I felt as I viewed this scene of the lodge nestled under the huge pines. I saw no one around, yet I could hear something. A buzzing, a humming?

Then, as I walked onto the porch, I saw a very fragile, slight woman hunched over a spinning wheel. She was focused on her work, guiding the wool into the wheel and making thread. It was so fascinating! I asked if she would mind if I just watched for a while.

She answered by saying, "As you like."

I did not feel exactly comfortable, so I stood near the railing of the porch and held onto it. I was silent for a few minutes. She said nothing and did not look my way. Finally, taking a chance and feeling braver, I asked her what she was weaving.

Her answer was this: "I Am Weaving Forgotten Realms."

I was taken aback by this statement. I did not know how to answer. I looked at my watch; my stomach was grumbling for dinner. When I looked up, my eyes caught those of the woman, and her smile was warm and intriguing as she motioned for me to come closer. I answered her call silently and walked through a Web I knew nothing about!

The woman was winding the new yarn around her arm as she spoke to me, saying, "Sit for a while. I can feel your curiosity and need. I suppose that you know who I am?" As she said this, she was pointing to her beautifully embroidered blouse. It was a spider's web on pure purple silk with silver threading and little jewels stitched on the junction points of the web design. It was hard not to keep staring at this work of art! I could hear the Seer speaking about how I was one of the gems on the web, and she had been noticing me. Looking up quickly, I said, "You have? I am honored. And yes! I do know that you are the Spider Seer!"

She laughed at my comment and then got serious and asked me, "Why are you afraid of me and Spider Medicine?"

Shaking my head, I said, "I'm not really sure. I guess that sometimes when I see a spider they just make me nervous, especially if they are large. But I have picked them up from time to time and taken them outside, or removed them from an area when I did not want them there! Of course, I put them into a napkin or something to carry them with; I do not relish being bitten!"

The Spider Seer slapped her knee with her hand and roared with laughter again! "Well, my dear, at least you are honest! Like so many of the Animal Seers-Keepers, there is an unbalanced picture of who they are and what their teachings are about. So many of your kind need to be retaught, yes, retaught!" She was smiling now and told me to sit in one of the rocking chairs and hold out my arms so that she could wind the yarn into a proper skein. I did as she requested and sat down on the rocker in some kind of a dream state.

"Ah! That makes it much easier!"

She was a petite lady with an hourglass-shaped figure. Her face was ageless; I wondered what she looked like when she was in actual spider mode? Forgetting that all these Seers were telepathic, I got an answer! "Later on I will show you!" said the Seer.

For now, the Spider Seer said, "Let's talk of weavers! In our metaphysical work, the 'Weave' is a force, a type of energy. Think about the atom; when an atom is examined, one discovers that it is nearly all empty space. It is actually the potential of energy waiting to be born. It is the invisible force that holds the world together. This is part of the vast space of our universe; this is the Weave. This is what shamanic healers, ancient native healers, have always known and worked with intuitively. This weave of creative force is what spider medicine can teach you to use. It can become your divine inspiration. Remember this: 'The spider weaves her web from within!' Her web is infinitely sensitive to vibration, and the smallest movement is felt reverberating over the entire web. What does this tell us? Well, foremost, to be certain with truth and love about that which we decide to weave! So many are affected when we weave. The master weavers throughout time have considered Grandmother Spider the Weaver of the cosmic web, which is the very fabric of the universe. She teaches us that a delicate web connects everything in the universe. When we ourselves have a weakness, the entire web is that much weaker, and therefore everything we do affects the existence as a whole. When we are stronger and more honorable, everything else is stronger and more honorable."

The Spider Seer stopped for a moment and took the yarn she had been winding around my arms and hands and tied it off into a neat bundle. It was a rich burgundy color, and I wondered what she would make with it. For now, though, I was glad to have my arms free and shook them out for better circulation.

The Seer looked at me and said, "You were patient with that winding; it is a good sign. Spiders are patient' weavers are patient."

I looked at her with my head tilted and said, "Thanks! I do want to show you my necklace. It is a piece of Baltic Amber, and it has a spider embedded within its center." The Seer asked if she might touch it. "Of course!" I said.

"So beautiful!" she told me. She held up the teardrop shape, the size of a large coin, to the light to examine it better. "Amazing!" She said, "It could be thousands of years old."

"I know!" I answered. "Pretty wild, huh? A native elder once told me that amber was a teardrop of blood from one of the Standing People, a Tree!"

The Seer nodded her head in agreement, smiled, and said, "I believe you have this piece for a reason: to help you learn what spider and the weave can teach. Do you wear it often?"

"Only sometimes," I answered.

"Well, that indicates to me," she said, "that you intuitively know when you are meant to use its energy. Did you know that amber itself is a wonderful gem? Even though it is made of resin, it is a gem. And it can aid one with psychic protection!"

"Wow!" I answered. "I will remember to use it that way. I do have several other pieces as well."

"Use the others for protection," she said. "Save the dear little spider here for your weaving work!" That made me smile.

"Now let us get into the study of spider, which is called, 'arachnology.' They are predatory invertebrate animals that have segments, eight legs, and no chewing mouth parts, and no wings. All spiders produce silk, a thin, strong protein strand extruded by the spider from spinnerets most commonly found on the end of the abdomen. Many species use it to trap insects in their webs. The silk also aids in climbing and can be formed into walls for burrows, to build egg sacs, to wrap prey, and temporarily hold sperm. Most species can inject venom to protect themselves or kill prey. There are some that have bites that can pose a health problem to humans. The female Black Widow Spider, latrodectus mactans, is particularly harmful to humans. Males almost never bite humans. The Black Widows received their name because the females frequently consume the male after mating, leaving them widowed!"

"*Oh!* My Goodness!" I blurted out. I got no response.

The Seer continued. "Most spiders construct their webs and then hang on it, waiting for an insect to get stuck upon it. Before the insect can extricate itself, the spider rushes to bite it and swathe it in a silken shroud, saving their catch for later. If the spider feels threatened, it will let itself down to the ground on a safety line of silk. Spiders have poor eyesight and depend mostly on vibrations that reach them through their webs to orient themselves to any prey or for safety. They are not aggressive, and ordinary intrusion will cause them to flee. When people think of webs, usually they have in mind the spiral-shape web. These are made by the Orb-type spider. This takes an average of thirty minutes to an hour to weave. There are other types of webs: bowl or dome-shaped, funnel, and cobwebs.

"Unlike insects, spiders have a two-section body instead of three, often giving them a figure eight appearance. This, in conjunction with its eight legs, unlike an insect, links it to the mysticism associated with the number eight, an infinity symbol. It is the wheel of life, flowing from one circle to the next. The difficulty is learning to walk those circles or hold in the middle. Therefore, spider teaches us about balance and how to be between past-future, physical-spiritual, and male-female. Spider teaches that everything you do NOW is weaving a thread of what you may encounter in the FUTURE. Spider is connected to the 'Tarot Seer Wheel of Fortune X,' which is an Ancient One working with rhythms and, as the wheel moves, it creates energies. Looking at spider on their web, we realize they are the creator of their universe. This shows us that we create from our thoughts and actions. Also it is helpful to reflect upon the spiral of the spider's web, which weaves together at a central point. This reminds us to ask, Are you weaving toward your goals, or are you scattered? What at this time are you focused on?"

As the Spider Seer stopped speaking, I was reeling with questions about my focus at this time. I realized that I was scattered and needed to gain clarity about what to focus my energy on.

I said to the Seer, "This spider study is posing many more questions for me!"

She answered, "It is quite all right and normal. By encountering the right questions, we are able to dream in the right answers." Then she went on with her knowledge. "Some say spider formed the first alphabet, which was part of the geometric patterns of their webs. American Indians used the image of spider etched onto shells as protective amulets against danger from wind, rain, and all natural weather phenomena that might threaten the spider's own fragile web. The 'Kiowa' American Indians, originally from Canada but who migrated to Southwestern Oklahoma, derive the myth of Spider Grandmother. She was a heroine who brought light into the world. She took fire and the sun from the eastern land of light. Then she tossed the sun up into the sky, keeping a small piece as the gift of fire to her people.

"The North American Pueblo natives have a legend of Spider Woman that mentions the crosswise divisions of Earth into four quarters. This was the goddess Spider Woman's first act of creation. To begin making the world, she first spun a thread from east to west, then another from north to south, so the point of crossing would determine the center of the Earth. Spider Woman produced two daughters, who made the Sun and the Moon. She made the people of the Earth from black, red, white, and yellow clay. Several times she destroyed the world and its inhabitants she had spun and then rewove it, as spiders do with their webs. She saved only those wise ones who were true and could manage to keep contact with her via the invisible strands spun into the tops of their heads!"

"Oh! I love this story!" I cried out to the Spider Seer.

She laughed, saying, "I thought you might! And of course there is more to tell," she continued. "Some Native American legends tell of Spider-Spinning-Woman as the 'Weaver of the Web of Fate.' She wove the universe every day and unraveled her web at night. They say the world will end when her web is finished!

"Now let's talk of Spiders and symbolism. Spiders symbolize patience, for their patient hunting with web traps. They are also a symbol of mischief and malice, for using poison and the slow death this causes. Also they are a symbol of possessiveness, in the way they spin their prey into a ball and then take it into a burrow for storage. Spiders have also been attributed by many cultures to the origination of basket weaving, knot work, weaving, and spinning. Spiders are pervasive throughout folklore and mythology. As symbols in religion, they are found in the Wyrd, the Old English-Old Norse cultures' type of Karma belief. The 'Mocha' people of ancient Peru often depicted spiders in their art. Some parts of the world eat large spiders! 'Arachnophobia' is an abnormal fear of spiders.

"The Egyptians have the 'Goddess Neith' connected to spider, through weaving. The name 'Neith' means weaver. Neith wove the world into existence on her loom. 'Neith the

Goddess of Weaving' was also goddess of domestic arts. She was the protector of women and the guardian of marriage.

"In more modern times, there lived an incredible spinner. This was Mohandas K. Gandhi, who lived in India from 1869 to 1948. After returning to India from South Africa, where he had enjoyed a successful legal practice, he gave up wearing Western-style clothing, which he associated with wealth and success. He began dressing to be accepted by the poorest person in India, advocating the use of homespun cloth, khadi. He was often found with his distaff, ready to do his own weaving. Gandhi and his followers adopted the practice of weaving their own clothes from thread they themselves spun and encouraged others to do so. At that time, Indians often bought their clothing from British industrial manufactures. It was Gandhi's view that if Indians made their clothes, it would deal an economic blow to the British establishment in India. Later on the spinning wheel image was incorporated into the flag of the Indian National Congress."

"How amazing. Gandhi changed the consciousness of the people with spinning! This is so powerful!" I said to the Spider Seer.

Nodding her head yes, she continued. "The Greeks have many myths relating to spider through the connection of weaving! The Greek 'White Goddess'—'Ino-Leucthea' was said to have rescued Odysseus from drowning by means of her 'divine veil.' In this act she was identified with Odysseus's spouse, Penelope, known as a 'Fate-Weaver,' whose name also meant 'veiled one.' Her reluctance to cut the thread of his life preserved Odysseus through many near-fatal adventures. The pre-Hellenic Penelope was connected to Odysseus's fate but also suggests that, as the great weaver, she was connected to every man's fate. In the myths, 'her many suitors' may have originally meant that 'all men try to woo the Goddess of Fate'! The Greeks also have: 'The Three Goddesses of Fate: 'One who spins the threads of life,' 'One who weaves the threads of life,' and 'One who clips the threads of life.'"

"I like that name, 'Goddess of Fate.' I can think of many contemporary persons who have been tempted by this goddess!" I simply could not help but saying that quite loudly.

The Seer answered by saying, "You are right about that! Probably the most widely known Greek myth," she continued, "is that of 'Arachne and Athena.' In this myth Arachne was a young princess from Lydia, who had offended Athena. Arachne was a gifted weaver. Not only were her finished products beautiful but the very act of her weaving was a sight to behold. Nymphs were said to abandon their doings to observe Arachne practice her magic. The people said she must have been trained by the patron 'Goddess of Weaving Athena' herself. Arachne scoffed at this. She did not like being placed inferior to the goddess. She proclaimed that Athena could not do better than her!

"Athena was perturbed at Arachne's bold statement. She decided to give the young woman a chance to redeem herself. Athena came to Archane disguised as an old woman and then warned her to be careful, not to offend the gods, lest she incur their wrath! But Archane was rude and would not listen. She told the old woman that she could have a contest with Athena for weaving. If she lost, she would suffer whatever punishment the gods deemed necessary!

"Athena then revealed her true form and the challenge began. They both wove beautiful tapestries. Even Athena was forced to admit that Arachne's work was flawless. But Athena, still angered at the challenge, tore the tapestry to pieces and destroyed the loom. She touched Arachne's forehead, making sure that she felt guilt for her actions. Arachne was ashamed, but the guilt was too deep for a mere mortal mind. Becoming unbearably depressed, Arachne hanged herself!

"Athena then took pity on Arachne. She brought her back to life, but not as a human. By sprinkling her with the juices of 'aconite,' Athena transformed the woman into a Spider, saying that she and all her descendants were to forever hang from the threads and would be forever 'great weavers'!"

"Oh, dear Spider Seer! I think I love this story best of all! They are getting better and better, and I am feeling so much more at ease about spiders!"

The Seer answered with this: "It has taken you awhile! But I must say you are almost there with your comfort level and knowledge. Just be patient."

"What do you mean?" I responded, "Almost there?"

The Spider Seer stood up at that point and said, "It's starting to get pretty dark now. Why don't you walk with me awhile?"

I nodded my head yes and said, "Sure!"

She put a few things into a small basket, which was beautifully made. I asked her if she had made the basket. She answered, saying, "Yes, but we will talk of basket weaving another time! I want us to get down to 'The Star Field' quickly!"

"The what?" I said.

"You will find out soon enough," said the Seer.

We picked up our pace, and the Seer handed me an apple to munch on as we walked. She said, "I've been hearing your stomach for some time now, but you never complained that you had missed your dinnertime, it is the least I can do!" Then she began talking of spider again as we walked, and, small as she was, she sure could walk fast! I had to work at keeping up with her.

"Spiders," she said, "mostly move and work in the dark areas or hidden places. They do their weaving, they do their work, in the dark of night. Then as the light of the day touches their webs, we see their beautiful creations! This is another thought to reflect on for those drawn to spider and their own creativity.

"A spider person tends to draw people into their 'Web.' Those who become close to spider are engrossed, enchanted, captivated, raveled in Spider's enigma. People love spider and find she is hard to turn away from, even when she wants them to be gone. She fascinates them so much that they willingly tangle themselves in her web in hopes of understanding her better. But the person who really gain's Spider's affection is the one who can escape!" The Seer had a good laugh after that!

This gave me pause for thought. I did not know what to say.

But stopping now, the Seer said, "There is nothing that needs to be said! Ah! Look up at this beautiful night sky! They are all out there. I see Venus in the eastern evening sky now!"

I lifted my head up to the sky where she was pointing. The dark summer evening was blazing with stars. What a sight! Following the Seer's pointing finger across the open field, I could hear the ocean's waves just over the cliff. I pulled on a sweater. It was breezy and cool. I wished I had worn pants rather than a thin skirt.

Coming back to the present, I saw the Seer needed some help spreading the magical-looking blanket of purple; it was similar to her blouse, with a web woven into the pattern. She sat down and patted the blanket for me to do the same. I followed her suggestion.

Looking around the hillside, I had the feeling that the stage here under the night sky had been set just for us; it was so quiet, so peaceful, and very special! "There must be millions of stars up there!" I said.

"There certainly are!" answered the Seer. "Remember earlier when I spoke of the native belief of Grandmother Spider in the legends of weaving the world? And then we spoke of the Egyptian Goddess 'Neith,' who was weaving the world also! It is all connected, my dear. Throughout time all cultures have spoken of this weave of connection. In present contemporary time, we are connected by the Internet, 'the Web,' through the computer that networks and weaves around the Earth. Because of this communication, the world is always accessible, smaller somehow. So when something happens on the other side of the globe, it feels as if it is happening to us as well. As healers and Seers, we need to be careful about what we put onto this network, the Web. It needs to be true work that harms none, done in love.

I was nodding my head yes at this. Then I asked, "What is it I need to know, Seer?"

She replied quickly, saying, "There is much for you to learn if you commit to 'wanting this knowledge with your heart,' and then the time may be right for you. With patience and persistence you will grow into a fine Seer!"

"Right for what?" I asked.

She said, "Remember when we spoke earlier of 'Weaving Forgotten Realms'? Well, this weaving is a force; I believe I said a creative force, which is part of what spider medicine is about. Let me explain. 'The Weave' is both a barrier and a gateway between raw magic and the world. When this weave is in place and protected, those of right heart and mind are allowed to learn to work the magical gateways to Otherworlds. The weave is in the 'Ley Lines of Mother Earth,' much like the longitude and latitude lines that surround her. There are many layers and strands that connect and permeate everything within these lines. They are connected by juncture points throughout the entire surface. These are the 'Power Points.' There are sacred places made at these points: cathedrals, temples, pyramids, and pagan places. One of the tasks that a Spider Seer Weaver does is to keep these ley lines intact, protected, and safe for the human realm to live upon. Our work is immense; our worry is great! Many humans walk the Earth, but in many cases, not respectfully. They are careless where they tread. So we need healers, Dream Seers, who can work these weaves, to repair, to give insight to the humans, about understanding what it is we all share and live upon. Our Mother Earth! Our Ancient Dreaming is in place; we have dreamt the light into place.

Now we are training those who will assist us in both preserving the beauty and helping with ascending to a paradise on Earth!"

The Seer stopped and looked at me, saying, "Are you still afraid?"

I answered, "Yes, but it is manageable. I can handle the fear!"

"Good!" she answered. "Now I will tell you something of 'The Weaves.' Healing Weaving is for the universe, which involves flows of earth, air, fire, water, and aethers. Warding Weaving is to weave protection or enchantment for an area, person, and thing. A Seer weaves a 'ward' and then ties it off, therefore providing a woven protection or enchantment. Gateway Weaving is to weave portals to travel from one world to another, alternate dimensions of time travel. Control Weaving is a type of trap work, to weave a sticky spot, in order to slow something down: prey, person, other. In order to trap them for a while and control them. Or keep them from a certain path with an illusion, like weaving a dark swirling mist-web to confuse the tribes!

"In order to do all these things takes many years training with a Spider-Seer-Weaver. And before one can even start, they must be of pure intention and heart, and then, after they are initiated, they are given the 'Weave Codes'!"

I felt awestruck as she spoke. This is what I said: "Dear Seer, of all the Animal Seers, I feel that your teachings are my truest calling!"

She smiled and said, "Oh! You say that to each of us!"

I replied loudly, "No! No! I do not!"

She said, "My dear daughter, I was joking with you! I too feel this to be your path. You must, however, go through this learning process with all the Seers, to be sure, to be true to yourself. You have plenty of time, and there are also many crossover paths! So just relax and enjoy the view. How do you like 'The Star Field'? There are many woven myths that are sprinkled up there, like woven nets of gossamer gleaming! One day I will tell you about the 'House of Twelve'!"

With that she stood up and was gone in a flash, into the night sky, I thought. I was feeling I had gotten a glimpse of her as a Spider, and I was not afraid! Now I had much Dreamtime-weaving to contemplate.

"This is good!" I heard her say.

SWAN

DREAM OF THE SWAN SEER

I was sitting alone in front of the fire; the others had gone. The patterns kept weaving and I was struggling to gather my wits. This should not be part of our pattern! I said in a mad voice, and then I looked around quickly to see if anyone was there. No! I guess not. Seems I am the only one who needs to decompress. But the scene came back again. With tears welling up in my eyes, I watched again: the dreaming in the fire.

Our afternoon dreaming task had been to work in small groups of four on leadership skills. We were to choose a topic that one of the four Dreamers would present to the others in their group, helping each other to find their voice and give feedback. Straightforward, simple. I chose to work with some of the Novice Dreamers. I have been studying for some time now and felt I could be of help to those not as versed. I noted, as the groups formed, that I did not know much about these Dreamers in my group. We found a quiet place to work by the small pond. Three women, one man. Smiling at everyone, I asked which topic our leaders should present. At first, no one seemed to know. I was about to suggest something, when the woman with the very short, very blonde hair, spoke out.

"Soul Retrieval!" she said rather loudly.

I thought to myself this was a rather ambitious topic for novices, but then again I should not be judgmental. Looking around at the others, I asked, "What do you think?" All agreed this would be fine. Then I asked, "Who would like to be the first leader to present?"

Again there was quiet. Finally the man said he would give it a try. He was big, very shy, with a reserved manner. I noticed that he had a slight stutter when he spoke. Seeing a bit of fear in his eyes about having to role-play a leader, I wanted to give him some reassurances. "Art, is that short for Arthur?" I said.

He smiled and said, "Why, yes."

I answered, "As I recall the Celtic Gaelic name 'Art, Arthur' means Bear. What a wonderful energy to have! I suppose that you knew this!"

He smiled and said, "I do recall that, but it seems to be taking on a new meaning for me now!"

We got ourselves organized about what, from soul retrieval, we would want a leader to outline for us. This part was tedious because the blonde woman Dreamer seemed to have views and objections about everything and the other woman did not seem at all interested in what we were doing. But we finally got a format. Art was ready to be the first leader presenting the soul retrieval topic.

Art was so nervous doing this process. I felt that I had to encourage and empower him as much as I could. He certainly seemed to know the topic; however, he got carried away on tangents, and then he would forget how to get himself back on track. Next, flustered, he would stutter. In between, the blonde would say cutting things like, "No, that isn't right! I would not do it that way! You are wrong!" I had to keep her at bay and keep a peaceful platform for Art. He was really having a hard time! I could see that the blonde knew various things, but she was just so full of herself! It was becoming a real problem.

Finally she cut him to the quick, saying, "This is a joke. What are you doing here?"

I stood up with darts in my eyes. I was furious at her! I stumbled some before deflecting an attack meant for me. Pulling power to myself, I projected my awareness toward her. Her mental powers and defenses were sealed. So instead I aimed for her heart and soul. "Play nice!" I said telepathically. Holding my palm outward toward her, I said out loud, "Enough!"

She got up and said, "Sorry, I don't know...." And she walked away.

The rest of us decided we needed a breather. Art stopped me before I walked away. He said, "I really want to thank you for backing me up. But also for reminding me of my Bear Medicine, which I realize I need to work on." He was smiling as he said this.

I just answered, "You are welcome." There was nothing else to say.

Trying to let go of the afternoon, I kept staring into the fire and slowly I began to see new weavings. A Dream walker in the Fire said, "Be careful. Do not get stuck on this!" Then in the fire I saw a Silver Swan painted on a standard, like the ones of the Medieval Knights. A silver swan! That felt good.

I had no idea why this image came, but there it was. Then I felt a hand on my shoulder. Turning, I came out of my dream. It was getting cool, the fire was mostly embers now. Once I stood up, I saw the Swan Seer was there.

"Are you OK?" she asked me.

"Oh sure. I am fine!"

"You do not seem so fine to me! It is hard, working with all these personalities and emotions. Why don't we walk awhile before dinner?"

I nodded and said, "Yes!"

She handed me some grapes to munch on.

The Swan Seer and I walked a bit without talking. It was late afternoon, and the sun was getting lower in the western sky. We were near the small pond with the iris blooming in purples and yellows. Some tiny ones were deep cobalt blue. So beautiful here; the surface of the pond was like glass.

I turned to the Seer and said, "This is where my group met earlier."

She looked at me and said, "I know."

Trying to hold back tears, I looked away. The sun seemed to reflect off the Seer. I noted a beautiful silver necklace with tiny Swans tooled in the silver. I told the Seer how much I admired the necklace.

She answered me with this: "'I am the Queen of Luck, the White Swan.' I quote this from a book called *Carmina Gadelica*, which is a collection of poems and hymns from a Celtic time long past. Celtic lore tells us Swans are faerie women in the shape of birds. As a mark of their noble lineage, they wore gold or silver chains, possibly much like this one." She was holding out her chain for me to see. I told her how beautiful it was. She nodded, then continued, saying, "Celtic Swan deities possess the therapeutic powers of the sun and the water. I will tell you a small story from *Carmina*. A woman found a wounded swan on a frozen lake and took it home. She set the broken wing, dressed the bleeding feet, and fed the starving bird with linseed and water. The woman had an ailing child, and as the wounds of the swan healed, the health of the child improved. The woman believed that her treatment of the swan caused the recovery of her child, and she rejoiced accordingly and composed a lullaby, which she named, 'Lullaby Taladh.'"

"Oh my, what a beautiful story!" I said to the Seer.

She smiled and said, "Thinking about what happened for you in your leadership group, I want to offer you this. First, it is not easy teaching others skills you may have; the most effective way is by example. You gave the Novice Dreamers a good example today. Even though it may have been hard on those involved.

"We must, as teachers, leaders, show others respect and courtesy. And when something is not right, we know this intuitively, and as a leader we must intervene. This is the only way; this is truth. So, my dear, you did what was needed; you set right the broken parts. It is up to the others involved to take away whatever the teaching was for them. You can do no more. Hopefully you will begin to see the healing take place in the others. That work is up to them."

My heart felt better. I said to the Seer, "I suppose that is what the Dream walker in the Fire meant when he said, 'Do not get stuck on this!'"

She laughed and said, "It certainly is! Now I have other things to tell you about Swan! The Celtic name for Swan is 'Eala.' Swan represents, music, love, purity, and the soul. Sacred to the Bards, the swan's skin and feathers were made into the ceremonial Bardic Cloak, named 'Tugen.' To the Druids, the Swan is the soul itself in The Otherworlds. Swan aids them in traveling to the Otherworlds. It is associated with their festival of 'Samhain' in the month of October, which is a gateway between the realm of the living and the dead. Swans combine the two elements of air and water.

"A Saxon chronicler told of a 'Swan Knight Lohengrin,' who came from the mountain where Venus lives in the Grail. He was referred to as 'The Knight of the Swan,' servant of women. His silver symbol became a special order of Knighthood in the fifteenth century, in Cleves.

"In Greece the Greek God Zeus, who was King of the Gods, turned himself into a Swan to mate with the earthly 'Leda.' She is named as one of the moons of Jupiter. Leda was also Queen of Sparta. 'Aphrodite,' the Greek Goddess of Love, and had a Swan-drawn chariot. Many works of art have been done with this swan theme, including *Leda With the Swans*, a painting by Leonard da Vinci, and a poem, 'Leda and the Swan,' by William Butler Yeats. In Irish lore Swans were often disguised as Faerie Women. 'The White Swans of the Wilderness' were the children of the 'Tuatha de Danaan,' who are said to have settled Ireland. Of course we have the famous ballet *Lebedinoe Ozero-Swan Lake* by Tchaikovsky. And there is the Danish faerie tale by Hans Christian Anderson, *The Ugly Duckling*. In India it was the Swan that laid the 'Cosmic Egg' on the waters, from which Brahma sprang!

"So, my daughter, as you can see the Swan has captured the hearts of many, bridging Eastern and Western cultures. Swan Medicine is about the artist, the poet, the Faerie realms, the Dreamer, the Mystic, and the child! Quite a list; quite a magical being!"

The Swan Seer stood with her head tilted, smiling quizzically at me as she twirled her Silver Swan Necklace. I thought to myself, She is a true standard bearer, the exact image on the banner of the Silver Swan that I had seen in the dreaming fire. I told her I had seen the Swan necklace image in the fire, and then I reached over and gave her a big hug. I then thanked her for helping me to put things in perspective. But especially to learn more about Swan Medicine and how to be a good leader!

"It was my pleasure! But..." she said, with a long pause.

"What?" I said.

Looking with dark black eyes, she said, "Aren't you hungry?"

"Starved!" I answered. And off we went, laughing.

WHALE

DREAM OF THE WHALE SEER

After the talk about all the Earth changes and futures that might happen, well, just thinking these things, I felt a little depressed. Some of the Seers had shared some scary dream scenarios last night at the evening circle. Why did they do that?

The Whale Seer stopped me afterward and said, "I would like you to meet me at the beach at the early morning tide." She was smiling broadly at me.

I agreed, nodded my head, and said, "Yes, of course!" I walked away, wondering what that was all about.

I was there now. Where was she? It was freezing out here at this hour. The sun had only just appeared. Feeling crabby about waking up so early, I could hear my stomach grumble, and…There she was. I had better snap out of my mood, I thought. The "Whale Seer" looked like a mermaid or nymph, walking up from the waves of the sea. So beautiful, I thought. I watched as she shook her long black hair and smoothed it back as she walked up to where I stood on the beach. Like last night, she gave me a big smile, and I let go of my moodiness. She pointed to some rocks close to where the grasses grow; we walked over there and were out of the wind.

Sitting down, I said, "We are facing the rising sun. Look at those orange and pink colors. This is perfect! You must be cold," I said, offering her my shawl.

"No, I am not," she said. "I have learned how to conserve my body energy and maintain comfort." She looked at me with piercing eyes. I had never had a personal conversation with her. I had heard from others that she was cool and did not mince words. I was not sure of this assessment but could see she was getting to the point.

Coming out of my daydreaming, I heard the Seer was saying, "I noticed your alarm last evening, after the Keepers shared their dreams of possible future Earth. Some of the dreaming was grim, the tales very sad, and—"

Interrupting her, I said, "Why did they have to tell us those things? Scary, awful things!"

"Do you believe them?" she said.

"Believe? Well, it was the Keepers, after all, telling the dreams. Of course I believe the things they tell us!"

The Whale Seer pierced my eyes as she said, "Do you recall how the Seers phrased their telling, before relaying various dreams of the future?" I shook my head no. She answered me, "We were all conscious of the words and phrasing each of us said, 'possible future' or 'might happen'…Earth changes. Are you recalling these words?"

Tracking back to last night, I saw and heard the words; she was right. "But why?" I said. "The Dreamers were upset from hearing these possible dreams! The Keepers kept us on edge; we were afraid of what might happen!"

"Well," said the Seer, "I suppose we did our job!"

Very puzzled, I said, "You made us upset and mad. What does that do for any of us?"

Looking at me with love, The Whale Seer said something I will never forget! "We brought you to the edge with the dream words we painted for you."

"The edge?" I said.

She answered, "Yes, I believe just a minute ago you said, Edge! When we are at the edge; decisions must be made. When at the edge of a cliff, do we back up? Do we climb down? Do we trust and fly off? The work of a Dream healer is difficult. One needs to know what it is they stand for, their personal belief. When the Dreamer can make their belief a vision, they begin to develop a powerful dreaming medicine. Once they are firm in themselves, a Dreamer can dream dreams for others, helping the seeker that may come to them, showing them how to dream-paint their own vision of dreams. In the larger picture of our beautiful Mother Earth, we, the Dreamers of this steading, are here to defend, guard, and give back to the Mother as best we can, for all that she gives us.

"I can sense that you are still wondering," she continued, "why we needed you to see those terrible 'possible dream futures.' Because, my daughter, there are those who may want to bring about awful Earth changes, and those who are so caught in power or greed that they simply do not want to do the work to protect the Earth and her inhabitants. We must realize there is a part of humanity that may be aligned with energies that may be dark. Dreamers must be realistic and not Pollyannas about this. We can not assume that because we just attempt to send light and love with our heads, then everything will magically be OK! No! Our work is not so flowery! Part of what we are teaching here is to 'Recognize how the Fear' of these things can get a grip on people. Fear, out of control, might breed into an awful mess of changes on our planet. Our work here as Dreamers is to recognize our own truth about fears. Then when we are out in waking life situations, we can utilize our gifts to determine the truth of a fearful situation as best as we can. If need be, we defuse areas that get out of control with good, positive words, deeds, and dreams of intention that are filled with positive actions. We do this both in the waking dream world and the dream world of healers who dream to make a positive difference, by seeing a situation resolved well. Remember it happens in the Dream world first!"

At this point in our conversation, I guess my mouth must have been gaping open, because the Whale Seer, laughing a bit, said, "Take a deep breath, my dear."

Out loud I said, "So, the Seers have given us a test of sorts; that we might begin to figure out our core beliefs? Is this the teaching?"

In a very kind voice, she answered, "Yes, and to learn very well about the power of the words that you use." I was nodding my head, thinking of how easily I had believed everything the Seers had said last night, without listening to all the words. Now I said, "Maybe I should be wary of other things the 'Seers' might say?"

Chuckling, she said, "Maybe so!"

The Seer was standing, looking out over the rocks toward the sea. I wondered if she longed to be in the cool blue waters.

Turning suddenly, the Whale Seer said, "There is one dream I would like to share that might illustrate how a Dreamer with Whale Medicine worked to hold and heal our Mother Earth. The Whales are the record keepers; they can live for a century or more. With their sonar and echo-location abilities, they are able to bring back memories and knowledge that can help us in our current life. This dream happened after the tragedy of '9/11' in New York in the year 2001. The title is: POWER POINT.

I found myself at Manhattan Island near the river. I heard mournful sounds of the Whale coming from the water. I looked closer and there she was, huge, thirty feet at least. Her cries cut right through my bones. She looked at me with sad huge eyes and said, "It is time to heal. Climb on my back!" She went on, "I have things to show you." I followed her instructions. We then dove beneath the water. I could see other whales that she was communicating with. We swam around Manhattan at a good speed. The whales cries were intense but sounded beautiful to me, soothing somehow.

"Now," she said, "we are going to the underground crystal caves that lie deep within the belly of Manhattan." The sight was incredible, shimmering, and iridescent.

Whale said to me, "You know this is a power point. Like other vortices around the world, this is a place of power." She continued, "The people are ready now; they need healing! The First Peoples of this land always knew of this power place. They honored it. It was Sacred to them.

"It is time," said Whale. "We will go deeply into the underground rivers. I will communicate with the other whales, and we will cause such a force in the water currents that we will send the water clear through the area that was the World Trade Center!"

I heard the sounds of the other whales. The water swirled and I could see the force of the water going through their blowholes and up to where the two towers had stood. The water circulated several times before it receded. Then there was calmness.

Whale told me, "The water cleanses and has the ability to create and rebirth. We are ready for this cleansing now. Watch! As the water recedes, you will see Manhattan Island in its original, pristine state. You will see it as the First People saw it, rich with natural beauty, sacred. Now, look!"

We watched as all the creatures, large and small, began to take up their life there.

"You know," she told me, "Man may build another building. But would it not be beautiful to keep some of this newly cleansed land free and open? This would provide a place for the Mother Earth part of Manhattan and her people to breathe. This place, this event of 9/11, has stirred our hearts open. This is now OUR HEART CENTER!"

The Whale Seer folded her hands in her lap. There was silence. I was still in the dream. Quietly the Seer said, "This is certainly a dream about people being brought to the edge. It is about our Dream Seer the Whale waiting patiently, ready to take us to the next level. For a time after this event, the people of the country felt a uniting of energies to heal and bring a harmony. Of course there was tremendous fear as well. The light workers, the healers, the Dreamers, had a tremendous task to keep things balanced. To mend the tears in the grid of the Ley Lines is hard work and it is constant; we as Dream Healers must always be mindful of this work. Our heart centers need to be clean and kept open; this is yet another part of a Dreamer's work. And as you know, the balancing work is still going on!"

"Oh! My Goddess!" I screamed. "How do we do all this?"

She answered, "The record Keepers, the Whales, are here for us; with their help we can receive the knowledge of the ancients, to begin to bring in an age of harmony and peace. This will be hard and will take constant commitment on the part of the Dreamers who commit to this work, but it will happen!"

Shaking my head, I said, "I don't know? I don't know! Why do you do it?" I asked the Seer.

Her answer was, "My dear child, because I must!"

Turning my stare away from her, the tears streaming down my cheeks, I was not able to speak. I knew her eyes were on me; she had been so definitive, direct. She knows her truth, I thought. She is right! But it is so hard; will I be able to develop commitment like this? Can I find my truth and strength to follow through and make a difference? Please, Goddess, hear me, help me to do what I must! I trust in you and the Dreaming.

We said nothing. Both of us in our own dreaming, we sat, just looking at the full sun in the morning sky casting an orange glow across the water toward us. Somehow, I knew the Whale Seer had received my Dreaming!

WOLF

DREAM OF THE WOLF SEER

Walking to the Grove for the evening gathering with some of the Seers of the Sanctuary, I felt an excitement building. I could hear the chatter from the group of Dreamers ahead of me. I walked slow, wanting to enjoy the crisp evening air and connect with the Full Moon that was just appearing over the eastern mountains. What an incredible sight. It was starting to illuminate everything in a silvery glow; I noted that the white birch trees looked especially magical.

Off in my own private dream with the birch and the Moon, it took me a minute to realize the drums were calling the Dreamers to the circle. Quickening my step, but looking to the night sky, I smiled at the jeweled stars in that purple-black canvas. There was one star formation that I recognized: The Dog Star Sirius. I remembered that wolf was represented by this star. Also that Sirius was thought to be the home of the ancient gods of Egypt and the home of ancient teachers of some Native American Clans. I wondered if the Wolf Seer would be teaching this evening. How perfect, the Full Moon and the wolf teacher. I felt a slight shutter as I selected my space among the Dreamers. The opening was underway.

As the drumming slowed and the Dreamers became ready to begin the evening program, there was a loud howl! It came from the nearby woods. Some Dreamers looked concerned, but I knew the sound to be the Wolf and smiled as I looked at Grandmother Moon above us, giving us her light. Now in the center of the circle, strutting about, was the man, or wolf? Taking off the pelt of a wolf from his head, we all marveled at the Wolf Seer!

We all stared at him in anticipation for what would be next! Slowly he pranced in front of us. Then, in a deep, sure voice he began. "In Norse legends, Odin's warriors had the ability to transform themselves into wolves, known as 'Ulfhednar' Wolf heads. Why, you ask. The reason is this: the warriors cultivated the ability to allow the 'Animal Spirit' to take over their body during a fight. This ability was helpful to them as they wore the pelt of the wolf upon their heads as they entered the battlefield. In ancient Norway, there was a theory of 'Spirit Possession'; this was called 'The Berserk Rage.' You may recognize that name!" The Dreamers all nodded to each other around the circle. The Wolf Seer continued. "The Berserk Rage usually referred to the possession of the animal spirit of either the wolf or a bear. I am sure you are curious as to why we would be interested in these pieces of myth from history. We are interested because it is important to know the background of an animal Seer's medicine! Of course in the time of Odin, conditions were harsh, and war was a constant. However, as

Dream healers we may be called upon to provide an image of healing for someone, for some sort of war your client, friend, may be engaging in. Possibly a war with health issues. When we as healers know specific traits or histories of certain animals, we can then access our dream memory bank and pull out what is needed to help someone. Our collection of stories is very important!" The Seer looked around the group for a few minutes.

"I will continue. The Greek name for wolf is 'Phaedrus.' Phaedrus was a philosopher from ancient Greece and Italy. In many cultures, wolves have an evil connotation. They may be viewed as fierce animals, devouring things. Noted as crafty or cruel, sometimes as warlocks assuming the form of werewolf. The 'Beowulf' story in Norse myth is about a great supernatural wolf being and a great warrior from Sweden who travels from Sweden to Denmark to end the terror of Grendel. Of course there is the interesting tale of 'Little Red Riding Hood,' a classic nursery rhyme from the Brothers Grimm; now this is a story! In the telling we have the safe world of the village versus the dangers of 'The Woods.' There are warnings about talking to strangers, and the wolf is the deceiver! My goodness, the wolf is bad!" The Wolf Seer moved around the Circle, stamping his feet and looking mean. We all laughed at his theatrics!

Looking up at the Full Grandmother Moon, the Seer said, "Wolf in the wild is quite something else. An independent spirit of the wilderness, friendly, social, and very intelligent. Their behavior is ritualistic and based on a hierarchical structure. Within the pack are 'Alpha Males' and 'Alpha Females,' and they often mate for life. Wolves are skilled in body language; often a glance or posture is all that is needed to determine dominance.

"Wolf will go out of its way to avoid trouble or danger. Sometimes they use their ally, the Raven, as spotters for food, and Ravens often follow Wolf. They have amazing stamina and strength. Their sense of smell is one hundred times greater than humans, which gives them great discrimination. Wolves are very protective of their family and pack. They are a cunning hunter and can pass invisibly through the night, avoiding traps and hunters."

"Wolf became the emblem of Saint Francis of Assisi. Saint Francis was a Franciscan Friar of the Roman Catholic Church in 1100 to 1200 who was the patron saint of animals and birds. It is said that he tamed a wild wolf who was wreaking havoc among the village. Saint Francis was able to connect with this wolf and named him Gubbio. The wolf became the friend and ally of the village. The wolf was used as an emblem on Saint Francis's banners.

Wolf is also in Egyptian lore. The Egyptian God Up-U'at, Ap-wat or Wepwawet, is one of the oldest known gods. A god of war and death, Up-U'at's image was on one of the four sacred standards of the pharaoh's."

The Seer stood still and looked around our circle. Then, reaching down and spinning the drumstick on the ground, he looked to see where it had stopped. The Wolf Seer was looking up at me. The stick was pointing to me! Oh! My Goddess I said to myself. What does this mean?

As if he had heard my thoughts, the Seer said, "It means, my dear Dreamer, that you will tell us why these bits of wolf information could be helpful." He picked up the drum stick and handed it to me, helping me to stand up at the same time.

Nervous and shaking a bit, I twirled the stick. A talking stick, I thought to myself. I had the floor, and all eyes were on me. I glanced about the circle, and shifted my body some. Speaking slowly, I said, "Body language can help us to get our healing messages across. Wolves are skilled at this, as the Seer has told us. So when Dreamers are working with dream healing, we can use a certain glance," and I glanced strongly about the circle, "and maybe growl a little to get our point across. Or use a long strong pause for the client to catch up. It is important to become the 'Alpha Wolf'! Then lead, teach what needs to happen. Remember these stories, and others; create your own! Have them handy in order to help another learn and heal themselves."

I stopped there. It was quiet in the group. I looked around. The Dreamers had been listening! I sat down quickly and smiled! Then I heard the beautiful drumming to thank me! The Wolf Seer said that was great! He gave me a warm smile and then began to move onto other Dreamers, so they might add to the group's thoughts, as well. But I was still in my "Alpha Female Wolf" mode...within my own little world. I realized that under the light of this full moon I was able to conquer a fear about speaking in front of a group. This was wonderful! I was very pleased with myself. Thank you Grandmother Moon! And a special thank you to you, Wolf!

Section Three:
Dreams of the Tree Seers

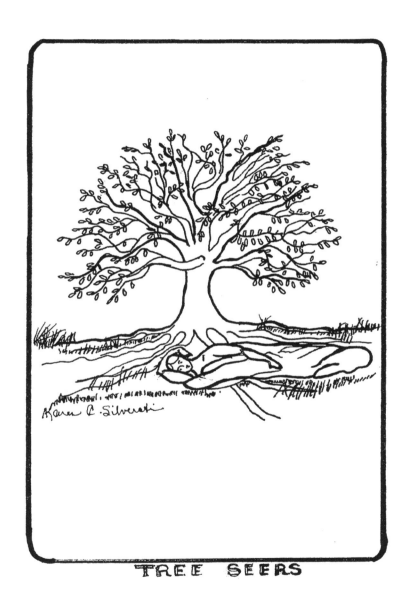

TREE SEERS

BIRCH

Karen C. Silverstein

"B" Beithe

THE BIRCH
LETTER "B," "BEITHE"
OGHAM: ⊣

STATISTICS FOR:

"The Birch" genus/species- *Betula pendula* (white birch); *Betula lenta* (black birch).

~Grows throughout much of North America and into Nova Scotia, also native to Europe, Himalayas, and China.

~Grows to a height of 35–80 feet tall.

~The Bark is white, grey, yellow , or blackish; with rivets of black lines and flaking pieces.

~The Leaves are usually oval and small with ragged edges, on alternate sides of the stalk.

~Number of species- approximately 12.

~Characteristic- Despite the slender beauty of the birch, it is actually hardier than the oak tree. It is able to thrive in places where the sturdy oak might die.

~~~~~~~~~

THE BIRCH: HOW USED IN THE WORLD

~The wood from birch is used in many artifacts, furniture (baby cradles), brooms, handles for tools, cloth; the bark has been used as paper and for making "birch-bark-canoes"; whole houses and fences have been made with this wood.

~Magical uses are many. Brooms were used by Celts to sweep away negativity and purifying just before the New Year. Birch cradles were thought to protect the newborn. Many farmers plant birch around their houses to protect from lightning.

~~~~~~~~~

MEDICINAL AND PSYCHOLOGICAL

~The Birch is used for healing. The parts used are: bark branches, leaves, sap, and wood.

Herbal teas can be made to break up kidney stones, astringents can be made for cleansing, and the inner bark and leaves can be made into a tea for rheumatism.

Birch sap can be harvested like maple sap to make "birch beer"; also the branches are used in the whiskey-making process. The sap is a natural shampoo. Also used for insect repellent.

The essential oil of birch can be made into "wintergreen oil"; the oil itself has numerous uses on the skin.

~~~~~~~~~

SACREDNESS AMONG THE GROVE

~The Birch is the first tree in the Ogham Alphabet: "Beithe"-"B"

~The Birch is associated with the "White Stag," beginnings, the Goddess, purification, renewal.

~ KEYWORD- New Beginnings

~Month- December 24 through January 20

~ Planet- The Sun

~The Birch stands on either side of "The Nameless Day" (December 23) within the Celtic calendar of the Grove and also next o the Yew tree; they both have a link to life and death.

~"FINGER TIP TREE" location- "Birch-Beithe"-"B" is on the top of the thumb.

DREAM OF "BEITHE,"
THE BIRCH TREE SEER

The north wind whistled hard through the wood in the storm of the night. I awoke several times and sunk deeper into the covers. Early rays of light were coming through the windows; I dressed quietly and went out onto the porch. Looking through the fields that led to the groves, I noticed the mist was clearing as the wind carried it out to sea. Walking some, with the wind caressing my face, I paused at the edge of the wood where tender sweet things grow, especially in the throws of late spring. I admired the tall fair ferns and maiden hair, and the gentle gentians of deep blue and azure.

"We must help," they whispered. Or so I thought I heard. The wind sighed, "They need you!"

"What is going on here?" I said quite loudly.

"The trees of the 'Birch Grove' call!" replied the wind!

I must be dream-walking, I thought to myself. Stopping to shake things out, I looked to the east where the sun brightens; there was a chill in the air. Wrapping my shawl tighter, I set off into the forest.

The crows were calling and putting on a sentry show, just ahead where the Birch grew thick. I followed their "cawing." Through the flutter of wings, I now heard, "They are feeling frightened and a bit weak!"

Now I had had enough and answered in a direct, strong voice, "Who is trying to converse with me, here in this wood? Show yourselves, I say!" Standing still and firm and with hands on my hips, I said, "*Well*. . .Who are you?"

The mist of the wood swirled but was silent. Then it came, "The Wind," but who can see the wind? Neither I nor you; yet I saw the leaves hanging and trembling, and I knew the wind was passing through. Now the Birches bowed their heads as the wind passed through. I stood firm and scanned this area of the Birch Grove. Off to one side was a crow; we stared eye to eye.

"So it is you!" I said with a laugh.

She cawed in recognition. Crow and I have had many interesting exchanges in the past, and now she seemed ready to speak again but instead turned her head to the stand of Birch nearby. There I saw the "White Stag," beautiful and strong with seven tines upon his head. We looked at each other and I knew there was magic afoot.

He is the one who spoke. "Some have been uprooted by the wind and storm of the night. It is good of you to come; they need you!" As he said this, he pointed his antlers toward the other side of the Grove.

Now I saw more Birch and the ones he referred too. Good of me to come…I thought to myself, I did not realize anyone had asked me. I looked with spirit eyes to the "White Stag" and saw that with his power he folded reality and bent the waking time, then opened us into something else. The magical land of the Grove.

Pulling my eyes away from him and looking to where he pointed, I heard him say, "When the fog clears, our most shy and 'Lady Like of Trees' will come." Just then in the sky, I saw streaks of lightning. The "White Stag" commented, "In Scandinavia, the Birch tree is sacred to the 'Thunder God Thor.'"

I turned now to the trees that had fallen, uprooted by the wind, he had said. There were three; a huge sadness over came me as I looked at these fallen trees. What can I do? Are they lost? Oh dear, I thought to myself. Staring at them through tear-stained eyes, I saw the fog and mist swirl as I walked closer to them in the Grove.

Catching me off guard I heard her…"The Lady of the Wood." She came through the fog quietly, shimmering and fluttering her dainty branches. She glowed now in the bright sunlight that came down around her. Her paper-white trunk marked with script in black upon the white. She was something to behold.

I wanted to speak, but the "White Stag" was there, saying, "The Birch is impressive not for size or age but for sheer beauty and its dogged resilience. Ah, Dreamer! Please may I introduce the 'Lady of the Wood,' our 'Birch Tree Seer'!"

Now the Birch Tree Seer held out her hand to me. I took it, saying to her, "I am so happy to meet you. I have looked forward to this for some time." She was quiet and pensive, with a hint of a smile; her handshake was firm. I felt gladdened to meet her. She seemed human yet she was otherworldly. I reminded myself that I was in the special place of the Nemeton. I focused to be back into the present.

"Come, Dreamer, I am pleased to meet you as well! Do not be saddened; their fate is now in the hands of the Goddess," she was saying as she pointed to the fallen Birch. "We will help them now in their transition," said the Birch Tree Seer. I just looked at her, my eyes glazed. The Seer said, "Do you not remember? You have done this before." I nodded my head as if I knew of what she spoke. The Seer smiled at me and patted my shoulder, then out of the Grove came others. The Seer exclaimed, "Welcome!" Looking at me, she said, "The Priest and Priestess have come 'to bless these dear trees'! One carries the wand-branch of the Rowan, and the other carries the wand-branch of the Apple. We are still between the worlds, as the sun has not fully risen. This is a most appropriate time for our 'Tree Blessing Ceremony.' We will make our wards strong to shield our work. Please do remember, dear Dreamer, that as an initiate, one needs to check their heart before proceeding into the work. If you have come in peace and love, 'The Way' shall be always open." She was looking for some acknowledgement, with her soft, gray eyes.

I answered, "I do understand and I feel peace and love."

"This is good, Dreamer!" She turned now to the others.

Silently, respectfully, I watched. The three, the Tree Priest and two Priestesses, were chanting and keening the passing of the fallen ones, offering their high regard for them with water and flower petals.

The Rowan Tree Seer was looking to the sun and said, "When we are troubled, it helps to look to the sun. With its light we remember that everyone is on the same journey under the sun. We arise and then we set; this is the way of the workings of the Goddess. But know, dear ones, we come again!" My hands trembled as he spoke, his never trembled at all.

Now the "Apple Tree Seer" came forward. She placed pieces of her fruit around the fallen Birches. "For your journey!" she said to the birches. The Seer leaned down and picked up one of the very small branches of birch; she then pulled out her blade and carved something onto it. Once she had finished, she held this up and walked around the trees for all to see. She was looking now at the fallen birches.

The Apple Tree Seer Speaks: "Dear Birch Seers, it is known that you hold the first position at the beginning of the 'Tree Ogham.' This serves to strengthen and set everything else in motion and its correct order. Throughout the cycle of life, death, and rebirth, the Birch can lead us all. Let me explain the 'Being of the Birch.' The physical makeup of these trees is very wispy, and each is strewn with light leaves, which allow much sunlight into the forest. Their roots are strong; their heart is big. The light leaves of the Birch are carried far by the wind and rot easily, giving good nutrition to the earth. The Birch contains a fertilization aspect that helps the other trees to establish themselves. The Birch can be thought of as a colonizer, or breaker of new ground.[3] The Birch is a tree that sacrifices itself for the benefit of others. We must remember this when we work with the 'Tree Ogham,' doing our magical workings, and use honor with the knowledge they provide."

The Apple Tree Seer then turned and walked toward me, holding the newly made "Birch Ogham" stick with the letter *B* carved upon it. She stopped in front of me and said, "This is the first lesson, and this symbol now goes to you!"

I put out my two hands in quiet disbelief and responded with, "I have much gratitude, and I thank you!" With tears streaming, I hugged her lightly.

"You are very welcome!" she replied and walked back to where the other Seers were blessing the fallen trees.

Now the "Lady of the Wood," the Birch Tree Seer was right next to me. "This would be a good time to walk the Grove a little. The Seers have more to do with their blessing ceremony and the 'Dryads' in the trees. And there is much I can tell you about myself and my kind."

We began our walk, with me feeling very sad. I knew there was much I needed to learn, but to begin my tree study with the passing of these trees made me wonder. I could still hear the keening as we got farther away. I tried to not hear it.

The Birch Tree Seer apparently read my thought and said to me, "You must listen! Their lamentations provide release. In our working and learning the way of the land, we come to know the way of the Goddess, and with her there is life and death. And we have rebirth each and every spring! You know this, Dreamer! So listen and be proud that you can hear and learn. One day you may be called to do the same."

I was wiping the tears from my cheeks, when she took me by the shoulders and said, "Dreamer! You are OK! You may not know your strength as yet. Have you a question or two to ask me?"

I laughed a little and said, "Strong, strength, you say. That does make me laugh!" We both did some more laughing and it helped. Finally I said, "Well, I do have one question for you. What is a 'Dryad'?"

The Birch Tree Seer had a very broad smile as she said, "Well, of course, this is something important to know! The Celts, the Druids, knew the life in all the trees was special and that it was assisted by the 'Dryads'-'Tree Spirits' that live in every tree. The word 'Dryad' actually comes from the Greek, and in Geek mythology 'Dryads' are 'tree nymphs.' The Nymphs are considered to be very shy creatures, except around the 'Goddess Artemis,' who was known to be a friend to the nymphs. In Greek the word 'drys'-'oak' is from the Indo-European root word 'derewo'-'tree' or 'wood.' But over time the term 'Dryad' has come to be used for all trees. So there you have it!" said the Seer, then she started again.

"For our work, from the Druids, in the month of March, incisions are made into the Birch bark, and the sugary sap is collected to make a cordial to celebrate the 'Vernal Equinox.' This was also a symbol to release the spirit 'Dryad' of the tree at the same time of the sun's own liberation of the spring season for man."

"Wow! I love that," I said. "There is always such beauty behind the teachings."

Again I heard the cries and keening from the other Seers. It made my spine tingle, but I tried not to show this. The Lady of the Wood had me walking again, and the sun was high into the morning sky, not a wisp of fog about now.

"We have much to cover, Dreamer, but best to start at the beginning! The first tree, as you have learned a bit about, is the first in the 'Beth-Luis-Nion' tree alphabet, which makes up the Ogham. This would be me, the 'Birch.' The birch tree is the tree of inception. It is indeed the earliest tree to put on new leaves at April first! And so it is the first in the alphabet lineup. The first month then begins immediately after the Winter Solstice, December twenty-fourth through January twentieth; this calendar date is considered by many Celts to be the month attributed to the Birch, the first moon of the Celtic year, the Birch Moon. 'Birch' in the Ogham is referred to as 'Beithe' and the letter is *B* in the alphabet. Then we learn that the attributes of this tree are about beginnings and opportunities. When a Dreamer decides to perform magical workings, they are wise to call upon Birch first. Birch at its best helps one to mentally and very carefully consider how to achieve the magic. This is where the skills of a Dreamer come in handy for journeying ahead for possible dream magic dress rehearsals and carefully selecting what is appropriate. Please know, these preparations will be recognized by those in the Otherworlds, who are very willing to assist us. So do ask!"

The Seer was checking me to see how I was listening; I smiled and let her know I was very much engaged. She continued as we walked to another part of the birch grove, which was so much bigger than I had realized.

"We can look at our magical endeavors as giving birth to a new idea. And when we look deeper, we see the deeper meaning in the Birch tree's physical attribute of 'colonizer,' which is a starter of new things on the physical level. The Birch is a very magical tree, even if I do say so myself. And I can be called upon to help start things and connect the Dreamer with the beings and goddesses of the wood!

"Remember then when starting 'new work,' 'new ideas,' use pieces of birch bark or pieces of my wood. Or maybe while dreaming a new idea, come to the 'Birch Grove' in the wood. Always the otherworld beings notice these things, and they may comply and bring the Dreamer good energy. It is said that in Ireland, when a girl is interested in being courted by a young man, she will give her lover a piece of birch as a sign of encouragement. This says, 'You may begin!'"

"Oh Seer, that is so nice! I love it!" I replied.

"Well now, keep it in your journal of stories for future use." She answered in a cheerful way and was about to continue, when we heard a stirring in the nearby trees and grass. We turned to find the "White Stag" standing there.

"Ladies, may I join you?" he said ever so politely. With those obsidian, dark eyes there was only "Yes!" to answer. The three of us continued our walk; I noticed that the Birch Tree Seer seemed very happy to have her companion with us.

The White Stag then said, "I've something to offer, if I may."

"Of course. Please share!" said the Birch Tree Seer.

The Stag continued, "Yes, well, Dreamer, our 'Lady of the Wood,' The Birch Seer, is associated with the element of water. She is a tree of the Sun and the planet Venus, and the herbal gender is feminine. The Birch is sacred to the God Thor and the Goddesses Diana and Cerridwen. Please know that Birch is very much a Goddess tree, the symbol of summer ever returning!" He paused and there was a sweet smile.

The Birch Tree Seer, in a laughing voice, said, "Stop! You cause me to blush!"

I looked at them both and realized they have danced many times together and that the Stag was her guardian true. We were now sitting near the small waterfall that ran through this part of the Grove. The day had grown with much light and love. The Stag had more to offer.

"There is an ancient poem by Gwion, called 'Cad Goddeu'-'The Battle of the Trees.' Here within, the Birch is mentioned as a 'very noble' tree. So Dreamer, please see how special our 'Lady' is regarded!"

"She is...The simple quality of her presence means much to me!" I had jumped up and spoken with enthusiasm.

The Seers both looked at each other and said in unison, "Oh! She is good!" I quickly blushed at that, and then the laughter came, first from them, and from me as well. We all looked at each other affectionately.

The Birch Tree Seer said she had things to share. "The ancient Hebrew mystics spoke of 'The Seven Pillars of Wisdom,' which for them correlated with the seven days of creation and the seven days of the week. They also aligned planets astrologically. These ideas were widespread and could be traced back into the time of the Babylonian beliefs. It is also said of their beliefs of 'The Seven Pillars of Wisdom' that the tree of the Birch was aligned with the 'Sun God' and its day was Sunday.

"In the work and training of a Druid, there are many levels of working. It is known that the first level comes with the 'Three Pillars of Wisdom,' which is the study of the 'Birch, Oak, and the Yew.' Also for the Celts, the Birch wood is one of the nine traditional firewoods to be added to the 'Belfire,' which burns at 'Beltane.' This is the Sun God returning to Mother Earth on the first of May each year. THE NINES TREES OF BELTAINE, an old Scottish rhyme for kindling the Beltane fire, says this:

Choose the willow of the streams, Choose the hazel of the rocks, Choose the alder of the marshes, Choose the birch of the waterfalls.

Choose the ash of the shade, Choose the yew of resilience,

Choose the elm of the brae, Choose the oak of the sun!

And nine trees listed, but one is missing as the ninth tree will forever be a mystery!

I clapped at the end of this rhyme and said to the Seer and the Stag how beautiful this was and how happy this made me feel!

The Birch Tree Seer said, "Why, you have come home, my child. This is why you feel as you do. Ah! But the hour is moving fast; we have much yet to cover. "

She stood up quickly from our perch among the rocks, and we were off again and soon in deep discussion. The Seer continued her tale of herself. "From a spiritual point of view, the Birch helps the Dreamer to prepare to give up something to help the common good. Birch is about being totally unselfish and being able to care for the needs of others so they may flourish. This commitment, brings one rewards of the heart"

The Seer put her hand on my shoulder and said, "Ah! Do not be sad, Dreamer. I know that you are thinking of the Birches who gave themselves to the wind earlier. Yes, they sacrificed themselves, but know that now the sun will come in stronger in that part of the Grove, and their roots are already propagating new shoots for the growing season. They are resilient and strong. The people will use her wood and bark, making baby cradles and rocking chairs, brooms, and so many things that are needed. All the while the people will remember to honor dear birch for the gifts that she provides and will keep her spirit alive in the artifacts and functional things that they make. Because, Dreamer, you will remind them to do so. It is your work now, you see!"

"However did you know, Seer, that I was thinking of the fallen Birch just then?"

She simply replied, "I am a Seer!" and continued her tale. "Now when you need to journey for your magical workings and you are not able to be in the Grove, just simply envision a 'Grove of White Birch' in a circle. To strengthen and give protection, use the warding of our branches laced together around this circle, and of course you may hold a few pieces of my wood! This way you may journey within the Grove circle to whatever it is that needs tending and feel confident that you have begun a new and true adventure for healing, magic, or information. When you have finished, do thank the members of the Grove of course, and close your 'circle of white birch' in your usual way. Remember the Birch is first in the Ogham, and your actions become the first movement toward whatever it is you are wanting to manifest. This movement begins the manifestation in the waking reality. This is what one might call a big thing! Big!" She was laughing some, and I realized that my mouth was just hanging open; there were no words for me to use right now. She must be laughing at this, I thought.

Then the White Stag said, "Yes, she is. Do not worry. There is much to take in. Give yourself some time."

"I am glad you have kept the Ogham stick of the Birch with you on our walk," said the Seer. Then she asked if she might hold it awhile; of course I gave it to her. She turned it over, admiring its beauty, and mentioned the fine carving that had been made of the Birches Ogham letter for 'Beithe.' "Yes! This is fine. I feel now that it has been charged and it contains the knowledge and power of the Birch. You may ask that it help you with understanding the magical working of the trees. Ask that the link that has been created between you and the Birch remain strong and true. Ask these things with a true, pure heart, and you will learn to be a 'Tree Seer of the Wood'!"

The Birch Tree Seer then put her hand to my face and said in a sweet voice, "You are a fine student, Dreamer! And you are honing your skills quickly. Always know I will be there for you when needed!" She then looked to the White Stag and said, "I take my leave now from the magical Wood!"

I heard water rushing and blinked my teary eyes. I was sitting near the waterfall, and the birches were off to the side. I could see how they then circled and grew into the white birch grove. Had I been dreaming? Well of course I was. And what an amazing dream it had been!

ROWAN

Karen L. Silverstein

"L" Luis

THE ROWAN LETTER "L," "LUIS" OGHAM:⊣

STATISTICS FOR:

"The Rowan" genus/species- *Sorbus aucuparia* (Europe Rowan); *Sorbus americanna* (North American Mountain Ash)

~Grows throughout the northern hemisphere; found in Europe, China, and North America.

~Grows to a height of 30–65 feet.

~Bark is a whitish gray, with flaking pieces. Leaves are deciduous, small, and rounded and are on alternate sides on the stalk. Flowers May through June. Red fruit in September through October.

~There are over 100 species. Botanically the Rowan is of the "Rose-family"-"Rosaceae." Some species may be considered a shrub.

~The Rowan can live to over 100 years.

~~~~~~~~~

THE ROWAN: HOW USED IN THE WORLD

~The wood of Rowan was made into all kinds of tools and handles for tools, used for small home furnishings like bowls, dishes, and other woodcraft. In the Middle Ages, bows were made of Rowan. Walking sticks are made of rowan to protect one on their journey, both physically and in the Otherworlds. Rowan is said to protect from lightning.

~Magical uses are many. The branches are often made into amulets, such as tying two equal pieces with red string to form a cross, an age-old amulet of protection. Often sewn into the kilts of Scottish Highlanders before battle. It has been said that Rowan wood can be carried and used to increase psychic powers. The branches are used as dowsing rods and magic wands. The leaves and berries can be added to incense to aid in divination and to increase psychic powers. Carrying the bark of Rowan brings good luck.

~~~~~~~~~

MEDICINAL AND PSYCHOLOGICAL

~The parts of Rowan that are used are the bark and berries (berries must be cooked before use). Used as: diuretic, astringent, haemostatic, digestive, and an expectorant.

The fresh juice of the berries is a mild laxative. The berries contain a high concentration of vitamin C. Pies and also bittersweet red wines were often made from the berries.

~~~~~~~~~

SACREDNESS AMONG THE GROVE

~The Rowan is the second tree in the Ogham Alphabet: "Luis"-"L"

~The Rowan is associated with the element of Fire, protection against lightning, vision, magic, the Green Dragon, and "Brigid."

~KEYWORD- Magic, psychic protection

~Month- January 21 through February 17

~Planet- Uranus

~The Birch and the Alder stand on either side of the Rowan tree within the Grove.

~"Finger Tip Tree" location- "Rowan-Luis"-"L" is the tip of the forefinger.

DREAM OF "LUIS,"
THE ROWAN TREE SEER

What can they be doing? I wondered as I saw the piles of thin branches strewn about the clearing in the Grove. In the center a fire was going strong, and the logs for the fire were close; the heat felt good on this blustery February 1 day. The "Imbolc" (Candlemas) would be tonight, "The Feast of the Black Maiden." I knew the preparations had been underway for days, but with my other obligations, I could not be involved until now. I wondered what the Seers needed me to do.

It did not take long to find out. I asked someone what they were doing with so many branches. "Come with me," he replied.

I had to step quickly to keep up with the other Dreamer! He then stopped next to a man of medium height in a green cloak; we waited patiently until he acknowledged us. When he turned around, his face was kind, but I could not read any particular expression. I noticed the dragon that was embroidered in blues and greens on his cloak. I said, "The dragon is just beautiful!"

In a rather dry voice, he answered with a simple, "Yes it is." Then he turned back to looking at the trunk of the tree, where he was standing. He said, "Can you read that?"

I looked to where he was looking and did not see anything to read. Nervously I answered, "I am not sure what it is I should read."

The Seer (because I realized that he was) turned to my fellow Dreamer and said, "Tell her!"

The Dreamer said, "He is reading the bark!"

I answered, "The bark?"

The Seer replied, "Why, yes! I am reading the patterns on the bark. This takes practice and time, and it has been part of my training. Possibly I will teach you this one day. In the meantime, I am pleased to meet you; I am the Rowan Tree Seer." He spoke so matter-of-factly, as if I had been there for hours with him.

I was startled a little, and it took me a few seconds to respond, but I made up the time with extra enthusiasm. "Very happy to meet you, Dear Seer!" And I reached out and shook his five-fingered hand with many gold rings on each.

His touch was warm and reassuring. He simply nodded his head and then picked up a five-pronged spear highly decorated with small red beads and a tree vine twisted onto the staff. Just then in the trees, a few "Druid Dhuhbs" (blackbirds) alighted and made a commotion. The Seer said, "They know this is a special day and night!" Quickly he started over to the other side of the fire.

I looked at my fellow Dreamer with question on my face. He simply shrugged his shoulders in an "I do not know" response; we both followed the Seer. Once on the other side, The Rowan Tree Seer greeted other Seers, and they spoke a few minutes while my friend and I waited. Then we saw one of the Seers remove a red blanket from a pile of sticks. They all looked this over carefully. I was puzzled as to what this was.

The Rowan Seer came over to us and escorted us to the others. He introduced both of us to the "Birch Tree Seer," "Alder Tree Seer," and the "Willow Tree Seer." They were all warm and cordial. Having already met the Birch Seer, I felt a comfort and received a nice hug from her. I really perked up from that.

We all turned our attention to the "Rowan Tree Seer." "Dreamers!" he was saying. I looked around and quickly saw that several other Dreamer friends had joined us. "Dreamers! I know you know that today and especially tonight are a special time in the Grove. It is 'IMBOLC'! Before we continue with our preparations, let me please give a simple explanation of this 'holi-day,' which is one of the Greater Sabots and marks the quickening of the year. This is the time in the changing seasons of our year when we celebrate and honor the transfer of the Goddess energy.

"We honor the 'Winter Goddess,' 'Cailleach Bheur'/'Berre,' which is Scottish. She is the 'Queen of the Faeries of Limerick.' We also honor the 'Birch Tree Seer' who supports this winter season.

"The Winter Goddess now transfers the energies of the winter season to the goddess who represents spring/summer.

"We honor the 'Spring and Summer Goddess,' 'Brighde'/'Brigit, which is Irish. She is the 'Queen of Heaven,' the goddess of wells and the water of life. We also honor the 'Willow Tree Seer,' who supports this spring/summer season."

Each of the Tree Seers mentioned nodded to us all as he spoke. The Rowan Seer paused; everyone was clapping and happy to have a better understanding of our celebrations. Now the Seer was trying to tell us something else; it took a few minutes for us to settle. Holding out his hands, he indicated silence to us. We all began to listen.

"The name 'Imbolc' is interesting; it comes from the name that is given to the belly of pregnant Ewes. 'Why should this be used?' you may ask…Well, it is because the fact of the Ewes becoming pregnant happens at the turn of the seasons, and the new calf and the milk that comes is very important to the Celts! Later on with the infusion of Christianity, this holiday came to be known as: 'Candlemas.' Candles were lit originally to honor Brigit and then later for the Virgin Mary. This is a time of the rebirth of the season."

The Rowan Seer was smiling at us all. I could feel the high magic that he possessed. I was very excited to be apart of this special time. The Rowan Tree Seer continued.

"We will have the actual ceremony at dusk later on; however, in the meantime I would ask the 'Alder Tree Seer' to share the 'Celtic Blessing' from *Carmen Gadelica*."

"This is an honor!" said the "Alder Seer." He recited:

We ask…

> "To save, To shield, To surround,
> The Hearth, The Home, The House, The Household.
> This Eve, This Night
> Oh! This Eve, This Night. And Every Night! Each Single Night!"

It was so moving. Everyone was feeling the spiritual essence coming through from the Seer who spoke and from the other Seers who were present. Each of us thanked the Alder Seer. Then he changed gears and said it was time to get moving.

The Willow Tree Seer said, "I need help to make the 'Fairy Goddess Wine,' which we will share later."

"How great that sounds!" I said, "What is it made of?"

The Willow Seer answered, "Why, with milk of course! Equal parts milk, honey, vanilla, and cinnamon."

Everyone clapped at that, and then we all got busy in preparation. The Rowan Seer asked me to help him with the "wattling," for the wattles.

"The Wattle? What is that?" I said in a high, cheerful voice.

"Come!" said the Seer. I followed him to where there were several others working with the branch pieces I had seen earlier. The Seer picked up a large, rectangular bunch of branches that was on a red blanket. He turned it over for me to view on all sides.

Finally, after looking awhile, I could see that it was woven branches. Then I asked him, "What is this for?"

He said, "They are called 'Wattles of Knowledge.' They are woven from the Rowan branches into these special mats. They will be used a little later by the Seers. They lie upon them as they journey into the new 'Imbolc' season of the year for any insights that may be helpful to us all! This is a good way for you, Dreamer, to become familiar with the Rowan wood and to practice your weaving skills. You will, of course, put good Dreaming energies into your work. What do you think?"

Laughing a bit, I answered, "This is great! I would love to help with this."

He smiled and said to find a comfy seat, which I did, and then he began showing me how to weave and interlace the Rowan branches in a certain way. It took me a little while to get the hang of it, but I really liked doing the weaving of these wattles. There were a few Dreamers like myself and a few Seers who sat in a circle with the Rowan Seer, wattling together. One of the Dreamers asked the Rowan Seer to reveal his story to us. We all cheered, "Yes, please!"

The Seer began his story and spoke with a full, sweet energy of life. "It is always helpful to begin at the start of things, and so I will!" said the Rowan Seer.

He was up now and walking within the circle we had formed for our work. His green robe was shining with the last rays of the western sun as he strolled about, stopping and leaning on his magnificently carved spear; I wondered about the battles he must have known. The green-and-blue dragon embroidered on the robe had eyes of red beads; I wondered if they were actually red Rowan berries and if the ones on his spear staff were the same; I decided that of course they were Rowan. Looking off to the woods and the Grove we were in, it only just dawned on me that most of the trees there were Rowans. How could I have missed this earlier! It was February, so there would be no red berries to see now but, of course, they were there, just waiting to show themselves ripe. I made a mental note to come through this way to check on the berries in the late summer; what a sight that must be.

I came back from my reverie to hear the Rowan Seer telling us: "My name is 'Luis,' in Gaelic of course; the name 'Luis' also means 'herb.' Also, the same word may stem from a root word meaning 'flame.' If you, however, remember that the 'flame' is what kindles the fire in the mind and soul to produce the 'divine light of inspiration,' you will then have a better image of the Rowan tree in the connection to magical properties and to its Druid association. I would venture to say it is a reference to my bright red berries! Still others say that the word 'Luis' in the Ogham means 'to swarm,' or 'a great many,' which may be in reference to its plentiful berries. In the Ogham alphabet, the word 'Ogham' comes from a Scottish-Gaelic name, 'Oidheam,' pronounced 'oy-am,' which means 'idea,' 'notion,' or 'hint.' It is therefore not connected to writing but rather to mental, abstract concepts. There are various sources of this Ogham alphabet. But for our work in the Nemeton, we will use *The Book of Ballymote* for sequencing of trees and also refer to the 'Beithe Luis Nion' alphabet. With that, I am 'Luis,' letter *L*, and the second tree in the Ogham! The word 'Rowan' may come from the Old Norse word 'runa,' which means charm or spell."

Now the Seer had stopped by the fire and was putting in a few logs; the flames lapped and there was hissing from the sap in the logs. I wondered if all the wood was Rowan for the fire.

The Seer continued with his walk and talk. "The Rowan tree has acquired many names, 'Mountain Ash' primarily, but there are many names as nicknames: Lady of the Mountain, Quicken, Quickbane, Quickbeam, Wicken Tree, Witchbane, and many more."

"In Scandinavian myth, there is a story of 'First Man and First Woman.' The First Man was formed from the Alder tree, and the First Woman was formed from the Rowan tree. The red berries from the Rowan are considered sacred by many cultures, most likely because of the symbolic images of creation, blood, life, death, and renewal."

Now the Seer stopped and went over to the red blanket. There he picked up a branch that had a section covered in red berries, dried some but still very red.

He continued, saying, "I save many branches such as this from the harvest time of the year, as you never know when you may need them. Now I would like to show you Dreamers something!" He was waving his hands for us to come forward to where he stood with his branch. He then handed the branch to one of my fellow Dreamers and told him to hold it steady, which he did. Then he asked me to pick off one or two berries and asked the others to do the same. He said, "Well, what is it you see?"

Those of us holding the berries examined them a minute, and then, slowly with voices of surprise, we said, "There is a star shape!"

"Yes! A five-pointed star, a pentagram." The Rowan Seer clapped loudly, and to the other Seers he said, "They are very observant for initiates! Good, very good! Dreamers, as you can see, the star shape is on the berry and also on the stalk from where it was picked." We all took a moment to look a little closer.

"As you all know, the pentagram has been considered an ancient symbol of protection, so carrying the berries would offer that protection. In Aegean/Mediterranean myths, the Rowan is connected to a tale about Zeus, in which Zeus had a cup that was stolen from Olympus. An Eagle was sent to recover the cup, and a battle raged. The legend has it that wherever a drop of blood or a feather fell during the battle, a Rowan tree subsequently sprouted and grew strong.

"The Celts associate the Rowan tree with Brigit/Bhrighde, whose arrows were made from the rowan. It can be noted that the tree is guarded by serpents and dragons. Guarding the red ripe berries was especially important dragon work. It has been said that berries heal the wounded and can add one year to a man's life! The Druids were known to kindle fires of Rowan for the opposing armies, with incantations spoken over them. In very old legends, a Rowan tree is often mentioned as an assembly point for warriors. In a poem known as 'The Wry Rowan,' the story tells of two thousand huntsmen that gather on a hillside that is covered with Rowan Trees![4] Rowan offers magic in Celtic legends.

"A forest that is mostly formed from the Rowan tree is rare indeed. Still, there lives a species of Rowan found only on the Scottish Isle of Arran that is not a hybrid but is instead a true genus of Rowan. Appropriate because 'Arran' was considered by the Celts to be the physical manifestation of the Otherworlds. Of course, this gives the island and everything growing on it a strong, magical link.

"In Celtic lore there are many tales of love, strife, and magic. I would like to share an excerpt from one in which the Rowan tree plays a grand part. It is the romance story of 'Diarmud and Grainne/ Grania. The lovers, the fugitives 'Diarmud and Grania,' were left in peace for a while. In their travels they came to the 'Wood of Dubhros.' There they saw for the first time the extraordinary 'quicken tree' of the Tuatha de Dnann, an ancient race. The tree had grown from a Rowan berry dropped accidentally by a musician of the Tuatha. In spring a cloud of bees continually hummed around the tree, and in summer, when the berries glowed red, clouds of birds fluttered. The more berries eaten, the more that there were. Any mortal who chanced to eat a berry enjoyed good health, youth, and beauty. They were sweet as honey to taste and more intoxicating than the strongest mead. If anyone ate more than one, he would likely loose his wits. Meanwhile, Grania began thinking about what she learned about the magic berries, and the more she thought of them, the more she wanted them!"

At that point the Seer stood up from where he had been sitting and was perfectly quiet, looking at each of us. Again he stoked the fire. There was some whispering among the Dreamers.

Finally after a long enough silence, I stood up and blurted out, "What happened?"

The Seer just smiled and shrugged his shoulders. I looked around and could not help saying, "That's it?" With my hands on my hips, I looked around for help.

Another Dreamer said, "There has to be more to this tale!" The Rowan Seer began laughing and the other Seers chimed in. I was confused and just threw up my hands.

The Rowan Seer said, "Well, I believe I hooked you all with a cliffhanger ending! It is up to you all to check out the rest of the story. All I will say is that some relate Grania to the 'Celtic Eve'!"

Now all the Seers were all really laughing! The other Dreamers and I finally joined in and confirmed that we would read the tale in its entirety. It was suggested that we all take some time to check out the weaving work we had been doing. All of us brought our work together and admired each others' handiwork. Our mats, or the 'Wattles of Knowledge,' were shaping up perfectly. It would not be long before we had them done. Then the Rowan Seer asked us to get back into our weaving, as he had more tales to offer.

Someone said with jest, "Sure hope we get the whole tale!" All of us thought that quite funny. We were feeling very good, being together like this.

The Seer continued. "The Rowan tree has been called 'Quicken Tree' due to its ability to grow high on mountain sides, clinging to outcrops of rock and fissures in the boulders. It can grow higher up the sides of mountains than any other native tree, sprouting and growing from the tiniest of crevices. Its life force energy is very strong and determined. It reflects power and vitality. Its message is *not* to give up, but to hold on strong to what you believe in and the power of your own life force!

"In ancient times it was valued as a protection against enchantment or unwanted influences or evil spirits. So sprigs of Rowan were placed over doorways and fixed to barns to protect animals. Rowan is valued for its ability to provide us with forewarnings. It gives us an increased awareness of enchantments from outside influences. Rowan strengthens one's personal power, psychic abilities, and one's life force. Rowan is the wood to use for making any magical tool, for divining, invocation, and accessing the spirit realms. It teaches us how to discriminate in our work for the healing good.

"The month of February, associated with Rowan and the Imbolc, is a good time to do magical initiations and healings. The branches of Rowan are used for many magical wands, including divining for water. The tree itself was often planted near graves to prevent the haunting of the area.

"The Rowan has many deities connected with its energy: Brigit, Aphrodite, Thor, and Cernunous. The gods of 'Dagda' and 'Lugh' assist the Rowan with courage and protection, especially in difficult circumstances, including war. 'Dagda' means 'good-god,' also 'all-father.' 'Dagda' has immense power and is armed with a magic club and with a cauldron. The cauldron was said to be bottomless. He was the 'High-King' of the 'Tuatha De Danann,' and he was the father to 'Brigit.'

"'Lugh' means 'long arm' or 'long hand' for his skill with a spear or sling. He is the son of 'Cian,' the father, and 'Ethniu,' the mother. Both came from the 'Mother Goddess Danu,' whose peoples were the 'Tuatha De Danann,' the ancient race.

"Rowan was used by the Druids in much of their work and used in all protection spells, especially from fire or lightning. Branches were woven and put onto hounds to increase their speed. So, as you can see, Dreamers, there are innumerable uses, and it would benefit you to look into these in more depth."

The Seer stopped walking around our circle, and he spoke in a much firmer voice than earlier.

"Dreamers, what we most need to understand is how the Rowan is connected with the 'Lord of the Hunt,' who is 'The Opener of the Way' and 'The Protector of the Way.' This is the spirit of the 'Green World,' who goes by many names. The most common names are 'Cernunnos,' 'Herne the Hunter,' and the 'Daghdha'/'Dagda.'

"'The Lord of the Hunt' is always depicted as being fierce, ugly, and aggressive, with horns and a club.[5] However, beneath the surface he is a caring, helpful, and docile being, willing to help you. If you are worthy! He is the 'Great Opener of the Ways' who will test but also direct those deemed worthy.

"In our work we come to realize that 'The Lord of the Hunt' represents the two sides of the 'Green World' and must be recognized and accepted by those of this world who wish to live in harmony. There is a harsh, threatening nature of the Green World but also a softer, gentle, beauty side to nature. Our reaction to them both is what brings us our wisdom. 'The Lord of the Hunt' will help one to understand this and how to access the energies of one's true higher aspect of self. It has been said that the Rowan can help one distinguish good from bad, friend from foe, and provide help from harm."

The Seer was next to the fire now and was silent a minute or two as he looked after the blaze. I thought to myself, What a good "fire keeper" he is. And I smiled to myself, remembering how he is related to the element of Fire! The warmth was nice, as it was really cooling now with the sun setting.

"Please remember that the Rowan is good for all rituals associated with empowerment. And should it be necessary, Rowan can be called upon for psychic attack. Call upon me in each season of the year, when I am only dressed in my branches, and when I am nurturing the buds that I carry, and when my red berries are full. Working with the Rowan throughout the four seasons helps one to understand how it goes through changes. The year is born, grows, wanes, dies, and is reborn. See how you feel, Dreamers, when you are cold, wet, dry, calm, or winded. Then there is morning, noon, afternoon, and night! How do you feel? You must experience things to understand your place in this 'Green World.' Find where you are needed to bring healing!"

Then he walked around the group of our "wattle-making Dreamers,' checking on everyone's finished work. The Seer was pleased with the results and said the Keepers would journey well upon them. He told all the Dreamers to find a piece of the Rowan wood that had not been used, a six-inch piece, not very thick. We all complied, and I wondered what was next. The Rowan Seer said, "Take out your blade and come to the fire and heat it just a little." He demonstrated with his own, as we all watched.

"OK!" he said. "Now please carve the two lines, with the crossed section over the top. Next carve the letter *L* for 'Luis' just above the Ogham glyph. Has everyone got that?" Then he walked about checking each person's work. When he was satisfied with all, he told us to bring our sticks to the fire. We were all so excited it took us a minute to be circled about the fire like he wanted us. Finally he was pleased with our formation. Then he asked the Seers who had been sitting with us throughout to join us now at the fire. The Rowan Seer asked us all to hold up our newly made "Luis Rowan" Ogham sticks, as if we all had long swords that touched together! Now he said, "With the power that is vested in me from the 'Dagda' and the 'Flame'! I now call for these new 'Luis' Ogham sticks to be charged! Dreamers it is time to know the way of Rowan and good workings for the Nemeton. So Mote Be It!"

None of us were prepared for that and now we, I, had my own "Rowan Stick"! My magic wand, I thought to myself. How great. I began talking to a few of the other Dreamers, all were exhilarated and happy but feeling tired too.

After the exuberance quieted down, the Seer came to the forefront, and he threw up his hands, saying, "That should be enough for today, ah! But there is so much more to tell... Maybe I should give you the tale of the—no. No! It is time to get ready for our evening's Imbolc ceremonies!"

Everyone in the circle was laughing and trying to shake his hand in thanks. It was a wonderful adventure being with him. I heard someone telling him that he was good at giving "cliffhanger stories" and it made the lessons fun. Everyone was having a grand time.

Now I saw the Willow Tree Seer, and many were gathered around her. Then I heard her offering the "Fairy Goddess Wine"! I clamored over to her to have mine. Then she asked if everyone had their wine. We were ready to have our toast. Looking around the group of Dreamers and Seers was satisfying. I saw the Seers who had the "Wattles of Knowledge," getting ready for their journeys. All was quiet, and only the crackling fire could be heard.

The Rowan Seer walked to the middle and stood upon a small Rowan wood trunk stump. He raised his glass and said, "Seers, Dreamers, Keepers of the Dream for All! A toast to the Goddesses, and may they now transfer the power energies from winter into spring/summer! Imbolc has come!"

How wonderful nature is. How grand the work of the land!

ALDER

Karen L. Silverstein

"F" Fearn

THE ALDER
LETTER "F," "FEARN"
OGHAM:▤

STASTISTICS FOR:

"The Alder" genus- *Alnus* (several varieties). Grows throughout much of Europe, Asia, and Africa, also found on the American West Coast.

~Grows to a height of 50–70 feet, with a conical shape.

~The Bark can be gray to dark brown in color and smooth. Leaves on most species are rounded with indented tips, on alternate sides of the stalk; develops a small pinecone-looking fruit. Usually found growing near water.

~~~~~~~~~

THE ALDER: HOW USED IN THE WORLD

~The wood from the Alder, when cut, appears bloodred in color. Dyes are made from the bark, fruit, and leaves. Many things are made from alder, as the wood is good for carving. It is very water resistant and lasts a long time in water. So it was used in bridges, jetties, and lake dwellings with the piles of alder wood sunk deep into the water. The Celts used Alder to make charcoal for metal working. The pith is easily pushed out of the green shoots to make whistles.

~Magical uses are many. Some whistles were made with three pieces of wood, each a different length and bound with twine; these were similar to a flute. Very good for calling in the Air elementals, Druid's termed this "Whistling up the wind."

~~~~~~~~~

MEDICINAL AND PSYCHOLOGICAL

~The bark of the Alder is an emetic and is used with water as a gargle for sore throats. The bark of alder was boiled with vinegar to kill lice and help itching as in poison ivy. Also used for dental needs, cleaning teeth, and curing inflamed gums and relieving tooth pain. The fresh leaves are astringent and were often applied to fresh wounds. Some say the heated leaves are good for rheumatism. Teas can be made from the bark to treat diarrhea, use as eye washes, and to treat coughs, and to ease the discomfort of childbirth.

~~~~~~~~~

SACREDNESS AMONG THE GROVE

~The Alder is the third tree in the Ogham Alphabet: "Fearn"-"F"

~Alder helps one to face up to things; its essence is invigorating. Alder may allow access into the fairy realms.

~The Alder is associated with the Raven and the Crow and the "God Bran"

~Month- March 18 through April 14

~KEYWORD- Protection, Determination.

~Planet- Saturn

~The Alder stands on either side of the Rowan and Willow within the Grove.

~"Finger Tip Tree" location- "Alder-Fearn"-"F" is the tip of middle finger.

DREAM OF "FEARN," THE ALDER TREE SEER

A pool can be found during the mistiness of the wood that some say is called "Mirror Lake," a special magic place; one that is good for scrying work. Many have been lost in attempts to find it! I had known about this for a while now and also knew I would need to find this place. With so many questions on my dreaming mind now from all the months training, I was feeling a quest to know what was ahead for me after the training and how I would then fit back into waking life. I felt strongly this was the time to find "Mirror Lake" and use my scrying and divining for my questions. These were my bedtime dream intentions as I listened to the rain outside. I planned for an early morning adventure, when I knew the mist would be thick. This of course was what is needed for the magic of "Mirror Lake." A bit intimidating, but somehow I also knew I would succeed!

Morning arrived quickly. I was happy to see the rain had stopped and that the foggy mist was lingering. I was glad or nervous and not sure which. I was remembering that "Dreaming Ahead" has been such an important skill to have learned here in the Nemeton and that the journey work helps one to find answers and be more prepared; this made me feel better. I learned from last night's Dreaming that the Raven would be my guide, and I was grateful. I knew he could help me find my way in the dense parts of the mist.

I dressed in warm gear. It was late winter but with spring in the air; this made me happy as I walked. The paths had snow remnants and were thick with mud as I followed the stream into the deep woods. Heading uphill and upstream made me winded in no time. Leave it to me, I thought as I trudged along. I seem to always pick the hardest path! Bantering silently to myself awhile and getting tired, I stopped to rest upon some rocks along the stream bank. As I got my bearings, I realized I had no idea how far I had come, or if I was even headed in the right direction for the mysterious "Mirror Lake." I began having visions of being lost in the wood, coming upon awful terrors!

Then I heard "caw, caw," and I jumped up! I did not see the Raven but knew he must be near. Thinking to myself about my Dream of the previous night, I scolded myself for not calling upon my guardian "Raven" when I started out. I really need to get myself together! That I blurted out loud, and then I began to move upstream again, battling the fog as I moved through the glen. I do like a challenge; as long as I can keep my will going, I know things will be fine. After all, I thought, the day is early and the sun will certainly brighten and burn off the fog at some point!

I stopped again to rest, and wondered what had become of the Raven.

"Not far," I heard in a flutter. I looked around the wisps of mist and the rustling branches. Where was he? "Hey, please, Raven, do not play games. OK, please come! I need your help, please!" I said this with all earnestness and crossed my fingers with light.

Another flutter and he was there, on one of the tree branches just in front of me. "Caw, caw, caw! At your service, dear Dreamer; all you need do is ask. Remember that!"

I was laughing and hopeful as I answered, "I will remember! I am glad you have come. Do you know where I am trying to go?"

He answered most matter-of-factly, "As I recall, I was in your dream. Let me see…something about 'Mirror Lake'…could that be it?"

I was laughing with him but was secretly relieved that he knew!

Then the wind picked up with a chill in the breeze; the mist was thicker than before.

The Raven had been reading my thoughts by the way he was speaking. "We just need to follow the stream awhile longer. You chose well to come this way, Dreamer, and I will be your eyes and guide you where the glen fog is the thickest ahead."

"Thank you! And—"

"OK! I hear you," he interrupted. "Let's be off!"

I was surprised at that but knew he was right. Sometimes I get carried away talking. The important thing is the task at hand, and I made a mental note to remember this for the future. I did not hear the stream water much anymore and wondered at that. I was not so sure where dear Raven had gotten to. Next thing I knew, I saw him on a tall, slender tree of fifty feet at least. It looked to me like a silver birch. I wasn't quiet sure. The ground here was boggy; the mist hung heavy, shielding much of the view. Here and there were shafts of sunlight. The morning earth creatures were chanting away; I heard many bird calls but did not recognize most of them. Sloshing around in the bog, I felt water seeping through my supposedly waterproof boots. At least it was warming up some.

"Caw, caw! Stop worrying about your wet feet; your soul has other lessons right now!" The Raven said this so quickly, but looking into his eyes, I saw only love there.

I answered succinctly, "Yes, I know. What are the lessons?" He quickly was in midair, but very slowly he flew around to the other side of the tree. I jumped to follow. On the other side of the wide trunk, there was an opening. What was it?

The Raven was on a branch just above. I was confused but the Raven began chattering something. Finally I just sat down on a fallen branch there. I thought I heard a doorway mentioned…?

Clearly now the Raven spoke. This time I heard, "Trees are used for doors and therefore are doorways! Dreamer, please meet the gatekeeper of this tree, 'The Alder Tree Seer.' He is here to welcome and to assist your work at this time."

I was tired, exhausted really, but this woke me right up! "Is it true? You are the Alder Tree Seer?"

He came from out of a fairy's dream, in green earth wear, young and ancient; he felt both soft and strong. He planted his long spear carved with dragons and ravens into the boggy ground in front of me. "I am who you say, 'The Alder Seer,' and Raven speaks highly of you, Dreamer!"

I stood up suddenly. He now asked me to be seated. His shield was of wood with silver inlay, laced with gold Celtic knot works. It was slung across his shoulder, and the warrior was calm and well spoken. I felt a comfort and said, "Happy to meet you, Alder Seer! Will you join me on my quest for 'Mirror Lake'?"

"I answer your call; my gateway has opened for you, as you braved the mists of this bog well. Now I would like to tell you about myself before we move on to 'Mirror Lake.' But first may I suggest that you remove those wet boots. You will actually feel warmer, and, as you can see, the sun is full out now and your boots can dry some as we talk."

I just nodded my head and then removed my boots. He had cut three branches with his knife and stuck two into the ground and gave me the smaller one. Then he inverted the boots and put one on each branch. Water tumbled down from each; I laughed at that. I looked around for Raven, but he wasn't there, so I asked the Seer about him.

"Ah, Raven! Well, he is my ally, that I say for sure. Off on important magic, I would guess. But there is more, and this is certainly a good place to begin my telling of me!" There was a huge laugh after that, which was contagious.

As I looked around, the sun was filtering onto the grasses. Still in some places the mist formed like hanging clouds. I could see under them but not above the puffy bluish-white mist, a world of the fairy beings and their dreamland. I heard a steady, drip, drip, drip....and came back from my daydreaming to see the drips of water falling from my boots.

"Are we back, Dreamer?" He handed me a cup of sweet milk to drink and dried fruit.

I was saying, "Thank you and Yes! I am back!"

"Good! Now listen if you will. In Welsh Myth there are stories from Gwydion of the 'Welsh Triads.' There is a magician who appears throughout one of these called the 'Fourth Branch of the Mabinogi.' Mabinogion is the title of eleven prose stories from medieval Welsh. In this Gwydion mentions 'Bran,' who is 'Bran the Blessed.' In Welsh, 'Bran' is 'Bendigeidfran'; this name literally means 'Blessed Raven/Crow.' He is son of 'Llyr' and 'Penarddun' and is a giant and king of Britain. One day he is mortally wounded in battle, and he had prophesied these events and what would follow his death. In his instructions, his followers were to cut off his head and to carry it where they went. The head remained alive and spoke to them, and they settled in the area of Harlech for seven years, living in peace and not corrupted. Then they traveled to the area called London and rested and were told to bury the head on the 'White Mount' or 'Bryn Gweyn.' It is said that this is the site now known as the 'Tower of London'!"

The Alder Seer was quiet and looking at me intently. He leaned upon the shield beside him.

My response was, "Oh, my God! What an incredible story. But what about the Raven?"

"Of course I knew you might want to know more!" he said with twinkling blue eyes. "You must understand that there are many layers here…Gwydion, in his stories, mentions that the name of 'Bran' meant 'Raven or Crow,' but he says the name also meant 'Fearn' in Irish, which translates to 'ALDER'! So 'Bran the Blessed' literally means 'Blessed Raven' and Alder tree!"

Standing up quickly, I knocked over one of the boots from its drying stick, saying, "Get out of here! What on Earth do you mean? I cannot…!"

The Seer just calmly picked up the boot and put it back on the stick as he said, "I did not intend for you to be upset. These things I say are true, as incredible as they may seem. However, we must take into account our work here and remember that things have many levels and are not always black and white. With our work we must become good at reading every color and layer!"

Settling I said, "So it is true! You and Raven are the same?"

He shrugged and said simply, "Well, something like that! But please know you are safe and there is much more to learn. Are you ready?"

I nodded my head yes. "I do not think anything can top this revelation!" Then I just collapsed onto the ground.

Then the Alder Tree Seer continued his story. "Now that we have some clarity, I will reintroduce myself! I am the 'Alder Tree Seer.' In Gaelic in the Ogham letters, I am 'Fearn' and letter *F*. The third tree in the Ogham alphabet, although some say I am the fourth, but this is semantics. I am the tree of 'Bran' and from the Stories of the 'Battle of the Trees' called 'Cad Goddeu.' Alder fought on the front line of the battles.

"The title given to the 'Alder' in the 'Word Ogham of Morainn' was 'Shield of Warrior Bands.' This means 'To Protect-Take Care Of,' which refers to the protection of the 'Spirit of the Alder tree itself.' Protection that I offer can be called upon in modern life, and though one may not have a physical wooden shield of alder wood, the protection will be provided. Remember that, Dreamer. If you should feel threatened, call upon me!"

Now the Seer was up and walking around the tree, stretching some and examining his spear. How many lives has he lived? How many causes and battles? A simple tree with roots and leaves, but a warrior as well. "Bran" on the front line! So much to take in; I had questions when I started out this morning. Now I had even more, but I was fine. Being there in this misty land of the fairies felt like a privilege that few would know! It occurred to me I would have more to share with those I came in contact with.

There was a stirring in the trees and a flutter of wings. The Seer had his arm stretched out, and the Raven glided gracefully onto this.

I said, "That is awesome!" I watched as Raven made himself comfortable there.

The Seer was now seated again, and the Raven stayed still on his arm. He picked up his telling of his tale. "The Celts also called upon Alder tree to do the 'guarding of the milk,' because the cow/cattle were a mainstay. Also of much importance was a 'Protection of the

Heart,' a literal shield of spiritual essence to protect one's heart or calling for another's. We come to realize there is more to the physical shield than the material implement of battle; the deeper purpose of the spiritual is the mainstay for our culture, for our work with the trees, and with the land.

"We must recall that Alder's place is at the front battle, and remember to use the Alder shield especially when journeying to the Otherworlds for protection.[6]

"The spiritual essence goes before the warrior! Be sure you know the Alder is about going forward, always taking on the challenge, being brave and bold. The Alder helps one take on the tests and come through them; the Alder is confident! Remember that Alder's advancing aspect is important, because when we break new ground and face up to things… We grow! In addition, as you proceed through your challenges, use the 'Alder-Shield' and strap it to your forearm, 'in front of your Heart'!"

The Seer had stood up with his shield and was very animated, showing exactly how to hold the shield. Then he had me stand up. He gave me the shield and had me practice placing it just right in front of my heart. He was saying, "Like this!" He gave a demonstration, then, handing it back to me, he went on to ask, "Do you feel the weight of it? Is your arm comfortable?" I nodded my head yes on both questions. He told me to move the shield around, out arm's length, and then to pull it back in front of the heart.

I did what he described. Large as it was, there was little weight and it felt easy to maneuver up, down, around. I liked doing the movements; it felt familiar somehow.

The Seer said, "Think of this shield as an extension of your arm, and feel comfort with it. Then with practice these movements will become an automatic reflex available to you whenever necessary. In fact this is an exercise assignment for you to continue a bit later. The feel of it will become so familiar that it will be there for you any time you choose, though in waking life the physical shield may not be seen, the wood of the Alder will be present for you, because you called on me to be there!"

I had been practicing my shield movement as he was speaking. When he stopped, I said, "Oh! Dear Seer, thank you. This is magical, being able to practice with your ancient shield!" I kept making swiping motions with the shield on my arm and then began moving about more boldly, half sprinting and dancing small jumps as if I were in an ancient battle! The Alder Seer became filled with laughter at my antics. "What?" I said, "I think I am doing well!"

He was still laughing when he said, "But you had best watch…your step!"

It was too late. In my zeal to use the shield with fancy footwork, I had backed up too far on the stream bank and gracefully plopped into the stream! I screamed, "*Oh!* My goodness! Oh it is cold."

Standing up quickly, the Seer held out his hand to help me up, all the while laughing. As I tried to dust off and wring out, he was saying, "Well done, Dreamer. Well done. You are a natural!" Now we were both laughing, and he gave me a blanket that he happened to have.

I began warming and drying some. Thank goodness the sun was out strong now and I did have the foresight to bring a change of clothes.

The Alder Seer said, "I would like to continue, as this is the perfect time to do so. Let me talk some about water!"

"Water!" I replied. "Yes, tell me about that!"

The Seer continued, "The Alder likes to grow near water and is often found half submerged in water. A Dreamer should always be aware of things both above and below the surface. I am sure, Dreamer, you have become familiar with this expression that so often helps us in our spiritual pursuits, 'As above, so below.' Looks to me like you just attempted to get a magician's firsthand look at the 'below side of things'!" He was laughing again.

I answered, "I always like to jump right into things!" I had changed my wet clothes and was warming up nicely now.

The Seer was anxious to keep going. "Knowing about above and below the surface is extremely important. When we check on the below, we then know what the land there is like and then devise a way to build a safe and secure foundation for whatever we are building. When Alder comes in contact with water, it turns black and hardens like stone, and it does not split when nailed." The Seer was up and rummaging through the grassy hillside at the edge of the stream. When he came back, he showed me the piece of alder wood he just found. He handed it to me, and I looked it over and tapped it upon rocks. Wet and black, it was definitely strong.

Continuing, the Alder Tree Seer asked me where was the small piece he had given me earlier. I handed it to him, and we checked the differences. Then he said, "You will need an Alder Ogham stick; I think this wet one will be perfect." He leaned over to get the stick and then took out his blade and began carving on it. He made three straight lines with a lintel top and the carved the letter *F* for the name "Fearn" for Alder. Looking it over a minute and making it a neat cut at either side, he then handed the Ogham stick to me, saying, "This is a nice one, Dreamer, and it will charge now as we finish up our Alder work of the day!"

I held it gently in both hands and told him, "I will treasure this and will use it for good in my Dreaming!"

With a smile and a small laugh, he said, "Ah! That you will, my lass!"

Now, he continued. "The Alder is amazingly resistant to water and will not decay. As a result, it was often used in construction of bridges and for foundations for homes located close to rivers. In our spiritual work, we may be involved with all kinds of things, and sometimes there may be situations of a psychic nature. Alder therefore can be counted on for its resistance quality; it is a powerful force in any psychic attack or battle. It has been said that 'Bran the Blessed' made his body into a bridge across Ireland to come to the aid of his sister, Branwen. In this battle the Welsh were victorious."

Smiling, he said, "Gather your things. Put on your boots; they have dried nicely."

I did as he said. And I asked him, "Where are we going?"

His only reply was, "Not far!"

It was near noon, I figured from the sun's position high in the sky. We walked along the stream in silence now, munching on snacks that he had for us. The movement felt good.

Before we left I had tucked my Ogham stick into my belt. I took it out and held it as we walked; it made me happy. We were walking over a bridge with mist very thick again; I wondered if it might rain.

Dashing to catch up to the Seer, I questioned him about the bridge. "Is this bridge made of Alder wood?"

He answered, "Of course!"

The foggy mist was so thick; I could hardly see in front of me. I made sure to know just where the Seer was. I asked another question: "How much farther?"

His only reply was, "Not far!"

I was getting tired and nervous at this trekking; I rubbed my newly received alder stick and put this back into my belt. I needed to pay attention!

Suddenly the Alder Tree Seer exclaimed, "Ah! The beauty of it!"

I looked ahead with my head up high, as I had only been looking down, being nervous walking in thick fog on a bridge, no less! The scene was of mist lingering over a house of some kind that was built off to the side of the bridge. When I looked closer, I saw that it was a round house of daubed and thatch materials; there were pots of red flowers, and the smell of wood smoke was sweet and rich. The Seer was next to the round house, talking with someone. I saw them embrace after he put down his shield and spear, leaning them against the house. I stopped in my tracks. I did not want to intrude. Turning myself to the left, I saw the mist was floating off as the sun shone through. I could not believe what I saw! I ran to the railing of the bridge, and there was the most beautiful lake I had ever seen.

Wanting to run and tell the Seer, I turned quickly and nearly knocked him over! But I could not prevent myself from saying, "You have brought me to Mirror Lake! I did not mean to bump into you, but I am so excited!" Then I noticed a woman standing with him, and I quieted down.

The Alder Seer said, "I do aim to please! Do you think it beautiful, dear Dreamer?"

"Think it beautiful? Are you crazy? It must be the most beautiful sight I have ever seen!" I ran next to the railing and looked at the still, mirror-like surface of the water and could see our images reflected. It was clear and bluish-green in color; I saw the clouds and mist reflected as I stared over the edge. Finally settling down, I turned to the Seer. He was smiling ear to ear and looked very young and handsome in his simple, green, woodland clothing.

"Dreamer," he said, "I would like you to meet the 'Priestess of Mirror Lake.'"

The Priestess took my hand and said to me, "I am honored that you have come!" She was an ancient one. Her blue and fern-green gown had embroidered work of seed pearls with moonstones and threads of silver laced through the bodice. She was petite, but strength radiated from her in ways I did not understand. She was young; she was ancient.

In a daydream, I was slowly bringing myself to say, "I am pleased to meet you as well, Priestess. I am so excited to be here!"

She nodded her head, saying, "I understand you may be interested in scrying. I can help with that. But first, the Alder Seer has a few things to show you. I will find you in a while."

I thanked her and told her I could hardly wait. I watched as she moved over the bridge and down to a ramp-way. She walked as if she floated. I wondered if this was real, but it did not matter...I loved it!

The Alder Tree Seer had been standing quietly by; now he spoke in excited tones. "Dreamer, I would like to show you the alder pilings that support the bridge and the round house. Come!"

We moved quickly toward the round house. It was of at least thirty feet in circumference, with neat and clean thatching, a fairy tale setting. I half expected elves to appear from under the planks of the wooden bridge. Next to the round house was a set of stairs that went down to the lake. They were narrow but easy to walk down. Halfway down, the Seer stopped and we looked underneath the house. He pointed out the floor design that radiated from the center, like the spokes of a wheel; the alder pilings supported the whole thing!

We walked farther down and now were on a kind of quay-boardwalk. From this vantage point, we were able to see beneath the bridge, and he explained the amazing engineering work required to build such a bridge. And of course it was made of Alder wood! The wood pilings were dug many feet below the water's silt, he told me. I could see the water up close now. There were ripples in some places, and it seemed to be teaming with fish and life. There were a few benches near the edge. The Seer seated himself; he motioned for me to have a seat. I was glad for the rest.

The Alder Tree Seer began, "Well, lass, you have come far today and are growing into an amazing Dreamer! I've a few more things to share before I am off. The Priestess will take care of you and help you with your scrying."

"I do not want you to go!" I said, full of emotion.

"I know," he said, "but we both have things that need tending, and you are doing fine! Remember this: Alder, that is me! Know that I can be very helpful during times of stress or tension. I can help soothe and protect. And should you need more, call on me for the protection of your heart to shield your heart! I am a tree with a masculine gender and can be helpful in making choices, offering spiritual guidance and of course protection.

"I would also like to explain that as one uses the tree workings of magical healings, it is beneficial to call upon the 'Daghdha' at the outset. He is the God of all the Trees. Remember Alder's name is derived from the Old English, 'Ealdor,' meaning chief; over time it became related to the office of 'alderman,' which is an elected government official. I am the tree on the 'front line'! My elements are both fire and water, quite a combination. I am a 'Chieftain Tree' and can help with the building of your magical work. Sometimes it is also helpful to know which tree grows next to which in the Grove as they may be helpful in your pursuits. For instance, the trees in the Grove next to me are 'Rowan'-'Luis' and also the 'Willow'-'Sail.'"

The Seer then got up and walked to the edge of the quay. Bending down and touching the water, he said, "She looks like glass but is so much more." Shaking out his hand, he said, "This about does it! We have had a very lovely day ,and I thank you for facing your challenges and coming to know your goodness of heart!" I was nearly to tears and wanted to speak, but he put up his hand and said, "Hush! No words are needed…Well now, the Priestess has come. Gather your questions, as I think scrying time is here! A time for Dreaming with the water."

The Priestess and I laughed together at his rhyming, and then we all heard a swoosh and a flutter. Then the Seer held out his arm, and the Raven alighted smoothly.

"Fare thee well, Dreamer!" said the Alder Seer. "And I have a song for you as I go!"

The Priestess took my hand as he backed away; it was a comfort.

I called out, "Where can I find you, dear Alder Seer. Where will you be?"

He answered, pure and simple, "Not far, not far, Dreamer!" His song was musical as he and Raven walked down the quay. "Let her hold you near, hold you near, as the Ravens come singing. The Ravens come singing. Oh Dear Mother of mine!"

In a flash he was up on the bridge. The Priestess was telling me something. I answered her absently mindedly, "Yes, I am coming!" But my Dreaming was still following the Alder Seer. "Thank you," I said quietly, holding onto my newly made Alder Ogham stick. I saw the Raven in the air and smiled sadly and happily and knew I was in the land of "The Fae."

"I am coming," I said to the Priestess.

WILLOW

"S" Sail

THE WILLOW LETTER "S," "SAIL" OGHAM: ⫞

STATISTICS FOR:

"The Willow" genus/species- *Salix chrysocoma* (weeping willow)

~Grows throughout North America, Europe, and China

~Grows to a height of 65 feet

~Leaves are narrow and have silky hairs on both sides

~Both male and female flowers are on the catkins

~~~~~~~~~~~

THE WILLOW: HOW USED IN THE WORLD

~The wood from the Willow is used in fence making and a large variety of baskets and artifacts. Also used for cookware and water jugs. The Native Americans used the willow for poles to construct their sweat lodges, covering the structure with animal skins. This is considered a sacred purifying ceremony.

The Magical uses are many; often rods are made of willow for divining purposes.

~~~~~~~~~~~

MEDICINAL AND PSYCHOLOGICAL

~The willow has been used for healing purposes through out the world, from the leaves, wood, and bark. The bark contains a source of a chemical that is used in the making of aspirin. The sap can be made into a gargle for nasal or sinus problems; also sap is used for eye drops. The leaves in a strong proportion can be made into shampoo to treat dandruff or skin irritations. Willow is known to be a good styptic, which can stop minor bleeding.

~~~~~~~~~~~

SACREDNESS AMONG THE GROVE

~The Willow is the fourth tree in the Ogham Alphabet: "Sail"-"S"

~Willow brings help with other world spirits; tides and linking; gives strength for new journeys.

~Willow associated with embracing change, a feminine tree.

~Keyword- Flexibility.

~Month- April 15 through May 12

~Planet- Moon.

~The Willow tree stands on either side of the Alder tree and Ash tree within the Grove.

~"FINGER TIP TREE" location- "Willow-Sail"-"S" is on tip of ring finger.

DREAM OF "SAIL," THE WILLOW TREE SEER

y bare feet were sinking into the moist ground and sloshing along the edge of the brook. My shoes were laced together and slung over my shoulder; it was easier walking like this, I told my Dreamer friend. Morning was coming up slowly in this part of the wood, a most advantageous time to find them, which is what one of the Keepers had said. "Make it your intent to look for 'The White Lady' in the wee hours. You will likely see them, hear them at least; it is up to you!" This is what the Keeper had said and all the information we were given. There was no time for questions; he was off to something else.

Mostly it was dark, with the sunlight beginning to peek through, and still, very still. As the cool air touched my cheek, I took in a breath of the mist. So quiet and so still, only the noise of twigs snapping while we walked; we must have been the only ones awake at this hour. Dreamers who had done this awhile back had given us general directions and reminded us to just think of the path work we were doing here in the Nemeton, and we would be protected and find our way. We knew our dream intent needed to be clear before we ventured out. So we most certainly did our Dream journey work.

There was a mystery, an uncertainty about the wood; somehow all the trees and plants looked alike, and this became overwhelming. I realized that my mind could be lead astray easily. Quickly and out loud, I said, "No! Don't go there!"

My Dreamer friend nudged me, saying, "Hey, it is OK! Let's just keep focused on the Dreaming we did already; that is our map! We can trust our Dreaming to bring us to the ford!" She was smiling at me with confidence.

I tried hard to smile back. We had paused on our watery path, deciding if this direction felt right.

My friend reached over and said, "Did you see that?" She was pointing across the brook, where the trees were not as thick. "Movement. There was something; I am sure of it!" said my friend as she held onto my arm.

I looked to where she was pointing and saw nothing. Apparently wanting to know the why of this, my friend was already heading across the shallow brook, her shoes still on. I dashed to keep up with her. We wound around briars and difficult thickets with thorns and red berries. Now my bare feet hurt from the undergrowth; but I would not dare stop for a second, for fear of loosing sight of my determined friend forging the way toward whatever she saw. The mist was thick, and I had not a doubt that we were being watched every step of the way. I told my friend this as we stopped at the top of the small hill just up from the brook.

She agreed and said, "The 'Old Ones' are at work."

I felt a chill on my back, but did not say a thing.

The wind shifted and we looked at each other; my friend and I said in unison, "You hear that too, right?" There was a soft, strange sound rising up, like a chant. But from where? Our eyes were wide with wonder and fright. We walked ahead ever so slowly, looking backward and all ways, staying close to each other for comfort. Again it came, soft and musical. We stopped and the mist drew back ...They stood in a circle around "The White Lady."

In disbelief my friend and I exchanged glances and gripped hands. We looked again to the grassy hill; there on the side where the water ran close was the source of the chanting. The wee folk, the Fairies, stood hand to hand about the most beautiful Willow tree I had ever seen.

My friend let go of my hand and nodded for me to follow. "The chanting music of the mist is what then led us to her, 'The White Lady.'" I spoke this to myself as we moved slowly toward them. Standing there so grand, so enchanting, close now. Was this real? I thought to myself.

They were in the middle of a ceremony, I was sure. I held out my arm in front of my friend, saying in a whisper, "Let's wait a minute!" We looked at each other and remained still. I took a quick look about and realized there had been a light snow here from the night. I put my shoes on the ground and quietly slipped them on. At least they are dry, I thought.

Patiently we stood, listening and watching but not comprehending what this was about. We did, however, use our etiquette of not interrupting their circle, as we knew from our own Dream workings of the importance of circle work. I thought to myself, If they want to interact with us, they will let us know. But of course I began to worry as to what we should say and—

Next thing I knew, my friend had nudged me. I focused to see "The White Lady" and the "Wee Ones" were silent now, and a slight of a path had been cleared; it seemed they were inviting us closer. My Dreamer friend and I exchanged glances and walked the path to fairy! Now we were just before the Willow. She stared at us both, no expression; I was not sure if she was Tree or Woman. My heart pounded. I waited a moment, thinking my friend would speak. I looked at her, and all she did was nod her head. Finally I knew it was me that needed to speak.

"Greetings! Dear Willow Seer!" I said in the strongest voice I could manage.

"And to you!" she replied.

I only nodded my head in reply. Then there was silence. Now I was worried. I mean, what would happen now? I could not even remember as to why we had come, like a veil had fallen over me. Oh my! I thought, I could blow this whole thing.

"Listen! Listen! Do you hear what she is saying?" My friend said softly. The Willow was swinging and swaying. My friend wanted to be sure I could hear the sweet voice of the Willow. Silently we leaned forward. The wind moved through the field and then her branches; there was a small creaking at first, then we heard her.

"Dear, dear!" said the Willow in a matter of fact way. "My new leaves have a dusting from the very last snow! Spring and summer are finally coming!"

My Dreamer friend and I laughed a quiet kind of laugh, and I said, "Dear Willow, you must be weary of winter!"

My friend said, "I am too!"

Looking at the grand tree, I noticed she certainly seemed cheerful now. "Look, the snow is already melting!" I offered. Then there was silence.

I glanced around with my peripheral vision and saw that many of the fairy folk had moved off; I wondered at that. I could feel the day growing warmer. All the while we were both glued to the Willow; she was very beautiful, with delicate new leaves of a pale, yellowish green. She shook now the last of the dewdrops that had been snow. It was wonderful watching her branches move and sway with the spring winds. I looked at her trunk gnarled and knotted, her wide roots above the short, brown grasses around the trunk. She is an ancient one who has seen much happen on this land, and yet she stood with a youthfulness and swayed with grace. How I yearn to be like her! I thought, I have so much to learn. I wonder if she will take my offering and have me as an adept. I wonder.

Coming back from my daydreaming, I heard my friend asking the Willow Seer about the Fairy folk and why were they going.

Suddenly in the quiet, we heard the now booming voice of the Willow Seer. "Going? Ah! They have tending to do, the 'Silent Watchers of the Forest.' Besides, is it not I that you have come to see?" At that there was a great rain of laughter. After a minute she added, "So you two have made it through the first part of the 'dream smoke'! Shall we continue?"

Of course we both nodded our heads yes and said, "Yes! Please, Willow Seer; there is so much we would like to learn."

The Willow Seer cocked her head some, and in her more human form, she shape-shifted and said, "Come!"

Before we began our walk with the Seer, we told her we had an offering of red ribbons to be used as braiding, to adorn her when she would like. She smiled, thanked us, and sighed some, holding the ribbons this way and that. We all moved a little closer to the edge of the brook, where she told us to find a comfortable place.

The Willow Seer speaks: "This is my temple, the land. There are those that care for this temple, the little ones, 'The Fairies' you call them. They are the 'Children of the Goddess'; mostly they remain hidden and should. Many are feminine and work to protect the light and help us to access this light, but only for the good of heart."

The Seer looked at us quizzically. She looked to be a child of thirteen, but her voice was that of the crone. I saw her again as the Willow tree. Tall and wispy beside the brook, throwing her branches over the sparkling water, with her long and narrow, sad, gray, weeping leaves. Some of the leaves were floating like little fleets of sunny canoes upon the flowing water. I detected motion off to the left; one of the Fairy beings was scampering behind the Willow.

"They protect me! Yes, the 'Wee Ones' do an amazing job. Most humans never even see or sense them. It is because you did acknowledge the 'Wee Ones,' along with your determination to move through the 'dream smoke,' that we sit together now. It was quite fun watching your journey here; the children and I enjoyed the show!" The Willow Seer had a really good laugh with that comment. I wondered how she was able to see us. But then I remembered I was now in the land of her magic and anything was possible for her!

I looked at my Dreamer friend. We both were a bit uneasy, wondering what was next.

"Ah! The 'in-between time' of day and seasons too, not quite Spring, but close!" The Willow Tree Seer was speaking from where we had paused on the knoll. Then she began walking in her human form, a creature of beauty and grace. My friend and I scampered to stay with her, and it was clear now that she had more to tell us. She stopped and turned to look us both in our eyes, saying, "In-between time,' between seed and new life; a most potent time of year! Tell me, Dreamers, what do you desire? What are you willing to sacrifice to have that desire filled?" Holding up the palm of her hand, she did not let us answer as she watched us exchange glances.

The Seer continued. "Let me think, maybe…Fear-For Love. Or Doubt-For Faith. Or Poverty Consciousness-For Abundance! Yes, that would cover the sacrifice-desire issues! Please do not answer this now; this is something for you both to Dream on! I will help you in the Dreamtime to have clarity with your desires; as new Dreamer-Seers it is very important to know what you want! How else may one fulfill their path work?"

My friend and I looked at each other wide-eyed and nervous now. I tried hard not to show this to the Willow Seer. She had moved quite ahead of us both in the wood along the icy brook and seemed to be looking around for something. Just then I spotted one of the Fairies whispering to the "White Lady." She was nodding her head, then she waved her arm for us to catch up. Of course we sped up to her. By the time we were close, the fairy was nowhere to be seen.

The Willow Seer said, "One of my Fairy companions came to assist us with where we will cross the ford. Once we cross, we will be on an island of fairy; it is here that we will continue with what I am destined to teach you! Know that there is much on this island that you will see and be curious about. However, once we come back, a veil may descend and it will be up to you to engage your Dreaming eyes to see what you need to see. You both may have different visions. There will be other things that you are not meant to know or understand at this time. Do you understand what I say? Are you ready to commit to truth and open your hearts to seeing differently?"

I looked at the Seer and began nodding my head slowly, meaning yes. In a firm voice, she said, "Words. I need out-loud words, please!"

My back shivered at that, and I looked at my friend. Quickly turning back to the Seer, we both said, "Yes! We are ready to commit!"

She looked at us both and then, with a half smile and loud voice, said, "Clear, articulate words. This is good; make that a practice for you both! Think about what needs saying, choose your words carefully, and speak them clearly."

I breathed a sigh of relief, but the next thing I knew, we were walking across the icy brook along a fallen tree trunk and some rocks. It was not far to the island, but concentration was needed as the logs underfoot were slippery and the water lapped close to the sides. I know I did not want to fall and then be freezing. Looking up for a minute, I saw the Willow Seer was on the land. She leaned some on the staff she was walking with; beyond her in the still dim light was a grove of trees. I wanted a better look but knew I had better cross completely first. My Dreamer friend had just gotten to the land. I quickened a little and carefully balanced and finally hopped off onto the island; my heart was racing.

I looked at the Willow Seer, and she said, "Returning will be much easier!" I wondered what she meant by that.

On the island we followed the Seer up a small hill. The wind blew and her hair caught some of the breeze and swirled in a graceful motion. Still barely daylight, it was hard to see too much. My feelings, however, were a calm anticipation and I felt thankful. We were now in front of the grove that was all willow trees, with their long branches cascading and intertwined about the circle of trees. Before we crossed through, the Seer came up to each of us. She straightened our clothing, smoothed our hair, and said nothing.

We waited a few minutes; there was a whispering in the leaves. Suddenly one of the Fairies was there, holding a basket made of willow, which he gave to the Seer. She thanked him and he was gone. She said to us, "He is a 'Gnome,' which is a fairy of the Earth element; he and his kind help to maintain the Earth, and they are great craftsmen."

I wanted to ask questions, but her forefinger was at her lips and she was shushing us both!

In a quiet voice, she said, "Once we cross into the 'Grove of Willows,' you will not speak until I let you know that you may!" She looked us both deep in the eyes and then went into her basket of willow and removed a willow wand for each of us and a candle, which she lit. After giving us another look, she lit her candle. With a nod of her head, we moved forward as she held away the drooping branches of a willow as if they were curtains for us to walk through.

The mist was everywhere; I knew there were others but could not see them. I stayed right behind the Willow Seer, slightly afraid, glad of my candlelight. My Dreamer friend was right next to me; that too was a comfort. My eyes were slowly adjusting to this misty dimness, and I noticed other sparks of light all around the grove and realized there were many candles lit. I told myself lit candles are a good thing and that we must be ready for some kind of ceremony.

In a moment we came to a standstill and were shown where we were to stand. There was the perimeter circle of Willows and an inner circle made up of the Fairies and some of the Keepers; we were a part of this circle. After a few minutes someone threw something onto the central fire, and it roared in a puff of blue and gold light, then simmered to a nice golden-red glow. I began to look about the space more carefully; I did not dare move anything but my eyes, and what I saw took my breath away! Between the mists were the proud Willows, their branches swaying some. The inner circle held the glimmer of the candles from the participants all dressed in finery and giving out incredible vibrations of joy and love. This beautiful place and image I will forever hold in my heart.

The Willow Tree Seer was now in the center, magnificent in her trailing silver-green gown and flowing, pale hair. In the background chanting musical sounds came as the Seer led us all in the opening ceremony, which in a whisper she called "Willows Enchantment." She stood next to an ancient well of water made from stone and led us all in the opening words of Dreaming; there was soft drumming along with the chanting.

Then in a language I did not understand, she spoke, sounding musical. As she continued, several beings at a time would walk toward her and then dip their willow branch into the well next to the Seer and then return to where they stood. Now there were Fairies next to me, and I was startled, but only momentarily. They led me to the well and helped me to dip my willow branch inside and then escorted me back to where I had been standing, telling me to keep the branch very still and to copy the motions of the "White Lady." I could feel an excitement growing as I waited patiently; my friend felt it too and squeezed my arm. Now the "White Lady" went to the well and put in her willow branch, and then, holding it to the side, she reached to her neck and removed her long, green mantel embroidered with silver symbols of the Moon and many other symbols. With perfect grace she bent in front of the well and spread out her green mantel.

Standing and looking about the circle, she said this: "Blessed Ones! We honor Brigit. May her green mantel forever keep the flow of the waters of life alive!"

Then she took her willow branch and sprinkled the water onto her mantel and onto herself. I looked around, and the others within the grove were doing the same thing. There was some laughter and chatter now. Of course my friend and I sprinkled ourselves with our willow branches, and we too began to smile and lighten up!

Now the Willow Tree Seer was holding up her hands, asking for quiet, saying it was time for all to be seated. She said, "Willows, Keepers, Fairies, Dreamers all! I have much to cover for our new Dreamer friends, and this will be a good review for the rest! We will reaffirm that the 'Blessed Ones' have not retreated entirely. The People of the Tuatha De Danaan and of the Celtic Goddess Danu are quite alive, yet!"

So excited and happy, I realized I was still standing! Everyone else had sat down; I did so quickly. The "White Lady" had been walking around our group as we settled; I noticed she leaned over and put on her "green mantel of Brigit." Sitting then on the edge of the stone well, she was ready to speak.

"Ah! Quiet! How nice. I begin by giving my mythical history, which covers the globe. Of course I will shorten things somewhat!" Laughter came from the crowd; the mood was lighter and happy.

"The Cailleach. This term is associated with the Celtic tradition as an aspect of the Lunar Goddess, especially the roots of willow. She is not a goddess of fertility or death or any one thing, but a deity that is transcendent. 'Cailleach' is connected to rivers, lakes, wells, marshes, the sea, and storms. Water! Also with mountains, rocks, megaliths, standing stones, the animals, trees, and plants. The Scottish call her 'Wife of Thunder'! 'The Cailleach' is an elemental power of winter; she comes into power when days shorten. She was called the 'Old Veiled One.' In Dream workings we need to be aware of the amazing force of 'The Cailleach.' She provides the anchoring and the rooting that is needed for the work in the Otherworlds, where so much of my work as the 'Willow Seer' takes place."

"Now, 'The White Lady'! Interesting name, 'The White Lady,' don't you think? There are various myths about this name given to the willow tree; many mention the small, pale leaves and pale bark. Most mention the female attributions given to the willow as graceful and beautiful. A Celtic descriptions of 'Willow' says this: 'color of a lifeless one.'[7] This shows us the connection of willow with the Otherworlds. Willow has the ability to allow us to experience the dwellers of the Otherworlds. The Celts have an unshakeable belief in life beyond waking reality; even though one may die to this world, they can remain very much alive in the Otherworlds. Let us look at the willow tree's relationship to life and death. The wood of willow to the Celts was very important; it was used in countless building of things. Annually it is chopped to the ground; this is a practice called 'pollarded.' Or it may have its head cut back. Yet it most assuredly grows back in the spring with a great number of new branches. The willow knows much about life, death, and rebirth.

"The White Lady sometimes refers to ghosts and the tree's association with ghosts. The Willow is known as the Tree of Enchantment and is associated with magic and witches. Willow is considered one of the seven sacred trees of the Druids. It is connected to the 'Triple Lunar Goddess,' who at one time represented the darker forces of the Moon. This is what came to be associated with witchcraft.

"From the Greeks in myth, at the temple at Delphi, 'Orpheus,' a Greek King of the Thracians, was depicted as receiving the mystic gift of eloquence by touching a 'Willow' in a sacred grove of Persephone. In Greek, 'Willow' is 'Helice,' and in Latin, it is 'Salix.' In Greek myth Poseidon preceded Apollo as 'Leader of the Muses' and was guardian of the Delphic Oracle. The Helicean Groves were sacred to him. According to 'Pliny the Elder,' Gaius Plinius Secundus, born AD 23 and who was a Greek historian and naturalist, a 'Willow Tree' grew outside the Cretan cave where Zeus was born.

"Also the 'Goddess Europe' has been depicted as seated in a Willow Tree with an 'Osier' basket in hand. 'Osier' is the name of a small shrub species of the genus *Salix*, the Willow.

"In Greece, Willows are sacred to the Goddess. Among those mostly widely associated with willow are Hecate, Circe, Hera, and Persephone, which are all considered Death aspects of the 'Triple Moon Goddess' and much worshiped by witches. In Greek myth 'Circe' is the 'moon-bride of the sun,' also called 'Belili,' the 'Willow Mother.'

"From the Hebrews we learn about "Sukkot"-'The Feast of the Tabernacles' in Jerusalem. In their ceremonies, a wand was used, called a 'thyrsus.' It was made from intertwined branches from the Alder, Palm, Myrtle, and Willow Trees, and it became a bough. This was used to honor the Moon Goddess and to chase out evil spirits.

"The Willow, sacred to the Moon Goddess, is a tree who loves water the most. Water is an element very connected with the Moon, which governs the oceans' tides and is associated with emotions as well. The Moon Goddess is the giver of dew and moisture generally. The Crane bird, a bird of the waters, and connected to feminine energies, is known to breed in 'Willow Groves.'

"In Greek myth there is a story of a 'Fairy' high in the mountains in Boeotia, Greece, called 'Mount Helicon.' This mount is known to have a 'Fairy' called the 'Fairy of Mount Helicon,' which took its name from 'Helice,' the Greek word for willow. Winds are known to blow strong there, and often poets are found in the willow groves, as the sound of the willows in the wind there gave inspiration to the Greek poets. Therefore 'Willow Tree' is sacred to poets."

The Seer held up her hands and said, "This is a good place to pause. Dream on what has been said."

Just then the wind picked up in the "Willow Grove," our place of dreaming with the "Willows of Enchantment." The Willow Tree Seer, pausing now, was walking slowly about our circle. She had her hands clasped behind herself, the wind ruffled her pale leaves and hair, and her gown of silver-green caught a breeze and twirled as she walked. There was a slight smile upon her pink lips, and it felt to me as if she were in a Dreamland of her own. The others in our group of Keepers, Fairies, and Dreamers seemed content to chat among themselves. I was only interested in watching the Seer, guessing about what would be next on this enchanted island.

It was brighter in the sky than when we started, and I had a view beyond the trees that made up the grove of willows. I could see a small hill close by; vivid green and lush with grasses, it had a very soft shape to it. I thought it curious that there were no trees growing there. I decided later I would go to investigate.

Hearing voices off to the left of my view, I turned and saw Fairies gathered. One reached to the drooping boughs of one of the trees and pulled them aside. It was like the Seer had done for my Dreamer friend and me at the start of this program, pulling the boughs to the side like a curtain. There was a sudden sparkling light. Slight and small she stood; I had to stand now to get a better view. People were oohing, and the voices were rising.

"Who is she?" I asked someone near.

They answered matter-of-factly, "Why, the Fairy Queen, of course!" They moved off to be closer; I was astounded and could do nothing for a minute. I looked to my Dreamer friend next to me; she was also stunned! Both of us looked to where the little Queen stood; one could not miss her as small as she was. The light around her was almost blinding.

"Is this real?" I asked my friend. All she seemed able to do was nod her head yes.

We both looked again. She was walking now, and the Willow Seer was with her; the Fairy Queen was a vision of iridescent hues, greens and watery blues. There were silvers woven in her garment, and she was adorned with pearls.

The Seer and the Fairy Queen were together next to the well. The Seer held up her hands for quiet and asked everyone to be seated. The Willow Seer said, "How fortunate we are to have this special guest! May I introduce to you the 'Fairy Queen' of this enchanted island. She has asked to share with us her connection with this land and the Willow trees! I am honored; I give you the 'Fairy Queen'!"

A platform of tree boughs had been put together for the Queen to stand upon; she was escorted now by several fairies that assisted her. Her loveliness and strength came through the light that she shed onto all in the circle. Everyone was excited, including me! Still in a speechless state, I watched as the small Queen began to command the group to attention. Here was I, in a glade in the woods of an island, with nature spirits and fairies and the Willow Seer. And to meet a Fairy Queen! This was truly amazing! Dreaming certainly has its benefits!

The "Fairy Queen" speaks: "Dreamers, Dreamers all! I am honored to be with you! I would like to assist the Willow Seer in explaining 'The Way'!"

The "Fairy Queen" may be small, but her voice was grand and musical. When she spoke, her green eyes scanned the circle, checking the Dreamers, leaving sparks of fairy dust as she moved back and forth on the platform. The pearls on her crown of silver were sparkling with iridescent light. Mist from the grove swirled near her and somehow seemed a part of her greenish-blue gown. A beauty from the forest. After a pause she continued.

"By that I mean the 'In-Between States' of being. 'The Way.' Awake in waking reality but not quite, still lingering from the Dreamtime state. 'The Way' of living a Dream makes one's days magical! How do you do that? I hear you all say. Easy for you! I heard that comment too. Well, your choice! There are certain windows of opportunity; this is one! You may open your hearts and eyes and learn, or you may stay where you are. Think of it this way: when in the wood watching a bird fly, we are impressed and wonder where it is going. We can keep our eyes glued and track him consciously. Or we may turn away for an instant, giving our attention to some distraction. When we turn back the bird has gone and we have lost the connection we had. Where do you want your attention? It is really that simple, and with practice one can find 'The Way'!

"Dream states are precious. The Willow Tree Seer and I are here to help you connect to these Otherworlds of being in Dreaming on a constant basis and we can show you worlds beyond what you ever thought possible and still keep you grounded in the waking reality of your life. This last part is important because where you spend much of your waking reality is where you are needed the most; the world needs the Dreamers and the Healers to be 'The Way Showers'!

"Well, Dreamers, what do you say? Are you ready to commit and step through the window? Do you know where your attention is? I cannot hear you!" said the "Fairy Queen" in a husky, deep voice.

Then there was a round of applause and laughter as the Dreamers responded loudly with "Yes!" The little Queen seemed pleased as she paced the platform. She looked to the Willow Tree Seer and then said, "Looks like we have some committed Dreamers!"

The Willow Tree Seer simply smiled.

Smiling and now completely still, the Queen continued, "Willows prefer to grow near water and fords; this gives the tree the feeling of being between the worlds. These 'In-Between States' and places are told in countless legends and stories. Many magical events, battles, and decisions are made at the fords, riverbanks, or beaches. The teaching is to remember these kinds of locales when you do your journey work with Willow! Use the images, see yourself crossing the riverbank, maybe carrying a willow basket or weaving a willow wattle fence. These vibrations help one tune with willow. They are symbols that will help with your healing workings."

I noticed the group around the circle nodding their heads yes. I too agreed that the use of the images would be helpful. The Queen began again.

"I need to explain the 'Ogham' for Willow, as it is an intricate part of this Celtic way of divination. One of the names given to the willow in the 'Word Ogham' is 'Alonglus,' meaning 'Strength of Bees.'[8] For the Celtic people, bees were considered to be from the Otherworlds and their ordered society was seen as a model for humans. Another word associated with the Willow tree in the Ogham is 'Cuchulain'-'Beginning of Loss,' referring to the realization of our own consciousness of the Otherworlds and the ability to let go of ties with this world. It is said that when one can truly do this, 'The Way' is opened to the other world realms."

The Fairy Queen was quiet. She motioned for a couple of her companions. They were next to her instantly. I felt the love and the respect they had for their Queen, and I watched the fairies assist her to the ledge of the well. What a perfect picture this all made, definitely something out of a fairy tale, I thought. All watched as she adjusted her skirts and her pearl accented crown. Now she began again.

"This term 'Beginning of Loss'-'Cuchulain' is about the ties with this world, letting them go and nonattachment. Wow! Easy to accomplish, right?" She looked around the group. There was mumbling in the background shadows; not a Dreamer came forth with an audible comment.

"Much as I suspected!" said the little Fairy Queen. "Yes! I know that you are able to give away objects you do not need. You all know this too! Remember the Willow Tree Seer is here to help. However, the real lessons come when we give away the abstract. For instance, correct attitudes, ideas, or bad habits. There may be unhealthy relationships with people or circumstances; these things are abstract and sometimes hard to even name. When we give away what is not right, not working in the makeup of our daily life, we begin to nurture our true soul nature. Then we heal and of course become more at one with the spirits of the Otherworlds. This is what our dear Willow Seer knows. She can help with giving away. Listen to her, and call upon her!"

The Fairy Queen, silent a minute, looked to the Dreaming crowd. Ever so slowly, she began anew. "Ah! There are, however, many tests! I can hear your questions...Will you really be able to give up a lifelong unhealthy relationship just like that? Gaining spiritual advancement; is this what I want? You may answer a quick yes! But when the time arrives to make the changes, it is usually difficult. Ponder this a moment as I move around the grove."

Now the Willow Grove was abuzz with the Dreamers commenting to each other about what the Fairy Queen had shared. The Queen was in conversation with the Willow Seer, a beautiful interchange with laughter slipped in. Other Keepers were also with them, shaking her hand and speaking softly. After a few minutes the drums sounded; it was time to be back in the circle.

The Fairy Queen was in the center now. The Willow Tree Seer was on one side, and a few of the Keepers were on the other. The Fairy assistants were right behind her. The Queen came forward and said this: "I have very much enjoyed sharing and being with you all! But alas my duty calls, and I've fairy dust to make and children to impress!" There was laughter all around. She smiled beautifully and after a moment held out her hand to the Willow Tree Seer. In a loving voice, the Queen said "My dear friend, I give the teachings back to your capable hands! Remember, Dreamers! Willow is here to help you with any dilemma!" Looking into the eyes of the Willow Seer, she said, "As long as you live, and even after, shine and be radiant!"

The Willow Tree Seer put her hands over her heart and bowed to the little Queen. She then said, "With many thanks from all of us here. I am deeply touched that you came!"

Then the "Fairy Queen" turned to the Dreamers and gave a blessing. "May your eyes be always open. May your hearts overflow. That which enchants will also protect. May this you always know!"

The Queen then threw up her hands and then blew kisses to the Dreamers as she and her entourage left the center stage of our "Willows of Enchantment" grove. I saw a couple of the fairies hold back the curtain like boughs of the Willow for their Queen. She paused a moment and, with fairy dust, waved a thank-you to us all.

Everyone was cheering; some had tears in their eyes. I sat back down. I too had tears in my eyes. Quickly I leafed through my journal to a clean page and began to make a sketch of this magnificent little "Fairy Queen," not ever wanting to forget her glow of iridescent hues, green-blues, and silvers with the mist encompassing her being. A tear dropped to my page and mingled with the dew drops that were her.

The Willow Tree Seer was at the front of the fire, which blazed and crackled. The fire keepers had certainly made sure we would have light and warmth for our enchantment here. The large "Weeping Willows" of the outer circle trembled in the breezes; this was a signal to the Seer, it seemed. She held up her hands as the soft drumming slowed.

"Apparently, Dreamers lead a charmed life! The Fairy Queen rarely gives so much of her time, but as I look around, I see the softening and the opening of 'The Way' beginning to take hold! We have all benefited from her enchantment."

The Seer was now down on the ground with knees and hands touching the Earth. There, in a trance and in a language I did not understand, she spoke to the lands beneath. I knew she was thanking our Mother Earth, the source of us all. She stood and the fire near her roared. The Seer was ready to speak.

"'Leave behind, leave behind, whispered the Willow on the bank.' I am here, Dreamers; Willow is here to help with this dilemma. I offer a foundation and a way to develop confidence with your skills. Dream journey work has one move beyond what is familiar and travel into unknown waters without fear. Remember the mention earlier of the 'Strength of Bees'? Bees know how to organize and to plan ahead; with our Dream work we can track ahead to the future, gain the information we need so we are more prepared for the unknown. Then with the suppleness that is a part of Willow, we can be flexible. Willow reminds us to bend and, when needed, to cut back, let go! This allows the new to surge and grow. Yes, change is hard, especially the relationship kind with those around us. In our Dreaming work, we are coming to the lessons of knowing our soul path, our desires. The Willow Grove can be of help; as one searches for truth and light in a dense forest, we may yearn for the open and expansive vistas. Remember there are things to be aware of in deep wooded areas. The gnarled roots may trip you. However, it would be good to sit with and Dream with those roots. What might be holding you back? The roots of the Willow may furnish you with a way to let go of an old holding pattern. Ask the tree how you might move onto the open place with more light. Remember the roots can help to keep you grounded, but know when it is your time to move and balance in the open light places."

The Willow Seer was quietly staring at us all, hands clasped. Then she began to move toward a large, tightly woven basket and pulled out several long, wet branches.

"These branches or stems have been used from ancient times by the Celtic peoples in the making of a boat called the 'Coracle.' The very foundation of these boats is willow, and the boats have the ability to carry us to new lands. What a craft this is! Both the boat and the ability!

"Earlier in your studies here on the Nemeton, I believe you learned about the Alder Tree. If you will recall, the Alder tree's wood was used for pilings in water. Now we have Willow's ability to build upon and make a floating craft. Wow, this is big!"

The group of Dreamers was laughing and talking some; there was an excitement building.

My friend said, with eyes glowing, "What will be next?"

The Willow tree Seer was ready to continue. "We turn to the woods over and over again to provide warmth and light for our homes and hearts. We turn to the waters of Mother Earth to sustain us in so many ways. With our Dream work we can call upon these same things to help us create a magical life.

"Keep in mind that the magician is always aware of what is both above and below the water.[9] Make this your practice too. Use your peripheral Dreaming capabilities as a kind of compass to help know where you are. When we connect to the worlds of the magician, he can help us to sail forth, move in a new direction. This is where I come in. Call upon me, the Willow, if you feel ready to sail!

Dreamers, on the average, have always been magicians! However, when in the early stages of novice Dreamers, one may wonder, can I be magical? Of course you must always answer, Yes! There is a vast paradox, that which is and yet is not, but is!

"Ready yourselves; we are about to take a Dream journey to the 'Lands of Willow.' Dreamers, please, if you would, summon this visual image. You are walking alone in the woods of the Willow. So many growing closely to the edge of the small river. It is a warm summer's day with the sun's noon rays reaching through the glen. Feeling energized by this special place, there are things on your mind that need sorting. Looking for a place to rest, you see through the brush; there is a glow around a large Willow. Drawn to this tree, you know it to be Grandmother Willow; she has beckoned you. Her enormous roots travel down the bank of the river. The river's edge is alight with verdant grasses and daisies. Willow's weeping boughs skim the top of the river's water. There is some creaking as you walk around her and then nestle into her trunk to rest; she is an Ancient One. You tell her thank you for allowing time to be with her and offer her tobacco, if you have this, or a simple piece of hair, as your appreciation.

"Sitting quietly, you note the sound of the river is soothing. There is more creaking, and then speaking in musical tones, the tree begins talking. You are in disbelief...but know it to be true!

"Braving up, you respond, 'Dear Grandmother Willow, I do hear you. But I do not quite understand, and I so much want to understand!'

"The Ancient One replies, 'Dear one, Dreamer that you are, open your eyes and heart a bit more. Yes! That is it. You have it, always did. At this juncture, trust is what is needed.'

"You smile and say, 'Thank you. I do believe I can hear you very well.'

"'This is good, Dreamer!' says the Grandmother Willow. 'You will need to take another bold step into the unknown and sail in waters uncharted by you; there will be gifts of this Dreaming. Be prepared to face what comes in these uncharted waters, no matter what. You are brave and able to show your strength. Remember 'the strength of bees'! You are protected and the magic waits! Dream through these waters, Dreamer, I am here.'"

The background drumming became very loud, then softened as the three beat recall came; I began to stir. Where am I? Confused for a minute or two, and looking around slowly, other Dreamers were stirring from their journey to the 'Lands of Willow.' I began to put the confusion aside as I realized I had just done some amazing journey work with the Grandmother Willow. I thought, I have come here to this grove to Dream and learn, and now I have just experienced a Dream within a Dream! This is definitely a magical place.

The Willow Tree Seer looked about and said, "Dreamers, where is your attention? We spoke about this a little earlier." Everyone was front and center now. "Yes! Just what I like! All eyes on me!" There was a ripple of laughter.

"Each of you traveled alone and far to the 'Lands of Willow.' Later on there will be time for these Dream reports. But the lesson for now was about 'your ability' to connect to the Otherworlds of Dreaming! It was important to be able to travel alone, be alone with the woods, the river, the Willow and feel in comfort doing this. As the Willow Tree Seer and a Keeper here in the Nemeton, please know that these efforts do not go unnoticed. Journeying calls attention and assistance from the realms of the 'Otherworlds.' Their task at hand is always to watch voyagers and to guide them on their way. As I look around you, I sense a glow around your auras. I can say quite assuredly I feel each of you has begun to open to the magic of 'The Way'! As a point of reference, the Willow is said to be an orphic, divination tree. Remember to use me this way."

The Seer was holding up her ring finger. Twisting her hand around, she said, "Who can tell me what this is?" There were a few crazy comments and laughing, none of which were the answer the Seer was seeking. "Come on now. Certainly someone must know!" she said, still turning her hand about.

Finally I raised my hand a bit; she caught the motion. "Yes, Dreamer, let us hear it!" she said with a confidence in her voice that I really did not feel.

I stood slowly and said, "I believe, your ring finger represents one of the 'Five Finger Tip Trees' and that the Willow tree is the tip part of that ring finger." I sat down fast, feeling the new attention; my face had surely gone red.

"Now that's what I am talking about! Thank you, Dreamer. I am happy to know that you have done some homework. This is exactly what the tip of my ring finger is. In the Ogham, the third finger tip represents the energy of 'Saille'-'Willow.' This becomes a wonderful tool to use when a certain kind of energy is needed. Looks as if many of you have a homework assignment on Finger Tip Trees!

"The time has been fast; the light is full-fledged daylight and time now to close! What a wonderful assortment of Dreamers and Dreaming we have had. I am happy that we could spend this time together within the 'Willows of Enchantment'!"

The Willow Tree Seer then gave a bow and to the group said, "May the Green Light of Fairy and Willow Light Your Way, Dreamers All!"

Mist began floating on the air shimmering with amber color. The drumming sounded the closing, and the sun's warmth was felt. I said quietly to myself, Thank you, and now I know extraordinary.

Putting my things together, I was about to leave, when the breeze fluttered the weeping boughs across the grove. Through the trees I saw the small hill I had seen earlier and knew I needed to see this closer. I walked to the edge where the willows stood guard. Pulling back the drooping boughs, I moved through the curtain to the outer world. Keeping my attention on the small grassy hill, it didn't take long; I was there. So green, so beautiful, only small, slight plants grew on it, and the shape was very rounded. Curious, I began to walk around this hill, admiring as I went, then...I stopped suddenly! A door? There is a door in the hill! I went closer to look, my heart racing! The door was shaped by a stone lintel that was held by upright slabs of stone. Along the side of these were pieces of stone laid horizontally in place without any mortar. The opening felt to be a part of the Earth. It felt like an entrance to her womb; could that be? So many thoughts raced through my head. I wondered if I should enter, but stood fast. I heard a voice and jumped. Having traveled far into Dreamtime, I was not aware that anyone had come.

Turning around, I discovered the Willow Tree Seer was right there. She said, "Permission must be gotten; there are words that must be said!"

With a sense of relief, I said, "Dear Seer, I am glad it is you! I got frightened! What do you mean, Permission?"

"Ah!" she answered. "There should be a little reverence and fright!"

"What is this place?" I said, moving around and touching the stone work on the outside of this hill.

The Seer cocked her head and said, "It is a 'Chamber,' a 'Sidhe,' a round barrow fortress belonging to the 'Aes Sidhe,' the prime magicians of the green isles of Ireland and of Scotland. It is of this world and not; it is part of the land of Fairy!"

I could not speak.

The Seer began to laugh. She said, "Not to worry, dear Dreamer. Not many come this far! I am, however, glad that you have!"

Finally I said, "But what is it for? Can we go in?"

She did not say a word but shook her 'Saille' finger at me. But then she said, "Not at this time, Dreamer! But there will be a time that you will know this 'Chamber.' For now we must go. However, keep me in mind with your finger tip!"

Then, before I knew what had happened, I was back at the main lodge, looking at my watch.

Someone said, "Breakfast is being served."

I recalled the Seer saying at the start that the return would be much easier. I need to do some Dreaming to fill in the blank spaces here!

ASH

Karen Silverstein

"N"   Nion

THE ASH
LETTER "N," "NION"
OGHAM:

STATISTICS FOR:

"The Ash" genus- *Fraxinus* (the Olive Family)

~Grows throughout North America and many places on the globe.

~Grows to a height of 80–130 feet tall

~Bark is smooth, greenish-gray, which cracks as it ages.

~Leaves are long and on opposite sides of its stalks, with as many as thirteen leaves.

~It has distinctive black buds. Its seeds are known as ash keys, which grow in bunches, each with a wing. The tree is often found growing near water.

~There are approximately 65 species.

~~~~~~~~~~~

THE ASH: HOW USED IN THE WORLD

~The wood from the ash is used all around the world in construction and for shelter. Also used for furniture, boats, agricultural implements, baskets, and all variety of items. Ash is one of the nine sacred woods used in the kindling of the Celtic Beltane fire celebrations in the spring. Ash is used for making mundane and magical tools.

~~~~~~~~~~~

MEDICINAL AND PSYCHOLOGICAL

~The Ash is used for physical healing and magical workings. The Leaves can be made into tea for a mild laxative and diuretic. The bark is known as a liver and spleen cleanser and can make the immune system stronger. Ash is known to keep away serpents and to protect against their bite. If there are no snakes to be found, Ash can be used instead to keep away nasty people or those who criticize, are impatient, or are psychic vampires.

~~~~~~~~~~~

SACREDNESS AMONG THE GROVE

~The Ash is the fifth tree in the Ogham Alphabet: "Nion"-"N"

~The Ash is associated with healing magic.

~KEYWORD- Integration

~Month- February 18 through March 17

~ Planet- Mercury

~The Ash tree stands on either side of the Willow and Hawthorn within the Grove.

~"FINGER TIP TREE" location- "Ash-Nion"-"N" is on the upper tip of the little finger.

DREAM OF "NION," THE ASH TREE SEER

Being a novice Dreamer in some ways is easy! I know so many things already and many times do not even have to work hard; I just know! This is what I am thinking to myself, sitting cross-legged in this circle. Boring!

I hear the Ancient One talking, but my attention wanders. The Ancient One is teaching other Tree Dreamers, Seers like me. I notice some of these Dreamers are busily taking notes. I would rather doodle in my journal and be in the nearby ocean, floating on the surf.

Suddenly I scream! "Where did the water come from?"

The Ancient One standing above me is holding a beautiful bowl carved from Ash, now dripping water.

As I look at her with the bowl curled under her left arm, she says this, "If you would rather be in the ocean water, go!" Blubbering through my surprise, I manage an apology. My attention has been brought back to the present. The Ancient One says, "Now that we are all here," she was looking at me, "you need to bring yourself together in a closer circle. Each of you has been studying and practicing your abilities. We will share with our circle what we have learned."

Fear is gripping me now! Learned? Practice? I scurry around my brain for the things I have been doing in regard to study. The memory banks of study are dim. I realize that I have no problem with wandering through these beautiful woods, catching the sun's rays, noticing the fairy mounds and the beings who reside in them…Drifting off a bit, I catch myself! Pay attention! I say to myself. Staring now into the sun, its warmth is comforting, I pause and listen.

The young Tree Dreamer next to me is demonstrating her ability to use the element of water to see, to scry, as divination. She is able to Dream with the water for future information. Wow! I think, she is good. Now I am really worried! What will I share?

I hear the Ancient Ash Tree Seer addressing me…"Your turn!" she says.

Staring into the sun now, I ask for help from my guides…At least I remember to ask for help.

Then quite suddenly I hear a voice saying, "I know how to make the element of fire flow through my hands!" The voice is my own. From the vantage point of my Dream body outside of myself, I watch this scene of me in quiet disbelief.

I tell the others in the circle: "First you grow your roots, the ones at the bottom of your feet deep, into Grandmother Earth. Next you travel back up the trunk of yourself and out through your branches to Grandfather Sky. You ask for spirit's help. Grandfather Sky directs you to Grandfather Sun. You hold your hands out to him."

I begin to feel confused. Slowly, slowly, I feel my Dream connection fading. I feel the Sun's energy withdrawing; I am not sure what is happening. However, I still see myself attempting to make fire spurt out of my fingers! Nothing, Nothing! The telling of this experience closes.

I am embarrassed and tearful now and long to run to the ocean. Ready to sprint, there is a hand on my shoulder. The Ash Tree Seer is saying, "All is not lost; look at your pinky finger!" As I look, I realize that there are ashes at the tip of my small finger; it is smoldering some! Looking at this and then the Ash Tree Seer, I am in awe.

The Ash Tree Seer tells me, "It is OK! Training and discipline are what is needed. But the ability is there. Could be you are meant to be an 'Ash Tree Seer'; of course this remains to be seen. As we check 'The Map of Your Hand' chart that we have all been studying, we see that the Ash resides at the top of the small finger, 'Nion,' and her letter is *N*." Stopping a few minutes and looking at me intently, The Ash Tree Seer goes on to say, "The Irish Gaelic word for Heaven is 'nionon' and relates to the Gaulish goddess 'On-Niona,' who was worshipped in Ash Groves." Her eyes are still on me as she finishes speaking.

Feeling a lot better now, I stand up. "What does this mean?" I ask the Seer. "What am I to do now?"

She answers, "You are to dig your roots in deeper, my dear. Going through the tests are not easy, my daughter. Natural ability is a gift; however, you must decide how you will manage this. Will you take the course as a 'wilder'? One who just does, without training, boundaries, or regard to who may be hurt in a backfire? I trust you will be ready now to commit and realize that you will be able to do wonderful, exciting, healing work. But know that it takes responsibility, time, diligence, and patience. Believe me, from here forward you will not be bored. Your task now is to integrate what you are learning from the three worlds: the lower world, middle world, and the upper world. Rewards and gifts come when we stay on the Dreaming path. Use your inner resources to strengthen your willpower to become a true Dream Tree Seer."

My mouth is open; I feel I'm in a daze. She is right; I had not thought about the regard for others; I have not been as smart as I thought. Finally, in a breathy voice, I say, "Dear Seer, I am ready to leave my 'wilder' stage. I am ready to commit."

The Ancient Seer is pointing now to a beautiful Ash tree nearby. Her face has no expression at all; her voice is very sharp.

"Go! Find your branch and make the tools that will serve your path; make your spear. Use the spear first as a weapon to cut away the parts of yourself that do not serve you now. Next, turn the spear over a few times, and it will become your wand. Your magical wand, for your magical workings. Next, thank from your heart the spear and the wand and give an offering. Be certain that you know which tool to use when. Thank the three worlds and the Dreamtime for connecting you to Grandfather Sun. For without their help, you would not be in this present space." The Seer pauses and looks me up and down; I feel nervous. Finally she continues.

"Next, go to the reflecting pool near the Ash tree. As you dream into this mirrored surface, ask for help! Ask for the ancient Goddess Bridgit. She is the guardian spirit of the water and the keeper of the Sacred Fire. She is waiting for you and can show you the way through the last winter month of the year. A usually wet month, when we need to rekindle our fire for spring."

The Ash Tree Seer turns abruptly. Looking to me briefly, she says something and then moves toward the others in our circle.

I am stunned! Slowly at first, but deliberately, I walk toward the beautiful Ash tree. The last words I hear from the Seer are about using the weaver's beam to pull your life threads together.[10] I can do this! I think to myself. I too can be a Tree Seer.

Remembering the Seer's instructions, I find a comfy place next to the reflecting pool and the Ash tree. Taking out my small carving knife, I find a fallen branch and begin to craft this into my tool of the spear and the wand; from time to time I look to the reflecting pool. I feel a comfort here and think about how I have been doing my work of late only with half a heart. I feel as if this shakeup from the Ash Tree Seer has given me a second chance, and now I have new fresh eyes.

As I work on my spear/wand, a message comes to me. I am told that the spear is not only a warrior's weapon but is the magician's symbolic weapon, which equates with the wand, which represents the will of the magician. The deliberate use of the Ash wand will set one onto their path. The "Spear of Ash" is for willpower. The Ogham letter "N"-"Nion" comes from a root word meaning, "A thing produced." It is sometimes referred to as the "Weaver's Beam." The Spear/Wand is a source to work healing with and for changing energy. I hear that some feel the Ash tree represents the World Tree-Axis Mundi with its roots very deep into the Earth. The spiral buds are linked to the spiral of life. The pole of a witch's broom was often made from Ash, offering protection and strength. In Celtic lore, the first man sprang from an Alder tree and the first woman descended from a Mountain Ash. In Celtic lands, Ash was often found growing near holy wells. In Scotland, oaths were sworn beneath the Ash, along with the Oak and Thorn. The Ash Tree helps with willpower, trust, and commitment.

I stop my daydreaming and realize I had just been given enormous amounts of information. Not quiet sure what to do with this, I just look over my handiwork of carving. I really like what I had just heard about willpower and commitment; I could really use some of that. As I turn my new tool over, I know I have made a good start here with my carving work, but there are still blemishes and rough spots to work on. I look into the reflecting pool and realize I need to really work on the blemishes and rough spots in my Dreaming path as well. That makes me smile, and as I look into the water. I think I see the face of the Ash Tree Seer smiling back at me from the water's surface! I turn around quickly, but nobody is there...I do hear laughter, and I laugh back. Then I begin again working on my new tools, including my Dream self.

Looking to the reflecting pool again, I remember to ask for the Goddess Bridget and give an offering from some of my packed sandwich, the bread of life, I think. Then the Dreaming becomes stronger, and I can feel the Goddess. She will help me with my threads, and I hear something about the "weaver's beam," knowing how to become one's own magician for self or another. I hear her say I can learn how to weave skillfully the threads that are my own gifts. She will guide me to finding my will to do so! I have so much still to learn!

HAWTHORN

Karen C. Silverstein

"H"   Huath

THE HAWTHORN
LETTER "H," "HUATH"
OGHAM: ⊢

STATISTICS FOR:

"The Hawthorn" genus/species- *Crataegus oxyancantha* (from Geek "kratos"-hardness; "akantha"-thorn).

~Grows throughout southern and northern Europe and eastern and central North America.

~Grows to a height of 45 feet.

~The bark is grayish-brown, flecked with small scales, and covered in sharp thorns. Leaves are on alternate sides of twisted stalks, giving a similar appearance to small oak leaves. Their fruit is berries.

~Number of species is at least eight.

~~~~~~~~~

THE HAWTHORN: HOW USED IN THE WORLD

~The wood is good for burning and is said to make the hottest of fires. All parts of the tree— berries, branches, seeds, and flowers—are used.

~~~~~~~~~

MEDICINAL AND PSYCHOLOGICAL

~The berries are used as a mix in a cardiac tonic. Its leaves and blossoms are made into a tea, used for anxiety, appetite loss, and poor circulation.

~The Greeks and Romans saw the Hawthorn as symbolic of hope and marriage, but in medieval Europe it was associated with witchcraft and considered unlucky.

~~~~~~~~~

SACREDNESS AMONG THE GROVE

~The Hawthorn is the sixth tree in the Ogham Alphabet: "Huath"-"H"

~The Hawthorn is associated with Otherworld workings and transitions.

~Month- May 13 through June 9

~KEYWORD- Intuition, prepare

~Planets- Mars and Venus

~The Hawthorn stands on either side of the Ash tree and Oak tree within the Grove.

~"FINGER TIP TREE" location- "Hawthorn-Huath"-"H" is on the thumb at the bottom of the nail.

DREAM OF "HUATH," THE HAWTHORN TREE SEER

This night, I had been told, was a "Spirit Night," of which there are three. Others are Midsummer and Samhain Eve. Maybe this is why I am so suddenly tired, I thought to myself as I scaled the last of the steps into the lodge; my room was close, thank goodness. I had felt anticipation for this day, not really knowing why.

One of the Keepers, speaking of energy this morning, said, "Everything a person draws, actually reflects a flow or a challenge to what they are drawing." What did this mean, anyway?

Closing my door, I got ready for a nap. I was feeling beyond tired. I had several quick Dream flashes of events and of messages being given to me but didn't have any idea what they meant. What was going on? I decided to light several candles around my room. As I was lowering the window shade, I could see the Dreamers making the bonfire ready for the Beltane Eve Festival. It looked beautiful from here, but first I needed to sleep!

Scooting down in my feather quilt, I heard a voice say: "She will come into her power within four years."

I drifted off to sleep; this is the dreaming that followed:

They approached by witch light; I was seated under a hedge, too afraid to move. The skies were mostly dark, but my spirit eyes could see plainly. But what am I doing here? I moved a bit for some comfort and scratched myself on the thorns of the hedge. Again I had a glimpse, small and quick; is it true? Had those been Fairies? Had they really come?

Someone was telling me, "Stay centered, removed from drama, stay connected to your resources. Do not succumb to temptation or doubt!"

"What on earth? What is that?" I said not so quietly, but then I turned, and out of the hedge itself, one of the Seers appeared. "Oh! Seer, I am sorry, I meant no disrespect!" She was not very tall. How did she come from the hedge? I wondered to myself. I noticed a sweet aroma, her smooth, oval face was ageless; her expression was nondescript.

"None taken, Dreamer!" answered the Seer. She had offered her hand to me and continued, saying, "No need to hide; you are safe. I am the Hawthorn Seer. Come with me now." She pulled me up from the hedge.

I felt another thorn graze my leg. She moved deftly ahead, but I kept up with the Seer, curious about where we were and what she wanted with me. Of course I knew I needed to learn about this Ancient One of Hawthorn, that is why I am here at the Nemeton. But Fairies? Not being able to hold my tongue, I blurted out, "They are not real, are they?"

"Are they or not? However, you will never see this place the same again. Now keep up with me!" The Seer had answered in matter-of-fact voice.

"I am unsure!" I said, running to keep abreast with her.

"Ah! The edges of reality do blur!" answered the Hawthorn Seer.

"It is just that…" My voice trailed off. We were now next to a mounded green hill, lit only by moonlight. There was activity all around, wood was being stacked near the bonfire, a pole was erected nearby, and the "Fey," as the Seer called them, were busily hanging ribbon garlands from the top. I noticed there was a grove of trees, semicircular in shape, just beyond the bonfire. We had stopped and the Hawthorn Seer was speaking to someone. Wondering what trees were in this grove, I moved a little closer to see them. The largest were definitely Oak, then I saw smaller ones, like the hedge I had started out from. Must be Hawthorn, I said to myself. And the other, I am not quite sure.

"That would be the Ash! Yes, Dreamer, the three, when growing together, are said to be the 'tree fairy triad' of Britain. You may have heard the expression, 'Oak, Ash, and Thorn'! This is often used to invoke the spirits of the "Fey"—the Fairies! Where the three trees grow together, one may see the fairies." The Hawthorn Tree Seer had come up to me without a sound. I was beginning to realize she knew much about magic, and I probably need to loosen up!

I responded cheerfully, "That is amazing! Everyone is so busy. I do know that it is Beltane Eve, but I had no idea about the Fairies being involved with the festivities."

There was no reply. The Hawthorn Seer moved her head slightly. She was shorter than I, with a very full feminine figure. Her auburn hair was arranged in a bun with ringlets around her face, with white flower blossoms tucked here and there. Her dress was white taffeta with russet embroidery in braided fashion at the hem and cuffs. The same braid edged the scooped neckline, but there were red berried jewels sewn into this.

Admiring her as I was, I was startled when she said, "I do know you are in a Dream, but it would still be best for you, Dreamer, to stay focused. I have Dream teachings to share!"

I know I turned bright red and wanted to say something, but it seemed we were off, and she was all business now. We walked a bit and came to the round green hill, not high, but covered with lush green grass and a few small plants. I could see the boughs of a full, white, flowering Hawthorn off around one side. We did not walk that way, no. Following the Seer, I climbed behind her partially up the hill. She stopped and looked around; taking her russet shawl off, she shook it high, and then it fluttered down onto the soft grass. Smoothing it some, she turned her hand in a gesture to be seated. I did! There was no talking for a few minutes; I looked around and took deep breaths to compose myself. In my scan from this hillside seat, I could not see the bonfire or the fairies; I supposed this was on purpose. Was I that unfocused to the Seer? I instantly resolved to be present!

The Hawthorn Seer said, "Dreamer, you are my only pupil for now. You must understand that the appearance of me, the 'Hawthorn Ancient One,' comes only spontaneously and infrequently in a Magician's work. And a Magician-Dreamer-in-training is what you are doing at this point. Time that you get this, Dreamer!" She looked at me hard; I held her gaze, and we understood each other. Satisfied, she looked away.

"You must know that I should never be sought after. No seeking of the energy of Hawthorn; never! Let me explain. If Hawthorn does come, it indicates something started on at another level is taking effect and there could be backlash that may arrive, so be prepared. In one's magical training, even though backlash is not wanted. Be thankful. Having some warning helps. But before I continue into the workings of Hawthorn, let me ask, are you aware of why we meet on this Beltane Eve?"

I knew that my eyes gave me away as not really knowing why. But I made a verbal attempt; in a clear voice, I answered, "I believe that the Hawthorn is very connected to the spring-summer seasons, and Beltane helps start this season."

She gave me a smile; I felt glad that I could say something. She adjusted her skirts and began.

"Well, that is a beginning. This is good, Dreamer. Beltane is an ancient Gaelic festival, celebrated for centuries in Ireland, Scotland, and the Isle of Man, also in other Celtic areas of Wales, Brittany, and Cornwall. This celebration actually marks the beginning of summer. It is known that the 'people of the Goddess Danu,' called the 'Tuatha De Danann,' and the Melesian races originated this festival. The great bonfires would mark a time of purification and transition. This then heralded the hope of a good harvest later in the year. The celebrations were accompanied with ritual acts to protect the people from any bad spirits from the Otherworlds. The fires are lit on a central hill for the evening festivities. The people make boughs to hang on the doors of their homes. These 'May boughs' are usually made from the branches of the 'Whitethorn'-'Hawthorn' tree."

My eyes were wide with interest. I felt confident. The Seer continued her magical telling.

"Part of the ceremony is about the 'May Queen and the Green Man.' There are a few versions, but the essence is that the 'May Queen's' beauty invokes a longing in the 'Green Man'; he attempts to catch her; this is forbidden! The Red Men catch him, and he is ritually killed by the 'Handmaidens' of the Queen. They strip him of his bulky winter form, and then he is thrown to the Red Men, who dance him around to a clockwise position and present him to the 'May Queen.' Looking at him, she takes pity on him and brings him back to life, in the form of a young, green sapling! There is singing and merriment, and he is then crowned at the base of the bonfire! Summer has begun its season of growth. All have been awakened by the 'May Queen and the Green Man.' As we look at this story, we can see the potent powers of death and then rebirth. The Hawthorn's role is the protection of the union of the Sun and the Moon, male and female. The Hawthorn promises cleansing, fulfillment, guardianship, transition, and fertility. Tall orders, but I do so willingly. I am blessed to have this honor."

The Seer stood quickly, but for a moment I thought I saw the glistening of a tear or two in her eye. Such a beautiful story; my eyes had also welled up. I waited; there was only silence. Then she walked some down the hill. I stood up and wondered, Is she abandoning me? Should I go also…No, her shawl is still here. Be calm, I said to myself, this Seer is not easy to know; yet I am here and she had said this was not something to happen often.

I could still see her; there was a split tree trunk in front of where she stood. Apparently it was an altar of sorts, as she began lighting candles there. Should I do the same? No. I stood fast; she turned and came partway up the hill. She looked into the night sky, now ablaze with starlight, consulting some, I was quite sure. After a brief moment, she walked toward me, her hands to her breast, and began once more.

"Inner Strength: finding it is key. Many times our way forward is obscured by heavy fog, things that want to deter us. One must be able to draw on their own inner strength and trust in their own steps. Directions for this are hard to find; instinct is what will guide one forward to calm." The Seer was seated again, with her knees up and arms around them.

"Let's go back to our earlier conversation, about possible backlash, because when it comes, inner strength is what we call upon!"

"Yes!" I answered, "That was just before the story of Beltane Eve."

She replied, "That is right. Now we will talk of the workings of Hawthorn. As a Dreamer- Magician, we learn that our weapons are energy and its magical use. The most important rule a Dreamer-Magician must have clear is this: Any magical workings that use new energies, started by the magician, will set up a chain of events, and the magician must always be prepared for any backlash.[11]

"What do you mean? I know this is your question here! A good example to give would be the Dream healing work one does for another. For instance, the Seeker, the person asking for Dream healing, may have a pre-set idea of what will happen if she consents to have the Dream healer journey to heal her condition, whether this be a physical or an emotional dream healing. This pre-set mind of the Seeker may not be the same as what comes in the Dreaming. The Seeker may not be prepared for the answers that are brought back by the Dreamer who has just journeyed and tracked for the Seeker's personal healing needs. The trained Dreamer-Healer is ready for this possibility with the Seeker. The trained Dreamer requires the Seeker to honor their dreaming by doing something in waking reality that is a physical action. The Dreamer is then ready with suggestions that provide support until the Seeker can work the results through on their own. Of course, at the onset of the healing session, it is made clear beforehand that the Seeker should have a support system in place within their home circle. It is not wise of a Dream healer to be the only support for the one seeking healing, as this may prove to be a drain upon the Healer. Make a note of this!"

There was a momentary pause from the Seer, with some staring at me, before she went on.

"In the process of the Dreaming for healing, upon conclusion of the Dreaming, the Healer provides the Seeker with the gifts of information obtained from within the dream. And not always are they shiny and beautiful. They always must be truthful and shared in a good way, never using hurtful words. Sometimes the truth found is not pleasant. The

Dreamer must find a way to share what she feels 'the Seeker can handle.' It is not necessary to give gory details; simply touch upon what is found with good words. This is a powerful way to help another in their process of healing themselves. The Dreamer must have ready suggestions for the Seeker: ideas that may help them change what they wish. This is part of the honoring. Always we speak to them about this, saying, 'If it were my dream...!' Which we know allows the Seeker to either take the suggestion or not. The Seeker, if they are honest, will have various forms of backlash because they have been moved off their center and the energy is at play. This should help illustrate the kind of situation that might produce what I like to call 'energy backlash'! The Seeker of the Dream healing has been given suggestions about what they might do for their follow-up and further their healing. These suggestions have been given to them by you the healer. The ball is now in their court.

"But what about the Dreamer-Healer ?" The Hawthorn Seer was looking right at me as she said this.

Suddenly I realized I should reply. "The Dreamer ? I do not I follow you here, Seer." I said this quickly; I was confused.

She laughed some and said in a much lighter tone, "I thought not! You must realize, Dreamer, that we are working with energy ,and when we move energy, there is a chain of events that affects not only the 'one who has sought healing'! The Dreamer, who provided the Healing Dream through her journeying, is affected by backlash at times too! We must be ready for the possibility of feeling out of sorts or irritable. What might we do? I will tell you. 'Dream track'! Reenter the Dream, track back to whatever it was you started with your energy work, and view the chain of events. Dream travel with your guardians. Were your defenses low in some area? Recall any energy of your own that may have leaked; bring that energy back to yourself. Be precise; do any clean-up. Leave no residue on yourself, wash your hands, shake them out, smudge if need be. Sometimes feelings of fear, tension, or depression may manifest. Hawthorn will then be contacted from the Otherworlds to show the Magician the things that must be seen, sometimes unpleasant things. The other world beings remind the Dreamer that this is the 'backlash,' and it is only temporary. To the less experienced Healer, these experiences may feel difficult. As we become more adept, we realize the temporary backlash is actually a positive indication that the earlier magical actions have been successful!"

The Hawthorn Seer paused and seemed to be checking on me. I smiled at her and let her know I was OK. The Seer then continued.

"Often to the newer Magician, this backlash feels like a 'psychic attack' from those trying to disrupt 'the work' at hand.[12] This is rarely the case. Replace this with positive affirmations.

"Now I will speak some of the Celtic Ogham and Hawthorn's position within this form of alphabet and divination. The Gaelic name for Hawthorn is 'Huath,' and its letter is *H*; it is the sixth letter in the Ogham. The letter *H* has a different function within the rules of Gaelic grammar, as neither consonant nor vowel. The same is said when working 'Tree Magic.' The Hawthorn should not be used by the Dreamer to invoke Otherworld journeys or rituals. The letter *H* increases the power of the other letters. The same energy applies when working with Hawthorn on a spiritual level. Once a Dreamer has set something to work, they must expect a period of disruption; do not let this be upsetting. This time can be used for the positive. It is time for the Dreamer to relax, reaccess and to contemplate. A time to 'Dream' the success of their magical workings. Although for the moment, things may appear to be confused."

The Hawthorn Seer was standing now, waiting for me to catch up with what she had said. I tried hard to show I was getting this. No room for doubt, I reminded myself.

She was ready to continue. "This may seem very contradictory, but please remember that: ENERGY IS NEUTRAL![13] And only appears negative or positive depending upon your reaction to it! Let me put this another way: Consider how your mood or attitude may spread energy to others. If you fear loss, your fear spreads. If you enthuse, enthusiasm spreads. The power that drives both scenarios is exactly the same. Your choice!

"Immediately after magical workings, while recharging, one should reflect upon what felt successful or where we felt lack. It is best to truthfully acknowledge these things. This is how we strengthen qualities for the next time you might need them. Call upon Hawthorn to increase and improve your spiritual aspirations through understanding the reason behind any suffering you may experience. Then be sure to know how to turn the whole experience into a positive, useful one."

The cracking sound of wood and the smell of wood smoke caught my attention The Seer stood up and was stretching. I did the same. I shivered some, as the air was now cooling.

The Seer leaned down and picked up her shawl. She threw it around my shoulders, saying, "You are an attentive, Dreamer! There is much about me that is serious, and there are many that stay away, not able to grasp what I am about. I have seen how you are able to be still, listen, and be ready to receive. This is a gift; not many have that stamina. You are beginning to find your place in the world." She smiled at me as she took her hand away from my shoulder.

Tears rolled down my cheeks; she wiped them softly away. I leaned into her and gave her a hug. "Thank you, dear Hawthorn Seer. I am honored to be with you this day!"

The Seer turned her head in the direction of the bottom of the hill, saying, "Let's move near to the altar; you may want to light a candle there for the evening's festivities."

We moved to the altar. I lit a white tapered candle. When I turned to the Seer, she was pulling over the second of two wooden chairs. There was a small campfire that was being stoked by the Fairy folk, and we were offered warm tea from one. She moved quickly, smiled sweetly, but did not speak. I found that I would really love to speak to her. Maybe later! The Ancient One was ready to begin once more.

"There is much myth that surrounds me. I am sure you have heard some about being both scary and unlucky, but sacred as well. Let me explain what I know to be true."

She took a minute and sipped on her tea, then adjusted the colorful lap blanket, provided to each of us by the Fairies, across her knees. "The Hawthorn has numerous names in the British Isles: 'Whitethorn, 'May blossom.' And its red fruit, haws, have been called 'pixie pears' because of its association with the fairy folk. As you know, the Pilgrims traveling to the New World took the name of 'Mayflower' for their famous ship. Isn't that interesting! In Ireland, Hawthorn is associated with Saint Patrick and still today is known as 'Saint Patrick's Thorn.' It has also been said of Hawthorn in legend that it may be the 'Glastonbury Thorn,' which flowered on the old Christmas Day, January 5, in the times of the Goddess of Avalon. It then would flower again in May. Myth tells of Joseph of Arimathea, who was Christ's uncle, had brought his staff of Hawthorn with him, which is said to be from the very same tree as the 'Crown of Thorns' worn by Christ. When Joseph arrived in England, he put his staff into the ground, and this then took root in the new soil, becoming what we now call the 'Glastonbury Thorn.' The 'Crown of Thorns' is a sacred but not lucky association, as you know! This crown was brought there so that Christianity would flourish in England, and so Joseph built the first Christian church in Britain at Glastonbury. It has also been told that somewhere nearby he also hid the Holy Grail, which has never been found since!"

The Seer had spoken this last part in an excited voice. I felt her enthusiastic energy and said to her, "This is an amazing story. I have only heard parts. Please go on!"

Smiling, she continued the history. "In ancient Greece, crowns of Hawthorn blossoms were made for wedding couples, and the wedding party all carried burning torches of Hawthorn. In Greek myth, the 'Goddess Cardea,' who presided over marriage and childbirth, was associated with the Hawthorn. She was known as the 'White Goddess' and was mistress of the 'God Janus'—the month of January is named for him—who guarded all doorways and portals. As such, 'Cardea' became known as the 'hinge of the door of the year.' In iconography she is depicted carrying a bough of Hawthorn as a protective emblem. The 'White Goddess Cardea' was used in Ireland as well, and her task was protecting the home with sacred Hawthorn. It has also been noted that 'Cardea' cast spells with the Hawthorn tree. In Greece there is a saying, 'May is an unlucky month!' Hawthorn is associated with this month and is used for purification. The month of May is when the temples and images of gods were washed, and then Hawthorn was burned as incense to purify. Hawthorn became known there as the 'Tree of enforced chastity'!"

The Seer stopped again. She took another sip of tea and munched on one of the small cakes that had been brought. They looked good, so I had some as well.

"I would like to tell a little more about the Gaelic word for Hawthorn," said the Seer. "The word 'Huath,' or 'Uath,' means 'frightful' or 'horrible.' Sounds awful, does it not! However, this actually indicates its magical virtues for those who work in magic. It must be remembered that working with Hawthorn requires a different tact than the other 'Ogham Trees.' When working magic, the trained Seer knows *not* to purposely call upon the Hawthorn as one might call upon another tree. You must know now,that Hawthorn is Not To Be Invoked by the Dreamer! Because the Otherworlds are the Only Ones Who Do! They send Hawthorn a warning that she might prepare for something, and the Hawthorn Seer always takes heed.

"Though Hawthorn is thought to be unlucky and has many superstitions surrounding it, the tree survives well. It is often found growing on Fairy Hills and thought to be a guardian of the 'Sidhe,' in Celtic myth. Hawthorn is thought to have been placed by the Fairies as a warning to humans. Despite its wild, gnarled appearance and formidable thorns, when in full bloom with its white sweet flowers in May, why, it is a sight to behold. Even if I do say so myself!"

The Seer was laughing, which was contagious! We both were very happy just then, and it was nice.

"The Hawthorn is often regarded as hostile and offensive due to its sharp thorns and tangled branches. However, these same branches can be defensive and protective, keeping at bay that which is trying to harm you. Much like a warrior, it is a protective tree and, after any difficulty, helps with backlash that may filter through. It is really a tree of good omen and hope. The Celts used Hawthorn on a physical level as a symbol for something hostile. The Celtic bards used this symbol in their practice of satire, the composition of verse describing an individual's bad points. This quaint means of attack was like talking in code and was thought to be a terrifying thing! This, to the Celts, was one of the worst things that might happen, to have one's character attacked. We must remember that there is tremendous power in the use of words, and this can be very damaging to someone. The use of satire was used by the Druids in the training of magicians. Only after many arduous years of training was one given the title of 'Bard' and then permitted to satirize others."

"Wow!" I said to the Seer. "You mean the bards would say the name Hawthorn to indicate a hostile deed of someone?"

"That is exactly the way the bards satirized a person. Of course, one needs to know the various meanings of the trees and also the context that this was done in! But, yes! You are correct, Dreamer."

The Seer said this with such a feeling of compliment to me I decided I would ask her something else. "Dear Seer, earlier you mentioned something I do not really know about, and I am curious."

She replied, "Yes! Go on!"

"I believe you said something like Hawthorn was planted or found growing on Fairy Hills and thought to be guardian of the 'Sidhe.' Could you tell me about this, please?"

"Why, dear Dreamer, we are seated upon a 'Sidhe,' just now!" She was chuckling at this!

"No way!" I responded, jumping up. "You mean to say this grassy hill is a 'Sidhe'? And the Hawthorn is here guarding this? I mean I guess I really do not know what this is!" Confused and out of breath from pacing and talking so fast, I suddenly slumped back down into my chair. I could hear chuckles still from the Seer; I did not see what was funny!

Then she stood and composed herself to say, "Dreamer, I have been patiently waiting for you to ask more about the wee ones! Now let me see how I can help you to believe more!"

I gave her a startled look. I thought I had come quite far in my belief in the Fairies. I could not answer, and I just sat firmly planted in my chair. The Hawthorn Seer was ready to explain.

"The name 'Sidhe' is a shortened name from the Scottish name 'Aossi'; this name means 'People of Peace.' The story of the 'Aes Sidhe' is centuries in the making and has been spread in many various tales throughout Scotland and Ireland. The myths tell of the Norse invaders who drove many Scottish inhabitants underground to live in the hills therein. It is said that they are a supernatural race. The 'Sidhe,' or the mounds in which they live, are made for the 'Fairy Race.' They are not part human and cute with butterfly wings as we think of fairies, *no!* This race is of far greater stature and power than we can conceive! Immortal and able to pass between worlds at will, with resources that are staggering and magical to a human. It is said that they are of the 'Tuatha de Danann,' the people of the 'Goddess Danu.' And they live on today and are visible only to those of pure heart who may have eyes to see them. They are blessed and I am one who holds the gates for their kind!"

The Hawthorn Seer had seated herself, and there was silence. In the wind I could hear the trees of the Grove and slight voices with laughter, and my nose perked at smells from the cook fires. I was here but not; I was in a Dream. But was this real? I had to know more!

I jumped up, almost knocking over the chair, saying, "*No* way! You mean I am here and able to be with an ancient race of fairies? I mean this is…is…Well, I just do not know what I mean!"

The Seer was up now too. "Magical! I think the word you are searching for is Magical! Looks like we may have a breakthrough, Dreamer. I will make a believer out of you yet! There is so much to take in here in one session; this is only a taste, and we have a festival to attend! Ah! There will be more insights gained there. But for now, I want to share these few things, and then we will go, as I know I am hungry and I can hear your stomach growling! Walk with me, dear."

We started away from the hill, the "Sidhe." I felt a touch of sadness. Here I was and did not even conceive of how precious this place was! The Seer linked her arm to mine as we walked slowly around the hill, then the bonfire came into view and she stopped.

"Discipline must be a part of every Dreamer's life; please use that as your guide when studying this intense path. Stay with it! You have a natural ability, and you will come into your own power in four years, no more. However, magic costs and one must be careful."

I blinked my eyes, trusting my heart to remember her teachings. We still were in eye contact; after a brief pause she continued.

"Hawthorn teaches us to tink differently. Its energy is designed to help one cope with fear, trepidation, and other difficult emotions. Hawthorn reminds one: Are you ready to take responsibility for spiritual progress? Please know that the Daghdha and I, as your personal guide, are there to help you."

We were silent awhile as we searched each others' eyes. With tears flowing, I began to thank her for this magical night of teaching. She pressed into my hand a stick; I looked at it in disbelief.

"Yes! May you find good use of this Ogham stick of the Hawthorn. My letter *H* is right there." And she pointed to that and the straight line symbols of the Ogham.

Then I said, "Oh, Seer, it is beautiful! Thank you!"

She answered, "You are most welcome, dear Dreamer. I believe it is time to witness the Fairies along with the 'May Queen and Green Man' firsthand, in the old way!"

We both laughed and moved toward the bonfire.

I awoke with a start from my afternoon nap. What was that? Was this a Dream? Where was that place? I got up quickly and went to the window. Dark now, the bonfire light filled the air with sparks of light and wood smells. I got ready to go; I was excited to be a part of the festivities. I was straightening the covers, when something tumbled to the floor. Reaching down, I picked up a stick—the Hawthorn Ogham stick! I traced the letter *H* carved into the wood. Sitting down, I thought to myself with a smile, That was real. I was there. I was Dreaming in two worlds, both real! This was going to be the start of a beautiful friendship, I decided as I remembered the Seer in her white taffeta dress with May blossoms in her hair... Of that I was certain.

OAK

Karen C. Silverstein

"D" Duir

THE OAK
LETTER "D," "DUIR"
OGHAM: ⊨

STATISTICS FOR:

~North American Oaks are divided into two groups, white and red oaks.

~"The Oak" genus/species- *Quercus alba* (white oak); *Quercus ruba* (red oak).

~Grows in most of the United States and many other parts of the globe.

~Grows to a height of 50–70 feet tall and 1–3 feet in diameter with a rounded crown.

~Leaves are 5–9 inches long. They are pointed, bristle tipped, and usually 7 lobed.

~The Oak is a "Keystone" species; more than five hundred other species of plants, animals, and insects are in symbiotic relationship with this marvelous tree.

~~~~~~~~~~

THE OAK HOW: USED IN THE WORLD

~The wood from the oak is widely burned, also used in construction worldwide. All parts, wood, leaves, bark and acorns, are used. Oak is used in spells for protection, strength, success, and stability, healing, and fertility. It is highly prized for health, money, potency, and for good luck. Acorns usually mature in two years and are a (nearly) untapped food source. They can be ground into flour and many other ways of cooking. Acorns have been a main food source for many nomadic tribes of prehistoric Europe. Oak is powerful for protection.

King Arthur's Round Table was said to have been made from a single slab of a giant oak.

~~~~~~~~~~

MEDICINAL AND PSYCHOLOGICAL

~The oak was used many ways for healing. From leaves and bark, a tonic can be made for astringent use on hemorrhoids. White Oak bark tea helps for sinus infection, unclogging congestion. Peeled acorns are made into potions to treat alcoholism, bad breath, and constipation. Oak is often used for divination workings.

~~~~~~~~~~

SACREDNESS AMONG THE GROVE

~The Oak is the seventh tree in the Ogham Alphabet: "Duir"-"D"

~The Oak is associated with protection, shelter, strength, and good luck.

~ Month- June 10 through July 7

~KEYWORD- Shelter, Protection

~Planet- Jupiter

~The Oak tree stands on either side of the Hawthorn tree and Holly tree within the Grove.

~"FINGER TIP TREE" location- "Oak-Duir"-"D" is on the lower tip of the forefinger.

DREAM OF "DUIR," THE OAK TREE SEER

Ah! The mighty Oak. The thought of this tree made me homesick. So long I had been away from my waking reality home, working at my training as Dreamer here in the Nemeton. In a flash I began to wonder, Are these memories of Oak from my current life, where a huge Oak of eighty feet stands as guardian? Or the life in which I roamed, Dreaming in the huge Oak Groves of County Forfarshire, Scotland? Each of these lives pulls and rewards me.

There was drumming now, I came back from my reverie. The Oak Seer, dressed as any ordinary man, was gathering the attention of the Dreamers. The nearby crow was cawing in his usual language. I looked and saw the mist was rolling in; crow always alerts me to change, and I thanked him for that. The mist thickened; I felt nervous. I was seated near one of the large granite boulders, a bit farther back than many of the Dreamers. I could hear and see everything perfectly well from my nesting place. I wasn't ready to be any closer to this Seer. I almost hoped the evening mist would engulf me; still I was here.

We, the Dreamer apprentices and novices, were told to gather in the Grove of the Oak, at the outlying ridge of the Nemeton. The note said to be there before dusk and ready to help with Dream circle preparation. I did what was asked, happily; yet I seemed to be holding a resistance to this program of 'Oak'! Was it fear? I was not sure. Now as I sat aside awaiting the opening ceremonies, I took in the view of the Oak Gove with wonder and anticipation of this beautiful place. One oak tree in particular was grander than the others, with huge sprawling limbs and a dense canopy. Its roots were as big as the branches, gnarled and twisted in different ways. Incredible, mighty, this Grandfather Oak, I was certain that it was this tree that the shape-shifted "Oak Seer" had come from.

The evening was warm, barely a stir in the leaves; it was Midsummer's Eve, and there would be celebration later on. Dreamers love to celebrate! Now, however, the drums were sounding, and we all joined hands in the opening of the evenings teachings titled: "Oak the Chieftain Tree."

He began speaking with a roaring voice; the far ends of the forest could certainly hear him talking and laughing; his charm was intoxicating. We all knew this large man to be the "Oak Tree Seer." He was different, he had shape-shifted, and I could not quite make out how he looked with the mist swirling. We all watched as he strode up and down under the canopy of the sprawling Grandfather Oak. Looking around the circle, all faces were glued to him; his charisma had captivated his audience. But me…feeling nervous. Why?

There was loud background drumming; the mist was lifting. The Oak Tree Seer was dressed in foliage; he wore a splendid leafy headdress of oak leaves and acorns. A mantel swung about his neck as he moved, made of the greenish cuttings of the inner bark of the oak. His torso lay bare in some places; other areas were covered with oak leaves that were sewn on like dragon scales. The Oak Man danced about, drinking and eating acorns, moving about in a riotous way, rejoicing in the Grove of the Oak, stopping at last near an old uprooted oak; the drumming was much too loud now. He paused next to the Grandfather Oak, laughing. He appeared a "Wild Man," almost hideous to look at. He is crude, crude! I said to myself.

There was silence now; he walked quietly around the uprooted oak. His feet were huge and left greenish footprints as strode about the grove. He seemed to be in contemplation; he felt crude to me. Most Dreamers were enthralled by his antics, waiting for what would be next. I sat in apprehension next to my boulder of granite laced with small garnets. I could hear the crow again; I stayed watchful.

The fire keepers had busied themselves earlier preparing a bonfire. I had not known that it was to be around this fallen oak. Someone came running in with a torch and lit the wood. Smoke puffed and sparks flew; the fire roared instantly. The Dreamers cheered and clapped, but where was he? After a few minutes, the cheering calmed.

He appeared as an "Oak Strewn Man" in the flames of the Oak. Walking from the flames, he spoke: "I speak through the Oak. I come from the land of enchantment, where one is free of ordinary conventions and free of space and time constraints!" He looked about the Dreamer crowd; he was somber and different.

I thought to myself, Has he been playing the Fool? Is he in disguise? I wasn't sure. I supposed this is why I felt nervous. I just am not sure about this Seer; he is not always what he seems. What had he said…"free of ordinary"? I suppose I may have trouble feeling free.

I stayed firm near my granite chair, thinking.

Someone near me said, "Certainly does like a grandiose entrance!" Another person said, "Maybe that is not it at all. Could be he is trying to get us to pay attention! Could be he wants to raise our present awareness in order to counterbalance the usual lack most people have in their attitude toward nature."

The bonfire had dimmed some. A few of the Keepers were standing near the Oak Seer, saying "Bravo! Bravo!" One said, "You have gotten our attention; let the magic continue!"

Then one of the Seers I had come to know and admire came forth, "The Hawthorn Seer." She had this to say: "As a fellow Keeper, who knows something about being outside the normal rule of things, and because of the order of the Ogham, I stand to one side of this tree, 'The Oak.' This has provided the opportunity to know him well. I am pleased to give this introduction on behalf of my colleague, the 'Oak Tree Seer.'"

There was a huge round of applause for this Seer. She was dearly loved by the Dreamers, and I knew that I would be happy to learn anything she might offer.

The Hawthorn Seer said, "The Oak, in Gaelic and the Ogham, is 'Duir.' The Ogham letter for oak is *D* and is the seventh tree in the Ogham. In the Gaelic poem of the 'Cad Goddeu'-'The Battle of the Trees,' one line says: 'The Door of the Druids.' This mention of 'Door' is synonymous for the 'Princely Oak.' The day of the week for Oak is Thursday, and it is associated with the number twelve. It is given that the Oak tree is associated with the Druids. Some Celtic scholars surmise that the root word of the word 'Druid' may lie in an old word for 'Oak.' Now let me tell you something about this 'King of Trees' and his association with Druid magic. Acquiring his knowledge is a very useful advantage for the Dreamer-Magician to have!"

With that comment the Seer seemed to be looking right at me. I turned away; my face, I know, was blushing. What is up with that? I thought to myself.

The Hawthorn Seer moved on. I heard her say, "The Oak tree has associations with Zeus, Jupiter, Hercules, Thor, and all thunder gods. To the Celtic peoples, oak has a very strong connection to the 'Daghdha'/'Dagda,' the Elder Chief of the Irish gods. The 'Oak King' is very connected to Midsummer Day, June twenty-first, and Solstice. The wood fuel of the Midsummer fires is always oak, and the fires of Vesta at Rome were always fed with oak and the need-fire is always kindled with an oak log. In Greece, the 'oak oracles' were introduced by the Achaean people, one of the main tribes that occupied ancient Greece from 1600 BC. They originally consulted the beech trees as the Franks did, but finding no beeches in Greece, they transferred their allegiance to the oak, which had edible acorns.

"'Oak' in the Celtic Ogham is considered one of the "Seven Chieftain Trees." Others are Ash, Holly, Hazel, Apple, Pine, and Yew. The calendar date from the Beth-Luis-Nion-Ogham Alphabet aligns the Oak tree with June tenth through July seventh. The Oak: 'I am a god who sets the head afire with smoke!'"

The Seer had said this last line with enthusiasm as she looked with affection toward the Oak Tree Seer. He of course was basking in the attention and waving his hands near the smoke of the fire. Everyone lightened with his joking display.

The Hawthorn Seer raised her hands to reposition the Dreamer's attention to what she had to say. "Dreamers! I've only a few more things to add before our 'Mighty Oak' has his due!"

The Oak Seer bowed and the Dreamers clapped loudly. The Hawthorn Seer continued.

"The name given in the 'Word Ogham of Morainn' for 'Oak' is 'Arddam Dossa.'[14] This is usually translated as 'highest or most exalted of bushes.' The word 'Dossa' can also mean 'sheltering defense' or 'protecting chief.' Be aware that the oak can be considered the highest of defenses, the 'exalted of chiefs' who offers protection! We must remember that ancient warriors of the Otherworlds, or warriors of this world, all at some point need shelter and the protection of a chief or king. The same applies to modern day warriors in the guise of magicians, as you are, Dreamers! Many go it alone for awhile, but eventually all need rest and protection. Which most certainly can be found in the shady branches of the majestic oak tree." The Hawthorn Seer now turned toward the "Oak Tree Seer." With love in her eyes and a heart singing voice, she said, "May we all come to know the 'Oak' as a place of rest, sheltering defense, and protection!"

The Seer went to the Oak Tree Seer, giving him a hug; he returned the embrace. She stepped back, clapping her hands, and said, "I present to you 'The Oak Tree Seer,' our 'High King of the Forest'!"

The entire group of Dreamers was standing, clapping, whistling, and very excited. I too had begun to smile and clap. I thought of some of the Seer's comments about a place of rest, protection…Suddenly I remembered something of childhood: seated beneath the shady branches of oak and feeling safe. Maybe I needed to look closer at myself and not prejudge this burly oak man.

By now the "Oak Tree Seer" was front and center. His clothing of oak was the same as earlier, still on the crude, wild side, but there was something different. I felt him to be natural a part of the landscape. Softly and in control, he spoke words of thanks to the Hawthorn Seer, saying, "My lady, you humble me!" He then gave her a gracious bow as if he were a knight.

I thought I remembered the word humble to mean "humus," which of course is earth. He spoke from the heart; he sounded like a king. I was impressed.

With a drumroll in the background, the clapping subsided as the "Oak Tree Seer" began his tale.

"Dreamers! Welcome to my Oak Grove! Some call me 'Chief,' some 'King,' and I am honored with these, but do not for a moment forget that it is the land that must be honored, the land that I am of and we all are from!"

The Seer was looking now at the Hawthorn Seer, wordlessly staring. There was a connection there I was sure, but you would not tell from the expressionless face of the "Lady."

The 'Oak Tree Seer' said, "Some of you may know that I, the Oak, am aligned with the realm of King, especially the 'High King.' I am bound to the land, the Goddess who connects us all. And as the Lady Seer has mentioned, I am at your command, as a 'protecting chief'! One deity you can consider to be you're 'protecting King' is the 'Daghdha,' the good god. It has been said that of all the trees, I, the Oak, am most closely connected with the Daghdha. I can tell you he has been my protector and console. He is the 'High King' of the 'Tuatha De Danannn,' a race of supernatural beings. Mighty in his powers and associated with a bottomless cauldron. The times he has been of assistance to me can not be counted! However, he may always be counted on! Call upon him."

The Seer was silent. He had moved near the bonfire and was adding oak logs that were stacked nearby; the fire crackled as he put them into the fire. Straightening up, he began a kind of prancing walk around the Grove. Oh no! I thought to myself. He has changed form; something is up. I nestled back against my granite chair.

He began to rearrange the mantel he wore and took off his leafy headdress of oak and acorns. He asked the Dreamers, "How do you like my hat?" He held this, twirling it this way and that.

Many funny comments flew back and forth. The one that caught my attention was, "Keep it on! It gives you a wild look!" Everyone laughed; I did too, but I thought of earlier when my comfort level of him was feeling his crudeness. I did not want to go there. No, not there!

Apparently the Seer thought otherwise, Next thing I knew, he said, "Perfect. I'll wear it! Now let's talk of this word you used, 'WILD'!"

"Oh! Goddess, help me," I said under my breath. It didn't matter; he went on. I scooted down into the rock, wondering where the mist was when you needed it!

Now the Seer strutted around the Grove, asking various Dreamers about his leafy outfit. I could feel some embarrassment of the women; I wished he would stop. What was this about anyway? Finally he found a place to sit on one of the tree stumps, quiet for a moment; thank goodness.

"Wild. I love it! Do you find me wild, I ask you? Do you, Dreamers, even know what the wild is? Do you? Or you?" He was pointing to various Dreamers as he spoke.

No one answered. There was a sense of uneasiness now. It was quiet except for the sparks the fire made, very quiet.

Slowly the Oak Seer began to walk; he then said, "First, let me give you some background. The Daghdha is an archetypal figure when working with oak on a spiritual level, but he is also very physical and graphic. On your own time you may want to read up on some of his antics. I will tell you this: he, like me, is associated with the rutting deer and is closely linked with the Earth on a physical level, which is emphasized in the many legends about him. These legends graphically detail his great appetite for food and sex, also detailing his crude appearance. The word for oak, used in the 'Beithe-Luis-Nion' Ogham, is 'Duir,' which sometimes is said as 'Dair,' a name common in Ireland. It's in names like 'Kildare,' of which at one time were huge Oak Groves used by the Celts as sacred sites. The word 'Dair' also has a second meaning that describes a rutting deer. Once again we can see the connection between deer and kingship. To the Celts, the noble stag was the 'King of Beasts.' Let us remember that a rutting stag was likely to turn on its attacker rather than run away, as deer usually do; therefore he was treated with respect and caution. The Daghdha legends also illustrate his close association with the 'Cauldron of Plenty' and the generous sharing of food, hospitality, and protection."[15]

The Oak Tree Seer stood still now, checking his audience for their reaction; slowly, silently his eyes spanned the Dreamers. Oh Goddess! I knew there was something here I was nervous about! I never have been comfortable with this subject matter, appetites, sex. I mean, what place does it have here! I would find out soon enough; the Seer was telling his Oak tale.

"Got your attention? Are you shifting some in your seats? Good, good! You should feel uncomfortable. But mostly the point is you should feel! OK! Feel! Oh, I know many of you newer Dreamers are surprised at best and confused when I speak of this emphasis on physical things. Here is the thing: how in the heck can we know where we are on this Earth if we do not explore the Physical? Think about that; think deeply. This may be a stumbling block for some of you who think we should only be dealing with spiritual matters. I need to tell you something: in order to experience one level fully, one must experience the other. I know, what does he mean? That is what you are thinking! I will explain. Listen closely; take notes if need be."

The Oak Seer paced some and then continued. "Dreamers! You must become deeply involved with the mundane events of your life! Do not live in your heads only! *No!*"

The group was quiet. I watched the 'Council of the Ancestor Keepers'; they were definitely holding the energy of the entire Grove caringly. For an instant my eyes caught those of the 'Ancient Keeper-The Moon Seer." I felt transference of love energy and was thankful. I suppose I was not the only one who felt discomfort here. As I scanned the people near me, I could see their apprehension and feel their reservations. I tried to shift love energy to them and could feel this transpire. Smiling to myself, I looked up, and the Oak Tree Seer was ready to go on.

"Dreamers, at this level in your path workings it is imperative to look inward. How do you feel about sexual desires, body functions and your constitutions? This is how you may come to truly know yourself and what you stand for. Should you find a wild side there, great! This is good; this is what it is to be living as an Earth being! The Earth has all kinds of attributes, including wild ones, and so do you. Yes! Dreamers, it is high time you know your 'Wild-Side'! Confused? Call upon me in your Dreaming; call upon the Daghdha. We can help to make clear these things as you begin to understand your physical side and your spiritual side, and our work then can continue with the balance of these.

Now, as these ideas begin to take hold, I know there are reservations. In our contemporary society, with many of you coming from puritanical upbringings, this for many presents challenges. Know this, a 'Dreamers Path' is a path connected with 'The Way of the Heart' and drawing upon your path working here allows one to overcome any drawbacks. And do not hesitate to ask for help!"

He turned slowly on his heel until he had taken in the full circle. Sending his eyes around, they landed on me. I drew back and lowered my eyes, but I felt understanding that I could not deny from the words the Seer had spoken. There was stillness now as each Dreamer was within their own dream, contemplating.

Suddenly the Oak Seer clapped his hands and said, "I need you! Each of you is needed and will be called upon as you go from this magical place of the Nemeton. Our work here is intense; the Keepers are willingly making you ready for the world...which needs the Dreamer Healers now, more than ever. There is more to tell. Come! Come in closer; let us form a tighter Dream circle to continue our work tonight."

The Seer had been waving his hands and got all of us to make a more compact circle; at first I was resistant but then realized I was being foolish and needed to stretch myself here. I grabbed my cushion and journal and found a comfortable space; this was sacred ground.

"These are difficult challenges here, I know. Once upon a time I too was confronted! But these challenges must be attended wholeheartedly; anything less would be inauthentic. We have another area to cover, about the Daghdha's attributes and those of me, the Oak Tree Seer. Attributes of generous hospitality and willingness to share the good things of this life, as symbolized by the ever-full cauldron. The Daghdha is associated with the magical 'Cauldron of Murias.' Its nature can feed all that come, whatever they desire; but cowards and liars would find the cauldron empty. A Dreamer must contemplate these challenges and answer, honestly, questions such as: Are you generous? Can you share with all kinds of people? Do you hold possessions, bad habits, or unneeded teachings because you do not take the time to let these go?

"Good questions! The answers need Dreaming upon, for most of you. Hold on to these in your journal and refer to them when you are ready to answer. These things must be worked out to be able to pass the tests with the level of Oak. There is a reward, however! Those of you who complete this test, the Daghdha will know, inviting you to his 'Cauldron of the Daghdha' and sharing what he has to offer. You cannot cheat! No! The cauldron will be empty to any who lie. To those who have learned to do their true work, it will appear full. Dreamers, you do have your homework cut out for you!"

The Oak Tree Seer walked to the bonfire, now low-burning embers. He piled on large oak logs; there was hissing and sparking and small chatter between the Dreamers. His tale of Oak began again.

"Let me be clear. The Oak, in regard to your Dream path work on the spiritual level, symbolizes the successful completion of your personal progress through the other trees up until Oak, within the Tree Ogham. Arriving at the 'Oak Grove' many serious lessons are behind you and you are wiser. Now is the time to 'Work' under the protection of the exalted King, which is me, 'The Oak'!

"The oak is associated with the planet Jupiter. In astrology Jupiter is referred to as uplifting energy. There is a dual nature to all planets, both positive and negative. The downside of Jupiter can be excessive or extravagant, self-indulgent behavior. These qualities are symbolized in mankind. The Oak also has these qualities, and it is up to the 'best in Oak' and the 'best in man' to integrate these.

"Oak can be an oracle to consult about what has transpired in an area where you may live. I am attuned to the long cycles of sacrificial kingships. Oak knows about the births, lives, and deaths in the service of the land and the people. Call upon me; I may be able to help with your questions!

"The Oak tree is a beautiful symbol of strength and royalty. During the seventh lunar month, June 10 through July 7, in the Grove of Oak, the Druids would carve a circle upon an elder Oak's bark. This carved circle was divided into four equal parts. This was done as protection against lightning. A practice still found today among some old foresters in Britain, lest the tree should fall. Oh Dreamers! Do you see how much I am loved!" The Seer stopped a moment and was prancing around, taking bows and carrying on with everyone! This was welcomed, as the lessons had been intense; we all laughed and lightened our moods. The Oak King picked up his thread and began again.

"Merlin, who was born in Carmarthen, Wales, lived among the oaks. Working from one of these magical Groves of Oak, it is said that he used one of the topmost branches to carve and fashion his magical wand. It has also been said that the Magicians of the Druids perform no rites without using the foliage of the Oaks. I must say, I do like that one!" Everyone had a good laugh. He raised his hands and immediately continued.

"The actions of the King and the Oak of the land were intimately connected to the fortunes of Ireland and Scotland for the Celtic peoples. If he, the King, behaved incorrectly, the land would suffer. This is certainly a huge responsibility to carry. But carry this, I do!"

The Oak Tree Seer was smiling at each of us, saying, "The lessons of Oak are a tall order, and, dear Dreamers, we really need to understand something here. There is a deep connection between the physical and the spiritual with your magical workings; at times this may be tricky to maneuver. Also there may be someone or something creating little fires of disruption in order to seek your attention and pull you off your path. You must work at being strong and keep yourself grounded at all times in this Earth plane! It is vital for your work and the good of all to keep securely anchored in this world. Make sure you do not let yourself drift into some fantasy world, traveling where you do not know how to navigate. You are very much needed here now!

"The Druids had much reverence for the Oak, especially an Oak in which Mistletoe would grow. Mistletoe grows in both the oak and the apple trees, and there is mystery surrounding this plant. The Mistletoe that grows on the oak produces white berries; the ancient Celts thought this to represent the sperm of the gods. So Oak became associated with male energy and procreative qualities of fertility. It has been said that the Druids, in great ceremony on the sixth day of the Moon, would gather this rare plant. The Elder Druid priest would be helped to climb the Oak tree and, with a golden sickle, then would cut the Mistletoe that then would fall into a white silken cloth held by other priests. This Mistletoe was then used with great reverence as an herb with special powers."

"Oh my gosh!" said one or two of the Dreamers. "That is an amazing story!"

"I know!" answered the Seer. "My life work is fascinating, is it not?" He had a huge roar of laughter from all. Finally, though, we all came back to some semblance of discussion again.

"Let me say this: 'who you are…is not the measure of your successes or failures; who you are is how you continue on immediately after your success or failures!' In the world of nature, we have all kinds of weather. Sunny days, ah yes! And stormy days, ah no! Now an Oak tree may sway and hold its ground through a storm; it may even loose a limb to lightning. But it does not then close its branches to those who seek shelter. No, it calls to those, animals or humans, 'Come, I can shelter and protect you. I offer you my humble hospitality'!"

The Seer was standing as he spoke. Around the circle I saw tears in many an eye. I know I was drying my tear-stained cheeks. This wild man of Oak was more than I had thought. He began again.

"Once one travels through the experience with Oak, we realize that we can become our own 'High King'! We understand that we have knowledge and experience, and finally we can now pass this to those who may come for shelter or protection. This is an awesome awareness to have acquired."

Just then there was commotion from the edges of the Grove, and the Oak Keeper walked over to speak with several of the fellows there. He then waved his hands, ushering them to come into the circle. In came men pushing wheelbarrows, four of them. The Seer then said, "How exciting! Just at the right time! Thank you, thank you, fellows. Yes, leave them right here in the center. Thanks!" And with that, the guys left our circle, smiling at us all.

Everyone was curious; we could not see the contents because each one was covered with a tarp. Dreamers were calling out, "What are the wheelbarrows for? What do you have covered up there? Come on! Tell us!"

The Oak man strutted about the circle; his leafy costume fluttered as he moved, a few oak leaves even falling to the ground. I wondered, How did he do this? Going back and forth as a creature of the natural world to someone looking as normal as your hometown school-mate? This was fascinating to me, and it seemed I was now feeling much more comfortable with this "Wild Chieftain Oak Man."

He stood now near one of the rustic red wheelbarrows and lifted the tarp a little. He said, "Perfect! But before we get into the mystery I have here for you, we need to discuss some tools. What I am referring to is 'Your Magical Weapons.'"[16] The Seer looked around for a response, and not having any come forth, including myself, he said, "Come now! Dreamers! Someone must have an idea here?" He seemed surprised and about to say something…

Shyly I raised my hand and ventured a quiet answer. I said, "Would you be referring to a wand, a magic wand?"

He turned on his large greenish feet and said, "Louder! We cannot hear you, Dreamer!"

This time I stood up and, with a deep breath upon rising, I said again, "A wand, a magic wand!"

The Oak Tree Seer smiled as he said, "Why, yes! This is part of what I mean! At least somebody had a partial answer. Thank you, Dreamer!"

I sat down fast. I was not ready for eye contact; my heart was racing, but I was glad I had gotten the nerve to answer.

The Ancient Oak Seer finally ceased his pacing of the Grove. He now said, "Well, since there seems to be a weak knowledge among us on this topic, we need to go into this right now. So please pay attention! 'The Magical Weapons of the Dreamer-Magician.' Two sets of weapons are important for your use: THE GREATER WEAPONS are Spear, Sword, Cauldron, Shield. The Greater Weapons are used for large group workings. THE LESSER WEAPONS are Wand, Knife, Cup, Stone. The Lesser Weapons are used for small or personal work, either inside or outside of self.

"These are the basic implements with which all ritual Work is carried out. Study these, become familiar with each one, know when which type of weapon is most appropriate. You must know this, Dreamers! Practice with your fellow Dreamers on their use."

The Seer was quiet, looking around as the Dreamers were taking notes in their journals. Looking at him, I felt he was dismayed at our progress here, but he said nothing to make anyone feel badly. He seemed to be ready now to move on.

"OK! Dreamers, please do get into this on your own time! There is, however, one of these weapons that we have learned something of here today. Who might know which weapon I refer to?"

A few people yelled out, "Cauldron, the Cauldron!"

He yelled back, "Now that is what I like to hear! Yes, correct! The Cauldron! At this point in your Dreamer training, some of you may become very drawn to the magical arts, and these tools of the magician will be like second nature to you. Not all of you will go in that way of path working. However, this is simply information that is helpful for a Dreamer-Magician to have under his belt. Also the actual physical weapons, if you intend that direction, will begin to make themselves known to you. They will appear when you are ready to know more and work with them. Please remember that NONE of these magical weapons are given freely, or without conditions. The Otherworld spirits are watching through the forest, and they take note of what it is you should have, and if you do not use them correctly, why…They simply just disappear from your use! A Dreamer-Magician must be pure in body, mind, heart, and spirit to earn what is rightfully yours. Think about these things. And know this: these are the same conditions of eligibility for 'High Kingship'!"

Everyone around the circle was buzzing with quiet talk; apparently this topic had really stirred up interest. I knew I need to learn more. Interestingly, I acquired a small knife years ago that has always felt magical to me. Although it has barely been used, it feels special to me.

With help of one of the other Keepers, the Oak Tree Seer pulled out a large wooden box. Now they were both passing out something to each of the Dreamers. I couldn't tell from where I was what this was. Why, it was a knife! As the Keeper gave one to me, along with sandpaper and a chisel tool, I looked them over, I said quite loudly, "What are we up to now?"

"Cauldrons, my dear, Cauldrons! This is the greater version of your 'Magical Cup.' This is the feminine principle, and this weapon has been searching each of you in your studies with the Oak. The teachings of Oak strive to balance both the male and the female energies. It is now time to fashion a 'Cauldron' for your own. Come! Take a look at what I have here, and then we will get to work!"

The Keepers helped the Oak Seer remove the tarps from the old red wheelbarrows. They were filled with oak rounds, rough bowls carved from pieces of oak. The Dreamers were thrilled; we each selected one that felt right to us and were instructed to get to work on making our own "Cauldron."

The Oak Tree Seer said, "Dreamers! You have all worked hard, and the Daghdha agrees you are ready to have one of your own for your magical workings. It is time to create a cauldron that will be meaningful to you on many levels of your dreaming work. Carve and sand away, and of course, please notice that it is made out of Oak. From the very Oak, that you see here—" He pointed to the fallen oak, which had now become part of the bonfire. "—which was taken down in a storm earlier this season. And in true Oak fashion, it is now gifting to you its beautiful wood. Oak is always reminding us of its generosity; remember that!"

All the Dreamers were laughing and talking as they settled in with their rounds of oak wood. I thought to myself, I will have my own "Cauldron"! Holding the rough hewn bowl, I kissed it for thanks. Suddenly as tears welled, I realized I was very happy and glad to know this amazing "Wild Oak Man"! Working on my carving, I invoked a little more freedom and joy for the physical in my life, to be a part of "my cup—my cauldron of plenty." I resolved now to really look at myself.

The Oak Tree Seer stood under the canopy of the huge Grandfather Oak. Looking at us, he said, "When you later admire these cauldrons, be reminded of the great strength and endurance of Oak. Oak tells us, 'Be of good courage and go forward with boldness!' Yes! Dreamers, you have done very well. I am thankful to each of you. And do not forget to call upon me, months from now, when you feel the need of protection or shelter!"

The Oak King strolled through the group of Dreamers crafting their personal "Cauldrons," stopping to chat and admire what he saw. Then he said, "I think we should all have enough time to at least smooth out the rough edges of your individual cauldrons before the evening ceremonies of Midsummer. Plenty of time! We will close our circle in about an hour. In the meantime, sand on!"

The Keepers gathered sitting together, talking and laughing as the Dreamers worked their oak wood. The firelight provided a warm orange glow' the mood was magical. I always love doing things with my hands. Ah! Another physical thing, I thought.

Looking up I saw the Oak Seer straight ahead. As our eyes met, I smiled, not so nervous now. Yes! In the Oak month, one can feel free as they please. I liked that thought. This was nice and felt right.

HOLLY

Karen C. Silverstein

"T" Tinne

THE HOLLY
LETTER "T," "TINNE"
OGHAM: ⊨

STATISTICS FOR:

"The Holly" genus/species- *Ilex opaca*

~Grows to a height of 65 feet but are usually trimmed to the size of an average shrub.

~The Holly grows throughout the globe in cooler climates. The brown bark is smooth; it is an evergreen tree with pointed leaves that are sharp. The trees produce red berries, which are poisonous.

~~~~~~~~~~

THE HOLLY: HOW USED IN THE WORLD

~The wood from the Holly burns well. All parts of the tree are used, but the berries are poisonous. The wood was used in the past for making spear shafts, and these were thought to hold magical powers. Holly is used as protection and for magic and can enhance other forms of magic in the workings. Often Holly is planted near a home for protection.

~~~~~~~~~~

MEDICINAL AND PSYCHOLOGICAL

~The Holly was used for many homeopathic remedies. The dried leaf can be made into a tea for fevers, bladder problems, and bronchitis. The juice of a fresh leaf can be used for jaundice. The juice can also substitute for quinine.

~~~~~~~~~~

SACREDNESS AMONG THE GROVE

~The Holly is the eighth tree in the Ogham Alphabet: "Tinne"-"T"

~The Holly is associated with a linking ability, evergreen aspect, progress, and protection.

~Month- July 8 through August 4

~KEYWORD- Progress, moves obstacles

~Planet- Mars

~The Holly stands on either side of the Oak tree and Hazel tree within the Grove.

~"FINGER TIP TREE" location- "Holly-Tinne"-"T" is on the tip of the middle finger.

DREAM OF "TINNE," THE HOLLY TREE SEER

Walking through the thinly scattered greenwood, I could hear the summer's south wind blowing. *"Follow, follow,"* I heard. But nothing was there as I looked around. Curious, I thought. Glad for my wrap, I shivered, pulling it closer. What got me out so early was beyond me right now; as I stood along the field's edge with the tree line of the wood to my left, I paused to see where to go. Again the wind blew; I could see the golden wheat fields ahead, with plants rippling in the early morning breezes. It looked like an ocean wave might, curling, rolling, rippling. Everything growing so beautifully, abundantly now at the height of summer. The evening would bring the "Lammas"/"Lughnasadh" festival. Tomorrow the first harvest of the season would be cut.

My ears picked up something, more than the rippling wheat; I turned toward my left, scanning the edge of the wood. There ahead was the fallen trunk of a tree covered in ivy vines and wild rose bushes. Next to this a small flock of starling birds were scurrying about. Again I heard, *"Follow, follow..."*

Intrigued, I walked toward the birds, though as soon as I arrived, they flew off! I looked skyward, asking, "What do you want?" No answer; now they were over the ridge. Turning my attention back to the fallen tree, I smiled at the beauty it contained with the ivy growing profusely. Shiny green, thick, large leaves that seemed to be protecting something there. I leaned down, looking closer, and smelled the wild roses. I picked one and put this in my hair. Just then I heard a different sound, something with a clinking noise. Distracted now from the ivy, I walked toward the sound.

Traveling to the sound of clink, clink, I walked through a fern glen, wet with morning dew. My imagination was expanding with the noises. Someone hammering something; maybe there are Dreamers mining for garnet. I laughed at this. But the garnet mine is the other side of the Nemeton. No! Maybe an old shoe cobbler? Talking to myself, I said, OK, now you are really over the top! But then I can attest to the fact that the fairy kingdom as alive and well, so...The clinking started to sound like clashing, and there were voices, excited voices, seemingly cheering.

Walking softly over the grasses that then became denser vegetation, I had to be more conscious of where I moved, as there was no real path. There were more oaks and hawthorns; the soil was sandy, even gravely. The noise level was increasing. I tried to go faster, but not wanting to be detected, I crouched down some. Scratching myself on a branch, I almost squealed but rubbed my arm instead. Moving away the branch, I saw that it was Holly with leathery, spiny leaves. "Ah, so it is you!" I said to the tree, still holding the branch. I noticed the tip was bursting a spray of new growth, green and glossy. Quietly I let the branch go behind me and saw that there were Hollies growing everywhere. Many were covered with bright red berries. It is beautiful; so I am in the "Holly Grove"! Realizing this, I finally looked ahead. I was still behind the foliage, but I could see quite clearly the small clearing. I took a deep breath and looked again…Is this "Sherwood Forest"?

In front of me were two men, or knights. I was not sure. They are sparring with each other, each having long spears. Clink! Clink! What on earth for? I mean, why are they doing this? Feeling angry, I mean, fighting…here? I looked around and half expected Robin Hood and Little John to pop out.

Next thing I knew, someone was saying, "Dreamer, Dreamer, you are just in time! The birds showed you the way, did they not? Oh! No matter, you are here. Come!"

Her voice was familiar. I knew it, but who is she? What is this place? Am I Dreaming? All these things ran through my head, and then I heard, "Of course you are! Dreaming, that is, and we have so much to Dream with!"

I did not answer her. She had gotten too far ahead of me. I moved quickly to be behind her, although reluctantly. She was saying that would be our spot, and she pointed to an area that had a green canopy type tent with colored flags around it. The chairs on the inside were filled with people, and some people standing, and all were happily cheering. I glanced to the open field and saw the two men running at each other with their lances or spears.

Feeling annoyed about the fighting, I stopped suddenly and stayed put. The woman in front of me was slight and airy feeling but was determined about where we were headed. She stopped and turned to look at me. In an instant it came to me: "Most Ladylike of Trees," the "Birch Tree Seer" with her shimmering and fluttering, dainty branches. Planted firmly to the ground, I said, "You are the 'Birch Tree Seer.' I know you!"

She turned around and, without a blink, said, "Yes, you know me, dear! However, in order not to miss this event, we must hurry." She motioned with her hand for me to follow and sprinted ahead. Her silvery gown and arms that seemed like thin branches were catching the morning light.

By the time I caught up to her, she was under the green canopy. Someone pulled two chairs out for us both. Various persons there greeted us warmly; it seemed were we expected. Not knowing what to do or say, I meekly looked around as I sat down. Someone handed me a cup of warm tea. What else was I to do? I took a sip. Beginning to get my bearings, I ventured glances to the field and around this lavish canopy. I saw familiar faces; although their names were not at the forefront, I knew I was seated with the dignitaries of the Nemeton, "The Ancient Keepers." Why had I been brought here was certainly not clear…A memory surfaced and something told me, *"Trust the dreaming."*

I took another look around, and the "Birch Tree Seer," sitting next to me, patted me on the shoulder and said, "Just enjoy the show!"

Enjoy the show? I sipped my tea; this did not bring any sense of calm. I looked around; no one else seemed distressed, and yet the men in the field were at each other. Curiously they looked to be enjoying this match; I mean, they were even laughing some! I began to study them closer before I asked more questions. The one to the right was a very big man. He had leaves for clothing that were covering his chest; his large feet were greenish, and his arms were bare. Upon his head was a helmet of sorts. As he moved closer to our tent, everyone cheered. I saw his hat more clearly before he danced off. Acorns! He had acorns woven into that headpiece! Surely this must be the "Oak Seer"!

I wanted to say something but decided to look over the other man instead. I turned to the left. This fellow was smaller, more wiry in his makeup. Although not as tall as the Oak Man, he was spry and quick. I watched as he maneuvered around the bigger fellow. With a twinkle in his eye, he now had the Oak man backing up toward our tent; he was on the offensive. As they both stopped and leaned against the narrow fence line of the tent, everyone held their breath, me especially so.

The smaller man said, "This makes two points for me!"

The Oak Man answered, "Points well taken, sir!" And before I could blink they were on the other side of the field!

"Do take your seat, dear. This will go on for a while."

Take your seat? I had not realized I was even standing. I turned to look at the "Birch Tree Seer," and with bewilderment, I asked her, "Is that the 'Oak Tree Seer'? And the other man is…who? Why are they doing this?"

Just then there was a round of applause. It seemed the Oak Seer had now taken a point, whatever that meant! Near the railing of the tent next to a brightly colored banner, I saw the "Apple Tree Seer." Dressed in red, she is the picture of a Goddess from Avalon, I thought to myself. I saw that her eyes met those of the opponent to the Oak Man. What goes on here? I wondered, turning back to the Seer next to me.

She had been speaking…"When you are ready, Dreamer, I will speak more!" The Birch Tree Seer had turned away.

I was embarrassed and said, "Oh, dear Seer, forgive me! I am confused with all that is happening here. Please do explain!"

"Explain! Why, there is not much to explain. This battle goes on every year, has been so from the beginnings of time. Dreamers must know this, and it is now your time to understand. Are you listening, Dreamer? No need to answer just yet…I would like you to observe, to feel. We will talk again in a minute. More tea?"

The 'Birch Tree Seer' had spoken with compassion; she did not scold my inattention, and I was relieved for that. I held out my cup and said, "Thank you…for the tea." I turned to look around the tent of emerald green, which was shielding the Sun's glare. The Ancient Keepers here were all dressed in their best; I felt as if I were a part of a royal court in the twelfth century British Isles. I laughed to myself, thinking, That is not so bad.

I could hear now more clinking coming from the center court. I turned to get a better look at the smaller man. Now who was he? He was dressed in shades of deep forest green; he wore green tights and a loose-fitting smock kind of a shirt of lighter green belted with leather. But shiny, small leaves with red berries were on this belt. I looked to his head and noted the headpiece was looped with the same shiny, green leathery leaves and red berries. The two knights, because for me that is how they seemed, were now up close. I saw this man in green easily now. His face was handsome, though flushed from this vigorous exercise.

Both cheeks red as apples, both green eyes twinkling, and for an instant he was looking at me with a wink, and then he was off. I could hear from across the field, "Point three for the Holly, dear sir!"

Why, of course! I said to myself. This is the "Holly Tree Seer"! Very excited with my realization, I turned to say so to the "Birch Tree Seer."

She had moved over to speak with the "Apple Tree Seer," and in her chair sat a different ancient one...He said, "You wanted to say something, did you?"

He looked me straight in the eyes, I knew this man! I was thankful to have that recall, but my answer was definitely flustered. "Oh! Seer, I didn't expect you there! Sorry, I am happy to meet you today, 'Rowan Tree Seer.'"

He smiled kindly and said, "Greetings to you, Dreamer! Now what was it you wanted to say?" He then sat back, crossing his legs. Dressed as a more contemporary man, he was not in tights. I mean, what man today wears tights, really?

I stopped my daydreaming activities and looked at him, feeling as if he had heard all my private thoughts. He smiled again. I looked away. Finally I answered him, "I simply realized that the shorter man in green is the 'Holly Tree Seer'! I have not actually met him yet in my workings here. I do hope I will!"

The "Rowan Tree Seer" looked at me with laughter in his eyes. "Of course you will meet him; this is why you are here, Dreamer! Are you enjoying the match?"

"Match? This is a match of what? I mean, nobody has told me why they are fighting." My voice had risen several octaves, and my hands were waving to express my frustration. Before he could say anything, I spit out another question or two. "For goodness sake, there are two tree men up against each other, and they seem to be enjoying this as well! For what? I mean, is this a battle of trees?" I had stood up and apparently called attention to myself. Someone started clapping, and a few others joined in. I sank down into my chair, embarrassed...I said quietly, "I just want to understand!"

I could tell the "Rowan Tree Seer" was trying not to laugh as he looked around. He slapped his knee and said, "She has spunk; we will give her that! Well, Dreamer, you have gotten part of it right!"

Then "The Birch Tree Seer" said, "'*CAD GODEAU'-'THE BATTLE OF THE TREES'!*" She looked at the Rowan Seer and said, "The match is about to close; the points are in the Holly's favor, six out of the nine. Let us all go to the front now, and our dear Dreamer can meet the contestants."

I wanted to find out more about this "Battle of the Trees," but apparently my questions would have to wait awhile. The "Rowan Tree Seer," smiling and offering his arm, said, "Shall we move to the front, my dear lady?"

I was impressed and put away any distress for now. I answered, "I would be honored, sir!" Once at the railing, all the others were clapping. I decided to get into the spirit. I felt like a lady in Avalon or Camelot! As I clapped, I realized this was yet another amazing adventure in my training as a Dreamer, here in the Nemeton. I finally relaxed and smiled in earnest.

Yes, this must be partly Sherwood Forest, I thought to myself as I watched the two Knights of the Trees bow and then shake hands with each other. I was glad they had not hurt each other. Apparently this was a game of sorts, done on a point system of nine points, and best out of—

I stopped daydreaming. Because then I saw the two walk toward the railing, and the "Oak Tree Seer" began to speak directly to the "Apple Tree Seer." The Oak Tree Seer speaks: "My heart is full from the season we have had, and the turning of the year is never easy for me! I have not given you away without a fair fight. I will hold my memories of walks in the moonlight, talks by the waters, of our Dreaming the future of the land who holds us all. In the Dreaming we meet my lady fair! We are now at the mid of the year, 'Lammas,' and now I give to you the man of the season who follows, 'The Holly Tree Seer'!"

With tears in my eyes, I looked at this ceremony and yearned to know more. With such empathy, I watched as the "Oak Tree Seer" leaned to kiss the "Lady of Apple"; she too was tearful. They embraced and stood back.

The Apple Tree Seer speaks: "We have helped many species to grow and produce fruits. Now the first harvest is upon us, the year turns, as we also must. We have set the seeds and have nurtured the Dreaming for our land!" She then turned toward the other man.

How does she do this? I wondered, stricken with a sadness I could not quiet explain. I watched as the "Oak Tree Seer" then took the hand of the "Holly Tree Seer" and put it over the smaller hand of the "Apple Tree Seer." He was full of enthusiasm, and she responded likewise. I admired her pale skin and the apple-rose glow of her cheeks and her smiling red lips. This was a fairytale image to hold. It was amazing to me how they were able to switch gears! Apparently involved in one relationship and then turning to the next. "The Holly Tree Seer" was ready to speak; his eyes glistened with tears that I saw clearly. I thought to myself, I guess the gear switching is not so easy. I looked at the "Apple Tree Seer"; she too had watery eyes. On they went with the ceremony.

The "Holly Tree Seer" speaks: "In a well-matched, fair fight, I have won, as I must each and every year! The turning comes and we move on to hold the future of the land. I thank you, dear 'Oak Seer,' for my due! You are a formidable foe, and more than this, a true friend I am honored to know! I shall watch over her well, and when the season of the time of falling leaves passes and you are in your winter branches, I shall be the protector and hold the 'Green of the Land.' My chariot of Holly awaits, dear 'Oak Man,' to take you into the land of the Dreaming!"

Watching the three then embrace and witnessing the audience cheering and clapping under the green canopy, it was all I could do to contain my sadness. I tried to mop my wet face with my hands.

The Birch Tree Seer was then handing me hankies, saying, "There, there! Change can be sad; Dreamers, however, know that change also provides new vistas and opportunities. Come! We have celebrating to do, and of course there are some who are waiting to meet you. As you are now ready, Dreamer, to progress in your Dreaming path!"

I looked at this amazing Seer. I was not able to hold back my thoughts and quickly said, "I am beyond sad…I feel devastation! How are they able to switch so easily their gears, from one way of being to another? How do these Keepers do it?"

We had been walking toward another part of the courtyard, in between the others who were there to celebrate. The Seer stopped and took both of my hands, saying, "Nature! Yes, nature, my dear, teaches us to turn with the seasons, and the 'Dreaming' teaches us with our training! To Dream ahead and therefore be prepared for what we may see ahead. Or to Dream to the past to uncover again the beauty of what has been. And the Keepers among us believe these timelines occur all at the same time! Ah! But that is an entirely different topic. Trust, dear Dreamer, that you will become more adept as we move on." She looked at me with smiling eyes and then let go one hand and pulled me along with the other. Again she said, "Trust!"

I could not say a thing; too much emotion to handle right now. I let her lead me, and she seemed fine about my not answering; I was glad.

The Birch Tree Seer was saying something else as we weaved through the crowd. "Where are they?" She had stopped to scan the people.

Standing idly by, looking over the scene, I realized everyone was having fun, talking, and eating interesting little cakes; my stomach rumbled.

The Seer heard this and said, "Of course you must be hungry, dear…Let's go to the buffet; we will find them there, no doubt!"

We came to a huge table with people helping themselves, complimenting the cooks, and taking more. The Birch Tree Seer had filled two plates for us both and then guided me to a place to sit. She then said, "I knew I would find you all at the feasting table!" She was half laughing as she put down our plates and gently but firmly pulled me close to the table.

Instantly the two men stood up. I was nervous; they were polite. One was talking: "So this must be the one you spoke of, 'White Lady'!"

He looked to me as he spoke, even though I knew he was addressing the Birch Tree Seer. I wished that his eyes would not look through me so, green as they were. I looked away, flushed and embarrassed. I heard another voice, one that I knew slightly.

It was the "Oak Tree Seer." He was cordially saying, "How nice to meet again, Dreamer! Have you met our lady here, the 'Apple Tree Seer'?"

Still so nervous, I hardly knew what to say. The Birch Tree Seer then put her hand gently on the back of my neck; I could feel a surge of energy. In a quiet, but clear voice, I said, "No, I have not, but I am happy to make your acquaintance."

I turned to the other man, who then offered his hand and said, "The pleasure is ours!"

Holding my hand momentarily, he, like the true knight he was, kissed the back of my hand. Oh! Dear! I thought to myself.

Just then the "Apple Tree Seer" came to the rescue and said, "Please, do be seated, both of you!" She then offered us wine to drink.

I hesitated and the "Oak Seer" said, "Go ahead. Drink. It will be good for you! May I now offer a toast to the turning of the seasons and to this new Dreamer who is learning the ways of the land!"

The man in green, the "Holly Tree Seer," added, "Here, here! To the 'Land of Dreams'!"

Everyone drank and ate. The food was great; I know my stomach was thankful. The four Keepers bantered back and forth. I had no idea what to say so remained silent. I did a lot of smiling and nodding though and hoped that was good.

After awhile, when the fruit pies had been eaten and we all felt a comfortable fullness, the dining conversation quieted. The Oak Tree Seer and the Apple Tree Seer stood and said they had things to attend too. Excusing themselves, they said they would find us later at the evening ceremonies. I smiled at them both.

The "Oak Man" stared hard at me and said, "Stay up with him on your walk, Dreamer!" He turned to leave with the "Lady Apple Seer."

"You'll do just fine!" she said to me and winked as they both strolled away.

Panic-stricken, I turned to the "Birch Tree Seer" with questions in my eyes.

"Oh yes! She will be just fine!" she answered as she patted the back of my neck. She had a broad smile and turned a little, eyes twinkling. I took a very deep breath and was about to ask the "White Lady" if she would be joining us, when she turned back to me.

She had a large satchel, and from this she gave me a journal; on the front was printed: "Notes from the Holly Tree Seer." She handed this to me along with a pen and said, "You both have so much ground to cover! I will find you later. Here, take the water with you." She leaned down and gave us each kisses on both cheeks and scampered off.

My heart was racing; I had barely spoken a word at our meal and had no idea what to say now! I could not help but stare at this handsome man who was young and ageless in his features. He was energetic and had such a sense of excitement for life. I wondered how I would keep up a walk with him, no less a conversation! Suddenly he was speaking, and I found myself still nervous.

"Well, it looks like it is you and I, Dreamer!" He stood up ready to go.

I remained in my seat for an instant, just looking...

"It's the tights, is it not? Contemporary Dreamers seem to have a block about my green costume!"

Not being able to hold back a smile with that comment, I laughed and so did he. The ice in me was melting some.

He was looking right at me. He had taken off his headpiece of holly and had folded this across his chest and said, "I am at your humble service! Let us stroll along the woodland path into the dense Grove of the Holly. I am told that is the best place to learn about me!" He laughed at what he had said and offered his left arm. I took it. He was so gallant, how could I not?

We walked some in silence through the crowd still lunching and socializing. The Seer greeted one after the other, and they all wished him good tidings. It was apparent how well liked this Keeper was.

The sounds of people began to fade, the forest sounds took their turn, and it was calming. Ahead I saw a small flock of starlings; they held their ground until we were upon them. "Must be good eating in that grass," said the Holly Seer.

I nodded and then told him, "I saw some when I started out this morning. I think it is this very same flock of starlings that made me aware of the path that eventually led me to find all of you!"

He smiled at me and said, "Very important, learning to read the signs and to trust in your intuition. Good work!" He pointed to the birds, saying, "They happen to be some of my gate keepers; it appears that they like you!"

The Seer was laughing and waved his hands at the birds; they fluttered some but did not leave. Then the Seer went over to a fairly small Holly tree covered in red berries. He spoke quietly to it for a minute and then returned with a fresh handful of shiny, green leaves that had many red berries. He then told me, "Only the female trees produce the red berries. Aren't they just lovely! She told me she wants you to have this corsage!" He then put the green and red spray into my hair. I was very touched. He walked off, checking this and that, not going far. Finally he said, "This will do fine!" He showed me where to sit alongside a fallen log. Continuing, he said, "We will stay here awhile and cover some basics."

My spray of holly had loosened; I took it out to look at it more closely. Finally I realized he was watching, and I said, "Thank you for this! She is very beautiful, the tree you got this from." I then folded my hands in prayer and bowed my head toward the Lady Holly. Then I pointed to where she stood, and the Seer and I admired her for a moment longer.

The Holly Tree Seer then began his lessons. "The eighth tree is Holly, which flowers in early July and produces berries shortly after. Traditionally, the Holly is King in the Forrest, ruling nature and its waning forces from midsummer to midwinter; then Oak King rules from midwinter until midsummer. Each battles for the hand of the fair Goddess. The mention of Holly appears in an old manuscript from the Irish, 'Romance of Gawain and the Green Knight.' In this story, there is a telling of the conquests that are fought by the immortal giant who is the Green Knight, whose club is made from a holly-bush. Another old tale from a Welsh myth, called 'Sir Gawain's Marriage,' says the Oak Knight and the Holly Knight fought every first of May until doomsday!

"From the old poem 'Cad Goddeu'-'The Battle of the Trees,' is a beautiful line about me, which says: "*THE HOLLY, dark green, makes a resolute stand; he is armed with many spear-points. Wounding the hand.*"

The Holly Seer had paused. I jumped up to say how beautiful that all was. "I think I am beginning to understand what happened earlier. This ceremony of a battle between you, the

Holly Tree Knight, and the Oak Tree Knight, has gone on forever in the way Celts believe in nature and how the transfer of the seasons is a transfer of a kind of power!"

"Why, yes, my dear Dreamer. You perceive some of what is happening here. Good. There is plenty more! Once Christianity began to take hold in the medieval times, various old customs were taken over. Saint John the Baptist, who lost his head on St. John's Day, took over the Oak King's titles and customs. So it seemed natural to let Jesus, as John's merciful successor, take over the Holly King's customs. Thus the Holly was glorified beyond the Oak. An example of this is seen in the 'Holly-Tree Carol,' a sentiment that derives from the 'Song of the Forest Trees': *Of all the trees that are in the wood; the Holly bears the crown.*"

"Wow!" I said to the Seer. "So many threads of history come from the trees."

The Seer smiled and said, "True, so true!" Then he continued. "The Holly is one of the seven 'Chieftain Trees' in the Ogham of Beth-Luis-Nion. Oak, Hazel, Ash, Pine, Apple, and Yew are the others. The name for the Holly in this Ogham is 'Tinne,' and its letter is *T*. In the thirteenth-month calendar form of the Beth-Luis-Nion, the Holly has the date between July eighth and August fourth. 'Holly-Tinne'-'I am a battle waging spear.' The word 'Tinne,' used in the Celtic Oghams, is thought to mean 'Fire,' derived from the word 'Tinder.' The wood of the Holly tree burns very hot, and its charcoal was used to forge swords, knives, and tools necessary for survival and protection. The old smithies and weapon makers were considered to be great magicians for their ability to use the elements of 'fire' and 'earth' to create these tools. It is believed this is the reason that the Druids associated the Holly with the element of 'fire.' Holly is aligned with the 'planet of Mars' and has the day of the week as 'Tuesday.'

"In another personification as the Holly King, we see he is often depicted as an old man dressed in winter clothing, wearing a wreath of a Holly on his head and walking with the aid of a staff made from a Holly branch. This is symbolic of the fertile interaction of the Goddess and God during nature's decline and darkest time of the year."

The Seer had stopped and moved to the edge of the tree line, then came back with a long holly branch. He adjusted his clothing and ruffled his hair. Then, putting back his holly wreath, he began to hobble in front of me. I started to laugh, saying he looked exactly as the old "Holly Man" that he had just described!

Next thing I knew, he shape-shifted once more. He seemed taller and his green eyes were surreal. He raised his right hand, and light burst forth in long rays from his hand! I could not believe what was happening. There was light coming from his hand! I was a little afraid but did not feel the need for flight, no, not yet. Deeply breathing in the afternoon air, I stayed motionless, waiting.

Seemingly in a trance, The Holly Tree Seer spoke: "There are boundaries between the waking world and the scared land, ones that I am obligated to uphold. These white beams of light—" He moved his hands around, and the light beams moved out to twenty feet! "—encompass our Earth and all her inhabitants. I help the Lady in her efforts to continually renew. She raises me up by her sheer faith in me. Many times I am confused and out of my depth, yet I do not question; I trust. I am bound to the Lady, the Goddess, and our Earth, as are the other trees of this sacred land. The Dreamers are an important part of our magical work; we communicate our needs to them, and they must share with us what the current humans need in healing. Together we Dream, we work, to make sure the peoples of the land do not reject her...the Goddess, as her work must be held in faith. Even when times may feel dark, we must know that the Goddess will endure. After storms, the sun always appears, as the moon lights the night sky and follows the day! It is so!"

The Seer slowly moved from his rooted place on the Earth, came out of a trance state, and was human once more. I must say I was relieved! Finally I took a breath. This all happened so unexpectedly; I do not mind saying I was shaken.

Apparently the Holly Seer realized this and approached me hesitantly. In a very calm and reassuring voice, he spoke. "There was not a better way for me to share what was needed, Dreamer! I have no intention of frightening you or hurting in any way. The fact of the matter is that I am a part of nature and the Goddess. Her power is awesome and can come upon one quiet unexpectedly! I believe that you need to experience a sampling of this power. I think that you got that!"

I slowly nodded my head and gave a small laugh. He seemed to breathe a sigh of relief; I felt that to be comforting and began to relax. The Ancient Holly continued.

"The Goddess is changeable. Why, just think of how the winds do blow, turning fast a loose leaf in the wind, while we look on, not knowing which way it might turn next. Yet we can count on her to bring us the water and the light that is needed for our plants to grow and produce. As the Holly Tree Seer, I have learned to balance and to be tolerant of changing conditions. I can endure the harshest of weather and yet still remain green! I have a strength few are able to develop. As such, I am who is called upon for protection in the second, darker half of the year when the snow can lay thick and the icicles stick to my leaves. The birds and other small creatures can find solace under my boughs."

The Seer stopped as he walked his path in front of me, then looked into my eyes with such compassion. I could not turn away.

"You must come to understand, Dreamer, that the Holly is the 'evergreen aspect' of the psyche. In Celtic myth of Holly, this is the Holy Spirit of God and is identified with the Earth Mother Goddess. It is she who holds the secret of life and death. Some say that she is identified with Morgan le Fay of the Arthurian legends, an enchantress who represents the mysterious powers of the female. And too, associated with the magic of the 'Sidhe' and the fairy kingdoms." He turned and began his pacing once more, stopping to touch another tree or a rock as he spoke.

"We must cover the use of my wood." He laughed as he beat upon his chest and then showed me the length of his arm, meaning his wood must be very strong! And I laughed as he acted this out.

"In the Word Ogham, it is stated that the wood of Holly is a mere third in the construction of the wheels for a chariot, and a third of the weapons use the wood of Holly. When we look at the Ogham symbol for Holly, we see that it consists of three upright notches. In the Word Ogham and other sources, there is a frequent reference to 'A Third'; the number three was very important to the ancient Celts.[17] Three is the number of levels of existence. It is the way everything manifests in this world. We know there is a left half and a right half. And that there is a 'part that is in between the two.' Here is the message a Dreamer needs to learn: the 'in between,' which becomes the 'Third,' is what we will work with in our Ogham magic. 'In Between the Magical Third' becomes key to our work.

"Now let's talk more about my wood! There is a passage from the story called the 'Cattle Raid of Cooley,' which deals with the repair of chariots. Here it states that chariots were made with the shafts of 'Holly,' as opposed to any other wood. Also from this legendary story we learn that Holly was used in making weapons. One story tells that the 'Warrior Nadcranntail' went into battle, taking with him nine spears of Holly, charred and sharpened.[18] The number nine is a magical number to the Celts.

"Reviewing the attributes of how Holly is used so far, we see the wheel of the chariot is made of Holly and lifts the chariot off the ground brining movement. This is good. Also a weapon made of Holly is the perfect instrument for clearing unwanted or hostile adversaries out of the way. In our work with Holly, we need these to move forward. Holly is an ancient symbol of protection."

The Holly Tree Seer became silent for a time, looking, just looking. . .I followed his gaze. This grove was sheltered from north to east and by a curve of the hill below; none on the path beyond would see this spot. It was a beautiful grove of both Holly and a few Oak. I could just picture a cottage in the hollow of the hill, facing south. Honeysuckle would grow well here, I was daydreaming. My Dream cottage was not to be for now. The Seer was in high gear and said we must walk a bit. I got up slowly, not wanting to leave this place, quiet and pure. Looking around, I noticed the starling bird guardians had vanished, or so it seemed. Maybe they had only quenched their light for the time being. Interesting. I have heard tell of such abilities. I smiled at the Seer. He seemed impatient. Was I being too slow? But he did smile back.

"We will walk this way!" he said in a smooth voice and pointed to the denser wood on the north side of the Grove. I realized that the movement felt good and I would be able to see another part of this magical Nemeton.

The Seer was very quiet as we walked. I was unsure about interrupting, but decided I would. I mean, there were many questions and things I did not understand. The wind whipped and I pulled my cloak closer. I thought, Here it goes. . .

"Dear Seer, may I interrupt your quiet?"

He responded with, "Interrupt. . .Yes, yes of course. Magicians and master Dreamers tend not to speak much. Continually planning moves ahead, much like chess players you see. Rehearsing for strategic purposes. This often takes intense mental focus. Not excluding you, my dear, no. What is it you wanted to say?"

"Oh! Well," I said, "I am wondering how I will ever learn all the things I need to know about the Tree Kingdom so that I can actually use this as practical magic once I have finished my training here. How will I know what I need on the spot for someone who may need help or healing? I mean—"

We had been walking side by side. Now the Holly Seer literally jumped in front of me! I was taken aback. He then, very loudly, said, "Stop it! Stop thinking of what you don't know! Think! Think, Dreamer!" His eyes glared.

The skin on the back of my neck was chilled, and my hands twisted and sweated. What had I done? With tears in my eyes, I said, "I am sorry! I just..."

He stepped closer and looked at me with those deep green eyes with deep black pools in their center. "It is nothing to be sorry for. This is about remembering who you are, Dreamer, and how far you have come while here on these sacred grounds. We each go through our trials and doubts, but we do not remain there. We cannot afford too! If you were not a worthy Dreamer, we would not be here together today. So think: who are you, Dreamer? And I will furnish your answer for now. You are an Ovate in training of the Ways of Dreaming, younger than some in the waking world but wiser than many. And when we do not know something, we DREAM and look to the Wisdom Keepers for answers. It has always been this way and will stay so. You must hold onto this, Dreamer!"

He moved off, suddenly walking ahead. I was stunned and did not know what to do. Thoughts raced: Did he not want to continue our studies? had I really said something bad? Then it hit me. The Seer had said, "Think! Who are you, Dreamer?" And here I was just thinking the worst! Why is it I pull in these negative thoughts? No, I will not go there! I wiped my eyes and ran my fingers through my snarled hair a couple of times. I held onto my little holly corsage as I walked. Feeling better, I caught up to where the Seer was standing next to an oak tree.

"Better, are we? I see you are holding your holly corsage; it can give one solace. Now let me say this: with our workings we mostly move things forward, many times having to compromise in order to just get things rolling. So we say yes! Yes! We try not to get caught in too much detail at that time; simply 'See the end result.' Flow is what we want. Adjustments can be made later.

"In our realms some are simply born into truth and love; they are the 'way showers.' But the world's collective energy of the negative elements works to erode this truth. Those born with this truth have overcome being susceptible to negatives, and part of their work is to liberate others from that negative control. You are one born with this truth! However, you have not yet accepted this fact, and it is time!"

The Holly Tree Seer turned away. I was happy to not have him stare just then, as the tears had come again, but these were for gladness, and I did not wipe them completely away. I pulled my emotions inward. I needed time to sort this out.

"What we have here is my honorable opponent!" said the Seer. He walked slowly around the huge oak tree, inspecting here and there.

I added, "He is very handsome and so big! His canopy stretches forty feet at least!"

The Seer was looking upward. "Ah! That it does. Mighty, this Oak, and proud!" He walked over to an outcropping of rocks. Dusting off some brush, he signaled for me to join him.

"Holly can be used as a substitute for the noble Oak. But as you have seen here today, Holly, who would be me, is a very important tree in its own right. In a Dreamer-magician's work at the beginning of their practice, it is preferable to begin with the Holly before the Oak. In training with tree magical workings, there is a word used for the magician to enact the 'Tainaiste.'[19] This refers to a part of the Dreamer's being that may be called upon to 'lay down its life as a substitute for the Oak King'!"

"You are kidding! Why?" I blurted this out without even thinking as I looked at the Oak tree and then back to the Holly Seer.

The Holly Seer was laughing and telling me to listen to the rest of the story! "As I was saying…This giving of life, Does *not* mean that you will be expected to give up your life in this world to complete some magical Working. But it does mean that you may be expected to sacrifice something in order to progress. If you think about this, you will see that this happens all the time in our day-to-day life. Please know that your 'Magical-Dreaming-Life' should simply be an extension of your mundane life."

I leaned back out of my intense forward pose and said, "Thank the Goddess for that! I suppose I do know what you mean about sacrificing, I have done this many times, and I am sure there will be more!"

The Seer was smiling and said, "Oh, I am certain there will be more. Now, the relationship between Oak and Holly is a complex one. Each of us involved with this work interprets this in their own way. To understand the double aspect of Oak and Holly, you must work with both until you form your own opinions of how they fit into both your magical life and your daily life. Once you have achieved this, you will have created the 'Trian Aspect,' which is the 'Third-In-Between Place.' This third aspect consists of the 'Trinity of Oak, Holly, and Self.' Now this takes time to be able to accomplish and feel comfortable with, but there are wonderful rewards for those who persevere."

"I sure do have my homework cut out for me!" I said with a positive tone. He was up now, picking up small, new, green acorns and rolled them around between both hands as he walked.

"The Holly is a symbolic tree that is powerful on the spiritual levels as you get to know me. Part of this symbolism lies in the fact that I am an evergreen tree. This demonstrates my ability to live and bloom despite harsh climatic changes and the turning of the seasons. Please know that I am a powerful symbol of life after physical death and of reincarnation on the physical level.

"Now, Dreamer, look to the grand Oak across from us, if you would please!"

I nodded my head and looked to the handsome Oak before us.

"We view the Oak, and it is grand! In our Dreamer training, we are learning 'to see' differently, and we see the King of the Trees is not an end in itself. There is a support system and yet a greater power behind the 'Oak High King.'"

I was not sure what he was getting at but did not interrupt and certainly did not blink an eye.

"The name for Holly in the Tree Ogham is 'Tinne.' There is an additional meaning to this word, which is 'Link,' as in chain. This is a valuable symbol of the Holly's link with the Oak. It is a link between his world and the Otherworlds. It is also the link that joins the 'Three Levels.' When we take note of the Holly tree's position in the Tree Ogham, the sequence is exactly halfway through the fifteen consonants. It is the pivotal point around which all other letters revolve. We should view this symbolically as the point between life and death, or of death and rebirth."

With the pause, I stood up, and the Seer who had been walking became still. I said to him, "I am overwhelmed. I knew when I saw you in battle this morning that there was something special, but this day has been even more than I could have ever thought. I especially admire the interconnection between you and the Oak!"

"Why, thank you, Dreamer! I have only a little more before we head back, as I am sure the others will be Dreaming our return soon. If we do not appear, they will search!

"I, the Holly, am often associated with the Winter Solstice, and my leaves and branches are used as ornamental decoration at that time of year. But right now is Midsummer, and I am intricately associated with the Celtic festival of 'Lammas,' when summer is half over and the harvest time is beginning. 'Lammas' means 'Loaf-Mass,' the meaning symbolizes the honoring of the grains used to make a loaf of bread. At this time of summer, the grain stands golden in the fields but has not yet been gathered in. The 'Lammas' festival expects us take a pause and realize this is a time of consequence, when we reap what we have sown. Will we reap a harvest of plenty or a harvest of disaster? Our past choices and actions will now come to light. What is it we have put into the Earth? This is a time to call in Holly and ask how Holly has guided us here. Whatever your answers, Holly reminds us of its strength to endure and the need to calm emotions if we are to reach wise decisions.

"As a point of reference when you begin using the magical workings of Holly, you may feel out of sorts. Let me make this clear: 'you are expected' to feel some disorientation during this time because you are creating a linking process. Do not be concerned; just know that you are now placing yourself in the 'In-Between States' of awareness of two things at once. As you know, this is not how humans normally function! However, it is imperative to gain the ability, the skill, to move from the physical world to the Otherworlds! As a Dreamer you know this. Of course you do know who it is that can be called upon for help. Why, me, of course!"

The Holly Seer then took off his crown of Holly and made a gallant bow, just as any noble knight might do. For me this was special, more than just a nobleman. I jumped up and down and clapped! "This has been the most wonderful day! I have learned so much and cannot wait to begin to practice what you have given me. Thank you! Dear Holly Seer!"

Of course, not being able to help myself, I dashed over to give him a hug! He was a bit shy about that, but still I was happy I did.

Next thing I knew, I heard voices calling for us. The Seer said, "Ah, saved! And he laughed hard, but then he gave me a hug in earnest.

The Oak Seer appeared with the White Lady Tree and the Apple Tree Seer. In unison they said, "There you are! It is time for us all to head over; a grand evening has been planed for this 'Lammas'!"

The Birch Tree Seer took my arm and said I could tell her about my days experience as we walked. I gave her a big smile and said, "It has been a big Dream day! Let me see... Where to start?!"

HAZEL

"C" Coll

THE HAZEL
LETTER "C," "COLL"
OGHAM:⊒

STATISTICS FOR:

"The Hazel" genus/species- *Corylus americana* and *Corylus avellana*

~The Hazel tree grows throughout the globe.

~Grows to a height of 30 feet tall.

~The bark is light brown to yellowish. The leaves grow on alternate sides of the stalk.

~~~~~~~~~~

THE HAZEL: HOW USED IN THE WORLD

~The wood from the hazel burns well. All parts—wood, branches, leaves, and nuts—are used. In ancient times the hazel was known as the tree of wisdom and was added to fire to gain wisdom. It is one of the sacred nine woods burned by the Druids at the Beltane fires in the spring. Hazel is called upon for protection and magic applications for manifestation, prosperity, fertility, and wisdom. Magic wands were often made of hazel and were used in divining the ley lines.

~~~~~~~~~~

MEDICINAL AND PSYCHOLOGICAL

The hazel made into a tea can be used as a drainage remedy and can help restore elasticity to the lungs. Hazelnuts, when eaten, are a good source of phosphorus, magnesium, potassium, copper, and protein. Powdered nuts can be added to mead or honeyed water to help coughs.

~~~~~~~~~~

SACREDNESS AMONG THE GROVE

~The Hazel is the ninth tree in the Ogham Alphabet- "Coll"-"C"

~The Hazel is associated with death, regeneration, transition, and rebirth.

~Month- August 5 through September 1

~KEYWORD- Wisdom

~Planet- Mercury

~The Hazel stands on either side of the Holly tree and Apple tree within the Grove.

~"FINGER TIP TREE" location- "Hazel-Coll"-"C" is on the lower tip of the ring finger.

DREAM OF "COLL," THE HAZEL TREE SEER

having the afternoon off, I went into the woods to relax. So much doing, studying, learning. As I walked among the trees, the chatter in my brain kept going. What about this, that, the other! Stopping for a moment to orient myself, something felt different on my path. I looked at my watch; it was only noon, and this made me smile. I looked up and connected with the sun streaming down. A beautiful clear blue sky, no heat or humidity, my hour of power, I thought to myself. Scanning the immediate area, I realized I was in a small clearing, a great place to rest and have my lunch.

Pulling off my backpack, I got my lunch out and sat leaning against the granite rocks. Thanking the sun and this beautiful retreat place, I begin to munch on my sandwich, relaxing. Looking about my space, suddenly my teeth clamped shut! My breath felt shallow. My eyes had focused on a tree in front of me. A stump of what was a tree. The tree, I saw now, was a woman hunching over as if in pain and sadness. I jumped up, knocking my lunch aside. After swallowing hard the lump of food in my mouth, I gasped and said, "Who would do such a thing?"

I ran over to this figure and saw the jagged edges of the tree bark; I was close now. There was fresh sap blood pouring down in various places. One spot was especially hard to look at. This was a round, saw-toothed blade left angling into the tree trunk skin. "Whoever did this was thoughtless!" I said out loud. I began to pry the round saw loose with a rock. Slowly it came out; the sap blood oozed more. It smelled sweet and raw. I picked up some dirt and put it on the open wounds of the trees trunk. With tears in my eyes, I said, "I am so sorry! So sorry!"

A voice answered me back, "You recognized me! I am one of your own. One who has been hurt by human needs, in the name of progress! No matter; it is only temporary!"

As I listened to this voice, I watched this amazing tree adjust herself. I watched as she shifted this way and that just a bit. You had to look intently, but you could see her getting her body comfortable to the state of her current condition. Time was literally standing still, and I was a part of this extraordinary glimpse of life in the making, after the life having been unmade. Through a misty silence now, again I heard the tree's voice.

"I will introduce myself, because you are one who is here for the 'Knowing' and cares about Mother Earth. I am the 'Hazel Tree Seer'; number nine in the Keepers of the Nemeton.

My name in the Ogham is 'Coll.' I am one of the three Tree Seers who bears fruit. The fruit I bear is hazelnuts, and they take nine years in the making! My branches are used by dowsers for locating hidden streams and buried metals. This must be part of why you stopped here today. You are being put in touch with your hidden talents of dowsing!"

Listening to her, my mind was reeling. Hidden talents? Nine years to make one nut!? I must be nuts, I said to myself. How can she even speak as she stands, oozing sap! How did I get involved with this? All I wanted was a little quiet time, is what I was thinking.

The Hazel Seer was answering me telepathically, "I know, I know. Rest and relaxation. A little fallow time; we all need it."

Confused and forcing a smile, I answered out loud, "There has been so much these past few days. So much learning, so much I do not understand. I am on overload, and I miss my waking reality home!" I realized how small my complaints were as she stood there with her trunk body cut open! How did she bear it? I wondered. Watching the sap blood dripping down one side of her, quickly I said, "I'm so sorry!" Patting more dirt into her wounds, the dripping slowed some.

The Hazel Tree Seer spoke out loudly. "I always come back, you know! I will prevail! This is also part of what you are here to learn: the hurts, the pains, the little deaths. All part of your teachings!"

"Little deaths?" I questioned.

"Yes," she answered. "The changes that come, the changes in people, family, friends, work. All little deaths! The one constant we all have is change!" Continuing, the Seer said, "I am sensing there is an afraid feeling for you as to what comes after your training here? In the Nemeton you are with like-minded Dreamers and the ancient Keepers, and we all look out for each other here. Projecting ahead you may be thinking, back in my own environment, what then? What am I meant to do then? Aha! I see the tears welling." She said to me softly, "It is OK, my daughter. We are all afraid of the unknown. However, as a Dreamer, we can play the 'Dream My Future' game and look at these dreams. This is helpful to see how various futures might feel."

It was quiet now in the wooded clearing, here in the afternoon. I had turned my face away from this Seer, not wanting her to see my anguish. Because of course she was right! I did admit to myself I was concerned about how I would manage in my regular waking reality. But this was the first time the words of these feelings had been said, and this was hitting me hard. Not knowing how to continue with her, I just said, "Where has the time gone?"

Completely ignoring my comment, the Hazel Tree Seer said, "I am referred to as the 'Fairest of Trees.' In Irish Gaelic the words are 'Cainiu Fedaif'; the deeper meaning of this expression lies in cainiu, to keen over a death, or to satirize someone.[20] It's attributed to the Goddess Brighid, following the death of her son, Ruadhan, during the Battle of Moytura. The modern Gaelic name for the Hazel tree is Calltuinn; it means 'the loss of something.' Brighid wept and wailed and keened with this death."

There was a long pause; I waited for the Seer to say more. Nothing! She stood quietly there, part woman and part tree; so quiet. I could feel and see the rays of the warm sun glistening on her oozing sap. "Why are you telling me this?" I asked the Seer. "Why?"

"I am the Tree Seer one can learn from about that illusive subject of Death! Little Deaths all preparing us for the larger. Do not look so startled, child! You will not be leaving anytime soon for the Otherworlds. The little deaths of change, in my Dreaming of your time now, may be what are ailing you. However, Brighid can be of much assistance to you. She can help you connect to your dowsing talents. Brighid holds the 'Fire Energy' of the hearth and home. You may call on her to help ignite her energy in your waking reality life of now, and she can be of assistance for Dreaming a future waking life. Think of her while you do the chores required to maintain your home. She will be there."

"But—" I tried to intervene.

The Hazel Tree Seer raised her branch-her arm, insisting on silence. "From where I stand, I see your path clearly. It is time now for you to find some of this clarity for your own." She bent down and gave me some of her hazelnuts. "Chew them!" I spoke not a word. Taking them, I began to chew. The Seer was saying, "We will invoke Brighid, and your task is to keep in mind 'her fire energy' to keep the hearth fire always tended within one's self and home. This, you see, is the deeper meaning of the Hazel tree. I know how to rest and mend, and I always prevail! I am the 'Fairest of Trees'!"

I stood up and collected more soil and patted this onto the open cut marks on her trunk. I found a loose branch and swept and tidied the area around her. Then I took out my small smudge shell and got the sage burning and smudged her all around her trunk. The Seer reminded me to smudge myself, and I did. I stood silent for a moment before her, then said, "I wish I could do more! I trust you are feeling better."

The Hazel Tree Seer then said, "You have done quite enough, my dear Dreamer! Please find a spot to sit and Dream with me awhile as I heal and you learn."

From my pack I got my blanket and put this right near the Seer's trunk. I told her thank you and that I would be delighted to Dream with her! As I settled into a Dream journey with the Seer, I began to feel calmness I had not had in some time.

The Hazel Tree Seer spoke her Dreaming: "I trust that the hazelnuts were tasty, Dreamer! Now, please know that my fruit can play an important role for you in linking with my energies, helping to recall useable information when needed. According to ledged, hazelnuts contain all wisdom.

"Now, having invoked Brighid to assist with possible future Dream lives to work you're Dreaming, you should know a little about her. There are many genealogies that say Brighid is a pre-Christian goddess of the Tuatha De Danann and the daughter of the Daghdha, the god of all the Celtic gods. His knowledge passed to her, Brighid the Keeper and the protector of the hearth and home.

"Dreamer, it is your time now to find some clarity around your future hearth and home. Begin now to Dream in your mind's eye what this home should look like, the way it should feel. Dream the hearth fire and tend the kindling there; add more hazel logs. Brighid is there. Do you see her? She is divine inspiration and can help with creating, firing up, any new endeavor. She will also help me along as the Hazel Tree, going through the little deaths of transitioning from one kind of life to another."

I could hear wind now around our woodland Dream place, and with the melody of the Seer's voice, I was quickly shaping a new dream for myself, for the future Dream life I would have. This was amazing to me, as I saw the fire within the hearth of a quaint home.

Brighid was there, gliding like an apparition and telling me this was only the foundation for this new life. I had much to do and flow with while here in the Nemeton now. "Keep these images," she told me, "and we will build and mold them as your Dreaming life moves on." Then she said, "There is something right here that is important for you to witness now. Please turn your Dreaming attention to the Hazel Tree Seer!"

I did as Brighid asked, and off to my right of the dense woodland I saw the Seer. She radiated a glow along with the sun, it seemed. I then saw her regenerate her limbs, her trunk, her higher branches. It was glorious! The late afternoon sun sparkled down, and she was healing herself! Incredible.

I blinked my eyes hard and sat up quickly. Out of my Dreaming, or was I?

There stood the most magnificent tree, all glowing in the light. The Hazel in all her wholeness and health! Then, in a whisper but with strength, the beautiful Hazel "Coll" Seer said, "I always prevail!"

APPLE

Karen Silverstein

Karen C. Silverstein

"Q"   Queirt

THE APPLE LETTER "Q," "QUEIRT" OGHAM:▤

STATISTICS FOR

"The Apple" genus- *Rosaceae* (The Rose Family)

~Grows throughout the Northern Hemisphere and many places on the globe.

~About 25 species of apple are native to temperate regions of the northern hemisphere.

~*Malus pumila*- The common native apple of southeastern Europe and Central Asia has numerous varieties developed from it.

~Sweet crab apple- *Malus coronaria*

~Common in Northeast America. Leaves have a pointed apex and a round base. Fruit is approximately one inch and has a yellow-green color. Grows as a shrub or small tree, often forming thickets. Their perfect flowers, fragrant pinkish-white, typically have five sepals and five petals.

~~~~~~~~~~~

THE APPLE: HOW USED IN THE WORLD

The wood is good for burning and carving, also in making furniture and utensils. The fruit is used to make jam, jelly, wine, cider, vinegar, and a huge variety of meals. Its bark was used for tanning hides.

MEDICINAL AND PSYCHOLOGICAL

~ "An apple a day keeps the doctor away!" Apples are rich in malic and tartaric acid, which help the body digest other foods. Apples have been used to treat diarrhea, dyspepsia, gout, liver problems, and indigestion. In northern Europe, warts were cured by rubbing them with two halves of an apple, which was then buried. As the apple halves decayed, so did the wart.

~~~~~~~~~~~

SACREDNESS AMONG THE GROVE

~The Apple is the tenth tree in the Ogham Alphabet: "Queirt"-"Q"

~The Apple is associated with awakening the Otherworld senses, re-birth, and protection.

~Month- not assigned

~KEYWORD- Rebirth and Love

~Planet- Venus

~The Apple stands on either side of the Hazel and Vine within the Grove.

~"FINGER TIP TREE" location- "Apple-Queirt"-"Q" is on the lower tip of the little finger.

DREAM OF "QUEIRT," THE APPLE TREE SEER

We had been sitting in the circle all afternoon, other Dreamers and I. All of us involved in-depth with book work, practical information we all needed. There was a restlessness drifting through our circle. The Keeper, who had been leading us, clapped her book together loudly. We all jumped!

"Enough!" she said, her eyes scanning the Dreamers. "We will close early. Some time off," she said.

There was a sigh from the group, as well as smiles. We need this, I said to myself.

After having put my things away, I knew I just needed to move, to walk, and head out through a quiet part of the steading. Trying to keep to myself, I picked up my pace. I knew I was missing lunch, but wasn't hungry. Running now through the forest, I started laughing! The movement just felt so good. The wind had picked up on this warm August day. Running so fast, I was a bit out of breath. Then I tumbled down on the open grassy area, like a schoolgirl. Laughing, I was truly enjoying the earth, sky, and warm wind. I stayed on my back, resting awhile, but then heard a small buzzing sound. Becoming curious, I tracked the sound to some bees, black and yellow striped, going from wildflower to wildflower. Following them, walking close, but not too close, then up a hill, I went into a small orchard. Such a beautiful spot with mountains in the background, and mist from the warm, humid day. Walking slowly through this small grove of trees, I realized they are all apple and enjoyed the peacefulness there; I was content.

"Si-si-si…" I heard a small voice, "Pis!" A whispering voice.

Looking about, I realized that the voice was coming from one sparkling, shining Apple tree.

In a quiet, raspy whisper, "Come here!" came from the tree.

Looking all about, as if someone else were there, I shrugged my shoulders!

"Come here!" said the Apple tree.

Moving next to her now, I could see and feel the sparkle and shiny glow that emanated from her. "That is better," she said. "Come sit next to me. I will shelter you!"

I thought to myself, interesting to hear this tree speak; however, in the Nemeton, this not out of the ordinary. I was tired though, and looking about I found a comfortable spot next to her trunk. I heard the bees again and noticed that they had made a hive within one of the knots on her trunk.

Her whispering voice said, "We support each other, the bees and I. They give me music, sweetness, and pollinate my flowers. I provide food and shelter for them, as I do for you."

I thought to myself, How perfect nature is.

Again her whispering voice said, "You must be hungry; try one of my apples!"

Searching the grassy area, I found one perfect apple and began munching; juicy and delicious. I felt relaxed and nodded my head to her. I did not seem to have words.

"Of course you know who I am, Dreamer, but introductions are always polite! I am 'The Apple Tree Seer.' My Ogham name is 'Quiert' and my letter is Q; I am number ten in the Ogham with the ancient Keepers of the Grove. I have been aware of you, Dreamer, and see that you have come far in your studies. It is time to reawaken and realize that you have always known these teachings from many different lifetimes. Now all coming together in this lifetime, with deeper meaning and soul purpose!"

The Apple Tree Seer stared at me awhile and I stared back, not quite getting what she had said about different lifetimes But she was beautiful with her ancient, twisted trunk and bright green leaves with branches drooping from the weight of her apple fruit. I felt calmness here. Coming back from my daydreaming, I saw she was shaking her branches some.

I paid attention to hear her say: "See the small knife near my trunk here? Pick it up along with another apple." I nodded and did as she said. "Take the knife and cut open the apple horizontally across."

"Like this?" I said.

She nodded. "Yes, yes! Cut me open and you will see nothing more beautiful than the center of me!" The juice squirted out and dribbled down my hands; I could smell its sweetness. The Apple Tree Seer said, "Lay the two halves on the ground." She was pointing now to the cut open apple. "What do you see?" she asked.

"A star, a five-pointed star!" I said with a questioning voice.

"Yes," she answered. "The five-pointed star of protection, the emblem of immortality. This represents the Goddess in her five stations from birth to death and back to birth again. Never forget this!" she told me. "Never! Your Dreamer training here is to become this kind of Goddess. I will be helping you to digest and assimilate my knowledge; I am the tree of knowledge."

The Seer had shape-shifted now into her human form. She had a swath of red-blonde hair and a gauze, silk gown in greens and reds, with a high-cut midriff edged in embroidery ribbons of small apples. She held a long, golden staff carved of an apple branch, with five golden apples at its crest. She stood looking at me as if this was completely normal, but with the hint of laughter on her lips. All I could do was just stand there and look at her and the apple I had cut open. I had to snap my concentration back to hear what she was saying.

"Some acknowledge the apple to be the forbidden fruit that Adam and Eve ate in the garden of Paradise, representing the beginning of knowledge and the loss of innocence. This led to Adam and Eve to being banished from the Garden of Eden. There are many stories around my dear fruit, with various cultures and religions using spins to their advantage. Now, the name for the 'apple tree' in Latin is 'malus,' which, most interestingly, is the root word for 'evil'!"

"No way! That is not fair!" I spurted out quickly.

"No reason for alarm, Dreamer. These tales simply add to the mystery of me! Now moving on…The 'apple tree' was designated by the Druids as one of the Seven Chieftain Trees for the Celts. This culture has always associated the Apple with the Goddess and love. Norse ledged holds that the gods ate apples to restore youth, and unicorns are said to live beneath the Apple and the Ash Trees. The Apple was considered a 'Dream Tree' in much of European folklore. The eating of Apples opens the gateways into the other realms and provides illumination and the gaining of knowledge. The Apple is used for the making of a magical wand. It is a favorite of witches at the Celtic Samhain festivals and is often used in making love spells. Apples are symbols of Avalon, the magical apple land, where Glastonbury is set within the Celtic Apple lands. In Arthurian legend, Avalon is derived from the Welsh word 'afal'-'apple.' Avalon's Queen is 'Morgan le Fay,' 'Morgan of the Fairies.' The original Morgan was a wise woman and healer, reminding us that all true healing may be derived from plants that grow upon earth. However, the knowledge of their uses and applications must come from the world of Spirit. In the Otherworlds 'Apple Tree' is a symbol of the earthly paradise in which it grows.

"The energy of apple represents a choice of beauty, life, and youthfulness. It is associated with the planet Venus, goddess of love, trust, and beauty. The apple was sacred to the Goddess Venus. There are accounts of the apple being adorned as Hesper, the evening star, on one half of the apple and as Lucifer, son of the morning star, on the other half of the apple."

The Apple Tree Seer had been moving about the apple tree as I sat at the tree's trunk simply mesmerized by her grace of movement and musical voice. Her gown of greens and reds fluttered with her hand gestures and walking. She stopped at times to check on the bees and their hive. Now she was reaching into the hive, and the bees swarmed a moment but then calmed, and she pulled out a comb of honey. She told me to collect a few apples and the knife, and then she proceeded to slice the apple, butter a few slices, and handed this to me. Sitting down she said, "Let's enjoy this snack a minute, and then I will explain about my seeds within my core."

We munched a few minutes on the apple-honey slices, which were amazing. I told her how much I loved them and thanked her too. Feeling as if I had always been here with her, I wondered what things we might have done in the past. I was very happy I had come today. Slowly it came to me that the Seer was speaking.

"The seeds! The seeds!" She was saying, "Take them out of the apple you cut into halves earlier and place them on the ground."

I felt like it took me forever, but I followed her request, placing them in the same star shape they had within the apple, just as she told me to do. Looking at the Tree Seer, I saw she was pointing to the two halves of the apple. When I looked, I saw that there were more seeds in the apple. I said to her, "Look! Ancient One, look! I've removed the seeds but more are there!"

I repeated the seed removal process. Watching now, I pointed and say loudly, "Look, look! More are coming back!" I was in disbelief and excited!

Calming now, I heard her sweet, whispering voice saying, "I know. I am your sheltering magical tree, These are your 'dream seeds,' and they are endless!"

Jumping up, I said, "What do you mean? The seeds will continue to be replaced though I continue to remove them?"

The Seer turned her head to one side and said, "Why, that is exactly what I mean, Dreamer. I will make a believer out if you yet!"

I walked back and forth under the canopy of the Apple, and the bees followed me. Then I went to the two apple halves and removed the seeds once more...just because! Again the seeds replenished themselves. Looking now to the Apple Seer who had seated herself quite regally next to her trunk, I then said, "This is awesome! I do not pretend to understand, but as a Dreamer I accept the truth of it, and I am enchanted to have seen this and meet you, dear Seer!"

I moved to her as she held out her hand, saying to me, "In time all things are made known! May the Goddess that resides in me be gifted to reside in you, dear Dreamer!"

I gave the Seer a warm hug. Just then we heard buzzing and saw the bees come out of their hive! I thanked the Apple Tree Seer for all she had taught me, and I thanked the bees. I told her that it was the bees that originally caught my attention and brought me here.

She answered me with a simple, "Yes, I know, dear Dreamer!"

Smiling to myself, I thought of the Goddess that resides within me!

VINE

"M" Muin

Karen C. Silverstein

THE VINE
LETTER "M," "MUIN"
OGHAM: ✝

STATISTICS FOR:

"The Vine" genus- *Vitis*

~Grows in most temperate climates throughout the globe.

~Grows to an average height of 4–5 feet when cultivated, higher in the wild.

~The five-pointed leaves meander on the branches, which are supported by the tendrils.

~~~~~~~~~~~

THE VINE: HOW USED IN THE WORLD

~The Vine is added to the Beltane fires and is one of the nine sacred woods. In magical uses Vine is considered a tree of joy and wrath, depending upon the quantity used. It is also considered a tree that can help with mental powers, rebirth, fertility, and happiness.

~~~~~~~~~~~

MEDICINAL AND PSYCHOLOGICAL

~The leaves from some vines can be made into tea for treating diarrhea, hepatitis, and upset stomach. Grape leaves can be used externally as poultices to treat rheumatism, headache, and fevers. The leaves and fruit from the vines can be used in spells to overcome complexes and to enhance ambition. The vine of the grape symbolizes resurrection, as its strength is a magical elixir known to dissolve boundaries with others.

~~~~~~~~~~~

SACREDNESS AMONG THE GROVE

~The Vine is the eleventh tree in the Ogham Alphabet: "Muin"-"M"

~The Vine is associated with hidden knowledge, overcoming adversaries, inspiration.

~Month- September 2 through September 29

~KEYWORD- Inspiration

~Planets- Venus and Mars

~The Vine tree stands on either side of the Apple tree and Ivy tree within the Grove.

~"FINGER TIP TREE" location- "Vine-Muin"-"M" is on the middle of the thumb.

DREAM OF "MUIN," THE VINE TREE SEER

Quiet, seemed the morning. Strange, I thought, not to hear the birds or even a soft wind; then the events of last evening came flooding with confusion as I lay motionless in my bed. Was I Dreaming still? There were things that need doing, but I could not recall what. Quietly I closed my eyes yet again.

I am the wind of the Sea

I am the dew drop of the Moon
I am the shining tear of the Sun
I am the sheath of grain from Earth
I am she, the Dreamer who seeks to learn the secrets.
"The Three Daughters of the West"…"The Triple Goddess"

Sitting wide awake now, I remembered this poem; I thought it beautiful. Where had it come from?

I threw my feet over to the cold floor, pulling a blanket around my shoulders; I heard the cool September breezes and then the Crow. I was back; the day would move forward now. Thoughts of last night and its intoxicating events began to fill my head.

There was a shift happening, even if it was not clear to me what the shift was. I dressed quickly and grabbed my wrap, realizing I was very hungry and wanted to get to the dinning lodge. Hints of secret Dreams pulled me: who was it inside my Dreaming? Feeling vague, I realized someone was knocking at the door.

I was startled. As I ran my hand through my hair, I called out, "Yes! Coming!" I opened the door to find the "Vine Tree Seer" standing there. I was quite surprised.

He handed me a cup of hot tea and said, "Good morning!"

I respond with, "Thank you," but I did not move from the threshold.

He saw my puzzled expression and added, "Thought I would check on you. Last night was engaging, to say the least. How are you feeling? Are you headed for breakfast? Let's walk awhile slowly."

"Yes, I am starving!" I answered, still confused as to why he was here. I mean, I barely had spoken with this Seer. Finally I added, "How do I feel? Well, I dimly remember last evening! I do know that there were Dreamers who were acting in a Dionysus way, but—"

The Seer interrupted with, "The wine. Yes, it was running freely, maybe not such a good idea for the newly consecrated Dreamers! And the playacting with Dionysus was interesting.

In Greek myth Dionysus is the God of Nature, God of Wine. It has been said that he produced the first wine from the grapevine and spread the art of tending grapes. He also had a dual side to his nature: on the one hand he could bring about joy and divine ecstasy and on the other hand, unthinking rage. Both of these reflect the nature of wine." The Vine Tree Seer paused as we walked away from my cabin.

I was thinking, Lot of information to digest so early in the morning. So I smiled a little and said, "I know I enjoyed the show and had few glasses of wine. I got home fine, but this morning I have hit foggy bottom!"

Smiling at me, the Seer walked on. His long strides had me hard behind him. We went through an open space and along a steep lane that twisted toward the sea. But I felt we would not go to the water now. I saw the dinning lodge off to the left before the rocky bluff in front of the shoreline. The bent grass whistled in the breeze.

It was a long time, I thought, before the "Vine Tree Seer" spoke, and when he did, it was about breakfast. He told me that he had arranged for a boxed meal, including some hot coffee, and then we would head for the south hill that looks over the sea. He told me there was something there I needed to see. Wondering at this some, I nodded my head in agreement; we collected our breakfast picnic and a blanket and got back onto the twisting dirt lane.

We greeted various Dreamers in passing, but we did not speak to each other. I was thankful, being tired still and a bit crabby and, I realized, out of breath as we climbed the rocky bluff of the south hill. Nearing the top, I could hear the gulls crying, and then we stopped at last on an ancient hilltop. I knew this to be the place of retreat; I felt safe. We stood in the tall autumn grasses dotted with yellow buttercups; smiling, I breathed in the morning air. Off to our right was a rocky cove and the beginnings of the inlet to the sea in the east. I saw the rambling green-gray marshes teaming with bird life. Looking to my left were the southeastern hills gently rolling one after the other. All were covered with grapevines, one hill after the other in greens and purple-greens as far as one could see!

With a huge smile on my face, I turned to see the Seer had picked a nice spot and was spreading the red blanket, anchoring the corners with stones he had found and then arranged his pack along with the picnic breakfast. Food! I thought to myself, and I ran over to join him.

"Hungry, Dreamer?" he said in his deep voice.

"I am famished!" I answered as I held out my teacup, which was now being filled with steaming black coffee from the thermos. I took a sip, hot as it was, but it tasted great. "Now that is what I am talking about!" I called out as I nestled into my pack lying on the blanket.

The Seer broke into a laugh as he handed me thickly buttered banana bread and hardboiled eggs. "A little coffee, a little food, and this Dreamer is set!" he said, laughing still.

I nodded my head in agreement; my mouth was full. From somewhere a breeze came. I kept my eye on him, a gentleman, tall and courtly. He could be a knight. I thought in the ancient world he probably was.

He spoke again, but more slowly, gesturing his arm upward. "I trust you are enjoying the view! My roots are here. My land, my vines are old and yet new; we flourish here on these southern hills!"

I answered before he could say more. "I love this place; I feel I know this place!" As if in a spell or a lucid moment, I knew this to be true.

The "Vine Seer" was looking at me intently. I felt him drawing upon his power, looking within. There was a lull; I searched for words and found none. He smiled and said quite simply, "Come!"

He offered his hand and pulled me up. The Seer dashed ahead toward the vines on the highest hill. I laughed as I stretched to catch up to him. Once at the top. I could see the Seer strolling between the long rows of grapevines, which were slightly tied with cord to the fencing that supported them. It must have been harvest time, as the grapes hung in dark burgundy clusters glimmering in the sunlight. The air was tranquil and sweet; I pulled off a few grapes to taste, and they were sweet as sugar, with a tang that stayed on my tongue. Smiling to myself, I searched around to find the Seer. Finally I spotted him examining the vines at the very crest of the hill.

As I approached, he said, "Were they to your liking?"

I answered quickly, "I love them!" and handed him a couple from my pocket.

Taking them, he rolled one over in his palm, checking it out, and then popped this into his mouth. He said, "It is early yet, not enough hard frost. Maybe by next week they will sweeten more and set, and the picking will begin. All are picked by hand; all technique is done the old way, as it has been so throughout several hundred years in my family, generation after generation. The vines are originally from the Burgundy region in France. We come from a lineage that can be traced back four hundred years."

The "Vine Tree Seer" held his hand up and pointed to an area away from the manicured grape vines. "We will head over there; a Dreamer needs to learn first about the vines in the wild!"

I was curious about that comment, but there was no time to ask anything. I needed to keep astride to where he was heading. As we got to the top of the high hill, we both turned to look back; the acres upon acres of grapevines were beautifully lined up. I saw a few crows overhead and then the gulls farther off. The ocean was there in its great expanse at the cliff's edge, glimmering now with the morning sunlight. I turned now to the Seer as he said, "A beautiful sight!"

We picked up our walking into the woodland, which bordered the vineyard. The canopy became thicker as we hiked inward, and the light was more diffused here. Leaves and small branches crunched as we walked; the Seer said nothing. I could tell he was intent on finding something; I decided to just enjoy the walk and pay attention to signs. There was nothing really in the way of divination in the landscape; I relaxed.

When I was twenty feet or so from the Seer, he stopped and flashed me a glance. I thought to myself, A stone face; he shows little emotion. Carved like granite rock was his face; very hard to read. I knew something was up, but what? I thought that a cold emotional exterior often belies inner warmth and steadfast integrity. Sometimes. I thought, at first glance we might miss the fact that the coldest demeanor one might meet may actually be the most reliable person, especially when the chips are down. Realizing that I was daydreaming with signs now from the Seer himself, I smiled to myself. Do not tip my hand as to my thoughts of him, I thought to myself. No need; just keep my cards close and pay attention. Whatever this was I was sensing about the "Vine Tree Seer" should be kept to myself. He has shown up to teach me today; I must be ready to listen!

A slight smile broke the hard lines on his face as he lifted his eyes and head skyward. He said to me in a matter of fact tone, "Yes, this one will do very nicely!" He was now walking around the base of an Apple tree, with huge knots upon its trunk and twisting branches that had a few bruised apples lingering there. It was not the Apple tree that he was examining, however, but a very large, old vine that traversed almost to the top of this thirty-foot ancient apple. The stone face expression slowly melted from the face of the Seer. And why not? I thought to myself, He is in his element here on this land.

Always to the point, the Seer motioned for me to come close; I did so quickly. He handed me the blanket and asked that I spread it out a little ways from the Apple and Vine trees. I got everything set up and pulled out my journal. "Come!" he said.

As I moved to where he stood under the Apple tree, I reached over to touch both the Apple and the Vine. "The vine is huge! Is the Apple tree OK with the vine wrapped around it so much?"

The Seer smiled and answered, "How do they look to you?"

I looked again at these two trees and said, "I feel that they are fine with this; they are happy!"

He laughed a dry laugh, saying, "And so it is! You discern correctly, dear Dreamer! The vine, if not disrupted, can grow to a very large size. And if you will notice—" He pointed to branches. "—there are many large meandering branches, which are incapable of supporting their own weight. The Vine relies on these long, thin but strong tendrils, which sprout from the main stem and then entwines itself around trees or sometimes structures to support its weight."

"That is amazing," I chimed in. "The Apple tree seems perfectly fine with this arrangement!"

"This is a natural arrangement, Dreamer; one that has been going on for some time in the wild. It is important for you to study the Vine in the wild, where it uses the host tree to support its growth. In our studies, this symbolizes the Vine's knowledge of the properties of the host tree, and that it is in harmony and sympathy with the tree. Actually understanding it so well that it is capable of living beside or on top of it! I see you are puzzled but smiling, Dreamer. Is there something you need to say?" I laughed at his comment, but he was right. I was puzzled with how they grew with each other and told him that. The Seer answered quickly with, "A bit later we will explore, through the use of 'Otherworld Journey-Dreaming,' what the two trees feel about their relationship and investigate both of their individual properties. This will greatly aid your new knowledge; in the meantime, please observe."

I nodded my head and answered, "I would really like that!"

We walked a few minutes around the two trees and then stood off to one side admiring them both. The Vine Tree Seer then lifted his right arm in a gesture for me to walk past him, saying, "After you, my dear!" Then we sat upon the red blanket. The Vine Tree Seer began his lessons with more intensity, twirling a small twig of the vine between his fingers as he spoke.

"In the 'Ogham' the word 'Vine' is 'Muin' and uses the letter *M*. From the 'Word Ogham of Morainn,' there is a reference to the Vine as 'highest of beauty' and also 'strongest of effort,'[21] meaning the vine can grow higher than the host plant that it may attach with. The Vine prefers to grow aloft, off the ground. In another reference from Morainn, 'Muin' means the back of man or ox, for they are the strongest in their efforts. The word 'Man' that is used in the text actually refers to 'Humankind,' not just the male of the species. Also, 'Muin' can mean 'To Teach.' In our Magical Workings of the trees, this is the meaning we will work with, using the strongest powers of man at this 'Level of Dreaming.'"

I stood up and stretched a bit, saying, "Muin-To Teach; I like this aspect! There are so many things for me to learn before I can teach, but I am very enthusiastic to do so. I do have a question now, if you would?"

The Seer, who was also standing, said, "Please, what is the question?"

"Well," I answered, "I noticed that the Vine does not seem to have any fruit. Is this grapevine or something else?"

"Come, Dreamer!" was the Seers reply. I followed him over to the tree twosome. "Glad to see that you are observant, Dreamer!" said the Vine Tree Seer. He was fingering the vine and its tendrils, showing me where fruit had been, saying that this was blackberry. Then he continued. "In this region the grapevine is not a native wild plant to the area, so what we have here can be referred to as 'The Bramble'-'The Blackberry.' Sometimes we might find 'The Raspberry' in combination with the Apple or another host tree. In ancient Europe, the grapevine was found in the southern countries. It was, however, carried north in migration and did well on the southern slopes of northern Gaul, Brittany, and Britain. In the more northern countries, the 'Bramble-Blackberry' bushes were native and were a substitute for grape wine in many areas. Blackberry wine is a very heady drink enjoyed by many. In the ancient times of the Celtic countries, there was a taboo against eating the blackberry. In Brittany the reason given was 'a cause des fees'-'because of the fairies.'"

The Seer stopped a moment, and I could not resist saying, "I love these fairies!"

"I can see that you do!" He responded without losing his story weaving.

"In Greece, the 'Vine' was sacred to the 'Thracian Dionysus,' the 'Vine God,' and was loved by the Greek 'Goddess Athaea'; her name means 'she who makes things grow.' The Vine was also sacred to the Egyptian God 'Osiris.' The 'Golden Vine' was one of the principle ornaments of the Temple of Jerusalem. It is said that the 'Vine Tree' is the tree of joy, exhilaration, and of wrath." The Seer was holding a few of the leaves from the Vine Tree, and then he asked me what I saw.

I began to touch the leaves as well. Finally I said, "I notice that the leaves are slightly hairy and that the newer tendrils really coil up tightly." I paused a minute to look at the Seer; he had that same stone expression, like earlier in the day. I looked again at the tree. Holding one of its leaves, I then counted the various points, saying out loud, "There seem to be five points to the leaves; that is what I see."

The Seer then clapped. "Exactly!" he said, and then we walked a bit around the Apple and the Vine. When he was satisfied with his musing, he said this: "As I do hope that you recall, from your studies with the Apple Tree, the apple fruit, when cut open, contains five points with the seed formation. Here we now have something mysterious, called 'Pentads' by the ancients, meaning the number five or in groups of five. This is pertaining to the British Goddesses, the 'deae matronae,' which have been prevalent since ancient Roman times. And in each of these various Goddess images are the 'Five-Pointed Leaves' sacred to the 'White Goddess'! These would include the Vine, Ivy, Bramble, Fig, and Plane, or 'Platanus,' a deciduous tree. There are various 'Five-Petaled Flowers' also sacred to her; these include the Briar-Rose, Primrose, and Periwinkle! I offer you this beautiful quote from 'Ecclesiastes': 'Like a Vine I budded forth beauty and my flowers ripen into glory and riches.' *M* for 'Muin,' which is the 'Vine'! Yes, we have intrigue and mystery with our work, Dreamer. So glad that you are paying attention!"

"Paying attention. Of course! I love the Dreaming lessons, and the mystery of it makes me even happier. What a beautiful quote...'I budded forth.' So beautiful!" I had answered the Seer rather quickly; he needed to hear my enthusiasm, as this was truth to me. He had quite a broad smile after that, no longer stoned faced. I was glad.

We strolled in the nearby woodland, not speaking, just enjoying the land. Of course I had questions bubbling, but I knew to give this gentle man a little space.

Circling back to the red blanket, the Vine Tree Seer said, "Please sit!"

Which of course I did. The leaves crunched underneath the blanket, and I chased a spider off the edge. But I got a nice message from the Spider, telling me to just remain on the web! I smiled and said finally, quite loudly, "Dear Seer, please do tell me more about the Bramble-Blackberry!"

"Learning to be a mind reader, are we?" said the Seer. "I was about to tell some of a Druid story with the 'Vine.'"

"That would be great!" I interjected.

The Seer remained standing and paced slowly in front of where I sat on the blanket. I could see the Apple tree beyond him and the twisted Vine, with a few leaves curling. I wondered what the blackberries would taste like. Beyond these was a very thick stand of trees; many of their branches seemed woven together. I wondered if the Bramble Vine was entwined there too.

He was ready now. I returned from my daydreaming to hear: "The Vine of the Celts' Druidic tree alphabet often refers to the Bramble-Blackberry bush. Blackberry is one of the few plants bearing blossoms and fruit at the same time. From Medieval Herbals there are mentioned many curative values. It has been said that the juice of the blackberry's virtue is to lift the spirits by restoring hope. Blackberry magic comes to us through 'country wisdom.' Here are but a few of the many tales: 'When in early spring the frozen dew covers the blackberry blossoms at dawn, farmers are said to rejoice, saying this is a 'Blackberry Winter'! For without this frost, the berries will not set. In essence then what appears to be threatening turns out to be a blessing for a very rich harvest!' There is an ancient legend which tells: 'Blackberries gathered and eaten within the span of the waxing moon at harvest time will assure protection from the forces of any evil runes.'

"The name of the 'Vine' is derived from the Latin word 'Viere,' which means 'to twist,' which is very descriptive of this plant. Vines are among the longest living plants. It has been said that in the Burgundy region of France there are still living grapevines of four hundred years.

"The Vine is actually a climbing shrub and not classified as a tree. Still, to the Celts, it belonged as one of the twenty trees in most Ogham alphabets. The Vine has been depicted by the Celts in ancient stories as growing over doorways. In one such story from the Welsh, 'First Branch of the Mabinogi,' we have this: 'The vine grew over the doorway of a round tower, which was said to be part of the Castle of Arianrhod. Within this castle was the "Seat of Annwn," described as the Otherworlds' lands of good and of plenty, and where souls were said to depart from this world, which is ruled by the King Arawn.' This is the center of the Celtic Mysteries on the astral plane. What do we have at the very entrance to this special castle? The Vine! Which of course is one of the guardians to the mysteries."

The Seer had paused momentarily, looking contentedly at me.

"Now the grapevine, though not native to the northern lands, came into play fairly early among the Celts. It has been said the grapevine in all likelihood was brought by the 'Danaan Peoples'—from the Greek story of Homer's *Iliad*, the tribe of 'Danaans'—when they invaded Ireland in ancient times. The vine was planted in sheltered southern regions and protected."

The Vine Tree Seer was quiet before he said, "We need now to talk in depth of the Grapevine, Dreamer!" He was more serious as he looked at me. I wondered if the "talk in depth of the grapevine" had something to do with the last evening's partying. But I said nothing. Still he was quietly staring at me; I realized that an emphatic point can be made in silence. Thinking about last night, I realized three glasses was one too many for me.

Before I could ask anything, the Seer rummaged from his pack a green bottle of Burgundy wine. He then held it to the light and checked it over; seemingly satisfied, he proceeded to use the corkscrew to open the bottle. Now he took in the aroma and smiled. Taking two small, clear wine glasses from his pack, he poured the wine into each glass. Outwardly I remained placid, inside I was cringing! Is this a drinking test? If so, I will fail! Small things; think of small talk to divert his attention to how I am feeling, I thought.

Too late. The Seer was conversing again. Handing me one of the wine glasses, the Vine Tree Seer said, "This bottle of Burgundy is three years old, from the vines of these southern slopes. I hope that you will like what is has to teach. Let us toast to you, Dreamer, a student of the Dreaming!"

We clinked our glasses, and I smiled as earnestly as possible. Then I took a sip. How could I not? "Thank you, Seer. What a lovely toast, and I like the taste!" I was speaking in a cheerful voice, and then, as I saw his eyes, dark and questioning, I blurted out, "The taste! That is the problem! I know I had a few too many glasses last night at the party. The Dreamers were doing skits about Dionysus and we—"

"Dreamer! OK, it is quite all right!" The Seer had stopped me from speaking. As my mouth stopped, the other words just hung in the air; I looked at him a little stunned.

He continued, "No need to explain anything; you all were just having fun! I have not invited you here today for any sort of reprimand, no! Relax! Let me give you a little more on Dionysus, as he became one of the most important gods in everyday Greek life and was associated with several key concepts. His association with death and rebirth can be seen symbolically in tending the vines. Each year the vines are pruned back sharply and left to become dormant through the winter, ready to bear fruit in the following spring. Another concept is that while under the influence of wine, we can connect with nature. In the mystery traditions, intoxication comes not from the plant but from the spirit of the plant, its divine essence. It has been noted that if careful, a man might become greater than him and do works he otherwise would not do. When I saw you enjoying the party last eve, I felt you to be prime for the 'lessons of the vine.' Nothing more than a teacher, a Keeper knowing that the student is ready for the lessons." The stoned faced man from earlier was full of smiles and laughter now.

I had been standing minutes before, but now I slumped down to the blanket, saying, "That's it? I mean, you do not mind the silly way I was last night?"

He was still laughing, but said, "We have much to cover before the day is out and bigger fish to fry!"

More laughter as I sat in amazement. Looking directly at him as he sipped his wine, I said, "OK! What does the wine-vine have to teach me?"

Answering instantly, the Seer said, "Bravo, Dreamer! To the 'Lessons of the Vine'! Yes, let's toast to that, exactly that!"

We then both clinked our glasses once more, with me taking only the smallest of sips, and I settled down upon the blanket to listen and learn about "The Vine."

The "Vine Tree Seer" speaks: "The vine may provide fruit, as from the blackberry and the grape, which are made into pleasing wines for drink. What needs to be understood as a Dreamer on the path of 'Magical Workings' is there is one who just drinks and there is one whose intention is to learn from the drink. Sometimes there can be amazing teaching during the divine inebriation the vine fruit provides, only if used carefully. Please keep this in mind: the fermented fruit of the vine can be a source of inspiration in the physical world. But in the Otherworlds one must *not* be involved with the drinking of wine. It is generally inadvisable to accept offers of drink, especially intoxicating drink, while involved with Otherworld Dreaming! There may be a price to pay. Do not do so! Should a situation arise with an offering of drink while in an Otherworld journey, be very careful whether to accept or to refuse. Ask: do I know and trust this person offering the drink? Please realize that the Otherworld part of you in this journey really does not require food or drink![22] Ask: why is it being offered? Ask: what kind of spirit are you? Are you being asked to provide something in return? The point is to learn what one can with care taken."

The Seer paused and checked for my reaction. My immediate thought was, I can get inspired while tipsy!

He smiled and said, "I heard that! Looks like we need to refine inebriation."

I had forgotten how easily some of the Keepers read thought patterns. I decided I had better pay attention, rather than cause attention. This ancient gentle man paid no mind to my thoughts now; he was already into another part of the Vine lessons.

"The Vine is a 'Teaching Tree,' but it also has the function of uniting and is often referred to as such, a 'Uniting Tree.' It is important to see how it grows. It is one of the few trees that grows in conjunction with another tree, then spreads itself across to join another tree and continues without limit. Doing so, it connects otherwise separate trees. By observing the growth patterns of trees in the wild of nature, we can then be taught something of great value. If we were to apply a few of these patterns to our ordinary lives, that would be something indeed. Become like the Vine, by uniting different properties of the trees within yourself. Next turn your gifts of knowledge into pleasing wine that can pass on inspiration to others.

"Another characteristic of the Vine is that it is a very strong tree that can bind to any other tree with little resistance from the host tree. This teaches us that one must strive to be strong both as an individual and when living and working with others. The Vine is strong in that its fermented fruit can cause a person to take leave of his or her senses and, in extreme cases, die. This same fermented fruit can be the source of inspiration. The teaching is to learn to use the wine properly, which is the real test of this tree. This requires much work with the Vine out in nature, learning from its roots, vine-trunk, and its fruit. In our magical workings with spirit, we are taught to strive for balance and to know how to use the 'In-Between' states of Dreaming; our aim should have us be role models and inspire others searching for their pathways."

The Seer was standing now, walking to the Apple and Vine combo. I propped my head up on my elbows and watched as he looked over the two trees. He was holding part of the Vine's trunk and traced its growth direction around the Apple tree. Then he spoke.

"The Vine is not choosey! As you can see, the Vine will happily attach itself to any tree that can support it. Showing us in our magical workings to be unbiased in attitudes toward other humans, to be glad to share one's knowledge and experience. The Vine in the natural world attaches itself and lives in harmony with other trees. Humans can learn much from this way of being.

"Interestingly the Vine has a close connection with the Apple tree, as does the Ivy, which we will learn about later. Important lessons can be found listening to the Vine while in the natural woods; be certain to listen to its host tree as well. Remember to call upon one's guides to help understand what it is that you hear while out in the woodlands.

"Another teaching to be had by Dreaming with the Vine is to actually envision oneself as the Vine. Imagine with the Vine or another tree as one goes through their day-to-day life interacting with family, friends, taking a walk, driving a car or at one's work place. When you interface your knowledge of the tree world into your daily routine, you will come to learn the importance of our human and plant world interconnections and how we can all provide support upon this web of life. Dream yourself as the Vine, budding new leaves and branches, then actually producing fruit. This is awesome work. The spiritual side of our Dream work is to do the linking and binding, just as the vine does in nature. Becoming the Vine can be a magical experience. Let us look at things this way: think of all the multiple relationships we have with people and how they weave and twist through our life. This is just how the Vine weaves and twists its way through the forest of trees and plant life. It is important to eat the fruits of the Vine, the grape and the berry. These are the gifts of much hard work in growth. However, Dreamer, we remember to use care and balance when doing so."

"I want you to know, dear Seer, that these lessons are so exciting to me! Why, I can feel myself—"

I would have continued, but the now smiling Seer held up his hand. Through a half laughing voice, with his head tilted to one side, he said, "Hey! Do you always talk so fast? A fellow can hardly get in a word edgewise!"

I giggled, saying, "What do you mean? Do I really talk so fast?"

"Come!" is all he said.

Of course I followed. We stopped at the base of the Vine and Apple trees; he told me to follow the thin roots that went into the Earth near the base of the trunk. He made sure I found the roots of the Vine and not the Apple. Then with a trowel tool, he began to dig up some of the thinner roots and showed me where to move away the soil to expose the root. Next he took out a pinch of tobacco for us each, and then with love and thankfulness, we asked the Vine if we might cut a portion for our magical workings. Once he sprinkled the tobacco, I did the same. He was satisfied that we could take some of the root, and then using a small knife, he cut a long stretch of about four feet. Once that was done, he handed me the Vine root and then quickly began to cover the root with soil and dried leaves. He dusted off his hands, and with his foot, he kicked around some of the leaves. We had not spoken; I did not even ask why he was doing this. I knew this would be unfolded to me.

Finally, he said, "That should do it; no one can even tell we were here! Come, Dreamer, we have work to do!"

I could not stand it any longer. I said, "What kind of work?"

"Now that we have been through the lessons, this is a good time to learn a little more about ritual. We will make a 'Sacred Cord' from the Vine root, which is to be worn by you in ritual.[23] This will indicate to the Otherworlds that you have reached an advanced stage in your 'Tree-Magic' studies, having gone now halfway through."

With tears, I moved close to the Seer and gave him a hug before he could say more. I said, "Thank you!" This was not the time to carry on; I did not say more.

The Seer only nodded. "Now, Dreamer, you are to enter a Dream journey and include the Vine Tree and its host, the Apple. Then you do the following; I will only tell you these instructions once. So please gather all your attention. Once you have begun your Dreaming work, I will be walking in the stand of trees ahead. You will quiet yourself and do a very fine job. I will come if you need me. Do not speak out loud; I will know without your voice of words.

"These are the instructions: First, measure this cord of the Vine long enough to wrap around your waist, allowing at least an additional two feet hanging down from each end. Second, in the middle tie a knot; think of the 'Vine Tree' in the Ogham and gather its energy there into the knot. Proceed to tie a total of eleven knots, one for each of the eleven trees you have worked with, using the same gathering energy for each specific tree. Working from the middle, move to the left side of the long cord and figure out equal distant spaces for ten more tree knots. Then, starting at the left bottom end of the cord, think of the first tree in the Ogham sequence of the trees—I do believe this to be the Birch—and gather its energy and tie a knot for the tree. Third, proceed with the rest of the trees until you meet up with the middle knot, which then will be the Vine! Now to the right side of the Vine will be empty cord space; this will be added onto in the same manner as you will do here today, at a later time with each of the trees. Add knots for each of the remaining nine trees as you, from this point, complete the study. In your study of the 'Tree Ogham,' with the Vine now, you have now gone just past the halfway point of the individual tree lessons. When you have completed the entire knot-tying, this brings the total to Twenty Ogham Trees. Do you understand this working, Dreamer?"

I nodded my head yes. Presenting a bubbly voice saying, "Yes! Of course, I can do this!" My inside voice, however, was feeling very shaky. Would I be able to remember the instructions for the way the cord should be made? More importantly, would I be able to gather the individual tree energy for each of the knots? Could I remember the trees? I was panic stricken just then and looked to The Seer, who was walking to the stand of trees. He turned and looked at me just a moment, and then I recalled what he had said: "call upon the Vine and the Apple for your journey Dreaming." Something released the sudden panic; I began to feel calmness. I thought of the Vine, how it weaves, twists, and links with the Apple. I thought of the Apple and the way her sturdy branches and roots support the Vine.

A smile came across my face. I thought, I may be able to do this after all! I looked up toward the trees. The Vine Tree Seer was there, just barely visible; it was enough, and he was a comfort. I looked more closely at my length of cord; it was time to get to work. I summoned my two trees again to assist me. Laying the cord upon the ground, I found its true center. I thought to myself, This will become my "Sacred Cord." Now I gathered the energy of the "Vine-Muin" and formed a fine knot into the center. This felt amazing, and the first one then became the next and on to each of the trees—the "Birch-Beithe," "Rowan-Luis,"

"Alder-Fearn," "Willow-Sail," "Ash-Nion," "Hawthorn-Huath," "Oak-Duir," "Holly-Tinne," "Hazel-Coll," "Apple-Queirt"—back to the middle the eleventh tree, "Vine-Muin."

I was just thanking the Vine and the Apple, when I was distracted by something. When I looked up, it was the Vine Tree Seer who had just lit a small fire in a small stone fire pit off toward the open space on the hillside. I smiled at the two trees where I had been sitting and again thanked them for their assistance. Standing and looking up to the sky, I began to realize it was now late afternoon. Where had the time gone? I suppose I had been deep into the Otherworlds where the concept of time is, well, isn't! I laughed with glee, feeling proud of what I had just done.

Picking up my newly made "sacred cord," I ran over to join the Vine Tree Seer near the fire. It was only a short distance, but I was surprised at how short of breath I seemed. Then I saw he had company. Stopping next to the Seer, I said under my breath, "Oh! They are here!"

"Come! Don't be shy now, dear Dreamer!" said the Vine Tree Seer. "The Keepers are here to support and to congratulate you on your achievement. Come!" He then took me by the hand and led me to the central area around the fire. Next he took my cord and then held this up for all to see; there was a round of applause for my work. I was stunned! I could not speak; the Keepers were clapping for me. I could not be sure because of the tears in my eyes, but I was fairly sure the Keepers were the first eleven Tree Seers. Of course this included the Vine Tree Seer.

What happened next was very moving for me. I had been to various ceremonies that had special focus, but now I was being told there would be a small ceremony for the honoring of my "midway point" on the tree-magic studies. A ceremony for me? Well, I could not believe it.

The "Vine Tree Seer" told me how the ceremony would go and he would be at my side to assist my weaving around the circle. The "Apple Tree Seer" would be on my other side to support me.

I saw the cord I had made being passed through the sage smoke above the fire; this was done by the Apple Tree Seer. Then it was passed to each of the Eleven Tree Seers; each of them held and blessed their knot on the cord. When finished, it came back to the "Vine Tree Seer," and he held the center knot, giving his blessing. Next he passed the cord through the smoke just slightly and then opened it to its length, holding it up horizontally. One of the Tree Seers then led me to stand directly in front of the Vine Seer.

I looked up at this amazing man as he said: "The work is done; the energy of the Seers has been lent to each of these knots. It is sealed and has now become this Dreamer's 'Sacred Cord.' You have done well, Dreamer. There is more to complete, but the first half of this task is always the hardest, and it is done. Please know, Dreamer, that this cord should be worn only during ritual or 'Magical Workings.' Let this cord serve as another mnemonic device in your 'Magical Workings,' where feeling the length of the cord will bring to mind the name, order, and meaning of each of the Tree Seers. May you continue to Dream Strong! May it be so!"

The Vine Tree Seer then reached over and gave me a hug. He tied my "Sacred Cord" around my waist. Offering his arm, he then walked me around the fire circle. Everyone there gave me words of praise and encouragement to finish the next set of trees. I was very proud to be a Dreamer as I walked about and relaxed slightly. However, this was one time that I was actually speechless. I suppose I just needed to be the one receiving at that particular time. Looking around the fire, the Keepers were enjoying themselves. I noticed that they too had on their "Sacred Cords," and I knew that they had at one time gone through a similar ceremony. This was truly something, and now I was following in some of their paths. Wow!

Just then the Vine Tree Seer was there, saying, "Now we really have something to toast to!" He handed me a wine glass filled with a beautiful Burgundy wine, no doubt from the southern hills. Smiling, I gladly took the glass. The Seer then said, "To you, Dreamer, and the midway marked by this eleventh tree, the Vine!"

We clinked glasses and I heard others saying, "Here, here! And to the next nine that she will do! Here! Here!" More clinking and much laughter.

Then I found my voice to say, "Is this a dream? Is it OK to accept this wine from you?"

The Vine Tree Seer thought that quite funny and clinked my glass again, saying, "She has been a quick study, and fun!" All the Seers were laughing as well. This made me glad. Let it please continue!

IVY

Karen R. Silberstein

"G" Gart

THE IVY
LETTER "G," "GORT"
OGHAM: ╪

STATISTICS FOR:

"The Ivy" genus/species- *Hedera helix*

~The growth of Ivy depends upon a host for its support. It has four or five pointed leaves, with its clinging tendrils that clutch for support.

~~~~~~~~~~~

THE IVY: HOW USED IN THE WORLD

~Most Ivy parts—leaves, bark, berries—can be used. There are some types that are poisonous; check this. Ivy is connected to the Winter Solstice and is used for decorating at the Yule Tide. Ivy is often used for weddings or hand fastings. In ancient times Ivy was woven into crowns for poets and for brides and grooms.

~~~~~~~~~~~

MEDICINAL AND PSYCHOLOGICAL

~The leaves can be used as a tincture for douche to treat female infections. Externally Ivy leaves can be made into poultices to heal nerves, sinews, ulcers, and infections. Tender Ivy twigs can be simmered into a salve to treat sunburn. Ivy is said to provide protection when growing near a house. Ivy is equated with fidelity and can be used in charms to bind love and luck.

~~~~~~~~~~~

SACREDNESS AMONG THE GROVE

~The Ivy is the twelfth tree in the Ogham Alphabet- "Gort"-"G".

~The Ivy is associated with warnings, evergreen strength, spiral ability, and reincarnation.

~KEYWORD- Warnings

~Month- September 30 through October 27

~Planets- Pluto and Moon

~The Ivy stands on either side of the Vine tree and Broom tree within the Grove.

~"FINGER TIP TREE" location- "Ivy- Girt"-"G" is on the middle of the forefinger.

DREAM OF "GORT," THE IVY TREE SEER

"Come quickly!" I heard as I darted through the forest, stepping over knotted roots, and dead, dried branches pulling on my skirts. There ahead was the swirling fog and the forest's edge. Over the twisted branches, I felt the mild rain as I ran. My eyes constantly on the greenest leaves of the forest, collecting the droplets.

"Come quickly!" I heard again; my attempt to move faster was hampered by the thick undergrowth and dense, profuse vines that covered the fallen trees. But I pressed on, needing to know. The sky was blue ahead. The tree stood alone on the rim of the forest like a sculpture, a gentle spiral, gray and smooth; twisted upper branches hung out to the sides. Peculiar, I thought. The leaves, as green and bright as they were, seemed not of the tree. Looking closer, I realized there was a movement there, and then I saw her.

She stepped away in diaphanous green silks and shining ivy leaves. The Goddess of the Tree. I looked at the tree, separate now from this being, and gazed at the tree itself. I observed that the once grand tree and smooth trunk was now a host for the shiny, verdant Ivy that clung and spiraled around the trunk and held to its branches.

Something shattered! I woke up!

Startled at this vivid encounter, I began to realize that in waking reality I was on a blanket next to the lake, having taken some time off. Standing up now, thinking I would go, I began commenting to myself how real this dream was. Looking a quick minute at the position of the Sun, I knew it wasn't too late. Rather than packing up, I pulled out my journal and began to reenter this dream and write it out. What does it mean?

But first a title. I looked from the lake to the edge of the wood, and there was the tree in my Dreaming! Covered in Ivy, I ran closer and knew that this was the Ivy Tree Seer. My journal was still in hand; I sat down and began to draw the tree as I saw it there and as I had seen it in my Dreaming. Once I had the rough sketching done, and the Dream written into my journal, I gave it this title: "Dream of the Ivy Tree Seer." Entranced, I began to recall what had happened. I had an afternoon nap by the lake and awakened with a vivid dream of the "Ivy Tree Seer." Then in waking reality, I reentered this Dream, and I found myself in front of the very tree of the Dream!

"Where am I? There or here?" I called out these words loudly and could hear them echo back to me. Feeling confused, I walked back to my things on the blanket. Thinking a little distance might help, I started to pack up.

I heard the wind and saw it travel across the top of the water, causing ripples and soft mysterious sounds. Half-forgotten stirrings of what happened made me slow down. For nights lately I had been dreamless. It happens and it is OK. Now this Dream!

"Well, I certainly hope you are not shattered too badly!" The hem of green silk drifted over my blanket. I looked up from my downward gaze to find the "Ivy Tree Seer" standing firmly in front of me. She spoke more softly now than before, saying, "Dreamer, did you forget the process? I believe one should ask, 'What do you want to know?' As I recall in your Dreaming and running to the request of 'Come quickly,' you pressed on, needing to know. What is it you need to know, Dreamer?"

"Oh my Goddess! You startled me. Where did you come from? Where am I?"

The Seer only hissed and said, "Do you usually answer a question with a question?" She stared hard, her long black hair twined about her down to her waist; I could see the shiny ivy spiraling in beautiful designs about her green silk gown. She was tall and slender, and I could feel vitality in her energy. Her emerald eyes held mine, and she was expecting an answer. What had she said?

Quickly tracking backward, I found the question...What do I need to know? Finally I muttered, "Why did you come to me in my dream? And why did you say, 'Come quickly'?"

Her answer was not in words as she looked me over and handed me a branch with ivy leaves on it. Turning and walking ahead, she moved her graceful head around once to say, "Come quickly!" Of course I followed; that is what one does while in the midst of training with magical Dream Seers. But I thought to myself, she has not answered my question either! Taking a deep breath, I twirled the ivy branch as we walked into the woods; it was cooler and darker here now that the sun had moved decidedly toward the west. I knew of course that my question would be answered in the form of teaching by this amazing Seer-Goddess who strode on ahead of me. Why had she come? Was I in waking life or still in my Dream, her Dream? I twirled the ivy branch a little more and could feel some stress.

Just then I tripped over a few fallen branches; down I went. The Seer stopped and checked on me, noting that I was fine. "I am clumsy sometimes!" I said.

Without feeling or any facial expression, she said, "You are not clumsy; you were not paying attention. Your focus was gone." I wanted to reply; there was nothing to say. I opened my lips and said nothing; she was right. Now she went on. "This is actually a good place to rest. Now please, Dreamer, pay attention, look around, and think about what comes into your view! Don't say anything just yet; I want you to focus. We will talk in a few minutes."

I smiled at the Ivy Tree Seer and rearranged where I should sit. I tucked the ivy branch into my belt and then cleared some dried leaves away from the fallen tree. Underneath was the greenest of greens, and I knew this to be ivy. Perfect for me to sit with, and hopefully I could find a better focus. The Seer was strolling not too far from me. I looked around and began to observe and understand the terrain better. I realized there were so many fallen trees, brambles and vines, and here I was in the middle. Every direction seemed to have obstacles, yet I knew that I had run through this spot earlier today…in my Dreaming, which allowed me some memory. I felt curiously easy, calm, and full of light energy.

The Ivy Tree Seer was back and sat across from me. "Tell me, Dreamer, what have you noticed?" she said in a firm, no-nonsense way.

I looked her in the eyes and then looked off to the sides of me, gesturing with my right hand as I spoke. "I feel calmness here, and I realize that I had run through this very spot earlier in my Dreaming. What I did not pay much attention to during the Dreaming itself is what I see now." I paused and looked at the Seer.

"Go on. What have you discovered?" she said simply. No smile, only intense emerald-green eyes.

"Now I see all the fallen trees and how thick the undergrowth is; there are vines, ivy vines, everywhere! I mean there are obstacles all over. I am, frankly, shocked at how I was able to get through all this in my Dream!" By now I was standing and became very animated as I spoke.

I stopped to hear the Seer say as she cocked her head to one side, "Are you feeling calm, Dreamer?"

I sat back down, my face flushed red, and I shook my head, saying, "I was only trying to describe how this feels to me…But I am all right."

Now she laughed. I was glad, at least I think so. Smiling some, she began to speak. "Since we are speaking frankly, as you said, I too am amazed that you got through the obstacles here. This tells me two things. One, you are a strong and determined Dreamer who will not let things get in her way. Two, sometimes a Dreamer needs to heed an obstacle; this is what you will learn about today."

I smiled at her and was happy she thought me determined. She was ready to continue.

"Now tell me, Dreamer, what is it you need to know from this Dream?"

I stood and paced a moment. Finally I answered, "I need to know what the urgency is for coming into the forest to meet the sculptured tree that holds the Ivy, which turns out to be you, dear Seer! Why do I need to meet you now? How did I plough through and not get hurt?"

The Ivy Tree Seer looked at me quizzically; she too stood up. I sat down. In her hand was a branch of Ivy; her emerald-green silks swayed with the breezes. She twisted her long, black hair back over her shoulders, which showed off her young-looking face. Knowing her to be ancient, I found myself wondering about her stories.

The Ivy Tree Seer said, "In my Dream of yours called 'The Ivy Tree Seer,' I find myself wondering where in waking reality do I give or receive warnings, and am I curious about this? Do I heed the warnings I receive? In my Dreaming I need to be aware of the main attribute of Ivy when it comes to me in a sleep or in a waking dream because 'The Ivy is a Warning Tree'!"[24]

She stopped for a moment and was patting the ivy branch across her hand. I wanted to respond but could see the timing was not right. She continued. "Have I made myself clear, Dreamer?"

I answered with a nod of my head, meaning yes. She replied with, "I am quite certain you barely know what I mean. Let me go back to the question of your Dreaming. In my Dream of yours, you were not hurt pressing through obstructions because you were under my protection. The timing was right for us to meet now; you are at a crossroads, Dreamer, and some paths may have danger. Not everything is the pretty picture you like to paint. It is time to be aware and to take heed of warnings when they come. Determination is good, when used with awareness. Now this is my Dream of yours. How are you feeling, Dreamer?"

I could hardly speak; I wasn't sure at all about warnings. What am I being warned about? Think! I said to myself, She is waiting for an answer. "How do I feel? I am totally confused. I thought I was doing well…Is there something I have missed a warning about? I mean—"

The Ivy Tree Seer put up her hand and said, "Well, I can see I have stirred up some interest here! This is good. Now to finish your Dream for now. Before we move more into study mode, please do tell me, Dreamer: How will you honor this Dream? And what will be your bumper sticker?" Very quietly she sat down and stared at me, expecting an answer.

Unsure about what to say, I took out the ivy branch from my belt and held it firmly. Finally, feeling a little strengthened, I said, "I would like to learn all I can about the Ivy; that will be my honoring. And for a bumper sticker I would say, 'Heed the Ivy'!"

Feeling pleased, I began to sit down on the green clump of ivy, but the Seer stopped me to say, "Before we are done, this branch will have the Ogham symbol of Ivy carved into it, and of course that will be part of your honoring, Dreamer!"

I sat there fingering the branch and was very happy about this new connection. The Seer apparently had additional plans, as she said to me, "Are you coming?" And she proceeded to march off back the way we had come through the woods. Catching up some, I focused because the fallen trees and twisted vines were a challenge; I did not want to fall again.

The Ivy Tree Seer found the blanket I had by the lake and motioned for me to sit with her. I noticed a white swan had graced the lake water, and we both watched it for a while. Then the Seer told me that the Swan often comes to assist her, along with the element of water. Nearby our blanket, a fire had been set into the stone circle pit. I wondered who had done this…but knew the powers that be often tended our needs here. A picnic basket was there, and the Seer handed me some bread and cheese; we sat and ate in silence for a while. This felt good, as the sun was low on the western horizon now, even though it was early September; afternoon into evening can be cool out here in the Nemeton.

Standing up now, she said, "I would like to show you something before it starts to get any darker this evening!" She offered her hand and pulled me up from the blanket. We then walked to where the tree of my Dream stood, and she told me to look it over. So beautifully sculptured was the host tree, and the ivy was happily twisting and growing abundantly around the tree. I noted this to the Seer.

She answered with: "Ivy's Latin botanical name is '*Hedera helix*'; this describes the spiral form of growth as 'Helix,' which means 'to turn around.' This term can be used when doing one's magical Dreaming path work. For sometimes we need to examine what it is we are doing and actually 'turn around' and notice what is taking place in a situation.

"Now look at the ivy that is growing close to the ground here." She pointed to several spots. "When you notice the difference in its appearance from the parts that grow around the tree, you will notice that the ground areas appear weak. Yet when it climbs in its growth, with the host tree or sometimes a wall for support, it grows increasingly stronger, and only the upright sections will produce flowers in the fall, with berries appearing in the spring."

The Seer stood back away from the trees and, looking upward, admired what she saw. I did the same thing. "That is amazing. And look how happy the Ivy seems! I wonder though about the host tree?"

"Yes," said the Seer. "It has given over life for the ivy, but please know that in nature there are certain givens that allow for this; contracts are made, and lives are played out."

I wanted to ask more about this, but the Seer quickly turned back toward the lake, having another lesson plan in mind for now. The swan was busily feeding upon the lake. She was a picture of grace and beauty. But I felt sadness about the host tree of Ivy.

Apparently the Seer knew, because she said, "Perseverance and patience are what you require now. In time you will gain wisdom with this. Ground yourself, Dreamer! We have much work to do!"

Well, that certainly shook me out of a Daydream! The Seer was certainly surprising in what she might do, and I did realize that her time with me was limited. I grounded by wiggling my feet into the grasses there and breathed very deeply for focus and concentration.

The Ivy Tree Seer said, "Ivy is not considered a proper tree. It usually depends on a host tree for its growth and support. And like the 'Vine,' the 'Ivy' is a binding and uniting plant. The leaves of ivy are a deep, waxy, forest green, and they stay evergreen, with four or five pointed lobes. It has thin, hairy, spindly stems-tendrils that clutch various surfaces and are strong enough to force their way through trees or even brick buildings. Sometimes Ivy can cause structural damage. When the host is a tree, it is not unusual for the Ivy to grow so thick that it eventually smothers and kills the tree.

"The word 'Gort' means 'Greenfields' or Gardens.'[25] It also means 'Standing Corn.' The importance of Ivy from a magical point of view is that although it appears very similar to the Vine, it is actually stronger. The Vine usually does not kill its host tree; the Ivy often does. The Ogham symbol notch for the Ivy are two slanted lines crossing the central stem, which is twice the number used as the symbol notch of the Vine. This demonstrates that the Ivy is more capable than the Vine of binding to a host tree. This ability to force its way through makes the Ivy a very powerful tree. This also gives the Ivy a sense of malice. In doing our magical Dreaming work, what does this indicate? Foremost it tells us to use caution with Ivy on the physical level, but even more care is required when working on the magical level."

The Seer was up now and walking at the lake's edge, picking grasses, stirring the smooth mirror surface with her hand. The mist was now curling from the water at the edges. I could tell she was familiar with this lake and its surrounds; she was a part of the beauty and it of her. I wondered about the things she had said having to do with caution. What kind of territory was this going to be? Should I be fearful? I didn't know.

The Ivy Tree Seer was back; she was refreshed. "I can feel your questions and uncertainty. Let me just say that fears arise when a new order of some kind is gaining influence, and this often results in an attempt to guard the old ways. The point is, Dreamer, you have now moved a bit more than halfway through the Ogham studies, and there are serious things to consider in your workings. The lesson of importance now is one of caution."

I said to the Seer, "I am beginning to understand, and it is amazing how you picked up on what I was thinking."

"This is what I do. Part of my training is to be ahead of the Dreamers' apprehensions when they are learning the ways. Now I would like to give some background history that will help to round out your lessons. Ivy and her teachings were used both by Greeks and Egyptians. Scared both to 'Dionysus' the Greek God of Wine and to the Egyptian God 'Osirus' God of the Sun. Vine and Ivy come next to each other at the turning of the year and are dedicated to resurrection, presumably because they are the only two trees in the Beth-Luis-Nion that grow spirally.

"In England the Ivy Tree has traditionally been the sign of the wine tavern. Ivy-Ale is still brewed at Trinity College and is a highly intoxicating medieval drink. Both Ivy and Holly were associated with the 'Saturnalia Festival,' an ancient Roman festival held in honor of the God Saturn, held December seventeenth through the twenty-third. The Holly became the club of Saturn, and the Ivy was the nest of the Gold Crest Wren, his bird. On Yule morning, which was the last of Saturn's merry reign, the first foot expected over the threshold had to be that of Saturn's representative, a dark man called the 'Holly Boy.' Elaborate precautions were taken to keep women away. From these times Ivy was associated with women, sometimes called the 'Ivy Girl.' Ivy also came to mean a shrewish wife, which may be a simile confirmed by the fact of the smothering or strangling of trees by the Ivy. In those times the 'Holly Boy' and the 'Ivy Girl' became opposing factions and were thought to represent the domestic war of the sexes.

"In one of the Greek myth stories of Dionysus, Tyrrhenian pirates captured Dionysus. He then magically changed the masts of their ship into serpents, himself into a lion, and the sailors into dolphins. Then he used his powers once more and wreathed everything with the Ivy.

"The Roman God Bacchus—in Greece, Dionysus—had the Ivy Vine dedicated to him and wore a crown of the Ivy. It is said the practice of wearing Ivy leaves as a crown was to prevent the adverse effects of intoxication. Because of Ivy's traditional connection with Dionysus, the Wine God, Ivy was believed to cure as well as to cause drunkenness. It has been found that certain varieties of Ivy do contain toxic substances that do confuse the mind."

All was quiet; I heard the flutter of swallows as I watched her. Change was on her face; a reflection on her alabaster skin, maybe distress or pain. She did not blink as her last words hung in the air. She walked to the fire and stirred the embers. With visions swirling of long ago Greek gods and Goddesses of different lands, I wondered of the things she had seen and at the warnings she must have given.

The Ivy Tree Seer turned and seemed renewed by the fire energy. Smiling as she glided in her green silks, she was beauty and grace. There was no doubt about her strength and power.

"Well, Dreamer, as we have had a cross-section of the Ivy, now we will talk about Ivy's connection with the Goddess. As I trust you realize, Ivy has a strong connection with the divine feminine. It has five-lobed leaves representing the 'Five Aspects of the Goddess': Birth, Initiation, Love, Repose, and Death. The Ivy with its five-pointed leaves is one of the 'Pentads' sacred to the White Goddess; the others are Vine, Bramble, Fig, and Plane. The White Goddess is also associated with the five vowels, A-O-U-E-I, Alin, Onn, Ura, Eadha, Idho. There is also reference to the 'Five-Fold Goddess' who is associated the white-leaf ivy. Ivy also has the attribute of fidelity. In times of old, women carried ivy to aid in fertility and general good luck. Ivy, wherever it is grown or proliferates, guards against negativity and disaster. There was a time when Ivy was not permitted in the Catholic Church because of its association with pagan Goddesses.

"Ivy has a spiral growth pattern that is linked with the spiral of life, death, and rebirth we all walk throughout our days. The sacred spiral also symbolizes reincarnation from lifetime to lifetime. Ivy travels everywhere; it spreads happily and thrives many times where other greenery may not. Its determination to reach through obstacles toward light and food is well known, and therefore Ivy is strength. The Swan is connected with the Ivy and is sacred to the Goddess and helps with communication between the Otherworlds. Both Swan and Ivy can be most happy in cold climates; both have strong perseverance.

"Druid and Greek priests presented newly married couples with a wreath of Ivy to confer a blessing of strength and eternal love on the union. During the eleventh lunar month, when the Ivy was flowering, it was used to decorate the sacred shrines and altars of the Druids. The evergreen aspect represents the immortality of the spirit and personal stamina, and is never indecisive."

Once more the Seer paused and went to the fire. I joined her and brought several logs to add. We built the fire high, banking it against the chill of the September evening. The stars were just slightly showing themselves; the moon had not yet made an appearance. Silently the Seer motioned for me to sit across from her next to the stone fire pit.

I decided to share this with her. "Over the last week, I had many wakeful nights, Dreamless nights. Many things have felt clouded to me. I realize how grateful I am to have this amazing Dream come through you. This experience has made me feel so alive!"

The Ivy Tree Seer was seated on a low tree limb, her silken skirts wrapped over her legs. She smiled broadly, looking like an impish young girl as she tossed incense into the pit. Blue smoke hissed and swirled; she laughed again. "Well, I am glad, dear Dreamer. We would not want you going around feeling clouded!" She laughed a big belly laugh, and I felt we had both come to know each other a little better.

"Now let's continue! We do not want to be out here too far into the night. Working with the spiritual level of Ivy, we find there is a teaching about how we use control. Ivy teaches us that we may not have the control we thought we did. The lessons in the Otherworlds often will point out danger or mistakes with what we are about to encounter. Many Dream seekers on this path feel they have acquired so much and are prepared, which is true. But herein lies the problems; the truth is you are in more danger now than when you first started! In the beginning of your magical work, you were incapable of anything that might cause harm. However, once you learn and progress, you gain powers and skills that could be used incorrectly or maybe indiscreetly. The lesson here with Ivy becomes one of 'responsibility and accountability' for the use of the knowledge you have gained. The Otherworld guides and guardians are there. However, at this point they may now not be inclined to step in. So we must remember, Dreamer, the responsibility lies with you! One must explain actions and intentions; you must know your subject work very well and use caution in all that you do. *Do not* be overly self-assured, because this is when you may unknowingly become a worry to yourself or others.

"The Ivy Tree is not one to consciously use while doing Otherworld journey work because you may get tangled and stuck. The tree wants you to know that you may be going in the wrong direction. The Ivy does this by placing itself as a dense thicket in your pathway, *DURING* an Otherworld journey. This sudden occurrence may indicate that your whole intention is wrong and needs to be changed or possibly abandoned. Do not look to work with Ivy frequently in your work. Should the Ivy appear often, it would be wise to stop and review your reasons for this kind of work. It would be to your advantage to really examine your waking life. Please remember that the Ivy is a true 'warning tree'!

"The positive aspects of Ivy are its natural pleasing oil scent. This becomes more meaningful once you realize you have narrowly averted some danger, with much thanks to the warning of the Ivy!

"Another lesson from Ivy is no matter how big and strong you think you are. The small-looking leaves and spindly vine of the Ivy seem harmless, even pretty, but they can take hold of you, maybe softly at first, but slowly bind and then restrict you! The 'Word Ogham of Aongnus' says, 'Ivy is the size of a warrior.'

"The lesson of Ivy is always to examine what you are doing and your motives. If you do not take heed, the Ivy will step in and squeeze you until you are incapable of doing anything. Ivy teaches us about caution and the need for discretion in all our Magical Dreaming work.

"A good exercise practice is to experience the Ivy, as you did with the Vine. Using journey work, notice how it feels to bind around another tree or object around you. Think about what this may mean in your physical waking reality of your daily life. For instance, if you were Ivy, what would you bind to and what would this be in your waking reality?

"Well, my dear Dreamer, there are many new things to reflect upon now. I think it would be wise to have us finish up for the evening. We can review questions in the morning if you like, but I feel some Dreaming with this and relaxing is what is called for now."

The Ivy Tree Seer was standing and stretching out her back; the wind stirred her hair. She stood bathed now in silver Moon radiance, a Seer Goddess. I was about to say something, when she spoke. "May I have the piece of Ivy stick you have been holding?"

I nodded my head yes. The Seer looked this over a moment and then took the small knife she had at her belt and shaved some rough loose pieces off. Then she laid this on one of the stones in front of the fire and began to carve into it. After a few moments, she smoothed the stick with her fingers and then she held this over the fire. Next from her pouch she took herbs or maybe sage and sprinkled this into the fire. Again she held the stick over the fire and through the smoke. Once that was done, she looked it over and then handed the stick to me, saying, "You have been a fine listener and good Dreamer. Your Dream was true, and that is what brought us together for these lessons. Use your knowledge well and show honor with your newly made Ivy Ogham stick. I will appear when you may need a warning or two. Now, however, it is time to head back to the lodge and join the other Dream searchers!"

With tears and my heart happy, I looked at my new "Ivy Ogham Stick." Touching lightly the finely carved symbol for Ivy, I reached over and gave the Seer a hug and thanked her profusely. It was a quiet walk back accompanied by the light of the Moon. Before we left the lake, we both gave our greetings to the Swan who now had her partner with her. What an amazing day into evening of Dreaming!

BROOM

Karen C. Silverstein

"nG" nGetal

THE BROOM/REED LETTER "nG," "N GETAL" OGHAM:

STATISTICS FOR:

"The Boom/Reed" genus/species- *Cytisus scoparius*; subfamily- *faboideae*.

~Grows as a shrub to about 1–3 feet in height

~The leaves are small and oval. In spring through summer the stems appear leafless due to the abundant yellow flowers that bloom, bursting open. The flowers are followed by pods that, when dried out, are full of seeds.

~~~~~~~~~~~~

BROOM/REED: HOW USED IN THE WORLD

~The Broom wood is used as the name suggests, for brooms, brushes, and baskets. In Scotland, Broom was used in the thatching of cottages. Since ancient times, fibers, cloths, and papers have been made by macerating the stems in water. The leaves and young tips are boiled to make a green dye.

~~~~~~~~~~~~

MEDICINAL PSYCHOLOGICAL

~The Broom was used to treat many ailments. The green tips were used as a diuretic. The sparteine found in Broom is now used for heart and circulatory disorders. Other preparations can treat gout, sciatica, and joint pain. In large amounts, the sparteine found in Broom can cause hallucinations; this may relate back to the idea of witches flying on their Brooms!

~~~~~~~~~~~~

SACREDNESS AMONG THE GROVE

~The Broom is the thirteenth tree in the Ogham Alphabet: "nGetal"-"nG".

~The Broom/Reed is associated with inner sight, searching, cleaning, and magical cleansing.

~Month- October 28 through November 24

~KEYWORD- Clean up

~Planet- Pluto

~The Broom/Reed tree stands on either side of the Ivy tree and Blackthorn tree within the Grove.

~"FINGER TIP TREE" location- "Broom/Reed-nGetal"-"nG" is on the middle of the middle finger.

DREAM OF "N GETAL," THE BROOM TREE SEER

Was I Dreaming? The music, melancholy, yet sweet, had me memorized. I looked around; no one was there. Was I awake? I pinched myself as a test of this place; was I there or here? The pinch hurt; I must be here. Again the sounds of pipes made their musical call. What was I to do? I looked around my room at the lodge; everything seemed as it should. The light was dim; it was early evening. Now I recalled that after a long day of Dreamer training, I had come back here to have a nap.

Turning now to look at my bed, I suddenly realized that I was there on the bed sleeping! With fright, I jumped back a little. I mean, I had never seen myself asleep…So if I was sleeping, then I must have been Dream walking! Confused, I began to think I should do something; go back to my body? Yes, that was it!

Then again I heard the music and turned to look at the door that was slightly open. I thought that odd, as I was sure I had closed this when I came back. I turned and looked at my physical self on the bed; I seemed content there, quietly breathing in breathing out. I wondered how I would get back to my sleeping self?

"Not hard!" I heard someone say.

Again the music came, haunting and pulling my heart. I turned quickly; holding my breath, I tried to say who are you? My words did not come.

She stood there wrapped in a tartan plaid of alternating greens and blues. Red hair streaked with silver rested regally upon her shoulders and cascaded to her mid back. She held a long staff that looked like a broom. As I looked closer, I saw it was woven with intricate threads of blues and greens, which held the shaft-stick to the gathered bristle straw pieces. Slowly she began to sweep on the floor an image of a pathway from the door entrance into my lodge room. Of course I realized that this was the "Broom Tree Seer," but what was she sweeping for? I looked at my body asleep upon the bed and wanted to go into it.

Apparently the Seer heard my thoughts. She said, "There will be time to return to yourself, Dreamer! It is not hard; one simply holds onto their silver cord and Dreams it so! No… Not yet! We have work that needs doing first. Yes, we are about to fly, Dreamer, using my 'Besom'!" She held up her Broom and motioned for me to come with her on her Besom, as she called her broom.

The music began again, and now I saw the "Piper." A fine-looking tall man walked upon the path the Seer had just swept in through the doorway. He was dressed in a tartan plaid kilt of blues and greens. It was held with the traditional kilt belt from which hung a black leather "sporran," a Gaelic word for pouch or purse. Three pipes hung over his left shoulder, with tassels of greenish threads hanging from them. The bag was held under the left arm, and the blowpipe with the reed between his lips was in his mouth, supplying the bag with air. His two hands held the downward pointed pipe, playing the notched holes on it. I felt myself to be in my ancient life in Scotland as the "Piper" played the most beautiful music I had ever heard. Turning now to the Broom Tree Seer, I definitely had questions!

She quickly spoke before I could. "Magical, is it not? Ah! The sound of it transforms for where we need to be! The Bagpipes have four reeds as a part of their design; other reed instruments have one or two. The beauty of this is the air in the bag provides a constant motion from blowing the mouthpiece and moves over all four reeds at the same time. Wonderful! The sound this makes is magic, and the reed is integral to this." The Broom Tree Seer looked at me with joy in her eyes, and again before a question of mine could be uttered, she was introducing me to her "Piper."

"Dreamer! I would like you to meet my 'Piper.' He is an especially wise Welsh magician and very gifted with music magic. He has been known to sing home the soul with enchantment when need should arise."

The Seer looked at him with endearment. I suddenly realized their connection ran very deep. Now the Seer was talking about her besom, saying that the bristles were female and the staff handle was male and that together the broom is a magical tool used in the cleansing of negative energy and debris of our psychic and physical lives. The voices were trailing off as I watched the "Piper" looking on lovingly to the Broom Tree Seer. Finally my own voice came through. "I am very pleased to meet you, Piper! The music you made with your bagpipes has transported me to a life I knew in Scotland; thank you!"

I held out my hand to greet him, and he caught it in both of his hands. Smiling warmly, he said, "Aye, Lassie, the pleasure is all mine. I am enchanted. You hold yourself well, Dreamer!"

I bore the compliment with a shaking of my head, as my face had turned quite crimson as he looked into my heart. I had no eyes for seeing anything, as tears welled to the rim. Turning away I removed my hand and started to speak about where it was the Broom Seer said we were to go. Looking around the lodge room, I knew I would soon be in a Dreamland I had never experienced before. I took a deep breath and sent love to my sleeping body for protection.

The Broom Tree Seer noticed this and nodded her head. She spoke something to the Piper, and he began his musical enchanting. She motioned for me to stand near her; I smiled, full of excitement. She put my hand onto the besom along with hers, saying, "We will be off to the 'enchanted grove'!"

The next thing I knew, we were flying through the air at rapid speed. I felt like Dorothy in the *Wizard of Oz*! We flew above the Nemeton at dusk; the aerial view was amazing. The vastness of the grounds was beyond comprehending. The beauty put me into thankfulness. My heart skipped some as the air currents picked up, and I began to laugh at the absurdity of this! Then I thought, Well, no more so than other trainings I have done.

Before I knew it, we were down and in the center of the Sacred Grove. My hair was strewn about my face; I was exhilarated as I looked about. The Broom Seer was already talking with other Tree Seers; she looked perfectly groomed, not a hair out of place. I watched from a slight distance as she adjusted her plaid leine on her shoulder. She looked to me now and put her hand out to come closer. She was fussing with something on her shoulder, a pin that held her plaid sash (leine) in place. The gold pin glittered in the evening light; the design was a downward pointed sword through the center of a circle; the entire pin was jeweled with emeralds and carnelian.

I said to the Seer, "Your pin is so beautiful!"

"Ah yes, it is that," she said. "It was gifted to me many years ago and is called the 'Tara Broach'!" She looked at me a moment. Red hair streaming down, her beautiful, oval face was young as one would be in their thirties, and yet the silver streaks were a mystery. I had to blink my eyes a few times out of my daydreaming, as I realized she was saying something.

"You enjoyed the ride over the Nemeton? I could hear you laughing some, Dreamer!"

I shook my head and laughed again at this recent experience. "I loved it! Thank you, Seer. I would love to go again!"

She laughed, saying, "Feeling like Harry are we?" She laughed more at my puzzled expression. "Like in Potter, Dreamer! Harry Potter!" Still laughing she was, and I joined her in that recognition.

Now she was all business, moving ahead with her working Dream. She lead me by hand to the center of the Grove where the fire had been kindled; smoke was wafting into the evening air. The Seer spoke softly with a few other Seers, who were standing there. Looking at me, she then said, "I believe you do know these Seers from previous work, Dreamer."

I nodded my head yes, saying, "Yes! It is good to see you, Ivy Tree Seer and Vine Tree Seer!" I shook their hands as they each greeted me in welcome.

The Vine Tree Seer spoke, saying, "This evening is a Dreamer's dress rehearsal for the turning of the Celtic Wheel of the Year for tomorrow night's festivities of the Sabbat of 'Samhain.' Which of course is about the dead returning to the spirit world; the time when the old God dies, returning to the Land of the Dead to await rebirth at the 'Yule' festival. This is also a time when the Crone Goddess goes into mourning for her lost son/consort, leaving her people in temporary darkness."

I answered quickly, "I am much honored to be here. What would you have me do?"

The Ivy Tree Seer said, "For the moment, please have a seat on the mat near us. The Broom Tree Seer will be opening our circle and then of course teaching to those who are open and clear."

Following her instructions, I sat upon the mat. Quietly, I looked around the full circle of Dreamers and Seers. In the distance beyond the trees, I heard whisperings of the bagpipes; I smiled to myself at the thought of seeing and hearing the "Piper" again. The Ivy Tree (Gort) Seer leaned over to tell me a few things.

"The word 'Sabbat' comes from the Greek word 'Sabutu,' which means 'To Rest.' Sabbats are the solar festivals that mark various points along the Celtic Wheel of the Year, usually when the sun reaches a point of balance or of extremes. Such as the solstices or equinoxes. Each Sabbat generally corresponds to some stage in the eternal, ever-renewing life of the Goddess and the God."

The Seer smiled and gave me a pat on my arm and then motioned to the center circle. There I could see the Broom Tree Seer calling upon the four quarters, invoking the deities and powers for the circle work with protection. Another Seer approached with a lit torch; this was the Ash Tree Seer. He walked the torch about the circle for all to see. After adding more wood to the central fire, he lit that as a ritual fire. Another Seer walked about the circle with the ritual offerings of libations for the spirits.

With that done we all now stood hand to hand as we said our opening: "May our doors and gates…" So very beautiful and moving; every time I say this, I feel such connection with our Goddess Earth Mother, and I feel chills along my spine.

The Broom Tree Seer speaks: "Greetings, Dreamers and Ancient Ones! This evening will be new for many, having not been part of a 'Samhain Sabbat,' and a renewal for the old-timers. Every turning of the year is a little different; this year we are delighted to have as our guest a wonderful 'Piper' who will enchant us all with his musical playing and accompany the drumming for the journey work!"

The Seer held out her hands and clapped. The entire audience of Dreamers was standing and clapping. The "Piper" then came into the circle with his bagpipes calling to us all; he was a classic image as he walked the circle, playing. His long, black hair was tied loosely back; his green-and-blue kilt swung back and forth as he moved. His yellow, saffron-colored shirt matched the thin yellow stripe woven into the blue-and-green plaid kilt. The pipes over his left shoulder vibrated softly. I felt that we all held our breath as he played; we most certainly were enchanted by him! The Broom Tree Seer bowed to the Piper, and he to her. Then he found the seat arranged for him near the fire. The Broom Tree Seer began anew.

"Now let me tell you how this evening will proceed. First, I will explain my placement in the Ogham, and at evening's end we will do our run-through for the Samhain to be held tomorrow evening. I will call upon the newer Dreamers to be a part of that ceremony."

I could feel myself getting nervous about any participation. I tried hard to move that feeling away so I would get the teaching benefit that I had come for.

The Broom Tree Seer speaks: "The Broom also may be referred to as the 'Reed.' From the 'Word Ogham of Morainn,' the Celtic name reads 'nGetal,' and the letters are *nG*. The Celtic words 'Luth Leighe' mean 'A Physician's Strength.' And from the 'Word Ogham of Aonghus,' we have 'Eitiud Midach,' meaning 'Robe of the Physician's.' The Celtic word 'Getal' means 'BROOM'! I know this is a lot from the dictionary, but just listen awhile and let these puzzle pieces fall into place.

"'nG' are the letters that represent 'Broom/Reed' in the Ogham; let me help here with a better understanding of the higher aspects of this composite letter. We must look back to two other 'letter trees' of the Ogham. First, 'N'-'Nion'-'Ash-Tree,' which is about healing magic, and the second letter, 'G,' is a period of lethargy or inertia representing 'Gort.'[26] When this is achieved, there is usually a backlash. The properties of 'Gort'-'Ivy Tree' are about caution; a cautionary tree and its presence should always be carefully noted during any magical Dreaming workings. What we need to understand about 'n-Getal'-'Broom/Reed' is that Broom is a combination of the letters *N* and *G*, the Ash and Ivy. Together they become a letter in the Ogham and a tree symbolizing the combined effects of these two trees."

The Seer scanned the audience a few minutes, searching for effect. Then she said, "Very powerful and very tricky! A Dreamer of magical Ogham workings has to know their material and know when which tree or trees are the best ones to use, given the circumstances of the work needing doing!" She scanned quietly, wanting her meaning to penetrate. You could hear a pin drop, it was so quiet.

"For our lesson, the examples would be these: you have started a new Magical Working, which might not be going well, or have now broken a spell of inactivity, or backlash has come that may be potentially dangerous or destructive. The 'Gort'-'Ivy Tree' will surely have come to you if you have made your proper connection with her, and she will provide a warning, having been invoked by the Otherworlds. Should this happen, you must then abandon the work. However! Now this is very important: check first to see if there is repair or healing needed due to the damage already caused. To *not* do this would be very dangerous! This is exactly when you call upon me, the Broom!"

The Broom Tree Seer began parading around the circle, pointing to herself, saying, "Yes! It is me that you need to call. And for what, you may ask? Why, I am the one who performs the essential 'Clean-up'! Yes, it is the Broom that comes to the rescue and cleans up the damage done. Please recall that in your physical lives it is broom that cleans up; every home has this essential tool! What we learn in our Ogham tree magic is that in our Dreaming world on the spiritual level, Broom is a correcting, healing tree energy used for any damage or injury inadvertently caused.

"The Reed/Broom was used for the thatching of roofs for Celtic houses. The Irish Celts also used the Reed for flying arrow shafts, which were said to be very swift. Sometimes the hollow stalks were filled with poison to make deadly arrows."

The Seer stopped for a minute, and everyone watched her as she moved to where the "Piper" sat. She asked him to play something soft; he stood up and began to play gladly. After a few minutes, she said to the "Piper," "May I?"

Nodding his head yes, he took off his bagpipes handed them to her. The "Piper" stood with his hands clasped behind his back, smiling broadly as the Seer held the pipes.

"This is a very beautiful and magical instrument! 'nGetel,' the Ogham name, relates to the mouthpiece of a bagpipe." She pointed to this. "The pipes of the bagpipes were originally made from Reeds!" She pointed to the pipes. Then from behind her on the ground, she picked up several Broom/Reed branches; after looking them over, she passed these to the audience for inspecting. One long piece she held onto and then handed this to the "Piper," saying, "Dearest 'Piper,' I believe there was something you wanted to share with these Dreamers!"

Wordlessly but smiling, the "Piper" walked to the center, holding the long Reed branch. Looking it over and tapping this into the palm of his other hand, slowly and shyly the "Piper" began to look out to the audience and speak.

"What if I were to tell you…" His voice trailed off. "There was a time, Dreamers, when I had choices to make; my way was not clear…" Again he stopped. He stirred on the edge of almost speaking but, not. Looking at us all straight on, he began, "This is a tale about mist and choices." Again there was quiet; the clouds stirred, and mist literally began to appear. The Dreamers were on the edge with anticipation! I could hear soft drumming nearby. The "Piper" went to the Seer and collected his bagpipes; he played softly, and this seemed to strengthen him.

Standing still, he began once more: "The mist comes often as the night does and hangs like a blanket of protection; it is a between the world's energy. Not quite air and not quite water, mysterious. The little ones know this; the mist is their cue. They are given safety to move about, to do their work of the 'Lands beneath the Forest.'

"On an eve much like we have here, with warm winds, hanging mist, and stars above beginning to show themselves, I wandered in the forest in my life before these times, estranged from family while I needed to work out situations there. I had done things I could not take back…I needed the distance then to Dream and maybe then find my way home. As I walked, I saw the edge of a hill where the mist hung heavily, the grasses there were greener than any other place, and there was an ancient, gnarled tree near the top. Of course I had to see this closer. Finally I walked to the tree and felt stillness there, and I knew this would make a fine encampment. Arranging my pack, I slumbered there and awoke into a magical Dream!" The Piper was silent, searching the crowd, then…

"Where I found myself in the 'Lands Beneath' teaming with life; time had no meaning here, and one could travel with a thought. As I moved through their realm, the 'wee ones'' work was taking place all around, mending of roots, setting of seeds, guiding of light through tunnels, holding of heat, movement of the winds through earth chambers, the channeling of the waters. There was an air of seriousness underneath the joking the Fairies did between each other. They knew I was there, but saw me not on their plane. I was a guest, was the message I had gotten; I am not sure why. It did not look like there would be much interaction.

"Finally, in loneness and desperation, I spoke to one who was near, not knowing if I would be even heard. 'How do I come to be here? For what purpose?' Feeling clumsy and large, I spoke in earnest to the wee man.

"He looked back at me immediately with unflickering dark eyes. 'I knew it 'twas not you that had no voice! You would come around eventually, I told the others; I did! I could tell by the feel of your colors. We will go now; things need righting!'

"He came close and touched me lightly on my arm. Through that touch we journeyed in a subterranean realm of the 'Lands Beneath.' Curiously I had no fear, only wonder. More curious was what he knew of me and my family, which he spoke of while we traveled. At my shock of what he knew, I felt time stand still. I realized we had stopped near a glen of water. There were small shrubs in flower, with a bright yellow glowing. A woman came and gathered certain branches; a man came with a long shaft of a branch. Together they tied the bristles and made a broom. With this they swept me down and plunged me into the waters and gave me new clothes. The man who had brought me here came to tell me he was called by the name Phen.

"'And what would you be called? he asked. Not knowing this, I felt lost; I could not answer and shook my head sadly. 'Do not worry,' he said. 'Your name will come; for now, watch and listen.'

"The next thing was more curious. Young fairy girls came through the bushes, arms laden with branches, threads, and animal skin. An older fairy crone began to use her knife, cutting holes into the animal skin, holes into the branches, which had been smoothed. Another crone was cutting threads to certain lengths. When they seemed satisfied that the pieces were ready, assembly began. For what purpose, I did not know. Phen came to me now, handing me a brew of warm tea; I gladly accepted this. After a few sips, I looked to the crone fairies and their work, and to my surprise they had finished their crafting. What they held was strange looking. Phen went to them, and they helped him put this contraption over his left shoulder. He shifted it back and forth; the crone fairies with needles in hand sewed adjustments. Phen seemed satisfied; next he began to blow into the long branch that leaned downward over his chest. The bag under his arm began to fill with air; the fairies made more adjustments with their knifes. Phen blew again, this time moving his hands along the downward branch with notched holes. I was startled to then hear mournful sounds, odd at first, but somehow hauntingly beautiful to me.

"At last I stood up; I needed to know what this thing was! 'Dear Sirs and Ladies, begging your pardon…May I know what this is?' Of course I wanted to then hide myself, but never being a shy one, the words were out and said!

"Phen smiled and answered most matter-of-factly. 'This, dear Sir, is your new instrument, and it is called the "Bagpipes"! As you saw, it was made by these fair ladies, from the skin of an animal, and the "Broom/Reed Tree" tied securely all about with dyed sinew, the color green for your healing.'

"Phen now held this instrument out in front of himself, the reed pieces hanging with green tassels dangling. I was flabbergasted and knew not how to answer! I mean, what was I to say?

"He stood there smiling still, a small but tough little man, and now insisted that I come forward to have a look! All I could do was look around the area; I noticed there were others now, many in fact. They all seemed to wait for what I would do. I could not be rude, although I did want to run.

"Slowly I walked up the crest of the hill to where they stood, then braving up, I asked this: 'What am I to do with this? And what is this about healing?' Time seemed to halt; as I looked around, all eyes were on Phen and me.

"One of the old crone fairies came over with her broom and swept a path in front of me and then made a circle with her sweeping. Looking up to me was a stretch, as small as she was, but her eyes held mine and she said to all: 'He is ready!'

"'Ready? Ready for what?' I said loudly.

"Phen came forward with the 'Bagpipes' and then placed them over my shoulder and positioned everything. I just let him do this. Then he took my fingers and showed me where the holed notches were, telling me to now blow into the long reed with my breath. He explained that the air would produce musical notes as I did this. I tried to follow what he said. I noticed now that he had a 'Bagpipe' of his own. He began showing me things on his instrument to copy as he did them. Slowly, very slowly, the bag filled with air, and the pipes vibrated some; it was not music for sure! I stopped for a moment to watch Phen; he played without effort, and it was beautiful. I tried again and realized that there was something to this. I liked it! This was much to my surprise. I did not quite know what to say.

"It was Phen who spoke, looking out to the realm of the Fairies. 'I told you all he had the voice. Now it is a matter of practice!'

"I laughed at this statement, saying, 'What am I to practice for? I admit the feel of this is good, but why should I practice?'

"One of the old crone fairies came forward to me, saying, 'Not many mortals are chosen for such a task as this, but the need is great and you have the ability. Although it seems you do not know this. You will learn the music of the "Fairy Pipers," and you will bring this to your kind. The Broom/Reed will help assist with your inner sight, and the music you will make can enchant and entice when needed. You will learn about this need as you heal; you will heal others! The art of "Piping" is a gift being passed on to those who are worthy and capable. Use this with clear intentions!'

"She moved away as quickly as she had come. My mouth hung open, I am sure. Phen then came to me and told me it was time to go back to the 'Lands Above' but that he would continue to teach me in the Dreamtime and I would become very well known for this, as well as healing myself and family!

"Phen put his hand on my arm, and I blinked, I had not said a word! Now I was back, nested under the old, gnarled tree. Back from my Dream! All I could think was, How did this happen? Was it real? Then I looked to the green grass and saw the 'Bagpipes' sitting there! My 'Bagpipes,' I thought. And I had not even thanked any of them! I then heard a small voice say, 'You are welcome, "Piper"!'

"I looked around to no avail; no one there. 'Piper'! He called me 'Piper'; Phen has given me a name!"

There was silence! Dreamers who usually have so much to say were quiet. Each still in the Dream, I thought to myself. I looked to the center space near the fire and saw the Broom

Seer talking with the "Piper" in whispers and with smiles on their lips. Suddenly I found myself standing, and I began a slow clapping with my hands; I looked about and others joined. Shortly the whole audience was clapping and cheering! Both the Broom Seer and the "Piper" hugged and then bowed time and again! This was an amazing story, and everyone was happy from this telling!

We all seated ourselves as the "Piper" enchanted us with his magical music. When finished, he bowed and then said, "Dreamers, I trust that you enjoyed my story concerning the music of the 'Fairy Pipers' who have passed their art onto me! Over the many lives in the Highlands, I have learned much from the Fairy Folk, and I still bid them honor. Now you have learned the Broom/Reed is very much a part of the pipes' components. And alas, the Boom Tree Seer has much more to share! What if I were to tell you another story? Ah, that must be for later!"

The "Piper" then bowed once more to the Broom Tree Seer and to us. Then his piping began, and his hips swayed the blue-and-green kilt as he walked the central circle and then went off into the deeper parts of the Grove. We all were still clapping and watching him even though he could barely be heard.

I looked to the center, and near the fire one of the Dreamers was using a beautiful broom around the edge of the stone fire pit. She worked it in a beautiful motion, and slowly the Dreamers' attention was brought back to the center, and they awaited the Broom Tree Seer's words. Looking at the sweeper, I realized she had done this intentionally to help us all shift to the next part of our work.

The Broom Tree Seer said, "The 'Piper' is a hard act to follow! Certainly many of you will enjoy his stories later tonight. Some may want to learn his craft of piping. You must be aware that the Fairy Folk teach us much. They are masters of living in a space of no-time, several universes at once, with multidimensional abilities. Here is a question, Dreamers, for you to ponder: if all time is now, am I immortal?

"In the Ancient world, the 'Traveling People' of Scotland and Ireland would camp in one location throughout the cold winter months. Come summer, they broke camp and spent the warmer months traveling from village to village or to various islands. The time to break winter camp was not determined by the calendar, but by the first yellow flowers of the BROOM! This illustrates to us today how important the 'Green World' is. The 'Green World' constantly gives us messages about time and when to travel or rest, teaching us in the nonphysical realms about the cycles of new beginnings.

"If we take a look at what we do know about the Ancient Celtic view of time, it soon becomes clear that trees and months simply do not enter into their concepts. To the early Celts, time simply was. Everything was here and now. The old writings legends make almost no references to past or future events. The narrative being almost entirely in the present tense. To the early Celts, the marking of time did not involve trees or any other form of Ogham. So we may assume putting a tree in line with a month happened randomly in the centuries that came later."

The Broom Seer was at the fire's edge, pausing and looking into the flames. From a round yellow vase, she pulled out several broom branches and looked them over a minute or so. Then she continued.

"I am reminded of the story of 'Blodeuwedd' from Welsh myth in the Fourth Branch of the Mabinogion. She was created for Llew Llaw Gyffes. Llew had been cursed by his mother, Arianrhod, to not ever win a bride of his own people. In Llew's distress, he called upon his uncle Gwyddion, the magician, and his uncle Math, Arianrhod's brother, to help him. Gwyddion was trained by Math, and they worked well with each other. Gwyddion and his brothers all fought in the 'Battle of the Trees.' Coming to Llew's predicament, they arrived at a solution to craft a beautiful bride for Llew. With their magical skills, they created her from the flower blooms of Oak, Broom, and Meadowsweet, along with six other plants and trees. She was made entirely of flowers and magnificent; her name, 'Blodeuwedd,' means 'flower face.' It is said she was aligned with the older legend of 'Cybele the Mother of All Living Things.' Part of the story tells of Blodeuwedd's fingers being 'Whiter than the ninth wave of the sea,' which proves her connection with the Moon; nine is the prime Moon number. The Moon draws the tides, and the ninth wave is traditionally the largest. Llew is very pleased with such a woman! Alas the story takes a turn; as time goes on, Blodeuwedd betrays her husband, Llew, for the love of Gronw. She is then punished by Gwyddion, who transmogrifies her into an Owl! Blodeuwedd thereafter becomes the 'Goddess of Wisdom.'

"The Goddess energy plays strongly in the workings of the Ogham. We see this in the pentad; let me explain. 'Arianrhod the Birth Goddess' and 'Arianrhod the Goddess of Initiation'; 'Blodeuwedd the Love Goddess' and 'Blodeuwedd the Goddess of Wisdom'; and 'Cerridwen the White Sow Goddess: these number five, and that forms a pentad. They are the same Goddesses in her five seasonal aspects.

"The Reed or Broom has always been associated with music. Since time began, pipes and flutes were made from reeds. In Greek mythology there is a connection with reeds through the Greek God Pan. The God Pan is a moon of Saturn, and the name 'Pan' means 'All-Everything.' Pan believed with music he could bring an end to care and worry and communicate between living and dead. In legend Pan had a contest to determine who could play the most skillful, sweetest music: Pan on his reed pipes or Apollo on his lyre. Pan was judged the winner, which Apollo considered an insult. In his rage, Apollo turned Pan into half a man and half a goat. The Greeks believe Pan was the god of the woodlands, pastures, herds, and fertility. Pan is thought to be the offspring of Hermes, and all hills, caves, oaks, reeds, and tortoises are sacred to him.

The Broom Seer was walking about the circle, taking a bit of a break, chatting here and there; some were asking questions. I noticed a power in her voice and how easily she was able to gain information from others without them even realizing this. I knew this is what very skilled magicians were able to do and that this gave them a sense of balance for what needed doing. I could tell the Seer was able to index things for when she might need them, to help on her path of heart and healing. I felt lucky to be able to observe and trusted that somehow I would learn from her for my own Dream Healing work.

She was ready now to continue. "In the ancient times of the Celts, true heroes were skilled not only in combat but also in the higher magical arts. As a Dreamer who is beginning to learn the magical arts, we must first and foremost recognize things about ourselves—like our feelings, thoughts, and emotions—and ask, do they belong to us? Are any damaging or dangerous? A Dreamer knows these must be dealt with as soon as they occur, and this may not be pleasant to do. This is the start of a Dreamer being very clear with themselves in their work."

"Another topic we must discuss is the importance of 'Magical Hygiene.'[27] Please know this is just as important as physical hygiene. With physical hygiene, to leave anything not done or untended may cause infection and disease. The same can be said of 'Magical Hygiene.' Healers need to remember that there are unseen life forms and they can attach themselves to things left by careless Otherworld travelers! These 'Otherworld Viruses' can take on a life of their own and become damaging."

The Seer, having paced the circle while speaking, was stopped. Her piercing eyes were deep green-black and shown like jewels; her jaw was set tight. I am sure the whole group was getting her message here with the extra energy she sent through her body language. I thought for a moment about these "viruses that may be left" and shuddered at the thought!

"The work of a Dreamer-Magician is serious; there is no room for working halfheartedly. One who works in this fashion will be weeded out in the Otherworlds. There are always consequences to be paid for carelessness!

"Now, a Dreamer may be wondering how to recognize these unwanted items and which to call 'debris' that may be floating around in the higher realms. Let me explain: the debris may come in the form of abstract things, such as incorrect or malicious thoughts, feelings, emotions, or mental actions. This is when a Dreamer's training becomes most important; because we learn through our journey work to recognize what truly belongs to us or to another. As Dreamers, we are empaths; we pick up things most easily. The Ivy Tree becomes important to make one aware; make sure to listen to the messages that come as warnings. Next we learn to call upon the 'Broom,' who has the gift of inner sight and can help you to search for things you have picked up on and then sweep them out!

"The message of Broom tells us that if we have had to use broom on some level, make sure to spend serious time checking any spiritual damage that may have been done inadvertently. Reflect, dream on what happened or went wrong and why. Then cleanse and heal where this is needed. Remember to check again on why Ivy and Broom had to be invoked in the first place. Be sure to note this and learn from any mistakes that will better your Magical-Dreaming capabilities.

"We all need help; make sure to call upon and invoke the 'Daghdha,' the 'Good God,' 'All-father,' and protector of the clans. Call your own personal guides as well for safe passage through the journey realms of the Otherworlds. Important work can be accomplished by using a linking process with these three trees: 'Broom, Ash, and Ivy." As you recall, Ash-Nion and Ivy-Gort make the Ogham letter *nG*. During ritual work, to perform linking, you would place the Ogham sticks of all three trees into the Earth itself within your ritually cast circle. This of course has been cast with your ceremonial knife for sacred ritual workings. As a trained Dreamer, you will begin to notice a reaction within the energy fields of your work. Pay attention now to the nuances; notice how it feels when one stick is removed or another one is put into our Mother. Change back and forth from Ivy to Ash to Broom; what do you notice? Practice this awhile and make notes. One will begin to feel the strong linking energy and feel how these trees support each other. A Dreamer must practice this; and time is the teacher. This is the only way to understand and learn the language of the trees fully."

The Broom Seer became quiet; she was turned to one side as the Ash Tree Seer handed her small pieces of broom sticks. She looked them over and stepped away from the fire. We were in a small break, so I went closer to follow what she was doing. She looked around herself and then skyward and quietly, slowly tossed into the air several of the branches. Very curious, I wanted to know why. So of course I came up to ask, but as I did, she tossed more into the air, and the wind picked up. I hesitated, then she looked at me and out came my words. "Dear Seer, why—"

I was interrupted by her answer before I finished the question. "I am, little Dreamer, well aware of your question! My purpose here with these pieces of Broom is to call and invoke the spirits of the Air!" The wind moved in several gusts now.

"May I ask why?" I tried for more information.

"Oh you may!" she said but did not say more.

I realized I had intruded on her sacred work, and stepped back, feeling ill at ease.

Others noticed the gusting winds, and the laughter was more hushed; the Dreamers were settling down for the Broom Seer once again. Before I could be seated, The Broom Seer called me to her and handed me a small bunch of broom pieces. She told me that once everyone was settled she wanted me to toss these pieces into the air as she had done earlier. I agreed that I could do this, feeling a tad nervous. The Seer then spoke to us all.

"Feeling the wind, are we?" She laughed, saying, "Still more to come!" She then nodded to me to toss my pieces of broom.

I took a deep breath and then flung these into the air. I felt as if I were in slow motion as I watched them toss and turn some and then drift down to the ground. In the meantime the wind kicked up huge gusts. I gripped onto my shawl; others were now standing and asking what was going on. The Seer seeming very pleased with my antics, laughed some, and then called out to the audience. "Magic! Magic, Dreamers! It is high time for you to know some of my bag of tricks. Now the tossing of the broom into the air is done to raise the wind, which helps one to invoke the spirits of the AIR! Which I do trust that you know are also called 'Sylphs' in the elemental world. The sylphs are most in line with our concept of the fairies and angels. They are part of the creative force of the air. As I am sure, you are aware of how their work can result in the tiniest of breezes to the mightiest of tornadoes. We all know that Air is the source of all life, and tonight, above all other nights, these spirits of Air, Fairy, and Angel will be most helpful! Just so you know, the other side to calming the Air spirits is for a Dreamer to take small bundles of broom, such as these." She showed us several tied bundles about five inches in length, each one of the five. Burn them to ash, and then bury the ash. However, tonight we need the wind stirring a bit more, for we are on the cusp of the Sabbat of Samhain!"

Everyone was very excited, to say the least. Dream magic was the thread that we all wanted to weave! Moving back to where I had been sitting earlier, I enjoyed the chitchat of the Dreamers for a while. Looking to the front, I could hear soft drumming, and we all then came back to center.

"Before we go further into Samhain, it is time for you each to receive your 'Broom Ogham Sticks'!" We cheered and clapped some at this announcement. The Broom Tree Seer held up her arms for quiet. We all paid her honor. She went to a basket that had been placed by the Ash Tree Seer and the Ivy Seer; it was large and intricately woven, made of broom, I was certain, and tied with a yellow ribbon. There within stood the branches of the broom tree.

One of the other Seers was stoking the fire pit and adding sage and herbs to the fire; broom was probably part of that mixture, I thought. The smoke lifted on the wind that came, floating about us. The drumming became louder, and we heard the "Pipes"! We all laughed some, smiling happily as the "Piper" entered our circle once more.

The Broom Tree Seer continued. "I would not think of not having our enchanter with us for the 'ceremony of the sticks'!"

We all lightened up as the "Piper" transported us into a magical journey within this grove of the Nemeton. Then one by one we were called by name to receive our "Broom Ogham Stick." I was the last and thanked the Seer gladly.

The Seer said, "We initiated thirteen Dreamers tonight, and thirteen is the number of 'nGetel,' the Broom! Be proud of how well you have done, how far you have come on your path! Dreamers: what is to be done now is to use your blade to remove some of the outer bark and then inscribe the proper letters of the Broom—'nG'—and the Ogham glyph into your stick; all the while do infusing with your spirit name! Awhile back you were asked to Dream on this and to have this name ready when needed. This is the time! Should you not be sure of this name, call upon the spirits of Air, the Fairy, or Angel beings to help you with this. This spirit name is something for you and spirit, only and once you have yours completed, go to the fire for the blessing that will be given to you and your new Broom Ogham Stick!"

We were high with excitement; things did simmer down some as we each got into our carving work. The work took very little time for me, and I had ready the spirit name for some time now. As I carved, I concentrated upon my own magical name. The Seer greeted each of us separately at the fire, pronouncing the blessings that were appropriate. Once done, we sat in circle awhile as the Seer told us something of what would happen for the Sabbat of Samhain taking place on the following eve.

The Seer speaks: "The 'Eve of Samhain' was a great spirit night for the Celtic people. The Broom/Reed Tree is associated with this festival. This would be comparable to our contemporary Halloween-All Hollows Eve. A time when the veil between the worlds is very thin, a night of divination and prophecy. Samhain is the festival to honor the dead but also a time of purification and turning of the 'Wheel of the Year.' The 'nGetal'- Broom/Reed Tree is ready for cutting in the month of November, with many uses on the physical plane. After Samhain Festival at the end of October, the Broom/Reed becomes the tree of 'Clean Up' of the dead souls. The Broom comes in and sweeps up![28]

"Some of you I know are interested in being involved in a ceremonial way tomorrow, so in about a half an hour, please meet me here by the fire. Please remember that the Broom is a cleaner! And it is now high time to physically embark upon the cleaning of your physical living area! All the while know that this chore becomes a way of magically cleansing our own psychic as we do this. Of course I expect you to first set a dream intention on what this might be for you personally. We receive wonderful results when we use this method of 'sweeping up spiritually' as we do our physical Broom sweeping work. In the meantime we will enjoy ourselves with the 'Feast of the Broom'! Congratulations, Dreamers!"

I now had my own Broom "nGetel" Ogham Stick! I tucked this work of a Dreamer's art into my belt. Very happy about this, I went to let the Seer know. She told me that I had studied well and to remember her when I had questions and she would be there for me. We heard the "Piper," and we both smiled at each other as we watched some of the Dreamers sitting near him.

The Broom Tree Seer said, "The 'Piper' will escort you a little later back to the lodge and your room there that still holds your sleeping body; we have not forgotten! When you are ready, remember your silver cord that connects your Dream body and back; you will be very safe and very sound!" She looked at me with those green eyes and said, "What is it, Dreamer?"

I answered, half laughing, "I had almost forgotten my other self in the lodge!"

She looked at me quizzically and said, "Oh! I see we may need another lesson on dream bodies; hold that Dreamer! " Off she went to join the others with the "Piper."

Now what did she mean by that? Curious, very curious! I heard the laughing and decided to join in the fun, and I trusted that I would not forget my other sleeping body!

BLACKTHORN

Karen C. Silvestri

"St" Straigh

THE BLACKTHORN LETTER "ST," "STRAIPH" OGHAM:

STATISTICS FOR:

"The Blackthorn" genus/species- *Prunus spinosa*

~Grows to a height on average to 12 feet tall; some have said traditionally Blackthorn never exceed 13 feet.

~The tree is native to Europe and naturalized in North America.

~The bark is light gray and scaly, and, just under the surface, a bright orange. The leaves are small, dark green ovals; the branches and twigs form thickets that are dense and thorny, twisting in all directions. The tree produces a great many sharp thorns; the flowers are white and scented, coming in the spring. The blackthorn produces blue-black, sometimes purplish berries in the summer, which ripen after the first frost; they are called "Sloe-berries."

~~~~~~~~~~~

THE BLACKTHORN: HOW USED IN THE WORLD

~The wood from the blackthorn is burned, but its main use is in the manufacture of walking sticks, shillelaghs, and other artifacts. The berries are harvested for making jam and used in gin making, "sloe-gin." At New Year, celebrants made Blackthorn crowns, which were burned in the New Year's fires. The ashes were used to fertilize the fields. Blackthorn is used at May Day to celebrate fertility. Wands were used at this time for wishing and divination. Blackthorn is used for protection and creating safe boundaries.

~~~~~~~~~~~

MEDICINAL AND PSYCHOLOGICAL

~The Blackthorn's leaves and fruit contain tannins, organic acids, sugars, and vitamin C. They can be made into tonics for mild diuretics and laxatives. The liquid from the boiled leaves can be used as mouthwash for sore throat, tonsillitis, and laryngitis. The dried fruits are used to treat bladder, kidney, and stomach disorders. Sloe berries help with indigestion, eczema, skin, and weak heart.

~~~~~~~~~~~

SACREDNESS AMONG THE GROVE

~The Blackthorn is the fourteenth tree in the Ogham Alphabet: "Straiph"-"ST"

~The Blackthorn is associated with second sight, transition, death, and the underworld.

~ Month- not assigned

~KEYWORD—Change, Prepare

~Planets- Saturn and Mars

~The Blackthorn tree stands on either side of the Broom tree and Elder tree within the Grove.

~"FINGER TIP TREE" location- "Blackthorn-Straiph"-"ST" is on the middle of the ring finger.

DREAM OF "STRAIPH," THE BLACKTHORN TREE SEER

We all know that it will come, but who likes to think of it? Surely not me! I really prefer to ignore the inevitable. Too much to do now: things that are fun and interesting to learn. There are roses I have not yet grown or enjoyed the scent of.

Smoke was drifting up from the fire. Sitting now deep in the wood with several other Dreamers, I suppose it must have close to midnight. So quiet, I could feel the silence of the void as I looked into the midnight-blue sky. I was enjoying my world.

One of the Dreamers broke the spell, saying, "Be ready! 'La Mere du Bois' is here!"

I wanted to ask what they meant, instead we all heard the high pitched crying, which I knew to be the "Kennings" for death! A chill ran down my back.

I looked past the stone campfire, to the edge of the wood, feeling the wind and seeing a motion rustling a small tree. The one with the delicate, oval, white-petaled flowers. Their musky scent caught my attention. The four of us stood up and slowly moved toward the tree.

The wind rippled; again a chill went down my back. Braving up and speaking out, I said, "Hey…What is going on? What is all this drama with the keening? I mean, really?"

All four of us laughed together; this did not relieve the tension! My friend reached toward the tree and pulled her hand away quickly. Putting her finger to her lips and sucking, she said, "There are thorns all over this thing!"

Then we heard someone saying, "Well of course there are! How else can I protect my 'sloe berries'?"

In unison we turned around toward the campfire to see a small, plump woman in a gray-ish linen gown embroidered with purple silk yarn threading around in a curious design. She leaned on a large, black, twisted staff that she suddenly picked up and shook at us, telling us she was ready, and of course we should be too! Her hair was tied up in a neat bun at the nape of her neck. Her hips swayed as she walked closer to the fire, leading herself with her twisted staff, which I assumed was made from the wood of the "Straiph" tree.

"Yes, yes! I am the Blackthorn Seer, and we have much to accomplish on this night. Ready or not, we will talk of death, 'Yours of course'! Now get yourselves situated; drink the hot coffee. The night will be long, and you must be awake to see!"

At least she had a smile on her face, I thought to myself. I won't let her brusque manner throw me off. I will simply acknowledge her as the oracle and Seer that she is known to be. Cannot say I relish her topic; I guess I had best get past that.

I looked at my Dreamer friends, two fellows and one woman. They also seemed nervous and were trying to deal with this. I wondered why we had been grouped together. I really did not know them. I supposed the Keepers had their reasons. We were kept so busy with lessons, there really was limited social time. I decided I would break the ice to bridge the distance with these Dreamers, figuring we would need the support from each other as the lessons from the "Blackthorn Seer" became known.

Leaning over to the man on my right, I said, "Look at the carving on her staff; certainly looks ancient!"

The Dreamer whispered back, "I know. And well used too. I think I will ask her about this, when I have a chance."

The "Blackthorn Seer" had a chair brought over for her; it too was carved and twisted of the same dark wood as the staff. She seemed to be settled now near the fire and asked us to do the opening of the circle for her. My woman Dreamer friend offered to lead us in our opening invocations. She did a fine, heartfelt opening, which the Seer praised her for. The Seer picked up her drum and asked us to be seated, as she would drum to help us be focused and centered for our work. While she did this, we could hear in the distance a soft keening, not as piercing as before, and then it trailed off; I was glad. I felt better to just hear the solitary drum! I could hear her swish around us as she drummed. I was trying hard for inner calmness, which did not seem to come to me.

The Dream camp scene became quiet. For a while it stayed too quiet; curious, I opened one eye to see if we were all still there. I breathed a sigh of relief to see my Dreamer friends. I could see the Blackthorn Seer seated in her chair; she held her Staff, which she was looking over. I hoped she did not see me looking. Too late!

"Nervous about the quiet are we, Dreamer? Ah! Something one needs to get used to. The waking world is full of babble! It is good to look to the void; there we can help to quell that ongoing monkey mind." She was looking to the black-blue sky and the far-off flecks of starlight. It felt to me that she had changed her tactics, using soft talk.

I was merely trying to hold onto what little power over myself I did have for focusing. I decided I was being tested here and would not let her distract me from my own inner flow of power. I only smiled some, giving a nod, and went back into myself deeper. With a stronger sense of purpose, I took a deep breath and put forth as much effort as she was; I trusted in myself not to be pulled.

Hearing soft drumming and a few voices, I opened my eyes to see that the Blackthorn Seer had a few other Seers with her now. They were the drummers, and I am not sure when they arrived. They consisted of The Oak Seer, The Willow Seer, and The Holly Seer; all were seated behind her, drumming. She was ready now, and I realized I was too, at least somewhat.

The Blackthorn Seer speaks: "We need to talk of the background from the ancient Oghams, for clarity on the nature of the Blackthorn, Me! From the 'Word Ogham of Morainn,' it is said, 'Aire Srabha'-'careful effort' and 'Tresim Ruamna'-'strongest of red.' And 'Straiph'-'sloe,' which gives strong red dye on metal.' These are curious quotes; they will begin to make sense as we get into the workings of the Blackthorn. Here is another, from the 'Word Ogham of Cuchulain'; it is said, 'Saigid NEL.I.A. & DDE, SUAS,' meaning 'an arrow's mist, smoke drifting up from the fire.'

"About my statistics: 'Straiph/Blackthorn' is a shrub rather than a tree, but a tree it is, as classified in the Ogham. The Blackthorn rarely reaches a height of thirteen feet, fifteen feet, and it is covered with strong, sharp thorns. They usually grow into dense, knotted, and impenetrable thickets. The fruit that it produces is a round, small, shiny, deep-purple berry known as 'Sloe-Berries.' The fruit is used in jam and as a flavoring in gin to produce the famous 'sloe-gin.'"

The Seer spoke with a deep, gravelly voice and walked up to each of us as she told her story. Looking into our eyes and soul too, I thought. Leaning some on her staff, she continued.

"Straiph-'ST' in the Ogham, is the last of the letters used in combination.[29] There are various versions as to why it is a combination letter. In various texts we are told: 'Where 'S' stands before 'D,' it is 'Straiph' that is to be written.' But as you will find in research, as with other double letters, this is never found in the manuscripts themselves. Confused? Yes! There is more.

"In 'Straiph,' we have the letter S, which comes from 'Sail'-'Willow,' and the letter T, which comes from 'Tinne'-'Holly.' Also the letter D, which comes from 'Duir'-'Oak'; as you should remember, the Holly tree often stands in for the Oak tree, standing in for the high king! The Oak in the background is not readily seen. When we put these letters together, S plus T equals ST, which equals 'Straiph'-'Blackthorn'; this becomes one of the Ogham letters.[30] Never have the Keepers said that learning the 'Tree Dreaming' would be easy! This path is not for those without perseverance!

"Remember the quote from the 'Word Ogham of Morainn': 'careful effort, strongest of red' and 'strong red dye on metal.' What could this mean?" said the Blackthorn Seer. Then she looked around for an answer; of course we were blank. She picked up again quickly, knowing we had not a clue!

"Here is another: 'the hedge of a stream.' Let me enlighten you, Dreamers! All of these quotes are clues, and all are to do with death and warriors! Yes, Dreamers, we are getting into death in a different way in our work together. Please remember that the color red is always synonymous with death in Irish legends. The strong red dye on metal is blood on the warrior's sword! The hedge of a stream is a description of tightly bunched warriors' spears, the hedge, as they advanced, the stream. These associations appear in a passage from one version of the 'Cattle Raid of Cooley,' which contains a warning to Cuchulain not to advance. Can you see what is going on here? Dreamers, wake up!

"We must begin to get used to these riddles; this is what the world of Dreaming and Magic is about! There are many of these riddle tests, and to become a true Dreamer, one needs to pass these tests. The bards of the Old World spoke to each other all the time in such fashion; this helped to keep what needed veiling safe from the ordinary world.

"Let us get into the two letters, *S* and *T*, which are of course the three trees: 'Sail'- 'Willow,' 'Duir'-'Oak,' and 'Tinne'-'Holly.' These are what make up 'Straiph.' Here is what is enlightening: as you will recall, the Willow has been described as the 'color of a lifeless one' and the hue of the lifeless,' owing to the resemblance of its color to a dead person. The Oak has been described as being a shelter of protection for warriors. When we recall the description of the Holly, it has been said that the Holly was the substitute for the real king, who was in fact expected to lay down his life on behalf of his people! From this amazing composite, we realize the significance of the Blackthorn. We must fully understand these components, before any use of its workings can be made."

It was quiet again. The Seer looked to the night sky, watching the heat lightening there. I liked her, but I did not like what she had come to teach us. Why was that? I thought. I sure do have a fear about death, mine! Well, there I have said this to myself at least. I know that what the Seer offers will be helpful; apparently there is no more time to put this topic on hold. If I had my way, that is just what I would do! I just keep thinking about the pain of it all, mine and others. Death is painful...OK, forget the pain; I do have the luxury of knowing that I am breathing! Pay attention; maybe I will find something useful.

I became dimly aware of conversation; blinking my eyes, I saw the Seer standing. She was saying something about an "electrical storm," pointing to the sky with the lightning streaking without any thunder sounds.

"Outwardly the heavens seemed shattered as we see the streaks of light, but with mounting tensions, something has to give. Release and discharge: that is what happens, and then the cycles reset. This is nature; this is human nature, and death is a part of the nature of life. The sooner we make peace with this, the easier it becomes. We prepare for this, and we waste no time."

I gulped and took a very deep breath. Prepare for this? I was not so sure about that! I tried to smile at my friends; they were definitely as worried as myself. I could tell the Seer was not concerned with our misgivings; on she went.

"Dreamers, the most important part of what you will learn with me is to confront your own deaths! I can tell you are excited about this. How will we do this? you may be wondering We will journey to this of course; that is what Dreamers do. But we will not try to see the actual death, *no!* The intention is to 'see the effects' on self, family, friends, and what is left behind. Personal things you have been involved with and doing. Oh I can tell you cannot wait to get into this Dream! Ah! We must first cover a few things in order to be best prepared. Trust me, I know. I have done this so many times, cannot even count the times!"

The Blackthorn Seer walked back to her drumming crew of Seers; I suppose this was to allow us time to think about "Dreaming our Death." Scary thought...I leaned over to one of the Dreamers saying so. She seemed even more out of sorts than I; we both vowed to look after each other as we went through this process. The thing she said though, got to me: "It is not me that I worry or am fearful for; it is my small child. Who will look after him?!"

All I could think of to answer was, "Make sure your life intention is for long life!" She did smile some at that.

The Seer was pouring coffee and then walked to her twisted, bent wood chair, which was really beautiful in its design. I wondered if she took this with her everywhere. How many other Dreamers had she helped through this tough subject matter? Did it get to her?

The air was cooler now; someone brought her a blanket. The drummers began again softly, and the Blackthorn Seer spoke out. "I have played a fine role in my time. I would like to tell you of Merlin, the ancient magician who used several sacred trees in his workings. I will give you a small outline here of some he called upon.

"'The Oak'-'Duir' was regarded as a male tree, with long life, wisdom, and kingship. Oak is associated with lightning and the Greek gods of Zeus and Jupiter, both gods of lightning.

"'The Apple'-'Quiert' was regarded as a female tree, the tree of the 'Goddess of Giving.' The fruit sometimes may be poisonous, if eaten at the wrong time, or unhallowed by the blessing of the Goddess or the Fairy Queen. We may come across the Golden Apple, as has been written of in myth.

"'The Thorn/Blackthorn'-'Straiph.' This tree consists of many trees, and all bear fruit and spines. The fruit of the Blackthorn is called 'Sloe.' These trees are sacred to the 'Goddess of Taking.' In the initiatory traditions of the Celts, the thorn tree was associated with seer-ship and second sight. It also marked the entrance to the Otherworlds or Fairy Realms, being the guardian with its thorns and thick growth of thickets, veiling what was needed. There are many myths from various traditions concerning thorns and sacrifice. Of course these include those of Christianity, which may have been a grafting onto earlier sacrificial myths and rituals.

"Remember earlier my mentioning of my height of thirteen to fifteen? Let us look at how this comes into our magical Dreaming work. In the ancient writings of 'O'Flaherty's and O'Sullivan's Beth-Luis-Nion,' there were omissions of two mythically important trees: 'Queirt'-'Apple' and 'Straiph'-'Blackthorn.' The explanation is as follows: The 'Beth-Luis-Nion' calendar is a solar one, expressing the year's course of the Sun. It is, however, ruled by the 'White Moon Goddess.' Her sacred number is thirteen in so far as it coincides with the solar year, but fifteen in so far as the moon falls on the fifteenth day of each lunation. Fifteen is also the multiple of three and five. The number three expresses the three phases of the Moon and the Goddess's aspects of Maiden, Nymph, and Hag/Crone. Five expresses the five stations of her year: Birth, Initiation, Consummation, Repose, and Death. Since only thirteen, twenty-eight-day months can be fitted into a year, two of the months must be shared between pairs of trees. For this reason in the calendar, we do not see the name of 'Queirt'-'Apple'; it is shared with 'Coll'-'Hazel' in the calendar months. The same sharing applies to 'Straiph'-'Blackthorn,' which is shared with the tree, 'Sail'-'Willow.' My numbers really are important!

"As you can see, I am a tree linked with warfare, wounding, and death. But I am also associated with the Scottish 'Goddess Cailleach,' the Crone of Death, and with the Irish Morrigan. It has been said that in Scotland, winter begins when the 'Cailleach,' the Goddess of Winter strikes the ground with her Blackthorn staff. Often in fairytales such as 'Sleeping Beauty,' Blackthorn forms a thick, impenetrable thorn bramble that hides the magic castle from intruders and princes alike. In order to prove worthy, the prince must cut through this thorn forest to rescue the princess. I am the tree of initiation into the mysteries of self-conquest and transcendence. Blackthorn opens the pathway to underworld initiation. Please realize, initiations are often reenactments of our own death and rebirth. The actions of fate may not be avoided, but you can count on me to help with these big transitions.

"In France the Blackthorn tree is called 'La Mere du Bois,' which means 'The Mother of the Wood'!"

I whispered, looking to my Dreamer friend, but my voice was heard by all. "That is what you said at the start of the evening!" I turned a little red, as I was suddenly embarrassed at my outcry. However, everyone laughed, even the Seers! I thought it was nice to see us all loosen up.

The Blackthorn Seer had a soft, red-lipped smile on her pinkish oval face; wisps of fine silver-gray hair blew across her forehead. She pulled the hair away with one hand as she adjusted her crossed legs and her skirts. Again she continued her tale.

"From ancient times, the Celts have felt the Blackthorn, whose Latin name is '*Bellicum*,' a necessary but an unlucky tree! Still today lingers a fear of 'the black rod,' which was carried as a walking stick by local witches. Some have heard say the rod can cause miscarriages. In the year 1670, in Edinburgh lived Major Weir, the Covenanter and self-confessed witch. He was burned at the stake, and his blackthorn staff was burned with him, as this was thought to be the chief instrument of his sorceries!

"Now that is a tale, Dreamers! There are many such as this, where my name comes to mind. Blackthorn is also the traditional timber with which bellicose Irish tinkers fight with at fairs. This weapon is called 'Shillelagh,' and the name may have been modeled after the old Northern French words 'Estrif' and 'Estriver.' This may very well be the same word as 'Straiph,' which was derived from the Breton peoples in Brittany, France.

"In Latin we have the words 'Strebloein' or 'Strabloein,' which come from the verbal root word 'Streph,' which means 'To twist,' 'To reeve with a windlass, to wrench, dislocate, and put on the rack.' These all give 'Straiph/ Blackthorn' its cruel connotation. Wow! Harsh, are they not? But do not worry, I am strong and can take it! Let us get into the why of these connotations.

"Since ancient times, the Celts, the Druids, had special magical means of communication through the development of the Ogham. The 'Straiph' was part of the finger alphabet on the hand: 'The Finger Tip Trees.' The hand was divided into sections with the various trees being allotted to a certain finger. It was expected that a young acolyte Dreamer would come to know these meanings by heart. The finger alphabet was used in the witch cult of medieval

Britain, especially in the Glastonbury area, which was the principle seat of the Old Religion and held strong well into the seventeenth century. From confessions of members of these covens at their trials in 1664, it appears that the chief or god of these witches was known as Robin. It was said that he sealed his initiates with a prick from a thorn needle made between the upper and middle joints of the 'physic finger'; this was considered to be the 'Alder Finger,' which is part of the 'Finger Tip Trees.' This is precisely the spot at which one would expect the prick, since the various covens' activities included both black and white magic. At that time it was said that the upper joints of the fingers belong to 'Coll'-'Hazel,' which is the tree of white magic and healing. The lower joints of the fingers belong to 'Straiph'-'Blackthorn,' which was the tree of black magic and blasting. Blasting may be considered a form of a curse or the sending of one, which might cause one to become confused or befuddled. It has been noted that these witches used the thorns of thorn trees for sticking into wax images of their enemies under Robin's direction.

"The Druids and the Bards frequently used the tree alphabet, the 'Finger Tip Trees,' in their magical workings. They developed various ciphers that were used to mystify and deceive all ordinary people who were not within the secret of their work. For instance one poet, Bard, might ask another in public: 'When shall we two meet again?' The answer might come back with the words misplaced and backwards or with countless letter rearrangements. In one verse we see the 'Straiph' tree as being concealed by referring to it as 'A Pack of Wolves'!

"Irish myth tells of the use of spell casters, which were referred to as 'Geis'; the plural is 'Geasa.' The word 'Geis' means a taboo, similar to being under a vow, a bond, or a spell, which can be compared with a curse. Important to know here is that the 'Geis' is thought to be tied with one's fate or destiny. The violation of one's 'Geis' may lead to some misfortune and, in some cases, to one's death! I am quite sure that this talk of 'Geis' spell casting has your curiosity piqued, knowing as I do your fondness for the contemporary Harry Potter novels! However, what you need to know here in these lessons is that the Blackthorn will give you a gift if you study in earnest; that is the gift of accepting your own death.[31] This is the ultimate transformation after all ,and when you come to terms with that, shape-shifting and magical spell working will be a snap!"

I looked at the Seer with my eyes in wide disbelief; so were the other Dreamers. Talk about transformation. She still had much to tell.

"Blackthorn's meaning is about change, but a change that will not be easy. Dreamers must use their inner strength and spiritual authority and be able to walk through this new doorway that is also about opportunity. A Dreamer learns to make a stand and meet any challenge. The Blackthorn has always been associated with spiritual authority, and its wood is most favored as staffs for witches and magicians. The wood is used in making wands, which is said to facilitate shape-shifting from human into animal form. These wands are also used to send any negativity of a curse back to their source!

"Four bodies of prose of Irish Mythology include: Mythological Cycle, Ulster Cycle, Fenian Cycle, and the Historical Cycle. All of them center on the exploits of the mythical hero 'Fionn mac Cumhaill' and his warriors, the 'Fianna Eireann.' The legend of 'Pursuit of Diarmuid and Grainne,' a tale from the 'Fenian Cycle,' concerns a love triangle between the great warrior 'Fionn mac Cumhaill,' the beautiful princess 'Grainne,' and her paramour 'Diarmuid Ua Duibhne.' These tales date from the tenth through the sixteenth centuries. The illustration here of shape-shifting and sacrificing can give us guidance on the makeup of 'Straiph.' In one passage of the story, the woman 'Sadhbh,' who was the mother of Oisin by Fionn mac Cumhaill and daughter of Bodb Derg, King of the 'Sid of Munster,' is found eating the fruit of the blackthorn tree. She then becomes pregnant and gives birth to a son with a curious lump across his head. The lump then turns into a snake, which is killed in compensation for another man's life! Another telling tale is a poem called 'The Sword of Oscar.' In the story the 'sloe-berries' are introduced again, and again there is the theme of one person then dying on the behalf of another. What is the lesson here, Dreamers?"

The Blackthorn Seer looked at the four of us, really thinking we might answer. I wanted to offer something but was not quick enough. Luckily she did not seem to mind our ineptness. But I had better be ready for the next time, I thought. Somewhat of a pause followed, but she did not lose her momentum as she sat down gracefully into her chair.

"Dreamers, let's look at the lessons. One of the most important things the Blackthorn tree represents is the warrior's death in the service of his or her High King, and on behalf of his or her people. The Word Ogham of Cuchulain makes reference to 'an arrow's mist' and 'smoke drifting up from the fire.' These quoted phrases are the kennings for death! If we were to precede with the word 'magician' as in the phrase above—'A magician's arrow mist' and 'a magician's smoke drifting up from the fire'[32]—we can begin to have a better description of what Blackthorn is teaching us, which is being the transformer! Magicians transform things and these lessons are about facing up to your own death, whether it be soon or long away. Sooner or later we all have to experience the transition from this world to the Otherworld. I want to emphasize, Dreamers, that it is better to be prepared, rather than not! Contemplating and meditating on one's own death is not as morbid as it may first appear. This is a practice used by many magical and spiritual disciplines. It is only neglected by the Christian Church in the West, which then contributes to the fear of death and dying.

"To help you all understand the meanings within the Blackthorn makeup, the other Seers and I have a small play to perform for you. Get more coffee and settle in for a new perspective and some fun!"

The Blackthorn Seer joined with the other Keepers and began their staging. The Dreamers and I drank the hot coffee and ate the sweet cakes and fruits provided on the camp table, and then sat down.

The Four Keepers approached in unison; we could hear the high-pitched keening as the wind also gave a stir of cool air. The "Blackthorn-Straiph Seer" had donned a black gown, like a judge might wear. The "Willow-Sail Seer" had a flowing transparent shawl wrapped about her, with a pale face that was almost transparent and looked lifeless. The "Oak-Duir Seer" held numerous branches and carried himself like a king would. The "Holly-Tinne

Seer" walked as if he were invisible, right next to the Oak, but he sure gave a sense of quiet support. They stopped in front of us and formed a semicircle.

The Blackthorn Seer, holding a lit candle, stepped forward, saying, "Let the 'Dream Theater of the Oak' begin! Come! 'Duir Seer,' how have you fared in the world so far? Speak!" She passed the candle to the Oak Seer.

The majestic Oak Seer stepped forward: "To give an account of my life: this you ask, and I must answer truthfully. I have had a tall order as High King of our sovereign land and mostly have done as the goddess has asked. I have given my shelter tirelessly to the warriors who needed safety. But the burden has taken a toll some days, and then the loneliness would set in. There were times I would have rather had fun than the serious concerns of state, to be the carefree boy. But the high emotions I have felt when knowing the people were cared for and were able to enjoy times of plenty and peace on the land, to see the gardens bloom with the damask pink roses, would bring tears to my eyes, making any burden I had worth all! So much still, I could have done better! Who will look after my domain, as I have? This change worries me. Who will wear my clothes, sleep in my bed, and wear this emerald ring and crown of gold? What is in their heart? Will they remember the lessons I have shared? Have I given enough love that I might be remembered? Blackthorn-Straiph Seer, how do you judge me now?"

Stepping out of the dark night, with the candle lighting her face, The Blackthorn Seer said, "It is not I that must judge! It is you! Think of what you might have omitted." She stepped back.

Holding the lit candle, the Oak-Duir Seer was slow to speak. The Blackthorn Seer handed him a branch of her black, twisting wood. He turned finally to look at the Holly-Tinne Seer and stared for a time.

"As the High King, I have been remiss! Nothing could have been accomplished well if it had not been for the help of the Holly Seer! No deeds could have been completed if it were not for his sacrifice and laying down of life for me. I owe him all; he is the spine and the structure while staying in the shadows. But it is he that stays evergreen, while I, at year's end, must retreat and die back. I cannot take the credit of this high land domain without acknowledgement of all that he has given. In every relationship there is a sharing of the work and there is one who may shine brighter for a time. What must be remembered is nature has its cycles with this and we all need to know which cycle of either shining or sacrifice we are in. I relinquish all but for him!"

The Oak Seer held out his hand to the Holly Seer, and they both embraced. The candle was given to the Holly Seer. The Holly-Tinne Seer speaks: "I thank you, my high king! Without blinking an eye, I would yet again be in your service. My heart is true; my words are clear for your work. It is I who sponsors you gladly!"

The candle flickered in the breeze as The Blackthorn Seer took it and walked slowly around the two Seers, waving a smudge and then nodding to the Holly Seer to disengage. The night air was very cool; I wrapped my shawl tighter around myself; in the blue-black air, something moved. We heard the piercing cry of keening. The Willow-Sail Seer seemed to float toward us. She truly looked like the lifeless one of death! The other Dreamers and I looked at each other and grasped hands.

The Blackthorn Seer had her staff held out in front of her with her left hand and the candle in her right hand. The Blackthorn Seer said, "Who sponsors this Seer in their time of transition?"

The Willow Tree Seer said, "It is I, The Sail."

The Blackthorn Seer said, "Duir Oak Tree Seer, having viewed how you have fared and coped, do you now find yourself worthy for this ultimate transformation?"

The Oak Seer speaks: "I have looked far within and feel sadness but excitement, and alas find myself worthy! Who is there for me?"

The Willow Tree Seer said, "It is I, the Willow-Sail, who is here for you and can show you the gateway to incredible realms! Please take hold of this branch, a gift of the Blackthorn; she will clear a path for you, and the Otherworlds will lie in secret no more!"

Then in a flash, the candle had gone out; the wind was gusting, and there was nothing to see but the blackness of the night. We were all in the void; I felt exhilaration but did not feel fear. There was deep silence for a while. Then after a few minutes, one of the Dreamers began clapping, and the rest of us joined. The four Keepers walked to the fire where the dimly lit coals now blazed welcome.

The Dreamers and I began laughing and giving hugs to the actors of this "Dream Theater of Oak." We all praised them and thanked each of them for bringing to light what each of us needs to face. They answered us with thanks, saying they had done their best with much "careful effort"!

The Blackthorn Seer now held high her twisted staff of the "Straiph"; then she spoke: "Dreamers! We are happy that you enjoyed our theater presentation! I do, however, have several other points that need mentioning." She paused and looked about until we were settled and attentive.

"It is not advised to visualize your own specific death during Otherworld journeying. The effects can be too traumatic. This is what the 'Word Ogham of Morainn' means by the phrase 'careful effort.' These journeys are real in the Otherworlds, and we must take care not to see the actual event. It is very acceptable to consider the effects of your death—not the death itself, but the effects on you and those you leave behind. Should you find this a difficult thing to do, call upon me, the Blackthorn, hold my sloe fruit or a branch, and I will provide support.

"From the 'Word Ogham of Aonghus,' we have the phrase 'increasing secrets.' This is a mental exercise to consider for the ongoing effects of one's own death. Shifting our sphere of existence from this world to the Otherworld is the most transforming thing any of us will ever do. Again call upon me to assist; I can help you to find more meaning and understanding with less fear.

"The spiritual lesson of the 'Straiph-Blackthorn Tree' is to accept the inevitability of your own death and to prepare for it. We can do this by having a very firm understanding of what the Otherworld means for you. Remember too that on this plane in waking reality it is about making sure all your debts—on all levels—are paid! Make sure that nothing is left unsaid or undone in this world. Make sure that there are provisions made for those left behind. And that in the Otherworlds you are able to face those who have gone before you. Of course this includes family, friends, loved ones; but it also includes those whom you may have tried to avoid in this world."

The Seer had been standing very still as she spoke, and she gave each of us special knowing looks with her words. Now she became quiet for a few minutes and began to walk around us toward the wood. When she came back, she had branches of "Straiph" for each of us and handed them to us without a word. Then she stepped back and continued.

"The rule is to be in a constant state of readiness for Death! Yes, be ready! Do things as soon as they need to be done. Say things when they need to be said. And make sure to repay debts and favors as soon as practical. Why? Because, Dreamers, tomorrow may be too late!

"Now you have enjoyed the theater, and this has given you a model to follow for your own personal journey with facing your death. We will be getting to that in just a bit, but beforehand I want to offer my help in providing energy for you to do this. So first we will take a quick journey to our own personal auras. Our intention is to look for flaws we may find, and I will help each of you to heal and correct these. You will travel with the branches of the 'Straiph,' which I have given to each of you. Call upon the Celtic God Don as we do this work; he is closely associated with death and is a very protecting father figure to have with you. The Celts thought him to be the collective father, and he can help us understand the death from which we are born and to which we return.

"OK Dreamers, the drumming has begun. Journey to the aura that surrounds your body; scan and check for any places that need healing. I will be with you!"

The drumming became mesmerizing; quickly I checked on my aura. The Blackthorn Seer was there. Working together we mended spaces in my aura, and then she sealed me with certain colors of healing light I had chosen and known only to me. This felt intense but, once done, very invigorating. When all of the Dreamers had completed this aura work, we were told that this was something we should continue on our own. The sealing done after the healing and correcting work is to prevent leakage so we will not pick up psychic matter that does not belong to us. The Seer told us that this becomes very helpful when we are at last ready for our magical transformation.

The group was in a fine mood now, and the Willow Tree Seer then came walking over with a silver tray, upon which rested wine goblets for us all. She said, "A toast to the Blackthorn Seer. And of course the beverage is 'Sloe-Gin' for each of us!"

The Holly Tree Seer said, "To a wonderful transition from this world to the Other, and to the Blackthorn Seer!"

We all laughed and cheered each other...Imagine that, I thought, cheering Death! But it felt right, and we each were becoming prepared in our own way. As I held my branch of "Straiph" wood, I looked forward to carving the Ogham letters *ST* into a magical Ogham stick to use for my work. I smiled at the thought of this; the Blackthorn Seer smiled back at me, knowingly.

All of us sat around the fire, and the Blackthorn Seer said if we were ready, a bit later they would drum for us to face our individual journey to death. But if we did not want to do this tonight, that was OK too. The Dreamers and I each looked at each other, and we all began to laugh. "What is so funny?" said the Blackthorn Seer.

I looked at her, still with laughter, and said, "After all this dress rehearsal, we feel like it is now or never. We will do it tonight!"

The Seers laughed and one said, "I like your spunk!"

We could hear the sound of quiet keening coming from somewhere in the wood. Looking at each other, we Dreamers were pensive. Then someone said, "It is always there, so what!" We all laughed; the blue-black night was still young.

ELDER

Karen C. Silverstein

"R" Ruis

THE ELDER LETTER "R," "RUIS" OGHAM:

STATISTICS FOR:
"The Elder" genus/species- *Sambucus ebulus*
~Grows native in Europe and naturalized in other areas.
~Grows to a height of 33 feet tall.
~The bark is light brown, and leaves grow alternately; it has creamy white, five-petaled flowers, with a sweet scent. Black berries are harvested in the autumn.

~~~~~~~~~~

THE ELDER: HOW USED IN THE WORLD
~The bark of the wood is used for making different colored dyes. It is thought to be unlucky to chop down an Elder tree, as it is watched over by the fairy folk. Magically it used in the powers of healings and visions. Good for protection, cleansing, and exorcism. Elder twigs were woven into headdresses to enable the wearer to see spirits. The month of Elder is associated with the Winter Solstice.

~~~~~~~~~~

MEDICINAL AND PSYCHOLOGICAL
~The Elder is said to have over 70 medicinal uses. The bark is used for headache and to promote labor. The leaves can be made into drinks, poultices, and salves. The flowers are made into a wash for sunburn. The berries are safe when ripe and are made into jams, teas, and wines. Elder is linked to the eternal turnings of life and death and rebirth, and to creativity and renewal.

~~~~~~~~~~

SACREDNESS AMONG THE GROVE
~The Elder is the fifteenth tree in the Ogham Alphabet: "Ruis"-"R"
~The Elder is associated with visions, rebirth, creativity, protection, and accepting death.
~KEYWORD- Cleanse, Renew
~Planets- Saturn and Venus
~Month- November 25 through December 22

~The Elder tree stands on either side of the Blackthorn tree and Fir tree within the Grove.

~"FINGER TIP TREE" location- "Elder-Ruis"-"R" is on the middle of the little finger.

DREAM OF "RUIS," THE ELDER TREE SEER

The whimsical little cottage could hardly be seen, covered as it was with plants, vines, and trees that seemed to grow from it. Thank goodness I found this place before dark, I thought. Looking at my watch, it was just past seven, darker in the woods here with the tree canopy so thick. I turned to look at the entrance, if you could call it that! For it was covered with many drooping branches covered in small white flowers; each branch intertwined with another so thickly that at first look you would not really see an entryway. Except there was light coming through the door that was partially opened. Should I go in? No, had better wait some. Just then there was a slight flutter as two crows landed in a nearby tree. From somewhere out of old Dreaming, I recalled that in Europe there is a bird called the "Rook," which is very similar to the crow, but smaller. I looked around, but no person seemed to be here. It was a warm night, no need for a wrap, but I put mine on anyway.

I was feeling so glad to have come alone to meet the Seer for my study, liking the idea of "one-on-one working." Here in the stillness, looking at the unbelievable growth of the forest with the little gardens blooming with flowers and various interesting vegetable plants tucked in between, made this all seem fairytale, Dreamlike, not the usual waking world. I thought to myself, I should be used to this! It was amazing to be in yet another area of this vast Grove of the Nemeton. I looked about the dense forest; with the evening sounds beginning, I felt a bit nervous alone here. So I took a deep breath. Do not take the wrong emotional path here, I said to myself. The Seer will be here in a moment, and she did say seven thirty p.m., and I am early.

I walked near the cottage with the branches hanging heavily with fragrant flowers. They were creamy white and consisted of five small petals, so beautiful. I turned a bunch over on the back and could see five green sepals form the shape of a star, like tiny star-shaped umbrellas!

I was feeling tired. So much was going on today, and it was quite a long hike into this part of the Grove. Leaning over, I took in the scent of the star-like flowers. I was thinking I would sit down next to this small tree, when I heard, "Not advised!" I jumped back, startled, but did not see anyone.

"Do not think to nap here, Dreamer! It is considered unwise to rest under her too long, for if you fall deeply asleep, you may never wake up!"

I was walking away backward from the tree and frightened, still not seeing anyone and wondering, What now?! I turned very fast and would have left had I not bumped into an old woman, looking like my grandmother, I thought. I could not breathe, not really, and certainly could not speak. She did not move; neither did I. After a moment of her scanning me, I took a breath, saying to myself, OK! You can do this! I almost gave her a greeting, but instead she handed me a basket tightly woven, with a white cloth inside it.

She spoke: "The dew will be arriving shortly, and we need to pick some petals and leaves before it collects. Put them into your basket, making layers between with the white cloth. Pick only the petals of this Elder Tree that fall off easily, and put them on one layer. Then pick the leaves and put them on another layer. Do not pick the leaves from the tip; pick down from the main stem, and not too many from one stem! The evening light is ample; this will not take us long."

All I could do was nod my head. I did not seem to have a voice. I got to work as the Seer instructed. At least I assumed she was the Seer. Dear Goddess, I hoped so! The flower scent was beautiful, and it was easy to pick them. I layered them along with the leaves just as she had said and shown me. Once or twice she nodded her head in approval. No words were spoken, and I was surprised, for I felt comfortable with her in this fairytale scene; it was good. I wondered what she meant about the napping under this tree. Her attire was that of a peasant out of a painting from Van Gogh's *The Potato Eaters*, with a plain dark dress and a white linen fitted cap over her head.

My basket was filling up and the Seer noticed. I could see she had put hers down now near the cottage door. As she reached for mine, she thanked me, saying, "Well done. The Keepers tell me you are prepared to work with me and that you know I am the 'Elder Seer' who watches over these parts of the Grove. Is this so?"

I was ready with a response, which surprised me. "Yes, Elder Seer, I am prepared and thankful you will have me!" She was stern and plain in her direct reply.

"Well, we will see how happy you are a little later on!" She gave a half-dry smile and turned toward the cottage. I waited a minute before moving. She turned and looked harshly, as if to say, what on earth are you waiting for! I did not wait; I caught up fast to the door of the cottage. The Seer pushed the door open. Various tree limbs moved with it; this did not seem to bother her, and I wondered why she did not trim them. She had picked up her basket and put it on the wooden table and now reached for mine.

The room was aglow from the fireplace, and every surface was covered with plants and herbs. Some hung from the rafters, drying, some looked like jars of jam, and some were full of dried leaves and pieces of plants in jars of all sizes. Others were in leather satchels or some were rolled in paper. In between jars and baskets were beautiful crystals and stones collected; there were shells and all manner of natural collections so fascinating to me. On the table were various tools for chopping, mortars, cutting utensils, and storing containers. There was a heady scent all about the room. To one side was an old-fashioned wood burning stove, with a cooktop and ovens beneath. Two pots were simmering something that smelled wonderful, and curiously the whole place felt very familiar.

I watched the Seer as she removed her shawl and hung this on a peg. Then she offered her hand to take mine. Then she stood at the table with her hands placed flat on the wood. Adjusting her head to the left, she stared at me. I did not know what she wanted or what to do with my arms, so I folded them in front of me and tried to smile. She told me to be seated there. I did but she did not sit. No! She stared!

Finally she said this: "The lesson of Elder is difficult; she not only asks that you accept death willing but that you have already realized and worked on how it is you would like to be remembered! Think on that, Dreamer! That is your task as you work here with me. How would you be remembered? What is it you need to do?" She put her left palm of her hand up in front of me, saying, "You will not answer this now! Now we will have soup, and then we will work on herbs that need tending. Close the window some, Dreamer, and you can wash your hands over there. If you have not brought with you night things, I have them, as you will spend the night here with me!"

All I could do was take a deep breath. The Seer had moved to the wood neatly stacked by the stove and put the small-sized pieces into the small door at the top of the cook surface. Next she went to the washstand with the white antique ceramic washbasin. She removed her white cap and combed out her white hair, then tied it back. She looked into the large oval mirror that was part of the wooden stand at the top. I felt her looking at me in the mirror reflection. After washing and drying her hands on the white linen towels, she made a gesture for me to do the same. As I stood, I straightened my skirts and smoothed my hair from my neck, twisting it into a loose braid.

When I had finished with the washing, the Elder Tree Seer handed me a knife and had me cut slices of cheese that lay on the cutting board on the table. Then she put out freshly baked bread, and I cut that into several slices too. It smelled great! When I had the bread done, she took the part not sliced and stood it upright with the cut part down onto the bread board. Next she began to ladle the soup into huge, blue ceramic bowls and carried each of them to the table. Just then at the open window, a crow alighted and cawed to let us know it was there. The Seer told me to put some of the crumbs onto the spirit plate she handed me and to place this on the window ledge, which I did. Of course the crow snatched them in a blink. She moved to the long end of the table and came with a cold pitcher of a purple juice, which I was certain must be Elderberry. Then, picking up a narrow basket, she told me to take out our silverware, which I did. We both sat down, and she handed me white linen napkins with a purple elderberry design.

Then she said, "Yes, Dreamer, we thank the Goddess for our bounty, we do! And let us eat!"

The Seer began to eat quickly. Everything smelled so good; I too began and really enjoyed the vegetable soup, hunks of a sharp cheese, and warm bread. The little, whimsical cottage was very comfy and home like. We did not talk, but that seemed OK. Once done, I began to clear the dishes to the small counter next to the sink. The Seer remained seated and watched me. I found a large napkin to wrap the bread in, and there was oiled cloth for the cheese. I would have done the dishes, but the Seer said, "Come now, the 'wee ones' will be here later and finish everything."

She went to the stove and took the soup pot off the burner, then she poured us each a cup of tea and motioned for me to follow. Walking through the little house to the back, we arrived at porch, which, to my disbelief, had a view of the sea in the distance!

Not being able to hold back my delight, I exclaimed to the Seer, "This is so special! You have your own little hideaway here. Whoever would think the ocean could be seen from this place in the Grove! I mean the forest and foliage is so thick and dense, it is hard to see more than several feet any which way! How did you ever find this place, dear Seer?"

She laughed for the first time; I was glad. Then she told me to sit in one of the rocking chairs there on the back porch. She also sat and began to rock back and forth, sipping her tea. "Find it? No, I did not find it. I Dreamt what I needed and then kept my faith in the ungraspable for a time. The garden of the forest was here, that I knew, and it was my garden of desire. The trick was finding the way in! I had no idea where the gate to this garden lay hidden; it was not clear. But the point was I desired this after I Dreamt it, and I knew I would find a gate to go through, and never doubted! After much work and love, this became what you and other Dreamers see now. A 'whimsical cottage,' as I believe you phrased it, deep in the wood, hidden from view, but what a view for those who go through the gate. I am glad that you like it, Dreamer. Look, the Moon is rising now in the eastern sky; she will wax until full, three days from now. Beautiful, is she not, over the waters?!"

The Elder Tree Seer was smiling, and I could feel how proud she was of this special cottage, the place where she did her work in Dreaming, healing, herbalism, and seer-ship. Not to mention all those that she must have touched and taught her skills to. I felt honored to be with her and thought I should say so. I did wonder at her saying something about the "whimsical cottage." I am quite sure I did not say that to her directly! Very interesting, I thought.

"Dear Elder Seer, thank you for having me here to apprentice. I am truly honored!" I bowed my head to her.

She acknowledged with a nod of her head, saying, "You are welcome, Dreamer; we must get going with our tasks if you are to learn anything. We will sit here a few minutes until the Moon is a bit higher. Have you any questions before we move inside?"

"I was wondering if this is where you make up your ideas for your work, here on this special porch."

The Seer smiled and then said, "New ideas are not made, no! They arrive on the east winds! But I suppose I do find myself out here dreaming about which way the wind is blowing, and then I look within and more likely than not the Dream-idea comes to light on the Easterly Wind! In many archaic traditions, man is understood to enter the world from the eastern direction, and like the Sun, follows a path to the west. And just as the Sun sets in the western sky and dies for the night, so man does follow the west. This direction has come to have an association with death for many ancient cultures."

Oh! My, I thought to myself. I was really just making polite conversation. How did she manage to bring us to her theme so quickly? I guess that is why she is the Seer and not me; I mean, I was almost forgetting why I was here. I was really pipe Dreaming with that. I did, however, smile at her and nod my head in a yes response.

She was up now, saying the Moon was where she needed to be and the night air was cooling quickly. She opened a cupboard and handed me a blue wooden tray and three white candles. We went back to the kitchen. I noticed everything had been tidied up, and there was more tea on the stove and a plate covered with a purple-and-white plaid napkin. Funny, I had not heard anyone doing any cleaning; strange, because this cottage was so small.

The Seer now arranged the three candles, which were about five inches tall and very thick in diameter, on the blue tray at the end of the long kitchen table. She had a small book of wooden matches in her hand, which she handed to me. Then she said this: "At the start of my magical working of the Tree Dreaming, I like to set the tone with an opening of the light before our invocations. What you see here is what I like to call 'A Celtic Triad.' These three candles are those that illume all darkness. They represent 'Truth, Nature, and Knowledge,' as well as the 'Triple Goddess.' Dreamer, please do us honor and light them with your heart light!"

I lit the candles gladly, and the Seer gave a beautiful invocation as we held hands, heart to heart. From somewhere in the background, we heard soft drumming and the melodious sound of a flute. I wanted to ask about that, but the Seer was ready to begin her lessons; I could do this later. But first she was pulling out twine and scissors and baskets of dried herbs. It appeared we would work and lecture at the same time. That was certainly fine for me.

The Elder Tree Seer said, "We have needed little formal introduction as to who I am, Dreamer. This is good and saves time, as we have so much to cover. Now the twigs and leaves we will be bundling up like so with this twine. And as we work, I will offer what I know to be true of myself. I like to move quickly, so you will need to keep up. If there are questions, keep them to the point."

I was a little stunned at this but kept this to myself; I would just do the best I could. I watched as she tied the twigs and leaves together with the purple twine, very neatly wrapped. I tried one myself but was corrected as she showed me that the twine needed precisely five circles pulled tightly around the top of the stems before tying it off with three knots. And as these were done, she taught me a certain blessing to be said. I felt like my hands were all thumbs for a while, then it became easier. The Seer said it would take a little time to get the knack of it but that I would.

She told me that these twigs and leaves were harvested at the first of spring when the leaves were young and that they would be used in many remedies. I thought to myself that these then were picked to dry about a month ago. I wondered who might need the herb bundles I was working on.

The Seer was talking now of her craft. "As this needs to be said: my name in the Celtic Ogham for 'Elder'–'Ruis,' and my letter is *R*. 'Ruis is Elder' and in the Word Ogham of Moraine, it is said, 'TINNEM RUICE,' which means 'Intensest of Blushes,' and it is the redding of a man's face through the juice of the herb being rubbed on it.[33] In the Word Ogham of Aonghus, it is said, 'ROMNAD DRECH,' which means 'Redness of Faces.' Curious, are they not? We will see more of these expressions later, so remember them.

"The Elder tree, which in Latin is *Sambucus nigra*, is a member of the Honeysuckle family and is one of the sacred trees of Wicca and Witchcraft. The word 'Elder' is derived from an old Anglo-Saxon word 'Aeld,' which means 'Fire.' This may be due to an association of one of the uses of the wood. Because the pith of an Elder branch is soft and pushes out easily and the tubes formed were once used as pipes for blowing up fires, later bellows were made from Elder for this use. From this followed the folk names: 'Pipe-Tree, Bore-tree, Eldrun, and Ellhorn.'

"The botanical name for the Elder, '*Sambucus*,' is adopted from the Greek word 'Sambuca,' which was actually a musical instrument used by the Romans. Elder was used because of its hardness. This was likely a type of wind instrument, similar in nature to panpipes or a flute. During various rituals, flutes or whistles made of Elder are used to summon the spirits.

"The Elder tree can grow to a height of thirty feet easily, sometimes more. It can be easily rooted from new growth from any of its pieces. The small white flowers are what then sets to growing the blue-black-purple elderberries, which grow profusely in bunches. Another tree of death; I know you are thinking…I just finished with the Blackthorn tree, and I faced up to my death! What else could there possibly be?"

The Seer paused with her craft work of the herbs and her talk, staring at me across the table. Did she want me to answerer? I could not, feeling very nervous; I looked away, hoping I would not be pressed. Slowly she let her gaze go from me and began her talk again. Silently I let out a sigh of relief, keeping my hands busy with the task of the elder bundles and deciding to focus my eyes on the tying for now.

"What we come to know is that death is not the end, merely a transition from one type of existence to another. From the Celtic peoples we have learned that it was important to them to have a good reputation, be brave, honorable, and truthful. That these things remain with us in our next existence is part of their belief.

"Looking at other ancient civilizations, several believed that to continue to exist in the Otherworlds, it was necessary for your physical remains to be kept intact in this world, as was so for the ancient Egyptians. The Celts had some similar beliefs, but they did not preserve the body to sustain life in the Otherworlds. The Celts used cremation, rather than burial. The memories of a person are what is important in the Otherworlds. It was important to be a strong, brave, and truthful person. In contemporary life today, people still have a desire to be remembered for the good they have achieved during their lifetime. Many feel it is wrong to speak ill of the dead."

Subtle energies seemed to shimmer light across the work table from the candles. I was daydreaming about those in my life that had passed and the good things I remembered of them. The Elder Seer was right about being remembered in a good way.

Her momentary pause of "the theme" was over: she was speaking again. "From ancient burial chambers in Europe, dating from as early as 2500 to 2000 BC, the Elder Tree has been found in various uses. The shape of the Elder-leaf was used as the shape of portholes between two contiguous slabs of burial chambers. The Elder-leaf shape of the funerary flints in megalithic long-barrows suggests its association with death is long standing. The Elder tree is a waterside tree in many locations, and it is able to keep its fruit well into December.

"Elder is often associated with witches and is thought to be an unlucky tree. Here is a little background on why that might be so. But I must tell you right off that these things are twisted hearsay, and I most certainly am not unlucky! It has been said that in the Bible that Judas was made to hang himself from the branches of the Elder. Also from the Bible, Jesus used Elder as the crucifixion tree. There are many tales in English folklore concerning elder; one such says 'that to burn the logs of Elder is to bring the devil into the house'!

"The creamy white flowers are at their best in Midsummer, and its five-petaled blooms make the Elder another aspect of the 'White Goddess.' There are some that give the number thirteen a connection with the Elder and even call it unlucky and the tree of doom . Now I really take offense to that!"

I laughed at the Seer's comment and watched her a minute as she pulled down another basket loaded with leaves and twigs for us to assemble. "How so?" I asked her.

"Well, let me tell you some of my amazing features, Dreamer! In magical workings I am a tree of Venus. The Celts' name for 'Venus' is 'Gwena.' Beautiful, is it not?! I am associated with the element of 'Air' and 'Water,' also with black horses, the rook and the crow, and ravens. As the Elder I am linked to the eternal turnings of life and of death, birth and rebirth, also to creativity and renewal. The Elder is sacred to the deities of Bran, Venus, Hel, Callech, and the White Goddess. I, as the Elder, am the Old Crone aspect of the 'Triple Goddess,' which is about wise old energy at the end of the year's cycle. And I am sometimes called the 'death tree' because of this! Now is that fair? I ask you! I represent the end/beginning and the beginning/end; this is how it is with life!" She just went on with barely a breath. "From the 'Beth-Luis-Nion Calendar' of thirteen months, the Elder tree is attributed to the dates of November 25 to December 22."

"In the tales of Greek myth, Pythagoras was a Pelasgian from Samos. And it was he who developed the doctrine of the 'Transmigration of Souls.' According to his biographer, Porphyriu, Pythagoras went to Crete, the seat of the purest Orphic doctrine, for initiation by the 'Idaean Dactyls.' It is here he underwent a death by thunderbolt! It is suggested that twenty-eight days passed between his thunderbolt death and his revival with mixture of milk and honey. This time period is thought to be the twenty-eight-day month of the letter *R*, the death-month ruled by the Elder Tree or the Myrtle. And then it was said that Pythagoras was reborn at the Winter Solstice festival as an incarnation of Zeus.

"The month of Elder includes the Winter Solstice, which is celebrated as the 'Sabbat of Yule,' a day to mark the return of the Sun. This is an excellent time to call upon the Sun God or Goddess. Please know that I, the 'Elder Tree Seer,' have the magical powers of healing, cleansing, offering, love, protection, prosperity, spirituality, sleep, exorcism, fairy magic, and of vision! In ancient times at Samhain, the last of the Elderberries were picked with solemn rites. The wine made from these berries was considered the last sacred gift of the Earth Goddess, and was valued and drunk ritually to help invoke prophecy and divination!

"Wood spirits are said to live in the Elder Forests, and it is the wood elves that come with flutes made of Elder wood and play their magical music for those of the forest to enjoy. In ancient Europe these spirits were believed to dwell within the Elder trees, and there are still taboos against burning it or cutting the trees. Elder was planted near houses for protection and as a shield against dark witches. I am a tree that is considered special to the 'Sidhe' and fairy realm. The Elder aids in fairy contact and protects against enchantment. There is a tale that tells: 'if you bathe the eyes with the dew' collected from the Elder tree, you will be able to see fairies and witches! In the Isle of Man, Elders are the main dwelling place for elves. In Scotland, if you stand under an Elder tree at Samhain, you can see the fairy host riding by.

"It was and still is unlucky to harm an Elder. Pieces of my tree are often used to bless a person or object by scattering leaves and berries over them and to the four directions. As a protection, my branches were hung in doorways of houses or in cowsheds. Elder was often buried in the graves to ward off evil spirits and is considered protection against the earthbound. In healing work, spells were often used to divert illness from a sick person into the physical Elder tree, which knows how to handle sickness. Small branch pieces were used and worn close to the body to protect against illness. It was thought, however, to be dangerous to place any piece of Elder in or near a child's cradle, because there was fear the tree fairies would see this as a sign they could take the child away.

There are many parts of northern Europe that consider the Elder tree to be home of a presiding spirit known as 'Dame Ellhorn.' In early England near Lincolnshire, it was considered risky to cut down an Elder tree without asking 'the Old Lady's Leave'! So, dear Dreamer, do remember to ask!"

The Elder Tree Seer stopped and then went to the rows of shelving opposite the stove in the kitchen; there she climbed a small wooden ladder and rummaged among an upper shelf for something. I jumped up and ran over to help her, as she was bringing down a large roll of oiled paper layered within a huge basket. I took this quite heavy basket over to our work table. She was not a very big woman, but she certainly had amazing strength and dexterity as she scurried up and down the ladder getting the things we needed. Finally she seemed satisfied that we had our supplies. Now that we had tied the twigs and leaves with the purple twine, the Seer opened a lid to one of the huge willow woven baskets, and we began to layer the herb packets into it, alternating with brown paper for the layers. Once this was done, she closed it with the wooden pin through a leather latch. Then we put this on one of the higher shelves with a label saying Elder-leaves-twigs/date.

The Seer smiled, saying, "Good!" And she began again after asking me to pour us some tea and to bring the plate with the cookies, which were shortbread with elderberries, of course. She suggested that we wash our hands before eating, as we had handled a lot of herbal mixtures.

We munched our delicious snack, and I asked her, "Was it the fairies and the elves that did our kitchen clean-up?"

She answered quickly, "Yes! And it was the same crew making the flute music on your behalf earlier in the evening!"

I laughed and said, "Thought so!"

The Seer began once more. "We have caught up with the leaves and the twigs for now, so let us get going with the petals; that is what you see here rolled in these oiled papers. We will unwrap them and put them into the jars. Next taking the petals picked earlier, we'll roll them back into these papers."

She disappeared for a time and then finally came back with a crate of jars and put them on the floor. I simply just looked around in awe of this whole experience. The Seer said, "To start, please begin to line up all the wide-mouthed jars onto the table, from the box on the floor; keep the lids with each one you open. I will be moving fairly fast depositing the petals, and you will do a shake down of each, like so! No lids on just yet! These petals can be made into an infusion for the treatment of colds or flu; often I will use these with peppermint and yarrow."

She gave me a demo as to how this should be done; it was easy enough. "Are you ready Dreamer?"

I answered, "Yes!"

We got to work, and the jars began to fill up. They really looked nice with the dried, now a creamy, off-white petals in each of the green glass storage jars. We set up at least thirty to forty bottle green glass jars When we had these ready, the Seer went to each, checking for too much or too little and made them all even. Then she said we could sit and do up the lids, for which she had rubber stoppers that had to be placed in between the jar and the lid. We also applied labels to each jar. As we worked on this, she began her talk of Elder once more.

"What is important to know, Dreamer, is that Elder can help after we encounter 'the initial-transition-of-death,' which the Blackthorn tree prompted. Again now we go over our life. Oh, I see that look in your eyes, Dreamer! Nothing to fear; we are simply going to have a life review; nothing more than that." She chuckled a little. I managed to give a shy smile that was all.

"What generally happens for most folks is a pop up of the prominent things we wished to have done differently or the things we did not get to do. Elder can help here to over-come any emotional feelings that linger. She reminds us that it is important now to accept what you have already done and that which you cannot change. From 'The Word Ogham of Aonghus,' we have 'the redness of face.' And from 'The Word Ogham of Cuchulain,' we have "BRUTHFERGGA .i.IMDERGADH,' which means 'arduous anger, punishment'!

Wow, these are harsh, Dreamer, but as I am sure you know, this is the way many people feel when they look at those things they feel they missed or Dreamed and did not do while in this waking reality!

"But Dreamer, please know that is the beauty of our work here! We can learn from any mistakes and make sure not to repeat them in the future. As Dreamers, we Dream ahead what we need and want, and we hold fast to receive what we truly want. That is key here, Dreamer: know what you want and do it! Yet still there will be things not accomplished, and Elder will show us how to use these various mistakes or things left undone, and give them a positive bent. Simply admitting them to yourself and sometimes to others and maybe making compensations for damage done, the healing begins. You see this is what is meant by Cuchulain when he refers to 'arduous anger and punishment.'[34] What we learn is we need to cut the cord from any regret and make changes toward positive healing.

Facing up to those aspects of yourself that you may have repressed. You realize that if you are to progress, one must meet the challenges and deal with as many as necessary. We must check ourself for bias, bigotry, unfairness, or selfishness. These things must be reconciled as completely as possible before the 'blushing elder' will go away. Once you have done this, you will feel confidence!"

The Elder Tree Seer paused and looked at me a moment, her head to one side; with sympathetic eyes she held my gaze. And I held hers.

Although I could feel slight tears coming to my eyelids, I did not let them spill. Finally I said to her, "I think I understand your message here, Seer, and I will do my best when I get to my review time."

She looked a moment more and said, "Good! I expect a high level of doing from you, Dreamer." Then she walked away and brought back more jars. It only took her a minute to pick up again on the tale of Elder. "Elder first helps us with the righting and purging, with a final cleansing of the various loose ends of our life. Then I come forward so you recognize the good things you have done, the achievements, the help you have provided for others. We come to understand this is more important than any wrongs we may have done. Elder then teaches us to 'sing our praises,' that this is quite all right. That it is OK to shine! It is very good to admit these good things to yourself, along with any of the wrong things. I come to help you walk in balance and to be proud of what you have done. Having our good points praised and recognized can also bring on the 'Blushing and reddening of face'! I have been Dreaming of you, Dreamer, and see that you will accomplish much in bringing the old ways back in a new light for our contemporary Dreamers and their families. I look forward to the day when I see your 'Blushing, reddening face'!"

The Seer was beside herself with laughter from her comment. All I wanted to know was: "You saw something? What did you see? I need to know! What was this? Please!"

After more laughter, the only thing I got in the way of an answer was, "What I saw? I am not at liberty to let on just yet, why it was... Well, I cannot say, Dreamer!" Reams of laughter for a bit, which was not funny to me! She said, "Now where was I? Oh! You should see your red face now, Dreamer! But that is neither here nor there. Let me see…Oh! Yes!"

I felt my face, and yes it felt red, but now the fun at my expense was now over, and we were onto the lessons. I guess I really did not mind, but I was sure curious as to what she saw of me!

"The Elder makes it clear to us that, after our cleansing and resetting, not only are we an individual, but we are family members and part of larger social groups that we have been involved with. I need to remind you too of the spiritual level and of the earth beings we are a part of. What is important to understand is not only have these groups affected us, but we too affect these groups! Think on that, Dreamer; we are all so connected. Connected now and in the future, and we are actually living our lives in a multidimensional way over time! Know we are remembered and inevitably affect someone.

"To understand this, let us look at how some of earth's great beings lived in just one incarnation, such as philosophers, religious leaders, thinkers, saints, and others.[35] People have used their lives as role models, and some of these persons have affected people for generations. Dreamer, we too have this ability! We will certainly leave a mark on those with whom we were part of, looming larger than we can know now. Now you may be wondering what this teaches us. Clearly this teaches us how closely we are linked. What affects one affects another, and this has been so for eternity; man, however, has been a tad slow on this important lesson! We simply affect each other whether forest family, animal family, or human family. One day we will be an actual elder—an older person, an influential member of a family, tribe, or community—and we will have information to share with the future generations. Remember it is the 'Elders who show us the way'!"

The Seer stood up now and got the oiled papers we had emptied, and then rolled these out onto the table. Next she showed me how to layer the petals we had picked earlier in the evening onto the paper, alternating their oval shape in order to fit in as many as was possible. When we had this done, we checked all them over so that they lay just so. The petals looked very beautiful, and their aroma was incredible. Then I held one end as the Seer began to slowly roll up this paper; from time to time we made adjustments, but finally it was rolled up to a thickness of several inches thick. I held the roll while the Seer produced a purple ribbon to tie at the two ends and in the center. This roll was put into the woven willow basket with the leather latch. Next the Seer came with a small dustpan, and we swept up the table and also the floor. Then she had some hot water from the stove kettle and had me wash the whole surface down with water and baking soda. The stove gave off a lot of heat, and the table was dry in no time. Now I watched her assemble some dishes to be used at breakfast, and then she declared to me we were about done. But she brought over one more bundle that was wrapped in the purple and white plaid cloth, tied with purple ribbon.

She said this: "Dreamer, you have worked hard this evening and done well. And I must say you were attentive to the lessons. Glad to see you were able to keep up with two things going at once; this is a good skill to have in life. Please open this. A present for you!"

She sat down across from me, and I was very excited. I took off the purple ribbon and unfolded the cloth to find the most beautifully carved Ogham stick, smooth, dark, blackish wood with the Letter *R* carved along with the Ogham script. I was very touched and quickly stood up and ran to give her a hug! I said, "This is amazing, and means so much coming from you! I will use this with good heart, dear Elder Seer! Did you carve this?"

She answered with, "I carved the script and the *R*. However, our fairy folk made ready the basic stick, and of course their blessing was given, as they have been watching you!" She started to laugh and then was pointing to me.

"What? What is it?" I said, wondering.

"Your face, dear, is very red and blushing!"

Of course she was right, but it was funny and I laughed too!

"Now just a few things…" she said, seriously. "It is important in your ritual workings of Elder to connect and link with the previous five trees. They are the ones who have gotten you to this point. We must realize how we support and affect each other. Please, Dreamer, tell me what these five trees are."

I was taken off guard for a minute and got very nervous, but with some focusing energy, I gave the tree list to the Seer. "I believe the five trees are: Blackthorn, Broom, Ivy, Vine, and Apple!" I had been looking into space but finally looked at the Seer.

She smiled and said, "You are correct. Now remember these for the linking you will do later!"

Silently I let out a sigh of relief as I smiled at her. I leaned back on my chair as the Seer continued.

"In a few minutes I will give you your things for the night and take you back to the sleeping porch to sleep for the night. I do have a dream journey for you to go off with, and of course you will begin to have a glimmer of that initial question that was asked of you, Dreamer. 'After accepting death, how is it you would like to be remembered? What will you choose at this young age of yours to focus on for your life?' Just keep this as an intent that you will be working on for some time hence, Dreamer!"

I only could nod my head as a yes. The Seer loaded my arms with a towel and night clothes, which all had the scent of the Elder flowers. Then we went to the porch. She left me for a while, and I got myself ready for bed and Dreaming. I walked to the kitchen to say good night and to get my new Ogham stick of "Ruis."

The Seer walked back with me then relayed this beautiful Dream. "I would like you to build a forest scene in your Dreaming work with these past five trees that you named earlier and, of course, the Elder tree. View the forest as a whole, and then the individual trees. View their ideas, emotions, and their symbolism. Next put down your roots, and then reach out your individual branches up to the sky! Can you feel the link with this forest, of the trees? Now begin to enjoy the life force they help each of us with by the amazing energy they are able to generate. This is your journey for the night, Dreamer! Sleep well, my Dear One; the night on the sleeping porch is always magical. The fairies are usually early risers, so do not be alarmed when you hear them getting breakfast ready. We will compare Dream notes in the morning!"

I thanked her immensely for the incredible lessons of the Elder and let her know that I felt very much at home here.

As she walked away, I thought I heard her say, but barely, "Of course you would feel at home here, dear girl. You have lived a life like this many a time."

FIR

"A" Ailm

THE FIR/PINE LETTER "A," "AILM" OGHAM: ✛

STATISTICS FOR:

"Fir/Pine" genus/species- *Abies balsamea* and *Pinus*.

~Grows in most of the United States and throughout the world, with a great many varieties.

~Grows to a height of 40–60 feet (in many varieties) and 1–1.5 feet in diameter.

~Bark is gray to a reddish brown and in scaly patches; the flat needles are 0.8–1.5 inches and usually blunt or notched at the tip; cones are cylindrical, purplish green (new), and are 2–4 inches long. Likes moist soils near lakes and streams and mountainous areas.

~~~~~~~~~~

THE FIR/PINE: HOW USED IN THE WORLD

~The wood from the Fir is burned widely as firewood. Also is used universally as construction lumber. In the past the Plains Indians of North America used the pine as lodge poles to frame their tepees. In many cases the number of poles used was 13 in order to honor the "Thirteen Moons of the Lunar Year."

~~~~~~~~~~

MEDICINAL AND PSYCHOLOGICAL

~The Fir/Pine has at least 33 species with proven medicinal properties. Used as an inhalant, pine resin is good for respiratory complaints. Many Native Americans burn pine needles, inhaling the fumes for headaches. An infusion made from pine needles is an excellent source of vitamin C. The sap and resin is used as a rubefacient, diuretic, and irritant.

~~~~~~~~~~

SACREDNESS AMONG THE GROVE

~The Fir/Pine is the sixteenth tree in the Ogham Alphabet: "Ailm"-"A"

~The Fir is associated with weaving, interdependence, relationships, will of magic, and eternal life.

~Month- not assigned

~KEYWORD—Will of magician

~Planets- Moon and Jupiter

~The Fir tree stands on either side of the Elder tree and Furze tree within the Grove.

~"FINGER TIP TREE" location- "Ailm-Fir/Pine"-"A" is on the very lowest part of the thumb.

DREAM OF "AILM," THE FIR/PINE TREE SEER

She came out of the center of the trunk, dripping with sap. Startled as we all were, we could not stop looking at her! We heard someone ask, "Who is she?"

The answer came back: "She is the Pine Tree Seer, number sixteen in the Nemeton."

Looking at her, I said, "Is she OK? She looks a mess!" There was a large assortment of needles and cones stuck to her dripping sap. She didn't seem to be bothered by her mess. Or the bugs that were stuck to her along with discarded dolls, shoes, wine bottles. It was incredible! There were even people's faces stuck to her like tired party masks! "Why?" I asked her, "Do you not take care of yourself? Wouldn't you feel better with some pruning?" I said.

She groaned some but answered strongly. "I am the Tree of Emotions. This mess you see is only temporary. I am here to help you with your sadness, anger, pain, grief. The things you need to release. Your pains and disappointments, stick them to me! My sap can take it! Use me as a bridge of release." She stopped speaking for the time.

She watched me and the other Dreamers as we attempted to understand what she said. Looking at her, beyond the "sticky things," we saw the beauty there, the strength of her trunk, the sturdiness of her roots. The afternoon's breeze had picked up and ruffled her pine needles, which caught the rays of the sun. My Dreamer friends and I all agreed that this was truly amazing! Now with baited breath, we awaited what else she may want to share with us.

The Pine Tree Seer said, "My lineage is ancient. Some of you here may follow in my path, and you must be able to use all your senses and know the Earth's cycles. What are you sensing now?" She had stopped abruptly. I began to notice my sense of smell and the scent of pine. Now we heard the Pine Tree Seer saying, "That scent is a powerful way to travel back on our timeline of our life path. For example, with the scent of cookies baking in an oven, we can be transported to another time in our life, as a child. Use this! But use it carefully."

The Pine Tree Seer continued. "I know how to run these!" She was pointing to the variety of stuff stuck to her sap! "I run these sticky things through my sap-my blood of my veins and recycle them back into the Earth and the Universe. Please, come to me! Use me this way. But ask my permission first, with respect. Use me some but do not use me up! Part of my job here in the Sacred Grove, the Nemeton, is to help others heal their soul. To find the parts of themselves that have gone missing due to disappointments, tragedies, losses, big or small. I guide you to find that little frightened child who may have run off, losing a part of himself. This may have happened from fear of abuse or lack of love. Through my work with you, Dreamer, we can find that specific time and place of pain and loss. We do this by Dreaming back in time, where we revisit these places of the past. We Dream to recycle this scene from the past. Together we release the 'sticky things' that are not a part of you now."

Our small group was enthralled by our lessons, and hardly realized it was dusk. The sun was setting quickly, and the afternoon's warmth was receding to cooler evening air. Turning my attention back to the Seer, I realized she was holding a beautiful basket.

"Made from the small 'runner roots' of the pines you see here," the Pine Tree Seer was saying, and demonstrating. "One gathers them just below the Earth's surface and pulls them out with the digging stick, then carefully tamps back the earth with thanks. I then coil the runners and keep them in the water until ready to do the weaving. My Pine family is happy to provide containers for many uses. It is always wise to provide an offering before the collecting."

Now she was reaching inside her basket filled with pinecones and pine needles. "Dusk, twilight," she was saying, "the perfect time to Dream journey!" The Seer motioned for us to come forward. Then she said, "Please, select a pinecone for use in your journey work. Connect with this pinecone and ask it to catch your emotions that need healing. Please take a pine needle as well. Now settle into your spot on the grass for our Dream journey. Next, just before the journey, take the pine needle and prick your finger! Please expect this to hurt; this is good."

There was a lot of whispering and chatting among the Dreamers. I could not imagine what she was trying to get across to all of us, but I did get comfortable in my spot and held the pine needle, quietly looking it over. Looking around, I noticed that I was not alone in my confusion.

The Pine Tree Seer spoke again: "You may choose to prick the lower part of your thumb, that is, if you like; but anywhere on your hand will be just fine."

She had paused and was walking around us now and had shape-shifted from the actual pine tree to a beautiful Pine Tree Seer who was all cleaned up! Her flowing gown was a textured material of deep forest green. She was extremely tall with long, lean limbs, and moved in grace without sound. Her hair was dark and long, adorned in small pinecones tied in amber-colored ribbons. Every time my eyes caught hers, I felt waves of light and compassion. My friends were just as touched as I was, and we were excited and ready for the lessons the Seer would share. The Seer was ready to continue.

"Should you want to learn deeply the path of the Pine Tree Seers, the area on the thumb of your hand is where the Pine energy resides. Please remember that my name is 'Ailm'/Fir-Pine in the Ogham of the Celts, and in your dreaming you may refer to me this way if you like. Whichever finger you use, the point is to feel the pain of the pricking, sense it! By feeling this slight pain, we can ready ourselves to Dream travel; we will then journey back in time to the place of that emotion. Pain, sadness, hurt, or disappointment; whatever this is for you, we will find that past Dream scene. Together then, with trust and patience, we will find what is there and bring it to the surface where it can be recycled. By doing these things, being true to yourself, you will be able to entice a part of your soul back to where you are now!

"Dreamers, before we do this Dream journey for your individual soul healing work, there are things that I must share with you about myself, important things that have strengthened me into the Keeper that I am. Be ready now to hear the tale of the Pine Tree Seer. Then after a small break, we will proceed with the journey work."

The Pine Tree Seer said, "As I believe you know, I am number sixteen in the Celtic Ogham, and I am called 'Ailm'; this name comes from a root word that can mean 'that which goes forward' and also 'will or desire.' The message from this says: do go forth and use your will, find your way with experimentation, try new things. In the Celtic Word Ogham of Cuchulain, this is referred to as the 'beginnings of the weaver's beam'![36] Now Dreamers, I trust that you realize this symbolizes the 'will of the magician.' This weaver's beam can be a wand or a spear; there are various levels here, and we need to learn what is needed at the appropriate time. Different species of trees are next to each other in the forest, and yet all the trees are interdependent with each other; this then makes up the vitality of the forest. What we come to trust in nature is that we all support each other and we all learn from each other's emotions. We learn which tree combinations complement and which ones do not seem to grow well together. We call upon the 'weaver's beam,' the will of the magician, to cultivate the best possible green forest!

"The Pine/Fir tree is associated with the Moon and the planet Jupiter and belongs to the triple aspect Goddess in Celtic lore. I, the Fir, am sacred to many Goddesses; Artemis and Diana are some. Also to the gods of Osiris and Attis, both of which were imprisoned in the Fir/Pine trees. The silver fir was a sacred tree to the Druids, who felt the tree stood for hope. In the Orkney area of Scotland, new mothers and their babies are 'sained' by whirling a fir-candle three times around their beds. The Pine/Fir is used for magic involving power, insight, and progression. I am a tree that works to understand relationships and provide new realizations. I can teach one how to learn from mistakes and how to make good choices.

"In an ancient forest in Loch Marcee in Northwest Scotland, which is part of the still surviving fragment of the Great Wood of Caledonia, stands an ancient Grove of the Druids. The 'Scots Pine' is there and is known as the 'wishing tree,' with ancient growth still there next to a healing well. For centuries people have come to this tree with the sick for healings.

"One species of pine, the 'bristle cone pine' of the White Mountains of California, are the oldest living things on earth. The eldest of these, named 'Methuselah,' has been dated to an age of 4,776 years and gives no indication of dying any time soon! The pine is a symbol of life's perpetuity through the darkest part of the solar year at winter, and yet it remains evergreen! Precisely why it is brought into homes each year as Christmas trees, boughs, and wreaths decorating and honoring life eternal.

"Now remember, Dreamers, my name, 'Ailm,' is an Irish word meaning 'that which goes forward and will and desire'![37] I am also a vowel tree; the sound of the letter A can express amazement, solution, or groaning from pain. But we must remember that a vowel tree spoken on its own has little meaning. Just as when we put letters together to form words, the Pine likewise can only be understood in working with the other trees. The meanings vary from tree to tree, as all are interdependent of each other, but best understood when the energies are woven together. This is why you need to learn how to use your will of the magician with your weaver's beam, your wand, made of Pine/Fir of course!"

The Seer was finished with her incredible tale about herself, and everyone had clapped loudly! I felt her high energy and vitality to be tremendous. We were all on a short break and were happily contemplating what we might find our journeys to take place momentarily. The Drum sounded from somewhere, making us realize then that there were several other Keepers along the outer circle. I thought about what the Pine Seer had said about their interdependence and how nice that felt. In a flash now, all was made ready to journey.

The Pine Tree Seer reminded us of our dream journey work intention: "Find those sticky, painful parts of yourself and bring them back for us to recycle! Note the timeline of the events, think about where in your body this lost piece may now feel at home. This is your intention! Take the time that you need; it is your life, and you are in charge here!" She stopped a moment and threw pine branches into the central fire pit; the flames lapped and hissed. Then she threw in pinecones that must have been coated in pine sap; the fire hissed even more. But the aroma was sweet and clean, and I could feel it pulling me to my Dream.

The Seer then said, "Dreamers, this is the time for your pine needle…Prick that finger! Feel that pain and travel with this into the past timeline of yourself!"

The Drumming was loud, and the Dreamers found their individual travel paths, yet we were all there to support each other. I heard the Pine/Fir Tree Seer say, "Call on me for questions and support in your Dream. You only need ask. Notice me in the scent of the wood; I am here!"

FURZE

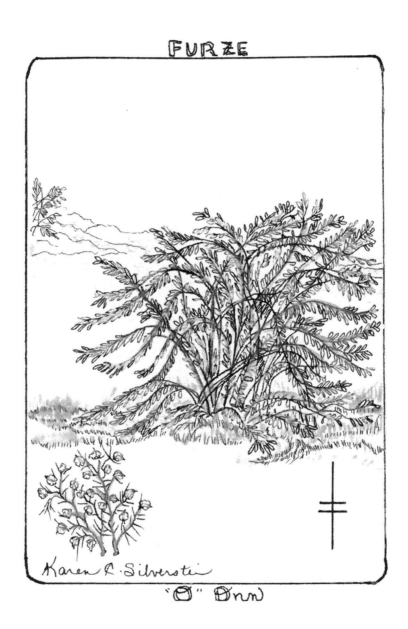

Karen R. Silverstein

"O" Onn

THE FURZE/GORSE LETTER "O," "ONN" OGHAM:✠

STATISTICS FOR:

~ "The Furze" genus/species- *Ulex europaeus*

~Grows native to Western Europe and Northwest Africa, but can be naturalized elsewhere.

~Its growth is more of a shrub of 4–5 feet, similar to the Broom tree.

~The yellow flowers are found mostly in the spring, but it has been known to bloom year around when temperate. It is covered with large thorns. It has large seed pods that replenish rapidly.

~~~~~~~~~

THE FURZE/GORSE: HOW USED IN THE WORLD

~The wood burns fiercely. It is a prolific plant found all over the British Isles. It has been said of Furze/Gorse: "I am ablaze on every hill." This is because it blooms so widely in spring and grows so rapidly that it is often burned down to allow new growth grass to take hold. Broom tree is for cleanup, but Gorse/Furze is called upon when strong magical hygiene is required. Gorse is used for protection and conflict.

~~~~~~~~~~

MEDICINAL AND PSYCHOLOGICAL

~The Furze/Gorse tree is not used much in medicine. The flowers, however, have been made into teas for treatment of jaundice or effective to clean the kidneys from gravel or stones. The ashes left from burning have been used as alkali-type soap. The yellow flowers make a golden dye.

~~~~~~~~~~~

SACREDNESS AMONG THE GROVE

~The Furze/Gorse is the seventeenth tree in the Ogham Alphabet: "Omn"-"O"

~The Furze/Gorse is associated with hope, fertility, vitality, and positive in all things.

~KEYWORD- Hope

~Planet- Mars

~Month- not assigned

~The Furze tree stands on either side of the Fir tree and Heather tree within the Grove.

~"FINGER TIP TREE" location- "Furze/Gorse-Onn"-"O" is on the lower forefinger.

DREAM OF "ONN,"
THE FURZE/GORSE TREE SEER

Walking up the hillside from the sea, I felt perfect on this bright, early spring morning. Soft winds blew the hair across my face, and the rolling waves could still be heard even way up here. I turned to look back at the sea; the clouds were lifting now, and the Sun was drifting through, a good time to sit for a while and look for Dream information in the clouds. Sitting there on the crest of some rocks, I was next to a beautiful, small tree of five feet or so, which was thickly covered in bright yellow flowers. They were highly scented and full of activity, as they were covered in bees! I moved a little away so the bees would not find me fascinating. I thought about their queen bee back in the hive and thought of the 'Melisa' bee, priestess of ancient times who worked tirelessly for Earth Mother, and still does. I munched on an apple and homemade muffins that I had brought from the lodge. I finished it and tossed the apple core under the small tree, an offering of sort, and watched the bees go to that.

Having plenty of time before meeting a few other Dreamers to work on Dream assignments, I spread out my shawl, and then myself too, and watched the clouds awhile. One of them appeared to look like a horse to me. My daydreaming wandered on.

Suddenly, though it was never asked...I drew a breath with a question; curious, but I did not know the question. Thinking of last night, I remembered that dusk seemed to come early and with so much mist; it covered me still, and I did not really recall our program! What was going on here? Searching, I attempted to ask the question finally that I felt to be lingering. I was not myself at all! Remembering too that I had a long Dream in the night, but all I could recall were the pictures, which were of smoke, so much smoke and flames. I watched a fire; barely moving, like a weightless spirit, I was. What is this and where am I? Weightless... Then I heard the bees stirring, awakening me to my place on the hillside. Looking again at the clouds, more shapes, but now grayish and swirling. I wondered what had happened to the nice, puffy white ones.

Something had me sitting up quickly; looking around, I realized there was a smell of smoke. Standing, I saw that the swirling gray clouds were actually smoke! What on earth? Where was the fire? The wind was blowing stronger. I grabbed my shawl and ran the last part of the hill, to the crest. Out of breath, I bent over a second...Oh! My Goddess! Looking straight ahead only a few hundred yards, an entire hillside was a blaze! Crashing down to my knees and crying, "Oh no! Help please! Don't let this whole hill be consumed!" Wrapping my hands around my knees with my head down, I felt helpless. Nothing to be done, I thought. It is finished! Looking from time to time at the fire blazing over the mass of trees, which I realized were Furze/Gorse, I felt despair. Seeing the yellow flowers melting like molten gold, I felt sadness for them, for the mountain; what a waste! As I stayed watching, back came that same weightless feeling from the Dream I had just remembered earlier. How long I remained like this, I was not sure; no sense of time. The question again began to form: What is this? What could have started the fire?

Finally I was standing and decided I must find my way back to the lodge; others must know about this disaster, or at least I could tell them. Looking at the hill now, I saw that the flames were calmer; in some places it was just smoldering, looking horrid and black. I heard the slight clinking of bells, but saw nothing. I started back down the hill and partway down met a curious animal. I heard the clinking and saw the bell that was around the neck of a sheep. I ran to it and gave it a hug, asking where it had come from and saying it had better be aware of the fire ahead. Somehow the aliveness of this animal lifted my mood. I told the dear thing that we were lucky to have been on this side of the hillside, or we might have been done for.

The sheep just stood there, near the tree with the yellow flowers, not minding me rattling on; much more interested in munching the new grass shoots there. It looked at me with knowing, sad eyes. I asked her where she had gotten her bell from; she must be long to someone! She just kept munching, and I realized what was important to her; turning, I saw the bees. Of course they were buzzing, doing their own munching, which was important to them. Thinking to get going, I said good-bye to the sheep and the bees. Turning to go, but instead of leaving, I stood firm, because someone was walking toward me.

I waved my hands and called out, "Hello! Over here!" Waving my hands again, I could not tell from this distance who they were, but I would be glad for the company after what I had just seen. I glanced back at the upper hillside where the fires were smoldering now. I thought to myself how quickly it all burned. By the time I turned around, the sheep was moving off toward the figure still moving toward me. He was squatted down now, petting the sheep. I decided to walk toward them. It was a man, tall and broad shouldered, who stood with an angular face and reddish-blonde hair. He was saying something about…"She needs to have her wool done, sheared, and then she ran off. She has the knowing, that one always did!"

I was confused by what he said—it made no sense—but I did say, "Hello!" And with politeness I introduced myself as one of the New Dreamers.

He took my hand and shook it, saying, "Hello, Dreamer, and yes I know who you are!"

I smiled at that but wondered how he could know me, thinking there was an air about him. He spoke again, saying, "I am 'The Seer Furze/Gorse,' and I had thought to be working with you a week from now, but this is fine, just fine!"

He had leaned back over and was ruffling the thick wool of the sheep. He said something about, "This one gets attached to her coat each year. Of course we can see why, beauty that it is, but she will be giving it up by day's end!"

I barely knew what to say and had not the slightest clue that I was to be working with the Gorse Seer, next week, let alone now! I thought of the Dreamer friends I was supposed to meet, wondering what had happened with that. I could feel him looking at me and knew his eyes sought mine. Finally I did look into them, and I gave a response. "Yes! Of course, Seer, I am happy to meet you!" I was able to relax some after that. Suddenly remembering the fire, I blurted out, "You must come with me! I need to show you the fire! Hurry!"

I began to run up the hill; the Seer was coming, but he certainly was not running. Did he not care? I flagged him on with my arm and kept on to the top. Quite out of breath and ahead of him, I rested and calmed myself. I did look to the hill across the way, only occasional flaming now, mostly smoldering and ashen; it made me sad and depressed. He certainly was taking his time.

The Seer arrived at the top of the hill with the sheep at his side, talking gibberish to it. But what was odd was that he looked ahead and then looked at me and he smiled! I mean, what was wrong with him? Couldn't he see the devastation across the way?

My mouth was hung open—I was sure of that—but all I could do was to look at him and then the ashen hillside and point. His answer came, but not what I expected!

"Really something, is it not? With the early spring heat, the wood was very dry; did not take long to get it kindling." He turned his hillside gaze toward me and would have said something more, but I did not give him a chance.

"You knew? This fire was set? You knew? I do not understand. Did others know? Why? Just tell me *why!*"

After my outburst and fit of anger, my face turned the color of red rowanberries, and I crumpled down to the grass. I was fit to be tied and did not want consoling…But after hearing the softness of his voice for a few minutes, I looked up, and with tears I said, "Please just tell me straight, as I so love this place, why would anyone want to burn any of it?"

"Hey there, Dreamer! Please know there is much you do not yet understand! But then this is why you have come here to us; you will learn and one day share with one younger than you the things a Seer comes to know! Now come, walk with me; let us look closer at the hillside that ablaze! It was all the older Furze you see, and they have had quite a nice life. But now their spines are sharp, and the branches thickly spreading where they were not needed. Come, it is easier to understand what I will say if you see the Gorse up close and personal, as they say! Don't be sad!"

He was very convincing, and of course I could not pretend to know much of what goes on here with the Keepers. I felt slightly uplifted that he portrayed me as being someone who might one day be able to share knowledge. Pulling up myself from the grass and mustering my courage, I took the hand he now offered to me. All I could say was, "I just want to understand."

The taller trees that we passed on our way were swaying together under the blue sky and may have been Ash. The gray, smoky clouds were moving off now, out to sea, I thought. I still had a hard time knowing that this fire had been set intentionally. There had better be a good reason, I thought to myself! The sheep walked along with us, its bell clinking as we moved. We were now in the thick of the last of the smoldering, charred wood, and we could only go so close, as it was extremely hot still.

Finally I said to the Seer, "So this is what Gorse looks like when you burn it down! It is awful and sad!"

The Furze/Gorse Seer had a somber mood now. Serious and cool, he said, "I like that you speak your mind, Dreamer. However, I do believe it is time for the lessons to begin, since you have taken this so to heart. First you must know that these fires honor the 'God of Jupiter' and the first fires of spring! In the old ways of the Celts, this was an honored festival time. The Furze is full of yellow-gold flowers in spring, and this typifies the young Sun at Spring Equinox, which is the time the 'furze fires' are lighted on the hills. This is done to burn away old prickles that are too rampart and thick; this then allows for the tender new shoots to sprout up from the stock of the roots. The sheep love to eat these shoots, and this process also encourages new grasses.

"From the ancient 'Welsh Triads,' which are historical observations, we have a poem called 'Cad Goddeu'-'The Battle of the Trees.' Many trees are referred to in the triad. In one reference to the Furze Tree it says, 'The furze not well behaved, until he was tamed.' This refers to the fact that the furze, that grows so rampantly, is burned to keep it in check, as I have said earlier. The Furze/Gorse at one time was grown as hedges by farmers, but it was difficult to keep, and little or nothing can grow near this tree, so this was another reason for the burning. It is still common practice today, and it is not unusual in rural parts of Britain to see entire hillsides blackened from recent burning."

The Gorse Seer had stopped near one of the trees at the very top of the hill; he was pointing to something on another hill a short distance away. I followed his finger and saw that the next hillside was covered in tall grass and small bushes and sheep. He said we would go there. I was glad to be away from the heated earth here and the gray ash that seemed to float everywhere.

It did not take us long to get to where the sheep were grazing, and the whole atmosphere felt better to me. The Seer informed me that this particular hill had been set ablaze last fall, as sometimes is done. Then he pointed out the fresh new bushes that were sprouting up from the old Gorse stock and showed me the sheep that were nibbling happily there. He introduced me to a few of the herders and then turned over the sheep that had followed us to them. Then he spoke with some other Dreamers and Keepers who would join us. Apparently this had been arranged, only I did not know. Where have I been? I wondered at not being myself. The Seer then got busy talking with a few of the Keepers.

The space here was set for a Dreaming circle, and I did not even have my journal! There was a light lunch being served; fixing a plate for myself, I took up conversation with my new companions. I was relieved to find out that they too seemed confused! I found that there were extra journals on the table and that we were in for quite a day according to what some seemed to know.

I excused myself to have a walk around and saw off to the side of the stone walls were a few Gorse Trees in full yellow bloom; that is where I went. I thanked the one in the middle of three, which were still there and had survived any burning! Even though I had heard the explanation and understood, I still felt sadness. Then I heard the soft drumming and knew it was time to start; I had better find a spot for myself. Turning to go, I saw "The Gorse Seer" was there. I smiled and hoped I did not look the sad feelings I felt. Although he did not say so, I think he knew.

All he said was, "Give this some time; there is still so much to the story of me!" He laughed and I did too.

I found my space, and the Seer found his at the front of our circle. After a beautiful opening by the Broom Seer, we all settled down. There were at least eight of us, which I noted in my journal, writing in their names when I knew them, filling in the others later.

The "Onn" Furze/Gorse Seer said, "I had thought to start next week, but it seems the early 'furze fires' have matched us together today. Today is good! Now I like to do the formal stuff early on, because it always helps weaving through later! Just so you all know, I am called 'Furze' by some or 'Gorse' by others; in the Ogham it is the same. My name being 'Onn' and my letter being O. I am number seventeen in the Ogham within the Grove and the second of the vowel letters used. Also, I am the first to bloom in spring; in fact I bloom in some places all year long! Yes, I am a prolific bloomer!

"At this level in your work, you all are becoming more familiar with the Ogham and its interesting phrases that give us keys to understanding. These are a few for Furze. From the 'Word Ogham of Morainn': 'CONGNAID ECH,' meaning 'Helper of Horses.' Also there is 'ONNAID,' meaning 'Wheels of a Chariot.' And another, 'ALITER COMGUINIDECH,' meaning 'Equally Wounding, Whin.' These will be explained as we move into the work.

"There are similarities between the Broom Tree and the Gorse Tree on both physical and mental levels. The characteristics and things said of the Broom can also be applied to the Gorse. References from the old texts of 'strength of warriors, wounding and chariots' emphasize the military aspect of the Gorse. Let's look deeper into this. As you recall, the Broom Tree is used for cleanup work following abandoned work. With Gorse it is different; it is cleanup but used in cases where resistance is felt, because 'the work' is being stopped."[38]

The tall man with the glint of golden light in his reddish hair looked composed, confident, as he looked about the group of Dreamers. There was no doubt that he was a Seer to be reckoned with, when needed. In my daydreaming, I viewed him as a fearless knight of the ancient ways, wearing a golden disk of the Sun hung about his neck, leading a charge against enemy lines. I could tell he had persistence about him underneath that easy manner' he did not let things influence him or take him off his course…This was my Dreaming. Coming back into the circle, there were several Dreamers now wanting to pursue with questions.

He was not taking them. He just said, "We will get to that later! Now I am sure you want to know what the definition of 'the work' is![39] As Dreamer-magicians, we have learned to apply our skills for healing that needs tending to; many times this is done in very abstract ways. Magic is partly about creating something that may not have had form. This implies creating an intelligence that was not there before. What we need to under- stand is the life form was there already but not activated. There are many scenarios. What a Dreamer-magician is trained to do is to work with this energy and activate it, abstractly. In some cases, what happens is a change in plan of what was supposed to happen, because of a mistake. Having now activated the life form with magical workings, this form may have taken on an intelligence of its own, and now it can be seen that you need to 'Stop the Work.' This intelligence may decide it does not want to be abandoned and may actually fight against you! My dear Dreamers! If this is what comes about, it is not Broom that is needed here for cleanup. No!" The Seer looked to the Broom Seer and said, "No insult intended!"

She looked back and, with a bright smile, replied, "None taken, Dear Sir!"

"What needs to be understood is, Broom in this instance is not severe enough to over- come this type of reaction. Dreamers, this is when you call upon me! Furze/Gorse is larger and more heavily armed with thick spines along its branches. A formidable tree that knows how to deal with such resistances."

The Seer had paused momentarily, and the Dreamers were abuzz with comments and looks to each other; we were intrigued. My curiosity was really piqued! I heard some cracking sounds and could see someone was adding wood to the nearby campfire.

"My wood catches for kindling quickly even when it is green. Although when cutting and gathering, one can be easily wounded, due to its many sharp spines!" The Seer was back on target. He had also been watching the fire keeper.

"Now, thinking back to the characteristics of the Broom, we spoke of the importance of 'Magical Hygiene.' This is just as important as the physical hygiene. We stressed the need to always do what is necessary for 'the cleanup' after any magical work. Gorse makes it clear to us that we may actually bring an intelligence or a consciousness that was not there before into our working area. We must use precautions both before our work and after that we do not leave anything halfway done! In our usual workings, and almost always, we have a situation of harmony with any forces that were invoked. To have to actually abandon the work will rarely be the case. However, should things go wrong, or something suddenly becomes unnecessary within the working, you have a changed situation. The criteria has changed, and there is not a quick fix. The first thing to do is to make a quick inventory of what was done, by going back into your dreaming work. Check what is no longer being used and do your cleanup using the Broom with this. Next a Dreamer must be able to determine if they feel any half-completed, independent intelligences floating about. This takes practice to develop solid Dreamer intui- tive capabilities to be able to know and recognize these energies. If you do feel something amiss, even if you only have a slight feeling, then it is important to 'Invoke Furze/Gorse'! I can be very powerful and will help you to complete the cleanup process most easily! When these processes are not adhered to these energies can mingle about and sometimes latch on to places or people where they do not belong. The rule of thumb is to 'not go where you do not understand the work'; this is not a game. Our code, as always, is search for the pure truth. Know thyself, Dreamer! Tread carefully."

The Gorse Seer checked each of us personally after his comments. He needed to be sure we had heard his words. I looked around at the other Dreamers; all were pensive and thinking over his words. This is very serious stuff, I thought to myself. This is definitely not for the weekend Dreamer! He seemed satisfied and continued.

"Novice Dreamers are often in a position in which they may have unintentionally invoked some unwanted life force.[40] Even if you only suspect you may have done this…Always be safe and use Gorse anyway. I see that you are all feeling nervous here. But do not fear! The novice Dreamer is rarely able of creating strong magic as to be worried about. Please know, Dreamers, that magic does have its own built-in safeguards. Know too, as with all skills, it takes time, practice, and learning to truly trust one's intuition to become comfortable with this magical level of working."

The Gorse Seer had us all break for a short while; the Dreamers were glad of this. We munched on snacks and spoke about energy that might be lurking. Some were making jokes about this, but in our hearts we all knew we were definitely in new territory and needed to pay attention with respect. I noticed the Gorse Seer near the campfire, smiling and talking with the Broom Seer, The Ivy Seer, and The Vine Seer. He looked my way a moment, and I noticed a glimmer in his eyes; I felt they were up to something for sure. The drumming started and we all got back to the work at hand.

The Furze Seer continued. "Welsh folklore says of Furze, 'good against witches'! Now, in the old ways, I was often used as a protective tree, and it was known that within the craft were both the dark energies and the light energies; this was common knowledge. The yellow flowers of the Furze are the first of the spring and are frequented by the first bees of the year, as the Ivy's flowers are the last. In the old Goddess religions, these things were known by all living close with Earth Mother and deeply connected to her cycles. The name 'ON-NIONA' is a Goddess worshipped by the Gauls in 'Ash-Groves.'

"Curious, aren't you!? Well, let me explain further. This name is actually a compound of 'ONN and NION,' the 'FURZE and ASH.' Very interesting how we all flow together in the Grove, is it not!? Now this information also reveals to us the date of the 'Goddess Festival of Onniona,' namely the Spring Equinox, which is at the close of the 'Ash month.' This is approximately March twentieth of each year. Ash, Furze, and the spring, when the hillsides are ablaze with 'Furze Fires'! I learned somewhere a simple old chant which you may want to use from time to time; it goes like this: 'Onniona, Onniona, Onniona, Onniona…O, oooo!' One simply repeats these words!"

All of the Dreamers cheered with this information. I felt everyone liked the idea of this Goddess who came into play. Still yet, I had a sad feeling for what had been burned; the Seer had us move on.

"I believe there has been some mention of the 'Finger Tip Trees' in your work with the other Tree Seers. In reference to the Furze, the location on the hand would be the forefinger at the bottom. Interestingly this is also the finger of the 'Jupiter God,' and as I have said to some, the spring 'Furze Fires' are burned in his honor as the god of shepherds.

"One of the main lessons of Furze/Gorse is that of 'Hope'! It survives the burning! My roots do not die. I survive and I do not give up!

"Gorse is one of the few plants that can flower all year around, especially when the winter is mild. This is mostly likely why it is traditionally linked to fertility. My wood burns easily and fiercely, even when green. Because of its thorns, like other thorny plants, I can be called on for vitality, and I can provide very strong psychic protection. Gorse will grow even in the poorest of soil. Now I would certainly say this is symbolic of finding the positive in all situations! Wouldn't you all agree?"

The Dreamers cheered again, liking all these characteristics. I thought to myself, I will be sure to remember the positive in all situations! The Seer allowed us a minute, smiling cheerfully.

"I am the Blaze on every hill! I am called 'Onn.' As was mentioned earlier, my bright yellow-gold flowers shine about every Spring Equinox and are just in time for the newly woken bees. The bees are sun-beings, and in many traditions they are the carriers of the soul. As 'Onn' I am thought to be as bright as the precious mineral of gold on the high hillside moors in times of old. This is certainly a nice analogy, because when we look at gold in its alchemical terms, many feel it to be a kind of Holy Grail. Again and again, attempts have been made to turn the base metal of lead it into the precious metal of gold. It is the process of transmutation with which the Dreamer strives to work for. Gold is an amazing natural conductor of electricity, an invisible power, so to speak. We cannot say exactly what electricity actually is or really see it as it travels through countless electrical lines, but there it is and has allowed humans countless benefits! I do not think any of us could imagine contemporary life without this transformative energy!

"What we are working with on the level of the Furze Tree is this process of transmutation. Changing the essence of something into something else; doing this for the good of the whole. What Furze helps us with is a kind of initiation on a spiritual level, so that we may continue with our path, which is 'The Work of the Earth's Keepers'! I am the Blaze on every hill!

"Considering the spiritual workings with Gorse, we come to a moral element that must be considered. The question is a hard one but must be reckoned with, and as a Dreamer on this path, one will not be able to move forward from here unless the reckoning is done!"

The Furze Seer took some extra time with his pause, seemingly very concerned for our attention. What could he possibly be getting at? I wondered.

"The question is this: How do you feel about deliberately killing a life force of which you have given an existence?[41] Does this go against any firmly held belief that you may have concerning violence or killing? Can you bring yourself to destroy something on one level, which may mean you will be called upon to destroy something on the other levels?"

There was a west wind that came through just then, and then silence. None of us spoke. I think we all just stared into space for a while; at least I am sure that is what I did. The sadness I had felt earlier in the day resurfaced, and slowly I thought of the Seer's question and thought, What are my beliefs? I heard some talking and then some laughter and came back into focus with our circle.

"Oh! This is serious stuff!" said the "Ivy Tree Seer." "But let me be frank here. You are Dreamers! And Dreamers know the way of nature and the cycles of life. And besides that, I can certainly be called upon to 'provide any warring' information you may need to prepare the way for your workings! So serious, yes! But let's not get too caught up in the drama here! Laugh when you can and even when you would prefer not!"

With that statement we all did laugh, and that lightened our mood. I did detect some nervousness from my fellow Dreamers. Only natural, I thought. I am nervous too.

The Gorse Seer began again. "This is a dilemma that will require a lot of careful thought, for one day you will be in a position to choose what should happen with a certain life force. It is important to already know what your belief is, and you must be prepared to act. I advise to listen very strongly to your intuition. On a mental level, you may be able to deliberately kill. Although a terrible thing, make sure you are in touch with your specific feelings in each and every case. This is extremely important because sometimes you may not 'feel anything wrong,' or other times the feeling may say, 'this is very wrong.' A Dreamer must practice paying attention to both. And, again, hone those intuitive skills you all have. 'Know thyself, Dreamer'! It is when we 'do not' that problems can occur for the Dreamer and this sometimes produces halfway done workings that are messy.

"One conclusion on these thoughts might be looked at this way: 'The problem is not whether it is 'morally right' to kill in some situations and not in others, no! We must decide how we feel about our morals and how it affects us spiritually. You may feel how can I judge? 'Who am I to say what will live or not?' Ultimately, this is something each of us must answer for ourselves."

The Gorse Seer looked at each of us with sympathy, knowing he had just given us much heavy information. But he did not allow us to linger in this. "The day is still bright and golden, and we will all supper here later when the sun does the setting for the night, and I am told that we can camp here by the fire for the night, if you choose. Provisions are being made for all of this. I feel it would be good to Dream further on your newly acquired information and intuitive skills here by the fire and as a group. This could be highly beneficial to all, and we have both Jupiter and Onniona that will look after our needs! Think on this; decide at supper!

"Now a few more things before we break for the day. I would like to suggest a journey that you can all use in your Dreaming for the night. Of course I am the featured actor in this Dream! However, do select a few other trees to be featured in your dream along with me, the Furze/Gorse.

"The Dream Title is 'The Challenge and Furze/Gorse.' The intended scenario will be: View the forest with the trees you have picked—select at least three. Get to know each of them and notice their feelings, characteristics, emotions. Next, choose a situation that needs cleanup in the forest, maybe something going on between different varieties. Become the Gorse who has now been called upon to 'Stop the Work' and negate the emotional experience that was going on between two different trees. Be the Furze tree that has to carry out the actual destruction. Or become the one who views this scene. Pay attention to what happens; this may take many forms of direct intervention, and it may be solved without much ado because the energy is subtle. Or it may turn into violent emotions that need dealing with because the energy has taken on a new form and fights against any stopping of their existence. This might even turn extreme! Once the actions you have taken are over, make sure about what has been done, go over the work. Should there still be things that have been left undone, do that cleanup! Do what is necessary in your view. Before returning from this journey, be very certain that you absolutely close off the veil between the Otherworlds! Make sure you *do not* come back with any stuff! Cleanse yourself with sage or something that you like to use, and cleanse your 'Onn Ogham Stick,' which you have traveled with. Now, as I said earlier, we will do this journey this evening; you will have the afternoon to contemplate. I wish you…Good Journeying, Dreamers!"

The Gorse Seer was finished and was answering questions from the Dreamers. I felt OK with the information, although it was intense.

Then the Furze/Gorse Seer added: "I look forward to morning Dream reports from all of you! Now time for some fun! A couple of the Seers and I have a play ready to go called *The Energy That Lingered*! Afterward it will be time for supper; thank goodness for that. I mean they barely give us anything to eat while we are here!" Everyone was hysterical with laughing now! This was good. I heard the Seer say, "Come this way. The theater has been set over here on the hill near the 'Furze Fire.' That is, the one blooming yellow flowers, not burning!"

We were all so happy for a break and of course very curious about this play!

THE ENERGY THAT LINGERED

HEATHER

Karen C. Silverstein

"U" Ur

THE HEATHER LETTER "U," "UR" OGHAM:⌗

STATISTICS FOR:
~"The Heather" genus/species- *Calluna vulgaris*
~Grows more as a bush than a tree, with an average height of 4-6 feet.
~The branches and stems grow in twisted fashion, forming huge thickets in the wild moorlands of Scotland and the British Isles. It can be naturalized in other areas. It produces small purple, red, pink,white and bluish flowers, all with a delicate aroma in spring. The bees are attracted for their pollen.

~~~~~~~~~~~~

THE HEATHER: HOW USED IN THE WORLD
~The Heather is sacred to the Summer Solstice and associated with the Sun. This tree is considered a feminine tree and is sacred to many goddesses. Used for magic for love, luck, and ritual power. It represents good fortune.

~~~~~~~~~~~~

MEDICINAL AND PSYCHOLOGICAL
~The Heather's flowering shoots are good for teas to treat insomnia, stomachaches, coughs, and skin problems. Heather tea can be used for urinary infections.

~~~~~~~~~~~~

SACREDNESS AMONG THE GROVE
~The Heather is the eighteenth tree in the Ogham Alphabet: "Ur"-"U"
~The Heather is associated with the new, renewal, creativity, and love.
~KEYWORD- Transitions
~Month- not assigned
~ Planet- Sun
~The Heather tree stands on either side of the Furze tree and Aspen tree within the Grove.
~"FINGER TIP TREE" location- "Heather-Ur"-"U" is located on the lower middle finger.

DREAM OF "UR," THE HEATHER TREE SEER

The Posters had been put up, saying:
~SOMETHING ENDS~SOMETHING BEGINS~
Are you up for what needs doing?
Tomorrow Go to the Moors
10:00 a.m. Until Done!
~ THE KEEPERS ~

This was certainly getting attention. In talking with a few other Dreamers, we all knew we would go, and of course we were intrigued by the come-on of the poster. I mentioned that this must certainly be the Heather Tree Seer. Someone said they had heard that her sweet scent could lure a Dreamer, but she was strict and stern as they come! We all shook our heads and laughed. I decided that I would just wait and see and not arrive prejudging anything.

Morning came quickly, and I was excited walking in the soft summer rain. The mist was trying to swirl thicker, but the sun seemed to be winning out. After breakfast, those of us heading early to the Moors had been given a packet containing scissors and other craft tools; we all joked about what we might be doing with the likes of these…Some said magic tools!

Once we were atop the last hill of Heather, and could see for miles around, again I was astounded by the immense beauty of this place called the Nemeton. Off to one side on the grass were a few Dreamers busily working. Arriving closer, it became clear that they were crafting all manner of things from the twisted stalks and roots of the Heather. Looking around, I could see ropes, brooms, brooches, and many other things. Smiling, I thought, this is good. I like to make things.

The scent is what I noticed first; the rain had been replaced by breezes, and I imagined that it was picking up the fresh, pink blossoms' scent of Heather on the Moors. But it was her. Like a Goddess she swayed forth, long fair hair hanging loose; she seemed so young. As she approached with a pale face and lips that seemed too red, I knew she was older. Not that it mattered. With perfect features, she moved herself among the Dreamers; the scent of Heather mingled in the air and hung there. I wondered what she must be thinking of me as she stared with her cornflower-blue eyes. Yes, it was the Heather Tree Seer. I smiled as broadly as I could, as I knew that this was her land, her domain.

Coming out of my musings, someone was speaking to me. Something about making "Spirit Dolls" for the Goddess and that we would soon be "Dressing the Heather Trees"! For some reason it was hard for me to turn my gaze away from the Heather Tree Seer. Of course I did and was really interested in what was going on here. My Dreamer friend suggested that I walk with her to where the ceremonial Dream circle had been set high on the heath. We set out on one of the paths; the Heather Tree grew there, twisting and sideways. More like a shrub, I thought. Beautiful in its denseness and the various colors, from white in some areas, to pale pinks, deeper pinks, and some even reddish pink. Walking along, enjoying the blooms on the Heath, I mentioned to my friend that this felt like the nearest to a fairyland as one might get! She agreed, saying that she was sure that her psychic senses had been heightened since she arrived last evening to help with preparations for today.

We passed a poster along the path way which read: ARE YOU READY FOR CHANGE? I laughed and said, "What is this all about?"

My friend smiled and said, "I cannot really say; I was told what to write and add the creative design on the posters. Do you like them?"

"*Oh!* I like them! Only I am a little leery of this change thing...I really am not fond of change."

She replied, "All I can tell you is the Heather Tree Seer seems earnest and straightforward, and I feel her so connected to the Goddess. I am sure whatever we learn from her will be a benefit to us. Now let me give you these pieces of twine and colored ribbons; we will show the others how to wind three threads of these together, using the colors of their choice. Then they will make wishes or prayers with them and then tie them to the 'Heather Trees... 'Dressing the Trees' is what this is called. Each Dreamer must add their particular dressing to the Heather in order for their energy to be felt on the Heath. Once done, we will begin the opening circle, and the teaching of The Heather Tree Seer will begin!"

I nodded my head in response and watched how she tied her three strands; it was easy enough. Then we set up our pillows and drums into the Dreamer circle and added the light to the central candle there on the altar near the fire. Ten o'clock was coming fast; my friend and I placed our own "Tree Dressings" into the heath. Next we arranged, at the start of the path, a table full of the twisted twine of Heather and the colored ribbons. Slowly at first they came, and then bunches of Dreamers all were happy to "Dress the Trees"! We counted ten Dreamers that would be a part of our study and at least five Keepers would be attending.

Finding our place in the circle with the other Dreamers felt like home to me. And like other class circles, the soft drumming began, but after a while there was something different; I couldn't put my finger on what. Then it hit me. The scent; she was here! She stood at the center of our ritual circle, in pink. From somewhere I remembered the expression..."Pretty in Pink"...Yes, this was the Heather Tree Seer.

It only took a moment for her to have a command of her audience; with all eyes on her, she led us through our opening circle with charm and grace. After our group settled, she offered this...

The Heather Tree Seer said, "The Growing of Plants. Do you Dreamers like tending plants? Do you enjoy their sprouting, flourishing, flowering, and fruiting?"

She paused a moment, looking around; it was quiet, with some head shaking. She moved about, shifting her pink chiffon, tossing her pale hair back, and said, "Dreamers, I have asked you a question! Do you like tending plants? Come on now!" She moved her arms in the gesture of saying come now! Of course the Dreamers responded, giving "yes, of course" replies like "I love growing plants"; all got very excited. The Seer was pleased at last with the Dreamer input and finally said, "Good! I thought as much. Now I intend for this to be a very participatory class; this is what gives us juice and energy. Please do stay up with me! What about when the plant begins to change, to mature, wither; what then? What do you do?"

She did not need to prompt the Dreamers; they had gotten the message and were now offering all kinds of advice. Some said the plant was in a new cycle, some said the plant needs to be pruned back, and others said the plant was in a time of being fallow.

The Seer had a big smile on her red lips and said, "Very good, Dreamers. Glad to see you are awake and in play! These are all good answers. What we need to remember with our Dream Workings with the Ogham is the green world, the world of the trees, teaches us cycles. In the Celtic way of magical work, each situation must be assessed and then a determination is made as to which Ogham Tree in the alphabet must be called upon. Which tree did the initiation? Which carried out the work? Which did the end work? And which tree is used to renew? Well, of course the last part of that question has its answer in me, 'The Heather Tree,' for renewal!"

Another pause while she waited for us to think a minute about all this. She was up and walking with authority, but she was headed away from the central circle. One of the Keepers brought her boots, pink rubber ones! Once they were on her feet, she hiked up her pink dress and said, "We go to the lower Heaths! I will talk along the way!"

Well, everyone scrambled then to catch up with her; we all laughed, making comments about the pink rubber boots. We did realize by now that there was never any set format to classes with the Keepers, so laughing was the best outlet. It was a little difficult to be right next to her, because ten Dreamers were a lot to be walking with. However, the Heather Tree Seer would stop along the path way to the lower Heaths, and we could hear her well enough, as her voice was strong and deep.

Some of the other Keepers had come along; the Furze Seer was one. He asked those he walked with if we recognized him in the plant cycle description the Heather Seer had given. I chimed in that he was the one doing the "end work"! He answered me, saying, "Glad to see you were paying attention!"

One of the other Dreamers wanted to know a little more about the word "fallow," which someone had offered earlier. The Furze Seer said, "I do believe you are right on course with that question; let's catch up to the Heather Seer and listen!"

We all turned our heads to where the Heather Seer, in her pink rubber boots and matching pink dress, stood on top of smooth granite rocks. Some of the Dreamers said, "You are a sight for sore eyes, Seer!"

Of course everyone was hysterical, but this was not to last, as the Seer replied, "Never mind that nonsense; get your eyes looking here!" She was pointing to the Heath on her left. I noticed that it looked threadbare, almost empty. The mood of the Dreamers had changed to concern; we all wanted to know why it looked this way, and what had happened.

Now that the Seer had our attention again. She leaned down with her hiked-up pink dress, and prodded the stalks of the few plants that were there, using the staff she walked with.

The Heather Tree Seer spoke with caring as she began to explain how the "Heath" comes to be what it is. "This is one of the 'fallow' parts of the Heath Grove, an older area needing some rest. The word 'fallow' has the meaning of 'plowed but left unseeded,' 'marked by inactivity.' Here we can witness how this amazing plant lies in waiting for the roots to be nurtured by the sun and, in time, will shoot out new growth. But for this current time when it lays awaiting, it is fallow. Heather grows in abundance and helps to form the vegetation known as 'Heath.' It thrives in full sun and usually reaches an average height of six feet and will bloom through early autumn. Heather is said to reach the height of its power at Midsummer, approximately June twentieth, the summer solstice, the longest day of the year! Which is about where we are now, Dreamers! The Heath was used in ancient times as a place of ceremony and ritual, a place close to the Goddess yet closely associated to the sun because of the openness and clear views to the sky. Heather is also connected to the planet Venus, and its element is water. It has been said that the source of the phrase 'Heathen' may actually come from the Heath and the way it was used in ancient times."

The Seer was down from the rocks, telling us she had more to show us. Other Dreamers and I marveled at her agility and admitted we liked the word heathen and its implied meaning. I thought to myself, I like this Seer! Now we were farther down the hill, and the vegetation was much denser. I was happy for the old pathway that we walked, for it would certainly be hard to walk on the branches of the Heather itself. I could hear the Seer saying the plants actually stay evergreen, and the small flowers of various colors are bell shaped. Many of us looked closer at the flowers.

She was on the move again, telling us about the Caledonian forest in Scotland and how the Heather grows on the peat bogs there much like what you see here. She told us a bit about the cutting of the peat and that it was dried and used as fuel. She had us all stop and look under the Heather she had pulled apart so we could see the peat. One of the Keepers added that in some places nearer the sea, if you dug down some, you would find water right under the peat bog. The Heather Seer said that she had a fine relationship with the peat and that they helped each other. We climbed back up one of the Heath hills. From this position, it was a beautiful sight, as the Trees were blooming in various shades of pink.

The Heather Tree Seer came to a small clearing and had us stop; she told us to catch our breath and to look around. She began again. "Tell me, Dreamers, what do you see?"

Someone answered, "I see pink, and all the hills are wearing pink!" "The scent is also wonderful," added another.

Finally I added, "I see so many bees; they are very busy!"

The Seer smiled and said, "Yes, the bees are busy and happy! The honey is made from the bees that feed on the pollen of the Heather; it has a wonderful, delicate flavor that's very popular with the people here."

She was looking to the sun and then said, "The bee travels from the Heather back to the hive in relation to the position and angle of the sun. Very amazing! The bee is regarded as a messenger from and to the Spirit world by the Celts. This, Dreamers, indicates Heather's close contact with the Spirit world and with healing. In ancient times the Danes brewed a powerful beer made from honey and heather. Many consider the Heather to be a feminine herb and constitution. Some say my crystal stones are the amethyst and peridot; these are nice. But also, I say, look in the Heather fields to find your own particular crystal in the rough! I admit to the feminine classification, which is fine with me!"

Everyone laughed for a while. Finally the Seer said, "Is it the pink boots? What!?"

More hysterics and then we were climbing the last of the hill. The path was not as steep; we were on a gentle slope, and now and again the Seer would stop and give us her story.

"I am sacred to many Goddesses: Isis, Venus-Erycina, Uroica, Cybele, Guinevere, and Butes, just to mention a few! In the old ways, it was common to find the wise women out here on the Heaths, communing with one of these Goddesses as part of the work they did as Healer-Dreamers. Now before we leave the thick of the Heaths and move into our deep workings at our Dreamer circle, there are a few things that a Dreamer should know about my domain. Heather here in the Heaths is not only home for me…No! I share this land with the Fey, and these are called specifically the 'Heather Pixies.' Now, I do know that in your contemporary world, which many of you are a part of, Heather Pixies would not seem likely! In that world there are many who doubt such things. I am here to tell you they exist! And if it were not for them care taking of the land as they do, we might all be far worse off than now. They are shy creatures and have clear or golden-colored auras and fine, translucent wings. They are attracted to the Heather for the strong canopy of branches and flowers that I provide for their homes in safety. The Heather Pixies are not averse to human contact but do not necessarily seek this out. Very caught up in their work at hand, they are, keeping the 'Heather-Heath' vibrant and strong. They do have a prankster nature, so do be aware, should you make their acquaintance."

We had walked the length and breadth of the heath, and we all collapsed when we got back to our ceremonial circle. Lunch was about to be served in a wonderful buffet camp setting; we were on break, and the Dreamers seemed glad of it. After lunching a bit, I found a quiet spot and began to make notes in my Dream journal; the day had certainly been rich and fun. I found myself smiling as I jotted down a few things.

Looking across the way, I saw the Heather Seer was sitting on a stool, and one of the Keepers was taking off her pink boots. There was much joking about this…I heard her say, "I like Pink! That is the way it is! But for now, bare feet feel the best." She had been brought a damp towel to freshen with and then was served her lunch at the table set for her and the Keepers; they were all in fine spirits.

Soon the drumming began, and our afternoon session was about to start. Some of the Dreamers had baskets filled with heather twine and twigs; we were all asked to collect some of this material to make "Spirit Dolls," which could be used for healing purposes. The larger pieces of wood were to be shaped into our Heather Ogham Sticks. For now the collecting was done; the making would be on our own time.

The Heather Seer started anew. "I trust you all ate and rested well! Now the lessons take a different tact. However, it is always good to see where one comes from and how the plants and trees grow. Yes this has provided a foundation for the story I will now tell! My Latin name is *Calluna vulgaris*. Which of you can say my Celtic name, I ask you."

The Heather Seer scouted the circle for a response; I was glad to see it came quickly; pronunciation was not my forte! One of the Dreamers offered the Celtic name for "Heather": "URA," and is pronounced "OOR"UH!

The Seer clapped and said, "Very good. Great! The name is also spelled without the 'A' as 'UR.' And my letter for the Ogham alphabet is the letter *U*.

"Here are a few examples from ancient text Oghams that will help us with insight to the workings of Heather within the Ogham systems. From 'The Word Ogham of Cuchulain,' on heather it is said, 'FORBHAID AMBI.I.UIR'-'Completion of lifelessness, the grave.'[42] Also 'The Word Ogham of Aonghus' says, 'SILAD CLAND'-'Growing of plants.'

"Now let that settle in a minute. As you recall, we spoke earlier about the 'growing of plants.' Yes! And yet we can see where this description has come from for the Heather, but we also realize the other descriptions of the Heather in these ancient scripts are very contradictory to the last one, 'Growing of plants'! Why is that? Just think a minute, and let me give you some additional information. As you may have noticed, the Celtic alphabet of the Ogham always has stories, twists, and turns; it simply is not just an alphabet!

"As we refer back to the words used above, 'Completion of lifelessness, the grave'! WOW! Morbid. They all sound morbid and also imply that the Heather is a tree of Death. Why NO! This is not the case with Heather. The word 'UR' means 'NEW' in both Irish and Scottish Gaelic; this begins to explain. Also the Celts have a strong belief in reincarnation. The actual dying and then being placed in your grave was seen as the first step toward 'UR,' something 'NEW'! Of course at first look this seems like a contradiction. There is a Gaelic euphemism for death that refers to something called 'The White Sleep.'[43] This is not a fear or superstition of death but actually a type of 'Kenning' to describe the state in which the dead person exists. For in waking reality, they are physically lifeless, dead, just waiting 'to awaken, to grow' into the Otherworlds. As you recall, 'The Word Ogham of Aonghus' reflects this belief when it is said, 'Growing of Plants.' And of course at first we felt this to be a contradiction to the other Word Ogham descriptions. Believe me, Dreamers, when I say it really takes a lifetime to understand all the nuances of this beautiful representation of Celtic life!"

Everyone was abuzz, agreeing with the Seer's last comment. I guess we all were comforted with her words, with the difficulty of understanding this ancient way. The afternoon had turned warm, and the Seer suggested a short break for lemonade and stretching the limbs, which felt great. I watched the Heather Seer as she walked off alone to the edge of the Moor; there she walked a short way into the pink Heather Heath and practically blended in with the same color of her dress. She held her hands out in front of her, palms up, and seemed to be doing a private ceremony. I had a flashback to ancient times and saw her doing something similar on the Heaths, but there was a huge gathering of women and men and a bonfire that had been stacked, yet not lit. I guessed the fire would be set in the evening. I wondered what the ceremony was about. How much has happened on this land; how different contemporary life is for me. Yet still here am I, and maybe things are not so different at that.

There was rattling now and Dreamers shifting around; I came back from my daydreaming. I had not seen the Heather Tree Seer walk back to the circle, yet she was right there and ready to go.

"In Irish and Scottish Gaelic, the word for 'Heather' is 'Fraoch,' and this means 'Fierce' or 'War-like'; again we see there is a contradiction to the description of 'Something New.'

"There are various qualities in the studies of the Ogham, with the use of the letters, with both contradictions and exceptions to their use. To understand the word 'UR,' this means 'NEW ,' let us refer to the letter 'Q'-'Queirt'-'Apple.' What we learn is that this letter is to be used when 'Coll,' Coll-Hazel, stands before 'U,' UR-Heather, or when 'Coll' stands before 'UR.' What we must remember is that one of the meanings of 'Coll'-'Hazel' is that of 'Destruction.' When it is combined with 'UR,' the meaning then reads like this: 'Destruction preceding something New!'[44]

"Confused, Dreamers? Let me explain it like this. Looking at the other descriptions of 'UR'-'Heather,' we have these words: Fierceness, war-like, destruction, the grave, the growing of plants, and something new! We see a pattern and start to understand that Heather represents 'a phase that follows destruction' and helps to bring in 'something that is new'! Patterns; we study the patterns, Dreamers.

"Like everything that we do, Dreamers, it takes practice to feel comfortable with your craft, and of course that is what is expected of you here in the Nemeton. If you were not highly trained and very capable already, you would not have been invited to apprentice here in the first place. So relax some but practice what you know, and know what you need to still learn!"

The Seer spoke to us with such a passionate voice that I could feel she felt us all very important. Sometime over the last several months, I had heard said, "The timing is now! The Dreaming is now! You are all needed Now!"

I got a chill on my neck, remembering this, and promised myself to study harder. The Seer had been silent only moments. Around the circle, other Dreamers were affirming their work, same as me.

"Who can recall the previous tree studied before me?" The Seer was asking this question as she now strolled about the outer rim of our Dream Circle. She held a few branches of pink blooming Heather, flipping them into her palm as she walked.

Someone called out, "It was the 'Furze/Gorse Tree'!"

She smiled and said good, but then asked the Dreamer the Celtic Ogham name of the Furze.

The Dreamer did not know, but fortunately someone else did. They said 'Onn'-'Furze.' The Seer answered this was correct; she did, however, clamp down and say, "Dreamers, at this point, you should know these Celtic names; I want you to know them! Practice!"

"Getting back now, the tree previous to me was 'Onn'-'Furze,' and this tree represents the destroying of something that was created, which was no longer necessary. An ending of a kind. What we know from modern science is that nothing is ever totally destroyed; it changes form, one form to another. In the cleanup work you learned to do with 'Onn,' what you destroyed has now taken another new existence. The important teaching here is, after serious cleanup from the assistance with 'Onn,' it is 'Ur'-'Heather' that the Dreamer knows to invoke to help grow something new. Always, Dreamers, we are working with the perpetual cycles of life, death, and rebirth!

"The transition from one state of being into another can sometimes be unpleasant and sometimes violent. This is why you call on me. 'UR'-'Heather' is very important to use after working with 'Onn'! Heather has amazing calming capabilities, which are a benefit to the situation and for you, the Dreamer, as well. My energy will help with cushioning the blows of tremendous change. After all, Dreamers, I smell very nice!"

The Seer tossed her head back and laughed with the group, but she picked up quickly again.

"Heather is about renewing and can help with any hesitation one might have had while working with Furze to destroy energy you may have created. There is a lot of responsibility with this type of work; have no doubt about that. Justifying something created and then causing the destruction of it most certainly makes a Dreamer aware of being accountable for their actions. Whatever the outcome.

"Let me shed some light on the Celtic magical system. A Dreamer alone is the only one responsible for their progress, development, and any actions taken. One must Dream and think very carefully on everything they are working with and Dream the possible scenarios of possible outcomes. This allows the Dreamer to make more informed choices in their workings. Working with 'Onn'-'Furze' to destroy is very serious. Every Dreamer must know that every action has a reaction, whether in ritual, spiritual, or physical realities. We must be accountable for all of these.

"In Celtic magic, one faces the consequences directly, rather than awaiting judgment from a higher being. The Celts do not believe in the concept of divine reward or retribution found in the faiths of Jews, Christians, and Muslims. Also there is no belief of 'the deeds' of one life affecting the next or the type of karma as in the Hindu belief system. What the Celts believe is each person is responsible for their own actions and any effects that may come. This is a very simple and fair way to look at life."

The Heather Tree Seer stopped and told us all she needed a moment, please. Then she went to where the other Keepers were gathered. After conversing awhile, she returned to say,

"They tell me all is ready! That is: 'The Furze Seer,' 'The Hazel Seer,' 'The Elder Seer,' 'The Blackthorn Seer,' and 'The Apple Seer' have made everything ready for the last part of our program today." She was looking at these Seers when she said, "And I do thank you all, as I could not have managed without your help!"

She clapped her hands to the other Seers and blew them sweet Heather kisses. Everyone cheered! Now the Seer informed us to walk with her to another part of the Heath and to bring our packet of craft things, including the stick we would make into a Heather Ogham. The mood was high energy, and I felt glad to be walking' my Dreamer friends said the same. We all tried to guess what would be next, and there were some very farfetched ideas that came around, with lots of fun and laughing. We walked the gentle, sloped path, and the Heather Seer picked up again with her story.

"In Irish myth we are told the legend of the 'Irish Triple Goddess'; one story tells of the death of 'Garbh Ogh,' who was an ancient giantess, and her carriage was drawn by elks. She decided to gather stones to heap herself a triple cairn and then began the work to set her stone chair in the womb of the hills at the season of 'Heather-Bloom.' It was there that she then did expire!"

We had all stopped at the crest of a hillside in full Heather bloom. Everyone was in rapture, listing to her telling made so vividly. And when she had almost stopped, her voice was only a whisper and then quiet! We all looked at each other, thinking the same thing… Could it be true?

Then the Seer said a curious thing as she threw back her pinkish mantel over her shoulder. "Why, this could be me…having come back to check on the blooms of the Heather!"

Of course we all just laughed, but I know I felt some nervousness from the others, including myself. The Keepers who were walking to the side just roared; really, they were beside themselves! I thought to myself, Maybe she is this Triple Goddess!

I turned to go forward on the path, but then saw the others looking to the hillside. The Heather Seer, standing there firm, was pointing to the hill, and then I saw it. The flat granite stones were neatly piled, holding up the earth cut away into the hill. And there was a cave-like entrance, dark and damp, held open with a huge stone lintel piece. The workmanship was precise and beautiful. If you looked one way, all you saw was the hill of the Heath in bloom with pink Heather. But once you rounded the turn, there it was: the "cairn." I got chills, just of the idea of this. But I was curious too and looked through the entrance, with the last of the western sunlight, to see inside this hillside cave. And there was a chair, most certainly piled with the same stones as the front entrance, and it was large…In fact I was amazed at the size of the interior of this "cairn"! I had a memory then of a wonderful trip I had made to the very most southeastern part of the Brittany coast of France, visiting a seaside village called Carnac, known for its megaliths and also Merlin. It was there I saw similar stone structures; I have had a fascination with these ever since.

Suddenly I realized everyone was way ahead of me, and I dashed to get caught up. The Seer saw me and said, "I was wondering where you were. Well, I've a few more tales to tell!

In Gaelic there is a 'Heather Goddess named Uroica,' and at Midsummer the Heather is passionate with its blooms of deep pinks and reds. So the Heather is thought to be a Midsummer tree and is associated with mountains and bees. The Goddess herself is a Queen Bee about whom male drones do swarm in the mid of summer. In another myth we are told that Venus fatally courted Anchises on a mountain to the hum of bees. Folktales say that 'White Heather' is thought to be lucky and is a protection in acts of passion. In Italy the Sicilian Mount Eryx is famous for the visit of 'Butes,' the bee master and son of the North Wind, who tends the bees on the hills of Heather. He was given a hero shrine that is tended and honored by the 'Nymphs' of the 'Goddess Erycina.' The Heather tree is also sacred to the Sicilian Goddess Venus-Erycina.

"In Egypt and Phoenicia Heather is also sacred. There is a story of Isis, whose brother Osiris is immured in a Heather Tree at Byblos. In Wales, from the Welsh poem by Gwion, 'Cad Goddeu'-'The Battle of the Trees,' a reference is made to the 'Heath-Heather' comforting the battered Poplars, calling this 'Heather-Ale,' which is a favorite restorative in Wales."

We had walked a distance past the way we had gone in the morning, and now the path had a downward turn. When it leveled some, the Heather Seer asked us to stop and gather on the rock outcropping to listen to more of her tale. It was late afternoon, and the sky was beginning to turn pinkish; I thought this must surely be in honor of our pink Seer!

"I would like you all to notice the growth of the Heather you see here. Can anyone tell me what they think of its growth?" There were all kinds of comments, from "so beautiful" to "so thick," and more. She just listened awhile, sitting gracefully, not giving away any thoughts through facial movements.

Finally I spoke out and said, "To me, this Heather looks much younger than much of the Heath that we have seen."

The Seer smiled and stood up, saying, "Now this Dreamer is observant; this is what I wanted you to notice! Remember the Heath we saw in the morning, which was fallow?... Well, this pink blooming area right here was much like that only one and a half year ago. Cycles; yes, the Heather may wind down to almost nothing, but I always rise up again!

"I would like to tell you about Heather on the 'Finger Tip Trees.' The finger designated as the Saturn finger is connected with the Heather Tree. Of course I have a story that tells of this. The Egyptian God Osiris, brother of Isis, was also thought of as Saturn; he is the one who was enclosed in a Heather tree. The Saturn finger is the third finger, and the Heather-'U' is the lowest vowel on the finger. The location is the bottom joint of the finger, the 'URA'-Heather, of which has been said is a suitable tree to use for the initiation of Scottish witches. According to Shakespeare, witches met on the 'Blasted Heaths'! This Saturn Finger is sometimes called the 'Fool's Finger,' and golden rings are worn upon this finger. To wear a ring on the 'Fool's Finger' was thought to naturally express the hope of resurrection. Because Saturn-Saturnalia, which equates with the 'The Fool,' is also the festive holiday of 'Saturnalia.' And each year someone is designated to play this part of 'The Fool,' who reigns for a week and then, on his last day as king, he is beheaded!" The Seer was silent quite suddenly, and she looked at us all for our reaction. At last speaking again, she said, "Do not be sad! The Fool rises up again unhurt! Very much like the Heather that always rises up again!"

The Seer had now jumped up and onto the path, saying, "They are probably ready for us by now! Is everyone together? Dreamers, stay together; the path gets very narrow and a bit steep before we reach the open grasses. Let us go down to the lowest part of the Heath, our own private Moor!"

The Heather Seer was leading the way, then the Dreamers followed, ten of us on the steep narrow path barely wide enough for a child. I said, "How they even call this a path!"

Someone answered me back, saying, "This is what keeps the place private and special!"

I turned around to find the voice to that comment and was very happy to see the 'Onn'-'Furze Seer' there, watching our backs of the single file line; this was a comfort, and I liked him and was glad he was there. Giving him a smile, I trudged forward. How much farther? I wondered .

At last the path opened some, and the Heather branches were shorter and did not poke out at us so much. The path was only a hillside now; the steep walking was over. Everyone was glad, a little tired, but happy we had gotten down without incident.

The Heather Tree Seer brought us to the crest of the hillside and spread her arms out over its edge. With a huge smile and pointing toward a grassy field surrounded by hills of Heather on all sides, she said, "This is for all of you!" In the middle was a huge bonfire around which were set tables of food. "Strolling musicians and bards too!" said the Seer.

Cheering with excitement! Someone said "Party Time!" All were ready to bolt down the last small hill.

"Not quite yet!" said the Heather Seer. "It will not be officially Midsummer until those last rays of light move off to the mountains. Then we will go have food and enjoy the festivities! Please have a seat. I have only a little more to share. You can do it, I know, so pay attention, please!

"What I would like you to remember as the most benefit to you in the lesson of Heather is to contemplate your personal positions in life and ask yourself, 'Am I ready to take on the responsibility of destroyer and then be the creator? Can I do this? Am I ready to handle such change?' Know too that what you may do may also be done to you! These are the areas I would suggest you to Dream journey with in your dreaming tonight.

"It would be well to carry forth from where you left off with Furze in your studies and apply that to your ritual working with the Heather. This will help you to better understand the huge energy consequences of these two trees. Destruction with Furze and then creation with Heather. I know that the words and the ideas seem clear enough; but trust me when I say, learn to Dream very carefully first, and tread slowly, as the implications that are involved have lasting effects. Talk with each other about this; find out what you feel and believe.

"The Celtic peoples do not have a 'creation myth' explaining how things came into being. They simply believe that creation is a perpetual process of life-death-rebirth. Heather has a special ability to give us positive energy to understand these natural rotations on our Earth. 'As above, so below'!

"I think that about does it, Dreamers! You have been a great group, and I have loved being with you all! Now, a bit later around the fire, we will fashion our 'Spirit Dolls' that we will toss into the Heath for blessing for the land and the Goddess and, of course, a little luck for ourselves! There will also be time to carve your 'Heather-UR'-Ogham Stick. I am Heather; now that you have come to know me, I will help you gain insights and find solutions and sweet inspiration that you may put to practical use!"

We were all thanking her, and she was giving us hugs. I must say her scent was still inspiring and sweet. Suddenly we heard something like a flat-based French horn blowing several times. We all held our ears and laughed!

"That would be the 'Conch Shell Horn'!" said the Seer. "It seems Midsummer has arrived!"

We all got down the hill to the blazing bonfire and the sound of flutes and other odd instruments. The Conch Shell Horn blew again and we all cheered! I realized then that we were now in a small cove area right next to the sea and that the main lodge was only over one Heather hill from here! Looking back to the bonfire, I joined the others and felt I had really stepped back into ancient time. So much to dream on, and so sweet the night. I looked over and caught a wink from the Heather Tree Seer. I held up my new Heather Ogham Stick to her and gave a gracious bow.

ASPEN

Karen C. Silverstein

"E" EADHADH

THE ASPEN
LETTER "E," "EADHADH"
OGHAM:

STATISTICS FOR:

"The Aspen" genus/species- *Populus balsamifera* (common popular) and *Populus tremuloides* (North American).

~Grows throughout northern Europe and North America.

~Grows to a height of 65 feet.

~The trunk is thin and sparse and trembles in the slightest breeze. The silver-gray bark has black spots on it.

~~~~~~~~~

THE ASPEN: HOW USED IN THE WORLD

~The wood of Aspen burns well. It has been used in construction and in making artifacts.

~~~~~~~~~

MEDICINAL AND PSYCHOLOGICAL

~The Aspen does not have many herbal uses. It is made into tea that is used chiefly as a tonic in treating fevers. An infusion can be made for treatment of chronic diarrhea. Sometimes called the "Balm of Gilead," the buds can be used as a stimulant or tonic for various ailments. The sap is made into ointments for various skin problems.

~~~~~~~~~

SACREDNESS AMONG THE GROVE

~The Aspen is the nineteenth tree in the Ogham Alphabet: "Eadhadh"-"E"

~The Aspen is associated with power, shielding-shadowing, protection, underworld, and death.

~KEYWORD- Shield, power

~Planets- Jupiter, Saturn, Sun

~Month- not assigned

~The Aspen tree stands on either side of the Heather tree and Yew tree within the Grove.

~"FINGER TIP TREE" location- "Aspen-Eadhadh"-"E" is on the lower part of the ring finger.

DREAM OF "EDHADH," THE ASPEN TREE SEER

Rushing to get there on time, we ran through the clump of trees, rather than the pathway. We did not want to miss the Dream Theater that would be presented by the Keepers at 4:00 p.m. My Dreamer friends and I had been practicing the Ogham technique of linking with other trees in our journey work. Now we had to scramble so we could be a part of the opening scene. The wind had picked up, and we could hear the trees as we crossed over their roots clattering in the breezes. Someone pointed out how silvery the narrow leaves were and said that these were the Aspens. Finally we saw the small, grassy, step-leveled amphitheater on the hill. The drumming was accompanied by flutes; we had to push through a bit to find seats on the grass step benches. I took a look around the amphitheater to the small semicircle stage and could see that this was a packed audience and an excited one. A bell tolled several times, and then a couple of Dreamer-actors strode across the stage with a large banner held at each end by the Dreamers. In bold greens and yellows it read:

"THE TREMBLINGS OF ASPENS"

The audience cheered and clapped; I was thankful to have arrived in time. I sat upon my grassy bench, and the air hushed some. Then onto the stage came Dreamers dressed as various trees, and some were as river water or marshes. Next one of the Keepers appeared dressed as a Druid Bard in leggings of green and a full, bellowing yellow shirt cinched in with a wide, brown leather belt. He then began to narrate a story, walking with confidence and with authority. I realized he was the "Furze Seer," and he seemed perfect for this role.

"Dreamers! May the Green World provide blessings in our deeds, in our words, in our wishes, and in our dreams! May the magic of the trees be held in our hearts now as a branch of glory for lives well lived!"

In a deep and raspy voice, he spoke slowly and distinctly, moving his staff in the air. "We enter a time of the ancient ones in a land of water and winds, marshes, and mountains, a place that time has forgotten. The sea has left her mark on the craggy, steep, rocky shores. Layer upon layers of rocky cliffs. You'll not see many of you here, as this place is much removed, as it should be. But the Old Ones knew, and they swore oaths with the earth here. An insulted chief would pick up a piece of sod and, holding it over his head, shout, 'Vengeance!' Midwives here gave newborn babes a small spoonful of earth as their first meal. Both salt and earth are placed on the corpse, as it too returns to this rocky earth mother. The land is remote and has a surround of water on almost all sides. Considered the gateway to the Otherworlds, in the old tongue it was called 'Alpae'; we know this as Scotland. It is the most northern reaches that we speak of, the Hebrides and the Orkneys, the sacred islands of old. In this climate one must be prepared; as the days and warmth of the sun are short, the winds come cool in the evenings, even in the mid of summer. But the sky is the bluest you'll ever see, and the magic is strong and true; the 'Isle of Skye' will forever be with you once you have come to know her!"

There was silence until the winds blew strong, and the Aspen tree Dreamers moved across the stage, fluttering their branches of silvery green. The Druid-Bard had stepped into the back of the stage and now moved forward with his arm held out, which was then joined by a smaller arm to his left. From under the Aspens, she walked out, tall and lean, in a mahogany, tanned leather vest, tight to her chest. Both arms bare but for the leather cuffs studded with silver, her auburn hair glistened in the sun, held with a leather diadem. Her skin was as white as the white marsh trefoils. Her waist was nipped in by an odd belt, which held a scabbard embroidered with the white-and-red trefoil flower design on soft deer skin leather; the handle of the sword it held glimmered in the afternoon's light. Is she a warrior? I wondered at this.

The drums got louder; she walked to the fore of the stage on her own, graceful and determined, she spoke outright, "I SHIELD! I SHADOW! My work as warrior woman would be remiss if I did not offer these Otherworld skills. I am 'Scathach,' Warrior Queen from the Isle of Skye!"[45]

This actor's part, I was told by my friend, was being played by the Aspen Seer. I loved the way she simply spoke out about who she was! Her high, determined voice seemed to electrify the Dreamer audience; we were excited for what might be next. We were not disappointed.

"My residence sits on the high stone cliffs above us: 'Dun Scaith'-'Fort of Shadows.' My name means 'Shadow' or 'Shadowy' but also means 'Shield'! 'SCATHACH' is pronounced 'SKY-AH,' which as you now know, is the island that we now stand upon, 'THE ISLE OF SKYE'!" There was a pause as she eyed the dreaming crowd momentarily.

"Please let us understand this: in the legend stories of the Ulster Cycle of Celtic mythology, is an interesting lad, the Ulster Hero 'CuChulainn.' Now he was quite well trained as a warrior physically and could certainly look after himself in the arts of combat. What he lacked, I did instruct, as to how to better access the Otherworld realms. For this work we were in need of the Aspen tree, as now are you, Dreamers! More depth of his story can be found in 'Scathach's instruction of this young hero 'CuChulainn' as it appears in 'Tochmarc Emire'-'The Wooing of Emer.'

"For this instruction we need to call upon my Otherworld skills of 'Shield Making.' Just as CuChulainn learned about the intricate parts of a warrior's life and how important a 'Shadow Shield' is to the workings of the craft, so shall you Dreamers learn this as you spend time on the 'Isle of Skye.' We will begin to learn the importance of this 'shield,' as we have now attained great knowledge from the previous Ogham trees!"

Just then the Seer who was "Scathach" bowed into the back of the stage. The Dreamers clapped with enthusiasm; we were off now on a wonderful Scottish adventure, and all were longing for more!

The Druid came forth again through the Aspen trees and the breezes and said this: "Aspen leaves tremble in the lightest wind and bring messages of weather changes and other changes. Often referred to as 'Whispering Aspen,' the leaves move with the smallest breath of the wind; some say the winds can symbolize the ability to endure and conquer. Aspen can grow to a height of sixty-five feet and is found usually near rivers, marshes, and water. It sprouts from a base clump, called multi-stemmed clones, also referred to as thickets. Aspen's pith has an interesting star shape to it, and the tree is found in many parts of the world."

The wind was coming stronger; I pulled on my shawl. The Dreamer actors used the wind to their advantage, coming up against the Druid as if to knock his footing. He stood firm.

"The Druid was pointing now to the opposite side of the stage, saying, "Some call her the 'Trembling Aspen' or the 'Whispering Tree.' Look, she comes! A symbol of courage and endurance, she knows how to work with the winds and weather! Her gift is knowing one can be flexible without snapping."

All faces turned toward the "Aspen Seer"; again the winds swirled, and the Dreamers playing wind and weather tested her. She only grew stronger. Tall and lean in green-silver and white silk trailing, she moved as if dancing with the breezes. Held about her white thin neck was a torque necklace of thick gold twisted with inlaid emeralds and aquamarine. Holding a white swan, she had the command of a Goddess Queen, so sure of herself. Incredibility stunning, just her presence caused one to want to bow down to her.

The Druid came closer, saying, "My lady, we welcome you!" He did bow elegantly, and the crowd all clapped and cheered. Someone brought out a stool and covered it in green velvet draping to the floor. Sitting regally a moment, she surveyed the Dreamer audience with barely a smile on her ruby heart-shaped lips; being satisfied with that, she put her swan down on the floor next to her, sitting it upon the green velvet folds that lay there. Her long white fingers looked like those of a piano player as she used them to remove her outer robe and held it out at arm's length for a handmaiden to take. Yet she never took her eyes, green as her emeralds, away from the audience.

Something made me suspect. Her airs and transforming presence, were they illusion? Surely she is real, but would she fade? I was not sure of my daydreaming.

The Druid moved to the center of the stage and offered his hand to her. She responded graciously, saying, "I thank you, dear Sir. I am ready to speak!" As the "Aspen Seer" stood, she towered over the Druid, who of course was being played by the "Furze Seer." I remembered then about the Aspen growing to sixty-five feet.

"Dear Lady, I had forgotten your height," said the Druid. "But how else might you keep guard over the forest, shielding us!" Everyone laughed, including the Aspen Seer!

"Well, I have much to say on shielding! Thank you!"

The winds were whipping up again; the Seer raised her long forefinger to the breeze and said,

"I can always tell you which way the winds are blowing; one only needs to listen to my chattering and trembling. It is not hard; it just takes time.

"As all my distinguished Seers have done, I too will talk of my Ogham name. My Ogham letter is *E*. My name is 'Eadhadh' and is pronounced as 'Eh-uh.' There have been several different spellings: 'Eadad,' 'Ebhadh,' 'Ebad,' and 'Eduath.' My name seems to have been in controversy from the ancient times of the Celts and Druids who seemingly were not in agreement about the magical meaning of the Aspen tree. Let me tell you of what I know. I am related to the element of the Air. Now I ask you, how can you grasp the air? You may breathe it but may not actually hold it; you may feel it but not really see it! Yet it is there, as the Aspen is, able to bend and flow with what needs doing. Part of my mystic is seeing beyond the obvious to new levels of Dreaming!

"From the 'Word Ogham of Morainn,' in Gaelic it is said, 'AERCNAID FERND-FID'- 'Distinguished Man or Wood.'[46] The 'Word Ogham of CuChulain' says of Aspen: 'BRATHAIR BETHI. i. E'-'Kinsman to the Birch, Aspen.'

"Confusing, I know, and not making much sense. Let's look at what 'Morainn' says. 'Distinguished Man or Wood.' This may refer to the physical bark of Aspen, which is quite distinctive. The silver-gray bark has black diamond shapes covering a lot of the surface. A deeper meaning may have to do with the level of attainment a student of Ogham has achieved through working the magical trees prior to and including the Aspen. Also the old root word for the word 'knowledge' and the word 'wood' are the same in Old Irish. So when we reread this, it becomes: 'Distinguished Knowledge.' Giving an entirely new flavor to the meaning. This would indicate that the person has advanced to an experienced level of knowledge. Having had a successful completion of studies that preceded this level of tree study, this is an indication of achievement."

The Aspen Seer had been speaking in a very proper voice, without much hand movement as she spoke. Clear and concise was her approach, standing tall and regal in front of her stool of green velvet. Now she moved to a small wooden table made of aspen with the bark still on the legs clearly marked with diamond shapes. Standing next to the table, she began to undo her hair, pulling out the pins that held her auburn locks in a fancy updo. The Dreamers began shifting and fussing with each other: "For goodness sake, what was she doing.... undoing her hair?" I of course wondered too: would there be other undoings? We all watched in amazement; she was beautiful to see, but what was this?

After a few moments, she spoke: "Yes! This is better!" She shook her head, and her auburn hair tossed about, then she took a large, silver comb from the table and combed as she walked and also talked.

"I am combing out my tangles of self-importance![47] This is lesson number one. I am only partly the personality you first saw. I have come to know at times there can be dangers that lurk with that personality. This combing of my hair helps me to temper myself and to balance with the more natural part of who I am!"

Once again the wind blew up strongly; I shivered some and realized evening was with us. As the Aspen Seer walked the stage and then went to the stool, someone handed her a light blue denim shirt. She put this on and rolled up the sleeves; she could have been a young woman from anyone's contemporary hometown just then. But of course as she moved with authority and sat onto the green velvet stool, I was instantly reminded that this was no ordinary hometown girl. Casually crossing her legs, she then searched the Dreamer audience for some time it seemed. But what was she looking for?

The Aspen Seer speaks: "I see all your fresh faces, full of wonder with the things you have come to know, anxious to work your magic. Hoping to do miracles, I am sure. Some of you may even be arrogant at this point, even cocky! Could that be you? Or you? Maybe it is you over there!"

The Seer was up now to the edge of the stage, turning from Dreamer to Dreamer; she made me nervous, and she made us all nervous!

The wind blew gusts across the stage, and the drummers in the background added drama. The Seer stood next to her stool; looking at the silver comb in her hand, she said in a softer voice now, "Always my ally, the wind. And now you, Dreamers, are feeling the winds of change with our Dream Theater. Yes, any one of us can fall into the trap of too much self-importance! In spite of the high level of achievement a Dreamer on the path of the Ogham gains by mastering the skills of the previous eighteen trees and now that of Aspen, the nineteenth tree, there are more dangers than before! The largest danger is usually the trap of self-importance. Let us understand why. The Dreamer at this level has arrived on the edge of much self-aggrandizement, and many times this produces unfocused work. This of course leads to mistakes in judgment, and that begins to upset the delicate balance of the whole.

"Could that be you, Dreamer? Are you feeling very grandiose? Think about this some. This may be what the 'Word Ogham of CuChulain' is expressing with the statement: 'Kinsman of the Birch.' Now please do recall that the 'Birch' is the first tree in the arrangement of the Ogham letters; so this reminds us all to not forget where we started from; let us be humble!"

The Seer was walking around the stage in between the Dreamers who played the parts of various trees; her skirt swirled silver and green as she moved. Stopping all at once, she said in a deeper, more serious voice, "The danger at this level is that we may assume we are protected, when not so. At the beginning levels of our magical Ogham workings, a Dreamer is safeguarded automatically, until they are more proficient. At this higher level, the powers that be assume you are now very in control and know how to perform with proficiency in a safe, balanced way within the 'Green World Laws.' Therefore the Aspen with its ability to 'Shield' reminds us to use protection and sometimes to use that shield to *protect you from yourself!*[48]

"The lesson of Aspen can be viewed as having achieved a degree of proficiency, and at this new level, one now requires experimentation in order to progress further. This is exactly why the safeguards of the lower levels are not here. It is assumed that the Dreamer now has the ability and the discernment to know what to use and when. This can be viewed as the teacher-student scenario; the teacher has attained much and now needs to explore more challenging dimensions. Using his time to his advantage, he chooses to leave the basic skills, which still must be taught to the novices, to his brighter, advanced students to teach. This allows him to do research that may then trigger new theories, advances, and discoveries. This then becomes a new, uncharted course of action that most certainly requires the Aspen's power to shield and protect!

"The additional warnings apply here about damage that might be accrued by those who may work recklessly at this very advanced level. Keeping the Aspen close now reminds one of their incredible responsibility and the power that one has accumulated through all the tree workings. Aspen is there to remind you to make sure you are capable of using control. Aspen also gives us courage to take calculated risks in our work. I give a warning here about being prepared to cope with any consequences: a Dreamer must be certain of the laws of magic and of course the purpose for which they are performing the work.

"It has been said of me, 'Eadhadh'-'Aspen,' that I am a 'Test Tree.' One who is willing to push the boundaries of knowledge. I trust that you Dreamers come to know this aspect of me!"

There was the sound of wings flapping, and we were all astounded as the white swan lifted herself close to the Seer! She leaned over, picking up this magnificent creature, petting it, and talking to it softly. The Seer then moved to the back of the stage; we all clapped and cheered, having enjoyed her so much! Then the bell tolled a few times, and we were now on a short intermission.

The early evening sky was in purples and bright pinks, making a striking contrast to the green amphitheater. A few doves flew overhead, and from this high point, I could just make out the ocean down below the hill, with mist that was curling from the water's edge. Off to one side, a refreshment tent had been set up; many were there having beverages or cookies. I was still deeply in the teachings of the Aspen Seer and did not feel like mingling just now. I walked down the dirt road awhile, quiet with my Dreaming. I came to a crossroad and looked both ways; I knew I did not have a lot of time, but I remembered something about "offerings were often made at the crossroads." So I offered mine, with a pinch of tobacco, for the strength of my work here and for the Keepers who teach and the Dreamers who strive so hard to learn!

Quickly then I retraced my steps in time for the tolling bell and got seated on the grassy steps of the theater. The torch lights had been lit. Soft drumming, and the lights shown on the set of the "Isle of Skye," with Dreamer actors as warriors now in the backdrop of the stage.

"Our ancestors believed that the wind was the messenger of the gods. Anything closely associated to it, like Aspen, was deemed sacred!" The "Warrior Queen Scathach" spoke these words as she stood next to the Aspen tree Dreamers on the stage, who trembled now with the breeze. "From the 'Cad Goddeu'-'The Battle of the Trees,' it is said: 'The long-enduring poplars,' aspen, 'in battle much broke.' Long enduring shields were made of her, as the Aspen was known to hold and protect until the battle's end. In my work I have trained many, even the great Ulster hero CuCuhlain! And they have let me know what has been most important, which of course I knew before they could have even dreamt what to tell me!"

Scathach walked about the set of the Isle of Skye, confidently holding and moving her decorated sword about in the air. She was a force to be reckoned with, is what was immediately felt by all. "A strong woman" would not even begin to describe her energy; she was fascinating!

"What I speak of is the ability to be the 'Spiritual Warrior'! A Dreamer has the ability to unite those who are at arms with the sacred land our Earth. A Spiritual Warrior understands what true power is and knows how to use it. They know about boundaries, balance, bravery, and how to build bridges of light. It is the Dreamer and the Spiritual Warrior in you all that can be honed with the training of the Aspen, who strives to heal and reach new territories. The Dreamer is the great healer of the heart and spirit of the world. With the knowledge of Aspen here on the Isle of Skye, we can use the bridges of light toward the realms of the Otherworlds, connecting this with our waking reality!"

She stopped speaking and slowly she returned her sword to her scabbard that hung at her waist; it looked heavy, but she maneuvered it with ease. That done, she looked at us all; her eyes were glistening under the lights of the stage. She held out her right arm and with a gesture, waved it, saying, "Use your time here wisely, Dreamers. Should you have questions of the warrior kind, I can always be found at the edge of the stone cliffs, in 'Dun Scaith'!"

The lights faded from her, and the Dreamers roared and clapped with enthusiasm for this "Warrior Queen." It took a few minutes for the audience to calm. Now the light shown to the left, and out of a swirling mist walked the one in the green leggings and yellow shirt, the Druid. And what he said was both a puzzle and beautiful.

"From a tale of long ago, the coppiced work had been done; it seemed never again to be green. The woods were still gray, at near end of winter sleep. They surely hold their seeds, their needs. No motion in the air, dare we hope? Yet walking the rocky cliff edge, it is seen small, timid in the cracks, but surely a speck so small, cannot be… Yes, it is the Aspen we see holding strong, holding on!"

The Druid Seer walked about the stage; a seemingly proud man versed by the lineages of old, he offered us all a sense of groundedness, which is so needed in the Dreaming. I sensed in him the age old magical practices of his ancestors—using herbs to heal, divination to see into the future—done mostly as a solitary craft, but true to the ways of the old wise ones. He seemed ready now to continue.

"Edhadh is considered a tree of old age and called the 'Shield Maker's Tree' by many. In Greece, according to Pausanias, it was first introduced into Greece from Epirus by Hercules. The Latin legend says he bound his head with 'poplar' in triumph after he killed the 'Giant Cacus.' The sides of the leaves next to his brow were whitened by the radiant heat it gave out. The myth then may account for the differences in leaf and ritual use between the Aspen, white poplar, and the black poplar, which was a funereal tree sacred to Mother Earth in pre-Hellenic Greece. There is a reference to the divinatory use of 'Black Poplar' and 'Silver Fir.' The 'Fir' apparently stood for hope, and the 'Poplar' for loss of hope.

"The 'Black Poplars' in ancient Rome had an association with the Priestess of Mother Earth at Aegira, and it was considered a tree sacred to heroes. In ancient Ireland, the 'Fe' was a word that meant measuring rod. This was a piece of wood used by coffin makers on corpses and was made of Aspen. It was presumed to be a reminder to the souls of the dead that this was not the end! In Mesopotamia, golden headdresses fashioned from Aspen leaves have been found in burial sites from the year 3000 B.C."

He stopped his oratory and, noting the soft drumming, walked to the back of the stage. He now gathered the Aspen Seer to him and escorted her to the front. She glided lightly next to him; though much taller, it seemed not to matter.

"There is more to the Lady's story, as she will so cleverly tell; I am called now to the shore, as the evening fires are about to be lit. I bid you farewell until later; near the cliffs is where you are all invited to come. Together there we will 'ride the wind'!"

The Druid gave the formal kiss on each cheek to the Aspen Seer, and he moved from the stage. As he left, the Aspen Seer looked after him with her head bent gently to one side, clapping her hands along with the Dreamer audience. Turning now to her Dreamer audience, she said, "One will not find a finer fellow! I will fill in the details a bit more and shore up any doubts you may have lingering. Then you will be tested some and earn your keep here! This is not the place for you as a weekend warrior or Dreamer. No! This is the real deal, and we will ride the wind, and it will be wild!"

The Aspen Seer was in a fine mood with laughter as she was speaking. Her dress was an interesting juxtaposition: silver-green silks, a torque necklace of gold, emeralds, and aquamarine, along with her denim blue shirt with rolled up sleeves, and auburn hair flowing. She was both ancient tree goddess and contemporary Seer, and we all liked that; it made her real.

There was a lot of chattering with the Dreamers; then the soft drumming was heard, and we settled into our space. The Aspen Seer continued.

"Some other known facts of me from various parts of the world. . .In Italy, close to the river Alpheus, in the district of 'Triphlia,' which means 'trefoil,' was a leper colony founded by the Goddess called 'Leprea.' The district later came under the protection of 'Zeus of the White Poplar.' Another name for leprosy is 'leuce,' which means 'the White Poplar.'

"In Wales from the 'Tales of the Mabinogion,' is the story of 'Culhwch and Olwen.' Now Olwen was the daughter of Ysbaddaden Chief Giant. Messengers of King Arthur sought after her as to be a wife to Arthur's cousin Cilydd, whose son 'Culhwch' was in need to be wed. She was sent for and after many a journey was found. It was said of her: 'Whiter were her breasts than the breast of the white swan, redder were her cheeks than the reddest foxgloves. Who so beheld her would be filled with love of her. Four white "trefoils" sprang up behind her wherever she went; and for that reason she was called "Olwen."' Some described the 'trefoil flowers' to be 'white as leprosy' and that the 'white leaves of the Poplar' were a prophylactic against all forms of leprosy."

All the Dreamers cheered at her telling of these tales; we all liked this kind of composite info on the Aspen! In the background the Dreamers playing the trees and the wind became very quiet for the moment. The Seer had been walking the stage in a lively fashion; now she sat on the edge of the stage, and all the spotlights were on her. She held up her left hand, and I noticed again her long, narrow fingers. She was looking at her ring finger, moving the golden ring set with large amber around in circles, taking it off, and holding it up for us to see. She said, "On the Finger Tip Trees, the fourth finger is called the 'Apollo Finger'; Apollo the Sun God is the patron of physicians and considered the God of Wisdom. This fourth, Apollo finger, is also called the 'gold finger' in German. In addition the 'Apollo finger' is connected with the Poplar-Aspen Tree. In Greece is a story of the Sun God Phaethon, and when he died, his sisters wept well for him. They were then metamorphosed into 'Poplars,' and their tears into pieces of 'Amber,' all sacred to Apollo!" She paused just a moment and then said, "In your workings with Aspen, please do remember all the rich history with the power of Apollo and the many others. You may want to think twice before pointing any finger at anyone!"

The whole audience stood up with lightheartedness, clapping and ready for more. The Seer was standing now, holding up her arms for quiet; finally there was a hush.

"You have all come a long way in your study of the Tree Ogham, and despite many a challenge, you have come through. Know you have gained the power to overcome all obstacles, including spiritual death and related transformations. You are able to let go of the past and yet retain useful knowledge from the past. Your abilities include an intuition to be able to help those in need, not fearing change.

"Aspen tree, from ancient times, was thought to protect one from disease and death. It is a tree associated with the underworld and the 'White Goddess' of death at the onset of the Winter season.

"You have come to know something of my 'Shielding and Shadowing,' and I trust you will use this! If you should feel unsure, simply seek me out; you are Dreamers with the ability to journey for answerers. Do that when needed! Aspen can help you reach the Otherworld realms most easily for all kinds of reasons, including communicating with those who have recently crossed. The Otherworlds, at this point in your magical workings, should be feeling more comfortable, and 'Journey Dreaming' must feel like second nature now. But never take any of this for granted! It is up to you to remember your trainings and safeguards now. My key word is 'Power,' but I do not abuse it! Never should you, Dreamers, never!"

There was complete quiet, not even a breeze; we all hung there with wonder and anticipation of our new paths. I could sense Dream fragments of times in the future and then times in the past. I had a momentary glimmer then of an ancient past…"Seven old crones dancing hand in hand, their circular dance to the rhythm of a maddening tune, on an island made of solid gray rock." A bell sounded then, and the last round of the drums, and I came back from my Dreaming.

The Aspen "Eadhadh" Seer jumped off the stage and had a large basket full of her branches; she handed these out to us all, laughing and hugging along the way. The Dreamers were still clapping and giving her thanks for an amazing "Tree Dreaming" performance. She then began to lead the way across the road, which lead to where the evening fires were blazing by the sea.

The Seer said, "We will have a grand time 'shield making,' and I am quite certain the 'Warrior Queen Scathach' will be there for instruction, and you will be tested on your warrior skills! This will be the perfect time to work on your Aspen Ogham stick and have it blessed. Of course there will be dinner, singing by the fire, and for those who are ready and daring, we will 'ride the wind' together!"

She was in high spirits, as we all were. What a great experience and teacher. Of course I was not the only one who quizzed her about the "WIND RIDING" as we walked down the rocky craggy cliffs of the "Isle of Skye."

YEW

Karen C. Silverstein

"I" IDHADH

THE YEW
LETTER "I," "IDHADH"
OGHAM:▤

STATISTICS FOR:
"The Yew" genus/species- *Taxus baccata*
~The Yew grows throughout the world.
~Grows to a height of 50 feet when not trimmed. It is considered the longest living tree.

~~~~~~~~~~~~

THE YEW: HOW USED IN THE WORLD
~The Yew is poisonous in all its parts; working with this tree requires much caution.

~~~~~~~~~~~~

MEDICINAL AND PSYCHOLOGICAL
~The Yew does not have any medicinal use.

~~~~~~~~~~~~

SACREDNESS AMONG THE GROVE
~The Yew is the twentieth tree in the Ogham Alphabet: "Idhadh"-"I"
~The Yew is associated with death, time travel, divination, rebirth, and eternity.
~KEYWORD- Knowledge
~Planet- Saturn
~Month- not assigned
~The Yew tree stands on either side of the Aspen tree and Birch tree within the Grove.
~"FINGER TIP TREE" location- "Yew-Idhadh"-"I" is on the lower part of the little finger.

DREAM OF "IDHADH," THE YEW TREE SEER

Joining the others, I entered the "Ovate Grove of the Yew." The trees were planted in a large semicircle with the opening side facing the northern hills. So very cold, this last day of the Celtic wheel of the year. We have not had any snow as yet, but it would not be long now; I could feel it in my bones. Tomorrow will be the Sabbat of the Winter Solstice, and finally the light will begin to increase again. A disquieting feeling was with me; I wasn't sure why. I had heard from others that had already been through these teachings that this would be a very interesting class with the Keeper of the last of the twenty trees Ogham, the Yew Tree Seer. I had been looking forward to it, until this afternoon.

We could not really see his face, since he was cloaked with a grayish robe and hood, but this was a Keeper, I was sure. He carried a silver branch that had silver bells attached to it. He strode past us, with the bells clinking, as we settled into the circle at dusk; we had learned early on in our trainings that the bells were one of the warnings to become silent. Keepers would be ready to recite a tale or maybe a poem, and the bells helped them with the inner realms and with the ensouling of their story.

I nested into a space exactly opposite the northern opening to the wooded hills. I liked to see the open sky, and just now dusk was coloring the clouds with mauves and oranges. Eagle flew overhead, giving its cries as a blessing to begin. The Yew Tree Seer was in front of the northern opening, seated along with six other Seers. These were the Seven Chieftain Tree Seers, consisting of the Ash Seer, the Oak Seer, the Holly Seer, the Hazel Seer, the Apple Seer, the Fir Seer, and the Yew Seer. One of them presided over the opening of our circle very beautifully, with protection for our workings. There was a heady smell of mugwort and sandalwood; we were all moved and excited to begin our lessons.

The sky of the night was darkening yet clear as the first stars began to show themselves, and the coldness seemed less so in among this sacred Grove of the Yew. I was impressed with the beauty of the altar and the way the fire shown its light on the Dreamers' personal objects displayed there, including deer antlers and bear claws and an eagle whistle made of eagle bone. There were many amazing crystals, so many beautiful things that would gather the evening's energies to be taken home later. I had brought with me my favorite six-faceted, clear quartz crystal, which I had placed on the altar of every class. A Dreamer in attendance to the Yew Tree Seer came to the alter and picked up a narrow basket that was woven from still green needled yew branches, with red berries here and there. She took this to the Oak Tree Seer who was seated on one of the seven wooden benches in the northern part of the circle.

As he held this basket, all the eyes of the Dreaming audience were on him. He spoke softly with the other Chieftain Tree Seers, and when they had all been consulted, he walked to the center and said, "Welcome, Dreamers! You have all traveled far with your Dreaming, working the Tree Ogham. To be here tonight for the last of the twenty trees, 'The Yew,' speaks so very highly of your efforts!

"Our intended focus this evening will be working with the ancestors of the Otherworlds, and in addition we will journey to our own personal life ancestors of this lifetime for clarity with our soul paths. It may not be easy; in fact it is likely there will be trouble spots. This important 'Soul Retrieval' or 'Soul Recovery' Dream work will test you all yet again! However, it is this hard work that will begin to unlock for you your ancestry knowledge, which is in each of us. We all hold this knowing, but few dare try to unlock it. The gatekeepers can be fierce, and often there are things we would rather not see from our past or reopen or even have a hint of. Yet we all have come with the knowing of certain wisdom at birth; it is up to you now to clear any clutter and work your true path!"

The Oak Tree Seer had spoken in a rather booming voice; there was not a sound as he was quiet now, searching the Dreamers' faces and auras. Checking, I thought, to see who was shook up, and if we were centered.

That disquieting feeling from earlier was back; my hands felt sweaty, and the breeze was cool. I turned myself toward my Dreamer friend and raised my eyebrows.

She shrugged and said in a whisper, "We will be fine! Let's just remember to remind each other to breathe; we will be fine!"

I wanted to say something; I didn't feel fine. But the Seer had picked up once more.

He had the Dreamer attendant take from him the green-needled yew basket he held, and then he sat down on his wooden bench. I had the feeling his bench was made of Oak and that each of these Seven Seers had benches made of their own wood. The Yew Tree Seer was in the center of the seven and had not said a word; I wondered when she would begin and what she would be like. I had not yet seen her around the grounds, not in her human form, but she was certainly growing in abundance in her tree form. With the evening's dim light, I could not get any feeling about her, not yet.

The "Ogham Staves" were being passed around from the basket held by the attendant to the class of Dreamers, which counted twenty. And there were twenty Staves, one for each of the Ogham Trees. We were told by another of the Keepers that each of these sticks (staves) had a simple note attached that was the message of that particular tree. We were told not to look at this until everyone had one, and then we were to select a fellow Dreamer as a partner to work our magical workings with for our evening work. Lastly we would read our own tree message. Once that was done, we would have a small break before the Yew Tree Seer spoke. Then later in the evening, we would do the necessary Soul Retrieval work with our partner, where we would use our stave to search our hearts for our soul path knowing and healing.

The Keeper, who had been speaking, sounded the drum softly and each of us read our message that was tied to the "stave of our tree."

The Dreamers were chatting and sharing their messages; they seemed to be in high spirits. I was glad to be holding my "Stave." Turning it over a few times, I noticed the finely carved workmanship of the Yew. Six inches in length, the bark kept on the stick, which was smooth, soft brownish-gray. Each Dreamer received the same Yew stave, but everyone's note would be a different tree for their personal work. I felt nervous; finally I opened the white vellum card attached with green ribbon, it read as follows:

"BEFORE REBIRTH MUST COME DEATH"~"THE YEW"

Setting the card facedown on the ground, I trembled! The night was dark, and deep into the wood, I was in the "Grove of the Yew"…I was afraid!

"Breathe! Just breathe! Remember what we said. You can do this."

Where was I? I heard a voice but could not decipher the words. Was I floating? Slowly I caught myself; I had spun out on a Dream of fear, and my Dreamer friend, thank the Goddess, was there supporting me, telling me to breathe! Finally I did. I looked at her.

She was so strong, saying, "You are at our 'Tree Dreaming' class; you can do this! Remember…We said breathe! I will help you through worries…Talk to me now!"

I saw her worried expression and felt bad; I certainly did not want her to get caught up in my stuff! Finally, with a weak laugh I said, "I am breathing! See…My breath! I do not know what triggered me so, but since you are my partner for the evening, please do look at my card!"

I turned over the card; my friend looked at it and without expression said, "Why this is nothing! You have yourself worked up, and for what? Was it not you who has quoted 'The White Queen' speaking to Alice about doing six impossible things before breakfast!? We can do this. Breathe!"

After that statement, I laughed; how could I not!? And she laughed, and then we began to think of all the amazing impossible things we have done with our Dreamer training. Finally we began to realize that this class session would only be another of those impossible things we could do! I said to my friend, "By the time we are done here, we will have the most amazing résumé!" This of course set us into another round of laughing. And so, by and large, we worked our way through the break, and now the bells sounded; it was time to move on. I felt better, I could do this!

There was stirring from the center of the Seven Seers; she moved forward. Was she young or old? I could not tell. She had black curly hair, tumbling and thick. She was not very tall in a forest-green straight tunic coming to the ankles. It clung to her tightly and was cut low at the neck. Her cleavage showed a single strand of garnet-red berry beads. A mantle of green and burgundy silk brocade hung over her left shoulder, intricately embroidered with yew and glyphs. She unraveled the chiffon burgundy scarf from her face entirely now, and more black hair cascaded. Her sleeves drooped long and swayed as she moved. On her left wrist was one very large garnet stone set into a large silver cuff bracelet; it radiated the light of magic.

As I looked at her eyes deep and black, which stood out on her ivory skin, I felt the piercing stare of an eagle. Who was this woman?

The Yew Tree Seer speaks: "I embrace you, dear Dreamers. This ancient 'Grove of the Yew' has been witness to much, and now we will witness you! This is the Grove of the Ovate level, one of three levels of training in the Druid traditions. The Ovates are responsible for understanding the mysteries of death and rebirth, for transcending time, divining the future, conversing with the ancestors to bring counsel to those in waking reality. The Ovates are expert 'time travelers'! Part of their training is tree lore, herbalism, and healing. You Dreamers should now know the tree is the supreme teacher of the mysteries of time.

"The tree that represents the ovate grade is the 'Yew,' the tree of death and rebirth and eternity. My direction is the north. My time of year is autumn and winter; time of day is dusk, evening, and midnight. It is here spirit is borne out of darkness, learning the 'spiritual intelligence of the night'!"

Her voice came as if through the trees, and from the sounds of silence now, I felt us all to be in trance, listening to a "Spirit of Earth." A warm fragrance was about her as she walked around us. She lured me. I was nervous and yet I was fine; I just breathed. I looked at my Dreaming partner for the evening, and she nodded her head to say OK. The Yew Tree Seer was now back in the front, with her back to the opening in the north and the firelight just in front of her. I felt her to be ancient. She did not look old; she looked like a "Sage" and was to be revered. She held up both arms, with her long sleeves bellowing, and began to turn around to each direction, incanting something I could not hear.

Now she was ready to continue. "Here now I will offer part of the chronicle of my life. It has been a long life, Dreamers, as you will now ascertain. The Yew tree lives the longest of all the trees we have studied in the Ogham. In fact it is believed that some Yew trees found in British churchyards may be as old as four thousand years. In England, Yew has been traditionally linked with death, graves, and afterlife; this must certainly be due to the fact that its needles are poisonous if eaten. I do believe that in waking reality four thousand years is old indeed! Always I am a symbol of everlasting life. The Yew was one of the only evergreens that existed in early Britain, Ireland, and Gaul. To come across this magnificent tree, acknowledging its slow growth, old age, along with its bright red berries and green needles in the dead of winter, led the early Britons and Druids, in particular, to regard the Yew as a symbol of both transformation and eternity. In centuries past, family burial vaults in England, Scotland, and Ireland were often constructed in churchyards beneath 'Yew Trees' to recall the prospect of immortal life.

"Despite the Yew's age, I am not a tall tree; I grow on average of about fifty feet. My growth is spreading in nature, and many times I have several trunks arising from the same root. I am an evergreen tree with needles, and bear red berries, which have a single seed within. You must take care around me as I am entirely poisonous in all my parts!"

The Yew Seer looked at us severely for a few minutes and then laughed, saying, "You are nervous now; I see the looks in your faces! Have I gotten your attention? Good, there is more, much more! In times past there have been no safe medicinal uses. However, modern science has produced a Taxol solution from the bark or needles of the Yew.[49] This formula has had success in the treatment of certain cancers. Now I think that a good thing.

"Should you handle the physical pieces of the Yew tree, be very certain to wear protective gloves and wash hands thoroughly after use. From *Macbeth*, Shakespeare recognized the relationship of Yew and Heckate and referred to the contents of her cauldron as 'slips of yew, silver'd in the moon's eclipse.' Elsewhere Shakespeare says of Yew, 'double fatal Yew' and makes Hamlet's uncle poison the king by pouring its juice, 'hebenon,' into his ear! Dreadful and awful…This is theater. Yet the waking reality is this tree is one to be mindful of, careful with! It is likely that the Latin name for the Yew tree, *Taxus*, is the root word for the word toxic.

"The Irish Druids had a poetic rite called the 'Dichetel do Chennaib'-'a recital from the finger ends,' of which the Ovate was required to be a master. A poem or prophecy was recited that was accomplished with the aid of a mnemonic contrivance of some sort in which the fingers played a principal part. For the Yew Tree on the 'Finger Tip Trees,' there is a strong connection with Mercury; the Mercury Finger, the little finger, is the Yew. It has been said that Mercury aids in the conducting of souls to the place presided over by the 'Death-Goddess-Heckate,' alias Mercury's mother Maia, to whom the Yew was sacred.

"I am the tree associated with death. There is more here to understand; as we enter the Ovate Grade, we come now to the Grove to experience a symbolic death. In the studies of the Ovate Grade, we travel beyond and through this frame of reference to approach the heart of sacred timelessness. Dreamers, what we learn is The Yew tree symbolizes the mystery of self-transformation, renewal, and rebirth."

The Seer had stopped speaking and all was silent; she was standing near the altar. She reached down and picked up the deer antlers that lay there; holding them in one hand, she admired and connected with them. Then quite suddenly she swung them around her; her body moved as in a dance. The antlers, sweeping wide in front of her, cast shadows in the firelight. There was power there; we were all enraptured. The drumming could be heard but only slightly.

Then the Yew Tree Seer said, "I give over these antlers to the Holly Tree Seer, one of the Keepers of the deer energy and who will now assist me in the telling of my tale as I make myself ready for consult of the Otherworld spirit beings."

Silently we looked on as she gave the deer antlers to the Holly Tree Seer. He had a tall wooden staff of at least six feet in height and stripped of its bark to which he attached the antlers and a small sprig of holly. Holding this out for all to see, it looked like a deer mask on a pole, eerie and beautiful at the same time. The Seer bowed graciously to the Yew Seer. We all watched her walk to the center of the opening of the Yew Grove, and she disappeared into the night.

The Holly Seer, holding the antler staff, looked after the Yew Tree Seer; longingly, I thought. He was also an evergreen tree with red berries; interesting. But he turned to us in short order, smiling, and said, "The evening is young yet; there is still much to share! Now tell me, Dreamers, are you mystified with her? Of course you are! But know that she is tough and expects you all to complete our evening lessons before she returns. As with all the Ogham, understanding the writings and symbolism is tricky; the Yew tree is not different.

"'The Word Ogham of Morainn' says of Yew, 'SINEM FEDHA'-'Oldest of Woods,' and 'I BUR'-'Service Tree, Yew.' 'The Word Ogham of Cuchulain' says, 'LUTH, NO LITH, LOBAIR.i. AES'-'Strength, or color, of a Sick man, People or an Age.' 'The Word Ogham of Aonghus' says, 'CAINED SEN NO ATLEAM AIS'-'Abuse for an Ancestor or Pleasing Consent.' These phrases are always confusing at first. Let us begin to understand the 'Word Ogham of Morainn'-'Oldest of Woods' and 'Ido-the Yew.' The Yew is so ancient that some feel it just is! In the Ogham we have learned it is the longest living tree, evergreen, and it is the only tree that is poisonous.

"There are levels of meaning here.[50] If you misuse the Yew tree physically, you will be poisoned physically. If you misuse the tree mentally, and claim you know more than it can actually tell you, in all likelihood you will poison yourself mentally. Often this is seen in the world of magic, with those who work the craft having aggrandizement out of control. Be mindful, Dreamers, as this is sad to see!

"The message here, Dreamers, in regard to the mental level of the Yew is that it exists, and there is nothing a Dreamer need do! Should you be able to develop the ability to understand the Yew, we caution to use this ever so wisely, just as you have done with the Aspen, which stands next in line with the Yew. Remember that the Yew stands in the circle of the nineteen trees that came before and sums up their energies as the twentieth tree, filled with love from all.

"An ancient Celtic word for 'Yew' is 'EO,' and it is the same for the word 'Salmon.'[51] The Celts believed 'salmon contained the sum of all knowledge within its body.' Eating the 'Salmon of Knowledge' would provide a person with all the answers they were looking for. The working with the Yew is very much the same; it contains all knowledge. But, Dreamers, be aware! This most certainly does not mean you only need this tree. No! One absolutely must go through the entire study process of each tree in order to obtain the knowledge. If you try to shortcut with only the Yew, there could be poisonous results. We must be mindful that in magical workings there are 'NO' safe shortcuts!

"This most certainly is what is referred to from 'Aonghu's' description: 'Abuse of Ancestors' or 'Pleasing Consent.' Understand that each tree is an ancestor, and the learning and knowledge gained takes time. Each ancestor must always be treated with respect. When you do this, the result is gaining pleasing assistance from the Otherworlds.

"The Yew is able to live far longer than human lives and therefore is an attribute in helping us to access our ancestral memory and bring this information to the present. Sometimes this entails the death of old ideas and thought forms so we may achieve rebirth.

"Yew was the 'death-tree' in all European countries and was sacred to Heckate in Greece and Italy. In Rome the black bulls were wreathed with Yew before their sacrifice to Heckate.

The Roman Emperor Claudius had a special edict recorded in the Suitonius: 'Now there is nothing better for the bite of a viper than the juice of the Yew'!

"The Yew is mentioned by Pausanius as the tree Epaminondas found on the bronze urn on Mount Ithome; the urn contained a tin scroll with the secret mysteries of the Great Goddess. In Ireland the Yew was 'The coffin of the Vine,' as wine barrels were made of Yew staves. In the romance of 'Naoise and Deidre,' Yew stakes were driven through the corpse of these lovers to keep them apart. But the stakes instead sprouted into trees!

"The small village of Dunure, Ayrshire, Scotland, has an interesting history. A common name in the area is 'MacIvor' or 'MacIver,' and could come from the Gaelic, meaning 'Son of the Yew.' The town derives its name 'Dunure' from an old Gaelic title meaning 'Fort of the Yew.' There are some that say this village with its ruined castle has a connection to King Arthur, and it may be the original Camelot. In another part of Europe, there is an account from 'Lucan Pharasalia III,' 372–417 BC, of a sacred grove in southern France, which reads as follows:

> According to local tradition, no birds ventured to perch upon the trees [of the sacred grove], and no wild beast made his lair beneath them; they were proof also against gales and lightning, and would shudder to themselves though no wind stirred….Superstitious natives believed the ground often shook, that groans rose from hidden caverns below, that Yews were uprooted and miraculously replanted. And sometimes serpents coiled about the Oaks, which blazed with fire but did not burn. Nobody dared enter this grove except the priests….

"Now in Scottish magic, when such things were worked, this was referred to as 'The Airts,' and this was much sought after by the common folk!"

The Holly Tree Seer looked at us all as he moved toward the fire, stopping now to kindle the charcoal in the fire; he had been speaking at a good clip, relaying the tales of Yew. It was deeper into the night, and the scene of the Holly Keeper holding a staff with deer antlers on it made me think we were in a distant century of the past. I was certainly becoming more familiar with multidimensional levels of existence within the Dreaming, and I liked it.

We were on a short break; everyone seemed glad. My Dreamer friend and I compared a few of our notes, and we had something to drink; the air was cooler now. I had coffee to warm with and to stay alert. It was good to move about. Someone said they had seen lightning and it may rain; I hoped not, as I liked when we did our work in the open air.

I saw that the Holly Seer was talking to the Hazel Tree Seer. She was a gentle soul I had worked with early on; as I remember, she told me I had a talent for dowsing and divining. I saw that she had put next to the fire a very large silver bowl; I wondered if divining would be in the near future? Just then another of the Keepers walked about with the silver branch of bells chiming, and there were drums sounding as well. The circle was restarting.

The Holly Tree Seer came forward and said, "I now transfer the staff of the deer to my lady, the Hazel Tree Seer!" They gave short bows of respect to one another. The Hazel Tree Seer moved to the silver bowl, holding the antler staff, which now included a sprig of Hazel.

She said, "Later we will have need of this silver bowl of water; sparkling pure and clean, it will assist us with the soul retrieval and the divining of our soul paths, doing our channeling. We all have this ability and can learn to develop this more. All art forms—visual, written, music, dance, scientific breakthrough—are forms of channeling from the source, the divine source of inspiration. When we journey with our soul recovery for ourselves later, in essence channeling is what we are doing, pulling from within our own being knowledge about our personal experiences. Which then become tools for our wisdom of knowing!"

The Hazel Tree Seer walked about us now holding the antlered staff; she gave me a sense of comfort of this place. She was ready to continue.

"There is a story that relates the relationship of the trees with the middle world between the 'world of the Sidhe,' the fairy-folk. It is called 'The Yew of the Disputing Son,' as translated by Caitlin Matthews; here we learn about the cause of a 'Battle of Mag Mucrama,' which was fought between Eogan Mac Ailill Olom and Lugaid Mac Con. There had been a killing of the fairy Eogabul and the raping and killing of Aine, the fairy woman. Fer Fis's revenge for the killing of his father and sister is very subtle. He fashions a 'Yew Tree' of such unparalleled growth and beauty that Ailill's son, Eogan, and his foster sons Lugaid Mac Con and Cian, all claim it for themselves. One battle leads to another, and the terrible slaughter that follows allows the 'Sidhe' to be fully avenged![52]

"Now, Dreamers, what we learn from this story is not only how central the 'Tree World' was to the early Celts, but also how the energy of the Yew Tree was used by simply just being! In the story, the Yew Tree was fashioned to stand firm in its growth and to give out beauty. The battle ensued as the warriors did themselves in by turning on each other; they poisoned themselves! The fairy of the 'Sidhe,' simply watched."

The Hazel Seer had been walking the circle of Dreamers as she relayed her tale. She stood now near the center where the other Seven Seers' benches were set. She turned her head to the sky; we all did and saw lightning there. I wondered how soon there might be rain, and I hoped it would not show.

The Seer began again, saying, "I am one of the Seven Chieftain Trees, the Watchers of Seven; we look after these Groves and the Green World, and our roots go deep with the ancestors." As she spoke, the wind swirled and there was change in the air as another strike of lightning came. Then, holding my breath, the thunder shook the Wood. A touch of light fell on the Grove of the Yews, and again a thunder shower came fast and hard. Yet, no rain; only fear was felt. A great mist rolled from the sides of the Grove. Were we under enchantments? I wondered, but I breathed, as did my friend.

An apparition, a ghost at first, but we all knew it to be her. She stood central now with the others. Each Keeper was like a rock, a megalith standing stone anchored perpendicular into the inner circle before the circle of Yews. Like spires to the natural lay of the land, those Seven Mighty Seers, holding the energy through wind and some rain now, stood firm. And from out of nowhere, the other "Thirteen" and then "Twenty Seers" stood strong. They had formed now as one within the one called the 'Yew'!

Quiet, too quiet, and then someone started to clap. As the realization hit all the Dreamers, we all clapped and some gave cheers! We had caught the message now, loud and clear: the Yew Seer was composed of all the others, as they of her. I clapped louder than many, happy to know this truth. We were all damp now, but not badly, from the rain. It was passing on now, the storm moving out and the stars shining close now. The soft drumming began, and a Keeper walked through with the silver bells; our chatting ceased and we focused now on the "Yew Tree Seer."

Smiling and cheerful in her forest-green tunic, she walked forward; playful, I thought. One of the Seers gave her the Staff with the deer antlers. I noticed that now it was adorned with the sprigs of each of the "Twenty Trees"; she fingered these a moment before speaking. The Dreamers were still clapping.

"Thank you! Thank you, Dreamers! Now I need to tell you the storm was a random thing! However, it certainly gave substance to my entry, don't you think?" She was laughing as she said this and looked around to the other Seers; everyone was in high spirits.

"Close as we are to the 'Side' here, there may have been something in play, but no matter; I have ascertained you are getting the lessons well; this is good. Now more seriously... The Druids had great reverence for the Yew Tree. It was used in the preparation of magical wands and in divination. But before the Druids were permitted to work any deeds, dangerous or not, to work with the Yew, they would already have had many years of extremely arduous training.

"An interesting fact comes to light while studying the Tree Ogham; one finds that the higher lessons have less to say about each tree, and that they have fewer uses.[53] Curious, is it not? The last example now comes with the Yew. We have discovered from our research that it really has little use, and really there is not much to be said of *me*! Let's think about this.

"We realize this is exactly what we were like as infants first entering the world. Important communications are much like childbirth. They enter the world with power, tenderness, joy, struggle, and revelation! The symbolism of the Yew is that it contains all properties and uses of the prior trees. This is the same as human babes, who contain all the knowledge of their ancestors.

"One of the most important lessons in magic is to identify one's ancestry and the inherent knowledge that resides in each of us. As Dreamers we use the tool of Soul Recovery, Soul Retrieval, and Past Life knowledge to unlock our mysteries. This helps to develop our abilities and potential healing use for our waking Dream world. Certainly exciting to know we can pull together parts of ourselves for a more complete whole!"

The Yew Seer had been standing still in the center, very animated with her body language and lessons; we all felt her enthusiasm. She walked among us now, chatting and looking at the staves the Dreamers had chosen in the luck of the draw early in the evening. She stopped, quiet now, just ahead of me and explained how we would conclude our evening.

"Dreamers, each of you should have your partner chosen by this time; once that is clear, you will pair off into ten groups of two each. One person will Dream Journey for their personal Soul Recovery; the other Dreamer will track and sit watch over the one who journeys. A specific intention for this must be set between you both, including a description of your 'Tree-Gate,' using the stave note that you had selected earlier. This tree-gate is your visual runway to take Dream-Flight from, which becomes the common ground between you. With the drumming we will journey for ten minutes and come back with the drum recall. Next we compare Dream notes with each other. After this the Dreamers switch roles so that the other person can do their Soul Recovery journey work. This will be exhilarating, and some may find things a struggle or intense. But persevere, Dreamers! And of course the Seers are all here keeping the watch and can help should you need this. At night's end we will share the Dreaming reports; it will be grand! Now the Hazel Seer has reminded me to say that the use of the silver bowl of water is yours for scrying if that divination method is helpful to you. A couple more things and a short break, and we will travel to our ancestry!

"From ancient stories of the Celts, this one seems fitting now. On 'Samhain Eve' in the 'Glen of the Yew,' the warriors realize they have come to an end of battle. They come to see that everything has been experienced and completed on one level. It begins to dawn on them that it is now the time for the next level. This is the same with the lessons of the Yew, meaning a final stage has been completed. But the realization most important now is the beginning of a new level. Once a Dreamer has been able to reach the level of the 'Yew Tree,' they then return to the beginning of the 'Humble Birch,' starting over to the next level of magical workings!"

The Yew Seer stood quiet now, only a few feet from me. The Dreamers were on break now, noisily talking and excited for this next and last part to their personal training. I could hear some talk of a major party that certainly needed to be arranged now that we would become graduates of the Tree Ogham! The Dreams were forming fast and furious around this; I knew I was at a milestone here.

Turning to say so to my friend, I found the Yew Seer instead! Startled a little, but not minding, I told her how exciting this class had been and all the classes. She smiled warmly, listening to my banter. She looked younger than when I saw her from a distance in the dim and sometimes eerie light of the night fire. Her eyes are what held me, although I did love her regal forest-green attire and the jewelry was exquisite up close. But the eyes were those of the Eagle and of the Old Ones; I felt her lend me strength through the ethers.

Standing rooted in front of me, holding the staff with the antlered deer in her left hand, no words were spoken until this: "May I know which stave you drew from my basket?" She asked this, but I felt she knew the answer.

"Why of course, dear Seer." I leaned down, picked up my card, and presented it to her: "BEFORE REBIRTH MUST COME DEATH!" - "THE YEW"

She looked at the card quietly, holding the white vellum paper with the green ribbon in her hands. I felt nervous; she was not. I felt unsure; she was not. Looking at me now, eyes more tender, she said, "All things human change; you are coming to know this, Dreamer. I would not have seen you with another card. You are not afraid now in the Grove of the Yew. You will do this walk; you are strong, Dreamer!"

She just stood there; all else stopped around me in my Dream. Sad and strange I felt, but happy too. As I looked at her, I felt a tear fall and cling then to my cheek. Is it wise to weep? I wondered.

The Yew Tree Seer tilted her head, saying, "No need to weep, Dreamer. Dream. That is what we do!"

She walked off and mingled with the others. Then the drumming started, and the silver bells, and we were off again into the night assisted by a clouded Moon and bright starlight. I smiled to myself at all that had transpired and wondered what my "Soul Recovery Dreaming" would bring of my ancestors.

I realized I was happy; I would have the "Tree Gate of the Yew" to travel with!

SECTION FOUR
Life After Learning

LIFE AFTER LEARNING—A DREAMER'S INITIATION

A few of the Keepers approached me…One of the Tree Seers hands me a red rose and says,

"For you. 'Tis the last rose of summer for your new 'parfume de reve,' your fragrant Dreams. My dear Dreamer, you have tended your garden well. Through your time here in the Grove, you are coming to understand that the Dreaming has brought forth many forgotten paths of learning."

One of the Animal Seers says, "You have made it through the 'Dreamer's Initiation'; this speaks highly of you and your developed skills. You have walked the paths with the Keepers, learning the overall teachings for the many and learning the intensely personal workings meant just for you. Much has been transferred by the Keepers to your body and bones, and some of this will take time to awaken. Our bodies always tell us the story through the places of wounds stored in our emotional bodies. A Shamanic Dreamer comes to know the laws of the work, and anything that is avoided, such as wounds, merely fester and grow in their insidious influence over us. Dreamer, you have come to know yourself deeper now and know that to heal any wounding one must tap into their own ancestral heritage before one can truly reach their full potential in 'The Work.' You have come to realize that it is through the Dreaming that you, Dreamer, have found the courage and the strategies to release what does not apply to you now from these heritages of past life Dreaming and to collect the parts that are appropriate for you now. May you continue to radiate your love and peace thorough your Dream walks this century!"

One of the Trump Seers says, "The Dream side encounters under rows of trees; the moon-washed nights, scanning the heavens for omens; the wind assisting the birds in their flight; the animals teaching you Dreaming in the night…All these encounters and more have helped you, Dreamer, to a new connection with 'The Shining Realms,' a place of being able to live in a state of heightened awareness. The Dream Keepers who have traveled through with you to our sanctuary, the Nemeton within the Grove, will come back and forth as needed. You are becoming aware now of living multidimensionally in all time spans; past, present, future Dreaming lives. Remember, Dreamer, the times when you experience the moonless night and the soulless day: this is when a Dreamer's skills may be the only shining light. Always hold onto your Dreams! In my Dream speak for you, I wish you the magic that you wish for yourself!"

The Three Seers give their embraces to me and walk off to others waiting. I feel as if in a trance. I nod my head, though barely speak a word. I am astounded by all the Dream wishes; I know that now my Dream world will become more personalized, but I have a worry at the edges of me about not having this world I had come to know and love as my daily routine.

The group of Keepers addressed many other newly initiated Dreamers like me. It is a warm end of a summer day; I look at the red rose I have been given and inhale its musty aroma and walk awhile among the flower gardens here. How could this training have skipped by so quickly? Who am I now? I keep asking!

Absorbed in such a way in my own daydreaming, I am slightly shocked when I hear someone saying, "Dreamer, Dreamer! Are you OK?"

I turn to find one of the Seers there offering me a seat on the garden bench...I slowly answer, "Yes, I am fine. Just caught up in the amazement of everything!"

The Seer looks me in the eyes, and I feel the gateway from within her eyes. Slowly, quietly, she begins to speak and hands me a small, reddish clay sculpture of a reclining goddess. The Seer says, "This is for you. It is 'The Sleeping Lady'; she is an oracle goddess for Dreaming and Healing. She was found in the Oracle Room of the Hypogeum Temple in Malta. This was one of the several 'Dream Incubation Temples.' Call on her and on me when you should need help and assistance."

I lean over and give the Seer a big hug and many thanks! I feel cheered by the Seer's presence and the gift.

She looks to me and says, "I did hear your daydreaming question earlier...'Who am I now?' May I offer you this, Dreamer: no need for hurrying, worrying about what may be now. For you are 'Here Now'! And the path is illuminated before you on this beautiful day or night. Beyond that, one knows nothing...but for the Dreaming, and that is what you are now, 'A Dreamer'! You are 'a maker,' and I believe all makers feel this way at times about dreaming the idea. The feeling is hazy at first; you know there is something that needs doing, and then you forge on! Drawing it, fashioning it, envisioning it. Upon waking, we each recreate our world every day."

The Seer stops speaking, and I am welled with teary eyes. Smiling at her, I nod my head yes to her words of wisdom. Then a few other Seers come over. Each of them give me support with these comments: "You are ready, Dreamer, and readiness is all!" Another says, "You are a Dreamer who has learned to change the past when needed and to script your future!"

The comment that strikes me the most comes from one of the Trump Seers; he says, "Dream Mastery is a journey not a destination. Remember that, Dreamer!"

I look back and say with laughter and strength now, "I love all of these!"

All The Keepers are there now along with the other initiated Dreamers, including me. The Keepers, standing now in a semicircle, arc before us with hands lifted to the blue summer skies. They say together: "We are in agreement; you are ready to be walking and teaching in the waking world the 'Great Dreaming Work.' From this point you are now both here and there, living multidimensionally within the Dreaming!"

The Keepers begin a chant along with the beautiful soft drumming, and I hear the words...

"Go now!

Go now!

Go now!"

THE KEEPERS WEAVE THROUGH REFLECTING USING DIVINATION

Journeying within the Nemeton sanctuary has been about Dream support. Dreamers have learned how a certain word, a deed, or even not doing affects and "mirrors" what is in our world. Trained Dreamers have come to know their hearts, truths, and passions. The work has taught how honoring and respecting our own boundaries and those of others helps to grow our imaginations and creativity. Dreamers, you have strengthened where you are in the present and where you see yourself in the future.

The tapestry of a Dreamer's life is always being woven in the mirror. It is our art! What does this "Dream Art" reflect for you? We have learned from the Keepers where the tapestry threads are strongly woven and where the weave seems weak. Looking at the tapestry, we can discover our immediate boundaries; we notice how the stitch looks. Have we selected the right colors? How does this illuminate the psychic fabric that we have been weaving?

As Dream Seekers you have come to know situations in your personal lives that have been reflected to you by the Keepers. These may be situations that need insight, help with confusion, help with feeling stuck, and of course, healing with your dreams. Now is the time to make use of the tools that have been gifted for you to use with your "Dream Path Work." The Dream messages will be received from individual Keepers that present themselves in the various "Keeper Images" or "Ogham Sticks" castings done in divination. This is very exciting! Using the images received, we can mend and add to the weaving of our own tapestry from these divination selections. And we come to know we are directing something very important while we dream weave for ourselves or another.

WORKING WITH THE KEEPER IMAGES *as DIVINATION*:

*Reading through the entire book first is best. Once completed, your personal "Dream Path Work" can take form.

*In all divination workings, it is best to have an INTENTION ready before you cast for an image to gain information for yourself. Write this intention into your journal.

A DREAMER'S DIVINATION RITUAL:

*Before you begin, be sure to set your space with cleansing first, such as smudging your space with sage or insense, call in protection from your animal guardians, angelic guardians, or others.

*Second, decide on a clear intention for your divination work.

*Third, honor yourself and the reflective weaving process. Be prepared; ask specific questions or just ask for guidance over the next month.

*If you receive a message that feels not right, pick again until you feel comfortable. This is your Dream Healing, and you must be able to work with this. The second image then becomes a support for the first image. You are your own Dream Director, never forget that! The following questions may be added to your own personal intentions:

- What is the sacredness among the Grove that I feel from this Seer?
- What has been reflected in the mirror from this Seer?
- What dream mask do I recognize in the mirror for myself?

As you proceed seeking answers, guidance, and destiny information for yourself, use the dream mirrors! These are the Seers the Keeper images and are gateways for your dreaming intentions. These workings help you, Dreamer, to weave the reflected divinations into your tapestry that is the "Dreamer Life," which you are living now!

♥THE DREAMY DIVINATIONS—SUGGESTIONS FOR SPREADS:

Selections of the "Keeper Images" can be done by randomly opening to a page, or with intention. Have your intention,question ready.

THE THREE FATES SPREAD: select one image from each of the Three Seers (Trump, Animal, Tree).

CAST A TRUMP KEEPERS SPREAD: select three to five images from the Trump Seers.

CAST AN ANIMAL KEEPERS SPREAD: select three to five images from the Animal Seers.

CAST A TREE KEEPERS SPREAD: select three to five images from the Tree Seers.

COUNCIL OF THE SEERS SPREAD: select two images from each of the Trump Seers, Animal Seers, and the Tree Seers.

♥THE FINGER TIP TREES-THE MAP OF YOUR HAND:

Learn the energy of the Trees that is contained within the palm of your hand.

OGHAM DIVINATION—CREATE YOUR OWN SET OF STAVES & CAST OGHAM STICKS:

To Begin:

1) Decide which Dream of the Tree Seers you most relate with. Choose at least three Tree Seers that you can make into Ogham staves-sticks. Ideally you may make a set of twenty staves for each of the Tree Seers.

2) Think about which physical woodland forest in waking reality you might travel to and visit. When there, walk through the woods. It is helpful to bring along a "tree guide" to identify the trees. Using your intuition, ask for a tree to present its presence to you. Once you have asked permission from this Tree Seer, you may want to draw a circle of protection about the circumference of the tree, using a branch or your knife you have brought with you. Sit awhile and Dream with this Tree Seer. When you are ready, ask permission of the tree, then use your knife and cut a small branch that you will use as your Ogham divination stick. Make sure you label the tree branch, using tape as temporary identification. Give thanks! Use this process for however many Ogham sticks you intend to collect.

3) Once you are home, you can cut into the sticks the appropriate Ogham letter. Some people like to peel off the bark first. I like to keep the bark on the sticks. This helps me to remember the bark textures and appearance. This is your choice. Cut your sticks to at least a six-inch length. Make them all of equal length.

4) After you have your bundle of Ogham staves labeled with the tree seer's alphabet (to label, use a sharp knife and carve into the stick the appropriate lines of the Ogham alphabet letter), write down on a small piece of paper the correct alphabet and match this to the tree name.

Example: ASH TREE-"NION"- "N"

5) Then roll your small identification paper around the twenty sticks and tie with a cord or ribbon.

Now you have a set of Ogham sticks that are accessible for your use at any given time. Keep them handy and at your fingertips! It is also helpful to record the Ogham alphabet into your dream journal.

DIVINATION WITH OGHAM

Casting for a Dream Reading:

1) Set your sacred space, smudge and call in your protection: animal guardians, angels, or goddess guardians. Set your intention and your question; be specific. Hold your Ogham Set while you do this.

2) Cast the sticks on the ground. Notice which Tree Seers fall next to each other. Which are separate? Make notations in your journal as to which Tree Seers you need to work together with concerning your intention, and which ones to work with separately.

3) Is there any pattern they make as you see them on the ground? Dream with this. What do these Tree Seers mirror for you at the present time?

4) Make sure to do your research and follow-up information. Of course it is important to honor the messages that come to you! And by all means, record the findings in your Dream Journal!

Map of Your Hand

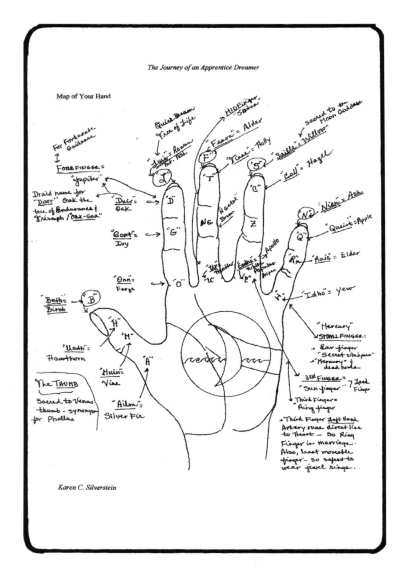

Ogham Hand Chart
Finger Tip Trees

5 Fingers—5 Main Letters

Main Letter	Finger	Main Trees	Support Trees
B	Thumb	Birch	Hawthorn
L	Forefinger	Rowan/Mt. Ash	Oak
F	Middle Finger	Alder	Holly
S	Ring Finger	Willow	Hazel
N	Small Pinky Finger	Ash	Apple

Signaling Keyboard (Druids)
-Use this in Energy work.
-Use these to send signals to another for healing or to find information.

♥CAST A TREE KEEPERS SPREAD:
-Randomly select Five Tree Keepers to help you with your question or intention.

RESOURCES USED FOR WRITING THIS BOOK:
THE TRUMP SEERS:
(BOOKS)
- Gareth Knight, *A Practical Guide to Qabalistic Symbolism* (Boston: Weiser Books)
- Gareth Knight, *Tarot and Magic* (Rochester, VT: Destiny Books)
- Cynthia Giles, *The Tarot History, Mystery and Lore* (New York: A Fireside Book)
- Arthur Edward Waite, *The Pictorial Key to the Tarot* (Boston: Weiser Books)
- Papus (Dr. Gerard Encausse), *Tarot of the Bohemians* (London: William Rider & Son)
- Mary K. Greer, *Tarot Mirrors — Reflections of Personal Meaning* North Hollywood,CA Newcastle Publishing)
- Angeles Arrien and J. P. Tarcher, *The Tarot Handbook* New York, NY Putnam Books)
- Emily Peach, *The Tarot Workbook* (New York: Sterling Publishing Co.)
- Manly P. Hall, *The Secret Teachings of All Ages* (Radford, VA Wilder Publications)
- Toni Allen, *The System of Symbols: a new way to look at Tarot* (London, Listansus Press UK)
- Pamela Eakins, PhD, *The Tarot of the Spirit* (Boston: Weiser Books)
- Ruth Ann and Wald Amberstone, *The Secret Language of Tarot* (Boston: Weiser Books)
- Margaret Starbird, *The Tarot Trumps and the Holy Grail* (Boulder, CO Woven Word Press)
- E. Valentia Straiton, *Celestial Ship of the North* (City: Kessinger Publishing)
- Barbara G. Walker, *The Woman's Dictionary of Symbols & Sacred Objects* (San Francisco: Harper Books)
- J. C. Cooper, *An Illustrated Encyclopedia of Traditional Symbols* (New York, NY Thames & Hudson)

(INTERNET RESOURCES)
-Wikipedia, The Free Encyclopedia, http://www.wikipedia.org
-Aeclectic Tarot (Solandia), http://www.aeclectic.net
-Pythagorean Tarot, "John Opsopaus," http://web.eecs.utk.edu
-Tarot Hermit, http://www.tarothermit.com

THE ANIMAL SEERS:
(BOOKS)
- Ted Andrews, *Animal Speak* (St. Paul, MN: Llewellyn Publications)
- D. J. Conway, *By Oak, Ash, & Thorn* (St. Paul, MN: Llewellyn Publications)
- Alexander Carmichael, *Carmina Gadelica, Vol. I & II* (USA Forgotten Books)
- E. Valentia Straiton, *Celestial Ship of the North* by:–(USA Kessinger Publishing)
- Jamie Sands and David Carson, *Medicine Cards* (Santa Fe, NM: Bear & Company Books)
- Philip and Stephanie Carr-Gomm, *The Druid Animal Oracle* (Shaftesbury, Dorset, UK Fireside Books)
- Barbara G. Walker, *The Woman's Dictionary of Symbols & Sacred Objects* (San Francisco: Harper Books)

- J. C. Cooper, *An Illustrated Encyclopedia of Traditional Symbols* (New York, NY Thames & Hudson)

(INTERNET RESOURCES)
-Wikipedia, The Free Encyclopedia, http://www.wikipedia.org

THE TREE SEERS:
(BOOKS)
- Steve Blamires, *Celtic Tree Mysteries* (St. Paul, MN: Llewellyn Publications)
- Helena Paterson, *The Celtic Lunar zodiac* (Boston, MA Charles E. Tuttle, Company, Inc.)
- Robert Graves, *The White Goddess* (New York: Farrar, Straus and Giroux)
- Alexander Carmichael, *Carmina Gadelica, Vol. I & II* (USA Forgotten Books)
- Caitlin and John Matthews, *Encyclopaedia of Celtic Wisdom* (Shaftesbury, Dorset, UK Element Books)
- Mara Freeman, *Kindling the Celtic Spirit* (San Francisco: Harper Books)
- Edain McCoy, *Celtic Myth & Magic* (St. Paul, MN: Llewellyn Publications)
- Miranda J. Green, *The World of THE DRUIDS* (London, UK Thames & Hudson Books)
- R. J. Stewart, *The Way of Merlin* (London, UK The Aquarian Press)
- Barbara G. Walker, *The Woman's Dictionary of Symbols & Sacred Objects* (San Francisco: Harper Books)
- Nathaniel Altman, *Sacred Trees* (New York: Sterling Publishing Co.)
- Roger Phillips, *Trees of North America & Europe* (New York: Random House)

(INTERNET RESOURCES)
-Wikipedia, The Free Encyclopedia, http://www.wikipedia.org.
-Controverscial.com, "In Worship of Trees" (George Knowles), http://www.controverscial.com
-OBOD Druid, FSA Scot (Susa Morgan Black), http://www.druidry.org
-Celtic Tree Lore, http://www.dutchie.org

♥VISIT US ♥ http://www.earthdreams.com e-mail karen@earthdreams.com
♥COLOR DIVINATION CARDS:
"JOURNEY OF AN APPRENTICE DREAMER" Available for $14.95 + S&H
Card Deck of the Dream Seers, the sixty four Keepers illustrated in the book

APPENDIX I.

⚡ THE LIGHTNING DREAM WORK GAME

an original dreamwork process developed by Robert Moss

Phase One: Telling the Dream

1. Choose who will tell a dream first.
2. Encourage the dreamer to tell the dream as clearly and simply as possible, without personal background or analysis.
3. Ask the dreamer to give the dream a title.

Phase Two: Asking the 3 Basic Questions about the Dream

The partner (or lead partner, if working in a group) now asks the dreamer three basic questions.

1. What did you feel when you woke up?
2. Reality check:
- What do you recognize from this dream in the rest of your life?
- Could any part of this dream be played out in waking life in the future?
3. What would you like to know about this dream?

Phase Three: Playing the "If It Were My Dream" Game

The partner now says to the dreamer, "If it were my dream, I would think about X".

Phase Four: Honoring the Dream

Dreams require action! The vital last part of the process is for the partner to ask the dreamer:

- What action will you take to honor this dream?

Try to guide the dreamer towards specific *action*. If the dreamer does not know what to do, the partner should suggest possible actions "if it were my dream". Some suggestions:

- write a bumper sticker from the dream
- go back inside the dream through dream reentry
- share the dream with someone else who may need its guidance
- write/paint/create to honor the dream

COPYRIGHT © ROBERT MOSS

For more on the Lightning Dreamwork, please read Robert Moss' books *Dreamways of the Iroquois* and *The Three "Only" Things* and visit www.mossdreams.com

ENDNOTE REFERENCES

[1] Susan Johnston Graf, *W. B. Yeats: Twentieth Century Magus*, Weiser Books (2000).

[2] J. H. Howard, Shawnee: Ceremonialism Native American Tribe USA.

[3] Steve Blamires, *Celtic Tree Mysteries*, Llewellyn Publications, St. Paul, MN.

[4] Ibid.

[5] Ibid.

[6] Ibid.

[7] Ibid.

[8] Ibid.

[9] Ibid.

[10] Ibid.

[11] Ibid.

[12] Ibid.

[13] Ibid.

[14] Ibid.

[15] Ibid.

[16] Ibid.

[17] Ibid.

[18] Ibid.

[19] Ibid.

[20] Ibid.

[21] Ibid.

[22] Ibid.

[23] Ibid.

[24] Ibid.

[25] Ibid.

[26] Ibid.

[27] Ibid.

[28] Ibid.

[29] Ibid.

[30] Ibid.

[31] Ibid.

[32] Ibid.

[33] Ibid.

[34] Ibid.

[35] Ibid.

[36] Ibid.

[37] Ibid.

[38] Ibid.

[39] Ibid.

[40] Ibid.

[41] Ibid.

[42] Ibid.

[43] Ibid.

[44] Ibid.

[45] Ibid.

[46] Ibid.

[47] Ibid.

[48] Ibid.

[49] Ibid.

[50] Ibid.

[51] Ibid.

[52] Text from Cormac Mac Culennain, the king-bishop of Casbel (d. 908), found in the twelfth century compilation, *Leabhar Laignech*

[53] Steve Blamires, *Celtic Tree Mysteries*, Llewellyn Publications, St. Paul, MN.

MY HEARTFELT ACKNOWLEDGEMENTS

I **offer this book with love for the magic in a Dreamer's life!**

What has made this book different and exciting?

My answer is the meeting of the Keepers from the Dreamtime. Yes! This has made a very rich and interesting journey for me over a good many years. For my life in both worlds, I thank the Keepers!

This work of my life simply would not have happened without my Earth-loving and grounded husband, Jay. He is a true Earth Keeper! His untiring patience and support are what have made this book become a physical presence in paper and ink! I love him truly in this life and our Paris life and many other lives, of which I am certain.

I am grateful to my teacher and friend Robert Moss, whose Dream Teacher training has broadened my view of the worlds that I hold dear. I thank him for the use of his "Lightning Dream Work" technique, which I have applied to my book. I am blessed for the times the Dream family has spent with him on a beautiful mountain in the Adirondacks of New York State.

I am forever grateful to the many Dreamers I have come to know and cherish as a Dream family. Most especially to the Dream Sisters of my monthly Woman's Dream Circle. I mention a few here. Especially to Irene D'Alessio, who has held space for me. And to Susan Breed, Donna Katsuranis, Jane Knox, Laurie Murphy, and Sherry Puricelli. Also thanks to Susan Morgan, Jan Johnson and Adelita Chirino all strong Dreamers. A special thanks to dear Gabby, a Dreamer of Heart who now has crossed to the Otherworlds, and thanks to her husband, Roger, who resides and dreams in this waking reality. All these Dreamers so faithful to the Dreaming.

Thanks also to Dr. Jeffrey Yuen, priest of Taoist lineage and doctor of Chinese Herbal Medicine; he has nurtured my body, mind, and spirit on "My Heart's Journey."

Thanks to the many Native American Teachings that I have come to honor, especially to Grandmother Rosy and Grandmother Twylah Nitsch.

Thanks to my friend Stephanie Adams, for without her technician's help, the book wouldn't be.

I thank my parents, Helen and Ralph Crockett, who nurtured in me a love for the arts and books.

A very special thanks to my son, Joshua, who organized the technical style with much patience and taught me so much computer friendly lingo!

A very special thanks to my daughter, Erica, who has given me so much encouragement and editing advice that I needed! In addition, thanks for building the new website!

Thank you to Team six at CreateSpace for all the good support and work!

This book has become an entirely novel approach to our ancient divination systems of learning.

It works, it is alive, and fun to use!

~GOODEARTHDREAMS
~KAREN~

Made in the USA
Charleston, SC
04 March 2013